good wine GUIDE 2004

ROBERT JOSEPH

A DK PUBLISHING BOOK

London, New York, Munich,
Melbourne, Delhi

A Penguin Company

Produced by RJ Publishing Services

Editor • Robert Joseph
Deputy Editor • J.D. Haasbroek
Associate Editor • Anastasia Edwards
Photography • Ciel Monmari, Steve Gorton, Ian O'Leary

Dorling Kindersley

Senior Editor • Gary Werner
Senior Art Editor • Sue Metcalfe-Megginson
Managing Editor • Deirdre Headon
Art Director • Peter Luff
DTP Designer • Louise Waller
Production • Sarah Sherlock

Sixth American Edition, 2003
2 4 6 8 10 9 7 5 3 1

Published in the United States by
DK Publishing, Inc., 375 Hudson Street,
New York, New York 10014

A CIP catalog record of this book is
available from the Library of Congress.

ISBN 0-7894-9638-0

Color reproduced by Colourscan, Singapore
Printed and bound in Italy by Graficom

See our complete
catalog at
www.dk.com

CONTENTS

INTRODUCTION 4

HE BASICS

NEWS 6
PERSONAL CHOICE 10
WINE ON THE WEB...16
TASTING AND BUYING 18
READING THE LABEL 24
COUNTRIES 28
THE GRAPES 48
STYLES 56
STORING 60
SERVING 62
INVESTING 66
VINTAGES 68
WINE AND HEALTH 72
FOOD AND WINE...76

–Z OF WINE

AN ENCYCLOPEDIA OF GRAPES, PRODUCERS, REGIONS, AND TERMS 97

VINE CHALLENGE AWARDS 2003

INTERNATIONAL WINE CHALLENGE...263

VINE LOVERS GUIDE TO THE WORLD

RESTAURANTS, WINE BARS, AND SHOPS...365

INDEX 393

INTRODUCTION

Welcome to the 19th edition of the Robert Joseph *Good Wine Guide* – an annually updated wine drinker's companion that is really four books in one. In the first section – *The Basics* – you'll find all the grounding you need to get through a dinner party among wine enthusiasts, set up a cellar, or choose a bottle in your local supermarket. There's guidance on grapes and regions, flavors and vintages. The relationship between wine and health and ideal marriages between food and wine are covered too, as are wine on the web, and the pros and cons of wine investment.

The A–Z of Wine – is an encyclopedia of some 3,100 wines, terms, regions, and producers, recommended examples, and the best way to pronounce the names of all those wines. So, you'll never have to pause before ordering a bottle of Ngatarawa from New Zealand.

Next comes a set of award-winning bottles from the 9,400 entries to the 2003 *International Wine Challenge*, the world's biggest wine competition. The examples that appear here are the 247 Gold Medal and Trophy winners as well as some 750 Good Value award winners chosen across a wide range of styles for the flavor and character they deliver for the price tag they bear.

The section that follows – *The Wine Lover's Guide to the World* – is a wholly new departure for the 2004 Guide, and includes recommendations for over 200 restaurants, bars, and shops across the globe. Whether you are in Boston, Barcelona, or Beijing, you'll be sure of finding a good, fairly-priced glass of wine.

Taken as a whole, the *Guide* should (as a reviewer wrote of a previous edition) be the "only wine book you need" when choosing, buying, or drinking wine in 2004.

The 2004 *Guide* owes much to Anastasia Edwards, its Associate Editor and J.D. Haasbroek, the deputy editor who kept the book on track and on schedule. I am also very grateful to the long list of people who generously helped with recommendations for *The Wine Lover's Guide to the World*. Michael Florence, Birgitta Beavis, Nathan Birley Richard Ross and Chris Mitchell were responsible for the *International Wine Challenge* content and Charles Metcalfe, Anthony Downes and most particularly Catharine Lowe, provided moral support. I also have to thank Piers Russell-Cobb and, at Dorling Kindersley, Deirdre Headon, Louise Waller and Gary Werner. Richard Davies at *Wine International* and and Kim Murphy at the *Wine Institute of Asia* were as indulgent as ever. These people share any credit for this book; the criticism should fall on my shoulders alone.

THE
BASICS

News

PALATES IN WONDERLAND

BITTER HARVESTS

As the winemakers and buyers of the world gathered at trade fairs in London and Bordeaux in May and June 2003, there was something missing: the buzz of excitement of previous years. Of course the visitors were politely interested in the new arrivals from familiar and novel regions and producers, and of course they joined in the gossip about who was about to take over, or be taken over by, whom. But they were all subdued by the awareness that these are very uncertain times for the wine world. At the traditional end of the scale, Bordeaux merchants were acknowledging a general lack of interest in their region's 2002 vintage – despite a drop in prices of 25 to 40 percent. The very top wines such as Latour, Margaux, and Lafite may have been snapped up, but other estates' efforts were wallflowers at the dance.

Chateau Latour 2002, one of the few Bordeaux of that vintage to attract buyers when it was offered early in 2003.

The 2002 vintage was, admittedly, neither a great one in Bordeaux, nor in most of the rest of Europe, but that was only part of the problem. Cellars were still full of unsold 2001 Bordeaux – and even some purportedly "historic" 2000s. Sales of European wines outside the continent were also handicapped by the unexpected muscle the euro had dramatically developed against the dollar, pound, and yen. A combination of SARS in Asia and Canada, shaky stock markets, and the uncertainty surrounding the Iraqi conflict simply compounded the lack of enthusiasm for pricey French wine. And then, of course, there was the anti-Gallic feeling which made ordering a bottle of Châteauneuf du Pape tantamount to treachery. Few Americans mourned the news that Beaujolais winegrowers were once again having to destroy their surplus wine.

But US wine producers were in no position to revel in the woes of their counterparts across the Atlantic; they had far too many problems of their own. At least the chateau owners of Bordeaux were able to pay their bills – unlike the respected Californian winery De Loach, which filed for Chapter 11 bankruptcy protection in May. According to the California Association of Wine Grape Growers, 70,000 acres of raisin, table and wine grapes were plowed under in 2002, in a smart reverse from what The New York Times described as the "planting

Yellow Tail, the Australian wine that leapt from nowhere to become one of the most popular wines in America.

frenzy of the 1990s." And that process was certain to continue in 2004. Elsewhere, matters were little better. In the Margaret River, in Western Australia, one of the finest wine regions on that continent, vineyards planted four or five years ago are now adorned with "for sale" boards.

COUNTING THE BUCKS

Among the beneficiaries of this global glut were dynamic producers with the skills required to create instant wine brands. The most dramatic example of this trend was an Australian wine called Yellow Tail (or [yellow tail] to be precise) which was launched exclusively in the US, with the ambition of selling 25,000 cases over the first 12 months. In the event, more than a million dozen bottles were bought that year and sales are now 150 times faster than was originally predicted. Yellow Tail sells for between five and eight dollars. Another success is on offer for rather less.

The story that galvanized most Californian winemakers and vendors in 2003 concerned a locally produced wine called Charles F. Shaw which carried a price tag (in that state) of $1.99 per bottle and an instantly-adopted nickname of "Two-Buck Chuck". Despite the fact that it could only be bought from one chain – Vinegar Joe's which has 100 stores in the state – the bargain-basement bottles flew off the shelves at an unprecedented rate. Over a million dozen were sold in December alone, often by customers who loaded 10 or 12 cases at a time into their RVs.

The Two-Buck Chuck phenomenon so impressed the California wine industry's leading analyst, Jon Frederikson, that he named Bronco Winery of the Year at the annual United Wine & Grape Symposium – to the evident discomfort of most of the 1,000 members of the audience.

Sauvignon grapes in New Zealand.

One reason for their annoyance was the fact that, despite being made from cheap grapes grown in the San Joaquin Valley, the Charles F. Shaw wine legally bears a Napa Valley label – because that's where Bronco bottles it. As a point of comparison, the average retail price of Cabernet Sauvignon that genuinely has been produced from Napa Valley grapes was calculated in 2003 at $52. There is a growing call for California to introduce appellation laws that offer consumers a clearer notion of precisely what they are getting when they pick up a bottle of wine.

FRENCH CRIES

Mind you, those are the kinds of rules that some would claim are currently acting like a millstone around the neck of France's winegrowers. In 2003 they saw their share of the global market fall almost everywhere, with sales to the UK, in particular, falling behind those of Australia. Reliable weather, and a readiness to cut prices and create new brands, are only part of the advantage the wine producers of North America and the Southern Hemisphere enjoy, however. By sourcing grapes and wines from throughout large parts of their countries, they can, like manufacturers of ketchup and soap powder, satisfy a rising demand for their wine. Yellow Tail bears a "South East Australia" appellation: the grapes from which it was made could have been grown in 90% of Australia's vineyards. New Zealanders are currently drinking blends of local and Chilean Sauvignon Blanc, following a frost-hit harvest in their own vineyards. In Europe, any such blending is traditionally frowned upon. So how are the Europeans reacting? Italy and Spain are both looking at ways to fight back, with the latter country creating a big new Catalunya appellation that will make it easier to produce large quantities of branded wine, and a relaxation of once-strict rules governing the irrigation and the varieties of grapes that are used in classic areas. Cabernet Sauvignon is, for example, now quietly accepted as an ingredient in Rioja. France, however, in this as in other matters, is stubbornly marching to the beat of its own drum. Plans to launch a national *Cépage de France* designation were quietly buried under political pressure from winegrowers in Southern France.

THE TURN OF THE SCREW

As was predicted in these pages last year, dissatisfaction with faulty natural corks continued to grow among wine producers. Of the 12,000 bottles opened at the International Wine Challenge, no fewer than 4.9% were tainted by faulty corks. While synthetic corks still have their fans, screwcaps are rapidly being adopted as the most reliable way to seal wine bottles – partly thanks to impressive recent tastings of Yalumba's Australian Rieslings with screwcaps from the 1970s and 1980s. In New Zealand, a screwcap-sealed 2001 Pinot Noir from Villa Maria took the top award at the annual Air New Zealand competition; and, in California, the Napa Wine Co., which bottles wines for boutique producers such as Pahlmeyer and Bryant Family, announced that it was installing a screwcap bottling line – while another supporter, Randall Grahm of Bonny Doon, held a funeral for the cork. More significantly, in Europe, the Spanish producer Torres, Paul Blanck in Alsace, and Michel Laroche in Chablis all now offer classic wines with screwcaps. Meanwhile, the cork manufacturers are simultaneously doing their best to play down the incidence of taint and claiming that new techniques would do away with it completely. Nobody is holding their breath.

Some of the 12,000 bottles that were tasted at the International Wine Challenge (see page 263). Nearly one in every 20 of these wines was spoiled by a moldy cork.

Personal Choice

This is a quirky list of wines out of the thousands I have tasted at the *International Wine Challenge,* and elsewhere, this year. Prices are rounded off to the nearest dollar. Stocks are often limited, so it is likely that, in some cases, the vintage mentioned may become unavailable during the lifetime of this guide. Prices will vary between retailers and between states. For stockists, try *www.wine-searcher.com*

REDS FOR DAILY DRINKING

Echeverria Family Reserve Cabernet Sauvignon 1999, Chile ($8)
Chile now offers some of the best-value wine in the world, and no style works better here than Cabernet, which can deliver extraordinary pure blackcurrant fruit. This is a perfect example, and very more-ish.

Bodegas Fontana Fontal Tempranillo Roble 2001, La Mancha ($8)
The region of La Mancha used to be better known for Don Quixote and windmills than good wine, but it's now a place to watch for richly intense wines like this raspberryish blend of the local Tempranillo, Cabernet, Merlot, and Syrah.

Ravenswood Lodi Zinfandel 2000, Lodi, California ($15) Lodi is part of the Central Valley that is usually associated with cheap, basic wine, but it doesn't have to be. Zinfandel-specialists Ravenswood shows what can be done here. Intense, ripe juicy, and delicious.

Grand'Arte Red 2000, Estremadura, Portugal ($15) The long-predicted Portuguese wine revolution has finally begun – with wine like this intense, plummy, tobaccoey modern spin on traditional grapes.

Domaine de Vougeraie, En Bollery Terres d'En Face, Bourgogne Grand Ordinaire 2000, Burgundy, France ($12) The "*Grand*" in "*Grand Ordinaire*" traditionally means "very", but this wine, made by Canadian Pascal Marchand, is anything but ordinary. It's an unusual spicy, berryish, lightly oaky version of Beaujolais Gamay grape.

EDS FOR SPECIAL OCCASIONS

Felton Road Block 5 Pinot Noir 2001, Central Otago, New Zealand ($25) This mountainous part of New Zealand's South Island arguably now makes the best New World Pinot Noir. Great, raspberryish, complex wine that's (happily) sealed with a screwcap.

Ridge Geyserville 2000, Sonoma, California ($25) Still one of the bargains of the California wine scene, and I make no apology for including it. Quintessential Zinfandel, with poetic, spicy character and velvety texture.

Quinta do Crasto Douro Touriga Nacional 2001, Douro, Portugal ($17) This small estate uses grapes that would once have gone into port to produce top-class table wine. Australian-style winemaking + Portuguese grapes = excitingly classy, tobaccoey wine.

Familia Zuccardi Q Tempranillo 2001, Mendoza, Argentina ($50) I thought this intense, strawberryish wine was a top-class modern Spanish wine (of which there are now plenty). Impeccably made, and both rich and stylish. Worth keeping.

Sadie Family Columella 2000, Swartland, South Africa ($35) Eben Sadie grew famous at the pioneering *Spice Route*. Now he's running his own *garage* winery and making ripe, smoky, peppery, beryish *Shiraz/Syrah* to put many examples from the Rhône to shame.

Masi Costasera Amarone Classico 1999, Veneto, Italy ($30) One of the most classic wine styles in the world – from one of the most accomplished producers. Raisiny, intense and very, very complex. Drink with good parmesan or cheddar.

Penfolds Grange 1998, South Australia ($200) Mediocre vintages of Australia's ultra-cult win are rare, but so are truly great ones like this. Ludicrously expensive; extraordinary intense, peppery wine that's packed with complex dark-fruit flavors. Drink in at least a decade.

Erraruziz Vinedo Chadwick 2000, Chile ($45) I tasted this recently-launched wine "blind" against top Bordeaux of the same vintage. When the wines were unveiled, the Médoc won on points – just – but I mistook the Chadwick for Chateau Margaux. What more can I say?

E&J Durand Cornas 2000, Rhône, France ($40) Cornas is many Northern Rhône fans' favorite village. The steep slopes here produce wonderful intense blackcurranty/peppery wines like this example – which has also benefited by some contact with spicy oak.

Leonetti Cellars Cabernet Sauvignon 2000, Washington State, USA ($50) Leonetti are long-established Cabernet-kings in Washington State, and this is a first class, complex wine with gorgeous berry fruit. Leave for five years or so to appreciate at its best.

WHITES FOR DAILY DRINKING

Clos d'Yvigne, Bergerac Blanc, Cuvée Nicholas 2000, Southwest France ($17) Bergerac uses the same grapes as Bordeaux to produce the same styles of wine at a lower price. Wines like this peachy, kiwi-fruity, subtly-oaked *Semillon-Sauvignon* blend from British-born Patricia Atkinson deserve to develop a reputation for themselves.

Bonterra Roussanne 2002, Mendocino, California ($12) This organic wine from the north of California is made from a grape variety more usually associated with the Southern Rhône. Spicy and floral, with just the right amount of oak. Drink with a dish prepared with ginger.

Houghton Verdelho 2002, Western Australia ($12) Curiously, nobody apart from the Australians seems to have explored the unfortified potential of this grape. When it is not subjected to the winemaking techniques of Madeira, it produces terrific, refreshing, limey stuff.

Albariño Martín Códax 2002, Rias Baixas, Spain ($13) This corner of northwest Spain is still the source of the most interesting whites. Stylish, peachy-appley wine with a deliciously creamy texture.

Michel Laroche Chablis 2002, Burgundy, France ($17) A perfect alternative to oaky Chardonnay – and a reminder of how this grape can taste when the flavor comes from the minerals in the soil rather than the barrel in which the wine was aged. Appley, stony, and rich.

Borgo deio Vassalli, Pinot Grigio, Isonzo dei Friuli 2002, Italy ($13) Italian Pinot Grigio is very fashionable at the moment. Sadly, far too many examples are dull and flavorless and only popular because they are an alternative to oaky Chardonnay. This creamy, peary example is an exception to that disappointing rule. Delicious and very Italian.

Vergelegen Sauvignon Blanc, 2002 Stellenbosch, South Africa ($11) Vergelegen's reds are terrific, but so is this gooseberryish-minerally example of a white grape that is making a home for itself in the Cape.

Gentilini Robolla 2001, Cephalonia, Greece ($6) Evidence of the exciting developments now to be found in the most ancient wine regions of the world. Fresh, lemony-limey flavors are impeccably supported by characterful mineral notes.

Domaine Caillaubert Chardonnay-Sauvignon Blanc, Vin de Pays des Côtes de Gascogne 2000, Southwest France. ($8) The – to traditionalists in France – curious notion of blending the grapes of Burgundy and the Loire pays off well with this fresh, appley-tropical wine.

Hazendal Wooded Chenin Blanc 2001, South Africa ($13) Controversial in South Africa, where the oak is thought to remove "varietal character", this wine impressed me hugely when I tasted it "blind" at the Swiss Wine Awards Competition there. Terrific, appley, toasty, and rich.

WHITES FOR SPECIAL OCCASIONS

Simi Russian River Reserve Chardonnay, Sonoma, California 1998 ($25) The Simi winery first gained fame with stylish efforts produced by former Mondavi winemaker, Zelma Long. It still offers surprisingly fairly priced wines like this Chardonnay that deserve credit for subtlety. Nutty and Burgundian, with just enough oak.

Franz Künstler Hochheimer Kirchenstück Riesling Auslese Trocken, Rheingau, Germany 2001 ($24) Franz Künstler was a pioneer producer of dry Rieslings in the Rheingau, but unlike most of his neighbors who, all too often, bottled seeringly acidic wines, he has always made ripe wines with rich, complex, appley-grapey flavors.

Monte Schiavo Verdicchio dei Castelli di Jesi Classico Riserva "Le Giuncare" 2000, Marche, Italy ($22) Classy Verdichio deserves to be better known. This is creamy and nutty, but with some tremendous wild herbs and floral character. Very complex wine.

Freie Weingärtner Wachau, Grüner Veltliner ($30) A set of Grüner Veltliners recently outclassed some top white Burgundies. This subtle, rich, white-plummy example gets my vote as a Puligny-beater.

Cuilleron la Petite Côte Condrieu 2001, Rhône, France ($40) In 2002 I was invited to take part in the first international Viognier Symposium at Yalumba, in South Australia. There were some great examples of this curious grape, but no producer outclassed Yves Cuilleron, producer of this glorious peachy-apricotty wine.

Picardy Chardonnay, Pemberton, Western Australia ($25) Picardy is best known for its Pinot Noir; my vote, though, goes to this Chablis-like wine which is one of the subtlest examples of the Chardonnay grape I have tasted in the New World.

Muré Clos St Landelin, Gewurztraminer Vendanges Tardives 2000, Alsace, France ($25Y) Vendanges Tardives might make you – reasonably – imagine a lusciously sweety wine. This, though, is dry enough to enjoy with spicy food. Exotically full of lychee flavor, but far less blowsy than many examples of this variety.

Pavillon Blanc du Château Margaux 2001, Bordeaux, France ($35) Technically, this is a humble Bordeaux Blanc, but there's nothing humble about the complex layers of peachy-peary flavor and the stony notes that support them. It's still quite oaky, and needs time, but it's so delicious that most bottles will probably be enjoyed in their youth.

Pierre Labet, Beaune les Mosnières 2001, Burgundy, France ($20) White Beaune is a rarity, and worth looking out for when there is a good example like this on offer. Pure pineapple and hazelnut Chardonnay character, with some mineral backbone.

SPARKLING WINES AND ROSÉ

Schramsberg Blanc de Noirs, Méthode Traditionelle 1994, Napa, California. ($20) This Napa Valley winery is one of the oldest in California – and one of the longest-established producers of Champagne-style fizz (their first Blanc de Noirs was a 1967!). This is rich, ripe, chocolatey wine with plenty of Pinot Noir character.

De Venoge Brut Select Cordon Bleu, France ($22) De Venoge is not a name that is well known among Champagne drinkers, but it's one to look out for. Great value, rich wine with the brioche flavor, lacking in other sparkling wines.

Dom Ruinart Rosé 1988, France ($75) Pink Champagne is too often associated with chorus girl's slippers, but at its best, it is very serious wine. Billecart Salmon, Roederer, and Dom Pérignon all make good examples, but this is my favorite at the moment. Raspberries, cherries, and toast. Drink with food instead of a red or a white wine.

Charles Heidsieck Champagne Charlie Blanc de Blancs 1982, France ($90) There are plenty of horribly expensive Champagnes on the market, but this 20-year-old example has a mature, nutty, praline biscuity character that only comes with age.

Seppelts Salinger 2000, Australia ($16) Back on form after a disappointing patch, this pioneering Aussie fizz is a delicious creamy mouthful, with just enough pineappley fruit.

Deutz Blanc de Blancs 1999, New Zealand ($18) A great, rich, slightly tropically-fruity, dry, pure Chardonnay, produced by the giant Montana in association with the Champagne house Deutz.

ROSÉ

Fetzer Valley Oaks Syrah Rose 2002, California ($9) This is the second year in a row that I've included this wine, but it deserves to be here; good New World rosé is so rare. This is dry, peppery, wild-berryish, and very refreshing. Rush to find a bottle.

Château de Flaugergues Cuvée Sélection Rosé 2002, Coteaux de Languedoc, France ($12) The Coteaux de Languedoc is developing a reputation for its reds, but it is also beginning to show Provence how it should be making pink wines. This is classily packaged wine with a lovely fresh, spicy character and the pepper of the *Grenache*.

Chateau du Seuil Bordeaux Rosé 2002, France ($12) Drawing off some partly-made Bordeaux before it has had the chance to extract all of the color from the grape skins, simultaneously helps to produce richer red wine and tasty, plummy-blackcurrant rosé like this.

SWEET AND FORTIFIED WINES

Horst Sauer Scherndorfer Lump Riesling Trockenbeerenauslese, 2002 Franken, Germany ($70)   Franken is best known for traditionally-shaped bottles of earthy *Silvaner*. The Sauer estate makes great wines from that grape – and this terrific, honeyed, pure Riesling.

Weinlaubenhof Kracher Chardonnay No 7, 2000, Austria ($32) Late-harvest Chardonnay is a true oddity, and making one takes true care and skill. Alois Kracher is a master-craftsman who contrives to produce a wonderfully luscious, seductive wine that still maintains the pineapple and hazelnut character of this variety.

Clos Dady Sauternes 2001, Bordeaux, France ($28)   Source of one of the more curiously-named sweet wines in Bordeaux (how can I resist refering to "sugar-dady"), this small estate is also one of the most interesting. Creamily honeyed, apricotty, and truly delicious.

Disznoko Tokaji 5 Puttonyos Aszi 1998 ($28)   Tokaji is still the only Hungarian wine to attract a following in other countries. This example is produced by an offshoot of the giant AXA insurance company, and made with the same care as its Pichon Longueville wines in Bordeaux. Intense, dried apricots, and mangoes.

Saussignac AC Chateau Grinou 2001, Southwest France ($20 - 37.5cl)   Monbazillac was once the poor neighbor of Sauternes, and little Saussignac was one step lower on the ladder. But to prove that's no longer the case, try this extraordinary rich but fresh wine that combines apricot and passion fruit. Beautifully made.

FORTIFIED

Martinez Vintage Port 2000, Douro, Portugal ($40)   Once a label that was used by a bigger port house for less exciting wine, Martinez has now been ushered into the spotlight. Truly classy vintage, plum-and-mulberryish, port that stands comparison with the biggest names.

Hidalgo Very Old Dry Amontillado, Jerez, Spain ($35)   Hidalgo is a star in the sherry firmament, and this delicious nutty wine is everything sherry can be. Drink with the very best olives you can find.

De Bortoli Show Liqueur Muscat, Australia ($15)   Most of Australia's fortified Muscats come from Rutherglen in Victoria. This grapey pruney, Christmas Puddingy effort is from the less exhalted Riverina.

Cantine Florio Targa Marsala Riserva 1996, Sardinia, Italy ($20) Good Marsala is a rarity; most examples of this style are reserved for the kitchen. But the Florio estate makes extraordinary complex, raisiny examples for luxuriant sipping.

Wine on the Web

NET WORKING

At the beginning of 2003, residents of South Carolina were forbidden to get themselves tattooed and to ship in a bottle of wine from another state for their personal consumption. By the middle of the year, the rules on wine-shipments had been relaxed, and efforts were being made to loosen the rules on body-decoration. Interestingly, the lawyer leading the fight for the tattooees has now been taken on by the wine lobby to liberalize inter-state wine shipments. And to judge by his record on another famous case, he doesn't give up easily: His name is Ken Starr. Wine producers and retailers throughout the nation are watching Starr's efforts closely. If he succeeds, a larger number of US citizens will, like their counterparts in most of Europe and Australia, be able to order wine online from a source hundreds of miles away. The implications for the wine market are huge. Where inter-state ship-

Wine-searcher.com – does for wine drinkers what google.com does for users of the rest of the web.

ping begins, a breakdown in the old three-tier system that prevents retailers from importing wine directly could well follow. Even if that is a long way off, it is highly likely that Wal Mart, which has only just gotten into selling wine, will follow the lead of its European counterpart Tesco, the world's biggest online grocer. Europeans now increasingly order their wine over the net, along with their detergent and their dogfood. And Wal Mart's European subsidiaries are busily learning how things are done over there.

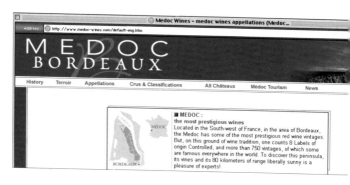

Traditional regions have learned to exploit the new medium.

For the moment specialist online retailers, like *wine.com*, are facing increasing competition from the combined efforts of established terrestial stockists and one of the most useful sites on the net, *winesearcher.com*, which will tell you precisely where to find almost any of the wines listed in the A-Z section of this *Guide*.

If *winesearcher* serves as a *google* for wine lovers, *winebid.com* is undoubtedly the *Ebay* of the finer wine world, especially now that it has broadened its scope to offer a wider range of classic Old World wines to go with all those cult Californians.

The early chat-rooms are still there – led by Robin Garr's veteran *wineloverspage.com* – but they have now been joined by news-based sites such as *wineblog.blogspot.com*. The free magazine content that was once offered online by wine retailers has now been replaced by a growing number of genuine magazines and subscription newsletters, led by *winespectator.com* and *decanter.com*, *Wine International*'s new *wineint.com* (with which I am associated), *erobertparker.com*, *jancisrobinson.com*, and Steve Tanzer's excellent *wineaccess.com*. And if these were not enough, countless wine regions, from the Médoc to the Napa Valley now have an informative presence online. Happy surfing!

News and views at wineblog.blogspot.com

For recommended websites, see page 395.

Tasting and Buying

SPOILED WITH CHOICES

Buying wine today has often become just like buying a gallon of paint. Just as the manufacturer's helpful chart can be daunting with its endless shades of subtly different white, the number of bottles and the information available on the supermarket shelves can make you want to give up and reach for the one that is most familiar, or most favorably priced.

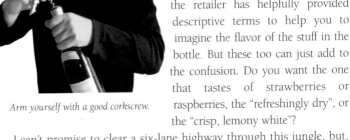

Arm yourself with a good corkscrew.

If you're not a wine buff, why should you know the differences in flavor between wines made from the same grape in Meursault in France, Mendocino in California, and Maipo in Chile? Often, the retailer has helpfully provided descriptive terms to help you to imagine the flavor of the stuff in the bottle. But these too can just add to the confusion. Do you want the one that tastes of strawberries or raspberries, the "refreshingly dry", or the "crisp, lemony white"?

I can't promise to clear a six-lane highway through this jungle, but, with luck, I will give you a path to follow when you are choosing a wine, and one from which you can confidently stray.

THE LABEL

Wine labels should always reveal the country where the wine was produced (see page 24,) and possibly the region and grape variety (see page 48) from which it was made. Both region and grape, however, offer only partial guidance as to what you are likely to find when you pull the cork.

Bear in mind the following:

1 Official terms such as Appellation Contrôlée, Grand or Premier Cru, Qualitätswein, and Reserva are often as trustworthy as official statements by politicians.

2 Unofficial terms such as Réserve Personnelle and Vintner's Selection are, likewise, as trustworthy as unofficial statements by the producer of any other commodity.

3 Knowing where a wine comes from is often like knowing where a person was born; it provides no guarantee of how good the wine will be. Nor how it will have been made (though there are often local rules.) There will be nothing to tell you, for instance, whether a Chablis is oaky, nor whether an Alsace or Vouvray is sweet.

4 "Big name" regions don't always make better wine than supposedly lesser ones. Cheap Bordeaux is far worse than similarly priced wine from Bulgaria.

5 Don't expect wines from the same grape variety to taste the same: a South African Chardonnay may taste drier than one from California. The flavor and style will depend on the climate, soil, and producer.

6 Just because a producer makes a good wine in one place, don't trust him, or her, to make other good wines, either there or elsewhere. The team at Lafite Rothschild produces less classy Los Vascos wines in Chile; Robert Mondavi's inexpensive Woodbridge wines bear no relation to the quality of his Reserve wines from Napa.

7 The fact that there is a château on a wine label has no bearing on the quality of the contents.

8 Nor does the boast that the wine is bottled at that château.

9 Nineteenth-century medals look pretty on a label; they say nothing about the quality of the 20th- or 21st-century stuff in the bottle.

10 Price provides some guidance to a wine's quality: a very expensive bottle may be appalling, but it's unlikely that a very cheap one will be better than basic.

A WAY WITH WORDS

Before going any further, I'm afraid that there's no alternative to returning to the thorny question of the language you are going to use to describe your impressions.

When Washington Irving visited Bordeaux 170 years ago, he noted that Château Margaux was "a wine of fine flavor – but not of equal body." Lafite on the other hand had "less flavor than the former but more body – an equality of flavor and body." Latour, well, that had "more body than flavor." He may have been a great writer, but he was evidently not the ideal person to describe the individual flavors of great Bordeaux.

Michelangelo was more poetic, writing that the wine of San Gimignano "kisses, licks, bites, thrusts, and stings...". Modern pundits say wines have "gobs of fruit" and taste of "kumquats and suede." Each country and generation comes up with its own vocabulary. Some descriptions, such as the likening to gooseberry of wines made from Sauvignon Blanc, can be justified by scientific analysis, which confirms that the same aromatic chemical compound is found in the fruit and wine.

Then there are straightforward descriptions. Wines can be fresh or stale, clean or dirty. If they are acidic, or overly full of tannin, they will be "hard"; a "soft" wine, by contrast, might be easier to drink, but boring.

There are other less evocative terms. While a watery wine is "dilute" or "thin," a subtle one is "elegant." A red or white whose flavor is hard to discern is described as "dumb." Whatever the style of a wine, it should have "balance." A sweet white, for example, needs enough acidity to keep it from cloying. No one will enjoy a wine that is too fruity, too dry, too oaky, or too anything for long.

The flavor that lingers in your mouth long after you have swallowed or spat it out is known as the "finish." Wines whose flavor – pleasant or unpleasant – hangs around, are described as "long"; those whose flavor disappears quickly are "short."

Finally, there is "complex," the word that is used to justify why one wine costs 10 times more than another. A complex wine is like a well-scored symphony, while a simpler one could be compared to a melody picked out on a single instrument.

TASTING

Wine tasting is surrounded by mystery and mystique. But it shouldn't be – because all it really consists of is paying attention to the stuff in the glass, whether you're in the formal environment of a wine tasting or drinking the house white in your local bar. The key questions are: do you like the wine? And is it a good example of what it claims to be? Champagne costs a lot more than basic Spanish Cava, so it should taste recognizably different. Some do, some don't.

See

The look of a wine can tell you a lot. Assuming that it isn't cloudy (which if it is, send it back,) it will reveal its age and hint at the grape and origin. Some grapes, like Burgundy's Pinot Noir, make naturally paler wines than, say, Bordeaux's Cabernet Sauvignon; wines from warmer regions have deeper colors. Tilt the glass away from you over a piece of white paper and look at the rim of the liquid. The more watery and brown it is, the older the wine (Beaujolais Nouveau will be pure violet.)

Swirl

Vigorously swirl the wine around the glass for a moment or so to release any reluctant and characteristic smells.

Sniff

You sniff a wine before tasting it for the same reason that you sniff a carton of milk before pouring its contents into coffee. The smell can tell you more about a wine than anything else. If you don't believe me, try tasting anything while holding your nose, or while you've got a cold. When sniffing, take one long sniff or a few brief ones. Concentrate on whether the wine seems fresh and clean, and on any smells that indicate how it is likely to taste.

What are your first impressions? Is the wine fruity, and, if so, which fruit does it remind you of? Does it have the vanilla smell of a wine that has been fermented and/or matured in new oak barrels? Is it spicy? Or herbaceous? Sweet or dry? Rich or lean?

Sip

Take a small mouthful and – this takes practice – suck air between your teeth and through the liquid. Look in a mirror while you're doing this: if your mouth looks like a cat's bottom and sounds like a child trying to suck the last few drops of Coke through a straw, then you're doing it right. Hold the wine in your mouth for a little longer to release as much of its flavor as possible.

Focus on the flavor. Ask yourself the same questions about whether it tastes sweet, dry, fruity, spicy, herbaceous. Is there just one flavor, or do several contribute to a "complex" overall effect?

Now concentrate on the texture of the wine. Some – like Chardonnay – are mouth-coatingly buttery, while others – like Gewürztraminer – are almost oily. Muscadet is a good example of a wine with a texture that is closer to that of water.

A brief look, then swirl the wine around the glass to release the aromas.

Does the wine smell fresh and inviting? Simple or complex?

Reds, too, vary in texture; some seem tough and tannic enough to make the inside of one cheek want to kiss the inside of the other. Tannin is necessary for a wine's longevity, but winemakers now distinguish between the harsh tannin and the "fine" (non-aggressive) tannin of wine carefully made from ripe grapes. A modern Bordeaux often has as much tannin as old-fashioned examples – but is far easier to taste and drink.

Spit

The only reason to spit a wine out – unless it is actively repellent – is to remain upright at the end of a lengthy tasting. On the other hand, if what you want is the taste, swallowing is an indulgence; you should have had 90 percent of the flavor while the wine was in your mouth. Some tasters swallow a few drops to experience the texture as the wine passes down the throat.

Pause for a moment or two after spitting the wine out. Is the flavor still there? How does what you are experiencing now compare with the taste you had in your mouth? Some wines have an unpleasant aftertaste; others have flavors that linger deliciously in the mouth.

SHOULD I SEND IT BACK?

Wines are subject to all kinds of faults, though far less than they were.

Acid

All wines, like all fruit and vegetables, contain a certain amount of acidity. Without it they would taste flabby and dull and rapidly go stale. Wines made from unripe grapes will, however, taste unpalatably "green" and like unripe apples or plums – or like chewing stalky leaves or grass.

Bitter

Bitterness is quite different. On occasion, especially in Italy, a touch of bitterness may even be an integral part of a wine's character, as in the case of Amarone. Of course, the Italians like Campari too.

Brettanomyces (Brett)

Bacteria in cellars can infect red wine in particular with "mousey," Band-aid-like, stable-floory, and metallic smells and flavors. "Brett" is suprisingly common and, in low concentration, can add complexity. It is also a – deliberate – feature of lambic ale.

Cloudy

Wine should be transparent. The only excuse for cloudiness is in a wine like an old Burgundy whose deposit has been shaken up.

Corked

Ignore cork crumbs on the surface of a wine. Corked wines are tainted by a chemical called trichloranisole – TCA – in concentrations as small as a few drops in a swimming pool. Badly tainted wines smell horribly mouldy; the flavor of faintly spoiled examples are merely flattened. All get worse with exposure to air. At least 5 percent of wines are corked. Stoppers made from tiny fragments of cork also give a taint of their own.

Crystals

Not a fault: fine white crystals at the bottom of the bottle are simply tartrates that fall naturally.

Maderized/Oxidized

Madeira is fortified wine that has been intentionally exposed to the air and heated in an oven. A maderized wine has been accidentally subjected to warmth and air. Oxidized refers to wine that has been exposed to the air – or made from grapes that have cooked in the sun. The taste is reminiscent of poor sherry or vinegar – or both.

Sulfur (SO_2/H_2S)

Sulfur dioxide is routinely used as a protection against bacteria that would oxidize (*qv*) a wine. In excess, sulfur dioxide may make you cough or sneeze. Worse, though, is hydrogen sulfide and mercaptans, its associated sulfur compounds, which are created when sulfur dioxide combines with wine. Wines with hydrogen sulfide smell of rotten eggs, while mercaptans may reek of rancid garlic or burning rubber. Aeration or popping a copper coin in your glass may clear up these characteristics.

Vinegary/Volatile

Volatile acidity is present in all wines. In excess, however – usually the result of careless winemaking – what can be a pleasant component (like a touch of balsamic vinegar in a sauce) tastes downright vinegary.

Reading the Label

INTRODUCTION

Labels are an essential part of the business of wine nowadays, but a century ago they barely existed. Wine was sold by the barrel and served by the jug or decanter. Indeed, the original "labels" were silver tags that hung on a chain around the neck of a decanter and were engraved with the word "claret," "hock," "port," or whatever.

Today, printed labels are required to tell you the amount of liquid in the bottle, its strength, where it was made, and the name of the producer or importer. Confusingly, though, labeling rules vary between countries and between regions. Labels may also reveal a wine's style – the grape variety, oakiness, or sweetness, for example. And lastly, they are part of the packaging that helps to persuade you to buy one wine rather than another. The following examples should help you through the maze.

CHAMPAGNE

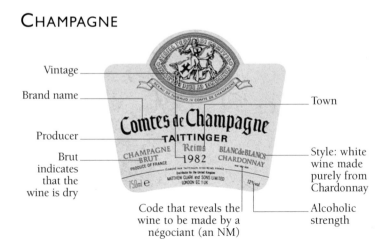

Vintage

Brand name

Producer

Brut indicates that the wine is dry

Town

Style: white wine made purely from Chardonnay

Alcoholic strength

Code that reveals the wine to be made by a négociant (an NM)

WHITES

Alcoholic strength

Producer

Region

Volume of contents

Address of importer

Brand

Grape variety

State of origin

One of more than 50 individual vineyards granted superior status

Region

Village

Appellation

Grape variety

Rich, sweet "botrytised" wine from specially selected grapes

Vintage

Producer

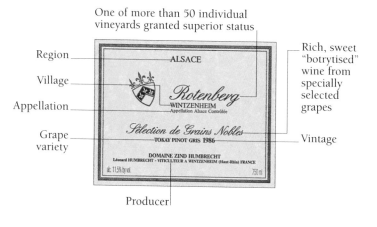

Town/ Region

Year firm was founded

Vineyard

Village

Quality level

Region

Producer

Vintage

Grape

Sweetness

Volume of contents

Official identity number

REDS

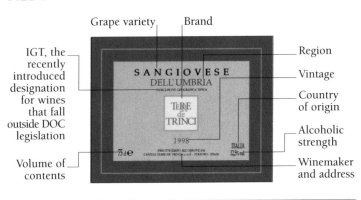

Grape variety Brand

IGT, the recently introduced designation for wines that fall outside DOC legislation

Region

Vintage

Country of origin

Alcoholic strength

Winemaker and address

Volume of contents

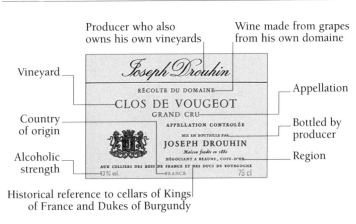

Producer who also owns his own vineyards

Wine made from grapes from his own domaine

Vineyard

Appellation

Country of origin

Bottled by producer

Alcoholic strength

Region

Historical reference to cellars of Kings of France and Dukes of Burgundy

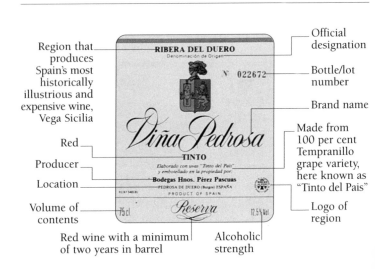

Region that produces Spain's most historically illustrious and expensive wine, Vega Sicilia

Official designation

Bottle/lot number

Brand name

Red

Producer

Made from 100 per cent Tempranillo grape variety, here known as "Tinto del Pais"

Location

Logo of region

Volume of contents

Red wine with a minimum of two years in barrel

Alcoholic strength

SWEET AND FORTIFIED

Paste made from "nobly-rotten" grapes

Producer

Wine name

A *puttonyo* is the "hod" of Aszú sweet grape paste used to sweeten tokaji – the number of puttonyos indicates the sweetness of the wine

Producer's crest

Country of origin

Volume of contents – smaller than standard wine bottle size

Alcoholic strength

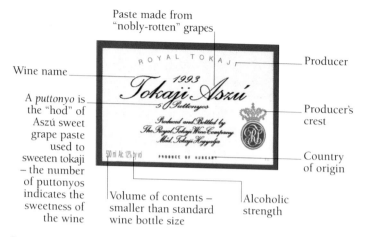

Style of sherry, Old Amontillado

Producer's crest

Producer

Produced and bottled in principal sherry town, Jerez

Brand name

Producer

"Traditional" means "unfiltered," like real vintage port. Other late bottled vintage is filtered so as to remove the need for decanting

History and credentials of producer

Vintage

LBV ports bottled 4 to 6 years after the vintage (rather than 2 for vintage port)

Unlike "tawny," which is matured in barrels

Bottling date – obligatory for LBV labels

Alcoholic strength

Company's name and address

Volume of contents

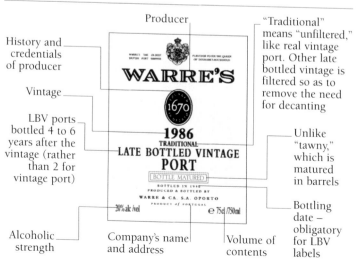

Countries

WHERE IN THE WORLD?

Whatever the grape variety, climate, and traditions, the local tastes of the place where a wine is made still largely dictate its style. Let's take a whirlwind tour of the most significant winemaking nations. (For more information on grapes, terms, and regions, see the A–Z, starting on page 97.)

AUSTRALIA

Reading the label: Late harvest/noble harvest – *sweet*. Show Reserve – *top-of-the-line wine, usually with more oak.* Tokay – *Australian name for the Muscadelle grape, used for rich liqueur wines.* Verdelho – *Madeira grape used for limy, dry wines.* Mataro – *Mourvèdre.* Shiraz – *Syrah.* Tarrango – *local success story – fresh, fruity, and Beaujolais-like.*

In recent years, Australian wines have overtaken those of France in several markets, including Britain, Ireland and the US. Quite an achievement for a country whose viticultural efforts were once the butt of a memorable Monty Python sketch – but not very surprising, given the Australians' 25-year master plan to dominate the global market for premium wine.

There are various explanations for Australia's success. The cooperation, competitiveness and open-mindedness of its producers has been crucial. Where else would almost a complete region like the Clare Valley decide, for quality reasons, to switch from natural corks to screwcaps? Just as important has been the readiness to explore and exploit new regions like Orange, Robe, Mount Benson, Young and Pemberton – and styles – such as Cabernet-Shiraz blends. Also invaluable has been the creation of a single regional appellation for South-East Australia that covers over 90 percent of the nation's vineyards and makes blending of large-volume branded wines like Yellow Tail and Bin 65 remarkably easy. A more controversial factor has to be the power of a quartet of giant companies –

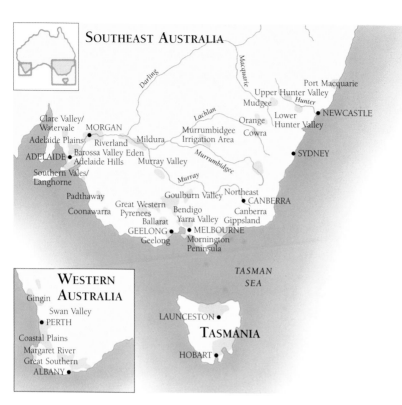

BRL Hardy, Mildara Blass, Orlando and Southcorp that collectively control over 75 percent of the country's wines.

AUSTRIA

Reading the label: Ausbruch – *late-harvested, between BA and TBA.* DAC (Districtus Austria Controllatus) – *denominated region.* Schilfwein/Strohwein – *made from dried grapes.* Smaragd – *Wachau wine with more than 12% alcohol.*

The source of wonderful late harvest wines, dry whites (especially Grüner-Veltliner), and increasingly impressive reds (St Laurent). Names to look out for include Kracher, Pichler and Willi Opitz.

CANADA

Reading the label: VQA (Vintners Quality Alliance) – *local designation seeking to guarantee quality and local provenance.*

Icewines, made from grapes picked when frozen on the vine, are the stars here, though Chardonnays and Cabernet Francs are improving fast. Okanagan in British Columbia seems to be the region to watch.

EASTERN EUROPE
After a bright start in the 1980's, the Eastern European wine industry is still coming to terms with life under capitalism surprisingly slowly.

Bulgaria
The pioneer of good Iron Curtain reds, Bulgaria remains a source of inexpensive Cabernet Sauvignon and Merlot, as well as the earthy local Mavrud. Efforts to produce premium wines have yet to pay off.

Hungary
Hungary's strongest hand today lies in the Tokajis, some of the best of which are being made by foreign investors. Already improving reds (especially from Villány and Eger) will be boosted by the arrival of Antinori from Italy. Also, look out for bargains from Hilltop Neszmély.

Romania, Moldova, and Former Yugoslavia
Still struggling to make a mark beyond their own borders with better than basic fare. Romania has inexpensive Pinot Noir, Moldova produces aromatic white and Croatia and Slovenia can offer interesting reds from local varieties.

ENGLAND AND WALES
Vineyards here are using recently developed German grape varieties to make Loire-style whites; high-quality late harvest wines; quirky reds produced under plastic poly-tunnels; and – most particularly – sparkling wines that win well-earned medals at the International Wine Challenge.

FRANCE

Reading the label: Appellation Contrôlée (or AOC) – *designation covering France's (supposedly) better wines.* Blanc de Blancs/Noirs – *white wine made from white/black grapes.* Cave – *cellar.* Cave des Vignerons de – *usually a cooperative.* Cépage – *grape variety.* Château – *wine estate.* Chêne – *oak barrels, as in* Fûts de Chêne. Clos – *(historically) walled vineyard.* Côte(s)/Coteaux – *hillside.* Crémant – *sparkling.* Cuvée – *a specific blend.* Demi-sec – *medium sweet.* Domaine – *wine estate.* Doux – *sweet.* Grand Cru – *higher quality, or specific vineyards.* Gris – *pale rosé, as in* Vin Gris. Jeunes Vignes – *young vines (often ineligible for* Appellation Contrôlée). Méthode Classique – *used to indicate the Champagne method of making sparkling wine.* Millésime – *year or vintage.* Mis en Bouteille au Château/Domaine – *bottled at the estate.* Moelleux – *sweet.* Monopole – *a vineyard owned by a single producer.* Mousseux – *sparkling.* Négociant (Eleveur) – *a merchant who buys, matures, bottles, and sells wine.*

Pétillant – *lightly sparkling*. Premier Cru – *"first growth", a quality designation that varies from area to area*. Propriétaire (Récoltant) – *vineyard owner/manager*. Réserve (Personelle) – *legally meaningless phrase*. Sur Lie – *aged on the lees (dead yeast)*. VDQS (Vin Délimité de Qualité Supérieur) – *"soon-to-be-abolished" official designation for wines that are better than* Vin de Pays *but not good enough for* Appellation Contrôlée. Vieilles Vignes – *old vines (could be any age from 20–80 years), should indicate higher quality*. Villages – *supposedly best part of a larger region, as in Beaujolais Villages*. Vin de Pays – *wine with regional character*. Vin de Table – *basic table wine*.

Still the set of benchmarks, against which winemakers elsewhere test themselves. This is the place to find the Chardonnay in its finest oaked (white Burgundy) and unoaked (Chablis) styles; the Sauvignon (from Sancerre and Pouilly Fumé in the Loire, and in blends with the Sémillon in Bordeaux); Cabernet Sauvignon and Merlot (red Bordeaux); Pinot Noir (red Burgundy and Champagne); Riesling, Gewurztraminer, and

Pinots Blanc and Gris (Alsace). The Chenin Blanc still shines most brightly in the Loire, and despite Australian successes, the Syrah (aka Shiraz) and Grenache are still at their finest in the Rhône. Other regions such as Jurançon and Arbois have grapes grown almost nowhere else.

France is, however, still handicapped by the unpredictability of its climate (especially in years like 2002) and by the unreliability of winemakers, too many of whom are still happy to coast along on the reputation of their region and on *Appellation Contrôlée* laws that allow them to get away with selling poor quality wine.

Alsace

> **Reading the label:** Sélection de Grains Nobles – *Sweet wine from noble rot-affected grapes.* Vendange Tardive – *late harvested.* Edelzwicker – *blend of white grapes, usually Pinot Blanc and Sylvaner.*

Often underrated, and confused with German wines from the other side of the Rhine, Alsace is slowly gaining in popularity. Its odd assortment of grapes make wonderfully rich, spicy, dry, off-dry and late harvest styles. There is also sparkling wine and a little red Pinot Noir. This is my bet to follow the success of its spicy red counterparts in the Rhône.

Bordeaux

> **Reading the label:** Chai – *cellar.* Cru Bourgeois – *level beneath Cru Classé, but possibly of similar quality.* Cru Classé – *"Classed Growth", a wine featured in the 1855 classification of the Médoc and Graves, provides no guarantee of current quality.* Grand Cru/Grand Cru Classé – *confusing terms, especially in St. Emilion, where the former is allocated annually on the basis of a sometimes less-than-arduous tasting, while the latter is reassessed every decade.*

For all but the most avid wine buff, Bordeaux is one big region with a few dozen châteaux that have become internationally famous for their wine. Visit the region, or take a look at the map, however, and you will find that this is essentially a collection of quite diverse sub-regions, many of which are separated by farmland, forest or water.

Heading north from the city of Bordeaux, the Médoc is the region that includes the great communes of St. Estèphe, Pauillac, St. Julien and Margaux, where some of the finest red wines are made. The largely gravel soil suits the Cabernet Sauvignon, though lesser Médoc wines, of which there are more than enough, tend to have a higher proportion of the Merlot. For the best examples of wines made principally from this variety, though, you have to head eastward to St. Emilion and Pomerol, Fronsac and the Côtes de Castillon, and

BORDEAUX

- SOULAC-SUR-MER

Gironde

Médoc

St. Estèphe

PAUILLAC • | Côtes de Blaye

St. Julien
Margaux
Listrac | • BLAYE
Moulis | Côtes de Bourg
| • BOURG

Haut-Médoc | *Dordogne* | Fronsac | Pomerol
| • LIBOURNE | Libournais
| St. Emilion
| Côtes de Francs
BORDEAUX • | Côtes de Castillon

Premières Côtes
Pessac-Léognan | de Bordeaux

Graves | Entre-Deux-Mers

Cérons | Loupiac
Barsac | Ste. Croix-du-Mont
LANGON • | Sauternes

Garonne

– – – AOC Bordeaux

to the regions of Bourg and Blaye where the Merlot is usually blended with the Cabernet Franc. It is here that most "garage" wines – limited in production; intense in flavour – are made.

To the south of Bordeaux lie Pessac-Léognan and the Graves, which produce some of Bordeaux's lighter, more delicate reds. This is also dry white country, where the Sémillon and Sauvignon Blanc hold sway. A little farther to the southeast, the often misty climate provides the conditions required for the great sweet whites of Sauternes and Barsac.

Each of these regions produces its own individual style of wine. In some years, the climate suits one region and/or grape variety more than others. The year 2002, for example was better for the Médoc than for St. Emilion. So beware of vintage charts that seek to define the quality of an entire vintage across the whole of Bordeaux.

BURGUNDY

Chablis
AUXERRE •
Sauvignon de St.-Bris
Irancy

Serein _Armançon_ _Seine_

DIJON •
Côte de Nuits
Gevrey-Chambertin Côte d'Or
Vosne-Romanée Clos de Vougeot
Nuits-St. Georges
Volnay • BEAUNE
Côte de Beaune
Pommard Meursault
Puligny-Montrachet
• CHALON-SUR-SAONE

Côte Chalonnaise

Mâconnais

Juliénas • MACON
Chénas St. Amour
Fleurie
Morgon
Moulin-à-Vent Beaujolais
• VILLEFRANCHE-SUR-SAONE

– – – AOC Burgundy

Coteaux du
Lyonnais • LYON

Saône

Burgundy

Reading the label: Hospices de Beaune – _wines made and sold at auction by the charitable_ Hospices de Beaune. Passetoutgrains – _a blend of Gamay and Pinot Noir._ Tasteviné – _a special label for wines that have passed a tasting by the_ Confrérie des Chevaliers de Tastevin.

The heartland of the Pinot Noir and the Chardonnay and Chablis, Nuits-St.-Georges, Gevrey-Chambertin, Beaune, Meursault, Puligny-Montrachet, Mâcon Villages, Pouilly-Fuissé and Beaujolais. The best wines theoretically come from the Grands Crus vineyards; next are the Premiers Crus, followed by plain village wines and, last of all, basic Bourgogne Rouge or Blanc.

The region's individual producers make their wines with varying luck and expertise, generally selling in bulk to merchants who are just as variable in their skills and honesty. So, one producer's supposedly humble wine can be finer than another's pricier Premier or Grand Cru.

Champagne

Reading the label: Blanc de Blancs – *white wine from white grapes, i.e., pure Chardonnay.* Blancs de Noirs – *white wine made from black grapes.* Brut Sauvage/Zéro – *bone dry.* Extra-Dry – *(surprisingly) sweeter than Brut.* Grand Cru – *from a top-quality vineyard.* Négociant-manipulant (NM) – *buyer and blender of wines.* Non-vintage – *a blend of wines usually based on wine of a single vintage.* Récoltant manipulant (RM) – *individual estate.*

Top-class Champagne has toasty richness and subtle fruit. Beware of cheap examples, though, and big-name producers who should know better.

Loire

Reading the label: Moelleux – *sweet.* Sur Lie – *on its lees (dead yeast), usually only applied to Muscadet.* Côt – *local name for the Malbec.*

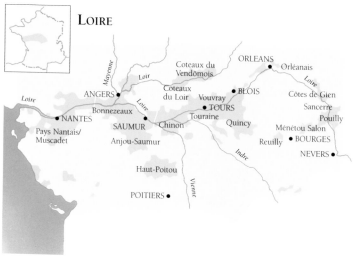

The heartland of fresh, dry Sauvignons and honeyed, sweet Quarts de Chaume, Coteaux de Layon and Bonnezeaux, and dry, sweet and sparkling Vouvray, all of which, like dry Savennières, display the Chenin Blanc at its best. The Chinon and Bourgeuil reds do the same for the Cabernet Franc.

Rhône

Reading the label: Vin Doux Naturel – *fortified wine, such as Muscat de Beaumes de Venise.* Côtes du Rhône Villages – *wine from one of a number of better sited villages in the overall Côtes du Rhône appellation, and thus, supposedly finer wine than plain Côtes du Rhône.*

With every year, as I – and others – have predicted, the popularity of this region continues to grow, helped in part by the success of wines made from red and white Rhône grape varieties in other countries ranging from Australia to Switzerland. Today, the world wants the ripe, spicy flavours of the Syrah, Grenache and Viognier, the value for money of Côtes du Rhône and the excitement of great good Condrieu, Chateauneuf du Pape, Côte-rôtie and also Hermitage.

Côte Rôtie
Condrieu VIENNE
Rhône
Côtes-du-Rhône
Hermitage
St. Joseph Crozes-Hermitage
Cornas
• VALENCE
Rhône Drôme
Clairette de Die
Chatillon-en-Diois
• MONTELIMAR
Côtes du Vivarais Coteaux du Tricastin
Côtes-du-Rhône-Villages
Béaumes-de-Venise
• ORANGE
Châteauneuf-du-Pape Gigondas
Vaqueyras
• CARPENTRAS
Tavel
• AVIGNON
Côtes du Ventoux
Coteaux de Pierrevert
Durance
RHÔNE
Côtes du Lubéron

The Southwest

Reading the label: Perlé or Perlant - *gently sparkling, used in Gaillac.*

THE SOUTHWEST

Côtes de / Haut-Montravel Bergerac • PERIGUEUX
• BORDEAUX Pécharmant • BERGERAC Dordogne
Côtes de Monbazillac
Duras
RODEZ •
ARCACHON Côtes du Cahors Lot
Marmandais
Côtes du Aveyron
Buzet • AGEN
MONT-DE-MARSAN Armagnac MONTAUBAN • Gaillac • ALBI
Côtes du
Frontonnais
Adour Côtes de • CASTRES
Madiran St. Mont • AUCH • TOULOUSE
BAYONNE Béarn MAZAMET •
Garonne
BIARRITZ CARCASSONNE •
PAU • • TARBES
Irouleguy Jurançon Limoux

A region producing Bordeaux-like Bergerac, Pécharmant and Buzet, sweet and dry Jurançon, Gaillac, Cahors, and Madiran. Despite their fame among French wine buffs, these were often pretty old-fashioned.

Today, a new wave of winemakers is learning how to extract fruit flavours from grapes like the Gros and Petit Manseng, the Tannat, Mauzac and Malbec. These wines are worth the detour for anyone bored with the ubiquitous Cabernet and Chardonnay and dissatisfied with poor claret.

The South

Reading the label: Vin de Pays d'Oc – *country wine from the Languedoc region. Often some of the best stuff in the region.* Rancio – *woody, slightly volatile character in Banyuls and other fortified wines that have been aged in the barrel.*

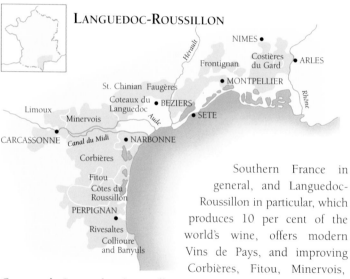

LANGUEDOC-ROUSSILLON

Southern France in general, and Languedoc-Roussillon in particular, which produces 10 per cent of the world's wine, offers modern Vins de Pays, and improving Corbières, Fitou, Minervois, Coteaux de Languedoc (especially Pic St. Loup) and Limoux (where Mouton Rothschild has a venture). An ideal climate and increasingly dynamic winemaking are raising the quality here and in Provence, where Cassis and Bandol now attract as much attention as rosé.

Eastern France

Reading the label: Vin de Paille – *sweet, golden wine from grapes dried on straw mats.* Vin Jaune – *sherry-like, slightly oxidized wine.*

Savoie's zingy wines are often only thought of as skiing fare, but, like Arbois' nutty, sherry-style whites, they are characterfully different, and made from grape varieties that are grown nowhere else.

GERMANY

Reading the label: Amtliche Prüfungsnummer (AP number) – *official identification number.* Auslese – *(usually) sweet wine from selected ripe grapes.* Beerenauslese – *luscious wines from selected, riper botrytis-affected grapes (Beeren).* Classic – *new designation for dry wine from a defined region.* Erste Gewächs /Lage– *top vineyard.* Erzeugerabfüllung – *bottled by the grower/estate.* Halbtrocken – *off-dry.* Hock – *British name for Rhine wines.* Kabinett – *wines that fulfill a certain natural ripeness.* Kellerei/Kellerabfüllung – *cellar/producer/estate-bottled.* Landwein – *equivalent of a French Vin de Pays.* QbA (Qualitätswein bestimmter Anbaugebiete) – *basic quality German wine.* QmP (Qualitätswein mit Prädikat) – *there are five ripeness rungs of QmP, rising from Kabinett, via Spätlese, Auslese, Beerenauslese to Trockenbeerenauslese plus Eiswein.* Schloss – *(literally "castle" or "Château") estate.* Sekt – *basic, sparkling wine.* Selection – *new name for dry wine from a quality site.* Spätlese – *second step in the QmP scale, late harvested grapes,.* Staatsweingut – *state-owned wine estate.* Tafelwein – *table wine, only the prefix "Deutscher" guarantees German origin.* Trocken – *dry.* Trockenbeerenauslese – *wine from selected botrytis-affected grapes.* Weingut – *estate.* Weinkellerei – *cellar or winery.* VDP – *group of quality-conscious producers.*

Led by younger producers like Ernst Loosen and Rainer Lingenfelder and Phillipp Wittmann, a quiet revolution is taking place here. Sugar-watery Liebfraumilch is becoming a thing of the past – as are the aggressively acidic dry wines of the 1980s and early 1990s. Today, expect to find rich dry and fruitily off-dry whites (ideally but not necessarily made from Riesling), classic later harvest styles, and a growing number of good reds (especially Pinot Noir). The Pfalz, Mosel and Baden are regions to watch.

ITALY

Reading the label: Abboccato – *semi-dry.* Amabile – *semi-sweet.* Amaro – *bitter.* Asciutto – *bone dry.* Azienda – *estate.* Classico – *the best vineyards at the heart of a DOC.* Colle/colli – *hills.* DOC(G) Denominazione di Origine Controllata (e Garantita) – *designation, based on grape variety and/or origin.*

Dolce – *sweet*. Frizzante – *semi-sparkling*. IGT, Indicazione Geografica Tipica – *new designation for quality* Vino da Tavola. Imbottigliato nel'origine – *estate-bottled*. Liquoroso – *rich, sweet*. Passito – *raisiny wine made from sundried grapes*. Recioto – *strong, sweet (unless designated Amarone)*. Vino da Tavola – *table wine. Now replaced by IGT for top wines*.

Three facts about Italy: (1) It is more a set of regions than a single country; (2) There is a tradition of interpreting laws fairly liberally; (3) Style is often valued as highly as content. So when it comes to wine, this can be a confusing place. Producers do their own frequently delicious thing, using indigenous and imported grape varieties and designer bottles and labels in ways that leave legislators – and humble wine drinkers – exhilarated and exasperated in equal measure.

New Zealand

This New World country has one of the most unpredictable climates, but produces some of the most intensely flavoured wines. There are gooseberryish Sauvignon Blancs, Chardonnays, and innovative Rieslings and Gewürztraminers, and impressive Pinot Noirs.

Hawkes Bay seems to be the most consistent region for reds, while Gisborne, Marlborough, Auckland, and Martinborough share the honours for white wine (though the last, like Central Otago, produces classy Pinot Noir).

NORTH ISLAND

Northland

Auckland • AUCKLAND

Bay of Plenty

Waikato

Gisborne/ Poverty Bay

Hawkes Bay

Wairarapa/ Martinborough

• WELLINGTON

Nelson Marlborough

PACIFIC OCEAN

Waipara

TASMAN SEA

Canterbury • CHRISTCHURCH

SOUTH ISLAND

Central Otago

• DUNEDIN

NEW ZEALAND

STEWART ISLAND

North Africa

Once the plentiful source of blending wine for French regions such as Burgundy, North Africa's vineyards have been hampered in recent years by Islamic fundamentalism. New investment is, however, now beginning to arrive from Italy and France (including a new venture in Morocco that is partly financed by Gérard Dépardieu).

Portugal

Reading the label: Adega – *winery*. Branco – *white*. Colheita – *vintage*. Engarrafado na origem – *estate-bottled*. Garrafeira – *a vintage-dated wine with a little more alcohol and minimum ageing requirements*. Quinta – *vineyard or estate*. Reserva – *wine from a top-quality vintage, made from riper grapes than the standard requirement*. Velho – *old*. Vinho de Mesa – *table wine*.

The sleeping beauty has woken. Portugal is belatedly introducing modern wine-making to its cornucopia of grape varieties, most of which are grown nowhere else (the Douro has over 80).

Innovators like Luis Pato, Jose Neiva, J Portugal Ramos, JM da Fonseca and Sogrape, with a little help from Australians Peter Bright and David Baverstock, and the ubiquitous Michel Rolland, are using varieties such as the Roriz and Touriga Nacional in regions like Estremadura and Alentejo as well as better-known Douro, Dão and Bairrada.

Portugal

SOUTH AFRICA

Reading the label: Cap Classique – *South African term for Champagne method.* Cultivar – *grape variety.* Edel laat-oes – *noble late harvest.* Edelkeur – *"noble rot", a fungus affecting grapes and producing sweet wine.* Gekweek, gemaak en gebottel op – *estate-bottled.* Landgoedwyn – *estate wine.* Laat-oes – *late harvest.* Oesjaar – *vintage.* Steen – *name for Chenin Blanc.*

The fastest improving country in the New World? No longer the source of "green" wines made from over-cropped and underripe grapes grown on virused vines, the Cape is now making terrific lean but ripe Rieslings and Sauvignons and reds made from Cabernet, Merlot and the local Pinotage. Thelema, Boekenhoutskloof, Saxenburg, Plaisir de Merle, Rust en Vrede, Rustenberg, Naledi/Sejana, Zandvliet, Vergelegen, Fairview, Eben Sadie, Kanonkop and Vriesenhof are names to watch – as are the up-and-coming regions of Darling, Malmesbury and Robertson.

THE CAPE

SOUTH AMERICA

Argentina

Reading the label: Malbec – *spicy red grape.* Torrontes – *grapey white.*

As it chases Chile, this is a country to watch. The wines to look for now are the peppery reds made from the Malbec, a variety once widely grown in Bordeaux and still used in the Loire. Cabernets can be good too, as can the juicy Bonarda and grapey but dry white Torrontes.

Chile

Reading the label: Envasado en Origen – *estate-bottled.* Carmenère/ Grand Vidure – *grape variety once used in Bordeaux.*

One of the most exciting wine-producing countries in the world, thanks to ideal conditions, skilled local winemaking, and plentiful investment. The most successful grapes at present are the Merlot and Cabernet, but the Chardonnay, Pinot Noir, Sauvignon and (the local) Carmenère, can all display ripe fruit and subtlety often absent in the New World.

SOUTHEASTERN EUROPE
Greece
After winning the confidence of a growing number of critics and wine-lovers in Britain, Greece's new wave of wine producers are beginning to make inroads elsewhere, both with "international" grapes and highly characterful indigenous varieties. Prices are high (so is demand in chic Athens restaurants), but worth it from producers like Château Lazaridi, Gentilini, Gaia and Hatzimichali.

Cyprus
Still associated with cheap sherry-substitute and dull wine, but things are changing. Look out for the traditional rich Commandaria.

Turkey
Lurching out of the vinous dark ages, Turkey has yet to offer the world red or white wines that non-Turks are likely to relish.

Lebanon
Once the lone exemplar of Lebanese wines overseas, Château Musar is now joined by the similarly impressive Kefraya and Ksara..

Israel
Over 90 per cent of Israel's wine is produced by Carmel, Barkan and – most impressively – by the Golan Heights Winery (under Gamla and Yarden labels), but small boutique wineries are now beginning to flourish.

SPAIN

Reading the label: Abocado – *semi-dry*. Año – *year*. Bodega – *winery or wine cellar*. Cava – *Champagne method wine*. Criado y Embotellado (por) – *grown and bottled (by)*. Crianza – *aged in wood*. DO(Ca) Denominacion de Origen (Calificada) – *Spain's quality designation, based on regional style. Calificada (DOC) indicates superior quality*. Elaborado y Anejado Por – *made and aged for*. Gran Reserva – *wine aged for a designated number of years in wood; longer than for Reserva*. Joven – *young wine, specially made for early consumption*. Reserva – *official designation for wine that has been aged for a specific period*. Sin Crianza – *not aged in wood*. Vendemia – *harvest or vintage*. Vino de Mesa – *table wine*. Vino de la Tierra – *designation similar to the French "Vin de Pays"*.

As elsewhere, the vinous revolution has arguably been most fruitful in regions that were previously overlooked. So, while traditionalists focused their attention on regions like Rioja, Navarra and Ribera del Duero and

SANTANDER

BILBAO ●

PAMPLONA ●

Navarra

Ampurdán

Costa Brava

Ribeiro Valdeorras

Rioja

Somontano

Ribera
del Duero

Ebro

BARCELONA ●

PORTUGAL

(see p41)

Duero

Cariñana

Penedes

Duero

Rueda

Terra Alto

Catalonia

MADRID ●

Tajo

Mentrida

Utiel

La Mancha

Requena

● VALENCIA

Valdepenas

Valencia

Yecla

Jumilla Alicante

CORDOBA

Guadalquivir

SEVILLE ●

Montilla

● GRANADA

Guadalete

Jerez

Málaga

CADIZ ●

SPAIN

early modernists such as Miguel Torres looked to the Penedés, some of the most exciting fireworks have been seen in Galicia (source of lovely, aromatic white Albariño) Tarragona, and Priorat, two areas that used to make thick red wine in which a spoon could stand unaided. Now, producers like Alvaro Palacios are making deliciously stylish wines that sell easily for $100 in New York (but are, perhaps for this very reason, rather harder to find in London).

Elsewhere, Rioja is improving fast (thanks often to the addition of a little Cabernet to the red blend) and increasingly good wines are coming out of Navarra, Somontano, Toro and Rueda. Ribera del Duero offers some great reds (Vega Sicilia, Pesquera and Pingus) but is still home to far too many disappointing but pricey victims of poor winemaking.

SWITZERLAND

Reading the label: Gutedel, Perlan, Fendant – *local names for the Chasselas.* Grand Cru – *top designation which varies from one canton to the next.* Süssdruck – *off-dry, red wine.*

The only place in the world where the Chasselas produces anything even remotely memorable – and the only one sensibly to use screwcaps for many of its wines. Other worthwhile grapes are the white (Petite) Arvigne and Amigne (de Vétroz) and the red Cornalin, as well as the Gamay, Syrah, Pinot Noir, and Merlot, a variety that is used to make white wines here.

USA

> **Reading the label:** Blush – *rosé*. Champagne – *any sparkling wine.*
> Fumé – *oak-aged white wine, especially Sauvignon (Blanc Fumé).*
> Meritage – *popular, if pretentious, name for a Bordeaux blend (white or red).*
> Vinted – *made by (a vintner, or winemaker).* White Grenache/Zinfandel,
> etc – *refers to the unfashionable rosé, slightly pink wines, sometimes also*
> *referred to as "blush".*

California

Despite the threat of the insect-borne Pierce's disease that threatens to
wreck its vineyards and a glut of cheap grapes, the best-known
winemaking state of the Union is still on a roll. The Napa Valley now
faces serious competition from Sonoma (now home to a serious E&J
Gallo winery) and southern regions such as Santa Cruz and Santa
Barbara. The Merlot grape has overtaken the Cabernet Sauvignon to
become the most widely-planted red wine grape but there is a growing

CALIFORNIA

trend towards making wines from the Pinot Noir (especially in Carneros and Russian River in Northern California and Santa Barbara further south) and from varieties traditionally associated with the Rhône and Italy.

Amid all this excitement, however, one problem remains. California may produce some of the very finest wines in the world, but its daily-drinking efforts still offer some remarkably poor value.

The Pacific Northwest

Outside California, head north to Oregon for some of the best Pinot Noirs in the US (at a hefty price) and improving, but rarely earth-shattering, Chardonnays, Rieslings and Pinot Gris. Washington State has some Pinot too, on the cooler, rainy, west side of the Cascade Mountains. On the east, irrigated vineyards produce great Sauvignon and Riesling, as well as top-notch Chardonnay, Cabernet Sauvignon, and impressive Syrah and Merlot.

New York and Other States

There are around 1000 wineries outside California, Oregona and Washington State. New York State produces good wines, particularly in the micro-climate of Long Island, where the Merlot thrives. The Finger Lakes are patchier but worth visiting, especially for the Rieslings and cool-climate Chardonnays. Elsewhere Virginia, Missouri, Texas, Maryland, and even Arizona can all offer wines to compete with California and occasionally some of the best efforts from Europe.

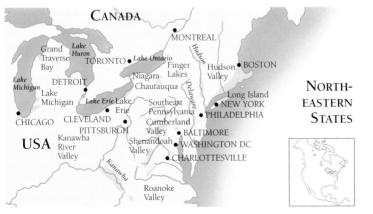

The Grapes

BLENDS OR SINGLE VARIETIES?

Some wines are made from single grape varieties – e.g. red or white Burgundy, Sancerre, German Riesling, most Alsace wines, and Barolo – while others, such as red or white Bordeaux, California "Meritage" wines, port, and Châteauneuf-du-Pape, are blends of two or more types of grape. Champagne can fall into either camp, as can New World "varietal" wines, which, though generally labeled as "Chardonnay," "Merlot," "Shiraz," etc., can often – depending on local laws – contain up to 25 percent of other grape varieties. Blends are not, *per se*, superior to single varietals – or vice versa.

WHITE WINE GRAPES

CHARDONNAY

The world's most popular and widely planted premium white grape variety, and the one whose name has become almost a synonym for dry white wine, is surprisingly hard to define. The flavor of any example will depend enormously on the climate, soil, and the particular type of clone. Burgundy, and the best California examples (Kistler, Peter Michael, Sonoma Cutrer), taste of butter and hazelnuts; lesser New World efforts are often sweet and simple and often very melony (a flavor which comes from the clone). Australians range from subtle buttery pineapple to oaky tropical fruit juice. Petaluma, Giaconda, Coldstream Hills, and Leeuwin show how it can be done. New Zealand's efforts are tropical, too, but lighter and fresher (Te Mata, Cloudy Bay).

Elsewhere, Chile is beginning to hit the mark, as is South Africa (Jordan). In Europe, look around southern France (James Herrick), Italy (Gaja), Spain, and Eastern Europe, but beware of watery cheaper versions.

CHENIN BLANC

Loire variety with naturally high acidity that makes it ideal for fresh sparkling, dry, and luscious honeyed wines; also raw stuff like unripe apples. Most California Chenins are semisweet and ordinary. South Africans call it Steen and use it for cheap dry and luscious sweet wines. There are few good Australians (but try Moondah Brook) or New Zealanders (try Millton).

GEWÜRZTRAMINER

Outrageous, oily-textured stuff that smells of parma violets and tastes of lychee fruit. At its best in Alsace (Zind Humbrecht, Schlumberger, Faller), where identically labeled bottles can vary greatly in their level of sweetness. Wines that guarantee luscious sweetness will be labeled as either *Vendange Tardive* or – the intensely sweet – *Sélection de Grains Nobles*. Try examples from Germany, Chile, New Zealand, and Italy, too.

GRÜNER VELTLINER

Fast-rising star, helped by the success of Austrian examples in a tasting against white Burgundy. Fleshy, limey, and capable of aging.

MARSANNE

A classic, flowery, lemony variety used in the Rhône in Hermitage; Australia (Chateau Tahbilk and Mitchelton); southern France (from Mas de Daumas Gassac); Switzerland (from Provins); and in innovative wines from California. At its best young or after five or six years.

MUSCAT

The only variety whose wines actually taste as though they are made of grapes, rather than some other kind of fruit or vegetable. In Alsace, southern France, and northeast Italy it is used to make dry wines. Generally, though, it performs best as sparkling wine (Moscatos and Astis from Italy, and Clairette de Die Tradition from France) and as sweet fortified wine. Look out for Beaumes de Venise and Rivesaltes in southern France, Moscatel de Setúbal in Portugal, Moscatel de Valencia in Spain, and Liqueur Muscat in Australia.

PINOT BLANC/PINOT BIANCO

As rich as Chardonnay, but with less fruit. At its worst – when over-cropped – it makes neutral wine. At its best, however (also in Alsace), it can develop a lovely cashew-nut flavor. When well handled it can also do well in Italy, where it is known as Pinot Bianco (Jermann), and in Germany (especially in Baden), where it is called Weissburgunder.

PINOT GRIS/PINOT GRIGIO

An up-and-coming Alsace variety also known as Tokay but unrelated to any other Tokay. Wines can be spicy and sweet or dry. The perfumed, aromatic qualities are associated with later-harvest examples. In Italy it is called Pinot Grigio, and in Germany, Grauerburgunder. Look for examples from Oregon (Eyrie), California, and New Zealand.

RIESLING

The king of white grapes. Misunderstood – and often mispronounced as Rice-ling rather than Rees-ling – it is often mistaken for cheap German wine made from quite different grapes. At its best, it makes dry and sweet, grapey, appley, limey wines that develop a spicy, gasoline character with age. Quality and character depend on soil – ideally slate – more than climate; and while the best examples come from Germany, in the Mosel (Maximin Grünhaus) and Rhine (Schloss Johannisberg), and Alsace (Zind-Humbrecht, Faller), this variety can perform well in such different environments as Washington State, Australia (Grossett, Tim Adams), and New Zealand (Matua Valley). Not to be confused with unrelated varieties such as Lazki, Lutomer, Welsch, Emerald, or White Riesling.

SAUVIGNON BLANC

The grape of Loire wines, such as Sancerre and Pouilly Fumé, and white Bordeaux, where it is often blended with Sémillon. This gooseberryish variety performs wonderfully in Marlborough in New Zealand (where

Muscat

Sauvignon Blanc

the flavors can include asparagus and pea-pods), in South Africa (Thelema), and in Australia (Shaw & Smith, Cullen). Chile has good examples (from Casablanca), and Washington State can get it right, as can California (Cakebread, Frog's Leap), but many examples are sweet or overburdened by oak. Oaked US versions, wherever they are produced, are usually labeled Fumé Blanc, a term first coined by Robert Mondavi. Only the best of these improve after the first couple of years.

SÉMILLON

In Bordeaux – in blends with the Sauvignon – this produces sublime dry Graves and sweet Sauternes. In Australia there are great, long-lived, dry pure (often unoaked) Sémillons from the Hunter Valley and (more usually oaked) Barossa Valley. Good "noble" late harvest examples have also been produced (by de Bortoli) in Riverina. Elsewhere in Australia, the grape is sometimes blended with Chardonnay. Progress is being made in Washington State and South Africa (Boekenhoutskloof), but most examples from California, New Zealand, and Chile are disappointing.

VIOGNIER

A cult grape, Viognier was once only found in Condrieu and Château Grillet in the Rhône, where small numbers of good examples showed off its extraordinary perfumed, peach-blossomy character, albeit at a high price. Today, however, it has been widely introduced to the Ardèche, Languedoc-Roussillon, and California (where it is sometimes confused with the Roussanne), and made with loving care (and often over-generous exposure to oak barrels) in Eastern Europe, Argentina, and particularly Australia (where Yalumba makes several good examples).

While examples of affordable Viognier are welcome, most lower-priced efforts are disappointing because this is a variety that performs poorly when asked to produce too much wine per acre. Clones of this grape vary widely, too. Buy with care.

Sémillon

Viognier

RED WINE GRAPES

BARBERA

A widely planted, wild-berryish Italian variety at its best in Piedmont, where it is increasingly successful in blends with Nebbiolo and Cabernet. Also good in Argentina, California, and Australia.

CABERNET SAUVIGNON

King of the Médoc and Graves (in blends with Merlot), and top reds from the New World, especially California, Chile, and Australia. Eastern Europe and southern France (Vin de Pays) have good value examples, and Spain is rapidly climbing aboard (in the Penedès, and Navarra). The hallmark to look for is blackcurrant, though unripe versions taste like weeds and bell peppers. There are also great Italian Cabernets. Good New World Cabernets can smell and taste of fresh mint, but like the best Bordeaux, develop a rich, leathery, "cigar box" character.

CARMENÈRE

A peppery-berryish grape once grown in Bordeaux and now almost only found in Chile and Italy (Ca del Bosco).

GRENACHE/GARNACHA

Freshly ground black pepper is the distinguishing flavor here, sometimes with the fruity tang of sweets. At home in Côtes du Rhône and Châteauneuf-du-Pape, it is also used in Spain (as Garnacha) in blends with Tempranillo. There are good "Bush" examples from Australia.

MALBEC

Another peppery Bordeaux refugee, used in France (for Cahors), the Loire, and Italy, where it generally produces dull stuff. It shines, however, in Argentina and is finding a new home in Chile and Australia.

Cabernet Sauvignon   *Malbec*

MERLOT

The most widely planted variety in Bordeaux and the subject of (enthusiastic over-) planting in California. In Bordeaux, where in some vintages it performs better than Cabernet Sauvignon, it is at its best in Pomerol, where wines can taste of ripe plums and spice, and in St. Emilion, where the least successful wines show the Merlot's less lovable dull and earthy character. Wherever it is made, the naturally thin-skinned Merlot should produce softer, less tannic wines than Cabernet Sauvignon (though some California examples seem to contradict this rule).

NEBBIOLO/SPANNA

The red wine grape of Barolo and Barbaresco in Piedmont now, thanks to modern winemaking, increasingly reveals a lovely cherry and rose-petal character, often with the sweet vanilla of new oak casks. Lesser examples for earlier drinking tend to be labeled as Spanna.

PINOT NOIR

The wild-raspberryish, plummy, and licoricey grape of red Burgundy is also a major component of white and pink Champagne. It makes red and pink Sancerre, as well as light reds in Alsace and Germany (where it is called Spätburgunder). Italy makes a few good examples, but for the best modern efforts look to California, Oregon, Australia, Chile, South Africa and, especially, New Zealand (Martinborough, Felton Road).

PINOTAGE

Almost restricted to South Africa, this cross between Pinot Noir and Cinsaut can – though rarely and only in the right hands, such as Kanonkop – make berryish young wines that may develop rich gamey-spicy flavors. Poorer examples can be dull and "muddy".

Nebbiolo   *Pinot Noir*

SANGIOVESE

The grape of Chianti, Brunello di Montalcino, and a host of popular IGT wines in Italy, not to mention "new wave" Italian-style wines in California and Argentina. The recognizable flavor is of sweet tobacco, wild herbs, and berries.

SYRAH/SHIRAZ

The spicy, brambly grape of the Northern Rhône (Hermitage, Cornas, etc.) and the best reds of Australia (Henschke Hill of Grace and Penfolds Grange), where it is also blended with Cabernet Sauvignon (just as it once was in Bordeaux). Marqués de Griñon has a great Spanish example, and Isole e Olena makes a fine one in Tuscany. Increasingly successful in California and Washington State and, finally, in South Africa. Surprisingly good, too, in both Switzerland and New Zealand.

TEMPRANILLO

Known under all kinds of names around Spain, including Cencibel (in Navarra) and Tinto del Pais (in Ribeira del Duero), and Tinta Roriz in Portugal, the grape gives Spanish reds their recognizable strawberry character. Often blended with Garnacha, it works well with Cabernet Sauvignon. So far, little used in the New World, but watch out for examples from Argentina and Australia.

ZINFANDEL

Until recently thought of as California's "own" variety, but now proved (by DNA tests) to be the same variety as the Primitivo in southern Italy. In California it makes rich, spicy, blueberryish reds (see Turley and Ridge Vineyards), "ports," and (often with a little help from sweet Muscat), sweet pink "White Zinfandel". Outside California, Cape Mentelle makes a good example in Western Australia.

Syrah   *Zinfandel*

OTHER GRAPES

WHITE

Albariño/Alvarinho Floral. Grown in Spain (delicious examples from Rias Baixas in Galicia) and Portugal, where it is used for Vinho Verde.

Aligoté Lean Burgundy grape, well used by Leroy.

Arneis Perfumed variety in Piedmont.

Bouvier Dull variety, used for late harvest wines in Austria.

Colombard Appley, basic; grown in S.W. France, US, and Australia.

Furmint Limey variety, traditionally used for Tokaji.

Kerner Dull German grape. Can taste leafy.

Müller-Thurgau/Rivaner Occasionally impressive; grown in Germany and England.

Muscadelle Spicy white grape used in white Bordeaux, but at its best when fortified (as "Tokay") in Australia.

Roussanne Fascinating Rhône variety that deserves more attention.

Scheurebe/Samling Grapefruity grape grown in Germany and Austria

Silvaner/Sylvaner Earthy, non-aromatic variety of Alsace and Germany.

Torrontes Grapey, Muscat-like variety of Argentina.

Ugni Blanc/Trebbiano Basic grape of S.W. France and Italy.

Verdelho Limey grape found in Madeira and Australian table wine.

Viura Widely planted, so-so Spanish variety.

Welschriesling Basic. Best in late harvest Austrians. Like Lutomer and Laszki and Italico, this "Riesling" is not related to the genuine Riesling.

RED

Bonarda Used in Argentina for juicy light wines.

Cabernet Franc Kid brother of Cabernet Sauvignon, grown alongside it in Bordeaux and by itself in the Loire and Italy.

Cinsaut/Cinsault Spicy Rhône variety; best in blends.

Carignan Toffeeish non-aromatic variety widely used in S. France.

Dolcetto Cherryish Piedmont grape. Drink young.

Dornfelder Successful, juicy variety grown in Germany.

Gamay The Beaujolais grape; less successful in the Loire and Gaillac.

Gamay Beaujolais/Valdiguié Pinot Noir cousin, unrelated to Gamay.

Mourvèdre (Mataro) Spicy Rhône grape; good in California and Australia, but can be hard and "metallic."

Petit Verdot Spicy ingredient of Bordeaux. Now being used on its own.

Petite-Sirah Spicy; thrives in California and Mexico. Durif in Australia.

Ruby Cabernet Basic Carignan-Cabernet Sauvignon cross.

Tannat Tough variety of Madiran. Better in Uruguay.

Touriga Nacional Plummy variety used for port and Portuguese wine.

Styles

STYLE COUNSEL

Wine can be separated into easily recognizable styles: red, white, and pink; still and sparkling; sweet and dry; light and fortified. To say that a wine is red and dry says little, however, about the way it tastes. It could be a tough young Bordeaux, a mature Rioja, or a blueberryish Zinfandel.

Knowing the grape and origin can give a clearer idea of what a wine is like, but it won't tell you everything. Winemakers vary as much as chefs. Some focus on obvious fruit flavors, while others – in France, for example – go for the *goût de terroir* – the character of the vineyard.

In a world that is increasingly given to instant sensations, it is perhaps unsurprising that it is the fruitlovers rather than the friends of the earthy flavor who are currently in the ascendant.

NEW WORLD/OLD WORLD

Until recently, these two philosophies broadly belonged to the New and Old worlds. Places like California and Australia produced wine that was approachably delicious when compared with the more serious wine being produced in Europe, which demanded time and food. Today, however, even the most expert palate can find it hard to tell which side of the Atlantic a wine was made.

Flying Winemakers, Consultants, and 'Garagistes'

These changes owe much to "flying winemakers" – mostly Australians – and consultants – such as Michel Rolland – who help to produce wine all over the world. Now you can choose between a Chilean white made by a Frenchman – or a claret bearing the fruity fingerprint of a winemaker who learned his craft in the Barossa Valley. Just as influential are the *garagistes* named after Bordeaux producers who make tiny quantities of intensely ripe and flavorsome wine in their garages.

Fruit of Knowledge

European old timers used to claim that the New World wines relied on alchemy (in the form of artificial flavors) for their fruity appeal. In fact, like the *garagistes*, the New Worlders simply pick the grapes when they are ripe (rather than too early), preventing them from cooking beneath the midday sun (as was traditional in Europe, where work stopped for a lengthy lunch). They pump the juice through pipes that have been cleaned daily rather than at the end of the harvest, ferment it at a cool temperature (overheated vats can cost a wine its freshness), and they store and bottle the wine carefully – all of which will help a wine made from even the dullest grape variety to taste fruitier.

COME HITHER

If the New Worlders want their wines to taste of fruit, they are – apart from a few reactionaries – just as eager that they can be drunk young. They squeeze the red grapes lightly, so as not to extract bitter, hard tannins, and they try to avoid their white wines being too acidic.

Traditionalists claim these wines do not age well, and it is certainly true that some garage wines of the 1990s seem to be fading faster than they should; but there is no question that the newer wave red Bordeaux of, say, 1985, have given more people more pleasure since they were released than the supposedly greater 1970 vintage, whose wines often remained dauntingly hard throughout their lifetime. A wine does not have to be undrinkable in its youth to be good later on; indeed, wines that start out tasting unbalanced go on tasting that way.

ROLL OUT THE BARREL

Another thing that sets many new wave wines apart has nothing to do with grapes. Wines have been matured in oak barrels since Roman times, but traditionally new barrels were only bought to replace ones that were worn out and had begun to fall apart. Old casks have little flavor, but for the first two years or so of their lives, the way the staves are bent over flames gives new ones a recognizable vanilla and caramel character.

Winemakers once used to rinse out their new casks with dilute ammonia to remove this flavor. Today, however, they are more likely to devote almost as much effort to the choice of forest, cooper, and charring (light, medium, or heavy "toast") as to the quality of their grapes. Winemakers who want to impress their critics take pride in using 100 percent new oak to ferment and mature their wine. Or more. Some of those Bordeaux *garagistes* have actually been going through two sets of new oak barrels to ensure that they get enough rich vanilla flavor.

Oak-mania began when Bordeaux châteaux started to spend the income from the great vintages of the 1940s on replacements for their old barrels – and when New World pioneers like Mondavi noticed the contribution the oak was making to these wines. Ever since, producers internationally have introduced new barrels, while even the makers of cheaper wine have found that dunking giant "teabags" filled with small oak chips into wine vats could add some of that vanilla flavor, too.

Today, wines without a flavor of oak are the exception to the rule. If you don't like that woody character, or simply want a change, opt for Riesling from almost anywhere, white Loire, and most New Zealand Sauvignon Blanc, Hunter Valley Semillon, Spanish "Joven" wines, French examples labeled as *Cuvée Tradition*, and New World wines describing themselves as "unwooded."

RED WINES – FRUITS, SPICE, AND... COLD TEA

If you enjoy your reds soft and juicily fruity, the styles to look for are Beaujolais; Burgundy and other examples of Pinot Noir; youthful Côtes du Rhône and Spanish reds; inexpensive Australians; young St. Emilion and Merlots from almost anywhere. Look too for Barbera and Dolcetto from Italy, and Nouveau, Novello, and Joven (young wines.)

The Kitchen Cupboard

Italy's Sangiovese is not so much fruity as herby, while the Syrah/Shiraz of the Rhône and Australia, the peppery Grenache, Malbec, and Carmenère, and – sometimes – the Zinfandel and Pinotage can all be surprisingly spicy.

Some Like it Tough

Most basic Bordeaux – especially examples from St. Estèphe – are more tannic, as are older-style wines from Piedmont and traditional South African Cabernets and Pinotages. The Cabernet Sauvignon will almost always make tougher wines than the Merlot or Pinot Noir.

WHITE WINES – HONEY AND LEMON

If dry wines with unashamedly fruity flavors are what you want, try the Muscat, the Torrontes in Argentina, basic Riesling and Chardonnay, and New World and Southern French Sauvignon Blanc.

Non-Fruit

For more neutral styles, go for Italian Soave, Pinot Bianco, or Frascati; Grenache Blanc; Muscadet; German or Alsatian Silvaner; and most traditional wines from Spain and Southern France.

Riches Galore

The combination of richness and fruit is to be found in white Burgundy; better dry white Bordeaux; and in Chardonnays, Semillons, and oaked Sauvignon (Fumé) wines from the New World.

Aromatherapy

Some perfumed, spicy grapes, like the Gewürztraminer, are frankly aromatic. Also try late-harvest Tokay-Pinot Gris – also from Alsace. Other aromatic varieties include Viognier, Arneis, Albariño, Scheurebe, Petite Arvine, and the increasingly exciting Grüner Veltliner.

Middle of the Road

Today, while few people want to buy wine labeled "medium sweet," there are plenty of New World Chardonnays, Alsace whites, and Vouvrays that hardly qualify as dry. The Loire can get honeyed semisweet – *demi sec* – wine right, as can Italy, where it is labeled as *abboccato*. Otherwise, head for Germany and *Kabinett* and *Spätlese* wines.

Pure Hedonism

Frankly sweet wine is making a comeback. Try Bordeaux, the Loire (*Moelleux*), Alsace (*Vendange Tardive* or *Sélection des Grains Nobles*), Germany (*Auslese, Beerenauslese, Trockenbeerenauslese*), Austria (*Ausbruch*), the New World (late harvest and noble late harvest), and Hungary (Tokaji 6 Puttonyos.) All of these wines should have enough fresh acidity to prevent them from being cloying, and the characteristic dried-apricot flavor that comes from grapes that have been allowed to be affected by a benevolent fungus known as "botrytis" or "noble rot."

Other sweet wines such as Muscat de Beaumes de Venise are fortified with brandy to raise their strength to 15% or so. These wines can be luscious too, but they never have the complex flavor of "noble rot."

PINK

Provence and the Rhône should offer peppery dry rosé, just as the Loire and Bordeaux should have wines that taste deliciously of blackcurrant. Sadly, many taste dull and stale. Still, they are better than California's dire sweet "white" or "blush" rosé. Look for youth and vibrant color.

SPARKLING

If you find Champagne too dry, but don't want a frankly sweet grapey fizz like Asti, try a fruity New World sparkling wine from California, New Zealand, or Australia. If you don't like too much fruit, try traditional Spanish Cava, Italian Prosecco, and French Blanquette de Limoux.

Storing

LAYING DOWN FOR BEGINNERS

THE RESTING PLACE

Not so long ago, when winemaking was less sophisticated and there were fewer ways to counter tricky vintages, there were two kinds of wines: the basic stuff to drink immediately, and the cream of the crop that was left in the barrel and/or bottle to age. So, a good wine was an old wine. And vice versa. Young wine and old wine had as much in common as hamburgers and *haute cuisine.*

Today there are plenty of wines that never improve beyond the first few years after the harvest, and are none the worse for that. On the other hand, some wines – German Riesling, fine red Bordeaux, and top Australian Shiraz and California Cabernet, for example – by their very nature, still reward a few years' patience in the cellar.

While many of us live in homes that are ill-suited for storing wine, one can often find an unused grate or a space beneath the stairs that offers wine what it wants: a constant temperature of 45°F–60°F (never lower than 40°F nor more than 68°F,) reasonable humidity (install a cheap humidifier or leave a sponge in a bowl of water,) sufficient ventilation to avoid a musty atmosphere, and, ideally, an absence of vibration (wines stored beneath train tracks – or beds – age faster.) Alternatively, invest in a fridge-like Eurocave that guarantees perfect conditions – or even adapt an old freezer.

RACKS AND CELLAR BOOKS

Custom-built racks can be bought "by the hole" and cut to fit. Square chimney stacks can be used, too. If you have plenty of space, simply allocate particular racks to specific styles of wine. Unfortunately, even the best-laid cellar plans tend to fall apart when two cases of Australian Shiraz have to be squeezed into a space big enough just for one.

If the size of the cellar warrants it, give each hole in the rack a cross-referenced identity, from A1 at the top left to, say, Z20 at the bottom right. As bottles arrive, they can then be put in any available hole and their address noted in a cellar book, in which you can record when and where you obtained it, what it cost and how each bottle tasted. (Is it improving or drying out?) Some people, like me, prefer to use a computer programme (Filemaker Pro or Microsoft Excel).

TO DRINK OR KEEP?

A guide to which corks to pop soon and which bottles to treasure for a few years in the rack:

Drink as Soon as Possible

Most wine at under $10, particularly basic Chardonnay, Sauvignon Blanc, Merlot, Cabernet, and Zinfandel; French Vins de Pays and all but the best white Bordeaux; cheap red Bordeaux and most Beaujolais. Nouveau/Novello/Joven reds, Bardolino, Valpolicella, light Italian whites; and almost all "blush" and rosé.

Less than 5 Years

Most inexpensive ($10-15) California, Chilean, Argentine, South African and Australian reds and whites; Petit-Château Bordeaux and Cru Bourgeois, and lesser Cru Classé reds from poorer vintages; basic Alsace, red and white Burgundy, and better Beaujolais; Chianti, Barbera, basic Spanish reds; and good mid-quality Germans. All but the very best Sauvignon from anywhere.

5–10 Years

Most Cru Bourgeois Bordeaux from good years; better châteaux from lesser vintages; all but the finest red and white Burgundy, and Pinot Noir and Chardonnay from elsewhere; middle-quality Rhônes; southern-French higher flyers; good German, Alsatian, dry Loire, and finer white Bordeaux; most mid-priced Italian and Portuguese reds; most Australian, California, and Washington State; South African, Chilean, and New Zealand Merlots and Cabernets on sale at under $30. Late harvest wines from the New World and medium-quality Sauternes.

Over 10 Years

Top-class Bordeaux, Rhône, Burgundy, and sweet Loire from ripe years; top-notch German and Bordeaux late harvest, Italian IGT, Barolo, and the finest wines from Tuscany; best Australian Shiraz, Cabernet, Riesling, and Semillon; and California Cabernet and finest Merlot and Zinfandel.

Serving

THE RULES OF THE GAME

"The art in using wine is to produce the greatest possible quantity of present gladness, without any future depression."

The Gentleman's Table Guide, 1873

The Romans used to add salt to their wine to preserve it, while the Greeks favored pine resin (which explains the popularity of pine-flavored Retsina today.) Burgundians often refer to Napoleon's taste for Chambertin, but rarely mention that he diluted his red wine with water. A century ago, the English used to add ice to red Bordeaux – and today, European skiers drink hot "mulled" wine, adding sugar, fruit, and spices, while sunseekers in Spain enjoy a refreshing chilled version in the form of *Sangria*. Today, Mouton Cadet is drunk in Asia with a dash of Sprite. And why not? Millions of American wine drinkers got their first taste of wine in the form of a "cooler" – a blend of wine, sugar, and flavored soda. A dash of soda pop would do many an acidic Bordeaux a world of good – it's just a pity when it's added to a classier glass of Médoc. It's well worth questioning accepted rules – especially when they vary between cultures. The advice that follows is based on common sense and experience – and offered only to help you to decide how you enjoy serving and drinking wine.

SOME LIKE IT HOT

Particular styles of wine taste better at particular temperatures. At many restaurants, though, white and sparkling wine are more often served too cold than too hot. Paradoxically, it is the reds that suffer most from being drunk too warm. Few of the people who serve wines at "room temperature" recall that, when that term was coined, there wasn't a lot of central heating. Be ready to chill a fruity red in a bucket of ice and water for five to 10 minutes before serving.

Red Wine

When serving red, focus on the wine's flavor. Tough wines are best slightly warmer. The temperatures given are a rule-of-thumb guide:

1   Light fruity reds: 50°F-57°F (an hour in the fridge).
2   Younger red Burgundy and Rhônes and older Bordeaux, Chianti, younger Rioja, New World Grenache: 57°F-62°F
3   Older Burgundy, tannic young Bordeaux, Rhônes, Zinfandel, bigger Cabernet Sauvignon, Merlot, Shiraz, Barolo, and other bigger Italian and Spanish reds: 62°F-67°F

Rosé

Rosé should be chilled at 54°F-57°F, or for five to 10 minutes in a bucket of ice and water.

White Wine

The cooler the wine, the less it will smell or taste. Subtler, richer wines deserve to be drunk a little warmer.

1   Lighter sweeter wines and everyday sparklers: 39°F-46°F (two or three hours in the fridge or 10-15 minutes in ice and water).
2   Fuller-bodied, aromatic, drier, semidry, sweet whites; Champagne; light Sauvignon; and Chardonnay: 46°F-53°F
3   Richer dry wines – Burgundy, Chardonnay: 54°F-57°F

Don't cook your reds – or freeze your whites...

THE PERFECT OUTCOME

The patented Screwpull is still the most reliable way to get a cork out of a bottle. The "waiter's friend" is the next best thing, especially the modern versions with a hinged section designed to prevent corks from breaking. Whatever corkscrew you choose, avoid the models that look like a large screw. These often simply pull through old corks. These fragile stoppers are often most easily removed using a twopronged "Ah So" cork remover. I find these really tiresome for younger wines, however.

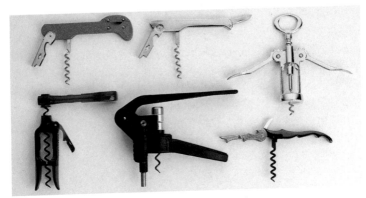

Good corkscrews all have spirals rather than screws.

WHICH GLASSES?

On occasions when no other glass was available, I have enjoyed great wine from the glass in my hotel bathroom. I suspect, though, I'd have gotten more out of the experience if something a bit more stylish had come to hand.

Glasses should be narrower across the rim than the bowl. Red ones should be bigger because whites are best kept chilled in the bottle rather than warming in the glass. If you like bubbles in your sparkling wine, serve it in a flute rather than a saucer from which they will swiftly escape. Schott, Spiegelau, and Riedel all produce attractive glasses that are specially designed to bring out the best in particular styles of wine. The Schott glasses have the advantage of being harder to break.

Wines definitely benefit from custom-designed glasses like these.

TO BREATHE OR NOT TO BREATHE?

After what may well have been a fairly lengthy period of imprisonment in its bottle, many a wine can be a bit sulky when it is first poured. Giving it a breath of air may help to banish the sulkiness and bring out the flavor and richness, which is why many people tend to remove the cork a few hours before the wine is to be served. This well-intentioned action, however, is almost a complete waste of time. (The contact with oxygen offered by the neck of the bottle is far too limited.) If you want to aerate a wine, you'd be far better off simply pouring it into a jug and back into the bottle just before you want to drink it. Broad-based, so-called "ship's decanters" not only look good, but also facilitate airing wine as it flows down the inside of the glass in a fine film. L'Esprit & le Vin make a special decanter for this purpose. Alternatively, small devices are now available that aerate wine to mimic the effect of decanting.

As a rule, young red and – surprisingly perhaps – white wines often benefit from exposure to air, especially when the flavor of a white has been temporarily flattened by a heavy dose of sulfur dioxide. Older red wines, however, may be tired out by the experience and may rapidly lose some of their immediate appeal.

Mature red Bordeaux, Rhône, and port, for example, may need to be decanted in order to remove the unwelcome mudlike deposit that has dropped to the bottom of the bottle. This initially daunting task is far easier than it seems.

Simply stand the bottle for up to a day before decanting it. Pour it very slowly, in front of a flashlight or candle, watching for the first signs of the deposit. Coffee filters suit those with less steady hands.

Decant red – or white – wine to bring out the flavor.

ORDER OF SERVICE

The rules say that white wines and youth respectively precede red wines and age; dry goes before sweet (most of us prefer our main course before the dessert); the lighter the wine, the earlier. These rules are often impossible to follow. What are you to do, for example, if the red Loire is lighter bodied than the white Burgundy? Can the red Bordeaux follow the Sauternes that you are offering with the foie gras? Ignore the absolutes, but bear in mind the common sense that lies behind them. Work gently up the scale of fullness, "flavorsomeness," and quality, rather than swinging wildly between styles.

LIQUID ASSETS

Investing in wine in the current market is probably no worse a bet than sinking your hard-earned cash into stocks and shares or most other commodities – and may well be rather wiser. $1500 of Dow Jones stock bought in 1997 fell in value to $1275 in 2002, while the same sum spent on 1996 Chateau Latour 'in futures' would have yielded a healthy profit in 2002 of $1125. Twelve months later, however, in early 2003, your claret would have dropped back from $2625 to $1875. But that's still better than plenty of high-tech stocks.

YOUTH BEFORE AGE

For most of the 20th century, the only wines worth investing in came from "blue chip" estates with long pedigrees such as the Bordeaux of Châteaux Latour, Cheval Blanc, and Haut-Brion; the Burgundies of the Domaine de la Romanée-Conti; and top port. Wines without the potential to improve in the cellar were not taken seriously, and a 10-year-old bottle from a good vintage would carry a significantly higher price tag than one made from grapes picked a couple of years ago.

Today, the auction rooms are full of newcomers, both among the wines and the bidders. There are Bordeaux from small estates (such as Clinet) and recently launched "microwines" or "garage" wines produced in tiny quantities, such as le Pin and Valandraud, and examples from New World regions such as the Napa and Barossa valleys. The common quality of these wines tends to be a rich, seductive, fruity, oaky character that was rarely encountered in traditional Bordeaux, which often required years to lose the tannic character of its youth. These immediately enjoyable young wines now often carry bigger price tags than earlier vintages. Their capacity to age is far less certain – and their ability to hold their value already dubious.

THE RULES

1) Wines command different prices in different countries **2)** Unlike works of art, wines don't last forever. **3)** Tread carefully among microwines with unproven potential. **4)** When buying futures/*en primeur*, deal with financially solid merchants. **5)** At auction, only buy wines that have been carefully cellared. **6)** Store wines carefully – and insure them. **7)** Follow their progress – read critics' comments and watch auction prices. **8)** Beware of falling reputations for wines and vintages. **9)** When bidding at auction, take note of the buyer's premium. (15-17.5%) and the possible increase in cost from local sales tax (VAT) and delivery charges. **10)** A diamond brooch is more easily converted into cash than a prize Bordeaux.

FRANCE
Bordeaux

Châteaux Angélus, Ausone, Cheval Blanc, Cos d'Estournel, Ducru-Beaucaillou, Eglise-Clinet, Figeac, Grand-Puy-Lacoste, Gruaud-Larose, Haut-Brion, Lafite, Lafleur, Latour, Léoville Barton, Léoville Las Cases, Lynch-Bages, Margaux, la Mission-Haut-Brion, Montrose, Mouton-Rothschild, Palmer, Pétrus, Pichon Lalande, Pichon Longueville, le Pin, Rauzan-Ségla, Valandraud. Vintages: 1982, 1983 (Margaux), 1988, 1989, 1990, 1995, 1996, 1998, 2000. 1999, 2001, and 2002 (top properties).

Burgundy

Drouhin Marquis de Laguiche, Gros Frères, Hospices de Beaune (from Drouhin, Jadot, etc), Méo-Camuzet, Romanée-Conti (la Tâche, Romanée-Conti), Gouges, Lafon, Leflaive, Leroy, Denis Mortet, Roumier, de Vogüé.

Rhône

Chapoutier, Chave, Guigal (top wines), Jaboulet Aîné "La Chapelle".

PORTUGAL (PORT)

Cockburn's, Dow's, Fonseca, Graham's, Noval, Taylor's, Warre's.

CALIFORNIA

Beaulieu Private Reserve, Bryant Family, Diamond Creek, Dominus, Duckhorn, Dunn, Harlan Estate, Grace Family, Matanzas Creek, Robert Mondavi Reserve, Opus One, Ridge, Spottswoode, Stag's Leap.

AUSTRALIA

Armagh, Clarendon Hills, Ch. Tahbilk 1860 Vines Shiraz, Henschke Hill of Grace, Cyril Henschke, Mount Edelstone, Penfolds Grange and Bin 707, Petaluma Cabernet, "John Riddoch", Virgin Hills, Yarra Yering.

Vintages

TIME WILL TELL

Thirty years or so ago, good vintages were rare. Today, physical, chemical, and organic ways to combat pests and diseases enable winemakers to produce good wines almost every year. Even so, some places are naturally more prone to tricky vintages. Northern Europe, for example, suffers more from unreliable sun and untimely rain than the warm, irrigated vineyards of the New World. A dependable climate does not necessarily make for better wine; grapes develop more interesting flavors in "marginal" climates – which is why New World producers are busily seeking out cooler, higher-altitude sites in which to plant their vines. It is not widely known that New World wine producers are allowed to improve a vintage with small amounts of younger or older wine. Doing so in France is illegal – though far from unknown.

IT'S AN ILL WIND

Some producers can buck the trend of a climatically poor year – by picking before, or after, the rainstorms, carefully discarding rotten grapes, or even using equipment to concentrate the flavor of a rain-diluted crop. In years like these, well-situated areas within larger regions can, in any case, make better wines than their neighbors. France's top vineyards became famous because of the way their grapes ripen. Even so, different varieties of vine can ripen differently from one year to another, depending where they are are grown. 2002, for example, was a better vintage for the Cabernet Sauvignon of the Médoc than the Merlot of St. Emilion and Pomerol. 1997 was, similarly, a fair-to-good vintage for red Bordeaux, but a truly spectacular one for Sauternes.

The following pages offer a general guide to the most significant vintages of this and the past century. Bear in mind, though, that the state of older wines will have been affected by the way they have been stored.

)VER 50 YEARS OF WINE...

2003 (SOUTHERN HEMISPHERE)

Despite fires in the former and frost in the latter, Australia and New Zealand produced small but good harvests. South Africa made its best wines in years. Impressive wines were produced in Chile and Argentina.

2002

There was little great Bordeaux (and decidedly less in St. Emilion than the Médoc) or Burgundy, and Europe was generally patchy or poor. Germany and England, however, did very well. California, Australia, and New Zealand were top class, and good wines were made in Chile and Argentina. Fires and intense heat spoiled South Africa's vintage.

2001

Good red, but great white Bordeaux. Better white than red Burgundies and Northern Rhônes. Good sweet Loires. Piedmont and Tuscany were great, as were Tokaji and top Germans. Chile and South Africa and New Zealand did well, and there were signs of brilliance in California.

2000

Good-to-great Bordeaux. Red Burgundy and Sauternes fared less well. Portugal produced fine table wines and vintage port. Italy saw its best results in the south, and there were great Tokajis. Australia's best wines were from Western Australia and the Hunter Valley.

1999

Variable red Bordeaux but fine Sauternes. Great red and white Burgundies and worthwhile Rhônes, Loires, and Alsaces. Other top wines were from Tuscany, Mosel-Saar-Ruwer, Tokaji, Coonawarra and Victoria, New Zealand, Chile, and Argentina.

1998

A mixed vintage throughout the northern hemisphere. Some great red Bordeaux, lovely Sauternes and Alsace, and fine white Burgundies (especially Chablis) and ports. California reds were varied.

1997

Now mature red Bordeaux and brilliant sweet whites. Great white Burgundy but variable reds. Alsace, Germany, and Austria made terrific wines, as did the port houses of the Douro and producers in the US, Australia, and New Zealand. Italy had a truly great year.

1996

Classic Bordeaux (especially Médoc, Graves, and Sauternes), white Burgundy, and the Loire. Patchy Alsace, Rhône, and Germany and fair in Italy, Spain, and Portugal. California, New Zealand, and Australia produced top-class red and white wines.

1995

Classy red Bordeaux and white Burgundy. Italian and Loire reds, Rhône, Alsace, Germany, Rioja, and Ribera del Duero are all good, as are Australia, New Zealand, South Africa, and North and South America.

1994

Unripe red Bordeaux, fine northern Rhône reds, fading red Burgundy, and great vintage port. Average-to-good Italian reds and Germans; California had a great vintage, and Australians were good to very good.

1993

Red Bordeaux is tiring now. There are excellent Tokaji, Alsace, and Loires (red and white), good red Burgundy and top-class whites. Wines were better in South Africa and New Zealand than in Australia.

1992

Poor Bordeaux but good white Burgundy. Fading red Burgundy. Taylor's and Fonseca produced great vintage port. Fine California Cabernets.

1991

Maturing Bordeaux and good Northern Rhône reds. Fine port and good wines from Spain, South Africa, California, New Zealand, and Australia.

1990

Great Bordeaux, Champagne, Germans, Alsace, Loire whites, red Rhônes, Burgundies, Australians, Californians, Barolo, and Spanish reds.

1985–1989

1989 Great red and good white Bordeaux and Champagne. Stunning Germans and red Loires; excellent Alsace. Good red and superb white Rhône, good red Burgundy. **1988** Evolving red Bordeaux and Italian reds, fine Sauternes and Champagne, Tokaji, German, Alsace, Loire reds and sweet whites, good Rhône, and red Burgundy. **1987** Fading red Bordeaux and Burgundy. **1986** Fine red and white Bordeaux, Australian reds, white Burgundy. **1985** Reds from Bordeaux, Rhône, Burgundy, Spain, Italy, Champagne, Port, Champagne, Alsace, and sweet Loire.

1980–1985

1984 South African and Australian reds, and Rieslings. **1983** Red Bordeaux, red Rhône, Tuscany, Piedmont, Sauternes, Madeira, port, Tokaji, Alsace. **1982** Red Bordeaux, Australian, Portuguese, and Spanish reds, Italian reds, Burgundy, and Rhône. **1981** Alsace. **1980** Madeira, port.

1970–1979

1979 Sassicaia, sweet Austrians. **1978** Rhône, Portuguese reds, Bordeaux, Burgundy, Barolo, Tuscany, and Loire reds. **1977** Port, sweet Austrians. **1976** Champagne, Loire reds and sweet whites, sweet Germans, Alsace, Sauternes. **1975** Top red Bordeaux and port, Sauternes. **1974** California and Portuguese reds. **1973** Napa Cabernet, sweet Austrians. **1972** Tokaji. **1971** Bordeaux, Burgundy, Champagne, Barolo and Tuscan reds, sweet Germans, red Rhône, Penfolds Grange. **1970** Port, Napa Cabernet, red Bordeaux, Rioja.

1960–1969

1969 Red Rhône, Burgundy. **1968** Madeira, Rioja, Tokaji. **1967** Sauternes, Châteauneuf-du-Pape, German TBA. **1966** Port, Burgundy, red Bordeaux, Australian Shiraz. **1965** Barca Velha. **1964** Red Bordeaux, Tokaji, Vega Sicilia, Rioja, sweet Loire, red Rhône. **1963** Vintage port, Tokaji. **1962** Top Bordeaux and Burgundy, Rioja, Australian Cabernet and Shiraz. **1961** Red Bordeaux, Sauternes, Champagne, Brunello, Barolo, Alsace, red Rhône. **1960** Port, top red Bordeaux.

1950–1959

1959 Red Bordeaux, Sauternes, Tokaji, Germans, Loire, Alsace, Rhône, Burgundy. **1958** Barolo. **1957** Madeira, Vega Sicilia, Tokaji. **1956** Yquem. **1955** Red Bordeaux, Sauternes, port, Champagne. **1954** Madeira. **1953** Red Bordeaux, Tokaji, Champagne, sweet Germans, Côte Rôtie, Burgundy. **1952** Red Bordeaux, Madeira, Champagne, Barolo, Tokaji, Rhône, Burgundy. **1951** Terrible. **1950** Madeira.

1940–1949

1949 Bordeaux, Tokaji, sweet Germans, red Rhône, Burgundy. **1948** Port, Vega Sicilia. **1947** Bordeaux, Burgundy, port, Champagne, Tokaji, sweet Loire. **1946** Armagnac. **1945** Port, Bordeaux, Champagne, Chianti, sweet Germans, Alsace, red Rhônes, and Burgundy. **1944** Madeira, port. **1943** Champagne, red Burgundy. **1942** Port, Rioja, Vega Sicilia. **1941** Madeira, Sauternes. **1940** Madeira.

ANNIVERSARY WINES

1904 Claret, port. **1914** Claret. **1924** Claret, port. **1934** Claret, port.

Wine and Health

BETTER RED THAN DEAD?

"Wine is fit for man in a wonderful way, provided that it is taken with good sense by the sick as well as the healthy."

Hippocrates

SAVOIR VIVRE

Around 2200 BC, a Sumerian clay tablet recommended wines for various ailments. In 1890, an Irish physician attributed the well-being of the French to red wine. A century later CBS television's *60 Minutes* "French Paradox" programme revealed that Gallic wine drinkers were healthier than Anglo-Saxon teetotallers. And, in 2003, a US government ban on references to the possible health benefits of wine on labels was finally lifted. Bottles of wine sold in America still have to carry strong health warnings – unlike bullets.

WHITE WINE AND LUNGS

In early 2002, a survey of 1,555 New Yorkers by Dr. Holger Schunemann of the University of Buffalo uncovered an apparent link between the consumption of white wine and better lung function. Anti-oxidants in the wine appear to prevent the creation of free radicals, harmful molecules that damage lung tissues. If further research supports these findings, white wine sales may get the boost red wine enjoyed when it was announced that it was good for the heart.

RED WINE AND HEALTHY BLOOD

Numerous credible reasons have been given for the link between wine and health, including the simple fact that alcohol relieves stress that might otherwise cause disease. (This would help to explain why moderate consumption of other alcoholic drinks also appears to be beneficial.)

However, a conference at the University Victor Segalen in Bordeaux in 2001 raised the possibility that the 200 phenolic compounds in red wine may be effective against a number of ailments, ranging from heart disease to cancer and Aids. Many of these compounds come from the skins and seeds that are used in making red wine, but discarded when producing white. White wine has a tenth as many of them as red.

RED WINE AND HEART DISEASE

According to Université de Bourgogne researchers, people who daily drink up to four glasses of red wine have higher levels of HDL (high density lipoproteins) – "good" cholesterol that escorts "bad" cholesterol away from artery walls. Prof. Ludovic Drouet of the Hopital Lariboisière in Paris believes wine also acts against the furring of arteries because polyphenols aid cell proliferation and hinder blood clotting. Heart attack victims are now advised to drink wine while convalescing. A report in the British Journal of Pharmacology additionally associated the relaxation of blood vessels and reduced blood pressure with red wine consumption.

Resveratrol, an antifungal compound found in high concentration in grape skins has been shown to improve the lipid profile of volunteers drinking three glasses of red wine a day for two weeks. Resveratrol appears to be 20 times more powerful as an antioxidant than Vitamin E. Prof. Joseph Vercauteren of the University Victor Segalen in Bordeaux suggests that the phenolic compounds found in red wine mop up damaging chemicals – free radicals – more effectively than vitamins C and E because they are fat soluble.

WINE AND AIDS

Red wine may also be used to augment the treatment of Aids, according to Dr. Marvin Edeas of the Hôpital Antoine Béclère in Clamart, who is studying the way the polyphenols rejuvenate blood. It may also be effective against diseases such as sickle cell anaemia and thalassaemia.

WINE AND FOOD POISONING

Wine of both colors counters both constipation and diarrhoea, while white wine in particular stimulates the urinary functions. A 2002 Spanish study – published in *Epidemiology* – suggests wine may be effective against salmonella and possibly against hepatitis A, while according to an Oregon study (reported in the *Journal of Food Science*), it combats both samonella and E. coli. It also kills cholera bacteria and combats typhoid and trichinella, the poisonous compound in "bad" pork. One researcher, Dr. Heinrich Kliewe, actually recommends that moderate amounts of wine can counteract some of the side effects of antibiotics.

WINE AND AGEING

Marie Antoinette apparently used to wash her face in red wine to protect the skin against wrinkles, and a Bordeaux health spa (at Château Smith-Haut-Lafitte) makes great use of extracts from grape seeds. Today, though, most researchers are more concerned with the way antioxidants in red wine appear to inhibit the effects of degenerative oxidation, such as strokes. Wine may also offer protection against Alzheimer's Disease; moderate wine drinkers in their 70s and 80s seem to remain more alert.

WINE AND VIRUSES

Apart from any beneficial effects of wine against the Aids virus, it may also combat other viruses. According to Drs. Jack Konowalchuk and Joan Speirs of the department of microbial hazards in Canada, the polyphenols in tannic red wine are effective against such viruses as those that cause cold sores, and may even act against genital Herpes 2.

WINE AND PREGNANCY

Despite the fears it arouses, the risks associated with drinking wine while expecting a baby are actually very low. Fetal Alcohol Syndrome is rare outside the poorer inner cities of the US. In 1997, the UK Royal College of Obstetricians and Gynaecologists reported that up to 15 units of alcohol per week should do no harm to a fetus.

WINE AND CALORIES

There is no difference in calories between a Muscadet and a red Bordeaux (around 110 per glass). More alcoholic wines, such as California Zinfandels, Australian Shirazes, and some red Rhones, with strengths of 14 per cent will have more calories, while sweeter, but less alcoholic German wines that weigh in at 9 per cent, have less than 80 calories. A Stanford University survey suggests the action of the wine on the metabolism somehow makes its calories less fattening.

WINE AND STROKES

A 2003 *Journal of the American Medical Association* report described research at Tulane University linking moderate wine drinking (2-3 glasses daily) to an almost 30 percent lower risk of stroke.

WINE AND CANCER

Alcohol has been linked to rare occurrences of mouth and throat cancer – but only among smokers. In fact, according to a British research team at the De Montfort University, there are clear indications that red wine may act against cancer. The study found that a tumor cell enzyme called CYP1B1 transforms the resveratrol naturally found in red wine into piceatannol, which, in turn destroys cancer cells. A separate study at Marshall University in West Virginia (published in *Cancer Letters* in February 2003) found that the amount of resveratrol in a glass of red wine killed human skin-cancer cells. Dr. Francis Raul of the University Louis Pasteur in Strasbourg believes that resveratrol inhibits the proliferation of human intestinal cancerous cells and the formation of tumors in mice predisposed to intestinal tumors. Prof. Djavad Mossalayi of the Victor Segalen University has tested it on normal and cancerous human cells and found it to be toxic to both. He thinks the action of wine on cancer cells may not be linked to its antioxidant properties but to the way it acts on the basic process of cell division. Red wine is also rich in gallic acid, an acknowledged anticarcinogenic. Wine's role in reducing stress may help against certain forms of cancer.

HANGOVERS

All alcohol is hangover fare. The best way to avoid this fate is to drink plenty of water before going to bed. Vitamin B (Berocca tablets from Roche) are useful on the morning after, as is toast with Marmite or Vegemite yeast paste, if these are available. Otherwise, go for protein and refreshing orange juice diluted with sparkling mineral water.

WINE AND ALLERGIES

Red wine, like chocolate, can inhibit a useful little enzyme called phenosulfotransferase-P, or PST-P, which detoxifies bacteria in the gut. An absence of PST-P is linked to migraine, which is why some people complain of headaches after drinking a glass or two of wine. Other people have found that red wine is also associated with episodic skin allergies. Sufferers from wine-related allergies may find that some of these conditions can come and go over time. Interestingly, there also seems to be differences in the effects of particular styles of wine. Chianti, for example, is claimed to have lower amounts of histamines. So, while awaiting the results of further research into wine-related allergies, it may be worth sampling small doses of various kinds of wine.

WINE AND ASTHMA

One side effect of wines that are heavily dosed with sulfur dioxide (used to combat bacteria in most dried, bottled, and canned foods) is an incidence of asthma attacks among those who are susceptible to this condition. Red wines in general, and New World and organic wines in particular, have lower sulphur levels. The highest levels of sulphur will be in sweet white wines and wines with low alcohol levels.

Food and Wine

MATCHMAKING FOR BEGINNERS

One of the most daunting aspects of wine has always been the traditional obsession with serving precisely the right wine with any particular dish – of only ever drinking red with meat and white with fish or shellfish. It may be reassuring to learn that some of these time-honored rules are just plain wrong. In Portugal, for example, fishermen love to wash down their sardines and salt cod with a glass or two of harsh red wine. In Burgundy they even poach fish in their local red.

On the other hand, the idea that a platter of cheese needs a bottle of red wine can be trashed in an instant. Just take a mouthful of red Bordeaux immediately after eating a little goat's cheese or Brie. The wine will taste metallic and unpleasant because the creaminess of the cheese reacts badly with the tannin – the toughness – in the wine. A dry white would be far more successful (its acidity would cut through the fat), while the Bordeaux would be shown at its best alongside a harder, stronger cheese. If you don't want to offer a range of wines, try sticking to one or two cheeses that really will complement the stuff in the glass.

Don't take anything for granted. Rare beef and red Bordeaux surprisingly fails the test of an objective tasting. The protein of the meat somehow makes all but the fruitiest wines taste tougher. If you're looking for a perfect partner for beef, uncork a Burgundy. If it's the Bordeaux that takes precedence, you'd be far better off with lamb.

The difference between an ideal and a passable food-and-wine combination can be very subtle. Most of us have after all happily quaffed red Bordeaux with our steak, but just as an avid cook will tinker with a recipe until it is just right, there's a lot to be said for making the occasional effort to find a pairing of dish and wine that really works. Like people who are happier as a couple than separately, some foods and wines simply seem to bring out the best in each other.

A Sense of Balance

There is no real mystery about the business of matching food and wine. Some flavors and textures are compatible, and some are not. Strawberry mousse is not really delicious with chicken casserole, but apple sauce can do wonders for roast pork.

The key to spotting which relationships are marriages made in heaven, and which have the fickleness of Hollywood romances, lies in identifying the dominant characteristics of the contents of both the plate and the glass. Then, learn by experience which are likely to complement each other, either through their similarities or through their differences.

Likely Combinations

It is not difficult to define particular types of food and wine, and to guess how they are likely to get along. A buttery sauce is happier with something tangily acidic, like a crisp Sauvignon Blanc, rather than a rich, buttery Chardonnay. A subtly poached fish won't appreciate a fruit-packed New World white, and you won't do pheasant pie any favors by pulling the cork on a delicate red.

What to Avoid

Some foods and their characteristics, though, make life difficult for almost any drink. Sweetness, for example, in a fruity sauce served with a savory dish seems to strip some of the fruitier flavors out of a wine. This may not matter if the stuff in your glass is a blackcurranty New World Cabernet Sauvignon, but it's bad news if it is a bone-dry white or a tough red with little fruit to spare.

Cream is tricky, too. Try fresh strawberries with Champagne – delicious; now add a little whipped cream to the equation and you'll spoil the flavor. Creamy and buttery sauces can have the same effect on a wine and call for a similarly creamy white – or a fresh, zippy one to cut through the fattiness.

Spices are very problematic for wine – largely due to the physical sensation of eating them rather than any particular flavor. A wine may not seem particularly nasty after a mouthful of chili sauce; it will simply lose its fruity flavor and taste of nothing at all – which, in the case of a fine red seems to be a pity. The way a tannic red dries out the mouth will also accentuate the heat of the spice. The ideal wine for most Westerners to drink with any spicy dish would be a light, possibly slightly sweet, white or a light, juicy red. Chinese palates often react differently to these combinations, however. They like the burning effect of the chili and see no point in trying to put out the fire with white wine.

Always Worth a Try

Some condiments actually bring out the best in wines. A little freshly ground pepper on your meat or pasta can accentuate the flavor of a wine, just as it can with a sauce.

Squeezing fresh lemon onto your fish will reduce the apparent acidity of a white wine – a useful tip if you have inadvertently bought a case of tooth-strippingly dry Muscadet. And, just as lemon can help to liven up a dull sauce, it will do the same for a dull white wine, such as a basic Burgundy or a Soave, by neutralizing the acidity and allowing other flavors to make themselves apparent. Mustard performs a similar miracle when it is eaten with beef, somehow nullifying the effect of the meat protein on the wine.

Marriage Guidance

In the following pages, I have suggested wines to go with a wide range of dishes and ingredients, taking the dominant flavor as the key point. Don't treat any of this advice as gospel – use it instead as a launchpad for your own food and wine experiments.

And, if no wine seems to taste just right, don't be too surprised. Heretical as it may seem, some dishes are actually more enjoyable with other drinks. The vinegar that is a fundamental part of a good relish, for example, will do no wine a favor. Even avid wine lovers might well find beer a far more pleasurable accompaniment.

Cooking with Wine

Finally, a word or two about how to make the best use of wine in the kitchen (apart from its role as refreshment following a vigorous session of egg-beating, and as a tranquilizer for the moments when sauces curdle and soufflés refuse to rise). The first (and most often forgotten) rule to remember is that wine that's not good enough to drink is probably not good enough to pour into the frying pan or casserole. At least, not unless you take a perverse pleasure in using and eating substandard ingredients. On the other hand, despite the advice of classic French recipes, your "coq au vin" won't be spoiled by your unwillingness to make it with a pricy bottle of Grand Cru Burgundy. A decent, humbler red will do perfectly well, though it is worth trying to use a similar style to the one suggested.

Second – and just as important – remember that, with the exception of a few dishes such as British sherry trifle or zabaglione, in which wine is enjoyed in its natural state, wine used as an ingredient needs to be cooked in order to remove the alcohol. So, add it early enough for the necessary evaporation to take place.

A

Almond Liqueur Muscats or Beaumes de Venise.
Trout with Almonds Bianco di Custoza, Pinot Blanc.
Anchovies
Fresh Anchovy (Boquerones) Albariño, Vinho Verde, Aligoté.
Salade Niçoise Muscadet, Vinho Verde, or Beaujolais.
Salted Anchovies Rioja red or white, Manzanilla or Fino sherry.
Tapenade Dry sherry or Madeira.
Apple
Apple Pie or Strudel Austrian off-dry white.
Blackberry and Apple Pie Late harvest Riesling, Vouvray demi-sec.
Roast Pork with Apple Sauce Off-dry Vouvray or Riesling.
Waldorf Salad Dry Madeira.
Apricot Late harvest Sémillon or Riesling, Jurançon Moelleux.
Arroz con Pollo (Chicken and Rice) Côtes du Rhône, young Zinfandel,
    Navarra or Rioja "Joven."
Artichoke White Rhône.
Artichoke Soup Dry Loire whites, Pinot Gris.
Arugula Pinot Grigio, young Viognier.
Asparagus
Asparagus Crêpes au Gratin Muscadet, Vinho Verde, Cider.
Asparagus Soup Fresh dry whites, Sauvignon Blanc.
Avocado
Avocado Mayonnaise Unoaked Chardonnay, Chablis.
Avocado Stuffed with Crab Champagne, Riesling Kabinett, Sauvignon Blanc,
    Pinot Gris, Australian Chardonnay.
Guacamole Fumé Blanc or unoaked Sauvignon Blanc.

B

Bacon Rich Pinot Gris or Alsace Riesling.
Bacon with Marinated Scallops Fino sherry or mature Riesling,
    Shiraz-based Australians, Zinfandel from the US, or a heavy Cape red.
Warm Bacon Salad New World Sauvignon Blanc, California Fumé Blanc, or
    a good Pouilly Fumé.
Banana
Flambéed Banana with Rum Jurançon, Tokaji, Pedro Ximénez sherry, rum.
Barbecue Sauce Inexpensive off-dry white or a simple, fruity Cabernet.
Spare Ribs with Barbecue Sauce Fruity Australian Shiraz, Grenache, or
    Zinfandel; spicy Côtes du Rhône from a ripe vintage; or an off-dry white.
Basil Slightly sweet Chardonnay (i.e., California, commercial Australian).
Pasta in Pesto Sauce New Zealand Sauvignon Blanc, Valpolicella.
Beans
Bean Salad Spanish reds – Rioja and Rueda – or New Zealand Sauvignon Blanc.
Boston Baked Beans Light Zinfandel, Beaujolais, dry rosé, or beer.
Refried Beans Côtes du Rhône, Beaujolais, dry Grenache rosé.
White Bean Stew (Estouffat) Young Corbières, light Merlot.

Beef

Beef with Green Peppers in Black Bean Sauce Off-dry German Riesling or characterful dry white, like white Rhône or Marsanne.

Beef with Scallions and Ginger Off-dry German Riesling or one of the more serious Beaujolais Crus.

Beef Stew Pomerol or St. Emilion, good Northern Rhône like Crozes Hermitage, Shiraz or Pinot Noir from the New World.

Beef Stroganoff Tough, beefy reds like Amarone, Brunello di Montalcino, Barolo, Côte Rôtie, or really ripe Zinfandel.

Beef Wellington Top Burgundy, Châteauneuf-du-Pape.

Boeuf Bourguignon Australian Bordeaux-style, Barolo, or other robust reds with sweet fruit.

Boiled Beef and Carrots Bordeaux Rouge, Valpolicella Classico, Australian Shiraz.

Bresaola (Air-Dried Beef) Beaujolais, Barbera, and tasty reds from the Languedoc.

Carpaccio of Beef Chardonnay, Champagne, Cabernet Franc, and Pomerol.

Chili con Carne Robust fruity reds, Beaujolais Crus, Barbera or Valpolicella, spicy reds like Zinfandel or Pinotage.

Corned Beef Loire reds from Gamay or Cabernet Franc.

Corned Beef Hash Characterful spicy reds from the Rhône or Southern France.

Creole-Style Beef Cheap Southern Rhône reds or Côtes du Rhône, Zinfandel.

Hamburger Zinfandel or country reds from Italy or France, e.g., Corbières.

Hungarian Goulash East European reds – Bulgarian Cabernet or Mavrud and Hungarian Kadarka – or Australian Shiraz.

Meatballs Spicy rich Rhône reds, Zinfandel, Pinotage, and Portuguese reds.

Panang Neuk (Beef in Peanut Curry) New World Chardonnay; New Zealand Sauvignon Blanc; or a spicy, aromatic white Rhône.

Pastrami Zinfandel, good Bardolino, light Côtes du Rhône.

Rare Chargrilled Beef Something sweetly ripe and flavorsome, but not too tannic. Try Chilean Merlot.

Roast Beef Côte Rôtie, good Burgundy.

Steak Pinot Noir and Merlot from the New World; Australian Shiraz; Châteauneuf-du-Pape; good, ripe Burgundy.

Steak with Dijon Mustard Bordeaux, Cabernet Sauvignon from the New World, or Australian Shiraz.

Steak and Kidney Pie/Pudding Bordeaux, Australian Cabernet Sauvignon, Southern Rhône reds, or Rioja.

Steak au Poivre Cabernet Sauvignon, Chianti, Rhône reds, Shiraz, or Rioja.

Steak Tartare Bourgogne Blanc; Beaujolais; Bardolino; or, traditionally, vodka.

Thai Beef Salad New Zealand or South African Sauvignon Blanc, Gewürztraminer, Pinot Blanc.

Beer (in a sauce)

Carbonnade à la Flamande Cheap Southern Rhône or Valpolicella.

Beet

Borscht Rich, dry Alsace Pinot Gris; Pinot Blanc; or Italian Pinot Grigio.

Black Bean Sauce
   Beef with Green Peppers in Black Bean Sauce Off-dry German Riesling
      or characterful, dry white like white Rhône or Marsanne.
Blackberry
   Blackberry and Apple Pie Late harvest Riesling, Vouvray demi-sec.
Black Cherry
   Black Forest Cake Fortified Muscat, Schnapps, or Kirsch.
Blackcurrant
   Blackcurrant Cheesecake Sweet, grapey dessert wines.
   Blackcurrant Mousse Sweet sparkling wines.
Blinis Vodka or good Champagne.
Blueberries
   Blueberry Pie Tokaji (6 Puttonyos), late harvest Semillon or Sauvignon.
Brandy
   British Christmas Pudding Australian Liqueur Muscat, tawny port, rich
      (sweet) Champagne, Tokaji.
   Crêpe Suzette Asti, Orange Muscat, Champagne cocktails.
Brie Sancerre or New Zealand Sauvignon Blanc.
Broccoli
   Broccoli and Cheese Soup Slightly sweet sherry – Amontillado or Oloroso.
Butter
   Béarnaise Sauce Good dry Riesling.
   Beurre Blanc Champagne Blanc de Blancs, dry Vinho Verde.
Butternut Squash
   Butternut Soup Aromatic Alsace Gewurztraminer.

C

Cabbage
   Stuffed Cabbage East European Cabernet.
Cajun Spices Beaujolais Crus.
   Gumbo Zinfandel or maybe beer.
Camembert Dry Sauvignon Blanc or unoaked Chablis.
Capers Sauvignon Blanc.
   Skate with Black Butter Crisply acidic whites like Muscadet or Chablis.
   Tartare Sauce Crisply fresh whites like Sauvignon.
Caramel
   Caramelized Oranges Asti, Sauternes.
   Crème Caramel Muscat or Gewürztraminer Vendange Tardive.
Carp Franken Sylvaner, dry Jurançon, Hungarian Furmint.
Carrot
   Carrot and Coriander Soup Aromatic, dry Muscat; Argentinian Torrontes.
   Carrot and Orange Soup Madeira or perhaps an Amontillado sherry.
Cashew Nuts Pinot Blanc.
   Chicken with Cashew Nuts Rich aromatic white, Pinot Gris, or Muscat.
Cauliflower
   Cauliflower Cheese Fresh crisp Côtes de Gascogne white; Pinot Grigio;
      softly plummy Chilean Merlot; or young, unoaked Rioja.

Caviar Champagne or chilled vodka.
Celery
   Celery Soup Off-dry Riesling
Cheddar (mature) Good Bordeaux, South African Cabernet, port.
Cheese (general – also see individual entries)
   Cheeseburger Sweetly fruity oaky reds – Australian Shiraz, Rioja.
   Cheese Fondue Swiss white or Vin de Savoie.
   Cheese Platter Match wines to cheeses; don't put too tannic a red with too
      creamy a cheese, and offer white wines – which go well with all but the
      hardest cheese. Strong creamy cheeses demand fine Burgundy; blue cheese is
      made for late harvest wines; goat cheese is ideal with Sancerre, Pouilly Fumé,
      or other dry, unoaked Sauvignons. Munster is best paired with Alsace
      Gewurztraminer.
   Cheese Sauce (Mornay) Oaky Chardonnay.
   Cream Cheese, Crème Fraîche, Mozzarella, Mascarpone Fresh light dry
      whites – Frascati, Pinot Grigio.
   Raclette Swiss white or Vin de Savoie.
Cheesecake Australian botrytized Semillon.
Cherry Valpolicella, Recioto della Valpolicella, Dolcetto.
   Roast Duck with Cherry Sauce Barbera, Dolcetto, or Barolo.
Chestnut
   Roast Turkey with Chestnut Stuffing Côtes du Rhône, Merlot, or soft and
      mature Burgundy.
Chicken
   Barbecued Chicken Rich and tasty white, Chardonnay.
   Chicken Casserole Mid-weight Rhône, such as Crozes-Hermitage or Lirac.
   Chicken Chasseur Off-dry Riesling.
   Chicken Kiev Chablis, Aligoté, or Italian dry white.
   Chicken Pie White Bordeaux, simple Chardonnay, or else a light Italian
      white.
   Chicken Soup Soave, Orvieto, or Pinot Blanc.
   Chicken Vol-au-Vents White Bordeaux.
   Coq au Vin Shiraz-based New World reds, red Burgundy.
   Curry Chicken Gewürztraminer, dry white Loire, fresh Chinon.
   Devilled Chicken Australian Shiraz.
   Fricassée Unoaked Chardonnay.
   Lemon Chicken Muscadet, Chablis, or basic Bourgogne Blanc.
   Roast/Grilled Chicken Reds or whites, though nothing too heavy –
      Burgundy is good, as is Barbera, though Soave will do just as well.
   Roast/Grilled Chicken with Sage and Onion Stuffing Italian reds,
      especially Chianti; soft, plummy Merlots; and sweetly fruity Rioja.
   Roast/Grilled Chicken with Tarragon Dry Chenin (Vouvray or perhaps
      a good South African).
   Saltimbocca (Cutlet with Mozzarella and Ham) Flavorsome, dry Italian
      whites – Lugana, Bianco di Custoza, Orvieto.
   Smoked Chicken Oaky Chardonnay, Australian Marsanne, or Fumé Blanc.
   Southern Fried Chicken White Bordeaux, Muscadet, Barbera, light Zinfandel.
   Tandoori Chicken White Bordeaux, New Zealand Sauvignon Blanc.
Chicken Liver (Sauté) Softly fruity, fairly light reds including Beaujolais,
   Italian Cabernet or Merlot, or perhaps an Oregon Pinot Noir.

Chicken Liver Pâté Most of the above reds plus Vouvray Moelleux, Monbazillac, or Amontillado sherry.

Chili Cheap wine or cold beer.

Beef Chili Robust fruity reds, Beaujolais Crus, Barbera or Valpolicella, spicy reds like Zinfandel or Pinotage.

Hot and Sour Soup Crisply aromatic English white, Baden Dry.

Szechuan-Style Dry, aromatic whites; Alsace Pinot Gris; Riesling; Grenache rosé; beer.

Thai Beef Salad New Zealand or South African Sauvignon Blanc, Gewürztraminer, Pinot Blanc.

Chinese (general) Aromatic white – Gewürztraminer, Pinot Gris, English.

Chives Sauvignon Blanc.

Chocolate Orange Muscat, Moscatel de Valencia.

Black Forest (Chocolate and Cherry) Gâteau Fortified Muscat or Kirsch.

Chocolate Cake Beaumes de Venise, Bual or Malmsey Madeira, Orange Muscat, sweet German, or fine Champagne.

Chocolate Profiteroles with Cream Muscat de Rivesaltes.

Dark Chocolate Mousse Sweet Black Muscat or other Muscat-based wines.

Milk Chocolate Mousse Moscato d'Asti.

Chorizo (Sausage) Red or white Rioja, Navarra, Manzanilla sherry, Beaujolais, or Zinfandel.

Cinnamon Riesling Spätlese, Muscat.

Clams Chablis or Sauvignon Blanc.

Clam Chowder Dry white such as Côtes de Gascogne, Amontillado sherry, or Madeira.

Spaghetti Vongole Pinot Bianco or Lugana.

Cockles Muscadet, Gros Plant, Aligoté, dry Vinho Verde.

Coconut (milk) California Chardonnay.

Green Curry Big-flavored New World whites or Pinot Blanc from Alsace.

Cod Unoaked Chardonnay; good, white Burgundy; dry Loire Chenin.

Cod and Chips (French Fries) Any light, crisp, dry white, such as a Sauvignon from Bordeaux or Touraine. Alternatively, try dry rosé or Champagne. Remember, though, that English-style heavy-handedness with the vinegar will do no favors for the wine. For vinegary fries, stick to beer.

Cod Roe (smoked) Well-oaked New World Chardonnay.

Lisbon-Style Cod Vinho Verde; Muscadet; light, dry Riesling.

Salt Cod (Bacalhão de Gomes) Classically Portuguese red or white – Vinho Verde or Bairrada reds.

Smoked Cod Vinho Verde.

Coffee

Coffeecake Asti.

Coffee Mousse Asti, Liqueur Muscat.

Tiramisu Sweet fortified Muscat, Vin Santo, Torcolato.

Coriander

Carrot and Coriander Soup Aromatic, dry Muscat.

Cilantro Dry or off-dry English white.

Coriander Seed Dry, herby Northern Italian whites.

Corn Rich and ripe whites – California Chardonnay.

Corn on the Cob Light, fruity whites – German Riesling.

Corn Soup with Chicken Chilean Sauvignon, Southern French whites, Soave, Chilean Merlot.

Corn Soup with Crab Sancerre, other Sauvignon Blanc.

Couscous Spicy Shiraz, North African reds, or earthy Southern French Minervois.

Crab Chablis, Sauvignon Blanc, New World Chardonnay.

Crab Cakes (Maryland-style) Rias Baixas Albariño.

Crab Cioppino Sauvignon Blanc, Pinot Grigio.

Crab Mousse Crisp dry whites – Baden Dry or Soave.

Deviled Crab (spicy) New World Sauvignon, Albariño.

Cranberry

Roast Turkey with Cranberry and Orange Stuffing Richly fruity reds like Shiraz from Australia, Zinfandel, or modern Rioja.

Crayfish

Freshwater Crayfish South African Sauvignon, Meursault.

Salad of Crayfish Tails with Dill Rich South African Chenin blends or crisp Sauvignon, white Rhône.

Cream When dominant not good with wine, particularly tannic reds.

Curry

Beef in Peanut Curry New World Chardonnay; spicy, aromatic white Rhône.

Coronation Chicken Gewürztraminer; dry, aromatic English wine; or a fresh Chinon.

Curried Beef Beefy, spicy reds – Barolo, Châteauneuf-du-Pape, and Shiraz/Cabernet – or off-dry aromatic whites – Gewürztraminer, Pinot Gris. Or try some Indian sparkling wine or cold Indian beer.

Curried Turkey New World Chardonnay.

Tandoori Chicken White Bordeaux, New Zealand Sauvignon Blanc.

Thai Green Chicken Curry Big New World whites or dry, Pinot Blanc from Alsace.

D

Dill Sauvignon Blanc.

Gravlax Ice cold vodka, Pinot Gris, or Akvavit.

Dover Sole Sancerre, good Chablis, unoaked Chardonnay.

Dried Fruit Sweet sherry, tawny port.

Bread and Butter Pudding Barsac or Sauternes, Monbazillac, Jurançon. Muscat de Beaumes de Venise or Australian Orange Muscat.

Mince Pie Rich, late harvest wine or botrytis-affected Sémillon.

Duck Pinot Noir from Burgundy, California, or Oregon, or off-dry German Riesling.

Cassoulet Serious white Rhônes, Marsanne or Roussanne, or try reds including Grenache and Syrah from the Rhône, berryish Italian reds, or Zinfandel.

Confit de Canard Alsace Pinot Gris or a crisp red like Barbera.

Duck Pâté Chianti or other juicy herby red, Amontillado sherry.

Duck Pâté with Orange Riesling or Rioja.

Peking Duck Rice wine, Alsace Riesling, Pinot Gris.

Roast Duck Fruity reds like Australian Cabernet, a ripe Nebbiolo, or Zinfandel.
Roast Duck with Cherry Sauce Barbera, Dolcetto, or Barolo.
Roast Duck with Orange Sauce Loire red or a sweet white like Vouvray demi-sec.
Smoked Duck California Chardonnay or Fumé Blanc.
Duck Liver
Foie Gras de Canard Champagne, late harvest Gewürztraminer or Riesling, Sauternes.

E

Eel
Smoked Eel Pale, dry sherry; simple, fresh white Burgundy.
Egg
Crème Brûlée Jurançon Moelleux, Tokaji.
Eggs Benedict Unoaked Chardonnay, Blanc de Blancs, British Bucks Fizz, Bloody Mary.
Eggs Florentine Unoaked Chardonnay, Pinot Blanc, Aligoté, Sémillon.
Spanish Tortilla Young, juicy Spanish reds and fresher whites from La Mancha or Rueda.
Eggplant
Stuffed Eggplant Beefy, spicy reds like Bandol, Zinfandel, a good Southern Rhône, or a full-bodied Italian.

F

Fennel Sauvignon Blanc.
Fig Liqueur Muscat.
Fish (general – also see individual entries)
Bouillabaisse Red or white Côtes du Rhône, dry rosé or peppery dry white from Provence, California Fumé Blanc, Marsanne, or Verdicchio.
Cumberland Fish Pie California Chardonnay, Alsace Pinot Gris, Sauvignon Blanc.
Fish Cakes White Bordeaux, Chilean Chardonnay.
Fish and Chips Most fairly simple, crisply acidic dry whites or maybe a rosé or Champagne (See Cod). Go easy with the vinegar.
Fish Soup Manzanilla, Chablis, Muscadet.
Kedgeree Aligoté, crisp Sauvignon.
Mediterranean Fish Soup Provençal reds and rosés, Tavel, Côtes du Rhône, Vin de Pays d'Oc.
Seafood Salad Soave, Pinot Grigio, Muscadet, or a lightly oaked Chardonnay.
Sushi Saké.
Frankfurter Côtes du Rhône or beer.

Fruit (general – also see individual entries)

British Summer Pudding Late harvest Riesling – German or Alsace.

Fresh Fruit Salad Moscato d'Asti, Riesling Beerenauslese, or Vouvray Moelleux.

Fruit Flan Vouvray Moelleux, Alsace Riesling Vendange Tardive.

G

Game (general – also see individual entries)

Cold Game Fruity Northern Italian reds – Barbera or Dolcetto – good Beaujolais or light Burgundy.

Game Pie Beefy reds, Southern French, Rhône, Australian Shiraz, Pinotage.

Roast Game Big reds, Brunello di Montalcino, old Barolo, good Burgundy.

Well-hung Game Old Barolo or Barbaresco, mature Hermitage, Côte Rôtie or Châteauneuf-du-Pape, fine Burgundy.

Garlic

Aïoli A wide range of wines go well including white Rioja, Provence rosé, California Pinot Noir.

Garlic Sausage Red Rioja, Bandol, Côtes du Rhône.

Gazpacho Fino sherry, white Rioja.

Roast/Grilled Chicken with Garlic Oaky Chardonnay or red Rioja.

Roast Lamb with Garlic and Rosemary Earthy soft reds like California Petite Sirah, Rioja, or Zinfandel.

Snails with Garlic Butter Aligoté and light white Burgundy or perhaps a red Gamay de Touraine.

Ginger Gewürztraminer or Riesling.

Beef with Onions and Ginger Off-dry German Riesling, one of the more serious Beaujolais Crus.

Chicken with Ginger White Rhône, Gewürztraminer.

Ginger Ice Cream Asti or late harvest Sémillon.

Goat Cheese Sancerre, New World Sauvignon, Pinot Blanc.

Grilled Goat Cheese Loire reds.

Goose A good Rhône red like Hermitage, Côte Rôtie, or a crisp Barbera; Pinot Noir from Burgundy, California or Oregon; or even off-dry German Riesling.

Confit d'Oie Best Sauternes, Monbazillac.

Gooseberry

Gooseberry Pie Sweet Madeira, Austrian Trockenbeerenauslese.

Goose Liver

Foie Gras Best Sauternes, Monbazillac.

Grapefruit Sweet Madeira or sherry.

Grouse

Roast Grouse Hermitage, Côte Rôtie, robust Burgundy, or good mature red Bordeaux.

Guinea Fowl Old Burgundy, Cornas, Gamay de Touraine, St. Emilion or mature Californian Merlot.

H

Haddock White Bordeaux, Chardonnay, Pinot Blanc, single-vineyard Soave, Australian unoaked Semillon.
  Mousse of Smoked Haddock Top white Burgundy.
  Smoked Haddock Fino sherry or oaky Chardonnay.
Hake Soave, Sauvignon Blanc.
Halibut White Bordeaux, Muscadet.
  Smoked Halibut Oaky Spanish white Rioja, Australian Chardonnay, oaked white Bordeaux.
Ham
  Boiled/Roasted/Grilled/Fried Ham Beaujolais-Villages, Gamay de Touraine, slightly sweet German white, Tuscan red, lightish Cabernet (e.g., Chilean), Alsace Pinot Gris, or Muscat.
  Braised Ham with Lentils Light, fruity Beaujolais; Côtes du Rhône; Rioja or Navarra Crianza.
  Honey-Roast Ham Riesling.
  Oak-Smoked Ham Oaky Spanish reds.
  Parma Ham (Prosciutto) Try a dry Lambrusco, Tempranillo Joven, or Gamay de Touraine.
  Pea and Ham Soup Beaujolais.
Hare
  Hare Casserole Good Beaujolais Crus or, for a stronger flavor, try an Australian red.
  Jugged Hare Argentinian reds; tough Italians like Amarone, Barolo, and Barbaresco; inky reds from Bandol or the Rhône.
Hazelnut Vin Santo, Liqueur Muscat.
  Warm Bacon, Hazelnut, and Sorrel Salad New World Sauvignon Blanc, California Fumé Blanc, or a good Pouilly Fumé.
Herbs (see individual entries)
Herring
  Fresh Herrings Sauvignon Blanc, Muscadet, Frascati, or cider.
  Roll-Mop Herring Savoie, dry Vinho Verde, Grüner Veltliner, Akvavit, cold lager.
  Salt Herring White Portuguese.
  Sprats Muscadet, Vinho Verde.
Honey Tokaji.
  Baklava Moscatel de Setúbal.
Horseradish
  Roast Beef with Horseradish California Pinot Noir or mature Burgundy.
Houmous French dry whites, Retsina, Vinho Verde.

I

Ice Cream (vanilla) Try Marsala, Australian Liqueur Muscat, Muscadelle, or Pedro Ximénez sherry.
Indian (general) Gewürztraminer (spicy dishes), New World Chardonnay (creamy/yogurt dishes), New Zealand Sauvignon Blanc (Tandoori).

J

Japanese Barbecue Sauce
  Teriyaki Spicy reds like Zinfandel or Portuguese reds.
John Dory Good, white Burgundy or Australian Chardonnay.

K

Kedgeree New World Sauvignon Blanc.
Kidney
  Lambs' Kidneys Rich, spicy reds – Barolo, Cabernet Sauvignon, Rioja.
  Steak and Kidney Pie/Pudding Bordeaux, Australian Cabernet Sauvignon,
    Southern Rhône reds or Rioja.
Kippered Herrings New World Chardonnay or a good fino sherry. Or, if
    you are having it for breakfast, Champagne, a cup of tea, or Dutch gin.

L

Lamb
  Casserole Rich and warm Cabernet-based reds from France, or California
    Zinfandel.
  Cassoulet Serious white Rhône, Marsanne or Roussanne, or reds including
    Grenache and Syrah from the Rhône, berryish Italian reds, or Zinfandel.
  Cutlets or Chops Cru Bourgeois Bordeaux, Chilean Cabernet.
  Haggis Beaujolais, Côtes du Rhône, Côtes du Roussillon, Spanish reds,
    malt whiskey.
  Irish Stew A good simple South American or Eastern European Cabernet
    works best.
  Kabobs Modern (fruity) Greek reds or sweetly ripe Australian
    Cabernet/Shiraz.
  Kleftiko (Lamb Shanks Baked with Thyme) Greek red from Nemea,
    Beaujolais, light Cabernet Sauvignon.
  Lancashire Hotpot Robust country red – Cahors, Fitou.
  Moussaka Brambly Northern Italian reds (Barbera, Dolcetto, etc), Beaujolais,
    Pinotage, Zinfandel, or try some good Greek wine from a modern
    producer.
  Roast Lamb Bordeaux, New Zealand Cabernet Sauvignon, Cahors, Rioja
    reserva, reds from Chile.
  Roast Lamb with Thyme Try a New Zealand Cabernet Sauvignon or
    Bourgeuil.
  Shepherd's Pie Barbera, Cabernet Sauvignon, Minervois, Zinfandel,
    Beaujolais, Southern French red.
Langoustine Muscadet, Soave, South African Sauvignon.
Leek
  Cock-a-Leekie Dry New World white, simple red Rhône.
  Leek in Cheese Sauce Dry white Bordeaux, Sancerre, or Australian Semillon.

Leek and Potato Soup Dry whites, Côtes de Gascogne.

Vichyssoise Dry whites, Chablis, Bordeaux Blanc.

Lemon

Lemon Cheesecake Moscato d'Asti.

Lemon Meringue Pie Malmsey Madeira.

Lemon Sorbet Late harvest Sémillon or sweet Tokaji.

Lemon Tart Sweet Austrian and German wines.

Lemon Zest Sweet fortified Muscats.

Lemon Grass New Zealand Sauvignon, Sancerre, Viognier.

Lemon Sole Chardonnay.

Lentils Earthy country wines, Côtes du Rhône.

Chicken Dhansak Sémillon or New Zealand Sauvignon.

Dhal Soup Try Soave or Pinot Bianco.

Lime Australian Verdelho, Grüner Veltliner, Furmint.

Kaffir Lime Leaves (in Thai Green Curry, etc.) Big-flavored New World whites or Pinot Blanc from Alsace.

Thai Beef Salad New Zealand or South African Sauvignon Blanc, Gewürztraminer, Pinot Blanc.

Liver

Calves' Liver Good Italian Cabernet, Merlot, or mature Chianti.

Fegato alla Veneziana Nebbiolo, Zinfandel, or Petite Sirah.

Lambs' Liver Chianti, Australian Shiraz, or Merlot.

Liver and Bacon Côtes du Rhône, Zinfandel, Pinotage.

Lobster Good white Burgundy.

Lobster Bisque Grenache rosé, fresh German white, Chassagne-Montrachet, dry Amontillado sherry.

Lobster in a Rich Sauce Champagne, Chablis, fine white Burgundy, good white Bordeaux.

Lobster Salad Champagne, Chablis, German or Alsace Riesling.

Lobster Thermidor Rich beefy Côtes du Rhône, oaky Chardonnay, or a good deep-colored rosé from Southern France.

M

Mackerel With Vinho Verde, Albariño, Sancerre, and New Zealand Sauvignon.

Smoked Mackerel Bourgogne Aligoté, Alsace Pinot Gris.

Smoked Mackerel Pâté Sparkling Vouvray, Muscadet.

Mallard Côte Rôtie, Ribera del Duero, or Zinfandel.

Mango Best eaten in the bathtub with a friend and a bottle of Champagne! Otherwise, go for Asti or Moscato.

Marjoram Provençal reds.

Marsala

Chops in Marsala Sauce Australian Marsanne.

Mascarpone

Tiramisu Sweet fortified Muscat, Vin Santo, Torcolato.

Meat (general – also see individual entries)

Cold Meats Juicy, fruity reds, low in tannin, i.e., Beaujolais, Côtes du Rhône, etc.

Consommé Medium/Amontillado sherry.

Meat Pâté Beaujolais, Fumé Blanc, lesser white Burgundy.

Mixed Grill Versatile uncomplicated red – Australian Shiraz, Rioja.

Melon Despite its apparently innocent, juicy sweetness, melon can be very unfriendly to most wines. Try tawny port, sweet Madeira or sherry, Quarts de Chaume, late harvest Riesling.

Mincemeat

Mince Pie Rich, sweet, late-harvest wine or botrytis-affected Sémillon.

Mint Beaujolais, young Pinot Noir, or try a New Zealand or Australian Riesling.

Thai Beef Salad New Zealand or South African Sauvignon Blanc, Gewürztraminer, Pinot Blanc.

Monkfish A light, fruity red such as Bardolino, Valpolicella, La Mancha Joven, or most Chardonnays.

Mushroom Merlot-based reds, good Northern Rhône, top Piedmontese reds.

Mushrooms à la Greque Sauvignon Blanc or fresh, modern Greek white.

Mushroom Soup Bordeaux Blanc, Côtes de Gasgogne.

Risotto with Fungi Porcini Top-notch Piedmontese reds – mature Barbera, Barbaresco, or earthy Southern French reds.

Stuffed Mushrooms Chenin Blanc, Sylvaner.

Wild Mushrooms Nebbiolo, red Bordeaux.

Mussels Sauvignon Blanc, light Chardonnay, Muscadet Sur Lie.

Moules Marinières Bordeaux Blanc or Muscadet Sur Lie.

New Zealand Green-Lipped Mussels New Zealand Sauvignon Blanc.

Mustard Surprisingly, can help red Bordeaux and other tannic reds to go with beef.

Dijon Mustard Beaujolais.

French Mustard White Bordeaux.

Steak with Dijon Mustard New World Cabernet Sauvignon or Australian Shiraz.

Wholegrain Mustard Beaujolais, Valpolicella.

N

Nectarine Sweet German Riesling.

Nutmeg Rioja, Australian Shiraz, or, for sweet dishes, Australian late harvest.

Nuts Amontillado sherry, Vin Santo, and Tokaji.

O

Octopus Rueda white or a fresh, modern Greek white.

Olives Dry sherry, Muscadet, Retsina.

Salade Niçoise Muscadet, Vinho Verde, or Beaujolais.

Tapenade Dry sherry or Madeira.

Onion

Caramelized Onions Shiraz-based Australians, Zinfandel from the US, or a good Pinotage.

French Onion Soup Sancerre or dry, unoaked Sauvignon Blanc; Aligoté; white Bordeaux.

Onion/Leek Tart Alsace Gewurztraminer, New World Riesling, or a good unoaked Chablis.

Orange

Caramelized Oranges Asti, Sauternes, or Muscat de Beaumes de Venise.

Crêpe Suzette Sweet Champagne, Moscato d'Asti.

Orange Sorbet Moscato or sweet Tokaji.

Orange Zest Dry Muscat, Amontillado sherry.

Oregano Provençal reds, red Lambrusco, serious Chianti, or lightish Zinfandel.

Oxtail Australian Cabernet, good Bordeaux.

Oysters Champagne; Chablis; or other crisp, dry white.

Oyster Sauce

Beef and Snow Peas in Oyster Sauce Crisp, dry whites like Muscadet or a Northern Italian Lugana or Pinot Bianco, white Rhône, Gewürztraminer.

P

Paprika

Goulash Eastern European red like Bulgarian Cabernet or Mavrud, Hungarian Kadarka, or Australian Shiraz.

Parmesan Salice Salentino, Valpolicella.

Baked Chicken Parmesan with Basil Chenin Blanc, Riesling.

Parsley Dry, Italian whites – Bianco di Custoza, Nebbiolo, or Barbera.

Parsley Sauce Pinot Grigio, Hungarian Furmint, lightly oaked Chardonnay

Partridge

Roast Partridge Australian Shiraz, Gevrey-Chambertin, Pomerol, or St. Emilion.

Pasta

Lasagne Valpolicella, Barbera, Teroldego, Australian Verdelho or Sauvignon.

Pasta with Meat Sauce Chianti, Bordeaux Rouge.

Pasta with Pesto Sauce New Zealand Sauvignon Blanc, Valpolicella.

Pasta with Seafood Sauce Soave, Sancerre.

Ravioli with Spinach and Ricotta Pinot Bianco/Grigio, Cabernet d'Anjou.

Spaghetti with Tomato Sauce California Cabernet, Zinfandel, Chianti.

Spaghetti Vongole Pinot Bianco, Lugana.

Tagliatelle Carbonara Pinot Grigio or a fresh, red Bardolino or Beaujolais.

Peach Sweet German Riesling.

Peaches in Wine Riesling Auslese, Riesling Gewürztraminer Vendange Tardive, sweet Vouvray.

Peanuts

Beef in Peanut Curry New World Chardonnay; an aromatic, white Rhône.

Satay Gewürztraminer.

Pepper (corns)

Steak au Poivre Cabernet Sauvignon, Chianti, Barbera, Rhône reds, Shiraz, or Rioja.

Peppers (fresh green, red) New Zealand Cabernet, Loire reds, crisp Sauvignon Blanc, Beaujolais, Tuscan red.

Peppers (yellow) Fruity, Italian reds – Valpolicella, etc.

Stuffed Peppers Hungarian red – Bull's Blood; Zinfandel; Chianti; or spicy, Rhône reds.

Pheasant Top-class, red Burgundy; good American Pinot Noir; mature Hermitage.

Pheasant Casserole Top class, red Burgundy; mature Hermitage.

Pheasant Pâté Côtes du Rhône, Alsace Pinot Blanc.

Pigeon Good red Burgundy, rich Southern Rhône. Chianti also goes well.

Warm Pigeon Breasts on Salad Merlot-based Bordeaux or Cabernet Rosé.

Pike Eastern European white.

Pine Nuts

Pesto Sauce New Zealand Sauvignon Blanc, Valpolicella.

Pizza

Fiorentina Pinot Bianco, Pinot Grigio, Vinho Verde, Sauvignon Blanc.

Margherita Pinot Grigio, light Zinfandel, dry Grenache rosé.

Napoletana Verdicchio, Vernaccia de San Gimignano, white Rhône.

Quattro Formaggi Pinot Grigio, Frascati, Bianco di Custoza.

Quattro Stagioni Valpolicella, Bardolino, light Chianti, good Soave.

Plaice White Burgundy, South American Chardonnay, Sauvignon Blanc.

Plum

Plum Pie Trockenbeerenauslese, Côteaux du Layon.

Pork

Cassoulet Serious white Rhône, Marsanne or Roussanne; or reds including Grenache and Syrah from the Rhône, berryish, Italian reds, or Zinfandel.

Pork Casserole Mid-weight, earthy reds like Minervois, Navarra, or Montepulciano d'Abruzzo.

Pork Pie Spicy reds, Shiraz, Grenache.

Pork with Prunes Cahors, mature Chinon, or other Loire red, or rich, southern French wine such as Corbières, Minervois, or Faugères.

Pork Rillettes Pinot Blanc d'Alsace, Menetou-Salon Rouge.

Pork and Sage Sausages Barbera, Côtes du Rhône.

Pork Sausages Spicy Rhône reds, Barbera.

Pork Spare Ribs Zinfandel, Australian Shiraz.

Roast Pork Rioja reserva, New World Pinot Noir, dry Vouvray.

Roast Pork with Apple Sauce Off-dry Vouvray or Riesling.

Saucisson Sec Barbera, Cabernet Franc, Alsace Pinot Blanc, or Beaujolais.

Spare Ribs with Barbecue Sauce Fruity Australian Shiraz, Grenache, or Zinfandel; spicy Côtes du Rhône from a ripe vintage or an off-dry white.

Szechuan-Style Pork Dry, aromatic whites; Alsace Pinot Gris; Riesling; Grenache rosé; beer.

Prawns White Bordeaux; dry, Australian Riesling; Gavi.

Prawn Cocktail Light, fruity whites – German Riesling.

Prawns in Garlic Vinho Verde, Pinot Bianco.

Prawn Vol-au-Vents White Bordeaux, Muscadet.

Thai Prawns Gewürztraminer; dry, aromatic Riesling; or New Zealand Sauvignon Blanc.

Prunes Australian, late harvest Semillon.
  Pork with Prunes and Cream Sweet, Chenin-based wines or good Mosel Spätlese.
  Prune Ice Cream Muscat de Beaumes de Venise.

Q

Quail Light, red Burgundy; full-flavored, white Spanish wines.
Quince Lugana.
  Braised Venison with Quince Jelly Rich and fruity Australian or Chilean reds; good, ripe Spanish Rioja; or a Southern French red.

R

Rabbit
  Rabbit Casserole Red Burgundy, New World Pinot Noir, or mature Châteauneuf-du-Pape.
  Rabbit in Cider Muscadet, demi-sec Vouvray, cider, or Calvados.
  Rabbit with Mustard Franken wine or Czech Pilsner beer.
  Rabbit in Red Wine with Prunes Good, mature Chinon or other Loire red.
  Roast Rabbit Tasty, simple, young Rhône – red, white, or rosé.
Raspberries New World, late harvest Riesling; Champagne; Beaujolais; demi-sec Champagne.
  Raspberry Fool Vouvray Moelleux.
Ratatouille Bulgarian red, Chianti, simple Rhône or Provence red, Portuguese reds, New Zealand Sauvignon Blanc.
Redcurrant (Cumberland sauce) Rioja, Australian Shiraz.
Red Mullet Dry rosé, California, Washington or Australian Chardonnay.
Rhubarb
  Rhubarb Pie Moscato d'Asti, Alsace, German or Austrian late harvest Riesling.
Rice
  Rice Pudding Monbazillac, sweet Muscat, Asti, or California Orange Muscat.
Roast Lamb with Garlic and Rosemary Earthy soft reds like California Petite Sirah, Rioja, or Zinfandel.
Rocket Lugana, Pinot Blanc.
Roquefort The classic match is Sauternes or Barsac, but almost any full-flavored, botrytized sweet wine will be a good partner for strong, creamy blue cheese.
Rosemary Light red Burgundy or Pinot Noir.
Rum
  Flambéed Banana with Rum Jurançon, Tokaji, Pedro Ximénez sherry, and rum.

S

Saffron Dry whites, especially Chardonnay.
  Bass in Saffron Sauce Riesling (German, Australian, or Austrian), Viognier.
  Paella with Seafood White Penedés, unoaked Rioja, Navarra, Provence rosé.
Sage Chianti, or country reds from the Languedoc. Otherwise Sauvignon
  Blancs are great, especially Chilean.
  Roast Chicken, Goose, or Turkey with Sage and Onion Stuffing Italian reds,
    especially Chianti; soft, plummy Merlots; fruity Rioja; and brambly
    Zinfandel.
Salami Good, beefy Mediterranean rosé; Sardinian red; Rhône red; Zinfandel;
    dry, aromatic Hungarian white.
Salmon
  Carpaccio of Salmon Cabernet Franc, Chardonnay, Australian reds, red
    Loire, Portuguese reds, Puligny-Montrachet.
  Grilled Salmon White Rhône (especially Viognier).
  Poached Salmon Chablis; good, white Burgundy; other Chardonnay; Alsace
    Muscat; white Bordeaux.
  Poached Salmon with Hollandaise Muscat, Riesling, good Chardonnay.
  Salmon Pâté Best white Burgundy.
  Salmon Trout Light Pinot Noir from the Loire, New Zealand; good, dry,
    unoaked Chardonnay, Chablis, etc.
Sardines Muscadet, Vinho Verde, light and fruity reds such as Loire,
    Gamay.
Scallops Chablis and other unoaked Chardonnay.
  Coquilles St. Jacques White Burgundy.
  Marinated Scallops with Bacon Fino sherry or mature Riesling.
  Scallops Mornay White Burgundy, Riesling Spätlese.
Sea Bass Good white Burgundy.
  Bass in Saffron Sauce Riesling (German, Austrian, or Australian), Viognier.
Seafood (general – also see individual entries)
  Platter of Seafood Sancerre, Muscadet.
  Seafood Salad Soave, Pinot Grigio, Muscadet, lightly oaked Chardonnay
Sesame Seeds Oaked Chardonnay.
Shrimp Albariño, Sancerre, New World Sauvignon, Arneis.
  Potted Shrimp New World Chardonnay, Marsanne.
Skate Bordeaux white, Côtes de Gascogne, Pinot Bianco.
Smoked Salmon Chablis, Alsace Pinot Gris, white Bordeaux.
  Avocado and Smoked Salmon Lightly oaked Chardonnay, Fumé Blanc, or
    Australian Semillon.
  Smoked Salmon Paté English oaked Fumé Blanc, New Zealand Chardonnay.
Smoked Trout
  Smoked Trout Paté Good, white Burgundy.
Snapper Australian or South African, dry white.
Sole Chablis, Muscadet.
Sorbet Like ice cream, these can be too cold/sweet for most wines. Try
    Australian fortified Muscats.
Sorrel Dry Loire Chenin or Sauvignon Blanc.
Soy Sauce Zinfandel or Australian Verdelho.
Spinach Pinot Grigio, Lugana.

Eggs Florentine Chablis or unoaked Chardonnay, Pinot Blanc, Sémillion.

Spinach/Pasta Bakes Soft, Italian reds (Bardolino, Valpolicella), rich whites.

Spring Rolls Pinot Gris, Gewürztraminer, or other aromatic whites.

Squab Good, red Burgundy; rich Southern Rhône; or Chianti.

Warm Squab Breasts on Salad Merlot-based Bordeaux or Cabernet Rosé.

Squid Gamay de Touraine; Greek, Spanish, or Italian white.

Squid in Batter Muscadet.

Squid in Ink Nebbiolo or Barbera.

Stilton Tawny port.

Strawberries – No Cream Surprisingly, red Rioja, Burgundy (or other young Pinot Noir). More conventionally, sweet Muscats or fizzy Moscato.

Strawberries and Cream Vouvray Moelleux, Monbazillac

Strawberry Meringue Late harvest Riesling.

Strawberry Mousse Sweet or fortified Muscat.

Sweetbreads Lightly oaked Chablis; Pouilly-Fuissé; or light, red Bordeaux.

Sweetbreads in Mushroom, Butter and Cream sauce Southern French whites, Vin de Pays Chardonnay.

Sweet and Sour Dishes (general) Gewürztraminer, Sauvignon Blanc (unoaked), or beer.

T

Taramasalata Oaked Chardonnay or Fumé Blanc.

Tarragon White Menetou-Salon or South African Sauvignon Blanc.

Roast/Grilled Chicken with Tarragon Dry Chenin Blanc, Vouvray, dry Chenin.

Thyme Ripe and fruity Provençal reds, Rioja, Northern Italian whites.

Roast Lamb with Thyme New Zealand Cabernet Sauvignon, Bourgeuil.

Toffee Moscatel de Setúbal, Eiswein.

Banoffee Pie Sweet Tokaji.

Tomato

Gazpacho Fino sherry, white Rioja.

Pasta in a Tomato Sauce California Cabernet, Zinfandel, Chianti.

Tomato Soup Sauvignon Blanc.

Tripe Earthy, French country red; Minervois; Cahors; Fitou.

Trout Pinot Blanc, Chablis.

Smoked Trout Bourgogne Aligoté, Gewürztraminer, Pinot Gris.

Trout with Almonds Bianco di Custoza, Pinot Blanc.

Truffles Red Burgundy, old Rioja, Barolo, or Hermitage.

Tuna

Carpaccio of Tuna Australian Chardonnay, red Loire, Beaujolais.

Fresh Tuna Alsace Pinot Gris, Australian Chardonnay, Beaujolais.

Turbot Best white Burgundy, top California or Australian Chardonnay.

Turkey

Roast Turkey Beaujolais, light Burgundy, and rich or off-dry whites.

Roast Turkey with Chestnut Stuffing Rhône, Merlot, or mature Burgundy.

V

Vanilla Liqueur Muscat.
  Crème Brûlée Jurançon Moelleux, Tokaji.
  Custard Monbazillac, sweet Vouvray.
Veal
  Blanquette de Veau Aromatic, spicy whites from Alsace or from the
    Northern Rhône.
  Roast Veal Light, Italian whites, or fairly light reds – Spanish or Loire;
    St. Emilion.
  Wienerschnitzel Austrian Grüner Veltliner or Alsace or Hungarian
    Pinot Blanc.
Vegetables
  Roasted and Grilled Light, juicy reds; Beaujolais; Sancerre; and Sauvignon
    Blanc. Unoaked or lightly oaked Chardonnay.
  Vegetable Soup Pinot Blanc, rustic reds such as Corbières, or southern
    Italian reds.
  Vegetable Terrine Good New World Chardonnay.
Venison Pinotage; rich red Rhône; mature Burgundy; earthy, Italian reds.
  Venison Casserole Australian Shiraz, American Zinfandel, South African red.
Vinegar
  Choucroute Garnie White Alsace, Italian Pinot Grigio, or Beaujolais.
  Sauerkraut Pilsner beer.

W

Walnut Tawny port, sweet Madeira.
Watercress
  Watercress Soup Aromatic dry Riesling (Alsace or Australia).
Whitebait Fino sherry, Spanish red/white (Garnacha, Tempranillo), Soave.

Y

Yams Depends on the sauce. When subtly prepared, try Pinot Blanc.
Yogurt Needs full-flavored wines, such as Australian Semillon or
    New World Chardonnay.

Z

Zabaglione Rich sweet Marsala, Australian Liqueur Muscat, or a fortified
    French Muscat.
Zucchini
  Zucchini Gratin Good dry Chenin from Vouvray or South Africa,
    young Verdicchio.

A–Z OF WINE

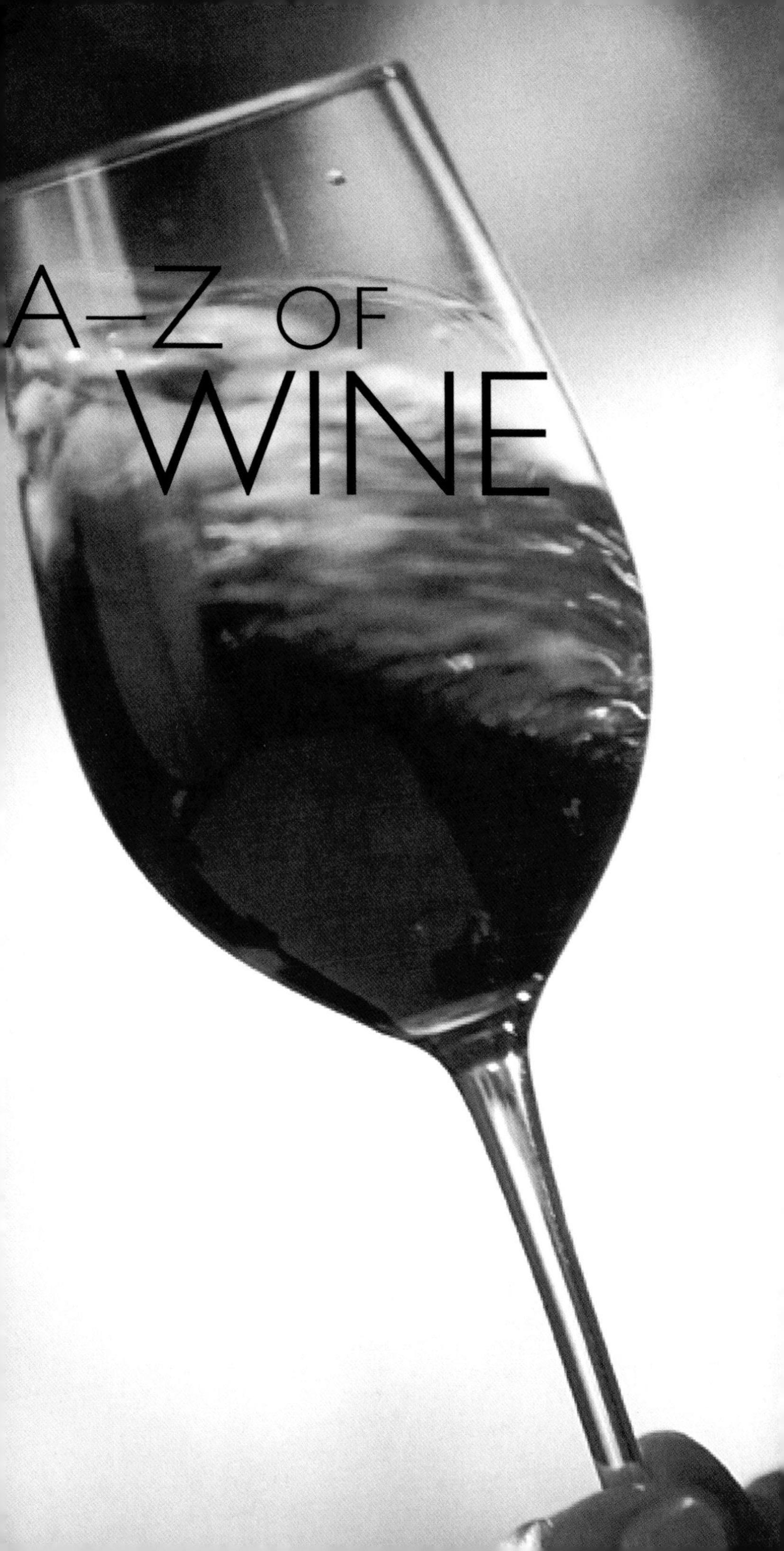

HOW TO READ THE ENTRIES

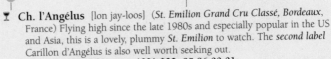

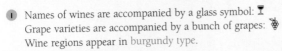

1. Names of wines are accompanied by a glass symbol: ▼
   Grape varieties are accompanied by a bunch of grapes: 🍇
   Wine regions appear in burgundy type.

2. Words that have their own entry elsewhere in the A–Z appear in italic.
   Recommended wines may also be cross-referenced. If you do not find an entry
   in the A-Z, it may very well be found in the index at the back of the book.

3. Throughout this section, examples are given of recommended vintages,
   producers, or wines which represent good examples of the region, style,
   or maker.

4. Recommended wines are accompanied by stars:

★★★★★	*outstanding in their style.*
★★★★	*excellent in their style.*
★★★	*good in their style.*

5. Prices are indicated using the following symbols:

   $ *under $7*   **$$** *$7–$15*   **$$$** *$15–$30*   **$$$$** *over $30*

6. Additional recommended vintages for particular wines may be listed in bold,
   where appropriate.

PRONUNCIATION GUIDE

All but the most common words are followed by square brackets [ ], which
enclose "sounding-out" pronunciation guides. These use the phonetic method,
with the accented syllable (if there is one) indicated by capital letters. For
example, **Spätlese** is pronounced as **SHPAYT-lay-zuh**. The basic sounds
employed in this book's pronunciations are as follows:

a *as in* **can**	**ah** *as in* **father**	**ay** *as in* **day**	**ur** *as in* **turn**
ch *as in* **church**	**kh** *as in* **loch**	**y** *as in* **yes**	**zh** *as in* **vision**
ee *as in* **see**	**eh** *as in* **get**	**g** *as in* **game**	**i** *as in* **pie**
ih *as in* **if**	**j** *as in* **gin**	**k** *as in* **cat**	**o** *as in* **hot**
oh *as in* **soap**	**oo** *as in* **food**	**ow** *as in* **cow**	**uh** *as in* **up**

Foreign sounds To represent sounds not common in English, the following
spellings are used: **eu** is a cross between **oo** and **a**; an italicized **n** or **m** is silent
and the preceding vowel sounds nasal; an **ñ** is like an **n** followed by a **y** (as in
Bourgogne); an italicized **r** is a cross between **r** and **w**; **rr** sounds like a rolled **r**.

A

☰ **Abacus** (*Napa*, California) Innovative (for California), high quality concept by the the *ZD* winery of blending tiny quantities of different red vintages.

☰ **Abadia Retuerta** [ah-bah-dee-yah Reh-twehr-tah] (Spain) Large venture close to *Ribera del Duero*, with Pascal Delbeck of *Ch. Belair* in *St. Emilion*. Several equally recommendable cuvées, including Palomar, Pago Negralato, Valdebon, and Campanario. ★ ★ ★ ★ Pago Valdebon 1999 $$

☰ **Abazzia Sant'Anastasia** [ah-baht-zee-yah San-tan-nah-stah-zee-yah] (*Sicily* Italy) New star in Sicily, with a *Super-Tuscan-* quality Cabernet – Litra – and fine *Chardonnay* – Baccante – as well as reds from the local Nero d'Avola.

Abboccato [ah-boh-kah-toh] (Italy) Semidry.

☰ **Abel-Lepitre** [ah-bel luh-pee-tre] (*Champagne,* France) The wine to look for here is the Réserve Blanc de Blancs Cuvée C.

Abfüller/Abfüllung [ap-few-ler/ap-few-loong] (Germany) Bottler/bottled by.

Abocado [ah-boh-kah-doh] (Spain) Semidry.

☰ **Abreu Vineyards** [Eh-broo] (*Napa*, California) Cult St. Helena winery with vineyards whose grapes go to such top *Napa* names as *Harlan Estate*. Only sells through its mailing list.

☰ **Quinta da Abrigada** [keen-tah dah ah-bree-gah-dah] (Alenquer, Portugal) Reliable estate making characterful wines.

Abruzzi/zzo [ah-broot-zee/zoh] (Italy) East coast region with often dull *Trebbiano* whites and improving *Montepulciano* reds. Castello di Salle; Farnese, Dino Illuminati; Gianni Masciarelli; Di Majo Norante; Eduardo Valentini.

AC (France) See *Appellation Contrôlée*.

☰ **Acacia** [a-kay-shah] (*Carneros*, California) Long-established, but often underrated producer of *Chardonnay* and *Pinot Noir, Viognier* and *Zinfandel*. Under the same ownership as *Chalone, Edna Valley*, and *Carmenet*.

☰ **Accordini** [a-kor-DEE-nee] (*Veneto*, Italy) New *Valpolicella* star with fine vineyards.

Acetic acid [ah-see-tihk] This volatile acid (CH3COOH) features in small proportions in all wines. Careless winemaking can result in wine being turned into acetic acid, a substance most people know as vinegar.

Acidity Naturally occurring (*tartaric* and malic) acids in the grapes contribute freshness, and help to preserve the wine. In reds and many cool region whites, the malic is often converted to lactic by a natural process known as *malolactic fermentation,* which gives the wines a buttery texture and flavor. In hotter countries (and sometimes cooler ones) the acid level may (not always legally) be adjusted by adding *tartaric* and citric acid.

☰ **Ackerman-Laurance** [ah-kehr-man Loh-ronss] (*Loire*, France) One of the Loire's oldest and most reliable sparkling wine producers. Privilège is the top wine. Now part of the huge Rémy Pannier group.

Aconcagua Valley [ah-kon-kar-gwah] (*Central Valley,* Chile) Region noted for blackcurranty *Cabernet Sauvignon. Michel Laroche* has just begun to make wine here. The subregion is *Casablanca.* Grapes from both are used by many Chilean producers. Concha y Toro, Errazuriz, Morande. ★ ★ ★ ★ 2001 Errazuriz Single Vineyard Syrah $$

☰ **Tim Adams** (*Clare Valley*, Australia) Highly successful producer of *Riesling*, rich peachy *Semillon*, and deep-flavored Aberfeldy *Shiraz* and intense peppery Fergus *Grenache*. ★ ★ ★ ★ ★ Clare Valley Riesling 2002 $$

☰ **Adanti** [ah-dan-ti] (*Umbria*, Italy) Star producer of spicy reds and herby Grechetto whites.

Adega [ah-day-gah] (Portugal) Winery – equivalent to Spanish *bodega*.

Adelaide Hills [ah-dur-layd] (*South Australia*) Cool region, with classy, lean *Riesling, Semillon, Sauvignon Blanc, Chardonnay,* sparkling wine, *Pinot Noir, Cabernet Franc* (Paracombe) and even *Zinfandel* (*Nepenthe*). Lenswood is a subregion. Ashton Hills; Chain of Ponds; *Grosett*; Heggies; Henschke; Mountadam; Nepenthe; Paracombe, Penfolds; Shaw & Smith; Geoff Weaver.

A

Adelaide Plains [ah-dur-layd] (*South Australia*) Little-known region pioneered by - second generation Italian-Australian - Joe Grilli's Primo Estate and Joseph labels. Ceravolo is another Italian name to look out for.

Ⴑ Weingut Graf [graf-ah-del-man] (*Württemberg*, Germany) Top estate, making good reds from grapes such as the *Trollinger*, Lemberger, and Urban. Look for Brüssele'r Spitze wines.

Ⴑ Adelsheim [a-del-sime] (*Oregon*, USA) Classy, long-lived *Pinot Noir*, *Chardonnay*, and *Pinot Gris*.

Ⴑ Age [ah-khay] (*Rioja*, Spain) Big, modern, highly commercial winery.

Agiorghitiko [a-gee-yor-jee-ti-koh] (Greece) Spicy, plummy, red grape grown in the Peloponnese for *Nemea*. Best at high altitudes.

Aglianico [ah-lee-AH-nee-koh] (Italy) The Nebbiolo of southern Italy? Thick-skinned, berryish-tobaccoey grape grown by the Ancient Greeks. Now used to make *Taurasi* and *Aglianico del Vulture* and shown at its increasingly impressive best by Cantine del Notaio and Antonio Caggiano.

Ⴑ Aglianico del Vulture [ah-lee-AH-nee-koh del vool-TOO-reh] (*Basilicata*, Italy) Licoricey-chocolatey wines made on the hills of an extinct volcano. Older examples are labeled as Vecchio (3 years+) and Riserva (5 years+). Armando Martino; D'Angelo; Basilium; Cantine del Notaio; Paternoster.

Ⴑ La Agricola (*Mendoza*, Argentina) One of this go-ahead country's most go-ahead wineries. The top wines are sold under the Familia Zuccardi "Q" range. Picajuan Creek and Santa Julia are labels that are also worth looking out for.

Agricola vitivinicola (Italy) Wine estate.

Ahr [ahr] (Germany) Northernmost *Anbaugebiet*, making light-bodied reds.

Ⴑ Aigle [eh-gl'] (*Vaud*, Switzerland) The place to find fresh, floral *Chasselas* (known here as *Dorin*). The *Pinot Noir* can be good too. Baudoux, Testuz.

Airén [i-REHN] (Spain) The world's most planted white variety. Dull and fortunately more or less restricted to the region of *La Mancha*.

Ajaccio [a-jax-yoh] (*Corsica*, France) Good reds, especially from the Sciacarello grape, come from this region named after the capital of *Corsica*. *Comte Peraldi* makes intense reds and whites. See also: *Gie Les Rameaux*.

Ⴑ Alban (*Central Coast*, California) *Edna Valley* winery with exciting *Rhône*-style reds and whites. ★★★★★ Seymour's Vineyard Syrah 2000 $$$$

Ⴑ Albana di Romagna [ahl-BAH-nah dee roh-MAN-yah] (*Emilia-Romagna*, Italy) Inexplicably, Italy's first white *DOCG*. Traditionally dull but improving white. Passita, sweeter whites are best. Celli; Umberto Cesari; Gruppo Cevico; Conti; Ferrucci; Fattoria Paradiso; Madonia; Uccellina; Zerbina.

Albariño [ahl-BAH-ree-nyoh] (*Galicia*, Spain) Spanish name for the *Alvarinho* and the peachy-spicy wine made from it in *Rias Baixas*. Lagar de Cervera; Martin Codex; Fefiñanes; *Pazo de Barrantes*; Salnesu; Valdamor.

Ⴑ Castello d'Albola [KAS-teh-loh DAL-boh-la] (*Tuscany*, Italy) Top Tuscan Estate belonging to the increasingly dynamic firm of *Zonin*.

Ⴑ Alcamo [ahl-Cah-moh] (Sicily) Distinctive, rich, dry white made from the local *Catarratto* grape. Rapitalà is the name to look for.

Alcohol This simple compound, technically known as ethanol, is formed by the action of yeast on sugar during fermentation.

Aleatico [ah-lay-AH-tee-koh] (Italy) Red grape producing sweet, *Muscat*-style, often fortified wines. Produces *DOC*s A. di Puglia and A. di Gradoli.

Alella [ah-LEH-yah] (*Catalonia*, Spain) *DO* district producing better whites (from grapes including the *Xarel-lo*) than reds. Marfil; Marqués de Alella; Parxet.

Alenquer [ah-lehn-kehr] (*Oeste*, Portugal) Coolish region producing good *Periquita* reds and *Muscat*-style *Fernão Pires* whites. Also making successful efforts from French varietals. Quinta da Boavista; Quinta de Pancas.

Alentejo [ah-lehn-TAY-joh] (Portugal) Province north of the Algarve with five *DOC*s: Borba, Portalegre, Redondo, Reguengos, Vidigueira. *JM da Fonseca* makes Morgado de Reguengo; *JP Vinhos* Tinta da Anfora and *Ch. Lafite* Quinta do Carmo. Alianca; Borba; Cartuxa; Cortes de Cima; Esporão; Herdade de Mouchao; Pera Manca; *Quinta do Carmo*; Redondo, Jose de Sousa; Sogrape.

Alexander Valley (*Sonoma*, California) *Appellation* in which *Simi*, *Jordan*, *Murphy-Goode*, and *Geyser Peak* are based. *Turley* makes big *Zinfandels* here too. Alexander Valley Vineyards; Arrowood, Ch. St Jean; Clos du Bois; Geyser Peak; Forefathers; Godwin; Goldsmidt; Jordan; Lancaster; Marcassin; Murphy-Goode; Rosenblum; Rockaway; Seghesio; Silver Oak; Simi; Stonestreet; Turley.

Algarve [ahl-garv] (Portugal) Huge, officially denominated region whose wines are worth drinking while in the region on vacation. Investment by UK pop star Cliff Richard and the use of Australian expertise are paying dividends.

⚚ **Caves Aliança** [ah-lee-an-sah] (Portugal) High quality modern *Bairrada*, *Douro*, and *Dão*. ★★★★ Quinta da Cortezia Touriga Nacional 2001 $$

Alicante (*Valencia*, Spain) Hot region producing generally dull stuff apart from the sweetly honeyed *Moscatels* that appreciate the heat.

⚚ **Alicante-Bouschet** [al-ee-KONT- boo-SHAY] Unusual dark-skinned and fleshed grapes traditionally used (usually illegally) for dyeing pallid reds.

⚚ **Aligoté** [Al-lee-goh-tay] (*Burgundy*, France) Lesser white grape at its best in the village of *Bouzeron*. G&J-H Goisot; Jayer-Gilles; A&P de Vilaine.

⚚ **Alión** [ah-lee-yon] (*Ribera del Duero*, Spain) New venture by the owners of *Vega Sicilia*, with fruitier, more modern wines.

⚚ **Alkoomi** [al-koo-mee] (*Western Australia*) Fine *Sauvignon* and *Riesling*.

Allan Scott (*Marlborough*, New Zealand) Well made whites.

⚚ **All Saints** (*Rutherglen*, Australia) Good producer of *Liqueur Muscat* and *Tokay*.

⚚ **Allegrini** [ah-leh-GREE-nee] (*Veneto*, Italy) Top-class producer of single-vineyard *Valpolicella* and *Soave*. Now often doing so without recourse to the *DOC/DOCG* system. ★★★★★ Amarone Allegrini 1999 $$$

⚚ **Thierry Allemand** [al-mon] (*Rhône*, France) Producer of classic, concentrated, single-vineyard *Cornas* from a small 6-acre (2.5-hectare) estate.

⚚ **Finca Allende** [ah-lyen-day] (*Rioja*, Spain) Excellent, pricey new wave *Rioja* bottled earlier for more fruit, freshness, density. Aúrus is the top wine.

⚚ **Allesverloren** [ah-less-ver-lor-ren] (South Africa) Old-established estate making solid wines, especially port styles, *Cabernet*, *Shiraz*, *Tinta Barocca*.

Allier [a-lee-yay] (France) Spicy oak favored by makers of white wine.

⚚ **Almaviva** [al-mah-vee-vah] (*Maipo*, Chile) Pricy red coproduction between *Mouton Rothschild* and *Concha y Toro*. ★★★★ Puente Alto 2000 $$$

Almacenista [al-mah-theh-nee-stah] (*Jerez*, Spain) Fine unblended sherry from a single *solera* – the sherry equivalent of a single malt whisky. Lustau.

⚚ **Aloxe-Corton** [a-loss kawr-ton] (*Burgundy*, France) *Côte de Beaune* commune with tough, slow-maturing reds (including the *Grand Cru Corton*) and potentially sublime whites (including Corton-Charlemagne). Louis Latour's pricey whites can be fine. d'Angerville; Arnoux; Bonneau du Martray; Denis Bousse; Capitan-Gagnerot; Chandon de Briailles; Marius Delarche; Drouhin; Michel Gay; Antonin Guyon; Jadot; Patrick Javillier; Daniel Largeot; Leflaive; Prince de Mérode; André Nudant; Comte Senard; Tollot-Beaut; Michel Voarick.

Alsace [al-sas] (France) Region whose warm microclimate makes for riper-tasting wines that are named after the grapes – *Pinot Noir*, *Gewürztraminer*, *Riesling*, *Pinot Gris*, *Pinot Blanc* (known as Pinot d'Alsace), *Sylvaner*, and (rarely) *Muscat*. In the right hands, the 50 or so *Grand Cru* vineyards should yield better wines. *Late harvest* sweet wines are labeled *Vendange Tardive* and *Sélection des Grains Nobles*. Albrecht; J Becker; Léon Beyer; Paul Blanck; Bott-Geyl; Albert Boxler; Ernest J & F Burn; Joseph Cattin; Marcel Deiss; Jean-Pierre Dirler; Dopff au Moulin; Faller; Hugel; Josmeyer; André Kientzler; Kreydenweiss; Kuentz-Bas; Albert Mann; Meyer-Fonné; Mittnacht-Klack; René Muré; Ostertag; Rolly Gassmann; Schlumberger; Schoffit; Bruno Sorg; Marc Tempé; Trimbach; Weinbach; Zind Humbrecht.

⚚ **Altano** [al-tah-noh] (*Douro*, Portugal) Appealing newish red table wine from the Symington Group of port fame. 99,00.

⚚ **Elio Altare** [Ehl-lee-yoh al-TAh-ray] (*Piedmont*, Italy) The genial, Svengali-like leader of the *Barolo* revolution and inspirer of *Clerico* and *Roberto Voerzio*. Tragically lost most of his 1998 harvest to moldy corks. ★★★★★ Barolo Vigneto Arborina 1998 $$$

A

I **Altesino** [al-TEH-see-noh] (*Tuscany*, Italy) First-class *Brunello di Montalcino*, *Cabernet* ("Palazzo"), and *Sangiovese* ("Altesi").

Alto Adige [ahl-toh AH-dee-jay] (Italy) Aka Italian Tyrol and Südtirol. *DOC* for a huge range of whites often from Germanic grape varieties; also light, fruity reds from the *Lagrein* and Vernatsch. Cant. Prod. di Cortaccia; Cant. Prod. di Termeno; Cant.Vit. di Caldaro; Gaierhof; Giorgio Grai; Franz Haas; Hofstätter; *Alois Lageder*; Maddalena; *Pojer & Sandri*;San Michele Appiano; Sta Maddalena; Niedermayer; *Tiefenbrunner*; Thurnhof;Viticoltori Alto-Adige.

🌿 **Alvarinho** [ahl-vah-reen-yoh] (Portugal) White grape aka *Albariño*; at its lemony best in *Vinho Verde* and in the *DO* Alvarinho de Monção.

I **Alvear** (*Montilla-Moriles*, Spain) Large producer of *Montilla*; quality is good.
Amabile [am-MAH-bee-lay] (Italy) Semisweet.

I **Castello di Ama** [ah-mah] (*Tuscany*, Italy) Brilliant small *Chianti* estate. Great single vineyard Vigna l'Apparita wines and very fine *Chardonnay*.

Amador County [am-uh-dor] (California) Intensely-flavored, old-fashioned *Zinfandel*. Look for Amador Foothills Winery's old-vine *Zinfandels* and top-of-the-line stuff from *Sutter Home* and *Monteviña*. Quady,Vino Noceto.

I **Amarone** [ah-mah-ROH-neh] (*Veneto*, Italy) Literally "bitter"; used to describe *Recioto* wines fermented dry, especially *Amarone della Valpolicella*. Accordini; Allegrini; Begalli; Brigaldara; Luigi Brunelli;Tommaso Bussola; Corte Sant' Alda; Masi;Angelo Nicolis; Quintarelli; Romano dal Forno;Tedeschi;Viviani; Zenato.

I **Amberley Estate** (*Margaret River*, Australia) Not one of the top stars of *Margaret River*, but a reliable name. ★★★ 1999 Semillon $$

I **Fattoria di Ambra** [fah-toh-ree-yah dee am-bra] (*Tuscany*, Italy) Leading *Carmignano* estate. Look out for single vineyard *Elzana* and *Vigne Alte*.

I **Bodegas Amézola de la Mora** [ah-meh-THOH-lah deh lah MAW-rah] (*Rioja*, Spain) Eight-year-old estate producing unusually classy red *Rioja*.

🌿 **Amigne** [ah-meen] (*Valais*, Switzerland) Unusual white grape that makes traditional (non fruit-driven) wines in Vétroz. *J-R Germanier; Imesch*.

I **Amity** [am-mi-tee] (*Oregon*, US) Maker of very high-quality berryish Pinot Noir, good dry *Gewurztraminer*, and *late-harvest* whites.

Amontillado [am-mon-tee-yah-doh] (*Jerez*, Spain) Literally "like Montilla." Often pretty basic medium-sweet *sherry*, but ideally fascinating dry, nutty wine. *Gonzalez Byass; Lustau; Sanchez Romate*.

I **Ampelones Vassilou** [am-peh-loh-nehs vas-see-loo] (*Attica*, Greece) Producer of good new-wave Greek wines.

I **Robert Ampeau** [om-poh] (*Burgundy*, France) Traditional Meursault producer whose Perrières is worth looking out for.

Amtliche Prüfungsnummer [am-tlish-eh proof-oong-znoomer] (Germany) Identification number on all *QbA/QmP* labels.

Anbaugebiet [ahn-bow-geh-beet] (Germany) Term for 13 large regions (e.g. *Rheingau*).

Anderson Valley (*Mendocino*, California) Cool area, good for white and sparkling wines including the excellent *Roederer*. Do not confuse with Anderson Valley, New Mexico. Edmeades; *Roederer; Steele;Williams Selyem*.

I **Anderson Vineyard** (*Napa*, California) Stag's Leap producer of intense blackcurranty Cabernet and rich, full-flavored Chardonnay.

I **Andrew Will** (*Washington State*) Superstar producer of some of *Washington State*'s – not to say North America's – best *Merlot, Cabernet Sauvignon*, and ("Sorella") Bordeaux blends.

I **Ch. Angélus** [on jay-loos] (*St. Emilion Premier Grand Cru Classé, Bordeaux*, France) Flying high since the late 1980s, this is a plummy, intensely oaky *St. Emilion* – though showing more elegance in 2002. The *second label* Carillon d'Angélus is worth seeking out.

A

Marquis d'Angerville [don-jehr-veel] (*Burgundy*, France) Long-established *Volnay* estate with rich, long-lived traditional wines from here and from *Pommard*. ★ ★ ★ ★ Volnay Taillepieds 2000 $$$

Ch d'Angludet [don gloo-day] (*Cru Bourgeois*, *Margaux*, *Bordeaux*, France) With a reputation built by the late Peter Sichel of *Chateau Palmer*, this is classy cassis-flavored, if slightly earthy, wine that can generally be drunk young, but is worth waiting for.

Angove's [an-gohvs] (*Padthaway*, Australia) *Murray River* producer with reliable, inexpensive *Chardonnay* and *Cabernet* and great brandy. Wine quality is now being helped by a move into *Padthaway*. ★ ★ ★ Kanarie Creek Chardonnay 2001 $

Weingut Paul Anheuser [an-hoy-zur] (*Nahe*, Germany) Strong estate with good *Riesling*, *Ruländer*, and *Pinot Noir*.

Finca la Anita [feen-kah lah an-nee-tah] (*Mendoza*, Argentina) Organic, small-scale winery to watch. Innovative wines include a tasty *Syrah-Malbec* blend.

Anjou [on-joo] (*Loire*, France) Dry and *DemiSec* whites, mostly from *Chenin Blanc*, with up to 20 percent *Chardonnay* or *Sauvignon Blanc*. The rosé is usually awful but there are good, light reds. Look for *Anjou-Villages*, in which *Gamay* is not permitted. Within Anjou, there more specific ACs, most importantly *Savennières* and *Coteaux du Layon*. M. Angeli; Arnault et Fils; Baudoin; Bise; *Bouvet-Ladubay*; Ch. du Breuil; Dom. du Closel; Deslesvaux; Donatien Bahuaud; Ch. de Fesles; Gaudard; Genaiserie; V. Lebreton; Ogereau; Ch. de Passavant; J. Pithon; Renou; *Richou*; Dme de la Sansonniere; Soucherie; Y. Soulez; Ch. la Varière.

Anjou-Coteaux de la Loire [Koh-toh duh lah Lwarh] (*Loire*, France) Lesser-known appellation for varied styles of Chenin Blanc, including luscious late-harvest examples. Do not confuse with *Coteaux du Loir*. Ch. de Putille.

Anjou-Villages [on-joo vee-larj] (*Loire*, France) Increasingly famous red wine appellation, thanks partly to Gérard Dépardieu's presence here as a (seriously committed) winemaker at Ch. de Tigné, and partly to the impressive quality of the juicy, potentially long-lived Cabernet-based red wines. Bablut; Closel; Ch. de Coulaine; C. Daviau; *Ch. de Fesles*; Dme Les Grands Vignes; Ogereau; *Richou*; Rochelles; Pierre-Bise; J-Y. Lebreton; V. Lebreton; Ogereau; de Putille Montigilet; Richou; Dom. de Sablonettes; *Pierre Soulez*; Ch. de Tigné.

Annata [ahn-nah-tah] (Italy) *Vintage*.

Annie's Lane See *Beringer Blass*.

Roberto Anselmi [an-sehl-mee] (*Veneto*, Italy) Source of classy dry *Soave* Classico wines, as well as some extremely serious sweet examples.

Antinori [an-tee-NOR-ree] (*Tuscany*, Italy) Pioneer merchant-producer who has improved the quality of *Chianti*, with his Villa Antinori and Pèppoli, while spearheading the *Super-Tuscan* revolution with *Tignanello*, *Sassicaia*, and *Solaia*, and producing around 15,000,000 bottles of wine per year. Now in *Piedmont* and S. Italy., and in joint ventures in California (*Atlas Peak*), Washington State, and Hungary ★ ★ ★ ★ Brunello di Montalcino Pian delle Vigne 1997 $$$; ★ ★ ★ ★ ★ Solaia 1999 $$$$ ★ ★ ★ ★ ★ Tignanello 1999 $$$$

Anubis (Argentina) Appealingly juicy reds come from this joint venture between Italian Alberto Antonini and Argentine Susana Balbo.

AOC (France) See *Appellation Contrôlée*.

AP (Germany) See *Amtliche Prüfungsnummer*.

Appellation Contrôlée (AC/AOC) [AH-pehl-lah-see-on kon troh-lay] (France) Official designation guaranteeing origin, grape varieties, and method of production and – in theory – quality, though tradition and vested interest combine to allow pretty appalling wines to receive the rubber stamp. Increasingly questioned by quality-conscious producers.

Aprémont [ah-pray-mon] (Eastern France) Floral, slightly *petillant* white from skiing region. Marc Portaz; B&C Richel; Ch. de la Violette.

Apulia [ah-pool-ee-yah] (Italy) See *Puglia*.

A

☂ **Aquileia** [ah-kwee-lay-ah] (*Friuli-Venezia Giulia,* Italy) *DOC* for easy-going, single-variety wines. The *Refosco* can be plummily refreshing. **Tenuta Beltrame;** *Zonin.*

☂ **Agricola Aquitania** [ah-gree-koh-lah ah-kee-tah-nee-ya] (*Maipo,* Chile) Estate founded by Paul Pontallier (of Ch. Margaux) and Bruno Prats (formerly of Ch. Cos d'Estournel), overlooking the city of Santiago. The top wine is Paul Bruno, and the second wine Uno Fuero.

Aragón [ah-rah-GONN] (Spain) Up-and-coming region in which are situated Campo de Borja, Cariñena, Somontano. Jalon; Grandes Vinos y Viñedos

✤ **Aragonez** [ah-rah-goh-nesh] (Portugal) Synonym for *Tempranillo.*

☂ **Arbois** [ahr-bwah] (Eastern France) AC region with light *Trousseau* and *Pinot Noir* reds and nutty dry Savignan (not to be confused with the Sauvignon) and *Chardonnay* whites. Also sherry-like *Vin Jaune,* sweet *Vin de Paille,* and sparkling wine. Aviet; Ch d'Arlay; Bourdy; Dugois; Fruitière Viticole; Lornet; Overnoy; la Pinte; J Puffeney; Rijckaert; Rolet; A&M Tissot; J Tissot. ★★★ 2000 Jean Rijckaert Arbois Pré Leveron.

☂ **Ch. Archambeau** (*Bordeaux,* France) Good-value Graves reds and dry whites

☂ **Ch. d' Arche** [dahrsh] (*Sauternes 2ème Cru Classé, Bordeaux,* France) Up-and-coming property.

☂ **Archery Summit** (*Oregon,* USA) A recent venture in Yamhill County in Oregon by Gary Andrus of *Pine Ridge* in Napa. Both Pinot Noir and Pinot Gris are impressive – if pricey. ★★★★ **Arcus Estate Pinot Noir 2000** $$$$

☂ **Viña Ardanza** [veen-yah ahr-dan-thah] (*Rioja,* Spain) Highly reliable, fairly full-bodied, long-lived, classic red Rioja made with a high proportion (40 percent) of *Grenache*; good, *oaky* white, too. ★★★ 1996 Rioja Reserva $$

☂ **d'Arenberg** [dar-ren-burg] (*McLaren Vale,* Australia) Excellent up-and-coming producer with memorably named, impressive sweet and dry table wines, and unusually dazzling fortifieds. ★★★★★ **The Hermit Crab Marsanne 2002 $$;** ★★★★ **The Twenty Eight Road Mourvedre 2001 $$**

Argentina Fast up-and-coming nation with fine *Malbec.* It is also good for its *Cabernet* and *Merlot,* which have a touch more backbone than many efforts from Chile; and there are interesting wines made from Italian red varieties. *Chardonnays* and grapey whites from the *Muscat*-like *Torrontes* are worthwhile too. La Agricola; Finca la Anita; Anubis; *Leoncio Arizu;* Balbi; *Luigi Bosca;* Canale; Catena (+*Zapata*); M Chandon (Paul Galard; Terrazas); Esmeralda; *Etchart;* Lurton; Morande; Navarro Correas; *Norton; la Rural;* San Telmo; Santa Ana; *Torino; Trapiche;*Weinert. ★★★★★ Nicolás Catena Zapata 1999 $$$

☂ **Tenuta di Argiano** [teh-noo-tah dee ahr-zhee-ahn-noh] (*Tuscany,* Italy) Instant success story, with top-class vineyards, and lovely juicy reds.

☂ **Argyle** (*Oregon,* US) Classy sparkling wine and still wines from Brian Croser (of *Petaluma*) Now (laudably) innovating with screwcaps.

✤ **Arinto** [ah-reen-toh] (Portugal) High quality white grape with good acidity and the ability to age in bottle. The flavor is lemony and peachy.

☂ **Arietta** [ahr-ree-yeht-tah] (Napa, California) Maker of classy Bordeaux blends which, unusually, mimic Cheval Blanc by marrying *Merlot* with *Cabernet Franc.*

☂ **Ch. d'Arlay** [dahr-lay] (*Jura,* France) Reliable producer of nutty *Vin Jaune* and light, earthy-raspberry Pinot Noir.

☂ **Leoncio Arizu** [Ah-ree-zoo] (*Mendoza,* Argentina) Variable, old-established producer. Also owns *Luigi Bosca*

☂ **Dom. de l'Arlot** [dur-lahr-loh] (*Burgundy,* France) Brilliant *Nuits-St.-Georges* estate under the same ownership as *Ch. Pichon-Longueville.* Delicate reds (especially*Vosne-Romanée*) and a rare example of white *Nuits-St.-Georges.*

☂ **Ch. d'Armailhac** [darh-mi-yak] (*Pauillac 5ème Cru Classé, Bordeaux,* France). The wines from this château come from the same stable as *Mouton-Rothschild,* and show similar rich flavors, though never the same elegance.

☂ **Dom. du Comte Armand** [komt-arh-mon] (*Burgundy,* France) The top wine from the Canadian-born winemaker here is the exceptional *Pommard* Clos des Epeneaux, but the *Auxey-Duresses* and *Volnay les Fremiets* are fine too.

🍇 **Arneis** [ahr-nay-ees] (*Piedmont*, Italy) Spicy white; makes good, young, unoaked wine. **Deletto; Ceretto; Funtanin; Malvira; Serafino; *Voerzio*.**

🍷 **Ch. l' Arrosée,** [lah-roh-say] (*St. Emilion Grand Cru Classé, Bordeaux*, France) Small, well-sited property with fruity intense wines.

🍷 **Arrowood** (*Sonoma Valley*, California) *Chardonnay, Merlot, Pinot Blanc, Viognier*, and *Cabernet* from former *Ch. St. Jean* winemaker. Now part of the *Mondavi* empire.

🍷 **Ismael Arroyo** [uh-Roy-oh] (*Ribera del Duero*, Spain) A name to watch for flavorsome reds. ★★★★ **Val Sotillo Gran Reserva** 1995 $$

🍷 **Arruda** (*Estremadura*, Portugal) Both a subregion and its eponymous co-op cellar, with a reputation for good value.

🍷 **Artadi** [ahr-tah-dee] (*Rioja*, Spain) Up-and-coming producer with particularly good *Crianza* and *Reserva* wines – and fast-rising prices. ★★★★ **Rioja Pagos Viejos Reserva** 1995 $$

🍇 **Arvine** [ah-veen] (Switzerland) Delicious, spicy white indigenous grape which has reminded some visiting Italians of their *Arneis*. **Bonvin; Chappaz; Provins; Rochaix**

🍷 **Bodegas Arzuaga** [Ahr-thwah-gah] (*Ribera del Duero*, Spain) One of the growing number of new-wave estates in Ribera del Duero, with large acreage of vines and emphatically modern winemaking that is catching the attention of US critics. ★★★★ **Ribera del Duero Reserva** 1997 $$

🍷 **Matteo Ascheri** [ash-sheh-ree] (*Piedmont*, Italy) Pioneering producer. Impressive single-vineyard, tobacco and berry *Barbera* wines, also *Nebbiolo, Syrah*, and *Viognier* and Freisa del Langhe. ★★★★ **Barbera d'Alba Vigna Fontanelle** 2000 $$

🍷 **Ashbrook Estate** (*Margaret River*, Australia) Excellent quality; look for *Chardonnay, Semillon, Verdelho, Sauvignon, Cabernet*.

Asciutto [ah-shoo-toh] (Italy) Dry.

Assenovgrad [ass-seh-nov-grad] (Bulgaria) Demarcated northern wine region with rich plummy *Cabernet Sauvignon, Merlot*, and *Mavrud*.

🍷 **Ashton Hills** (*Adelaide Hills*, Australia) Small up-and-coming winery producing good Pinot Noir as well as subtle, increasingly creditable *Chardonnay* and *Riesling*. ★★★★★ **2002 Riesling** $$

Assemblage [ah-sahm-blahj] (France) The art of blending wine from different grape varieties. Associated with *Bordeaux* and *Champagne*.

Assmanhausen [ass-mahn-how-zehn] (*Rheingau*, Germany) If you like sweet Pinot Noir, this is the place to come looking for it.

🍷 **Asti** (*Piedmont*, Italy) Town famous for sparkling *Spumante*, lighter *Moscato d'Asti*, and red *Barbera d'Asti*. **L'Armangia; *Bava*; Bera; Bersano; Contratto; Giorgio Fogliati; *Fontanafredda*; Gancia; Martini.**

Astringent Mouth-puckering. Associated with young red wine. See *tannin*.

Aszu [ah-soo] (Hungary) The sweet syrup made from dried and "nobly rotten" grapes (see *botrytis*) used to sweeten *Tokaji*.

🍷 **Ata Rangi** [ah-tah ran-gee] (*Martinborough*, New Zealand) Estate with high-quality *Pinot, Chardonnay*, and *Shiraz*.

🍷 **Atlas Peak** (*Napa*, California) Antinori's US venture is proving more successful with Cabernet than with Sangiovese.

Attica (Greece) Demarcated region round Athens; produces a lot of *retsina*.

🍷 **Au Bon Climat** [oh bon klee-Mat] (*Santa Barbara*, California) Top-quality producer of characterful and flavorsome *Pinot Noir* and particularly classy *Chardonnay*. ★★★★★ **Pinot Noir Knox Alexander** 2000 $$$

🍷 **Dom. des Aubuisières** [day Soh-bwee-see-yehr] (*Loire*, France) Impeccable wines ranging from richly dry to lusciously sweet. ★★★★ **Vouvray Sec 'Le Marigny'** $$$

Auckland (New Zealand) All-embracing designation which once comprised a quarter of the country's vineyards. Often derided region, despite the fact that some vintages favor it over starrier areas such as *Marlborough*. **Collards; Coopers Creek; Goldwater Estate; Kumeu River; Matua Valley; Sacred Hill; Stonyridge.**

Aude [ohd] (Southwest France) Prolific *département* and traditional source of ordinary wine. Now *Corbières* and *Fitou* are improving as are the *Vins de Pays*, thanks to new grapes (such as the *Viognier*) and the efforts of producers like *Skalli Fortant de France, Mont Tauch, Val d'Orbieu*, and *Domaine Virginie*.

Ausbruch [ows-brookh] (Austria) Term for rich *botrytis* wine which is sweeter than *Beerenauslese* but less sweet than *Trockenbeerenauslese*.

Auslese [ows-lay-zuh] (Germany) Traditionally sweet, but now sometimes *Trocken* – dry – wine from selected ripe grapes, usually affected by *botrytis*. Third rung on the *QmP* ladder.

☤ **Ch. Ausone** [oh-zohn] (*St. Emilion Premier Grand Cru Classé, Bordeaux*, France) Ancient (Roman) hillside pretender to the crown of top *St. Emilion*. Until the wine-making was taken over by *Michel Rolland* in 1995, the wine lacked intensity. Today they are first among equals. The 2000, 2001, and 2002 were all arguably wines of the vintage. Now experimenting with (previously illegal) *Petit Verdot*.

Austria Home to all sorts of whites, ranging from dry *Sauvignon Blancs* and increasingly impressive *Grüner Veltliners* (that are good enough to beat top white Burgundies in blind tastings) to ripe *Rieslings*, and especially luscious *late harvest* wines. Reds are increasingly successful too – particularly the Pinot-Noir-like *St. Laurents*. Hanstschia Angerhof; Bründlmayer; Feiler-Artinger; Freie Weingärtner; Holler; Juris; Jurtschitsch; Knoll; *Alois Kracher*; Alois Lang; Münzenrieder; Neumayer, Nicolaihof; *Willi Opitz*; Pichler; Johan Tschida; *Prager*; Ernst Triebaumer; Umathum.

🐝 **Auxerrois** [oh-sehr-wah] (France) Named after the town in northern *Burgundy*, this is the Alsatians' term for a fairly dull local variety that may be related to the *Sylvaner, Melon de Bourgogne*, or *Chardonnay*. South Africa's winemakers briefly planted it under the misapprehension that it was *Chardonnay*. In Luxembourg it is called the *Luxembourg Pinot Gris*.

☤ **Auxey-Duresses** [oh-say doo-ress] (*Burgundy*, France) *Côtes de Beaune* village best known for buttery whites, but producing rather more rustic, raspberryish, reds. A slow developer. Robert Ampeau; Dom. d'Auvenay; Dom Chassorney; *Coche-Dury*; Comte Armand; Jean-Pierre Diconne; Louis Jadot; Olivier Leflaive; Michel Prunier; Vincent Prunier; Guy Roulot.

AVA (US) Acronym for American Viticultural Area. American *appellation* system. It makes sense in smaller, climatically coherent *appellations* like *Mount Veeder* and *Carneros*; less so in larger, more heterogenous ones like *Napa*.

☤ **Quinta da Aveleda** (*Vinho Verde*, Portugal) Famous estate producing fair-quality dry *Vinho Verde* and varietal reds.

Avelsbach [ahr-vel-sbarkh] (*Mosel*, Germany) Ruwer village producing delicate, light-bodied wines.

☤ **L'Avenir** [lah-veh-near] (*Stellenbosch*, South Africa) A new and fast-rising star in the *Cape*, thanks to a – for the region – historically unusual obsession with ripe fruit. The big fruit-salady *Chenin Blanc* is a star, as are the rich *Cabernet* and one of South Africa's best *Pinotages*. Some people will find the *Chardonnay* just a touch too hefty. ★★★ Chenin Blanc 2002 $$

☤ **Avignonesi** [ahr-veen-yon-nay-see] (*Tuscany*, Italy) Ultra-classy *Vino Nobile di Montepulciano, Super-Tuscans* such as the *Grifi Merlot* and the innovative 50&50 which is a blend of Avignonesi's Merlot and Sangiovese from the nearby Capanelle estate. There are also serious *Chardonnay* and *Sauvignon* whites – plus exemplary *Vin Santo*. ★★★★★ 50 & 50 Decennale 1998 $$$$ ★★★★★ Vin Santo Occhio di Pernice 1990 $$$

☤ **Avontuur** [ah-fon-toor] (*Stellenbosch*, South Africa) Increasingly dynamic estate. ★★★ Baccarat 2000 $$

☤ **Ayala** [ay-yah-lah] (*Champagne*, France) Underrated producer which takes its name from the village of Ay. ★★★ 1996 Ayala Brut Millesime $$$

Ayl [ihl] (*Mosel*, Germany) Distinguished *Saar* village producing steely wines.

Azienda [ad-see-en-dah] (Italy) Estate.

B

⚮ **Babcock** (*Santa Ynez*, California) Classy single-vineyard *Chardonnays* (*Mount Carmel*), Pinot Noirs, Sangioveses, and Sauvignon Blancs.

⚮ **Babich** [ba-bitch] (*Henderson*, New Zealand) Family winery with wines from *Auckland*, *Marlborough*, and *Hawkes Bay*, source of the rich "Irongate" and Patriarch *Chardonnays*. The *Sauvignon Blanc* and *Pinot Gris* are good too.
★★★★ Marlborough Riesling 2001 $$$ ★★★★ Marlborough Pinot Gris 2002 $$$

⚮ **Quinta da Bacalhôa** [dah ba-keh-yow] (*Setúbal*, Portugal) The innovative *Cabernet-Merlot* made by *Peter Bright* at *JP Vinhos*. ★★★ 2000 $

⚮ **Masia Bach** [mah-see-yah bakh] (*Penedes*, Spain) This producer's specialty is unusual sweet and dry white

⚮ **Bacchus** [ba-kuhs] White grape. A *Müller-Thurgau-Riesling* cross, making light, flowery wine. **Denbies; Tenterden.**

⚮ **Dom. Denis Bachelet** [dur-nee bash-lay] (*Burgundy*, France) Classy, small *Gevrey-Chambertin* estate with fine cherryish wines.

⚮ **Backsberg Estate** [bax-burg] (*Paarl*, South Africa) *Chardonnay* pioneer, with good, quite Burgundian versions. A pioneer with screwcaps too, with the 2003 *Sauvignon Blanc*.

Bad Dürkheim [baht duhr-kime] (*Pfalz*, Germany) Chief *Pfalz* town, producing fine whites and reds. *Kurt Darting;* Fitz-Ritter; Karl Schäfer.

Bad Kreuznach [baht kroyts-nahkh] (*Nahe*, Germany) The chief and finest wine town of the region, giving its name to the entire lower *Nahe.* Paul Anheuser; von Plettenberg.

⚮ **Baden** [bah-duhn] (Germany) Warm southern region of Germany, with dry (*Trocken*) whites and good *Pinot Noirs*. The huge *Winzerkeller* cooperative makes good wines, as do: Becker; Ehrenstette; Dr Heger; Jechtingen; Karl Heinz Johner; R Zimmerlin.

⚮ **Baden Winzerkeller (ZBW)** [bah-den vin-zehr-keh-luhr] (*Baden*, Germany) Huge co-op; reliable but perhaps a trifle dull.

⚮ **Badia a Coltibuono** [bah-dee-yah ah kohl-tee-bwoh-noh] (*Tuscany*, Italy) One of Italy's best *Chianti* producers. Pure *Sangiovese* and *Chardonnay*. Great mature releases.

⚮ **Badia di Morrona** [bah-dee-yah dee Moh-ROH-nah] (*Tuscany*, Italy) Fine estate with a notable *Super-Tuscan* in the shape of the N'Antia Cabernet-Sangiovese blend. ★★★★ Colli dell'Etruria Centrale Vigna Alta 1999 $$

⚮ **Baga** [bah-gah] (*Bairrada*, Portugal) The spicy red variety of *Bairrada*.

⚮ **Ch. Bahans-Haut-Brion** [bah-on oh-bree-on] (*Graves*, Bordeaux, France) The *second label* of *Ch. Haut-Brion.*

⚮ **Bailey's** (*Victoria*, Australia) Traditional, good Liqueur *Muscat* and hefty, old-fashioned *Shiraz.*

⚮ **Bairrada** [bi-rah-dah] (Portugal) *DO* region south of *Oporto*. Revolutionary producers like *Sogrape*, *Luis Pato*, and *Alianca* are proving what can be done. Look for spicy blackberryish reds and creamy whites.

Baja California [bah-hah] (Mexico) Home to Santo Tomas, Casa de Piedra, and *LA Cetto*. ★★★★ LA Cetto Nebbiolo Reserva Limitada 1999 $$

Balance Harmony of fruitiness, *acidity*, *alcohol*, and *tannin*. Balance can develop with age but should be evident (even if hard to discern) in youth.

Balaton [bah-la-ton] (Hungary) Wine region frequented by *flying winemakers*, and producing fair-quality reds and whites. Chapel Hill.

Anton Balbach [an-ton bahl-barkh] (*Rheinhessen*, Germany) Potentially one of the best producers in the *Erden* region – especially for *late harvest* wines.

⚮ **Bodegas Balbás** [bal-bash] (*Ribera del Duero*, Spain) Small producer of juicy *Tempranillo* reds, *Bordeaux*-style *Cabernet* blends, and a lively rosé.

⚮ **Balbi** [bal-bee] (*Mendoza*, Argentina) A subsidiary of the huge Allied Domecq, and producer of good, inexpensive modern wines, including appealing *Malbecs* and dry rosés. ★★★ Reserve Barbaro 1999 $$

B

☰ **Ch. Balestard-la-Tonnelle** [bah-les-star lah ton-nell] (*St. Emilion Grand Cru Classé, Bordeaux*, France) Good, quite traditional *St. Emilion* built to last.

☰ **Balgownie Estate** [bal-Gow-nee] (*Bendigo*, Australia) One of Victoria's most reliable producers of blackcurranty *Cabernet* in Bendigo. *Chardonnays* are big and old-fashioned, and *Pinot Noirs* are improving. ★★★ **Cabernet Sauvignon 2000 $$; ★★★ Chardonnay 2001 $$**

☰ **Bandol** [bon-dohl] (*Provence*, France) *Mourvèdre*-influenced plummy, herby reds, and rich whites. Ch. de Pibarnon; *Dom. Tempier;* Dom. Tour de Bon; Pradeaux; Ch. la Rouvière; Dom. Vannières.

☰ **Castello Banfi** [ban-fee] (*Tuscany*, Italy) Dynamic US-owned producer with great *Brunello* and *Vini da Tavola*. ★★★★★ **Poggio alle Mura 1997 $**

Bannockburn (*Central Otago*, New Zealand) South Island area that's hitting the bull's eye with its Pinot Noirs. Akarua; Felton Road; Mt Difficulty; Olssens.

☰ **Bannockburn** (*Geelong*, Australia) Made famous by Gary Farr of *By Farr* experience at *Dom. Dujac* in *Burgundy* to produce concentrated *Pinot Noir* and *Shiraz* at home. The big *Chardonnay* and *Bordeaux* blends are impressive too.

☰ **Bannockburn by Farr** See *By Farr.*

☰ **Banrock Station** Successful branded wine from *BRL Hardy*

☰ **Banyuls** [bon-yools] (*Provence*, France) France's answer to *tawny port*. Fortified, *Grenache*-based, *Vin Doux Naturel,* ranging from off-dry to lusciously sweet. The *Rancio* style is more like *Madeira.* L'Etoile; Dom. Mas Amiel; Dom. du Mas Blanc; Clos de Paulilles; *Dom. de la Rectorie;* Dom. la Tour Vieille; Vial Magnères.

☰ **Antonio Barbadillo** [bahr-bah-deel-yoh] (*Jerez*, Spain) Great producer of *Fino* and *Manzanilla.* ★★★★★ **Obispo Gascon Palo Cortado $$$**

Barbaresco [bahr-bah-ress-koh] (*Piedmont*, Italy) *DOCG Nebbiolo* red, with spicy fruit, depth, and complexity. Approachable earlier (three to five years) than neighboring *Barolo* but, in the right hands – and in the best vineyards – of almost as high a quality. Gaja; Marchese di Gresy; Rino Varaldi; Castello di Neive; *Paitin; Pelissero; Alfredo Prunotto;* Albino Rocca; la Spinetta

☰ **Cascina la Barbatella** [kah-shh-nah lah bahr-bah-teh-lah] (*Piedmont*, Italy) Rising star, focusing its attention firmly on the *Barbera* (as Barbera d'Asti and single-vineyard Vigna di Sonvico and Vigna dell'Angelo) as well as a good Cortese-*Sauvignon* blend called Noè after one of its makers.

🐝 **Barbera** [Bar-Beh-Rah] (*Piedmont*, Italy) Grape making fruity, spicy, characterful wine (e.g. B. d'Alba and B. d'Asti), with a flavor like cheesecake and raisins. Now in *California, Mexico*, and *Australia* (at *Brown Bros.* and "*I*").

Barbera d'Alba/d'Asti [Bar-Beh-Rah Dal-bah / Das-Tee] (*Piedmont*, Italy) Up-and-coming designatios thanks to some great estates: GD Vajra; Vietti; Scagliola; Roberto Voerzio.

☰ **René Barbier** [Ren-nay Bah-bee-yay] (*Penedès*, Spain) Dynamic producer of commercial wines and, more significantly, leading pioneer in *Priorat.* ★★★★ **Priorat Clos Mogador 1997 $$$**

Barco Reale (*Tuscany*, Italy) The lighter, younger, *DOC* red wine of the *DOCG* region of *Carmignano.* ★★★ **2002 Tenuta di Capezzana $$**

☰ **Barca Velha** [bahr-kah vayl-yah] (*Douro*, Portugal) Portugal's most famous red, traditionally made from port varieties by *Ferreira*, now getting a quality boost. Also look out for Reserva Especial released in more difficult years.

☰ **Bardolino** [bar-doh-lee-noh] (*Veneto*, Italy) As if to prove that local politics still hold sway in the Italian wine industry, Bardolino was recently promoted to *DOCG* status. Can be cherryish and *Beaujolais*-like – or dull – Also comes as Chiaretto Rosé. Best young unless from an exceptional producer. *Boscaini;* Fabiano *Masi;* Portalupi.

☰ **Gilles Barge** [bahzh] (*Rhône*, France) Son of Pierre who won an international reputation for his fine, classic *Côte Rôtie.* Gilles, who now runs the estate, has also shown his skill with *St. Joseph.*

☰ **Guy de Barjac** [gee dur bar-jak] (*Rhône*, France) A master of the *Syrah* grape, producing some of the best – and most stylish – *Cornas* around.

B

☒ **Barolo** [bah-Roh-loh] (*Piedmont*, Italy) Noble *Nebbiolo* reds with extraordinary berryish, floral, and spicy flavors. Old-fashioned versions are dry and tannic when young but, from a good producer, and year, can develop extraordinary complexity. Modern versions are oakier but more accessible. *Elio Altare; Batasiolo; Borgogno; Chiarlo; Domenico Clerico; Aldo Conterno; Giacomo Conterno; Conterno Fantino; Fontanafredda; Gaja; Ettore Germano; Bruno Giacosa; Elio Grasso; M Marengo; Bartolo Mascarello; Giuseppe Mascarello; Pio Cesare; Oddero; Pira & Figli F Principiano; Ratti; Sandrone; Scavino; Vajra;* Vietti; Gianni Voerzio; Roberto Voerzio;. ★★★★ 1997 Barolo Monforte D'Alba Aldo Conterno 'Cicala'

☒ **Baron de Ley** [bah-Rohn Duh lay] (*Rioja*, Spain) Small estate whose French oak-aged wines, can be worth waiting for. ★★★ 1997 Rioja Reserva $$

☒ **Baron Philippe de Rothschild / La Baronnie** (*Bordeaux*, France & Chile) This Bordeaux merchant is the name behind the improving, but generally unexciting, branded Mouton Cadet and a range of fair AC wines from *Pauillac*, *Margaux* etc. The Chilean Escudo Rojo and expensive Almaviva (the latter a joint venture with Concha y Toro) is better and Opus One (with Mondavi) is fine. Baron Arques, a venture in Limoux is improving. ★★★★★ 1999 Almaviva $$$$; ★★★ 2000 Escudo Rojo $$

Barossa Valley [bah-ros suh] (Australia) Big, warm region north-east of Adelaide which is famous for traditional, old-vine *Shiraz* and *Grenache*, "ports", and *Rieslings* which age to oily richness. *Chardonnay* and *Cabernet* make subtler, classier wines along with *Riesling* in the higher altitude vineyards of the *Eden Valley* and *Adelaide Hills*. *Barossa Valley Estate; Basedow; Bethany; Wolf Blass; Grant Burge;* Charles Cimicky; E&E; Elderton; Groom; Hardy's; Henschke; Heritage; Steve Hoff; Kaesler; Krondorf; Peter Lehmann; Melton; Orlando; Penfolds; Rockford; St. Hallett; Torbrek; Turkey Flat; Yalumba.

☒ **Barossa Valley Estate** (*Barossa Valley*, Australia) Top end of *BRL Hardy* with good old-vine *Barossa* reds. ★★★★★ E+E Black Pepper Shiraz 1999 $$$

☒ **Daniel Barraud** [Bah-roh] (*Burgundy*, France) Dynamic producer of single-*cuvée Pouilly-Fuissé*.

Barrique [ba-reek] (France) French barrel, particularly in *Bordeaux*, holding about 58 gallons (225 liters). Term used in Italy to denote (new) barrel aging.

☒ **Jim Barry** (*Clare Valley*, Australia) Producer of the dazzling, spicy, mulberryish (some might say, over-concentrated) *Armagh Shiraz* and great, floral Watervale Riesling. ★★★★★ 1999 The Armagh $$$$

Barsac [bahr-sak] (*Bordeaux*, France) AC neighbor of *Sauternes* with similar, though not quite so rich, *Sauvignon/Semillon* dessert wines. *Ch. Broustet; Ch. Climens; Ch. Coutet; Ch. Doisy-Dubroca; Ch. Doisy-Daëne; Ch. Nairac.*

☒ **Ghislaine Barthod-Noëllat** [jee-lenn Bar-toh] (*Burgundy*, France) Top class *Chambolle-Musigny* estate.

☒ **De Bartoli** [day bahr-toh-lee] (*Sicily*, Italy) *Marsala* for drinking rather than cooking from a revolutionary producer who has voluntarily removed his Vecchio Samperi from the DOC system.

☒ **Barton & Guestier** [bahr-ton ay geht-tee-yay] (*Bordeaux*, France) Highly commercial *Bordeaux* shipper.

☒ **Barwang** [bahr-wang] (*New South Wales*, Australia) *McWilliams* label for cool-climate wines produced near Young in eastern *New South Wales*.

☒ **Basedow** [baz-zeh-doh] (South Australia) Producer of big, concentrated *Shiraz* and *Cabernet* and ultra-rich *Semillon* and *Chardonnays*.

Basilicata [bah-see-lee-kah-tah] (Italy) Southern wine region chiefly known for *Aglianico del Vulture* and improving *IGT* wines. Basilium.

Basket Press Traditional winepress, favored for quality reds by Australian producers such as *Chateau Reynella*.

☒ **Bass Philip** (*Victoria*, Australia) Fanatical South *Gippsland* pioneer Philip Jones's fine *Burgundy*-like *Pinot*.

☒ **Von Bassermann-Jordan** [fon bas-suhr-man johr-dun] (*Pfalz*, Germany) A traditional producer with fabulous vineyards and fine *Trocken Rieslings*.

B

✗ **Ch. Bastor-Lamontagne** [bas-tohr-lam-mon-tañ] (*Sauternes, Bordeaux,* France) Remarkably reliable classy *Sauternes;* inexpensive alternative to the big-names, often offering comparable levels of richness and complexity. Fine in 2001.

✗ **Ch. Batailley** [bat-tih-yay] (*Pauillac 5ème Cru Classé, Bordeaux,* France) Traditional estate that belongs to the merchant house of Borie-Manoux.

✗ **Bâtard-Montrachet** [bat-tahr mon-rah-shay] (*Burgundy,* France) Biscuity-rich white *Grand Cru* that straddles the border between the appellations of *Chassagne* and *Puligny-Montrachet.* Often very fine; invariably expensive. Cailot; Colin-Deleger; Joseph Drouhin; Jean-Noel Gagnard; Gagnard-Delagrange; Dom. Leflaive; Ch. de la Maltroye; Pierre Morey; Michel Niellon; Ramonet; Sauzet.

✗ **Batasiolo** [bat-tah-see-oh-loh] (*Piedmont,* Italy) Producer of top-class *Barolo,* impressive cherryish *Dolcetto,* fresh *Moscato,* intense berryish *Brachetto,* and a subtle *Chardonnay.* ★★★★ 1998 Barolo Cerequio $$$

✗ **Dom. des Baumard** [day boh-marh] (*Loire,* France) Superlative producer of great *Coteaux du Layon, Quarts de Chaume,* and *Savennières.*

✗ **Bava** [bah-vah] (*Piedmont,* Italy) Innovative producer making good *Moscato Barbera,* reviving indigenous grapes such as the rarely grown raspberryish *Ruche* as well as a rather wonderful traditional curious herb-infused *Barolo Chinato Cocchi.* Try it with one of Roberto Bava's other enthusiasms: dark chocolate.

✗ **Béarn** [bay-ar'n] (*South West,* France) Highly traditional and often dull region. Lapeyre is the name to look out for.

✗ **Ch. Beau-Séjour (-Bécot)** [boh-say-zhoor bay-koh] (*St. Emilion Grand Cru Classé, Bordeaux,* France) Reinstated in 1996 after a decade of demotion. Now making fairly priced, greatly improved wine.

✗ **Ch. Beau-Site** [boh-seet] (*St. Estèphe Cru Bourgeois, Bordeaux,* France) Benchmark *St. Estèphe* in the same stable as *Ch. Batailley.*

✗ **Ch. de Beaucastel** [boh-kas-tel] (*Rhône,* France) The top *Châteauneuf-du-Pape* estate, using organic methods to produce richly gamey (for some, too gamey – see *Brettanomyces*) long-lived, spicy reds, which reflect the presence in the blend of an unusually high proportion of Mourvèdre. "Hommage à Jacques Perrin" is the top label. There are also rare but fine creamy-spicy (*Roussanne-based*) whites. The Coudoulet Côtes du Rhône are a delight too. ★★★★★ 2000 $$$$

✗ **Beaujolais** [boh-zhuh-lay] (*Burgundy,* France) Light, fruity *Gamay* red; good chilled, for early drinking. Currently hard to sell (17% of the 2001 vintage had to be destroyed) and criticize (a recent suggestion by a well-informed critic that some Beaujolais was "shit" led to a court case and a hefty fine). *Beaujolais-Villages* is better, and the 10 *Crus* better still. With age, these can taste like (fairly ordinary) *Burgundy* from the *Côte d'Or. Beaujolais Blanc,* which is made from *Chardonnay,* is now mostly sold as *St. Véran.* See *Crus: Morgon;* Chénas; Brouilly; Côte de Brouilly; Juliénas; Fleurie; Regnié; St. Amour; Chiroubles; Moulin-à-Vent..

✗ **Beaujolais-Villages** (*Burgundy,* France) From the north of the region, fuller-flavored and more alcoholic than plain *Beaujolais,* though not necessarily from one of the named *Cru* villages. Duboeuf; Dubost; Foillard; Ch. es Jacques; Janin; Large; Pivot; Dme des Terres Dorées. ★★★ 2000 Beaujolais-Villages Vieilles Vignes Mommessin $

✗ **Beaulieu Vineyard** [bohl-yoo] (*Napa Valley,* California) Historic winery getting back on its feet after years of neglect by its multinational owners. The wines to look for are the Georges de Latour Private Reserve *Cabernets,* which have been consistently good, and the new Signet range. Recent vintages of the Beau Tour *Cabernet Sauvignon* show improvement too. ★★★★ Zinfandel Napa Valley Signet Collection $$$

B

Beaumes de Venise [bohm duh vuh-neez] (*Rhône*, France) *Côtes du Rhône* village producing spicy, dry reds and sweet, grapey, fortified *Vin Doux Naturel* from the *Muscat*. Dom. des Bernardins; *Chapoutier*; Dom. de Coyeux; Durban; de Fenouillet; *Paul Jaboulet Aîné*; la Soumade; *Vidal-Fleury*.

Ch. Beaumont [boh-mon] (*Haut-Médoc Cru Bourgeois, Bordeaux*, France) A good Cru Bourgeois that seems to be slightly underperforming at the moment.

Beaune [bohn] (*Burgundy*, France) Large commune that gives its name to the *Côte de Beaune* and produces soft, raspberry-and rose-petal *Pinot Noir*. As in *Nuits-St.-Georges*, there are plenty of *Premier Crus*, but no *Grands Crus*. The walled city is the site of the famous *Hospices* charity auction. Reds are best from *Michel Prunier, Louis Jadot, Bouchard Père et Fils* (since 1996), *Ch. de Chorey*, Albert Morot, and *Joseph Drouhin* – who also make an ultra-rare white. Other good producers: Robert Ampeau; Arnoux Père et Fils; *Pascal Bouley*; Dubois; Génot-Boulanger; Germain (Ch. de Chorey); *Michel Lafarge*; Daniel Largeot; Laurent; Maillard; Albert Morot; *Jacques Prieur*; Rapet Père et Fils; Thomas-Moillard; *Tollot-Beaut*.

Ch. Beauregard [boh-ruh-gahr] (*Pomerol, Bordeaux*, France) Estate producing juicy oaky *Pomerol*.

Ch. Beauséjour-Duffau-Lagarosse [boh-say-zhoor doo-foh lag-gahr-ros] (*St. Emilion Premier Grand Cru Classé, Bordeaux*, France) Traditional tough, tannic *St. Emilion*.

Beaux Frères [boh frair] (*Oregon*) *Pinot Noir* winery launched by wine guru Robert Parker and his brother-in-law (hence the name).

Graham Beck (Robertson, South Africa) Associated with *Bellingham* and producer of some of South Africa's best sparkling wines. A Coastal Range of still wines are looking good too, as the "Estate" multi-regional blend.
★ ★ ★ ★ ★ The Ridge Syrah 2000

Beerenauslese [beer-ren-now-slay-syh] (Austria/Germany) Sweet wines from selected, ripe grapes (Beeren), hopefully affected by *botrytis*.

Ch. de Bel-Air [bel-Ehr] (*Lalande-de-Pomerol, Bordeaux*, France) Impressive property making wines to make some *Pomerols* blush.

Ch. Bel-Orme-Tronquoy-de-Lalande [bel-orm-tron-kwah-duh-la-lond] (*Haut-Médoc Cru Bourgeois, Bordeaux*, France) Highly old-fashioned estate and wines. Under the same ownership (and philosophy) as *Rauzan Gassies*. Made a good 2000, but still has plenty of room for improvement.

Ch. Belair [bel-lehr] (*St. Emilion Premier Grand Cru Classé, Bordeaux*, France) Classy, delicate, long-lived *St. Emilion* with a successful 2002. Don't confuse with the *Lalande-de-Pomerol Ch. de Bel-Air* (or any of the countless lesser Belairs scattered around *Bordeaux*).

Bellavista (*Lombardy,* Italy) Commercial Franciacorta producers of classy sparkling and still wines. The Riserva Vittorio Moretti, which is only produced in top years, is the star of the show.

Albert Belle [bel] (*Rhône*, France) An estate that has recently begun to bottle its own excellent red and – oaky – white Hermitage.

Bellet [bel-lay] (*Provence*, France) Tiny *AC* behind Nice producing fairly good red, white, and rosé from local grapes including the Rolle, the *Braquet*, and the *Folle Noir*. Pricey and rarely seen outside France. Ch. de Bellet.

Bellingham (South Africa) The first winery to produce a dry *Chenin Blanc* in the Cape, this is now a highly commercial winery that is focusing increasingly on quality. *Cabernet Franc* is a particular success. Look for the Premium range.
★ ★ ★ ★ Spitz Cabernet Franc 2000 $$

Bendigo/Ballarat [ben-dig-goh] (*Victoria*, Australia) Warm region producing big-boned, long-lasting reds with intense berry fruit. *Balgownie*; Blackjack; Heathcote; *Jasper Hill; Mount Ida; Passing Clouds*; Water Wheel.
★ ★ ★ ★ Passing Clouds Graeme's Blend 1999 $$

Benziger [ben-zig-ger] (*Sonoma*, California) Classy wines from the family behind *Glen Ellen*. ★ ★ ★ ★ ★ Cabernet Sauvignon Sonoma County Reserve 1999 $$$$

B

Ⓨ Berberana [behr-behr-rah nah] (*Rioja*, Spain) Producer of a range of fruitier young-drinking styles, as well as the improving Carta de Plata and Carta de Oro and Lagunilla *Riojas*, plus sparkling Marquès de Monistrol.

Ⓨ Bercher [behr-kehr] (*Baden*, Germany) Dynamic estate, producing impressive, modern, *Burgundy*-style reds and whites.

Bereich [beh-ri-kh] (Germany) Vineyard area, subdivision of an *Anbaugebiet*. On its own indicates *QbA* wine, e.g. *Niersteiner*. Finer wines are followed by the name of a (smaller) *Grosslage*, better ones by that of an individual vineyard.

Ⓨ Bergerac [behr-jur-rak] (France) Traditionally *Bordeaux*'s "lesser" neighbor (and occasional source of wine illegally sold under that appellation). The wines, though still often mediocre, can be better value than basic red or white *Bordeaux*, while the best *Monbazillac* can sometimes outclass basic *Sauternes*. Côtes de Bergerac can be sweeter. Saussignac and Pécharmant are sub-appellations, as is Montravel. Ch. Belingard; Clos Dalmain; Court-les-Muts; des Eyssards; Grinou; la Jaubertie; Payral; de Raz; Tour des Gendres.
★★★ Bergerac Sec Chateau Le Payral 2002 $

Ⓨ Bergkelder [berg-kel-dur] (*Cape*, South Africa) Huge firm best known for its *Stellenryck* wines. Its cheaper *Fleur du Cap* range is likeable enough and the best of the *JC Le Roux* sparkling wines are first class.

Ⓨ Beringer Vineyards [ber-rin-jer] (*Napa Valley*, California) Big, once-Swiss, now Australian-owned (Fosters) producer, increasingly notable for its single-vineyard *Cabernet Sauvignons* (Knights Valley, *Howell Mountain*, *Spring Mountain*, and Private Reserve), *Cabernet Francs*, and *Merlots*; *Burgundy*-like *Chardonnays*; and "Nightingale" *late harvest* wines. ★★★★★ **Knights Valley Alluvium Red 1999 $$$**

Bernkastel [berhrn-kah-stel] (*Mosel*, Germany) Town and area on the *Mittelmosel* and source of some of the finest *Riesling* (like the famous Bernkasteler Doktor), and a lake of poor-quality stuff. Heribert Kerpen; Dr Loosen; Pauly-Bergweiler; JJ Prum; Von Kesselstadt; Selbach -Oster; J. Wegeler Erben.

Ⓨ Bernardus (*Monterey*, California) Producer of rich, unsubtle, fairly-priced, unashamedly New World-style *Sauvignon Blanc*, *Chardonnay*, and *Pinot Noir*.

Ⓨ Beronia [beh-roh-nya] (*Rioja*, Spain) Good, traditional reds and more modern whites from this small *Gonzalez-Byass* owned bodega.
★★★ Tempranillo Elaboracion Especial 2000 $$

Ⓨ Dom Bertagna [behr-tan-ya] (*Vougeot*, France) Estate offering the rare, (relatively) affordable *Premier Cru Vougeot* alongside its *Clos de Vougeot Grand Cru*. ★★★★ Chambolle-Musigny Les Plantes 2000 **$$$**

Ⓨ Bertani [behr-tah-nee] (*Veneto*, Italy) Producer of good *Valpolicella* and innovative wines such as the Le Lave Garganega-*Chardonnay* blend.

Ⓨ Besserat de Bellefon [bes-ser-rah duh bel-fo'hn] (*Champagne*, France) Elegant, light Champagnes of good quality but not always for long keeping.
★★★★ NV Besserat de Bellefon Cuvee des Moines Rose $$$

Ⓨ Best's (*Victoria*, Australia) Under-appreciated winery in *Great Western* making delicious concentrated *Shiraz* from old vines, attractive *Cabernet*, *Dolcetto*, *Pinot Noir*, *Colombard*, and rich *Chardonnay* and *Riesling*.
★★★ Great Western F H T Shiraz 1999 $$

Ⓨ Bethany [beth-than-nee] (*Barossa Valley*, Australia) Impressive small producer of knockout *Shiraz*. ★★★★ Shiraz 2000 $$;
★★★★ Bethany GR6 Reserve Shiraz $$

Ⓨ Bethel Heights (*Oregon*, California) Long-established winery, now a rising star, with good *Pinot Noir* and particularly impressive *Pinot Blanc* and *Chardonnay*.
★★★★ Pinot Noir Willamette Valley West Block Reserve 2000 $$

Ⓨ Dom. Henri Beurdin [bur-dan] (*Loire*, France) The estate at which you'll find benchmark white and rosé *Reuilly*.

Ⓨ Ch. Beychevelle [bay-shur-vel] (*St. Julien 4ème Cru Classé, Bordeaux*, France) A fourth growth that achieves the typical cigar-box character of *St. Julien* but fails to excite. The *second label* is Amiral de Beychevelle.

B

☰ **Léon Beyer** [bay-ur] (*Alsace,* France) Serious producer of lean long-lived wines.

☰ **Beyerskloof** [bay-yurs-kloof] (*Stellenbosch,* South Africa) Beyers Truter (of Kanonkop) produces some of South Africa's top *Cabernet* and *Stellenbosch Pinotage.* ★★★★ Beyerskloof 2000 $$

☰ Bianco di Custoza [bee-yan-koh dee koos-toh-zah] (*Veneto,* Italy) Widely exported *DOC.* A reliable, crisp, light white from a blend of grapes. A better-value alternative to most basic *Soave.* Gorgo; Portalupi; *Tedeschi;* le Vigne di San Pietro; *Zenato.*

☰ **Maison Albert Bichot** [bee-shoh] (*Burgundy,* France) Big *négociant* with excellent *Chablis* and *Vosne-Romanée,* plus adequate wines sold under a plethora of other labels.

☰ **Biddenden** [bid-den-den] (*Kent,* England) Producer showing impressive mastery of the peachy *Ortega.*

Bierzo [bee-yehrt-zoh] (*Castilla y León,* Spain) Up-and-coming region close to Galicia. Fresh whites made from the local Mencia grape are worth looking out for. Drink young. Pérez Caramés; Descendientes de J. Palacios.

☰ **Bienvenue-Batard-Montrachet** [bee-yen-veh-noo bat-tahr mon ra-shay] (*Burgundy,* France) Fine white *Burgundy* vineyard with potentially gorgeous biscuit-like wines. Carillon; Henri Clerc; Dom Leflaive; *Sauzet.*

☰ **Weingut Josef Biffar** [bif-fah] (*Pfalz,* Germany). *Deidesheim* estate that is on a roll at the moment with its richly spicy wines.

☰ **Billecart-Salmon** [beel-kahr sal-mon] (*Champagne,* France) Producer of the stylish winners (the 1959 and 1961 vintages) of the Champagne of the Millennium competition held in Stockholm in 1999 at which I was a taster. Possibly the best all-arounder for quality and value, and certainly the *Champagne* house whose subtle but decidedly ageable *non-vintage, vintage,* and rosé I buy without hesitation. Superlative.

☰ **Billiot** [bil-lee-yoh] (*Champagne,* France) Impressive small producer with classy rich sparkling wine.

Bingen [bing-urn] (*Rheinhessen,* Germany) Village giving its name to a *Rheinhessen Bereich* that includes a number of well-known *Grosslage.*

Binissalem [bin-nee-sah-lem] (*Mallorca,* Spain) The holiday island's demarcated region. José Ferrer's and Jaime Mesquida's are the best producers.

Bio-Bio (Chile) The coolest, wettest and most southerly wine region in Chile.

☰ **Biondi-Santi** [bee-yon-dee san-tee] (*Tuscany,* Italy) 19th century *Brunello di Montalcino* pioneer whose wines haven't always lived up to its prestige. There ahve been big recent improvements, however, notably with the single vineyard Greppo. ★★★★ Brunello di Montalcino 1998 $$$

Biscuity Flavor of savory crackers often associated with the *Chardonnay* grape, particularly in *Champagne* and top-class mature *Burgundy,* or with the yeast that fermented the wine.

☰ **Bischöfliche Weingüter** (*Mosel-Saar-Ruwer,* Germany) Large and historic *Mosel* estate, now making top quality again.

☰ **Bitouzet-Prieur** [bee-too-zay pree-yur] (*Burgundy,* France) If you like classic *Meursault* and *Volnay* built to last rather than seduce instantly with ripe fruit and oak.

☰ **Dom. Simon Bize** [beez] (*Burgundy,* France) Intense, long-lived, and good-value wines produced in *Savigny-lès-Beaune.*

☰ **Blaauwklippen** [blow-klip-pen] (*Stellenbosch,* South Africa) Recently sold, large estate, veering between commercial and top quality. The *Cabernet* and *Zinfandel* are the strongest cards, but the *Chardonnay* is improving fast.

☰ Blagny [blan-yee] (*Burgundy,* France) Tiny source of unsubtle red (sold as Blagny) and potentially top-class white (sold as *Meursault, Puligny-Montrachet,* Blagny, Hameau de Blagny, or la Pièce sous le Bois). Ampeau; Chavy-Chouet; *Jobard;Thierry Matrot.*

B

�*ϒ* **Blain-Gagnard** [blan gan-yahr] (*Burgundy*, France) Creamy, modern *Chassagne-Montrachet*. ★★★★ Chassagne-Montrachet Clos St.-Jean 2000 $$$

Blanc de Blancs [blon dur blon] A white wine, made from white grapes – hardly worth mentioning except in the case of *Champagne*, where *Pinot Noir*, a black grape, usually makes up 30–70 percent of the blend. In this case, *Blanc de Blancs* is pure *Chardonnay*.

Blanc de Noirs [blon dur nwahrr] A white (or frequently very slightly pink-tinged wine) made from red grapes by taking off the free-run juice, before pressing to minimize the uptake of red pigments from the skin. Paul Bara; *Duval-Leroy (Fleur de Champagne)*; Egly-Ouiriet.

�*ϒ* **Paul Blanck** [blank] (*Alsace*, France) Top-class *Alsace* domaine, specializing in single *Cru* wines. Now heroically pioneering screwcaps.

�*ϒ* **Blandy's** [blan-deez] (*Madeira*, Portugal) Brand owned by the Madeira Wine Company and named after the sailor who began the production of fortified wine here. Excellent old wines. Younger ones are less exciting.

�*ϒ* **Blanquette de Limoux** [blon ket dur lee-moo] (*Midi*, France) *Méthode Champenoise* sparkling wine, which, when good, is appley and clean. Best when made with a generous dose of *Chardonnay*, as the local *Mauzac* tends to give it an earthy flavour with age.

�*ϒ* **Wolf Blass** (*Barossa Valley*, Australia) Part of the huge Mildara-Blass operation (and thus owned by Fosters), this brand was founded by a German immigrant who prides himself on producing "sexy" (his term) reds and whites by blending wines from different regions of *South Australia* and allowing them plentiful contact with new oak. ★★★★★ Platinum Label Shiraz 2000 $$$ ★★★★★ Platinum Label Clare Valley Cabernet Sauvignon $$$

☙ **Blauburgunder** [blow-boor-goon-durh] (Austria) The name the Austrians give their light, often sharp, *Pinot Noir*.

☙ **Blauer Portugieser** [blow-urh por-too-gay-suhr] (Germany) Red grape used in Germany and Austria to make light, pale wine.

☙ **Blaufränkisch** [blow-fren-kish] (Austria) Grape used to make refreshingly berryish wines that can – in the right hands – compete with the reds of the *Loire*. ★★★★ Hans Igler Blaufrankisch 2000 $$

☙ **Blockheadia Ringnosii** (*Napa*, California) Despite the wacky name and label, this is a source of serious *Sauvignon* and *Zinfandel*.

☙ **Quinta da Boavista** [keen-tah dah boh-wah-vees-tah] (*Alenquer*, Portugal) Starry estate producing a range of red and white wines, including Palha Canas, Quinta das Sete, and Espiga. ★★★★★ Touriz Quinta da Boavista 2001 $$

☙ **Bobadilla** [booh-bah-dee-yoh] (*Jerez*, Spain) Fine Sherry *bodega*

☙ **Boccagigabbia** [Bbok-kah-ji-gah-bee-yah] (*Marche*, Italy) Top class estate, producing delicious *Pinot Noir* (Girone), *Cabernet* (Akronte), and *Chardonnay*.

Bocksbeutel [box-boy-tuhl] (*Franken*, Germany) The famous flask-shaped bottle of *Franken*, adopted by the makers of *Mateus* Rosé.

Bodega [bod-day-gah] (Spain) Winery or wine cellar; producer.

☙ **Bodegas y Bebidas** [bod-day-gas ee beh-bee-das] (Spain) One of Spain's most dynamic wine companies, and maker of *Campo Viejo*.

☙ **Bodegas y Viñedos del Jalón** [bod-day-gas ee veen-yay-dos del kha-lohn] (Calatayud, Spain) Good value reds and whites, especially Poema Garnacha, made by Scotswoman Pamela Geddes. ★★★ 2001 Poema $

Body Usually used as "full-bodied", meaning a wine with mouth-filling flavors and probably a fairly high alcohol content.

☙ **Boekenhoutskloof** [BOO-kurn-ohts-kloof] (*Franschoek*, South Africa) Marc Kent's little winery is the source of the Cape's – and one of the worlds' – best Semillons. The Syrah and Cabernet are terrific too. Porcupine Ridge is the second label. ★★★★ Porcupine Ridge Cabernet Sauvignon 2002 $$

☙ **Jean-Marc Boillot** [bwah-yoh] (*Burgundy*, France) Small *Pommard domaine* run by the son of the winemaker at *Olivier Leflaive*, and offering really good examples from neighboring villages *Puligny-Montrachet* and *Volnay*. ★★★★ Puligny-Montrachet Champ Gains 2000 $$$

B

Jean-Claude Boisset [bwah-say] (*Burgundy*, France) Dynamic *négociant* that now owns a long list of *Burgundy négociants*, including the excellent *Jaffelin* and the improved though still far from dazzling *Bouchard Aîné*. Boisset also makes passable wines in *Languedoc-Roussillon*.

Boisson-Vadot [bwah-son va-doh] (*Burgundy*, France) Classy, small *Meursault domaine*.

Bolgheri [bol-geh-ree] (*Tuscany*, Italy) Increasingly exciting and recently officially recognized region that was originally made famous by red superstars such as *Antinori's Sassicaia* and *Ornellaia*. Other impressive producers now include: *Belvedere*, *Grattamacco*, Tenuta dell'Ornellaia, Le Macchiole, and Satta, and there are some top-class whites made from the *Vermentino*.

Bolla [bol-lah] (*Veneto*, Italy) Producer of plentiful, adequate *Valpolicella* and *Soave*, and of smaller quantities of impressive single vineyard wines like Jago and Creso. ★★★ Le Origini Amarone della Valpolicella 1997 $$

Bollinger [bol-an-jay] (*Champagne*, France) Great family-owned firm at *Ay*, whose full-flavored wines need age. The luscious and rare *Vieilles Vignes* is made from pre-*phylloxera* vines, while the nutty *RD* was the first late-disgorged *Champagne* to hit the market. The 1988 RD is a current star. ★★★★ Bollinger Special Cuvee $$$

Bommes [bom] (*Bordeaux*, France) *Sauternes commune* and village containing several *Premiers Crus* such as la Tour Blanche, Lafaurie-Peyraguey, Rabaud-Promis, and Rayne Vigneau.

Bonarda (Italy, Argentina) Several red grapes in northern Italy use the name of Bonarda: most make quite rich, deep wine of no great complexity. The Bonarda grown in Argentina may be the same as one or more of these, or it may be different again. Properly ripe Argentine Bonarda can be very good.

Ch. le Bon-Pasteur [bon-pas-stuhr] (*Pomerol*, *Bordeaux*, France) The impressive private estate of **Michel Rolland**, who acts as consultant – and helps to make fruit-driven wines – for half his neighbors, as well as producers in almost every other wine-growing region in the universe.

Domaine de la Bongran [bon-grah] Good, innovative, Mâcon-Clessé from Jean Thévenet.

Henri Bonneau [bon-noh] (*Rhône*, France) *Châteauneuf-du-Pape* producer with two special *cuvées* – "Marie Beurrier" and "des Celestins" – and a cult following. ★★★★★ 1999 Corton-Charlemagne

Dom. Bonneau du Martray [bon-noh doo mahr-tray] (*Burgundy*, France) Largest grower of *Corton-Charlemagne* and impressive producer thereof. Also makes a classy red *Grand Cru Corton*.

Bonnes Mares [bon-mahr] (*Burgundy*, France) Rich *Morey St. Denis Grand Cru*. Dom d'Auvenay; Bouchard Père; Clair Daü; Drouhin; Dujac; Fougeray de Beauclair; Groffier; Jadot; Laurent; Roumier; de Vogüé.

Ch. Bonnet [bon-nay] (*Bordeaux*, France) Top-quality *Entre-Deux-Mers château* whose wines are made by *Jacques Lurton*.

F. Bonnet [bon-nay] (*Champagne*, France) Reliable producer under the same ownership as *Charles Heidsieck*. ★★★ 1996 $$$

Bonnezeaux [bonn-zoh] (*Loire*, France) Within the *Coteaux du Layon*, this is one of the world's greatest sweet wine-producing areas, though the wines have often tended to be spoiled by heavy-handedness with sulfur dioxide. Ch. de Fesles; Dom. Godineau; Les Grandes Vignes; René Renou; Sasonniere; Ch. la Varière.

Bonny Doon Vineyard (*Santa Cruz*, California) Randall Grahm, sorcerer's apprentice and original "Rhône Ranger", also has an evident affection for unfashionable French and Italian varieties, which he uses for characterful red, dry, and *late harvest* whites. He is also a screwcap pioneer, having recently announced the funeral of the natural cork. ★★★★ 2000 Le Cigare Volant $$$; ★★★★ 2001 Malvasia Ca'Del Solo $$

B

🍷 **Bonvin Jean** [bon-van] (*Valais*, Switzerland) Top producer of traditional local varieties.

🍷 **Bonterra** *Fetzer's* recommendable organic brand.
★★★ 1999 Sangiovese $$

🍷 **Tenuta Bonzara** [bont-zah-rah] (*Emilia Romagna*, Italy) *Cabernet Sauvignon* and *Merlot* specialists producing "*Super-Emilia-Romagnans*".

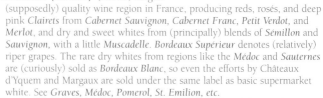

Borba [Bohr-bah] (*Alentejo*, Portugal) See *Alentejo*.

🍷 **Bordeaux** [bor-doh] (France) Largest (supposedly) quality wine region in France, producing reds, rosés, and deep pink *Clairets* from *Cabernet Sauvignon, Cabernet Franc, Petit Verdot*, and *Merlot*, and dry and sweet whites from (principally) blends of *Sémillon* and *Sauvignon*, with a little *Muscadelle*. *Bordeaux Supérieur* denotes (relatively) riper grapes. The rare dry whites from regions like the *Médoc* and *Sauternes* are (curiously) sold as *Bordeaux Blanc*, so even the efforts by Châteaux d'Yquem and Margaux are sold under the same label as basic supermarket white. See *Graves, Médoc, Pomerol, St. Emilion, etc.*

🍷 **Borgo del Tiglio** [bor-goh dehl tee-lee-yoh] (*Friuli*, Italy) One of the classiest wineries in this region, hitting the target with a range of varieties that includes *Sauvignon Blanc, Chardonnay, Malvasia,* and Tocai Friulano.

🍷 **Giacomo Borgogno** [baw-gon-yoh] (*Piedmont*, Italy) Hitherto old-fashioned *Barolo* producer that is now embracing modern winemaking and producing fruitier, more immediately likeable wines.

Palacio de Bornos [pah-lah-thyo day bor-noss] (*Rueda*, Spain) Leading producer of unusually good Spanish *Sauvignon Blanc* and *Verdejo*.

🍷 **De Bortoli** [baw-tol-lee] (*Yarra* and *Riverina*, Australia) Fast-developing firm that startled the world by making a *botrytized*, peachy, honeyed "Noble One" *Sémillon* in the unfashionable *Riverina*, before shifting its focus to the very different climate of the *Yarra Valley*. Top wines here include trophy-winning *Pinot Noirs* and impressive *Shirazes*. Windy Peak is a second label.
★★★★ 1996 Rare Dry Botrytis Semillon $$

🍷 **Bodega Luigi Bosca** [bos-kah] (*Mendoza*, Argentina) Good producer with good *Sauvignons* and *Cabernets*.
★★★ 2000 Pinot Noir $$

🍷 **Boscaini** [bos-kah-yee-nee] (*Veneto*, Italy) Innovative producer linked to *Masi* and making better-than-average *Valpolicella* and *Soave*. Look out for individual-vineyard wines such as the starry Ca' de Loi Valpolicella.
★★★ 2000 San Ciriaco $

🍷 **Boscarelli** [bos-kah-reh-lee] (*Tuscany*, Italy) The star producer of *Vino Nobile de Montepulciano* is also the place to find its own delicious Boscarelli *Super-Tuscan* and the exciting new De Ferrari blend of *Sangiovese* with the local Prugnolo Gentile.

🍷 **Boschendal Estate** [bosh-shen-dahl] (*Cape*, South Africa) The place to find some of the *Cape's* best sparkling wine and one of its most European-style Shirazes. Watch out for the new *Pinot Noirs* too.
★★★ 2001 Merlot $$

🍷 **Ch. le Boscq** [bosk] (*St. Estèphe Cru Bourgeois, Bordeaux*, France) Improving property that excels in good vintages, but still tends to make tough wines in lesser ones.

🍷 **Le Bosquet des Papes** [bos-kay day pap] (*Rhône*, France) Serious *Châteauneuf-du-Pape* producer, making a range of styles that all last. The pure *Grenache* example is particularly impressive.

🍷 **Botobolar** (*Mudgee*, Australia) Organic winery making characterful reds and whites.

Botrytis [boh-tri-tiss] Botrytis cinerea, a fungal infection that attacks and shrivels grapes, evaporating their water and concentrating their sweetness. Vital to *Sauternes*, the finer German and Austrian sweet wines, and *Tokaji*. See *Sauternes, Trockenbeerenauslese, Tokaji*.

B

Bott-Geyl [bott-gihl] (*Alsace*, France) Young producer, whose impressive *Grand Cru* wines suit those who like their *Alsace* big and rich. The oaked ("*barriques*") *Pinot Gris* is quite unusual.

Bottle-fermented Commonly found on the labels of US sparkling wines to indicate the *Méthode Champenoise*, and gaining wider currency. Beware, though – it can indicate inferior "*transfer method*" wines.

Bouchaine [boo-shayn] (*Carneros*, California) Much improved *Carneros Chardonnay* and Pinot Noir.

Pascal Bouchard [boo-shahrr d] (*Burgundy,* France) One of the best small producers in *Chablis*.

Bouchard Aîné [boo-shahrr day-nay] (*Burgundy,* France) Once unimpressive merchant, now taken over by *Boisset* and improving under the winemaking control of the excellent Bernard Repolt.

Bouchard-Finlayson [boo-shard] (*Walker Bay,* South Africa) *Burgundy*-style joint-venture originally launched by Peter Finlayson and Paul Bouchard, formerly of *Bouchard Aîné* in France, and now formerly of Bouchard-Finlayson. The vineyards at Hermanus are among the southernmost in the world. ★ ★ ★ ★ ★ Tete de Cuvée Galpin Peak Pinot Noir 2001 $$$$

Bouchard Père & Fils [boo-shahrr pehrr ay fees] (*Burgundy*, France) Traditional merchant with great vineyards. Bought in 1996 by the *Champagne* house of *Henriot*. The best wines are the *Beaunes*, as well as the La Romanée from *Vosne-Romanée*. Also doing wonders in *Chablis* at *William Fèvre*. ★ ★ ★ ★ Corton Charlemagne Domaine 2000 $$$$ ★ ★ ★ ★ ★ Meursault Perrières 2000 $$$

Vin de Pays des Bouches du Rhône (*Midi*, France) Dynamic region around *Aix en Provence*, focusing on *Rhône* and *Bordeaux* varieties. Top wines here include the great *Dom. de Trévallon*. Dom. des Gavelles.

Pascal Bouley [boo-lay] (*Burgundy*, France) Producer of good, if not always refined, *Volnay*.

Bouquet Overall smell, often made up of several separate aromas. Used by Anglo-Saxon enthusiasts more often than by professionals.

Henri Bourgeois [on-ree boor-jwah] (*Loire,* France) High-quality *Sancerre* and *Pouilly-Fumé* The top wine is called "la Bourgeoisie". Also owns Laporte and is now making wine in New Zealand. ★ ★ ★ ★ Sancerre La Porte du Caillou 2001 $$

Ch. Bourgneuf-Vayron [boor-nurf vay-roh] (*Pomerol, Bordeaux*, France) Fast-rising star with deliciously rich plummy *Merlot* fruit.

Bourgogne [boorr-goyñ] (*Burgundy*, France) French for *Burgundy*.

Bourgueil [boorr-goyy] (*Loire*, France) Red *AC* in the *Touraine*, producing crisp, grassy-blackcurrant, 100 percent *Cabernet Franc* wines that age well in good years. Amirault; Boucard; *Caslot-Galbrun;* Domaine de la Chanteleuserie; Cognard; Delaunay; *Druet.*

Ch. Bouscassé [boo-ska-say] (*Madiran*, France) See *Ch. Montus*.

Ch. Bouscaut [boos-koh] (*Pessac-Léognan, Bordeaux*, France) Good, rather than great *Graves* property; better white than red.

J. Boutari [boo-tah-ree] (*Greece*) One of the most reliable and long-established names in Greece, producing good, traditional red wines in Nemea and Naoussa.

Bouvet-Ladubay [boo-vay lad-doo-bay] (*Loire,* France) Producer of good *Loire* sparkling wine and better *Saumur-Champigny* reds. "Les Non Pareils" are top-quality mini-cuvées. ★ ★ ★ Saphir Brut 2000 $$;

Bouvier [boo-vee-yay] (Austria) Characterless variety used to produce tasty but mostly simple *late harvest* wines.

Bouzeron [booz-rron] (*Burgundy*, France) *Côte Chalonnaise* village known for *Aligoté*.

B

☪ **Bouzy Rouge** [boo-zee roozh] (*Champagne*, France) Sideline of a black grape village: an often thin-bodied, rare, and overpriced red wine, which can occasionally age well. Paul Bara; *Barancourt;* Brice; Ledru.

☪ **Bowen Estate** [boh-wen] (*Coonawarra*, Australia) An early *Coonawarra* pioneer proving that the region can be as good for *Shiraz* as for *Cabernet.*

☪ **Domaines Boyar** [boy-yahr] (*Bulgaria*) Privatized producers, especially in the *Suhindol* region, selling increasingly worthwhile "Reserve" reds under the Lovico label. Other wines are less reliably recommendable.

☪ **Ch. Boyd-Cantenac** [boyd-kon-teh-nak] (*Margaux 3ème Cru Classé, Bordeaux*, France) A third growth performing at the level of a fifth – or less.

🍇 **Brachetto d'Acqui** [brah-KET-toh dak-wee] (*Piedmont*, Italy) Eccentric *Muscatty* red grape. Often *frizzante.* Banfi; *Batasiolo;* Marenco.

☪ **Braida** [brih-dah] (*Piedmont*, Italy) A big producer whose range includes *Barberas* galore and some highly recommendable *Dolcetto* and *Chardonnay.*

☪ **Dom Brana** [brah-nah] (*Southwest*, France) One of the best producers of *Irouleguy.*

☪ **Ch. Branaire (-Ducru)** [brah-nehr doo-kroo] (*St.-Julien 4ème Cru Classé, Bordeaux*, France) A reliable – and steadily improving – estate.

☪ **Brand's Laira** [lay-rah] (*Coonawarra*, Australia) Traditional producer, much improved since its purchase by *McWilliams.* Delving into the world of *Pinot Noir* and sparkling *Grenache* rosé.

☪ **Ch. Brane-Cantenac** [brahn kon teh-nak] (*Margaux 2ème Cru Classé, Bordeaux*, France) Often underachieving *Margaux*; made a better wine than usual in 1999 and 2002. The unprepossessingly named second label Ch. Notton can be a good buy.

☪ **Branon** [brah-no'n] (*Graves, Bordeaux*, France) The first "Garage Wine" in the Graves, made in 2000 by Jean-Luc Thunevin and given an orgasmic response by critics who enjoy intensity and oak. Predictably pricey. Not successful in 2002.

🍇 *Braquet* [brah-ket] (*Midi*, France) Grape variety used in *Bellet.*

Brauneberg [brow-nuh-behrg] (*Mosel*, Germany) Village best known for the *Juffer* vineyard. Fritz Haag; Max Ferd Richter; Dr. H. Thanisch.

Brazil Large quantities of light-bodied wine (including *Zinfandel* that is sold in the US under the Marcus James label) are produced in a rainy region close to Puerto Allegre. The Palomas vineyard on the *Uruguayan* border has a state-of-the-art winery and a good climate but has yet to make exciting wine.

☪ **Breaky Bottom** (Sussex, England) One of Britain's best, whose *Seyval Blanc* rivals dry wines made in the *Loire* from supposedly finer grapes.

☪ **Marc Bredif** [bray-deef] (*Loire*, France) Big, and quite variable, *Loire* producer, with still and sparkling wine, including some good *Vouvray.*

☪ **Breganze** (*Veneto*, Italy) Little-known *DOC* for characterful reds and whites. Maculan is the star here.

☪ **Palacio de Brejoeira** [breh-sho-eh-rah] (*Vinho Verde*, Portugal) Top class pure *Alvarinho Vinho Verde.*

☪ **Bodegas Breton** [breh-tonn] (*Rioja*, Spain) Small, new-wave producer to watch for his Dominio de Conté single-vineyard wine.

Brett(anomyces) Hard-to-eradicate bacterial fault encountered increasingly frequently nowadays. Makes wines smell/taste of Band-aid or stable floors. In low levels (including some top Bordeaux and Rhône estates) it is detested by some (usually New World) tasters, tolerated by others (who claim that it adds complexity), and is probably unnoticed by the rest.

☪ **Ch. du Breuil** [doo breuh-yee] (*Loire*, France) Source of good *Coteaux de Layon*, and relatively ordinary examples of other *appellations.*

☪ **Weingut Georg Breuer** [broy-yer] (*Rheingau*, Germany) Innovative producer with classy *Rieslings* and high-quality *Rülander.*

☪ **Bricco Manzoni** [bree-koh man-tzoh-nee] (*Piedmont*, Italy) Non-*DOC* oaky, red blend made by Rocche dei Manzoni from *Nebbiolo* and *Barbera* grapes grown in *Monforte* vineyards that could produce *Barolo.*

Brick House (*Oregon*) A small organic slice of *Burgundy* in Yamhill County. The *Gamay* can be as good as the *Pinot* and the *Chardonnay*.

Bricout [bree-koo] (*Champagne*, France) A cleverly marketed range of good-to-very-good wines including the Cuvée Spéciale Arthur Bricout.

Bridgehampton (*Long Island*) Producer of first-class *Merlot* and *Chardonnay* good enough to worry a Californian.

Bridgewater Mill (*Adelaide Hills*, Australia) More modest sister winery and brand to *Petaluma*. ★★★★ Bridgewater Mill Shiraz 2000 $$

Peter Bright Australian-born Peter Bright of the *JP Vinhos* winery produces good Portuguese wines, including Tinta da Anfora and Quinta da Bacalhoa and a growing range of commercial fare in countries such as Spain, Italy, and Chile under the Bright Brothers label. ★★★ Baga Gran Castas 2001 $$

Bristol Cream (*Jerez*, Spain) See *Harvey's*.

Jean-Marc Brocard [broh-kahrr] (*Burgundy*, France) Very classy *Chablis* producer with well-defined individual vineyard wines, also producing unusually good *Aligoté*. ★★★★ Chablis Grand Cru Bougros 2001 $$$

Brokenwood (*Hunter Valley*, Australia) Long-established source of great *Sémillon*, *Shiraz*, and even (unusually for the *Hunter Valley*) *Cabernet*. Wines are now produced in other parts of Australia (the Shiraz below is a McLaren Vale-Padthaway blend. Look for the Hunter Valley "Cricket Pitch" bottlings. ★★★★ 2000 Shiraz $$$

Castello di Brolio (*Tuscany*, Italy) Historic *Chianti* estate now being revived. Look out for Castello di Brolio, Rocca Guicciarda and Casalferro, a blend of Sangiovese, Cabernet and Merlot. Wines labeled Barone Ricasoli are generally not from the estate. ★★★★ Chianti Classico 2000 $$

Brouilly [broo-yee] (*Burgundy*, France) Largest of the 10 *Beaujolais Crus* producing pure, fruity *Gamay*. *Duboeuf*; Cotton; *Sylvain Fessy*; Laurent Martray; Michaud; Piron; Roland; Ruet; Ch. des Tours.

Ch. Broustet [broo-stay] (*Barsac 2ème Cru Classé*, *Bordeaux*, France) Rich, quite old-fashioned, well-oaked *Barsac* second growth.

Brown Brothers (*Victoria*, Australia) Family-owned and *Victoria*-focused winery with a penchant for new wine regions and grapes (including several from Italy). The sparkling wine, the *Shiraz*, and the *Liqueur Muscat* are good, and The *Orange Muscat* and *Flora* remains a delicious mouthful of liquid marmalade. ★★★★ Brown Brothers Family Reserve Riesling 1998 $$

David Bruce (*Santa Cruz*, California) Long established *Zinfandel* specialist whose fairly-priced *Petite Sirah* and *Pinot Noir* are also worth seeking out.

Bruisyard Vineyard [broos-syard] (*Suffolk*, England) High-quality vineyard.

Alain Brumont (*Madiran*, France) Leading producer of modern wines from the traditional Tannat grape. Look for Ch. Montus and Domaine Bouscassé.

Le Brun de Neuville [bruhn duh nuh-veel] (*Champagne*, France) Little-known producer with classy *vintage* and excellent rosé and *Blanc de Blancs*. ★★★ Cuvee du Roi Clovis $$$

Willi Bründlmayer [broondl-mi-yurh] (Austria) Oaked *Chardonnay* and *Pinots* of every kind, *Grüner Veltliner*, and even a fair shot at *Cabernet*. ★★★★ Grüner Veltliner Qualitätswein Trocken Kamptal Alte Reben 2001$$$

Lucien & André Brunel [broo-nel] (*Rhône*, France) The Brunels' "Les Caillous" produces good, traditional, built-to-last *Châteauneuf-du-Pape*. ★★★ 1999 Les Cailloux Châteauneuf-du-Pape $$

Brunello di Montalcino [broo-nell-oh dee mon-tahl-chee-noh] (*Tuscany*, Italy) *DOCG* red from *Sangiovese*. *Altesino*; *Argiano*; *Villa Banfi*; Barbi; Biondi-Santi; *Tenuta Caparzo*; Cerbaiona; *Costanti*; Lambardi; Mastrojanni; Col d'Orcia; La Poderina; *Poggio Antico*; Talenti; Val di Suga.

Brut [broot] Dry, particularly of *Champagne* and sparkling wines. Brut nature/sauvage/zéro are even drier, while *"Extra-Sec"* is perversely applied to (slightly) sweeter sparkling wine.

Bual [bwahl] (*Madeira*) Grape producing soft, nutty wine – wonderful with cheese. *Blandy's*; *Cossart Gordon*; *Henriques & Henriques*.

B

Ⴑ Buçaco Palace Hotel [boo-sah-koh] (Portugal) Red and white wines made from grapes grown in *Bairrada* and *Dão*. They last forever, but cannot be bought outside the Disneyesque hotel itself.

Bucelas [boo-sel-las] (Portugal) *DO* area near Lisbon, best known for its traditional bone-dry white wines. Few are of great interest. *Caves Velhas*.

Ⴑ Buena Vista [bway-nah vihs-tah] (*Carneros*, California) One of the biggest estates in *Carneros*, this is an improving producer of California *Chardonnay, Pinot Noir*, and *Cabernet*. Look out for Grand Reserve wines.

Bugey [boo-jay] (*Savoie*, France) *Savoie* district producing a variety of wines, including spicy white *Roussette de Bugey*, from the grape of that name.

Ⴑ Reichsrat von Buhl [rike-srat fon bool] (*Pfalz*, Germany) One of the best estates in the Pfalz, due in large part to great vineyards like the *Forster Jesuitengarten*. ★★★★ Riesling Spätlese Forster Jesuitengarten 2001 $$

Ⴑ Buitenverwachting [bite-turn-fur-vak-turng] (*Constantia*, South Africa) Showpiece organic *Constantia* winery making tasty organic whites.

Bulgaria Still relying on its country wines and affordable *Cabernet Sauvignons* and *Merlots*. *Mavrud* is the traditional red variety and *Lovico, Rousse, Iambol, Suhindol*, and *Haskovo* the names to look out for.

Ⴑ Bull's Blood (*Eger*, Hungary) The red wine, aka Egri Bikaver, which helped defenders to fight off Turkish invaders, is improving now thanks to winemaker *Tibor Gal*.

Ⴑ Bernard Burgaud [boor-goh] (*Rhône*, France) Serious producer of *Côte Rôtie*.

Ⴑ Grant Burge (*Barossa Valley*, Australia) Dynamic Shiraz specialist and – since 1993 – owner of *Basedows*. All the biblically-named wines are good, but the oaky Meshach gets the attention. ★★★★ Shadrach 1998 $$

Burgenland [boor-gen-lund] (Austria) Wine region bordering *Hungary*, climatically ideal for fine sweet *Auslese* and *Beerenauslese*. *Feiler-Artinger; Höpler; Anton Iby; Kollwentz-Römerhof; Helmut Lang; Kracher; Münzenrieder; Nittnaus; Opitz; Umathum; Wachter.*

Ⴑ Weinkellerei Burgenland [vine-kel-ler-ri boor-gen-lund] (*Neusiedlersee*, Austria) Cooperative with highly commercial *late harvest* wines.

Ⴑ Bürgerspital zum Heiligen Geist (*Wurzburg*, Germany) One of *Wurzburg's* ancient charitable institutions, making often very good wine.

Ⴑ Alain Burguet [al-lan boor-gay] (*Burgundy*, France) One-man *domaine* proving how good plain *Gevrey-Chambertin* can be without heavy doses of new oak. ★★★ 2000 Gevrey Chambertin Cuvée Tradition $$

Burgundy (France) Home to *Pinot Noir* and *Chardonnay*; wines range from banal to sublime, but are never cheap. See *Chablis, Côte de Nuits, Côte de Beaune, Mâconnais, Beaujolais*, and individual villages.

Ⴑ Leo Buring [byoo-ring] (*South Australia*) Label used by the Southcorp (*Penfolds* etc.) group, specializing in ageable *Rieslings* and mature *Shiraz*.

Ⴑ Weingut Dr. Bürklin-Wolf [boor-klin-volf] (*Pfalz*, Germany) Impressive estate with great organic *Riesling* vineyards and fine, dry wines.

Ⴑ Ernest J&F Burn [boorn] (*Alsace*, France) Classy estate with vines in the Goldert *Grand Cru*. Great traditional *Gewurztraminer, Riesling*, and *Muscat*.

Buttery Rich, fat smell often found in good *Chardonnay* (often as a result of *malolactic fermentation*) or in wine that has been left on its *lees*.

Buzet [boo-zay] (*Southwest*, France) Eastern neighbor of *Bordeaux*, using the same grape varieties to make generally basic wines. Buzet; co-operative (Baron d' Ardeuil); Ch. de Gueyze; Tissot.

Ⴑ Byington [bi-ing-ton] (*Santa Cruz*, California) Fine producer of *Chardonnay* (Spring Ridge Vineyard) and *Pinot Noir*, and a rare example of good California Semillon.

Ⴑ Davis Bynum (*Sonoma*, California) Producer of interesting single vineyard *Pinot Noir* and *Chardonnay*.

Ⴑ Byron Vineyard [bi-ron] (*Santa Barbara*, California) Impressive *Santa Barbara* winery with investment from *Mondavi*, and a fine line in *Pinots* and subtly oaked *Chardonnays*. ★★★★ Nielson Vineyard Chardonnay 1999 $$

C

Ⓧ **By Farr** (*Geelong, Victoria*, Australia) Gary Farr's winery was previously known as Bannockburn by Farr. It's a good source of Pinot Noir, Chardonnay, and Viognier. ★ ★ ★ ★ **Viognier 2000 $$**

C

Ⓧ **Ca' del Bosco** [kah-del-bos-koh] (*Lombardy*, Italy) Classic, if pricey, *barrique*-aged *Cabernet/Merlot* ("Maurizio Zanella") blends and fine *Chardonnay/Pinot Noir* ("*Pinero*"), and *Pinot Bianco/Pinot Noir/Chardonnay Méthode Champenoise Franciacorta*. Look out also for the new Carmenero, made from the *Carmenère*.

Ⓧ **Luis Caballero** [loo-is cab-i-yer-roh] (*Jerez*, Spain) Quality *sherry* producer responsible for the *Burdon* range; also owns *Lustau*.

Ⓧ **Château La Cabanne** [la ca-ban] (*Pomerol, Bordeaux*, France) Up-and-coming *Pomerol* property.

Ⓧ **Cabardès** [cab-bahr-des] (*Southwest, France*) Recent appellation north of Carcassonne using Southern and Bordeaux varieties to produce good, if mostly rustic, reds. Confusingly, some are Cabernet-Merlot dominated, while others lean toward the Rhône. Cabrol; Pennautier; Salitis; Ventenac. ★ ★ ★ ★ L'Esprit de Pennautier, Chateau de Pennautier 2000 $

Ⓧ **Cabernet d'Anjou/de Saumur** [cab-behr-nay don-joo / dur soh-moor] (*Loire*, France) Light, fresh, grassy, blackcurranty rosés, typical of their grape, the *Cabernet Franc*.

🍇 **Cabernet Franc** [ka-behr-nay fron] Kid brother of *Cabernet Sauvignon*; blackcurranty but more leafy. Best in the *Loire*, Italy (where it sometimes seems to be a synonym for Carmenère), and increasingly in Australia, California, and Washington. It is of course, a partner of the *Cabernet Sauvignon* and particularly *Merlot* in Bordeaux, where it performed unusually well in 2002. See *Chinon* and *Trentino*.

🍇 **Cabernet Sauvignon** [ka-ber-nay soh-vin-yon] The great blackcurranty, cedary, green peppery grape of *Bordeaux*, where it is blended with *Merlot*. Despite increasing competition from the *Merlot*, this is still by far the most successful red varietal, grown in every reasonably warm winemaking country on the planet. See *Bordeaux, Coonawarra, Chile, Napa*, etc.

Ⓧ **Cabrière Estate** (South Africa) Reliable produce of *Cap Classique* sparkling wine. The wines are sold under the Pierre Jordan label

Ⓧ **Marqués de Cáceres** [mahr-kehs day cath-thay-res] (*Rioja*, Spain) Modern French-influenced *bodega* making fresh-tasting wines. A good, if anonymous, new-style white has been joined by a promising oak-fermented version and a recommendable rosé (*rosado*), plus a grapey *Muscat*-style white.

Ⓧ **Ch. Cadet-Piola** [ka-day pee-yoh-lah] (*St. Emilion Grand Cru Classé, Bordeaux*, France) Wines that are made to last, with fruit and *tannin* to spare.

Ⓧ **Cadillac** [kad-dee-yak] (*Bordeaux, France*) Sweet but rarely luscious (non-botrytis) *Sémillon* and *Sauvignon* whites. Ch. Fayau is the star wine. Its d'Yquem-style label is pretty chic too. Carsin; Cayla; Fayau; du Juge; Manos; Memoires; Reynon

Ⓧ **Villa Cafaggio** (*Tuscany*, Italy) Characterful *Chianti Classico* and *IGT* Toscana wines from an estate that has never taken its eye off the ball. San Martino is based on *Sangiovese*, Cortaccio on *Cabernet* and the top Chianti is *Riserva* Solatio Basilica. ★ ★ ★ ★ **Chianti Classico Riserva Basilica 2000**

Ⓧ **Cahors** [kah-orr] (*Southwest, France*) Often rustic wines produced from the local *Tannat* and the Cot (*Malbec*). Some are *Beaujolais*-like, while others are tannic and full-bodied, though far lighter than in the days when people spoke of "the black wines of Cahors". Ch. de Caix; la Caminade; du Cèdre; Clos la Coutale; Clos de Gamot; Gautoul; de Hauterivem; Haute-Serre; Lagrezette; Lamartine; Latuc; Prieuré de Cenac; Rochet-Lamother; Clos Triguedina. ★ ★ ★ ★ 2000 Château Croze de Pys Cahors Domaines Roche $$

C

Y **Ch Caillou** (*Bordeaux*, France) *Second Growth* Barsac property making elegant and increasingly good wine. As always in Bordeaux, there is an unrelated property of the same name in Graves, a Le Caillou in Pomerol, and a dry white, Caillou Blanc, from the Médoc's Ch. Talbot.

Y **Cain Cellars** (*Napa*, California) Spectacular *Napa* hillside vineyards devoted to producing a classic *Bordeaux* blend of five varieties – hence the name of the wine.★★★★★ Cain Five 1998 $$$$

Y **Cairanne** [keh-ran] (*Rhône*, France) Named *Côtes du Rhône* village known for good peppery reds. Dom d'Ameilhaud; Aubert; Brusset; Féraud-Brunel; Oratoire St-Martin; Richaud; Tardieu-Laurent; les Vins de Vienne.

Y **Cakebread** (*Napa*, California) Long-established producer of rich reds, very good *Sauvignon Blanc*, *Chardonnay*, and *Pinot Noir*.

Calabria [kah-lah-bree-ah] (Italy) The "toe" of the Italian boot, making Cirò from the local Gaglioppo reds and *Greco* whites. *Cabernet* and *Chardonnay* are promising, too, especially from *Librandi*. Watch out for new wave *Aglianico*.

Y **Calem** [kah-lin] (*Douro*, Portugal) Quality-conscious, small *port* producer. The specialty *Colheita tawnies* are among the best of their kind.

Y **Calera Wine Co.** [ka-lehr-uh] (*Santa Benito*, California) Maker of some of *California's* best, longest-lived *Pinot Noir* from individual vineyards such as Jensen, Mills, Reed, and Selleck. The *Chardonnay* and *Viognier* are pretty special too. ★★★★ Central Coast Pinot Noir 2000 $$$

California (US) Major wine-producing area of the US. See *Napa*, *Sonoma*, *Santa Barbara*, *Amador*, *Mendocino*, etc, plus individual wineries.

Y **Viña Caliterra** [kal-lee-tay-rah] (*Curico*, Chile) Sister company of *Errazuriz*. Now a 50-50 partner with *Mondavi* and co-producer of *Seña*.

Y **Callaway** (*Temecula* California) An unfashionable part of California, and a deliciously unfashionable style of – unoaked – *Chardonnay*.

Y **Ch. Calon-Ségur** [kal-lon say-goor] (*St. Estèphe 3ème Cru Classé*, *Bordeaux*, France) Traditional *St. Estèphe* now surpassing its status. Fine in 2000.

Y **Quinta de Camarate** (*Estremadura*, Portugal) Rich, supple red from the ever-reliable company of José Maria da Fonseca.

Y **Ch Cambon la Pelouse** (*Bordeaux*, France) Excellent *Cru Bourgeois Médoc*. 2000 and 2001 are particularly good, and good value too.

Y **Cambria** (*Santa Barbara*, California) Huge operation in the *Santa Maria Valley* belonging to the dynamic *Kendall Jackson* and producing fairly priced and good, if rarely complex, *Chardonnay*, *Pinot Noir*, *Syrah*, *Viognier*, and *Sangiovese*. ★★★★★ 1997 Julia's Vineyard $$

Y **Ch. Camensac** [kam-mon-sak] (*Haut-Médoc 5ème Cru Classé*, *Bordeaux*, France) Improving property following investment in 1994.

Y **Cameron** (*Oregon*, US) John Paul makes terrific *Pinot Noir* in this Yamhill estate – plus some impressive *Pinot Blanc*.

Campania [kahm-pan-nyah] (Italy) Region surrounding Naples, known for *Taurasi*, *Lacryma Christi*, and *Greco di Tufo* and wines from *Mastroberadino*.

Y **Campbells** (*Rutherglen*, Australia) Classic producer of fortified *Muscat* and concentrated Bobbie Burns reds. ★★★★ Bobbie Burns Shiraz 2001 $$$

Y **Campillo** [kam-pee-yoh] (*Rioja*, Spain) A small estate producing *Rioja* made purely from *Tempranillo*, showing what this grape can do. The white is less impressive. ★★★ 1996 Reserva $$

Y **Bodegas Campo Viejo** [kam-poh vyay-hoh] (*Rioja*, Spain) Go-ahead, if underrated, *bodega* whose *Reserva* and *Gran Reserva* are full of fruit. Albor, the unoaked red (pure *Tempranillo*) and white (*Viura*) are first-class modern Spanish wines. ★★★ Dominio de Montalvo Reserva 1996 $

Canada Surprising friends and foes alike, British Columbia (Okanagan) and Ontario are producing good *Chardonnay*, *Riesling*, improving *Pinot Noirs* and intense *Icewines*, usually from the *Vidal* grape. Paul Bosc; Cave Springs; Chateau des Charmes; Henry of Pelham; Hillebrand; Inniskillin; Jackson-Triggs; Konzelmann; Magnotta; Mission Hill; Pelee Island; Peller Estates; Pilliteri; Reif Estate; Stoney Ridge; Sumac Ridge; Thirty Bench; Vineland Estates.

C

Ⅰ **Bodegas Humberto Canale** (Argentina) Cool climate *Pinot Noir* and *Sauvignon Blanc* lead the field. *Malbec* and *Merlot* are improving very impressively too. ★ ★ ★ ★ Black River Cabernet Franc Reserve 2001 $$

Ⅰ **Canard Duchêne** [kan-nah doo-shayn] (*Champagne*, France) Improving and often fairly priced subsidiary of *Veuve Clicquot*.

Ⅰ **Canberra District** (New South Wales, Australia) Confounding the critics, a small group of producers led by Clonakilla, Doonkuna, Helm's, and Lark Hill are making good *Rhône*-style reds and *Rieslings* in high-altitude vineyards here. This also the source of Seppelt's Salinger sparkling wine.
★ ★ ★ ★ 2000 Lark Hill Exultation $$$

Ⅰ **Candido** [kan-dee doh] (*Apulia*, Italy) Top producer of deliciously chocolatey *Salice Salentino* and Cappello di Prete and Immensum *IGT*s
★ ★ ★ 1998 Salice Salentino Riserva Candido $

Ⅰ **Canépa** [can-nay-pah] (Chile) Good rather than great winery, making progress with *Chardonnays* and *Rieslings* and oaky reds.
★ ★ ★ Winemaker's Selection Malbec 2002 $$

🍇 **Cannonau** [kan-non-now] (*Sardinia*, Italy) A red *clone* of the *Grenache*, producing a variety of wine styles from sweet to dry, mostly in *Sardinia*.

Ⅰ **Cannonau di Sardegna** [kan-non-now dee sahr-den-yah] (*Sardinia*, Italy) Heady, robust, dry-to-sweet, *DOC* red made from the *Cannonau*.

Ⅰ **Ch. Canon** [kan-non] (*St. Emilion Premier Grand Cru Classé, Bordeaux*, France) Back on track after a tricky patch in the 1990s. The keynote here is elegance rather than power.

Ⅰ **Ch. Canon de Brem** [kan-non dur brem] (*Canon-Fronsac, Bordeaux*, France) A very good *Fronsac* property.

Ⅰ **Canon-Fronsac** [kah-non fron-sak] (*Bordeaux*, France) Small *appellation* bordering on *Pomerol*, with attractive plummy, *Merlot*-based reds from increasingly good value, if rustic, petits *châteaux*. Ch. Canon-Mouieux; Ch. Moulin Pey-Labrie.

Ⅰ **Ch. Canon-la-Gaffelière** [kan-non lah gaf-fel-yehr] (*St. Emilion Grand Cru Classé, Bordeaux*, France) High-flying estate run by an innovative, quality-conscious German who, in 1996, created the instant superstar *la Mondotte*. Rich, ultraconcentrated wine.

Ⅰ **Ch. Canon-Moueix** [kan-non mwex] (*Canon-Fronsac, Bordeaux*, France) A characteristically stylish addition to the *Moueix* empire in *Canon-Fronsac*. A wine to beat many a pricier *St. Emilion*.

Ⅰ **Ch. Cantemerle** [kont-mehrl] (*Haut-Médoc 5ème Cru Classé, Bordeaux*, France) A *Cru Classé* situated outside the main villages of the *Médoc*. Classy, perfumed wine with bags of blackcurrant fruit.

Ⅰ **Ch. Cantenac-Brown** [kont-nak brown] (*Margaux 3ème Cru Classé, Bordeaux*, France) Under the same ownership as Ch. Pichon Baron but less impressive. Good in 2002 though.

Canterbury (New Zealand) Waipara, here in the South Island, produces aromatic Riesling, Pinot Blanc, and Chablis-like Chardonnay. Chancellor; Giesen; Pegasus Bay; Melness; Mark Rattray; St. Helena; Sherwood Estate; Waipara Springs; Waipara West. ★ ★ ★ ★ Waipara West Chardonnay 1999 $$

Cantina (Sociale) [kan-tee-nuh soh-chee-yah-lay] (Italy) Winery (cooperative).

Ⅰ **Capannelle** Good producer of rich *Super-Tuscan* wine near Gaiole.

Cap Corse [kap-korss] (Corsica, France) 17 villages in the north of the island produce great, floral Muscat as well as some attractive herby dry Vermentino. Antoine Arena; Dom de Catarelli; Clos Nicrosi.

Cap Classique [kap-klas-seek] (South Africa) Now that the term "*Méthode Champenoise*" has been outlawed, this is the phrase developed by the South Africans to describe their Champagne-method sparkling wine.

[Wine label:] Clonakilla — 2000 — CANBERRA DISTRICT — SHIRAZ — % Alc/Vol — PRODUCT OF AUSTRALIA — 750

C

Ⴔ **Ch. Cap-de-Mourlin** [kap-dur-mer-lan] (*St. Emilion Grand Cru Classé, Bordeaux,* France) Good mid-range stuff.

Ⴔ **Caparzo** [ka-pahrt-zoh] (*Tuscany,* Italy) Classy, *Brunello di Montalcino* estate producing wines that age brilliantly.

Cape (South Africa) The area that includes all of South Africa's vineyards. See *Stellenbosch, Paarl, Franschhoek, Darling, Malmesbury, Walker Bay, Robertson, Tulbagh, Swartland, Worcester,* etc.

Ⴔ **Cape Mentelle** [men-tel] (*Margaret River,* Western Australia) French-owned winery, founded, like *Cloudy Bay,* by David Hoehnen. Impressive *Semillon-Sauvignon, Shiraz, Cabernet,* and a wild berryish *Zinfandel,* to shame many a Californian. ★ ★ ★ ★ Zinfandel 2000 $$

Ⴔ **Capel Vale** [kay-puhl vayl] (Southwest coast, Western Australia) Just to the north of *Margaret River.* Good *Riesling, Gewürztraminer,* and *Shiraz.*

Ⴔ **Capezzana** [kap-pay-tzah-nah] (*Tuscany,* Italy) The early home of *Cabernet* and *Sangiovese* blends. ★ ★ ★ ★ ★ Ghiaie della Furba 2000 $$$

Capsule The sheath covering the cork. Once lead, now plastic or tin. In the case of "flanged" bottles, though, it is noticeable by its transparency or absence.

Carnuntum (Austria) Wine region east of Vienna and mostly south of the Danube. A relatively warmish climate means that reds are looking increasingly good, especially from the *Zweigelt* grape.

Ⴔ **Conde de Caralt** (*Penedes,* Spain) Good *cava* and attractive still wines. The company is owned by *Freixenet.*

Ⴔ **Caramany** [kah-ram-man-nee] (*Midi,* France) New *AC* for an old section of the *Côtes du Roussillon*-Villages, near the *Pyrénées. Vignerons Catalans.*

Carbonic Maceration See *Macération Carbonique.*

Ⴔ **Ch. Carbonnieux** [kar-bon-nyeuh] (*Graves Cru Classé, Bordeaux,* France) Since 1991, the whites have greatly improved and the raspberryish reds are among the most reliable in the region.

Ⴔ **Carcavelos** [kar-kah-veh-losh] (Portugal) *DO* region in the Lisbon suburbs producing usually disappointing fortified wines.

Ⴔ **Cardinale** (California) *Kendall-Jackson's* top line, produced by a former star Mondavi winemaker from grapes grown on mostly hillside vines.

Ⴔ **Ch. la Cardonne** [kar-don] (*Bordeaux,* France) *Cru Bourgeois* whose quality is improving since its sale by the Rothschilds of *Ch. Lafite.*

Ⴔ **Carema** [kah-ray-mah] (*Piedmont,* Italy) Wonderful perfumed *Nebbiolo* produced in limited quantities largely by Cantina dei Produttori Nebbiolo.

Ⴞ **Carignan** [kah-ree-nyon] Prolific red grape used in *Corbières, Minervois,* and *Fitou,* and making either dull, coarse wine or richer spicier stuff when vines are old and yields low. In Spain it is known as *Cariñena* and Mazuelo, while Italians call it Carignano. ★ ★ ★ ★ Abbotts Cordis 2001 $

Ⴔ **Carignano del Sulcis** [ka-reen-yah-noh dehl sool-chees] (*Sardinia,* Italy) Dynamic *DOC* spearheaded by the Santadi cooperative.

Ⴔ **Louis Carillon & Fils** [ka-ree-yon] (*Burgundy,* France) Great modern *Puligny* estate. ★ ★ ★ Puligny-Montrachet Les Perrières 2000 $$$

Ⴔ **Cariñena** [kah-ree-nyeh-nah] (Spain) Important *DO* of Aragon for rustic reds, high in alcohol and, confuzingly, made not from the *Cariñena* (or *Carignan*) grape, but mostly from the *Garnacha Tinta.* Also some whites.

Ⴞ **Cariñena** [kah-ree-nyeh-nah] (Spain) The Spanish name for *Carignan.*

Ⴔ **Carmel** (Israel) Huge producer offering a wide range of pleasant but generally unremarkable wines.

Ⴞ **Viña Carmen** [veen-yah kahr-men] (*Maipo,* Chile) Quietly developing a reputation as one of the best red wine producers in Chile. Increasingly organic.

Ⴞ **Carmenère** [kahr-meh-nehr] (Chile) Smoky-spicily distinctive grape that, although almost extinct in Bordeaux, is still a permitted variety for claret. Widely planted in Chile where it has traditionally been sold as *Merlot.* Much Italian *Cabernet Franc* may also turn out to be Carmenère. See *Ca del Bosco.* Look for examples like the Santa Inès Carmenère, *Carmen* Grand Vidure, or *Veramonte Merlot.* ★ ★ ★ ★ 1865 Viña San Pedro 2000

C

Ⅰ **Carmenet Vineyard** [kahr-men-nay] (*Sonoma Valley*, California) Unusual winery tucked away in the hills and producing long-lived, very *Bordeaux*-like but approachable reds, fairly-priced *Chardonnay*, and also (even more unusually for California) good *Semillon-Sauvignon* and *Cabernet Franc*.

Ⅰ **Les Carmes-Haut-Brion** [lay kahrm oh bree-yon] (*Bordeaux*, France) Small property neighbouring *Ch. Haut-Brion* in *Pessac-Léognan*. Particularly good in 1999 and 2000.

Ⅰ Carmignano [kahr-mee-nyah-noh] (*Tuscany*, Italy) Nearby alternative to *Chianti*, with the traditional addition of more *Cabernet* grapes. See *Capezzana*.

Ⅰ **Quinta do Carmo** [Keen-tah doh Kar-moh] (*Alentejo*, Portugal) The Ch. Lafite Rothschilds' best foreign venture to date. Rich, tastily modern reds. ★★★ **1998 $$**.

Carneros [kahr-neh-ros] (California) Small, fog-cooled, high-quality region shared between the *Napa* and *Sonoma Valleys* and used by just about everybody as a source for cool-climate grapes. Producing top-class *Chardonnay*, *Pinot Noir*, and now, *Merlot*. Some of the best examples are from from Hudson and Hyde vineyards. *Acacia; Beaulieu Vineyard; August Briggs; Carneros Creek; la Crema; Cuvaison; Domaine Carneros; Domaine Chandon; Fisher; Kistler; Paul Hobbs; Macrostie; Marcassin; Mondavi; Mumm Cuvée Napa; Patz & Hall; Pine Ridge; Ramey; Saintsbury; Shafer; Swanson;* Truchard.

Ⅰ **Domaine Carneros** (*Napa Valley*, California) *Champagne Taittinger's* US sparkling wine – produced in a ludicrously incongruous replica of their French HQ. The wine, however, is one of the best New World efforts by the Champenois. ★★★★ **Le Rêve 1996 $$$**

Ⅰ **Carneros Creek** (*Carneros*, California) Produces ambitious *Pinot Noir* under this name and somewhat better (and cheaper) berryish Fleur de Carneros.

Ⅰ **Caronne-Ste-Gemme** [kah-ronn-sant jem] (*Bordeaux*, France) Reliable Cru Bourgeois that delivers value – even in poorer vintages.

Ⅰ **Carpineto** [Kah-pi-neh-toh] (*Tuscany*, Italy) High-quality producer of *Chianti*, and *Chardonnay* and *Cabernet* that are sold under the Farnito label.

Ⅰ **Carr Taylor** (*Sussex*, England) Sparkling wines are the best buys.

Ⅰ **Ch. Carras** [kar-ras] (*Macedonia*, Greece) Greece's best-known estate, left behind by more modern producers. Now in new hands.

Ⅰ **Herdade de Cartuxa** [har-dah-day de car-too-shah] (*Alentejo*, Portugal) Huge estate recently handed over to a charity by its owner. Pera-Manca is the top red. Whites are creamily complex

Ⅰ **Les Carruades de Lafite** [kah-roo-ahd-dur la-feet] (*Pauillac, Bordeaux*, France) The second label of *Ch. Lafite*. Rarely (quite) as good as *les Forts de Latour*, nor *Ch. Margaux's Pavillon Rouge*.

Ⅰ **Ch. Carsin** [kahr-san] (*Premières Côtes de Bordeaux*, France) Finnish-owned, Aussie-style estate with particularly tasty whites from Sauvignon Gris. ★★★★ **2000 Chateau Carsin Cuvee Prestige $$**

Ⅰ **Carta Vieja** [kah-ta vee-yay-ha] (Chile) Family winery making good reds and decent whites.

Ⅰ **Quinta do Carvalhais** [keen-tah doh car-vay-yash] (*Dão*, Portugal) Single estate which, under the forward-looking ownership of *Sogrape*, is showing how good *Dão* can be.

Casa [kah-sah] (Italy, Spain, Portugal) Firm or company.

Casablanca [kas-sab-lan-ka] (*Aconcagua*, Chile) Cool region in *Aconcagua*, producing especially impressive *Sauvignons*, *Chardonnays*, and *Gewurztraminers*. *Caliterra; Viña Casablanca; Concha y Toro; Errazuriz; Santa Carolina; Santa Emiliana; Santa Rita; Veramonte; Villard*.

Ⅰ **Viña Casablanca** [veen-yah kas-sab-lan-ka] (*Casablanca*, Chile) Winery in the region of the same name. ★★★★ **Casablanca Santa Isabel Merlot 2000 $$**

Ⅰ **Casanova di Neri** [kah-sah-NOH-vah dee NAY-ree] (*Tuscany*, Italy) Fine producer of *Brunello* and *Rosso di Montalcino*. ★★★★★ **Brunello di Montalcino 1998 $$$**

C

Casse Basse [kah-seh-bas-say] (*Tuscany*, Italy) Soldera's hard-to-find and pricey *Brunello di Montalcino* is developing a cult following in the US.

Caslot-Galbrun [kah-loh gal-bruhn] (*Loire*, France) Top-class producer of serious, long-lived red *Loires*.

Cassegrain [kas-grayn] (*New South Wales*, Australia) Variable, but often impressive, wines from the Hastings Valley on the east coast and elsewhere.

Cassis [ka-sees] (*Provence*, France) Coastal *appellation* producing (variable) red, (often dull) white and (good) rosé. **Clos Ste. Magdeleine; la Ferme Blanche.**

Castel del Monte [Ka-stel del mon-tay] (*Puglia*, Italy) Interesting southern region where Rivera makes excellent Il Falcone reds and Bianca di Svevia whites. Grapes grown include the local Aglianico, Pampanuto, Bombino Bianco and Nero, and Nero di Troia. ★★★ 1999 Cappellaccio Riserva $$

Castelgiocondo [kas-tel-jee-yah-kon-doh] (*Tuscany*, Italy) High-quality *Brunello* estate owned by *Frescobaldi*. ★★★★★ 1998 $$$

Castellare [kas-teh-LAH-ray] (*Tuscany*, Italy) Innovative small *Chianti Classico* estate whose *Sangiovese-Malvasia* blend, Nera I Sodi di San Niccoló, *Vino da Tavola*, is worth seeking out.

Castellblanch [kas-tel-blantch] (*Catalonia*, Spain) Producer of better-than-most *Cava* – but catch it young.

Castell de Remei [kas-te'y day reh-may-yee] (*Costers del Segre*, Spain) International grape varieties - *Merlot, Cabernet, Chardonnay, Sauvignon* - dominate at this property. Whites are good, reds better.

Casteller [kas-teh-ler] (*Trentino-Alto Adige*, Italy) Pale red, creamy-fruity wines for early drinking, made from *Schiava*. See *Ca'Vit*.

Castello di Ama [kas-tel-loh-dee-ah-mah] (*Tuscany*, Italy) Producer of great single-vineyard *Chianti Classico* (esp. the Bellavista Riserva) plus the stunning Vigna l'Apparita Merlot. ★★★★★ **Bellavista 1990 $$$**

Castell'sches, Fürstlich Domänenamt [kas-tel-shs foorst-likh Doh-mehn-en-ahmt] (*Franken*, Germany) Good *Auslese Scheurebe* and Rieslaner and dry *Silvaner*. Dornfelder reds are interesting, too.

Castillo de Monjardin [kas-tee-yoh deh mon-har-deen] (*Navarra*, Spain). Navarra rising star with good *Chardonnay, Pinot Noir*, and *Merlot*.

Cat's pee Describes the tangy smell frequently found in typical *Müller-Thurgau* and unripe *Sauvignon Blanc*.

Catalonia [kat-tal-loh-nee-yah] (Spain) Semi-autonomous region including *Penedés, Priorato, Conca de Barberá, Terra Alta*, and *Costers del Segre*.

Catena [kat-tay-nah] (Argentina) Dynamic Nicolas Catena produces wines at various price levels and labels, including Alamos, Esmeralda, and now, the ambitious Catena Zapata. ★★★★★ **Nicolás Catena Zapata 1999 $$$**

Cattier [Kat-ee-yay] (*Champagne*, France) Up-and-coming producer with good nonvintage wines.

Dom. Cauhapé [koh-ap-pay] (*Southwest*, France) *Jurançon* producer of great *Vendange Tardive* and dry wines from the *Manseng*. ★★★★★ **Jurançon Sec 'Chant des Vignes' 2001 $$$**

Cattier [Kat-ee-yay] (*Champagne*, France) Up-and-coming producer.

Cava [kah-vah] (*Catalonia*, Spain) Sparkling wine produced in *Penedés* by the *Methode Champenoise* handicapped by dull local grapes. Avoid *vintage* versions and look instead for Anna de *Codorníu* and *Raimat* Cava – both made from *Chardonnay* – or such well-made exceptions to the earthy rule as *Juvé y Camps, Conde de Caralt, Cava Chandon*, and *Segura Viudas*.

Cava (Greece) Legal term for wood- and bottle-aged wine.

Cavalleri [kah-vah-yah-ree] (*Lombardy*, Italy) One of the top sparkling wines in Italy.

Cave [kahv] (France) Cellar.

Cave Spring (*Ontario*, Canada) One of Canada's most reliable producers, with especially good Chardonnay. ★★★★★ **Niagara Riesling Icewine 1999 $$$**

C

Y **Ca'Vit** [kah-veet] (*Trentino*, Italy) The umbrella name of a group of coops.

Y **Caymus Vineyards** [kay-muhs] (*Napa Valley*, California) Producer of concentrated Italianate reds (including a forceful *Zinfandel*) and a characterful *Cabernet Franc*. Liberty School is the *second label*.

Y **Dom. Cazes** [kahrs] (*Midi*, France) Producer of great *Muscat de Rivesaltes*, rich marmaladey stuff to outclass most *Muscat de Beaumes de Venise*.

Y **Cellier le Brun** [sel-yay luh-bruhn] (*Marlborough*, New Zealand) Producer of *Méthode Champenoise* sparkling wine. ★★★ 2001 Terrace Road Sauvignon Blanc $$

🍇 **Cencibel** [sen-thee-bel] (*Valdepeñas*, Spain) Alternative name for *Tempranillo*.

Central Coast (California) Geographically varied set of regions south of San Francisco, including *Santa Barbara*, *Monterey*, *Santa Cruz*, and *San Luis Obispo*. Hardly surprisingly, the wines vary widely. ★★★ 1998 Alban Viognier

Y **Central Otago** [oh-tah-goh] (*South Island*, New Zealand) "New" region attracting a similar cult following to *Marlborough* (and investment by actor Sam Neil). *Gewurztraminer* and *Riesling* flourish, but Pinot Noir is king. Akarua; Black Ridge; Chard Farm; *Felton Road*; Gibbston Valley; Mt Edward; Mt Difficulty; Olssens; Quartz Reef; Rippon; Two Paddocks.

Central Valley (California) Huge irrigated region controlled by giants which make three-quarters of the state's wines without, so far, matching the efforts of similar regions Down Under. New vineyards and a concentration on cooler parts of the region are paying off for the *Sauvignon Blanc* but I doubt the potential of the increasingly widely planted *Merlot*. Smaller-scale winemaking is beginning to help (this is wine-factory country), but good wines are still the exception to the rule. *Quady's* fortified and sweet wines are still by far the best wines here.

Central Valley (Viticultural Region) (Chile) The region in which most of *Chile's* wines are made. It includes *Maipo*, *Rapel*, *Maule*, and *Curico*, but not *Casablanca*, which is in *Aconcagua*, further north.

Cépage [say-pahzh] (France) Grape variety.

Y **Cepparello** [chep-par-rel-loh] (*Tuscany*, Italy) Brilliant pure *Sangiovese IGT* made by Paolo de Marchi of *Isole e Olena*. Well worth laying down for a decade or more. ★★★★ 1999 Cepparello Isole e Olena $$$$

Cerasuolo [chay-rah-soo-woh-loh] (*Abruzzo*, Italy) Rosato wine made from the *Montepulciano* grape in *Abruzzo*.

Y **Ceretto** [cher-ret-toh] (*Piedmont*, Italy) Producer of good modern *Barolos* and increasingly impressive single-vineyard examples, plus excellent La Bernardina varietals (Syrah, Pinot Noir, etc.)

Y **Ch. de Cérons** [say-ron] (*Bordeaux*, France) One of the best properties in little-known *appellation* of *Cérons*.

Y **Ch. Certan de May** [sehr-ton dur may] (*Pomerol*, *Bordeaux*, France) Top-class *Pomerol* estate with subtly plummy wine. Made a great 2000.

Y **Lagar de Cervara** [lah-gar day chair-vair-rah] (*Rias Baixas*, Spain) One of the best *Albariños*. The wine is elegant, peachy-apricoty and firm.

Y **LA Cetto** [chet-toh] (*Baja California*, Mexico) Producer of tasty *Cabernet* and spicy-soft *Petite Sirah* good enough to give wines on the US side of the border a run for their money. ★★★★ Nebbiolo Reserva Limitada 1999 $

Chablais [shab-lay] (*Vaud*, Switzerland) A good place to find *Pinot Noir* rosé and young *Chasselas* (sold as *Dorin*).

Y **Chablis** [shab-lee] (*Burgundy*, France) When not over-priced, *Chablis* offers a steely European finesse that New World *Chardonnays* rarely capture. *Petits* and, more particularly, *Grands Crus* should (but do not always) show extra complexity. A new Union, des Grands Crus de Chablis, founded in 2000, is already beginning to improve quality. Bessin; *Bichot*; Billaud-Simon; Pascal Bouchard; *J-M Brocard*; La Chablisienne; D Dampt; René Dauvissat; D&E Defaix; J-P Droin; Joseph Drouhin; Durup; William Fèvre; Laroche; Louis Michel; Moreau-Naudin; S. Mosnier; Gilbert Picq; Raveneau; Servin; Tremblay; Verget; Vocoret.

C

  La Chablisienne [shab-lees-yen] (*Burgundy*, France) Cooperative making wines from *Petit Chablis* to *Grands Crus* under a host of labels. Rivals the best estates in the *appellation*. ★★★★ Chablis Grenouille 2000 $$$

  Chacoli / Txacoli [shab-koh-lee] (*País Vasco*, Spain) Mostly white, acidic wine from the *Basque* country. Good with the local fish-and-red-peppers.

  Chai [shay] (France) Cellar/winery.

  Chain of Ponds (*South Australia*) Enterprising Adelaide Hills winery. ★★★★ Ledge Adelaide Hills Shiraz 2000 $$

  Chalk Hill (*Sonoma*, California) Producer of rich *Chardonnay*, stylish *Sauvignon Blanc*, lovely berryish *Cabernet*, and great *Sauternes*-style whites. Chalk is ideal soil for Chardonnay. Here though, the only chalk around is in the name of the winery. ★★★★ Estate Vineyard Chardonnay 1999 $$

  Chalone [shal-lohn] (*Monterey*, California) Under the same ownership as *Acacia*, *Edna Valley*, and *Carmenet*, this winery is one of the big names for *Pinot Noir* and unusually *Burgundian*, long-lived *Chardonnay*.

  Chalonnais/Côte Chalonnaise [shal-lohn-nay] (*Burgundy*, France) Source of lesser-known, potentially good value but often rustic *Burgundies* – *Givry*, *Montagny*, *Rully*, and *Mercurey*. The Bourgogne Rouge can be a good buy.

  Chambers (*Rutherglen*, Australia) Competes with *Morris* for the crown of best *Liqueur Muscat* maker. The Rosewood is great.

  Ch. Chambert-Marbuzet [shom-behr mahr-boo-zay] (*St. Estèphe Cru Bourgeois*, *Bordeaux*, France) Characterful *Cabernet*-based *St. Estèphe*.

  Chambertin [shom-behr-tan] (*Burgundy*, France) Ultra-cherryish, damsony *Grand Cru* whose name was adopted by the village of Gevrey. Famous in the 14th century, and Napoleon's favorite. Chambertin Clos-de-Bèze, Charmes-Chambertin, Griottes-Chambertin, Latricières-Chambertin, Mazis-Chambertin, and Ruchottes-Chambertin are neighboring *Grands Crus*.
    Pierre Amiot; *Bachelet; Alain Burguet*; Bruno Clair; Pierre Damoy; *Drouhin; Dugat-Py; Dujac; Engel; Faiveley; Groffier*; Raymond Launay; *Leroy*; Denis Mortet; Bernard Meaume; *Jean Raphet; Roty*; Henri Rebourseau; *Armand Rousseau*; Jean Trapet.

  Chambolle-Musigny [shom-bol moo-see-nyee] (*Burgundy*, France) *Côte de Nuits* village whose wines can be like perfumed examples from the *Côte de Beaune*. Georges Roumier is the local star, and *Drouhin*, *Dujac*, and *Ponsot* are all reliable, as are *Bertagna*, *Drouhin*, Anne Gros, Ghislaine Barthod, Dominique Laurent Mugnier, de Vogüé, and *Leroy*. ★★★★★ Chambolle-Musigny Amoureuses 2000 $$$

  Champagne [sham-payn] (France) Region producing what ought to be the greatest sparkling wines, from *Pinot Noir*, *Pinot Meunier*, and *Chardonnay*. See individual listings.

  Didier Champalou [dee-dee-yay shom-pah-loo] (*Loire*, France) Estate with serious sweet, dry and sparkling *Vouvray*.

  Champy [shom-pee] (*Burgundy*, France) Long-established, recently much-improved *Beaune négociant*. ★★★★ Bonnes Mares 2000 $$$

  Clos la Chance (*Napa*, California) Up-and-coming producer of good-value *Chardonnay*.

  Dom. Chandon [doh-mayn shahn-dahn] (*Napa Valley*, California) *Moët & Chandon's* California winery now competes with its counterpart in Australia.

  Dom. Chandon [doh-mine shon-don] (*Yarra Valley*, Australia) Sold as *Green Point* and proving that Australian grapes, grown in a variety of cool climates, can compete with *Champagne*. Now joined by a creditable, *Chablis*-like, still Colonades *Chardonnay*.

  Dom. Chandon de Briailles [shon-don dur bree-iy] (*Burgundy*, France) Good *Savigny-lès-Beaune* estate. ★★★★ Corton Grand Cru Clos du Roi 1999 $$

  Chanson [shon-son] (*Burgundy*, France) *Beaune* merchant now improving since its purchase by *Bollinger*. ★★★★ Beaune Bastion 1er Cru $$$

  Ch. de Chantegrive [shont-greev] (*Graves*, *Bordeaux*, France) Large modern *Graves* estate with excellent modern reds and whites.

C

Chapel Down See Curious Grape.

Chapel Hill Winery (*McLaren Vale*, Australia) Pam Dunsford's impressively rich reds and whites (from *McLaren Vale* and elsewhere) are balanced by a leaner, unoaked *Chardonnay*. ★★★★ **McLaren Vale Shiraz 1999 $$**

Chapelle-Chambertin [shap-pell shom-behr-ta'n] (*Burgundy*, France) See *Chambertin*.

Chappellet (*Napa*, California) Innovative winery with the courage to make wines such as an oaked *Chenin Blanc*, Tocai Friulano, and "Moelleux" *late-harvest* wines rather than stick to mainstream *Chardonnay* and *Merlot*.

Chapoutier [shah-poo-tyay] (*Rhône*, France) Family-owned merchant using more or less organic methods. Not all wines live up to their early promise but credit is deserved for the initiative of printing labels in braille. Now making wine in Australia. ★★★★ **Hermitage La Sizeranne 2000 $$$**

Chaptalization [shap-tal-li-zay-shuhn] The legal (in some regions) addition of sugar during fermentation to boost a wine's *alcohol* content.

Charbono [shar-boh-noh] (California) Obscure grape variety producing spicy, full-bodied reds at *Inglenook*, *Duxoup*, and *Bonny Doon*.

Chardonnay [shar-don-nay] The great white grape of *Burgundy*, *Champagne*, and now just about everywhere else. See regions and producers.

Vin de Pays du Charentais [shar-ron-tay] (*Southwest*, France) Competing with its brandy-producing neighbor Gasgogne, this region now makes pleasant light reds and whites. Blanchard.

Charmat [shar-mat] The inventor of the *Cuve Close* method of producing cheap sparkling wines. See *Cuve Close*.

Ch. des Charmes [day sharm] (*Ontario*, Canada) Good maker of *Pinot*, *Chardonnay*, and *Icewine*. ★★★★ **1997 Paul Bosc Estate Riesling Icewine $$$**

Charta [kahr-tah] (*Rheingau*, Germany) Syndicate formed in the *Rheingau* using an arch as a symbol to indicate (often searingly) dry (*Trocken*) styles designed to be suitable for aging and drinking with food. Recently reborn with (thankfully) less rigorously dry aspirations, as part of the *VDP*.

Chartron & Trébuchet [shar-tron ay tray-boo-shay] (*Burgundy*, France) Good small merchant specialising in white *Burgundies*.

Chassagne-Montrachet [shah-san mon-rash-shay] (*Burgundy*, France) *Côte de Beaune* commune making grassy, *biscuity*, fresh, yet rich whites and mid-weight, often rustic-tasting, wild fruit reds. Pricey but sometimes less so than neighboring *Puligny* and as recommendable. *Carillon*; *Marc Colin*; Colin-Déléger; *Jean-Noël Gagnard*; *Henri Germain*; *Ch. de Maltroye*; *M. Morey*; *Michel Niellon*; *J. Pillot*; *Roux*; *Ramonet*.

Ch. Chasse-Spleen [shas spleen] (*Moulis Cru Bourgeois*, *Bordeaux*, France) *Cru Bourgeois château* whose wines can, in good years, rival those of a *Cru Classé*. A slightly dull patch in the 1990s but is now back on track.

Chasselas [shas-slah] Widely grown, prolific white grape making light wine, principally in Switzerland, eastern France, the Loire (Pouilly sur Loire), and Germany. Good examples are rare outside Switzerland, but it can develop attractive floral character there. **Pierre Sparr**.

Ch. du Chasseloir [shas-slwah] (*Loire*, France) Good *Muscadet domaine*

Château [sha-toh] (*Bordeaux*, France) Literally means "castle". Some châteaux are extremely grand, many are merely farmhouses. A building is not required; the term applies to a vineyard or wine estate. Château names cannot be invented, but there are plenty of defunct titles that are used unashamedly by large cooperative wineries to market their members' wines.

Château-Chalon [sha-toh sha-lo'n] (*Jura*, France) Like *Château Grillet*, this is, confusingly, an appellation. Unlike *Château Grillet*, however, here there isn't even a vinous château. The name applies to top-flight *Vin Jaune*. Berthet-Bondet; *Durand-Perron*; *Jean Macle*.

Chateau Hornsby (Alice Springs, Australia) Producer in Alice Springs where nature never intended vines to grow. Wines aren't wonderful but the winery is great for the Ayer's Rock tourist trade. The 2001 vintage was picked on 01/01/01.

C

Y **Chateau Ste. Michelle** (*Washington State*) Dynamic winery, with commercial *Merlot, Syrah, Sauvignon*, and *Riesling*. Joint ventures with *Dr. Loosen* and *Antinori* are proving fruitful. Columbia Crest is a good associated brand.
★ ★ ★ ★ **Eroica Riesling 2000 $$$**

Y **Chateau Woltner** (*Napa*, California) Producer of a range of unusually Burgundian single-vineyard *Chardonnays*, whose style owes much to the winemaker's experience in France.

Y **Châteauneuf-du-Pape** [shah-toh-nurf-doo-pap] (*Rhône*, France) Traditionally these are considered to be the best reds (rich and spicy) and whites (rich and floral) of the southern *Rhône*. There are 13 varieties that can be used for the red, though purists favor *Grenache*. Pierre André; *Ch. de Beaucastel*; Beaurenard; Henri Bonneau; Bosquet des Papes; Lucien & André Brunel; Cabrières; Chapoutier; la Charbonnière; Clos des Mont-Olivet; Clos des Papes; Delas; Font de Michelle; Fortia la Gardine; Guigal; Jaboulet Aîné; la Mordorée; La Nerthe; du Pegaü; Rayas; Réserve des Célestins; Tardieu-Laurent; Vieux Télégraphe.

Y **Jean-Claude Chatelain** [shat-lan] (*Loire*, France) Producer of classy individual *Pouilly-Fumés* and *Sancerre*.

Y **Jean-Louis Chave** [sharv] (*Rhône*, France) Gérard Chave and his son Jean-Louis run the best estate in *Hermitage*. These are great wines but they demand patience and are easily overlooked by those looking for richer, more instantly accessible fare. ★ ★ ★ ★ ★ **1999 Hermitage $$$$**

Y **Ch. Chauvin** [shoh-va'n] (*Bordeaux*, France) Improving *St-Emilion Grand Cru Classé* making wine of increasing complexity. A property to watch.

Y **Dom Gérard Chavy** [shah-vee] (*Burgundy*, France) High-quality estate.
★ ★ ★ ★ ★ **Puligny-Montrachet Les Folatières 2000 $$$**

Y **Chehalem** [sheh-hay-lem] (*Oregon*) Top class Yamhill producer of *Pinot Noir, Chardonnay*, and *Pinot Gris*, and benefitting from collaborating with the go-getting Patrice *Rion* from *Burgundy*. ★ ★ ★ ★ **Corral Creek Vineyard Pinot Noir 2000 $$$**

Y **Chenas** [shay-nass] (*Burgundy*, France) Good but least well-known of the *Beaujolais Crus* – supposedly with a naturally woody flavor (Chêne = oak). Louis Champagnon, Daniel Robin, Hubert Lapierre, Bernard Santé, and Duboeuf make worthy examples.

Y **Dom. du Chêne** [doo-shehn] (*Rhône*, France) Small estate producing rich ripe *Condrieu* and top-class *St. Joseph*. The best *cuvée* is "Anais."

Chêne [shayn] (France) Oak, as in *Fûts de Chêne* (oak barrels).

🍇 **Chenin Blanc** [shur-nah-blo'n for France, shen nin blonk elsewhere] Honeyed white grape of the *Loire*. Wines vary from bone-dry to sweet and long-lived. High acidity makes it ideal for sparkling wine, while sweet versions benefit from *noble rot*. French examples are hugely improved, and are both riper than they used to be, and suffer less from an excess of *sulfur dioxide*. When they are good, they are very good indeed. Also grown in South Africa (where it was known as *Steen*), in New Zealand (where it is lovingly – and successfully – grown by *Millton*), and Australia (where it is skillfully oaked by *Moondah Brook Steen*). It is generally disappointing in California (but see *Chappellet*). See *Vouvray, Quarts de Chaumes, Bonnezeaux, Saumur.*

Y **Ch. de Chenonceau** [sheh-non-soh] (*Loire*, France) Tourist attraction château that also produces high quality still and sparkling *Chenin Blanc*.

Y **Chéreau-Carré** [shay-roh kah-ray] (*Loire Valley*, France) Producer of excellent single estate Muscadets including Ch. du Chasseloir, Ch. du Coing and Comte Leloup de Chasseloir. ★ ★ ★ ★ **Grand Fief de la Cormeraie 2000 $**

Y **Ch. Cheval Blanc** [shuh-vahl blon] (*St. Emilion Premier Grand Cru Classé, Bordeaux*, France) Supreme *St. Emilion* property, unusual in using more *Cabernet Franc* than *Merlot*. A truly great 2002. Petit Cheval is the – first class – *second label*. ★ ★ ★ ★ ★ **2000 $$$$**

C

⊻ **Dom. de Chevalier** [shuh-val-yay] (*Graves Cru Classé, Bordeaux*, France)
Great *Pessac-Léognan* estate which proves itself in difficult years for both
red and white. Fine in 2002 ★★★★★ 1998 Blanc, Pessac-Léognan $$$$
Chevaliers de Tastevin [shuh-val-yay duh tast-van] (*Burgundy*, France)
A brotherhood – *confrérie* – based in *Clos de Vougeot*. Wines approved at
an annual tasting carry a special "tasteviné" label. (See the *Beaune* label).

⊻ **Cheverny** [shuh-vehr-nee] (*Loire*, France) Light floral whites from
Sauvignon and *Chenin Blanc* and now, under the new "Cour Cheverny"
appellation, wines made from the limey local *Romarantin* grape. Caves
Bellier; François Cazin; Ch de la Gaudronnière.

⊻ **Robert Chevillon** [roh-behr shuh-vee-yon] (*Burgundy*, France) Produces
long-lived wines. ★★★★★ 1999 Nuits St-Georges Aux Chaignots $$$

⊻ **Chianti** [kee-an-tee] (*Tuscany*, Italy) (*Classico/Putto/Rufina*) Sangiovese-
dominant, now often *Cabernet*-influenced, DOCG. Generally better than
pre-1984, when it was usual to add wine from further south, and to put dull
white grapes in with the black. Wines labeled with insignia of the *Classico*,
Putto, or the *Rufina* areas are supposed to be better too, as are wines from
Colli Fiorentini and *Colli Senesi*. Trusting good producers, however, is a far
safer bet. Castello di Ama; Antinori; Carobbio; Frescobaldi; Castellare; Castell'in
Villa; Isole e Olena; Fonterutoli Felsina; La Massa; Barone Ricasoli; Riecine;
Ruffino; Rocca di Castagnoli; Selvapiana; Castello dei Rampolla; Villa
Vignamaggio; Castello di Volpaia.

⊻ **Chiaretto di Bardolino** [kee-ahr-reh-toh dee bahr-doh-lee-noh]
(*Lombardy*, Italy) Berryish, light reds and rosés from around Lake Garda.
Corte Gardoni; Guerrieri Rizzardi; Nicolis e Figli; Santi.

⊻ **Michele Chiarlo** [mee-Kayleh Kee-ahr-loh] (*Piedmont*, Italy) Increasingly
impressive modern producer of *single-vineyard Barolo, Monferrato,
Barbaresco* and *Barbera*. ★★★ 2000 Barbera d'Asti Superiore $$

⊻ **Chignin** [sheen-ya'n] (*Savoie*, France) Fresh red (made from the *Mondeuse*)
and white wines that go especially well with cheese. A&M Quénard.

⊻ **Chile** Rising source of juicy, blackcurranty *Cabernet* and (potentially even
better) *Merlot, Carmenère*. See individual entries.

⊻ **Chimney Rock** (*Stag's Leap District*, California) Producer of serious, fairly
priced *Cabernet*. ★★★★ Cabernet Sauvignon 2000 $$$

⊻ **Chinon** [shee-non] (*Loire*, France) An *AC* within *Touraine* for (mostly) red
wines from the *Cabernet Franc* grape. Excellent and long-lived from good
producers in ripe years; otherwise potentially thin and green. *Olga Raffault*
makes one of the best. Otherwise: Philippe Alliet; Bernard Baudry; Couly-
Dutheil; Delauney; Ch. de la Grille; Charles Joguet; Logis de la Bouchardière.

⊻ **Chiroubles** [shee-roo-bl] (*Burgundy*, France) Fragrant and early-maturing
Beaujolais Cru, best expressed by the likes of Bernard Méziat. Emile
Cheysson; Georges Duboeuf; Hubert Lapierre; André Mètrat; Bernard
Méziat; Alain Passot; Ch de Raousset.

⊻ **Chivite** [shee-vee-tay] (*Navarra*, Spain) Highly innovative producer
outclassing many big name *Rioja bodegas*. The new winery was opened by
the King of Spain. ★★★ Gran Feudo Viñas Viejas Reserva 1998 $$

⊻ **Chorey-lès-Beaune** [shaw-ray lay bohn] (*Burgundy*, France) Modest
raspberry and damson reds once sold as *Côte de Beaune Villages* and now
appreciated in their own right. Allexant; Arnoux; Ch. de Chorey; Drouhin; Gay;
Maillard; Tollot-Beaut. ★★★ 2000 'Les Confrelins' Arnoux Père et Fils $$

⊻ **JJ Christoffel** [kris-tof-fell] (*Mosel*, Germany) Fine Riesling producer in
Erden and Ürzig. ★★★★★ 1992 Urziger Würzgarten Riesling Spätlese $$

⊻ **Church Road** (*Hawkes Bay*, New Zealand) A Montana subsidiary with a
range of premium *Hawkes Bay* wines. Look out for the Tom red Bordeaux
blend that is only made in top vintages. ★★★★ 1998 Tom $$$

⊻ **Churchill** (*Douro*, Portugal) Dynamic young firm founded by Johnny
Graham, whose family once owned a rather bigger *port* house. Good White
Port. Red: ★★★★★ Vintage Port 1997 $$$

C

⚱ **Chusclan** [shoos-klon] (*Rhône*, France) Named village of *Côtes du Rhône* with the best rosé of the area. ★★★ Ch Signac Cuvée Terra Amata 2000 $$

⚱ **Cinque Terre** [chin-kweh-TEH-reh] (*Liguria*, Italy) Traditionally dull but improving dry, and sweet, holiday whites. Forlini e Cappellini; la Pollenza.

🍇 **Cinsaut/Cinsault** [san-soh] Spicy red grape with high acidity, often blended with *Grenache*. One of 13 permitted varieties of *Châteauneuf-du-Pape*; also used in S. Africa and in the blend of *Ch. Musar* in the *Lebanon*.

⚱ **Cirò** [chih-Roh] (*Calabria*, Italy) Thanks to the efforts of pioneering producer Librandi, these southern reds (made from Maglioppo) and whites (made from Greco) can be well worth buying. Caparra & Siciliani; Librandi.

⚱ **Ch. Cissac** [see-sak] (*Haut-Médoc Cru Bourgeois*, *Bordeaux*, France) Traditional *Cru Bourgeois*, close to *St. Estèphe*, making tough wines that last. Those who dislike *tannin* should stick to ripe vintages like 2000.

⚱ **Ch. Citran** [see-tron] (*Haut-Médoc Cru Bourgeois*, *Bordeaux*, France) Improving – though still not dazzling – *Cru Bourgeois*, thanks to major investment by the Japanese.

⚱ **Bruno Clair** [klehr] (*Burgundy*, France) *Marsannay* estate with good *Fixin*, *Gevrey-Chambertin*, *Morey-St.-Denis* (inc. a rare white), and *Savigny*. ★★★★ 1999 Marsannay Les Longeroies $$.

Clairet [klehr-ray] (*Bordeaux*, France) The word from which we derived *claret* – originally a very pale-colored red from *Bordeaux*. Seldom used.

🍇 **Clairette** [klehr-ret] (*Midi*, France) Dull white grape of southern France.

⚱ **Clairette de Die** [klehr-rheht duh dee] (*Rhône*, France) The dry Crémant de Die is unexciting sparkling wine, but the "Méthode Dioise Traditionelle" (previously known as "Tradition") made with *Muscat* is invariably far better; grapey and fresh – like a top-class French *Asti*. Cave Diose; Jaillance.

⚱ **Auguste Clape** [klap] (*Rhône*, France) The supreme master of *Cornas*. Great, intense, long-lived traditional wines. ★★★★★ 1998 Cornas $$$$

⚱ **La Clape** [la klap] (*Languedoc-Roussillon*, France) Little-known *cru* within the *Coteaux de Languedoc* with tasty *Carignan* reds and soft, creamy whites. Ch Camplazens; Pech-Céleyran; Pech-Redon. ★★★★★ 2000 Ch Camplazens Premium $$.

Clare Valley [klehr] (South Australia) Slatey soil region enjoying a renaissance with quality *Rieslings* that age well, and deep-flavored *Shiraz*, *Cabernet*, and *Malbec*. Also the region that took the matter of corked wine into its own hands – by bottling over half of its 2000 *Riesling* with *Stelvin* screwcaps. Tim Adams; Jim Barry; Leo Buring; Grosset; Knappstein; Leasingham; Penfolds; Petaluma; Mitchells; Mount Horrocks; Pike; Sevenhill; Wendouree.

⚱ **Clarendon Hills** (*Blewitt Springs*, South Australia) Now – almost – living up to the over-generous praise given by US critics to its ultraconcentrated wines. The Australis and *Merlot* are good, but the old-vine *Grenache* and the whites are more interesting. ★★★★★ Blewitt Springs Vineyard Old Vines Grenache 1999 $$$

Claret [klar-ret] English term for red *Bordeaux*.

Clarete [klah-reh-Tay] (Spain) Term for light red – frowned on by the EU.

⚱ **Ch. Clarke** (*Bordeaux*, France) *Cru Bourgeois* Listrac château improving fast (especially in 2001) as more *Merlot* is introduced.

Classed Growth (France) Literal translation of *Cru Classé*, commonly used when referring to the status of *Bordeaux châteaux*.

Classico [kla-sih-koh] (Italy) A defined area within a *DOC* identifying the supposedly best vineyards, e.g., *Chianti* Classico, *Valpolicella* Classico.

⚱ **Henri Clerc et fils** [klehr] (*Burgundy*, France) Top white *Burgundy* estate.

⚱ **Ch. Clerc-Milon** [klehr mee-lon] (*Pauillac 5ème Cru Classé*, *Bordeaux*, France) Juicy member of the *Mouton-Rothschild* stable. ★★★★ 2000 $$$

⚱ **Domenico Clerico** [doh-meh-nee-koh Klay-ree-koh] (*Piedmont*, Italy) New-wave producers of a truly great *Barolo* and *Dolcetto*. Also of note is Arte, a delicious *Nebbiolo-Barbera* Piedmontese answer to all those hyped "*Super-Tuscans*". ★★★★★ Barolo Ciabot Mentin Ginestra 1998 $$$.

C

Climat [klee-mah] (*Burgundy,* France) Individual named vineyard – not always a *Premier Cru.*

⚚ **Ch. Climens** [klee-mons] (*Barsac Premier Cru Classé, Bordeaux,* France) Gorgeous, but delicate, *Barsac* that easily outlasts many heftier *Sauternes.*
☆ ☆ ☆ ☆ ☆ 2001 $$$.

⚚ **Cline** (*Carneros,* California) A winery to watch for innovative Rhône-style wines, including a delicious *Roussanne* and a bizarrely wonderful sweet *late-harvest Mourvèdre.* California needs mavericks like this.
☆ ☆ ☆ ☆ Los Carneros Vineyard Syrah 2000 $$

⚚ **Ch. Clinet** [klee-nay] (*Pomerol, Bordeaux,* France) Starry property; lovely, complex, intense wines.

Clone [klohn] Specific strain of a given grape variety. For example, more than 300 clones of *Pinot Noir* have been identified.

Clos [kloh] (France) Literally, a walled vineyard.

⚚ **Clos de Gamot** [kloh duh gah-moh] (*Southwest,* France) One of the most reliable producers in *Cahors.* ☆ ☆ ☆ ☆ Vignes Centenaires 1998 $$

⚚ Clos de la Roche [kloh duh lah rosh] (*Burgundy,* France) One of the most reliable *Côte d'Or Grands Crus. Drouhin; Dujac; Faivelay;* Lecheneault; *Leroy;* Perrot-Minot; Ponsot; Jean Raphet; Louis Rémy; *Rousseau.*

⚚ **Clos Haut-Peyraguey** [kloh oh-pay-roh-gay] (*Bordeaux,* France) A small *First Growth Sauternes* property now producing high quality once again.

⚚ **Clos de Mesnil** [kloh duh may-neel] (*Champagne,* France) *Krug's* single vineyard *Champagne* made entirely from *Chardonnay* grown in the Clos de Mesnil vineyard.

⚚ **Clos de l'Oratoire** [kloh duh loh-rah-twar] (*Bordeaux,* France) *St Emilion* property under the same ownership as Canon-la-Gaffelière and La Mondotte. The wine is very good, but usually less flamboyant than its siblings.

⚚ **Clos de Tart** [kloh duh tahr] (*Burgundy,* France) Fine *Grand Cru* vineyard in *Morey-St.-Denis,* exclusive to Mommessin. Wines repay keeping.
☆ ☆ ☆ ☆ 2000 $$$$

⚚ **Clos de Vougeot** [kloh duh voo-joh] (*Burgundy,* France) *Grand Cru* vineyard with more than 70 owners of mixed quality. **Amiot-Servelle; Robert Arnoux;** *Bertagna; Bouchard Père et Fils;* **Champy;** *Jean-Jacques Confuron; Joseph Drouhin; Engel; Jean Grivot; Anne Gros; Jean Gros; Faiveley; Leroy;* Méo Camuzet; *Mugneret-Gibourg; Jacques Prieur;* Prieuré Roch; *Jean Raphet;* Henri Rebourseau; *Dom. Rion;* Ch. de la Tour.

⚚ **Ch. Clos des Jacobins** [kloh day zha-koh-Ban] (*St. Emilion Grand Cru Classé, Bordeaux,* France) Rich long-lasting, if not always complex, wine.

Clos des Lambrays (*Burgundy,* France) *Grand Cru* in *Morey-St-Denis.*

Clos des Mouches (*Burgundy,* France) A *Premier Cru* vineyard in *Beaune. Drouhin* owns most of it, and makes flagship reds and whites.

⚚ **Clos des Mont-Olivet** [kloh day mon-to-lee-vay] (*Rhône,* France) *Châteauneuf-du-Pape* estate with a rare mastery of white wine.

⚚ **Clos des Papes** [kloh day pap] (*Rhône,* France) Producer of serious *Châteauneuf-du-Pape,* which – in top vintages – rewards cellaring.

⚚ **Clos du Bois** [kloh doo bwah] (*Sonoma Valley,* California) Top-flight producer whose "Calcaire" *Chardonnay* and Marlstone *Cabernet Merlot* are particularly fine. ☆ ☆ ☆ ☆ ☆ Alexander Valley Reserve Chardonnay 2001 $$$

⚚ **Clos du Clocher** [kloh doo klosh-shay] (*Pomerol, Bordeaux,* France) Reliably rich, plummy wine. ☆ ☆ ☆ ☆ 2000 $$$

⚚ **Clos du Marquis** [kloh doo mahr-kee] (*St. Julien, Bordeaux,* France) The *second label* of *Léoville-Las-Cases.* ☆ ☆ ☆ ☆ 2000 $$

⚚ Clos du Roi [kloh doo rwah] (*Burgundy,* France) *Beaune Premier Cru* that is also part of *Corton Grand Cru.*

C

⊼ **Clos du Val** [kloh doo vahl] (*Napa Valley*, California) Bernard Portet, brother of Dominique who used to run *Taltarni* in Australia, makes stylish *Stags Leap* reds – including *Cabernet* and *Merlot*. They develop with time.

⊼ **Clos l'Eglise** [klos lay-gleez] (*Pomerol, Bordeaux*, France) Spicy wines from a consistent small *Pomerol* estate.

⊼ **Clos Floridène** [kloh floh-ree-dehn] (*Graves, Bordeaux,* France) Classy, oaked, white *Graves* made by superstar *Denis Dubourdieu*.

⊼ **Clos Fourtet** [kloh-for-tay] (*Bordeaux*, France) Shifting from one branch of the Lurton family to another, this long-time under-performer is now part of André Lurton's portfolio. Watch this space.

⊼ **Clos Malverne** (*Stellenbosch*, South Africa) Small, quality-conscious estate making particularly good *Pinotage* and a *Merlot-Pinotage* blend called Auret. The *Shiraz* is showing increasing promise. ★★★★ **Shiraz 1999 $$**

⊼ **Clos Mogador** [klohs-moh-gah-dor] (*Priorato*, Spain) *René Barbier's* rich, modern, juicy red from Priorato. A wine whose quality, fame – and price – have all helped to revolutionize the Spanish wine scene.

⊼ **Clos Pegase** (*Napa*, California) The architectural masterpiece-cum-winery is worth a visit. The wines are improving. ★★★★ **Napa Valley Cabernet Sauvignon 1999 $$**

⊼ **Clos René** [kloh ruh-nay] (*Pomerol, Bordeaux*, France) Estate making increasingly concentrated, though approachable, wines.

⊼ **Clos St. Denis** [kloh san dur-nee] (*Burgundy*, France) Top *Grand Cru* vineyard in *Morey St. Denis*. **Dujac; G Lignier; Ponsot.**

⊼ **Clos St.-Landelin** [kloh San lon-duhr-lan] (*Alsace*, France) The sister label to *Muré*; fine, impeccably-made, long-lived wines, across the board. Unusually good *Pinot Noir.* ★★★★★ **1999 Riesling Vorbourg $$**

⊼ **Clos Uroulat** [oo-roo-lah] (*Southwest*, France) Top Jurançon producer, with limited quantities of impeccably made dry and sweet examples.

⊼ **Cloudy Bay** (*Marlborough*, New Zealand) Under the same French ownership as *Cape Mentelle*, this cult winery easily sells out every vintage of its *Sauvignon*, despite a steady increase in production. The Te Koko white Bordeaux-lookalike is showy but good, as are the *Chardonnay* and *Pelorus* sparkling wine are impressive, and the rare *late-harvest* wines. The *Pinot Noir* is a recent success.

⊼ **Clusel-Roch** [kloo-se rosh] (*Rhône*, France) Good, traditional *Côte Rôtie* and *Condrieu* producer. ★★★★★ **1999 Côte Rôtie Grandes Places $$$**

⊼ **la Clusière** [kloo-see-yehr] (*Bordeaux*, France) Recent, tiny-production (250–300 case) *St. Emilion* microwine from the new owners of *Ch. Pavie*.

⊼ **JF Coche-Dury** [kosh doo-ree] (*Burgundy*, France) A superstar *Meursault* producer whose basic reds and whites outclass his neighbors' supposedly finer fare. ★★★★★ **2000 Meursault $$$**

⊼ **Cockburn-Smithes** [koh burn] (*Douro*, Portugal) Unexceptional Special Reserve but producer of great *vintage* and superlative *tawny port*. ★★★★ **10 Year Old Tawny $$$.**

⊼ **Codorníu** [kod-dor-nyoo] (*Catalonia*, Spain) Huge sparkling winemaker whose Anna de Codorníu is good *Chardonnay*-based *Cava*. The Raventos wines are recommendable too, as are the efforts of the *Raimat* subsidiary. The California offshoot Codorníu Napa's sparkling wine is *Cava*-ish and dull despite using *Champagne* varieties. The *Pinot Noirs* are more impressive.

⊼ **BR Cohn** (*Sonoma*, California) A reliable source of Sonoma Valley *Cabernet*.

Colares [koh-lah-raish] (Portugal) Coastal wine region west of Lisbon famous for the ungrafted vines grown in its sandy soils. The wines are rare and getting rarer; the style is tannic and dark, and bottle age is needed.

Colchagua Valley [kohl-shah-gwah] (*Central Valley*, Chile) Up-and-coming subregion. *Bisquert; Casa Lapostolle; Undurraga; Los Vascos.*

⊼ **Coldstream Hills** (*Yarra Valley*, Australia) Founded by lawyer-turned-winemaker and wine writer *James Halliday*, but now in the same stable as *Penfolds*. Stunning *Pinot Noir*, *Chardonnay*, fine *Cabernets*, and *Merlots*.

Colheita [kol-yay-tah] (Portugal) Harvest or vintage – used to describe a single-vintage *tawny port*. Disdained by British-owned port houses, who prefer tawnies to be blends of vintages, and only sell Colheitas in Portugal.

Marc Colin [mahrk koh-lan] (*Burgundy*, France) Family estate with affordable wines from St. Aubin and a small chunk of (rather pricier) *Le Montrachet*. ★★★★ 2000 St.-Aubin Chateniere $$$

Michel Colin-Deleger [koh-lah day-lay-jay] (*Burgundy*, France) Up-and-coming *Chassagne-Montrachet* estate.

Collards [kol-lards] (*Auckland*, New Zealand) Small producer of lovely pineappley *Chardonnay* and appley *Chenin Blanc*.

Collegiata [koh-lay-jee jah-tah] (*Toro*, Spain) Rich, red wine from the *Tempranillo* produced in a little-known region.

Colle/colli [kol-lay/kol-lee] (Italy) Hill/hills.

Colli Berici [kol-lee bay-ree-chee] (*Veneto*, Italy) Red and white *DOC*.

Colli Bolognesi [kol lee bol lon yeh see] (*Emilia-Romagna*, Italy) Up-and-coming region for *Merlot* and *Cabernet Sauvignon* reds and fresh white *Sauvignon Blanc* and the local *Pinot Bianco* and Pignoletto. Bonzara; Gaggioli; Sandoni; Tizzano; Vallona.

Colli Euganei [kol lee yoo-gah-nay] (*Veneto*, Italy) Hills near Padova where Vignalta produces its Gemola *Cabernet-Merlot*. Other wines are less impressive.

Colli Orientali del Friuli [kol-lee oh-ree yehn-tah-lee del free-yoo-lee] (*Friuli-Venezia Giulia*, Italy) Lively, single-variety whites and reds from near the *Slovenian* border. Subtle, honeyed, and very pricey *Picolit*, too.

Colli Piacentini [kol-lee pee-yah-chayn-tee-nee] (*Emiglia-Romagna*, Italy) A very varied *DOC*, covering characterful, off-dry Malvasia sparkling wine and the Bonarda-*Barbera*-based Guttiunio. la Stoppa; la Tosa; il Pociarello.

Vin de Pays des Collines Rhodaniennes [kol-leen roh-dah nee-enn] (*Rhône*, France) The *Vin de Pays* region of the northern *Rhône*, using *Rhône* varieties, *Gamay* and *Merlot*. St. Désirat Cooperative; G Vernay.

Collio [kol-lee-yoh] (*Friuli-Venezia Giulia*, Italy) High-altitude region with a basketful of white varieties, plus those of *Bordeaux* and red *Burgundy*. Refreshing and often restrained. Borgo Conventi; Borgo del Tiglio; L. Felluga; Gravner; Jermann; Puiatti; Schiopetto; Venica & Venica; Villa Russiz.

Collioure [kol-yoor] (*Midi*, France) Intense *Rhône*-style *Languedoc-Roussillon* red (often marked by the presence of *Mourvèdre* in the blend) and, since 2003, white. A good group of producers here are beginning to attract attention. Ch. de Jau; Dom du Mas Blanc; Clos de Paulilles; de la Rectorie; la Tour Vieille.

Colombard/French Colombard [kol-om-bahrd] White grape grown in *Southwest* France for Armagnac and light, modern whites by *Yves Grassa* and *Plaimont*. Also planted in Australia (*Primo Estate* and *Best's*) and the US.

Jean-Luc Colombo [kol-lom-boh] (*Rhône*, France) Enologist guru to an impressive number of *Rhône* estates – and producer of his own modern, oaky *Côtes du Rhône* and *Cornas*.

Columbia Crest (*Washington State*) Winery associated with *Ch. Ste. Michelle*. ★★★★ Columbia Valley Reserve Merlot 1999 $$$

Columbia Winery (*Washington State*) Producer of good, fairly priced, *Chablis*-style *Chardonnay* and *Graves*-like *Semillon*, subtle single-vineyard *Cabernet*, especially good *Merlot*, *Syrah*, and *Burgundian Pinot Noir*. ★★★★ Syrah 1999 $$

Commandaria [com-man-dah-ree-yah] (Cyprus) Rare raisiny dessert wine.

Commune [kom-moon] (France) Small demarcated plot of land named after its principal town or village. Equivalent to an English parish.

Vin de Pays des Comtés Rhodaniens [kom-tay roh-dah nee-yen] (*Rhône/Savoie*, France) Fresh, aromatic whites are the stars here (*Sauvignon*, *Viognier*) plus some juicy *Rhône* reds (*Grenache*, *Syrah*).

Vin de Pays des Comtés Tolosan [kom-tay toh-loh-so'n] (*Southwest*, France) Fast-improving blends of *Bordeaux* and indigenous grapes.

C

Ⓣ **Bodegas Con Class** (*Rueda*, Spain) Good *Sauvignon Blanc* and Verdejo/Viura.
Conca de Barberá [kon-kah deh bahr-beh-rah] (*Catalonia*, Spain) Cool source of *Torres's* impressive Milmanda *Chardonnay* and Grandes Muralles.

Ⓣ **Viña Concha y Toro** [veen-yah kon-chah ee tohr-roh] (*Maipo*, Chile) Steadily improving, thanks to an investment in *Casablanca*. Best wines are Don Melchior, Marques de Casa Concha, Trio, Casillero del Diablo, and *Almaviva*, its joint venture with *Mouton Rothschild*.

Ⓣ **Condado de Haza** [kon-dah-doh deh hah-thah] (*Ribera del Duero,* Spain) Impressive new venture from the owner of *Pesquera*.

Ⓣ **Conde de Caralt** [kon-day day kah-ralt] (*Catalonia*, Spain) One of the best names in *Cava*. Catch it young.

Ⓣ **Condrieu** [kon-dree-yuhh] (*Rhône,* France) One of the places where actor Gerard Dépardieu owns vines. Fabulous, pricey, pure *Viognier*: a cross between dry, white wine and perfume. Far better than the hyped and high-priced *Ch. Grillet* next door. **Ch. d'Ampuis; Patrick & Christophe Bonneford; Louis Chèze; Gilbert Chirat; Yves Cuilleron; Pierre Dumazet; Philippe Faury; Pierre Gaillard; Michel Gerin; Etienne Guigal; de Monteillet; Antoine Montez; Robert Niero; Alain Parent (& Gerard Dépardieu); André Perret; Phillipe & Christophe Pichon; Hervé Richard; Georges Vernay; Francois Villand; Gerard Villano.**

Confréries [kon-fray-ree] (France) Promotional brotherhoods linked to a particular wine or area. Many, however, are nowadays more about pomp and pageantry, kudos and backslapping, than active promotion.

Ⓣ **Jean-Jacques Confuron** [con-foor-ron] (*Burgundy*, France) Innovative producer with good *Nuits-St.-Georges, Vosne-Romanée,* and *Clos Vougeot.*

Ⓣ **Cono Sur** [kon-noh soor] (Chile) *Concha y Toro* subsidiary with a range of varietals, including a classy *Pinot Noir* from *Casablanca*. Back on form after the arrival of a new winemaker (in 1998). The Isla Negra wines are good too.
★★★★ **Cono Sur 20 Barrel Merlot 2001 $$$**

Ⓣ **Ch. la Conseillante** [lah kon-say-yont] (*Pomerol, Bordeaux,* France) Brilliant property with lovely, complex, perfumed wines.

Consejo Regulador [kon-say-hoh ray-goo-lah-dohr] (Spain) Administrative body responsible for *DO* laws.

Consorzio [kon-sohr-zee-yoh] (Italy) Producers' syndicate.

Constantia [kon-stan-tee-yah] (South Africa) The first New World wine region. Until recently, the big name was *Groot Constantia*. Now *Constantia Uitsig, Klein Constantia, Buitenverwachting,* and *Steenberg* support the enduring reputation, but better wines are often easier to find elsewhere in the Cape. *Klein Constantia's late-harvest* Vin de Constance is the region's flagship, recalling the days when Constantia wines were talked of in the same breath as *Port* and *Bordeaux*.

Ⓣ **Aldo Conterno** [al-doh kon-tehr-noh] (*Piedmont,* Italy) Great, traditional producer of single-vineyard *Barolo* (esp. Gran Bussia) and similarly top-class *Barbera*. Other varieties are well handled too, particularly Grignolino and Freisa. Nobody does it better.

Ⓣ **Giacomo Conterno** [dja-ko-mo con-tehr-noh] (*Piedmont,* Italy) Aldo's (see above) older brother is even more traditional, and makes splendid Barolos of immense proportions and lifespan. His son Roberto is now taking over the winemaking.

GRAN BUSSIA

1995

BAROLO
DENOMINAZIONE DI ORIGINE CONTROLLATA E GARANTITA

RISERVA

IMBOTTIGLIATO DAL VITICOLTORE NELL'AZIENDA AGRICOLA
PODERI ALDO CONTERNO
MONFORTE D'ALBA - ITALIA
75 cl e   ITALIA   14%

Ⓣ **Conterno Fantino** [kon-tehr-noh fan-tee-noh] (*Piedmont,* Italy) Another brilliant Conterno. ★★★★★ **Barolo Bussia Soprana 1998 $$$$**

Ⓣ **Viñedos del Contino** [veen-yay-dos del con-tee-no] (*Rioja,* Spain) CVNE-owned *Rioja* Alavesa estate whose wines can have more fruit and structure than most. ★★★★ **Viña del Olivo 1999 $$**

C

Controliran (Bulgaria) Bulgarian version of *Appellation Contrôlée*

Coonawarra [koon-nah-wah-rah] (*South* Australia) Internationally acknowledged top-class mini-region, stuck in the middle of nowhere, with a cool(ish) climate, terra rossa (red) soil, and a long-brewed controversy over where precisely its boundaries ought to be drawn. (There are nearby "islands" of red soil whose wines have been excluded from the Coonawarra designation.) The best Coonawarra reds are great, blackcurranty-minty *Cabernet Sauvignons* and underrated *Shirazes*. Whites are less impressive; big *Chardonnays* and full-bodied *Rieslings*. *Bowen Estate; Hardy's; Katnook; Lindemans; Mildara; Orlando; Petaluma; Parker Estate; Penfolds; Penley Estate; Ravenswood (Hollick); Rosemount; Rouge Homme; Yalumba; Wynns.*

⍫ **Coopers Creek** (*Auckland,* New Zealand) Individualistic whites including a *Chenin-Semillon* blend, *Chardonnay, Sauvignon,* and *Riesling*.

⍫ **Copertino** [kop-per-tee-noh] (*Apulia,* Italy) Fascinating berryish wine made from the "bitter-black" *Negroamaro*. ★ ★ ★ ★ **Cantina Sociale 2000 $$**

⍫ **Corbans** (*Henderson,* New Zealand) Big producer (encompassing *Cooks*) making wines in several regions. Good, rich, *Merlot* reds (even, occasionally, from *Marlborough*). ★ ★ ★ ★ **Private Bin Gisborne Chardonnay $$**

⍫ **Corbières** [kawr-byayr] (*Languedoc-Roussillon,* France) Region where a growing number of small estates are now making tasty red wines. **Ch. d'Aguilhar; Aiguilloux; Caraguilhes; des Chandelles; Etang des Colombes; Grand Caumont; Hélène; de Lastours;** *Mont Tauch;* **Pech-Latt; Vignerons de la Méditerranée; Meunier St. Louis; d'Ornaisons; les Palais du Révérend; St. Auriol; St. Estève; Celliers St. Martin; Salvagnac; Villemajou;** *la Voulte Gasparets.*

⍫ **Ch Corbin** [cor-ba'n] (*Bordeaux,* France) *St-Emilion Grand Cru Classé* sometimes (but not consistently) making wine of richness and density.

⍫ **Ch Corbin-Michotte** [cor-ba'n mee-shott] (*Bordeaux,* France) *Grand Cru Classé St-Emilion* property that often has a fruity edge on *Ch. Corbin*.

⍫ **Ch Cordeillan-Bages** [cor-day-yo'n Baj] (*Bordeaux,* France) A *Pauillac* château now an hotel under the same ownership as *Ch. Lynch-Bages.*

⍫ **Cordier** [cor-dee-yay] (*Bordeaux,* France) Large shipper which also owns châteaux including Clos des Jacobins, Meyney and Cantemerle.

⍫ **Cordoba** (*Stellenbosch,* South Africa) Producer of wines high on the *Helderberg,* (so far) over-enthusiastically described as a local *"First Growth."*

⍫ **Cordon Negro** [kawr-don nay-groh] (*Catalonia,* Spain) Brand name for *Freixenet's* successful *Cava*. The matte-black bottle and generous marketing must account for sales. Not a sparkling wine I voluntarily drink.

⍫ **Corino** [koh-ree-noh] (*Piedmont,* Italy) Up-and-coming winery, winning applause for its Barolo. ★ ★ ★ ★ **Barolo Vigneto Rocche 1998 $$**

⍫ **Coriole** [koh-ree-ohl] (*McLaren Vale,* Australia) *Shiraz* specialist that has diversified into *Sangiovese*. The *Semillons* and *Rieslings* are pretty good, too.

⍫ **Corison** [kaw-ree-son] (*Napa,* California) Winery specializing in juicy *Cabernet*.

Corked Unpleasant, musty smell and flavor, or, quite often, simply a deadening of flavor caused by (usually invisible and often unsmellable) mold in the cork. At the 2003 International Wine Challenge, 4.9 percent of over 12,200 bottles, were spoiled by bad corks. Visit: **www.corkwatch.com.**

⍫ **Cornas** [kaw-re-nas] (*Rhône,* France) Smoky, spicy *Syrah; tannic* when young, but worth keeping. *Thierry Allemand; de Barjac; Chapoutier; Auguste Clape; Jean-Luc Colombo; Courbis; Eric & Joël Durand; Durvieu; Jaboulet Aîné; Juge; Jacques Lemercier; Jean Lionnet; Robert Michel; Michel Rochepertuis; de St. Pierre; Serette; Tain Cooperative; Tardieu-Laurent; Noël Verset; Alain Voge.*

⍫ **Fattoria Coroncino** [kawr-ron-chee-noh] (*Marche,* Italy) One of the best producers of *Verdicchio Castello dei Jesi Classico Superiore.*

Corsica (France) Island making robust reds, whites, and rosés under a raft of *appellations Vins de Pays (de l'Ile de Beauté)* are often more interesting.

⍫ **Dom. Corsin** [kawr-san] (*Burgundy,* France) Good *Pouilly-Fuissé* and *St. Véran* estate. ★ ★ ★ ★ **Pouilly Fuissé 2000 $$**

C

⊥ **Cortes de Cima** [kawrtsh-day shee-mah] (*Alentejo*, Portugal) Estate making good reds from local grapes plus a *Syrah* called Incognito.

⚜ **Cortese** [kawr-tay-seh] (*Piedmont*, Italy) Herby white grape used in *Piedmont* and to make *Gavi*. Drink young.

⊥ **Corton** [kawr-ton] (*Burgundy*, France) *Grand Cru* hill potentially making great, intense, long-lived reds and – as *Corton-Charlemagne* – whites. Bertrand Ambroise; *Bonneau du Martray; Chandon de Briailles; Dubreuil-Fontaine; Faiveley;* Laleur-Piot; *Louis Latour (white); Leroy;* Maillard; Nudant; Jacques Prieur; Tollot-Beaut; Thomas Moillard.

⊥ **Corzano & Paterno** [kawrt-zah-noh eh pah-tehr-noh] (*Tuscany*, Italy) Fine Chianti Colli Fiorentini and Vin Santo.

⊥ **Corvo** [kawr-voh] (*Sicily,* Italy) Brand used by Duca di Salaparuta for its improving reds and whites. ★★★★ Duca Enrico 1999 $$$

⊥ **Ch. Cos d'Estournel** [koss-des-tawr-nel] (*St. Estèphe 2ème Cru Classé Bordeaux,* France) Recently sold *estate* making top-class wines with *Pauillac* richness and fruit. Spice is the hallmark. A very fine 2002.

⊥ **Ch. Cos Labory** [koss la-baw-ree] (*St. Estèphe 5ème Cru Classé, Bordeaux,* France) Good, traditional, if tough, wines.

Cosecha [coh-seh-chah] (Spain) Harvest or *vintage.*

⊥ **Cosentino** (*Napa,* California) Producer of serious, long-lived reds.

⊥ **Cossart Gordon** (*Madeira,* Portugal) High-quality brand used by the *Madeira Wine Co.* ★★★★★ 10 year old Bual $$$

⊥ **Costanti** (*Tuscany,* Italy) Serious *Brunello di Montalcino* producer with classy, long-lived wines. ★★★★★ Brunello di Montalcino 1988 $$$$

Costers del Segre [kos-tehrs del say-greh] (*Catalonia,* Spain) *DO* created for the excellent *Raimat,* whose irrigated vineyards helped to persuade Spain's wine authorities to allow other producers to give thirsty vines a drink.

Costers de Siurana [kos-tehrs deh see-yoo-rah-nah] (*Priorato,* Spain) One of the stars of *Priorat.* Grape varieties for the Clos de l'Obac include *Syrah, Cabernet, Merlot,* plus local *Garnacha, Cariñena,* and *Tempranillo.* ★★★★★ Priorat Clos de L'Obac 1998 $$$

⊥ **Costières de Nîmes** [kos-tee-yehr duh neem] (*Midi,* France) An up-and-coming region whose whites and *Syrah*-based reds can match the best of the Northern Rhône. Ch. de l'Amarine; de Campuget; Dom. des Cantarelles; Mas de Bressades; Ch. Mourges du Grès; de Nages; Tuilerie de Pazac; Valcombe. ★★★★★ Ch. de Nages Cuvée Joseph Torrès 2000 $$$

⚜ **Cot** [koh] (France) Red grape of *Cahors* and the *Loire* (aka *Malbec*).

⊥ **Cotat Frères** [koh-tah] (*Loire,* France) One of the few *Loire Sauvignon* producers to achieve superstar status in the US. The Cotats' *Sancerres* repay aging and deserve their success. ★★★★★ 1999 les Monts Damnés $$$

Côte Chalonnaise [koht shh-loh-nays] (*Burgundy,* France) Region south of the *Côte d'Or,* considerably bigger, and the source of much basic *Burgundy* as well as some rather better wines. Principal villages are Bouzeron, Mercurey (the region can also be called the Région de Mercurey), Montagny, Givry, and Rully.

Côte d'Or [koht dor] (*Burgundy,* France) Geographical designation for the finest part of Burgundy, encompassing the *Côte de Nuits* and *Côte de Beaune.*

⊥ **Côte de Beaune (Villages)** [koht duh bohn] (*Burgundy,* France) The southern half of the *Côte d'Or.* With the suffix "*Villages*", indicates red wines from one or more of the specified *communes.* Confusingly, wine labeled simply "*Côte de Beaune*" comes from a small area around *Beaune* itself and often tastes like wines of that *appellation.*

⊥ **Côte de Brouilly** [koht duh broo-yee] (*Burgundy,* France) *Beaujolais Cru:* distinct from *Brouilly* – often finer. Floral and ripely fruity; will keep for a few years. *Duboeuf;* Pivot; Ch. Thivin.

C

⚥ **Côte de Nuits (Villages)** [koht duh nwee] (*Burgundy*, France) Northern, and principally "red" end of the *Côte d'Or*. The suffix *"Villages"* indicates wine from one or more specified *communes*.

⚥ **Côte Rôtie** [koh troh tee] (*Rhône*, France) Smoky yet refined *Syrah* (possibly with some white *Viognier*) from the northern *Rhône appellation* divided into "Brune" and "Blonde" hillsides. Most need at least six years. Ch. d'Ampuis. *Barge*; Bonnefond; *Burgaud*; Champet; *Cuilleron*; *Clusel-Roch*; Gallet; *Gasse*; Gentaz-Dervieux; *Gerin*; *Guigal*; *Jamet*; *Jasmin*; *Ogier*; *Rostaing*; Saugère; L. de Vallouit; *Vernay*; *Vidal Fleury*; *F. Villard*.

Côte(s), **Coteaux** [koht] (France) Hillsides.

⚥ **Coteaux d'Aix-en-Provence** [koh-toh dayks on prov vons] (*Provence*, France) A recent *AC* region producing light floral whites, fruity reds, and dry rosés using *Bordeaux* and *Rhône* varieties. **Château Calissanne**; Ch. Revelette; Mas Ste.-Berthe; Ch. Vignelaure.

⚥ **Coteaux d'Ancenis** [koh-toh don-suh-nee] (*Loire*, France) So far, only *VDQS* status for this region near Nantes, producing light reds and deep pinks from the *Cabernet Franc* and *Gamay*, and also *Muscadet*-style whites.

⚥ **Coteaux de l'Ardèche** [koh-toh dahr-desh] (*Rhône*, France) Light country wines, mainly from the *Syrah* and *Chardonnay*. A popular place with *Burgundians* to produce affordable alternatives to their own white wine.

⚥ **Coteaux Champenois** [koh-toh shom-puh-nwah] (*Champagne*, France) Overpriced, mostly thin, still red or white wine. *Laurent Perrier's* is not bad.

⚥ **Coteaux du Languedoc** [koh-toh doo long-dok] (*Midi*, France) A big *appellation*, and a source of fast-improving rich reds such as *Pic St. Loup*.

⚥ **Coteaux du Layon** [koh-toh doo lay-yon] (*Loire*, France) *Chenin Blancs*; some dry wines; sweet *Bonnezeaux* and *Quarts de Chaume*. **Perre Aguilas**; Patrick Baudoin; Dom. des Baumard; Ch. Pierre Bise; Ch. du Breuil; Cady; Delesvaux; des Forges; Godineau; Guimoniere; Ch. la Plaisance; Ch. des Rochettes; de la Roulerie; des Sablonettes; Ch. Soucherie; la Varière.

⚥ **Coteaux du Loir** [koh-toh doo lwahr] (*Loire*, France) Clean, vigorous whites from a *Loire* tributary.

⚥ **Coteaux du Lyonnais** [koh-toh doo lee-ohn-nay] (*Rhône*, France) Just to the south of *Beaujolais*, making some very acceptable good-value wines from the same grapes. **Descottes**; *Duboeuf*; Fayolle; Sain Bel Co-operative.

⚥ **Coteaux du Tricastin** [koh-toh doo tris-kass-tan] (*Rhône*, France) Southern *Rhône appellation*, emerging as a source of good-value, peppery-blackcurranty reds. **Dom. de Grangeneuve**; de Rozets; du Vieux Micoulier.

⚥ **Coteaux Varois** [koh-toh vahr-rwah] (*Provence*, France) Inexpensive, fruity reds, whites, and rosés. **Defends**.

⚥ **Côtes de/Premières Côtes de Blaye** [koht duh/pruh-myerh koht duh blay] (*Bordeaux*, France) A ferryride across the river from *St. Julien*. Poor winemaking prevents many *estates* from living up to their potential. Premières are usually red; Côtes, white. **Ch. Bertinerie**; Gigault; Haut-Sociondo; les Jonqueyres; Segonzac; des Tourtes.

⚥ **Côtes de Bourg** [koht duh boor] (*Bordeaux*, France) Clay-soil region just across the water from the *Médoc* and an increasingly reliable source of good-value, *Merlot*-dominated, plummy reds. **Brulesécaille**; Falfas; Fougas; Guerry; les Jonquières; Maldoror; Repimplet; Robin; Roc-de-Cambes; Rousset; Tayac.

⚥ **Côtes de Castillon** [koht duh kass-tee-yon] (*Bordeaux*, France) Region where the *Merlot* is often a lot more lovingly handled than in nearby *St. Emilion*. **Ch. d'Aiguilhe**; de Belcier; Cap de Faugères; Champ de Mars; Côte Montpezat; Grande Maye; Lapeyronie; de Parenchère; Pitray; Poupille; Robin.

⚥ **Côtes de Duras** [koht duh doo-rahs] (*Bordeaux*, France) Inexpensive *Sauvignons*, often better value than basic *Bordeaux* Blanc. **Amblard**; Duras Cooperative; Moulin des Groyes.

⚥ **Côtes de Francs** [koht duh fron] (*Bordeaux*, France) Up-and-coming region close to *St. Emilion*; increasingly good reds. **Charmes-Godard**; de Francs; la Claverie; la Prade; *Puygeraud*; Vieux Chateau Champs de Mars.

C

☨ **Vin de Pays des Côtes de Gascogne** [koht duh gas-koñ] (*Southwest*, France) Armagnac-producing region where dynamic producers *Yves Grassa* and the *Plaimont* cooperative used modern winemaking techniques on grapes that would in the past have been used for brandy. *Ugni Blanc* and *Colombard* are giving way to *Sauvignon Blanc*. **Grassa; Plaimont.**

☨ **Côtes de Provence** [koht dur prov-vonss] (*Provence*, France) Improving, good-value, fruity whites and ripe, spicy reds. The famous rosés, however, are often carelessly made and stored, but vacationers rarely notice that the so-called pink wine is a deep shade of bronze and decidedly unrefreshing. A region with as much appeal to organic winemakers as to fans of Mr Mayle's rural tales. **Dom. la Bernarde; la Courtade; d'Esclans; Commanderie e Peyrassol; Gavoty; de Mireille; Ott; Rabiega; Richeaume; Vanniéres.**

☨ **Côtes de St. Mont** [koht duh san-mon] (*Southwest*, France) Large *VDQS* area encompassing the whole of the Armagnac region. *Plaimont* is the largest and best-known producer.

☨ **Vin de Pays des Côtes de Tarn** [koht duh tarn] (*Southwest*, France) Fresh, fruity, simple reds and whites, mostly for drinking in-situ rather than outside France. **Labastide-de-Levis Cooperative.**

☨ **Vin de Pays des Côtes de Thau** [koht duh toh] (*Languedoc-Roussillon*, France) Fresh whites to drink with seafood in the canalside restaurants of *Sète*. **Les Vignerons des Garrigues.**

☨ **Vin de Pays des Côtes de Thongue** [koht duh tong] (*Languedoc-Roussillon*, France) Up-and-coming region between Béziers and Toulouse. **Domaines d'Arjolle, Condamine, l'Eveque, Teisserenc, and Deshenrys**

☨ **Côtes du Frontonnais** [koht doo fron-ton-nay] (*Southwest*, France) Up-and-coming, inexpensive red (and some rosé); characterful wines. **Ch. Baudare; Bellevue la Forêt; Cave de Fronton; le Roc; Viguerie de Beulaygue**

☨ **Côtes du Jura** [koht duh joo-rah] (France) *Vin Jaune* and *Vin de Paille* are the styles to look for in this area close to Arbois, as well as sparkling wine and Poulsard and Trousseau reds. *Ch. d'Arlay;* Jean Bourdy; Couret; Delay.

Côtes du Luberon (*Provence*, France) A region that boasts starry properties: **Val-Joanis, Vieille Ferme, Ch. de la Canorgue and Ch. de l'Isolette.**

☨ **Côtes du Marmandais** [koht doo mahr-mon-day] (*Southwest*, France) Uses the *Bordeaux* red grapes plus *Gamay*, *Syrah*, and others to make pleasant, fruity, inexpensive wines. **Ch. de Beaulieu; Les Vignerons de Beaupuy; Cave de Cocument.**

☨ **Côtes du Rhône (Villages)** [koht doo rohn] (*Rhône*, France) Spicy reds mostly from the southern *Rhône* Valley. The best supposedly come from a set of better *Villages* (and are sold as *CdR Villages*), though some single *domaine* "simple" *Côtes du Rhône*s outclass many *Villages* wines. *Grenache* is the key grape, though recent years have seen a growing use of the *Syrah*. Whites, which can include new-wave *Viogniers*, are improving. Red: **95 96 Beaucastel (Coudoulet); Dom. de Beaurenard; Cabasse; les Goubert;** *Grand Moulas; Guigal;* **Richaud; la Soumade; Ste. Anne.**

☨ **Côtes du Roussillon (Villages)** [koht doo roo-see-yon] (*Midi*, France) *Appellation* for red, white, and rosé of pretty variable quality. *Côtes du Roussillon Villages* is generally better. **Brial; des Chênes; Fontanel; Força Réal;** *Gauby;* **de Jau; Vignerons Catalans.**

☨ **Côtes du Ventoux** [koht doo von-too] (*Rhône*, France) Steadily improving everyday country reds that are similar to *Côtes du Rhône*, but often a touch better value. **Louis Bernard;** *Brusset; Jaboulet Aîné;* **Pascal; Perrin; la Vieille Ferme.** ★★★★ Côtes du Ventoux Grande Réserve, Louis Bernard 2001 $$

☨ **Côtes du Vivarais** [koht doo vee-vah-ray] (*Provence*, France) Light southern *Rhône*-like reds, fruity rosés, and fragrant light whites.

Cotesti [kot tesh-tee] (Romania) Easterly vineyards growing varieties such as *Pinots Noir, Blanc, Gris,* and *Merlot*.

☨ **Cotnari** [kot nah-ree] (Romania) Traditional and now very rare white dessert wine. Has potential.

C

☒ **Bodegas el Coto** [el kot-toh] (*Rioja,* Spain) Small *estate* producing classy, medium-bodied El Coto and Coto de Imaz reds.

☒ **Quinta do Côtto** [keen-tah doh kot-toh] (*Douro,* Portugal) Ports and intense, tannic, berryish red table wines – labeled as Grande Escolha – produced in a more southerly part of the Douro River than most other vintage *ports.*

☒ **Covey Run** (*Washington State,* USA) A *Yakima Valley* property making good *Merlot, Cabernet,* and *Chardonnay.*

☒ **Coulée de Serrant** [koo-lay duh seh-ron] (*Loire,* France) Great dry *Chenin* from a top property in *Savennières* run by *Nicolas Joly,* a leading champion of "biodynamique" winemaking. The Becherelle vineyard is fine too. Fans believe these wines need to be decanted well in advance.

☒ **Paul Coulon et Fils** [Koo-lon] (*Rhône,* France) Serious *Rhône* producer. *Coulure* [koo-loor] Climate-related winegrowing disorder. The condition causes reduced yields (and possibly higher quality) as grapes shrivel and fall off the vine.

☒ **Couly-Dutheil** [koo-lee doo-tay] (*Loire,* France) High-quality *Chinon* from vineyards just behind the *château* in which Henry II of England imprisoned his wife, Eleanor of Aquitaine. ✶✶✶✶ Clos de LOlive 1999 $$$

☒ **Viña Cousiño Macul** [koo-sin-yoh mah-kool] (*Maipo,* Chile) The most traditional producer in Chile. Reds are more successful than whites. ✶✶✶ 1995 Finis Terrae $$

☒ **Pierre Coursodon** [koor-soh-don] (*Rhône,* France) Maker of superlative traditional *St. Josephs* that need time but develop layers of flavor and complexity that are lacking in many a pricier *Hermitage.*

☒ **Ch Couhins-Lurton** [koo-ans loor-to'n] (*Bordeaux,* France) A *Graves Classed Growth* making notable *Sauvignon Blanc.*

☒ **Ch la Couspaude** [koos-pohd] (*Bordeaux,* France) This *St-Emilion Grand Cru Classé* has started to make wines in the fashionably rich, extracted style, and has won much critical acclaim because of it. Oak is used in extravagant amounts.

☒ **Ch. Coutet** [koo-tay] (*Barsac Premier Cru Classé, Bordeaux,* France) Delicate neighbor to *Ch. Climens,* often making comparable wines: Cuvée Madame is top flight.

☒ **Ch. Couvent-des-Jacobins** [koo-von day zhah-koh-ban] (*St. Emilion Grand Cru Classé, Bordeaux,* France) Producer of plummy-spicy wines.

Cowra [kow-rah] (*New South Wales,* Australia) Source of good, commercial, fruit-salady *Chardonnay,* but little of really great quality.

☒ **Dom. de Coyeux** [duh cwah-yuh] (*Rhône,* France) One of the best producers of *Côtes du Rhône* and *Muscat de Beaumes de Venise.*

☒ **Craggy Range** (*Hawkes Bay,* New Zealand) New kid on the block, with lots of US money behind it and good wines from here and elsewhere. Fine *Sauvignon Blanc* and promising *Pinot Noir.*

☒ **Cranswick Estate** (*Riverina, NSW,* Australia) Successful producer making reliable, fairly-priced wines under its own and the Barramundi label and some great *late-harvest* whites.

☒ **Quinta do Crasto** [kin-tah doo crash-too] (*Douro,* Portugal) An up-and-coming small port producer with good red table wines, too. Slightly more international in style than some. ✶✶✶✶ 1998 Douro Reserva $$

☒ **Cream Sherry** (*Jerez,* Spain) Popular style (though not in Spain) produced by sweetening an *oloroso.* A visitor to *Harvey's* apparently preferred one of the company's *sherries* to the then popular "Bristol Milk". "If that's the milk," she joked, "this must be the cream."

Crémant [kray-mon] (France) Term once used in *Champagne,* denoting a slightly sparkling style due to a lower pressure of gas in the bottle. Now used only elsewhere in France to indicate sparkling wine made by the traditional method, e.g., Crémant de *Bourgogne,* de *Loire,* and d'*Alsace.*

☒ Crépy [kray-pee] (*Savoie,* France) Crisp floral white from *Savoie.*

C

Criado y Embotellado (por) [kree-yah-doh ee em-bot-tay-yah-doh] (Spain) Grown and bottled (by).

Crianza [kree-yan-thah] (Spain) Literally keeping "con Crianza" means aged in wood – for less time than, and thus often preferable to, the *Reservas* and *Gran Reservas*, which are highly prized by Spaniards but can, to modern palates, taste dull and dried-out.

ℐ **Crichton Hall** [kri-ton] (*Rutherford*, California) Small winery specializing in top-class *Chardonnay*.

ℐ **Criots-Batard-Montrachet** [kree-yoh ba-tar mon rah-shay] (*Burgundy, France*) See *Montrachet*.

Crisp Fresh, with good *acidity*.

ℐ **Lucien Crochet** [loo-see-yen kroh-shay] (*Loire*, France) Top maker of red and white *Sancerre*. The *Cuvée Prestige* wines in both colors are – unusually for this appellation – worth keeping. ★★★★★ Sancerre La Croix du Roy 2000 $$$

ℐ **Ch. le Crock** [lur krok] (*St. Estèphe Cru Bourgeois, Bordeaux*, France) Traditional property that, like *Léoville-Poyferré*, its stablemate, has shown great recent improvement but still tends towards toughness.

ℐ **Croft** (Spain/Portugal) *Port* and *sherry* producer making highly commercial but rarely memorable wines. The *vintage port* is up to scratch.

ℐ **Ch. La Croix** [la crwah] (*Pomerol, Bordeaux*, France) Producer of long-lasting traditional wines.

ℐ **Ch. la Croix-de-Gay** [la crwah duh gay] (*Pomerol, Bordeaux*, France) Classy *estate* whose complex wines have good, blackcurranty-plummy fruit.

ℐ **Ch. Croizet-Bages** [krwah-zay bahzh] (*Pauillac 5ème Cru Classé, Bordeaux*, France) Underperformer showing some signs of improvement. Successful in 2001.

ℐ **Croser** [kroh-sur] (*Adelaide Hills*, Australia) Made by *Petaluma* in the Piccadilly Valley, this is one of the New World's most *Champagne*-like sparkling wines. A relationship with Bollinger helped pave the way for an LD (Late Disgorged) answer to that house's RD. ★★★★ 1992 LD $$$

🍇 **Crouchen** [kroo-shen] (France) Obscure white grape known as Clare Riesling in Australia and Paarl Riesling in South Africa.

ℐ **Crozes-Hermitage** [krohz ehr-mee-tahzh] (*Rhône*, France) Up-and-coming *appellation* in the hills behind supposedly greater *Hermitage*. Smoky, blackberryish reds are pure *Syrah*. Whites (made from *Marsanne* and *Roussanne*) are creamy but less impressive. And they rarely keep. Red: *Dom Belle; Chapoutier; Colombier; Combier; Delas; Alain Graillot;* Dom. du Pavilion-Mercure; Pochon; Sorrel; Tain l'Hermitage Cooperative.

Cru Bourgeois [kroo boor-zhwah] (*Bordeaux*, France) Wines beneath the *Crus Classés*, supposedly satisfying certain requirements, which can be good value for money and, in certain cases, better than more prestigious *classed growths*. Since around half the wine in the *Médoc* comes from Crus Bourgeois (and a quarter from *Crus Classés*), don't expect the words to mean too much. A new classification of the Crus Bourgeois was due to be announced as we went to press. In any case, the best Crus Bourgeois do not rely on their classification to attract customers. *d'Angludet; Beaumont; Chasse-Spleen; Citran; Fourcas-Hosten; Haut-Marbuzet; Gloria; la Gurgue; Labégorce; Labégorce-Zédé; Marbuzet; Meyney; Monbrison; de Pez; Phélan-Ségur; Pibran; Potensac; Poujeaux; Siran; Sociando-Mallet; la Tour Haut-Caussin.*

Cru Classé [kroo klas-say] (*Bordeaux*, France) The *Médoc* was split into five categories of crus classés, from first (top) to fifth growth (or *Cru*) for the 1855 Great Exhibition. The *Graves*, *St. Emilion*, and *Sauternes* have their own classifications. Some wines are better than others of the same classification.

ℐ **Weingut Hans Crusius** [hans skroos-yuhs] (*Nahe*, Germany) Family-run *estate* prized for the quality of its highly traditional wines.

Crusted Port (*Douro*, Portugal) An affordable alternative to *vintage* port – a blend of different years, bottled young, and allowed to throw a deposit. *Churchill's; Graham's; Dow's.* ★★★ Dows Crusted Port (bottled 1999) $$$

C

℉ **Yves Cuilleron** [Kwee-yehr-ron] (*Rhône*, France) Rising star producing great (red and white) *St. Joseph* and *Condrieu*. If you want to experience great late-harvest *Viognier*, this is the place.

℉ **Cullen** (*Margaret River*, Australia) Brilliant pioneering *estate* showing off the sensitive winemaking skills of Australian Winemaker of the Year (2000), Vanya Cullen. Source of stunning *Sauvignon-Semillon* blends, *claret*-like reds, a *Burgundian*-style *Chardonnay*, and the spicy recently-launched *Malbec-Petit Verdot-Merlot* Mangan. ★★★★★ Mangan 2001 $$$

Cultivar [kul-tee-vahr] (South Africa) South African for grape variety.

℉ **Ch. Curé-Bon-la-Madelaine** [koo-ray bon lah mad-layn] (*St. Emilion Grand Cru Classé, Bordeaux*, France) Tiny *St. Emilion* estate next to *Ausone*.

Curico [koo-ree-koh] (Chile) Region in which *Torres, San Pedro,* and *Caliterra* have vineyards. Now being eclipsed by *Casablanca* as a source for cool-climate whites, but still one of Chile's best wine areas for red and white. *Caliterra; Echeverria; la Fortuna; Montes; Miguel Torres; Valdivieso.*

℉ **Curious Grape** (*Kent*, England) Large, unusually dynamic, English wine producer that used to be called Chapel Down and includes the once-independent Carr Taylor and Lamberhurst wineries.

℉ **Cuvaison Winery** [koo-vay-san] (*Napa Valley*, California) Reliable Swiss-owned winery with high-quality *Carneros Chardonnay*, approachable *Merlot,* and now good *Pinot Noir*. Calistoga Vineyards is a *second label*.

Cuve close [koov klohs] The third-best way of making sparkling wine, in which the wine undergoes secondary fermentation in a tank and is then bottled. Also called the *Charmat* or *Tank method*.

Cuvée (de Prestige) [koo-vay] Most frequently a blend put together in a process called *assemblage*. Prestige *Cuvées* are (particularly in *Champagne*) supposed to be the best a producer has to offer.

℉ **Cuvée Napa** (*Napa*, California) The well-established California venture launched by *Mumm Champagne*, and still offering significantly better quality and value for money than the parent company back in France.

℉ **CVNE** [koo-nay] (*Rioja*, Spain) The Compania Vinicola del Norte de Espana (usually referred to as "koo-nay") is a large high-quality operation run by the owners of *Contino* and producing the excellent Viña Real in *Crianza, Reserva, Imperial,* or *Gran Reserva* forms in the best years, as well as a light *CVNE Tinto*. Some recent releases have been slightly less dazzling.

Cyprus Shifting its focus away from making ersatz "*sherry*". Even so, the best wine is still the fortified *Commandaria*.

℉ **Didier Dagueneau** [dee-dee-yay dag-guhn-noh] (*Loire*, France) The iconoclastic producer of steely, oak-aged *Pouilly-Fumé*, and even *late-harvest* efforts that upsets the authorities. Look out for the "Pur Sang" (made from rare, ungrafted vines) and oak-fermented "Silex" bottlings.

℉ **Serge Dagueneau et Filles** [sayrj dag-guhn-noh] (*Loire*, France) Another good Pouilly Fumé Dagueneau. ★★★★ Pouilly Fumé 2002 $$$

℉ **Romano dal Forno** [roh-mah-noh dal for-noh] (*Veneto*, Italy) Innovative estate for top-class Valpolicella (with some particularly good *Amarones*).

℉ **Ch. Dalem** [dah-lem] (*Fronsac, Bordeaux*, France) Rich, full-bodied *Fronsac*. Successful in 2002.

℉ **Dalla Valle** (*Napa*, California) One of the leading lights in the new trend toward Italian flavors, this small winery makes a delicious *Super-Tuscan* look-alike in the shape of the *Sangiovese-based* Pietre Rosso.

℉ **Dallas Conte** [dah-lass con-tay] (Chile) Joint venture between Australian *Mildara Blass* and Chilean *Santa Carolina*, focusing on commercial *Chardonnay* (from Casablanca) and *Cabernet*.

℉ **Dalmau** [dal-mou] (*Rioja*, Spain) Rich, modern red from the *Marques de Murrieta*. Not for purists. ★★★★ Rioja Dalmau Reserva 1996 $$$

℉ **Dalwhinnie** [dal-win-nee] (*Pyrenees, Victoria*, Australia) Quietly classy producer close to *Taltarni*, whose reds and whites are made to last.
★★★★ Moonambel Cabernet Sauvignon 2000 $$$

D

⟰ **Dāo** [downg] (Portugal) Once Portugal's best-known region – despite the traditional dullness of its wines. Thanks to pioneering producers like *Sogrape* and *Aliança*, and better grape varieties such as the *Touriga Nacional*, both reds and whites are improving very, very rapidly. Sogrape's Quinta dos Carvalhais and Duque de Viseu are particularly recommendable. *Aliança*; Boas Quintas; Duque de Viseu; Porta dos Cavaleiros; Quinta dos Roques; Casa de Santar.

⟰ **Darioush** [dah-ree-oosh] (*Napa*, California) Recently launched, Iranian-backed venture with high hopes – and a *Viognier* that is far more impressive than those of many of its neighbors. ★★★★ **Napa Valley Shiraz 1999 $$$**

Darling (South Africa) Up-and-coming western region, pioneered by Charles Back of *Fairview* and *Spice Route*, and by Darling Cellars.

⟰ **Kurt Darting** [koort dahr-ting] (*Pfalz*, Germany) New-wave producer who cares about ripe flavor. *Rieslings* are terrific, but so are other varieties. Great *late-harvest* wines. ★★★★ **Durkheimer Michelsberg 2002 $$**

D.A.S. (Austria) New designation, introduced in the *Weinviertel* as the forerunner of a French-style appellation system in which regions supercede grape varieties.

⟰ **Ch. Dassault** [das-soh] (*St. Emilion Grand Cru Classé, Bordeaux,* France) Named after the fighter plane manufacturer, this is good, juicy *St. Emilion*.

⟰ **Ch. de la Dauphine** [duh lah doh-feen] (*Fronsac, Bordeaux,* France) Like *Ch. Dalem*, this is proof that *Fronsac* really can match *St. Emilion*, whose reputation this region once rivaled.

⟰ **Domaine d'Auvenay** [Dohv-nay] (*Burgundy,* France) *Estate* belonging to Lalou Bize Leroy, former co-owner of the *Dom. de la Romanée-Conti*, and now at *Dom. Leroy*. Great, if pricey, long-lived, examples of *Auxey-Duresses, Meursault, Puligny-Montrachet*, and *Grands Crus of the Côtes de Nuits*. ★★★★★ **Meursault Narvaux 2000 $$$**

⟰ **René and Vincent Dauvissat** [doh-vee-sah] (*Burgundy,* France) One of the best *estates* in *Chablis*. Watch for other Dauvissats though, the name is also used by the *La Chablisienne* cooperative.

⟰ **Ch. Dauzac** [doh-zak] (*Margaux 5ème Cru Classé, Bordeaux,* France) Rejuvenated, following its purchase in 1993 by André Lurton of *Ch. la Louvière*.

Dealul Mare [day-al-ool mah-ray] (Romania) Carpathian region once known for whites, now producing surprizingly good *Pinot Noir*.

⟰ **Etienne & Daniel Defaix** [duh-fay] (*Burgundy,* France) Classy traditional *Chablis* producer, making long-lived wines with a steely bite.

⟰ **Grof Dégenfeld** [dehg-en-feld] (*Tokaj*, Hungary) Large new Tokaji producer. **Dégorgée (dégorgement)** [day-gor-jay] The removal of the deposit of inert yeasts from *Champagne* after maturation.

⟰ **Dehlinger** (*Sonoma*, California) *Russian River Pinot Noir* and *Chardonnay* specialist (with some great single-vineyard examples) that is proving highly successful with *Syrah* and *Cabernet Sauvignon*. ★★★★ **1997 Russian River Valley Late Bottled ReserveChardonnay $$**

Deidesheim [di-dess-hime] (*Pfalz*, Germany) Distinguished wine town noted for flavorsome *Rieslings*. *Bassermann-Jordan*; A. Christmann; Josef Biffar; Reichsrat von Buhl; JL Wolf.

⟰ **Deinhard** [dine-hard] (*Mosel*, Germany) See *Wegeler Deinhard*.

⟰ **Marcel Deiss** [dise] (*Alsace,* France) Small property producing some of the best wine in the region, including some unusually good *Pinot Noir*.

⟰ **Delaforce** [del-lah-forss] (*Douro*, Portugal) Small *port* house with lightish but good *vintage* and *tawny*. ★★★ **1995 Quinta da Corte Vintage Port $$$**

Delaire (South Africa) Quality-conscious winery with fruit carefully ripened at high altitudes and South Africa's first black oenology graduate as deputy winemaker. Great *Merlot* and *Cabernet*. ✶✶✶✶ Botmaskop.2000 **$$$**

Delamotte [del-lah-mot] (*Champagne,* France) Established among the *Chardonnay* vineyards of the Côte des Blancs in 1760, and now a subsidiary of *Laurent-Perrier* (and thus in the same group as *Salon*), this can be one of the best sources for *Blanc de Blancs Champagne.*

Delas Frères [del-las] (*Rhône,* France) *Négociant* with great *Hermitage* vineyards, now flying high since its purchase by *Louis Roederer.* ✶✶✶✶✶ Hermitage Cuvée Marquise de la Tourette 1999 **$$$$**

Delatite [del-la-tite] (*Victoria,* Australia) Producer of lean-structured, long-lived wines. The *Riesling* and, more particularly the *Gewurztraminer,* are the stars, but the Devil's River red is fine too.

Delbeck [del-bek] (*Champagne,* France) Underrated little producer, whose wines are strongly *Pinot*-influenced.

Delegats [del-leg-gats] (*Auckland,* New Zealand) Family firm that has hit its stride recently with impressively (for New Zealand) ripe reds, especially plummy *Merlots.* Look for the "Reserve" wines. The *second label* is *"Oyster Bay".* ✶✶✶✶ Reserve Cabernet Sauvignon Merlot 2001 **$$$**

Philippe Delesvaux [Dels-voh] (*Loire,* France) Quality-conscious *Coteaux de Layon estate* with some good red too.

Delgado Zuleta [dayl-gah-doh thoo-lay-tah] (Sanlucar, Spain) Old-established Manzanilla producer ✶✶✶✶ La Goya Manzanilla Pasada.

Delheim Wines [del-hime] (*Stellenbosch,* South Africa) A commercial *estate* with lean, quite traditional reds and white.

DeLille Cellars (*Washington State*) A small producer of very classy *Bordeaux*-style reds and whites under this and the Chaleur Estate labels.

DeLoach Vineyards (*Sonoma,* California) *Russian River* winery with rich *Chardonnay* and huge single-vineyard *Zinfandels.* Had to request protection from bankruptcy in 2003 and is now planning to reduce output.

André Delorme [del-lorm] (*Burgundy,* France) Little-known *négociant* based in the Côte Chalonnaise and specializing in sparkling wines.

Demi-sec [duh-mee sek] (France) Medium-dry.

Demoiselle [duh-mwah-zel] (*Champagne,* France). A new *Champagne* name to watch with attractive, light, creamy wines.

Denbies Wine Estate [den-bees] (*Surrey,* England) Part tourist attraction, part winery, the largest wine *estate* England has so far produced. Sweet wines are the best of the batch so far. ✶✶✶✶ Special Late Harvest **$$$**

Deutscher Tafelwein [doyt-shur tah-fuhl-vihn] (Germany) Table wine, guaranteed German as opposed to Germanic-style EC *Tafelwein.* Can be good value – and often no worse than *Qualitätswein,* the supposedly "quality" wine designation that includes every bottle of *Liebfraumilch.*

Deutsches Weinsiegel [doyt-shus vine-see-gel] (Germany) Seals of various colors – usually neck labels – awarded (over-generously) to supposedly higher quality wines. Treat with circumspection.

Deutz [duhtz] (*Champagne,* France, and also Spain, New Zealand, California) Reliable small but dynamic producer at home and abroad, now owned by *Roederer.* The *Montana Marlborough* Cuvée from New Zealand was created with the assistance of *Deutz,* as was the *Yalumba "D"* in Australia. Maison Deutz is a 150-acre cool-climate vineyard joint venture in California with Nestlé and *Deutz* where, unusually, a bit of *Pinot Blanc* goes into the – generally – excellent blend. The *Cuvée William Deutz* is the star wine.

Devaux [duh-voh] (*Champagne,* France) Small producer with a knack of producing fairly-priced wine and unusually good rosé and *Blanc de Noirs.*

Devil's Lair (*Margaret River,* Australia) A Southcorp subsidiary (like *Penfolds, Lindemans* and *Rosemount* etc.) concentrated, rich, dense wines, especially *Pinot Noir, Cabernet-Merlot,* and *Chardonnay.* ✶✶✶✶✶ Margaret River Cabernet Sauvignon 1999 **$$$**

D

Dézaley [days-lay] (*Vaud*, Switzerland) One of the few places in the world where the Chasselas (here called the *Dorin*) makes decent wine. **Pinget.**

Diabetiker Wein [dee-ah-beh-tih-ker vine] (Germany) Very dry wine with most of the sugar fermented out (as in a Diat lager); suitable for diabetics, but daunting for others.

Ⴘ **Diamond Creek** (*Napa Valley,* California) Big Name producer with a set of very good vineyards (Gravelly Meadow, Red Rock Terrace, and Volcanic Hill); toughly intense red wines which demand, and now – more than in the past – repay patience. ★★★★ **1995 Cabernet Sauvignon Volcanic Hill $$$$**

Ⴘ **Diamond Mountain** (*Napa Valley,* California) High altitude (700m) vineyard made famous by the 60-year-old Martin Ray winery. ★★★★ **Diamond Mountain Vineyard Merlot 1999 $$$$**

Ⴘ **Diamond Valley** (*Victoria,* Australia) Producer of one of Australia's – and the New World's best examples of *Pinot Noir.*

Schlossgut Diel [shloss-goot deel] (*Nahe,* Germany) Wine writer Armin Diel makes sublime *Rieslings* and pioneering oaked *Rülander* and *Weissburgunder.* ★★★★★ **Riesling Eiswein 2001 $$$$**

❦ **Dimiat** [deem-yaht] (Bulgaria) White grape said to be named after a town on the Nile Delta, but now producing simple, aromatic wine in Bulgaria.

Ⴘ **Dieu Donné Vineyards** [dyur don-nay] (*Franschhoek,* South Africa) Variable producer of quality varietals in the Franschhoek valley.

Ⴘ **Dom. Disznókó** [diss-noh-koh] (*Tokaji,* Hungary) Estate belonging, like *Quinta da Noval,* to *AXA.* Top-class modern *Tokaji* and dry lemony *Furmint.* ★★★★★ **Tokaji 5 Puttonyos Aszu 1998 $$$**

DLG (Deutsche Landwirtschaft Gesellschaft) (Germany) Body awarding medals for excellence to German wines – far too generously.

DO (Denominac/ion/ão de Origen) (Spain, Portugal) Demarcated quality area, guaranteeing origin, grape varieties, and production standards (everything, in other words except the quality of the stuff in the bottle).

Ⴘ *DOC (Denominación de Origem Controlada)* (Portugal) Replacing the old RD (Região Demarcada) as Portugal's equivalent of Italy's *DOCG.*

DOC (Denominacion de Origen Calificada) (Spain) Ludicrously, and confusingly, Spain's recently launched higher quality equivalent to Italy's *DOCG* shares the same initials as Italy's lower quality *DOC* wines. So far, restricted to *Rioja* – good, bad, and indifferent. In other words, this official designation should be treated – like Italy's *DOCs* and *DOCGs* and France's *Appellation Contrôlée* – with something less than total respect.

DOC(G) (Denominazione di Origine Controllata [e Garantita]) (Italy) Quality control designation based on grape variety and/or origin. "Garantita" is supposed to imply a higher quality level, but all too often it does no such thing and has more to do with regional politics than with tasty wines. (Giving a DOCG to *Bardolino* recently was particularly odd.) The IGT designation for quality wines previously sold as Vino da Tavola has helped to put DOC and DOCG into perspective as an indication of the region in which a wine was produced and its likely style.

Ⴘ **Ch. Doisy-Daëne** [dwah-zee dai-yen] (*Barsac 2ème Cru Classé, Bordeaux,* France) Fine *Barsac* property whose wines are typically more restrained than many a *Sauternes.* The 2000 is a star. The top wine is L'Extravagance.

Ⴘ **Ch. Doisy-Dubroca** [dwah-zee doo-brohkah] (*Barsac 2ème Cru Classé, Bordeaux,* France) Underrated *estate* producing ultrarich wines at often attractively low prices. **90 95 96 97 98 01**

Ⴘ **Ch. Doisy-Védrines** [dwah-zee vay-dreen] (*Barsac 2ème Cru Classé, Bordeaux,* France) Reliable *Barsac* property.

❦ **Dolcetto (d'Alba, di Ovada)** [dohl-cheh-toh] (*Piedmont,* Italy) Grape producing anything from soft everyday red to very robust and long-lasting examples. Generally worth catching quite young though. Like *Barbera* and *Shiraz,* often benefits from decanting. *Bests* use it to good effect in Australia. **Altare; Bava; Elvo Cogno; Aldo Conterno; Cortese; Vajra.**

D

Dôle [Dohl] (Switzerland) *Appellation* of *Valais* producing attractive reds from *Pinot Noir* and/or *Gamay* grapes. Germanier.

♈ **Dom Pérignon** [dom peh-reen-yon] (*Champagne*, France) *Moët et Chandon's Prestige Cuvée*, named after the cellarmaster who is erroneously said to have invented the *Champagne* method. Impeccable white and (rare) rosé. (*Moët* will disgorge older *vintages* to order.) ★★★★ 1995 $$$$

Domaine (Dom.) [doh-mayn] (France) Wine estate.

♈ **Domecq** [doh-mek] (*Jerez/Rioja*, Spain) Producer of (disappointing) *La Ina Fino* and the rare, wonderful *511A Amontillado* and Sibarita *Palo Cortado*.

♈ **Ch. la Dominique** [lah doh-mee-neek] (*St. Emilion Grand Cru Classé*, *Bordeaux*, France) High-flying property; one of the finest in *St. Emilion*.

♈ **Dominus** [dahm-ih-nuhs] (*Napa Valley*, California) *Christian Moueix* of *Ch. Petrus's* concentrated wine that is built to last. ★★★★★ 1999 $$$$

♈ **Domus** [doh-moos] (Chile) Star winemakers Ignacio Recabarren and Ricardo Peña's *Maipo's* estate makes good *Chardonnay* and better *Cabernet*.

♈ **Donauland** [doh-now-lend] (Austria) Varied wine region associated with good *Grüner Veltliner* but without a specific style of its own.

♈ **Hermann Dönnhoff** (*Nahe*, Germany) Brilliant winemaker who crafts great *late-harvest* wine and *Eiswein* from his Hermannshöhle vineyard.

♈ **Donnafugata** [don-na-foo-gah-tah] (*Sicily*, Italy) Large, modern winery making balanced, reliable wines from both local and international varieties. (Also, incidentally, the village at the heart of the novel and recently re-released Visconti film of *The Leopard*.)

♈ **Doonkuna** [doon-koo-nah] (*Canberra District*, Australia) Small winery making decent red wine. ★★★★ Chardonnay 2000 $$

♈ **Dopff "Au Moulin"** [dop-foh-moo-lan] (*Alsace*, France) *Négociant* with fine *Grand Crus*. ★★★★ 1999 Riesling Schoenenbourg $$$

♈ **Dopff & Irion** [dop-fay-ee-ree-yon] (*Alsace*, France) Not to be confused with Dopff "Au Moulin" this subsidiary of the Pfaffenheim cooperative is also a name to watch. ★★★★ Gewurztraminer 2000 $$$

♈ **Vin de Pays de la Dordogne** [dor-doyn] (*Southwest*, France) To the east of *Bordeaux*, this improving region offers light *Bordeaux*-style wines.

♈ **Girolamo Dorigo** [Jee-roh-lah-moh doh-ree-goh] (*Friuli-Venezia Giulia*, Italy) Classy Collio Orientali del Friuli producer with good reds (made from grapes such as the local Pignolo and *Refosco*) and even more impressive whites including a *Chardonnay*, *Verduzzo*, and *Picolit*.

⚲ **Dorin** [doh-ran] (*Vaud*, Switzerland) Name for the *Chasselas* in the *Vaud*.

⚲ **Dornfelder** [dorn-fel-duh] (Germany) Sadly underrated early-ripening, juicy, berryish grape that is beginning to attract some interest among pioneering winemakers in the southern part of Germany.

Dosage [doh-sazh] The addition of sweetening syrup to naturally dry *Champagne* after *dégorgement* to replace the wine lost with the yeast, and to set the sugar to the desired level (even *Brut Champagne* requires up to four grams per liter of sugar to make it palatable).

Douro [doo-roh] (Portugal) The port region and river whose only famous table wine was *Ferreira's* long-established *Barca Velha*. Now, however, led by port houses like *Quinta do Cotto*, *Ramos Pinto*, and *Niepoort*, and firms like *Sogrape*, there's a growing range of other stars to choose from. Alianca, Barca Velha; Quinta do Cotto; do Crasto; da Fonte; Duas Quintas; do Fojo; da Gaivosa; Lemos & Van Zeller; Niepoort; Redoma; de Portal; de las Rosa; do Vale; do Vallado; Doña Maria; Vale da Raposa; Vallado.

Dourthe [doort] (*Bordeaux*, France) Dynamic *négociant* whose Dourthe No.1 offers unusually reliable, good value (especially white) Bordeaux.

Doux [doo] (France) Sweet.

♈ **Dow** [dow] (*Douro*, Portugal) One of the big two (with *Taylor's*) and under the same family ownership as *Warre*, *Smith Woodhouse*, and *Graham*. Great *vintage port* and similarly impressive *tawny*. The *single-quinta* Quinta do Bomfim wines offer a chance to taste the Dow's style affordably.

D

Ⓘ **Drappier** [drap-pee-yay] (*Champagne*, France) Small, reliably recommendable producer. ★★★★★ **Carte d'Or 1998 $$$**

Ⓘ **Jean-Paul Droin** [drwan] (*Burgundy*, France) Good, small *Chablis* producer with approachable "modern" wines. ★★★★★ **Chablis les Clos 1999 $$$**

Ⓘ **Dromana Estate** [droh-mah-nah] (*Mornington Peninsula*, Australia) Viticulturalist Gary Crittenden makes good, if light, *Chardonnay* and raspberryish *Pinot Noir*, as well as an impressive range of Italian varietals sold under the "I" label.

Ⓘ **Domaine Drouhin** [droo-an] (*Oregon*) Top *Burgundy* producer's highly expensive investment in the US that's increasingly producing world-class reds – thanks to Veronique Drouhin's skill and commitment and some of *Oregon*'s best vineyards. ★★★★ **Pinot Noir 2000 $$$**

Ⓘ **Joseph Drouhin** [droo-an] (*Burgundy*, France) Probably *Burgundy*'s best *négociant*, with first-class red and white wines that are unusually representative of their particular *appellations*. Also look out for the rare white *Beaune* from its own Clos des Mouches, top-class *Clos de Vougeot*, and unusually (for a *négociant*) high-quality *Chablis*. The Marquis de Laguiche *Montrachet* is sublime.

★★★★★ **Marquis de Laguiche 2000 $$$$**

Ⓘ **Pierre-Jacques Druet** [droo-ay] (*Loire*, France) Wonderfully reliable *Bourgueil* producer making characterful individual cuvées. ★★★★ **Bourgueil Vaumoreau 2000 $$**

Dry Creek (*Sonoma*, California) A rare example of a California *AVA* region whose wines have an identifiable quality and style. Look out for *Sauvignon Blanc* and *Zinfandel*. *Beaulieu Vineyard; Collier Falls; Dry Creek; Duxoup; Gallo Sonoma; Nalle; Pezzi-King; Quivira; Rabbit Ridge; Rafanell; Turley.*

Ⓘ **Dry Creek Vineyard** (*Sonoma*, California) Eponymous vineyard within the *Dry Creek AVA* making well-known *Fumé Blanc*, great *Chenin Blanc*, and impressive reds.

Ⓘ **Dry River** (*Martinborough*, New Zealand) Small *estate* with particularly impressive *Pinot Noir* and *Pinot Gris* and delicious *late-harvest* wines.

Ⓘ **Duboeuf** [doo-burf] (*Burgundy*, France) The "King of *Beaujolais*", who introduced the world to the penny-candy flavor of young *Gamay*. Duboeuf offers good examples from individual growers, vineyards, and villages. These include reliable *nouveau*, good straightforward *Mâconnais* white, single *domaine Rhônes*, and now large amounts of commercial rather than fine Vin de Pays *Viognier*. ★★★★ **Moulin à Vent 2001 $$**

Ⓘ **Dubreuil-Fontaine** [doo-broy fon-tayn] (*Burgundy*, France) Quite traditional *estate*, producing full-flavored red and white individual cuvées from the *Corton* hillsides. ★★★★ **Savigny les Vergelesses 1999 $$**

Duca di Salaparuta [sah-la-pah-ROO-tah] (*Sicily*, Italy) Huge producer of good, reliable wines. The brand name is Corvo.

Ⓘ **Duckhorn** (*Napa Valley*, California) Once the producer of dauntingly tough *Merlot*, Duckhorn is now making far more approachable examples of this and other varieties. Decoy, the second label, offers an affordable, earlier-drinking taste of the house style, while the unusual Paraduxx *Cabernet-Zinfandel* is a delicious and immediately likeable novelty.

Ⓘ **Ch. Ducru-Beaucaillou** [doo-kroo boh-ki-yoo] (*St. Julien 2ème Cru Classé, Bordeaux*, France) "*Super Second*" with a decidedly less obvious style than peers such as *Léoville-Las-Cases* and *Pichon-Lalande*. Especially good in 1996, 1997, and (brilliantly in) 1998 and 1999 after a disappointing patch in the late 1980s and early 1990s. The 2002 is fine too.

E

☖ **Dom. Bernard Dugat-Py** [doo-gah pee] (*Burgundy*, France) Superstar *Gevrey-Chambertin estate* with great vineyards, from which M. Dugat makes delicious and unusually fairly priced wines *Grand Cru*.
★★★★★ Charmes-Chambertin 2000 $$$$

☖ **Ch. Duhart-Milon-Rothschild** [doo-ahr mee-lon rot-sheeld] (*Pauillac 4ème Cru Classé, Bordeaux*, France) Under the same management as *Lafite* and benefiting from heavy investment.

☖ **Dom. Dujac** [doo-zhak] (*Burgundy*, France) Cult *Burgundy* producer Jacques Seysses makes fine, long-lived, and quite modern wines from *Morey-St.-Denis* (including a particularly good *Clos de la Roche*), which are packed with intense *Pinot Noir* flavor. Now helped by Gary Farr of the excellent *Bannockburn* in Australia, and investing in vineyards in southern France.

☖ **Dulong** [doo-long] (*Bordeaux*, France) Reliable *négociant* that shocked some of its neighbors by producing *International Wine Challenge* medal-winning multi-regional *Vin de Table* blends under the "Rebelle" label.
Dumb As in dumb nose, meaning without smell.

☖ **Dunn Vineyards** (*Napa Valley*, California) Randy Dunn makes tough, forbidding *Cabernets* from *Howell Mountain* for patient collectors. Give them time, though; eventually, they yield extraordinary spicy, berryish flavors.
★★★★★ Howell Mountain Cabernet Sauvignon 1999 $$$$

Durbach [door-bahk] (*Baden*, Germany) Top vineyard area of this *Anbaugebiet*. Andreas Laible; Wolf-Metternich.

☖ **Ch. Durfort-Vivens** [door-for vee-va'ns] (*Margaux 2ème Cru Classé, Bordeaux*, France) Never really starry, but sometimes very classic, elegant wine, now with a new generation in charge. Recent vintages show decided improvement.. A wine for people who want an alternative to Parker-Power.

☼ **Durif** [dyoor-if] See *Petite Sirah*.

☖ **Jean Durup** [doo-roop] (*Burgundy*, France) Modern *estate* whose owner believes in extending vineyards of *Chablis* into less distinguished soil. Wines are good rather than great. The best are sold as Ch. de Maligny.

☖ **Duval-Leroy** [doo-val luh-rwah] (*Champagne*, France) Previously popular among retailers and restaurateurs to whom it supplied excellent own-label Champagne. Now notable for producing a Champagne for vegetarians and vegans. Fleur de Champagne and Cuvée des Rois are worth looking out for.
★★★★★ Blanc de Chardonnay 1996 $$$

☖ **Duxoup Wine Works** [duk-soop] (*Sonoma Valley*, California) Inspired winery-in-a-shed, producing fine *Syrah* from bought-in grapes.

E

☖ **E&E** (*Barossa*, South Australia) Top wine produced by *Barossa Valley Estate*.
★★★★★ E+E Black Pepper Shiraz 1999 $$$

☖ **Maurice Ecard** [Ay-car] (*Burgundy*, France) Very recommendable *Savigny-lès-Beaune* estate with good *Premier Cru* vineyards.

☖ **Echeverria** [eh-che-veh-ree-yah] (*Maule*, Chile) Impressive Curico producer with good *Cabernets*, *Chardonnays*, and *Sauvignon Blancs*.

☖ **Echézeaux** [eh-shay-zoh] (*Burgundy*, France) *Grand Cru* between *Clos de Vougeot* and *Vosne-Romanée* and more or less an extension of the latter *commune*. *Flagey-Echézeaux*, a village on the relatively vineless side of the Route Nationale, takes its name from the "flagellation" used by the peasants to gather corn in the 6th century. Grands-Echézeaux should be finer. *Dujac; R Engel; Grivot; Henri Jayer; Jayer-Gilles; D. Laurent; Mongeard-Mugneret; Mugneret-Gibourg; de la Romanée-Conti; E. Rouget; F. Vigot.*

☖ **L' Ecole No. 41** [ay-kohl] (*Washington State*) Superlative producer of classy *Chardonnay* and *Merlot*, as well as some lovely rich *Semillon*.
★★★★ Seven Hills Vineyard Syrah 2000 $$$

E

Edelfäule [ay-del-foy-luh] (Germany) *Botrytis cinerea*, or *"noble rot"*.

Edelzwicker [ay-del-zvick-kur] (*Alsace*, France) Generic name for a blend of grapes. The idea of blends is coming back – but not the name (see *Hugel*).

Eden Valley (Australia) Prime region for lean, limey *Riesling*; but the complicated geography and geology here means that the valley can also produce good reds.

Edes [ay-desh] (Hungary) Sweet.

☂ **Edmunds St. John** (*Alameda*, California) Producer with his heart in the *Rhône* – and a taste for rich, spicy *Syrah* and *Zinfandel* reds.

☂ **Edna Valley Vineyard** (California) Long-standing maker of rich, buttery *Chardonnay* in the *AVA* of the same name. In the same stable as *Chalone*, *Carmenet*, and *Acacia*.

Luís Felipé Edwards (Chile) High quality from an ex-pat Aussie winemaker. Look out for the lemony *Chardonnay*. ★ ★ ★ ★ ★ Terraced Shiraz 2001 $$$

Eger [eg-gur] (Hungary) Region of Hungary where *Bull's Blood* is made. Tibor Gall

☂ **Dom. de l'Eglise** [duh lay glees] (*Pomerol, Bordeaux*, France) Fairly priced, mid-line, wines.

☂ **Ch. l'Eglise-Clinet** [Lay gleez klee-nay] (*Pomerol, Bordeaux*, France) Terrific small estate that has gained – and earned – recent superstar status.

☂ **Egri Bikaver** [eh-grih bih-kah vehr] (*Eger*, Hungary) See *Bull's Blood*.

☂ **Cave Vinicole d'Eguisheim** [Eh-gees-hime] (*Alsace*, France) Dynamic cooperative with grand cru vineyards (including Hengst and Speigel) and alternative brands: Wolfberger and Willm. Look for the Sigillé wines.

☂ **Eikendal Vineyards** [ehk-ken-dahl] (*Stellenbosch*, South Africa) Understated wines (esp. *Chardonnay*) from the *Helderberg*.

Eiswein/Eiswein [ice-vine] (Germany/Austria/Canada) Ultraconcentrated *late harvest* wine, made from grapes naturally frozen on the vine and often picked a long time after the rest of the crop. (Some German vintages are harvested in the January of the following year!) Hard to make (and consequently very pricey) in Germany but much easier and more affordable in *Canada* where "Icewine" is a huge success. Unlike other top-quality sweet wines, Eiswein does not rely on *noble rot*. In fact, this characteristic is normally absent because winemakers need frozen grapes in a perfect state.

Eitelsbach [ih-tel-sbahk] (*Mosel*, Germany) One of the top two *Ruwer* wine towns, and the site of the famed Karthäuserhofberg vineyard.

Elaborado y Anejado Por [ay-lah-boh-rah-doh ee anay-hahdo pohr] (Spain) "Made and aged for."

Elbling [el-bling] (Germany) A popular grape in Medieval Germany, nowadays this highly acidic white grape is found in the upper Mosel Valley and in Luxembourg for (mostly) sparkling wine.

☂ **Elderton** (*Barossa Valley*, Australia) Highly commercial maker of big, rich, competition-winning wines, especially *Shiraz* and *Cabernet*. ★ ★ ★ ★ ★ Ashmead Barossa Cabernet Sauvignon 1999 $$$

Elever/éleveur [ay-lur-vay/ay-lur-vuhr] To mature or "nurture" wine, especially in the cellars of the *Burgundy négociants*, who act as éléveurs after traditionally buying in wine made by small estates.

Elgin [el-gin] (South Africa) Coolish – *Burgundy*-like – apple-growing country which is increasingly attracting the interest of big wine producers. Watch out for the *Paul Cluver* reds and whites from *Neil Ellis*. May eventually overshadow all but the best parts of *Stellenbosch* and *Paarl*.

Elk Cove (*Oregon*, USA) Organic Willamette Valley winery with sound range of whites. ★ ★ ★ ★ Viognier 2000 $$

☂ **Neil Ellis** (*Stellenbosch*, South Africa) One of the most reliable winemakers in the Cape – and a pioneer of the new region of *Elgin*. ★ ★ ★ ★ ★ Vineyard Selection Cabernet Sauvignon 2000 $$

Eltville [elt-vil] (*Rheingau*, Germany) Town housing the *Rheingau* state cellars and the German Wine Academy, producing good *Riesling* with backbone.

Elyse Wine Cellars (*Napa*, California) *Zinfandel* specialist with *Howell Mountain Vineyards*. Look out too for Cabernet and a Nero Misto spicy *Zinfandel-Petite Sirah* blend. ★★★★ Howell Mountain Zinfandel 2001 $$$

Emilia-Romagna [eh-mee-lee-yah roh-ma-nya] (Italy) Region around Bologna best known for *Lambrusco*; also the source of *Albana*, Sangiovese di Romagna, and *Pagadebit*.

Enate [eh-nah-tay] (*Somontano*, Spain) Dynamic modern winery specializing in varietals, including particularly successful Chardonnays. ★★★★ Cabernet Sauvignon Reserva 1998 $$

En primeur [on pree-muh] New wine, usually *Bordeaux*. Producers and specialist merchants buy and offer wine *en primeur* before it has been released. In the US and Australia, where producers like *Mondavi* and *Petaluma* sell in this way, the process is known as buying "futures."

Ch. l'Enclos [lon kloh] (*Pomerol, Bordeaux*, France) Gorgeously rich, fairly priced wines.

René Engel [On-jel] (*Burgundy*, France) Producer of rich, long-lived wines in *Vosne-Romanée* and *Clos Vougeot*. ★★★★★ Clos Vougeot 2000 $$$$

English wine Quality has improved in recent years as winemakers have moved from semisweet, mock-Germanic to dry mock-*Loire* and, increasingly, sparkling, aromatic-but-dry and *late harvest. Breaky Bottom; Thames Valley Vineyards; Nyetimber, Bruisyard; Three Choirs; Carr Taylor;* Chiltern Valley.

Enoteca [ee-noh-teh-kah] (Italy) Literally wine library or, now, wine shop.

Entre-Deux-Mers [on-truh duh mehr] (*Bordeaux*, France) Once a region of appalling sweet wine from vineyards between the Dordogne and Garonne rivers. Now a source of basic *Bordeaux* Blanc and principally dry *Sauvignon*. Reds are sold as *Bordeaux* Rouge. Both reds and whites suffer from the difficulty grapes have in ripening in cool years. Ch. Bonnet; Fontenille; Sainte-Marie; Tour-de-Mirambeau; Turcaud.

Erath Vineyards [ee-rath] (*Oregon*, US) One of *Oregon's* pioneering *Pinot Noir* producers, now better than ever.

Erbach [ayr-bahkh] (*Rheingau*, Germany) Town noted for fine full *Riesling*, particularly from the Marcobrunn vineyard.

Erbaluce [ehr-bah-loo-chay] (*Piedmont*, Italy) White grape responsible for the light dry wines of the *Caluso*, and the sweet sun-dried *Caluso Passito*.

Erbaluce di Caluso [ehr-bah-loo-chay dee kah-loo-soh] (*Piedmont,* Italy) Dry, quite herby white made from the *Erbaluce* grape. Also used to make sparkling wine. ★★★★ 1998 Cieck, Calliope $$$

Erden [ehr-durn] (*Mosel-Saar-Ruwer,* Germany) In the *Bernkastel Bereich,* this northerly village produces some of the finest, full crisp *Riesling* in the *Mosel,* and includes the famous Treppchen vineyard. *JJ Christoffel; Dr Loosen;* Mönchhof; Peter Nicolay.

Ermitage [ehr-mee-tahj] (Switzerland) The Swiss name for the *Marsanne*.

Errazuriz [ehr-raz-zoo-riz] (*Aconcagua Valley,* Chile) One of Chile's big name producers and owner of *Caliterra*. Wines have been improved by input from *Mondavi*. Look out for the "Wild Ferment" *Chardonnay* and *Syrah*. The top wine, Don Maximiano and the recently-launched Chadwick are among Chile's very best reds. ★★★★ Don Maximiano Founder's Reserve 2000 $$$ ★★★★ Chadwick 2000 $$$

Erstes Gewächs [air-shtes geh-vex] (Germany) First Growth: a new (2000) classification of the (hopefully) *Rheingau's* best vineyards, and part of Germany's drive to be seen to be doing better. The classification generously includes 35 percent of the vineyards. The jury is still out on the wines.

Erzeugerabfüllung [ayr-tsoy-guhr-ap-few-loong] (Germany) Bottled by the grower/estate.

E

Ⓧ **Esk Valley** (*Hawkes Bay*, New Zealand) Under the same ownership as *Vidal* and *Villa Maria*. Successful with *Bordeaux*-style reds and juicy rosé. ★★★★ 2000 Reserve Merlot/Malbec/Cabernet Sauvignon $$

Ⓧ **Esporão** [esp-per-row] (*Alentejo*, Portugal) Revolutionary *Alentejo* wines (including some fascinating varietals) made with help from Australian-born, Portuguese-based *David Baverstock*. ★★★★★ Esporao Aragones 2001 $$ ★★★★★ Esporao Touriga Nacional 2001 $$

Espum/oso/ante [es-poom-mo-soh/san-tay] (Spain/Portugal) Sparkling.

Ⓧ **Est! Est!! Est!!!** [ehst-ehst-ehst] (*Lazio*, Italy) Red named after the repeated exclamation of a bishop's servant when he found a good wine. Apart from the ones made by *Falesco*, today's examples rarely offer much to exclaim about.

Esters Chemical components in wine responsible for all those extraordinary odors of fruits, vegetables, hamster cages, and trainers.

Ⓧ **Estremadura** [ehst-reh-mah-doo-rah] (Portugal) Huge area producing mostly dull wine. Quintas da Pancas and Boavista show what can be done.

Estufa [esh-too-fah] (*Madeira*, Portugal) The vats in which *Madeira* is heated, speeding maturity and imparting its familiar "cooked" flavor.

Eszencia [es-sen-tsee-yah] (*Tokaji*, Hungary) Incredibly concentrated syrup made by piling around 22 kg of *late harvested*, *botrytised* grapes into *puttonyos* and letting as little as three liters of syrup dribble out of the bottom. This will only ferment up to about four percent alcohol, over several weeks, before stopping completely. It is then stored and used to sweeten normal *Aszú* wines. The Czars of Russia discovered the joys of Eszencia, and it has been prized for its effects on the male libido. It is hard to find, even by those who can see the point in doing anything with the expensive syrup other than pouring it on ice cream. The easier-to-find *Aszú Essencia* (one step sweeter than *Aszú 6 puttonyos*) is far better value.

Ⓧ **Arnaldo Etchart** [et-shaht] (*Cafayate*, Argentina) Big producer, benefiting from advice by *Michel Rolland* of *Pomerol* fame, and also investment by its French owners Pernod Ricard. The key wine here, though, is the grapey white *Torrontes*.

Ⓧ **l'Etoile** [eh-twah] (*Jura*, France) Theoretically the best *appellation* in the *Jura*. *Chardonnay* and *Savagnin* whites and sparkling wines can be good, and the *Vin Jaune* is of interest. Ch de l'Etoile; Michel Geneletti; Montbo

Ⓧ **Etude** [ay-tewd] (*Napa*, California) The recent purchase by *Beringer-Blass* has given thoughtful superstar consultant Tony Soter a new winery and access to new vineyards – and the chance to increase production. But he'll still be making small quantities of Pinot Noir from individual sites and clones (especially under the Heirloom label). Apart from these, there are good rich *Napa Cabernets* and *Carneros Chardonnays*. ★★★★ Cabernet Sauvignon 1999 $$$

Ⓧ **Ch. l' Evangile** [lay-van-zheel] (*Pomerol*, *Bordeaux*, France) Under the same ownership as Lafite Rothschild, and one of the top wines of 2000 and 2001. A classy and increasingly sought-after property that can, in great *vintages*, sometimes rival its neighbor *Pétrus*, but in a more *tannic* style.

Ⓧ **Evans Family/Evans Wine Co** (*Hunter Valley*, Australia) Len Evans's (founder and ex-chairman of *Rothbury Vineyards*) own estate and company. Rich *Chardonnay* and *Semillon* as characterful and generous as their maker. See also *Tower Estates*.

Ⓧ **Evans & Tate** (*Margaret River*, Australia) Much improved producer with good *Chardonnay* and *Shiraz* (including an impressive *International Wine Challenge* trophy winner). ★★★★ Margaret River Shiraz 2001 $$$

Ⓧ **Eventail de Vignerons Producteurs** [ay-van-tih] (*Burgundy*, France) Reliable source of *Beaujolais*.

Ⓧ **Eyrie Vineyards** [ai-ree] (*Oregon*) Pioneering *Pinot Noir* producer in the *Willamette Valley*, whose memorable success in a blind tasting of *Burgundies* helped to attract *Joseph Drouhin* to invest his francs in a vineyard here.

F

Ⅼ **Fabre Montmayou** [fab-re mon-mey-yoo] (*Mendoza*, Argentina) Luján de Cuyo winery to watch for rich *Michel Rolland*-influenced reds.

Ⅼ **Fairview Estate** (*Paarl*, South Africa) Progressive estate where Charles Back – both under his own name and under that of Fairview – makes wines such as the wittily named and labelled "Goats do Roam". See also *Spice Route*.

Ⅼ **Joseph Faiveley** [fay-vlay] (*Burgundy*, France) Impressive modern *négoçiant* with particular strength in vineyards in the *Côte de Nuits* and *Nuits-St.-Georges*. ★★★★ 1998 Nuits St Georges Clos de la Maréchale $$$$

Ⅼ **Falchini** [fal kee-noh] (*Tuscany*, Italy) One of the key producers of *Vernacchia di San Gimignano*.

Ⅼ **Falerno del Massico** [fah-LEHR-noh del mah-see-koh] (*Campania*, Italy) Modern producers such as Villa Matilde are leading the renaissance of a region famous among Ancient Roman wine drinkers. Reds and whites from local varieties: *Falanghina* (white) Piedirosso, Aglianico and Primitivo (red).

Ⅼ **Falesco** [fah leh-skoh] (*Lazio*, Italy) Producer of fine Montiano, *Merlot*, *Grechetto*, and *Est Est Est*.

Ⅼ **Ch. Falfas** [fal-fas] (*Côtes de Bourg, Bordeaux*, France) One of the best estates in the *appellation* – and a fine example of biodynamic winemaking.

Ⅼ **Théo Faller/Domaine Weinbach** [tay-yoh fal-lehr vine-bach] (*Alsace*, France) Family domaine of quirky character and very high quality. The wine style is rich and concentrated, and the wines benefit from bottle age. Several are named after the family. The Cuvée Laurence is a regular success.
★★★★ Gewurztraminer Cuvée Theo 2001 $$$

Ⅼ **Bodegas Fariña** [fah ree-nah] (*Toro*, Spain) Top producer in Toro, making cask-aged (Gran Colegiata) and fruitier, non-cask-aged Colegiata.
★★★★ Gran Colegiata Campus Viñas Vieja 1999 $$$

Ⅼ **Far Niente** [fah nee-yen-tay] (*Napa Valley*, California) Well regarded producer of sometimes over-showy *Chardonnay* and *Cabernet*.

Ⅼ **Ch. de Fargues** [duh-fahrg] (*Sauternes, Bordeaux*, France) Elegant wines made by the winemaker at *Ch. d'Yquem* – and a good alternative.

Ⅼ **Farnese** [fahr-nay-say] (*Abruzzo*, Italy) Dynamic producer with unusually good *Trebbiano d'Abruzzo*. ★★★★ Casale Vecchio Rebbiano d'Abruzzo 2002 $

Ⅼ **Gary Farrell** (*Sonoma*, California) A Russian River *Chardonnay, Pinot Noir,* and *Merlot* maker to watch.

Fat Has a silky texture which fills the mouth. More fleshy than meaty.

Fattoria [fah-tor-ree-ah] (Italy) *Estate*, particularly in *Tuscany*.

Ⅼ **Faugères** [foh-zhehr] (*Midi*, France) With neighboring *St. Chinian*, this gently hilly region is increasingly the source of really exciting red, though many still taste pretty rustic. Ch. des Adouzes; Gilbert Alquier; Ch. Chenaie; des Estanilles; la Closerie; Grézan; Cave Cooperative de Laurens; la Liquière; de Météore; Moulin Couderc; des Peyregran; du Rouge Gorge; St. Antonin.
★★★★ Chateau Grezan Cuvee Arnaud Lubac 2001 $$$ ★★★★ Abbaye Sylva Plana, la Closerie 2001 $$$

Ⅼ **Bernard Faurie** [fow-ree] (*Rhône*, France) Tournon-based producer who makes intense perfumed wines with great longevity.

Ⅼ **Bodegas Faustino** [fows-tee-noh] (*Rioja*, Spain) Big *Rioja* producer with traditional (*Gran*) Reservas, fair whites and *cavas*.

꩜ **Favorita** [fahvoh-ree-tah] (*Piedmont*, Italy) Traditional variety from *Piedmont* transformed by modern winemaking into delicate floral whites. Conterno; Villa Lanata; *Bava*.

Federspiel [fay-dur-shpeel] (*Wachau*, Austria) Local quality category (the middle one of three) for high quality dry wines. The rough equivalent of Kabinett. See also *Steinfeder* and *Smaragd*.

Ⅼ **Weingut Feiler-Artinger** [fih-luh arh-ting-guh] (*Rust*, Austria) Superlative innovative producer of dry and, especially, *late-harvest* wines.
★★★★ Ruster Ausbruch Essenz Welschriesling 2000 $$$

F

⟁ **Fattoria di Felsina Berardenga** [fah-toh-ree-ah dee fehl-see-nah beh-rah-den-gah] (*Tuscany*, Italy) Very high-quality *Chianti* estate.

⟁ **Livio Felluga** [feh-LOO-gah] (*Friuli*, Italy) Estate with terrific range of pure varietals and blends (e.g. *Terre Alte: Sauvignon, Tocai and Pinot Bianco*).

⟁ **Felton Road** (*Central Otago*, New Zealand) This is an instant superstar, producing New Zealand's – some of the New World's – top *Pinot Noirs*. Fans argue over the respective merits of the Block 3 and Block 5. There is also some very stylish *Riesling*. ★★★★★ 2000 Block 5 Pinot Noir $$$

⚘ **Fendant** [fon-don] (Switzerland) See *Chasselas*.

⚘ **Fer** [fehr] (*South-West*, France) Tannic grape used to make *Marcillac*. *Fermentazione naturale* [fehr-men-tat-zee-oh-nay] (Italy) "Naturally sparkling" but, in fact, indicates the *cuve close* method.

⚘ **Fernão Pires** [fehr-now pee-rehsh] (Portugal) *Muscat*ty grape, used to great effect by *Peter Bright* of the João Pires winery.

⟁ **Ch. Ferrand** [feh-ron] (*St. Emilion, Bordeaux*, France) Not to be confused with *Ferrand Lartigue*, this is a big estate, producing rather tough wines.

⟁ **Ch. Ferrand Lartique** [feh-ron lah-teek] (*St. Emilion Grand Cru, Bordeaux*, France) Small five-acre estate producing full-bodied rich wines.

⟁ **Luigi Ferrando** (*Piedmont* Italy) Producer in the Carema *DOC* of good *Nebbiolo*-based wines that are attractively light and elegant in style.

⟁ **Antonio Ferrari** [feh-rah-ree] (*Piemonte*, Italy) Small family estate that still has (tiny) stocks of an astonishingly fine port-and-curry-spice 1978 Piemontese Salice Salentino

⟁ **Ferrari** [feh-rah-ree] (*Trentino*, Italy) A sexy name for sexy *Champagne*-method sparkling wines. The Riserva del Fondatore is the star of the show.

⟁ **Ferrari-Carano** (*Sonoma*, California) Improving winery best known for its oaky, crowd-pleasing *Chardonnay, Cabernet Sauvignon, Zinfandel*, and rich *Merlot*. All these are good in their unsubtle way, but Siena, the Italianate *Sangiovese*-Cabernet blend, and the *Syrah* are both more interesting.

⟁ **AA Ferreira** [feh-ray-rah] (*Douro*, Portugal) Associated with *Sogrape*, this traditional Portuguese *port* producer is as famous for its excellent *tawnies* as for its *Barca Velha*, Portugal's best traditional unfortified red.
★★★★ Duque de Braganca 20 Year Old Tawny $$

⟁ **Gloria Ferrer** (*Sonoma*, California) New World offshoot of *Freixenet* (the people behind *Cordon Negro*) making unmemorable sparkling wine and somewhat more interesting *Chardonnay* and *Pinot Noir* from its *Carneros* vineyards.

⟁ **Ch. Ferrière** [feh-ree-yehr] (*Margaux 3ème Cru Classé, Bordeaux*, France) Once small, now rather bigger, thanks to the convenience of belonging to the same owners as the *Margaux Cru Bourgeois, Ch. la Gurgue* – and the legal right to swap land between estates in the same appellation.

⟁ **Ch. de Fesles** [dur fel] (*Loire*, France) Under the same ownership as Chateaux Varennes, Chamboureau, and Guimonière, this estate produces classic *Bonnezeaux, Coteau du Layon, Anjou Villages* and even *Anjou Rosé*.
★★★★ Coteau du Layon 2000 $$$

⟁ **Sylvain Fessy** [seel-van fes-see] (*Burgundy*, France) Reliable small *Beaujolais* producer with wide range of *crus*.

⟁ **Henry Fessy** [on-ree fes-see] (*Burgundy*, France) Consistent *négociant*, vineyard owner and producer of *Beaujolais*.

⚘ **Feteasca** [fay-tay-yas-cah] (Romania) White grape giving fair, peachy wine. F. Regala is slightly better than F. Alba. Red F. Neagra also exists.

⟁ **Fetzer** [fet-zuh] (*Mendocino*, California) Confusingly, this big producer offers different blends in the UK and US – which explains why the name is more respected in the UK. Fortunately, the whole world can buy the excellent "*Bonterra*" line which is the best commercial organic wine in the world. The Valley Oaks Syrah is Rosé is one of the only pink wines ever to win a Gold medal at the International Wine Challenge – and the only one to do so two years running. ★★★★ Valley Oaks Syrah Rosé 2002 $

F

☥ **Feudi di San Gregorio** [foy-di dee san gray-gor-yoh] (*Campania*, Italy) The Fiano grape at its best, with sweetish Privilegio at the top of the tree. Other varieties are also excellent, including Serpico, a complex Aglianico-Merlot blend. Subtle, elegant wines right across the board.

☥ **Nicolas Feuillatte** [fuh-yet] (*Champagne*, France) Quietly rising star with good-value wine. ★★★ **Premier Cru Rosé $$$**

☥ **William Fèvre** [weel-yum feh-vr] (*Burgundy*, France) Quality *Chablis* producer that is now under the same (Henriot) ownership as *Bouchard Père & Fils*, and showing similar improvements in quality: Oak use, in particular, is more delicate. ★★★★ **Chablis Valmur 2000 $$$**

☥ **Viña William Fèvre** [weel-yum feh-vr] (*Maipo*, Chile) M. Fèvre's efforts in Chile are improving too – but less rapidly ★★★ **Gran Cuvee Pinot Noir 2002 $$$**

☥ **Ch. Feytit-Clinet** [fay-tee klee-nay] (*Pomerol*, *Bordeaux*, France) A *Moueix* property with good, delicate wines.

☥ **Fiano** [fee-ah-noh] (Italy) Herby white grape variety used to make Fiano di Avellino in the south.

☥ **Les Fiefs-de-Lagrange** [fee-ef duh lag-ronzh] (*St. Julien*, *Bordeaux*, France) Recommendable *second label* of *Ch. Lagrange*.

☥ Fiefs Vendéens [fee-ef von-day-yi'n] (*Loire*, France) Surviving VDQS region close to Muscadet and offering a wide range of grape varieties – and fresh, light wines that are well worth buying in ripe vintages.

☥ **Ch. de Fieuzal** [duh fyuh-zahl] (*Pessac-Léogan Grand Cru* Classé, *Bordeaux*, France) *Pessac-Léognan* property returning to form and producing great whites and lovely raspberryish reds. Abeille de Fieuzal is *second label*.

☥ **Ch. Figeac** [fee-zhak] (*St. Emilion Premier Grand Cru*, *Bordeaux*, France) Forever in the shadow of its neighbor, *Cheval Blanc*, and often unpredictable in its evolution. One of the most characterful *St. Emilions*. Good in 2002.

☥ **Walter Filiputti** [feel-lee-put-tee] (*Friuli-Venezia Guilia*, Italy) Top-ranking winemaker with his own label since 1995. Filiputti's crusade is to prove Pignolo the greatest red grape in Friuli; he makes a range of other varieties as well.

☥ **Granxa Fillaboa** [gran-shah fee-yah-boh-wah] (*Galicia*, Spain) One of the best *Albariño* producers in *Rias Baixas*.

☥ **Filliatreau** (*Loire*, France) Exemplary producer of Saumur Champigny which shows how tasty the *Cabernet* Franc can be – and how it can age.

☥ **Ch. Filhot** [fee-yoh] (*Sauternes*, France) Rarely among the most complex examples of Sauternes, this is nonetheless one of the most reliable sources of well-made, good value wine. ★★★★★ **2001 $$$**

Finger Lakes (*New York State*) Cold region whose producers struggle (sometimes effectively) to produce good *vinifera*, including *Pinot Noir* and *late-harvest Riesling*. Hybrids such as *Seyval Blanc* are more reliable. *Fox Run; Heron Hill; Lamaroux Landing; Wagner.*

Fining The clarifying of young wine before bottling to remove impurities, using a number of agents including *isinglass* and *bentonite*.

Finish What you can still taste after swallowing.

☥ **Fino** [fee-noh] (*Jerez*, Spain) Dry, delicate *sherry* which gains its distinctive flavor from the *flor* or yeast which grows on the surface of the wine during maturation. Drink chilled, with tapas, preferably within two weeks of opening. *Lustau; Barbadillo; Hidalgo; Gonzalez Byass.*

☥ **Firestone** (*Santa Ynez*, California) Good producer – particularly of good value *Chardonnay*, *Merlot*, *Sauvignon* and *late-harvest Riesling* – in southern California.

F

♆ **Fisher** (*Sonoma*, California) Top-class producer of single-vineyard *Napa Cabernets* and *Carneros Chardonnays* from hillside sites.

♆ Fitou [fee-too] (*Midi*, France) Long considered to be an upmarket *Corbières* but actually rather a basic southern *AC*, making reds largely from the *Carignan* grape. The wines here may have become more refined, with a woody warmth, but they never quite shake off their rustic air. Ch. d'Espigne; Lepaumier; Lerys; de Nouvelles; *Mont Tauch*; de Rolland; Val d'Orbieu.

♆ Fixin [fee-san] (*Burgundy*, France) Northerly village of *Côte de Nuits*, whose lean, tough, uncommercial reds can mature well. New-wave winemaking and later harvesting are thankfully introducing friendlier fare. Dom Bart; Vincent Berthaut; *Bruno Clair*; Michel Defrance; Derey Frères; Fougeray de Beauclair; Pierre Gelin; André Geoffroy; J-P Guyard; *Louis Jadot*; Philippe Joliet; Denis Philibert.

Flabby Lacking balancing acidity.

♆ **Flagstone** (South Africa) Bruce Jack is one of the most dynamic players in South Africa. The winery is on the Capetown waterfront, but the generally recomendable wines come from various regions.

♆ **Ch. La Fleur** [flur] (*St. Emilion, Bordeaux*, France) Small *St. Emilion* property producing softly fruity wines.

♆ **Ch. la Fleur de Gay** [flur duh gay] (*Pomerol, Bordeaux*, France) *Ch. Croix de Gay*'s best wine and thus heavily sought after. Good in 2000 and 2001.

Fleur du Cap (South Africa) Reliable but dull wines. The new Unfiltered Collection has more personality.

♆ **Ch. la Fleur-Pétrus** [flur pay-trooss] (*Pomerol, Bordeaux*, France) For those who find *Pétrus* a touch unaffordable, this next-door neighbor offers gorgeously accessible *Pomerol* flavor for (in *Pétrus* terms) a bargain price.

♆ Fleurie [fluh-ree] (*Burgundy*, France) One of the 10 *Beaujolais Crus*, ideally fresh and fragrant, as its name suggests. Best vineyards include La Madonne and Pointe du Jour. Dom. Bachelard and Guy Depardon are names to watch. J-M Aujoux; Berrod; P-M Chermette; M Chignard; Després; *Duboeuf*; Ch. Labourons; Dom de la Madone; A Métrat; Andre Vaisse.

♆ **Finca Flichman** (Argentina) New ownership, by Portugal's *Sogrape*, should help this old-established company. Quality is interesting.

Flor [flawr] Yeast which grows naturally on the surface of some maturing *sherries*, making them potential *finos*.

🍇 **Flora** [flor-rah] A cross between *Semillon* and *Gewürztraminer*, best known in *Brown Brothers Orange Muscat* and Flora.

♆ **Flora Springs** (*Napa Valley*, California) One good, unusual *Sauvignon Blanc* (Soliloquy) and classy *Merlot, Cabernet Sauvignon* & *Cabernet Franc* blend (Trilogy). ★★★★ 1996 Rutherford Hillside Reserve Cabernet $$$

♆ **Emile Florentin** [floh-ron-tan] (*Rhône*, France) Maker of ultratraditional, ultra*tannic*, chewy *St. Joseph* from a vineyard dating back to the 16th century. ★★★★ St. Joseph le Clos 1998 $$$

Flying winemakers Young winemakers contracted by overseas customers make better and more reliable wine than wineries' own teams can manage. Often, European cooperatives' wines are transformed by picking riper grapes and keeping tanks and pipes clean.

♆ **Vinha do Fojo** (*Douro*, Portugal) Critical acclaim for this table wine sent prices soaring. It's dense and good, but having to look to its laurels.

♆ **Ch. Fombrauge** [fom-brohzh] (*St. Emilion, Bordeaux*, France) *St. Emilion* that is improving since its purchase by the owners of *Malesan*.

♆ **Ch. Fonbadet** (*Bordeaux*, France) Reliable, good value *Pauillac* Cru Bourgeois. Made an attractive 2001.

♆ **Ch. Fonplégade** [fon-pleh-gahd] (*St. Emilion Grand Cru Classé, Bordeaux*, France) If you like your *St. Emilion* tough, this is for you.

♆ **Ch. Fonréaud** (*Bordeaux*, France) Attractively approachable *Listrac*.

♆ **Ch. Fonroque** [fon-rok] (*St. Emilion Grand Cru Classé, Bordeaux*, France) Property with concentrated wines, but not always one of *Moueix*'s very finest.

F

Fonseca Guimaraens [fon-say-ka gih-mah-rans] (*Douro*, Portugal) A subsidiary of *Taylor's*, but independently making great *port*. Often beats supposedly classier houses' supposedly finer vintages. ★★★★★ 1984

JM da Fonseca Internacional [fon-say-ka in-tuhr-nah-soh-nahl] (*Setúbal Peninsula*, Portugal) Highly commercial firm whose wines include Lancers, the *Mateus*-taste-alike sold in mock-crocks.

JM da Fonseca Successores [fon-say-ka suk-ses-saw-rays] (*Estremadura*, Portugal) Unrelated to the *port* house of the same name and no longer connected to *JM da Fonseca Internacional*. Family-run firm, which, with *Aliança* and *Sogrape*, is one of Portugal's big three dynamic wine companies. Top reds include Pasmados, *Periquita* (from the grape of the same name), *Quinta da Camarate*, Terras Altas Dão, and the *Cabernet*-influenced "TE" *Garrafeiras*. Dry whites are less impressive, but the sweet old *Moscatel de Setúbals* are luscious classics.

Dom. Font de Michelle [fon-duh-mee-shel] (*Rhône*, France) Reliable producer of medium-bodied red *Châteauneuf-du-Pape* and small quantities of excellent, almost unobtainable, white.

Fontana Candida [fon-tah-nah kan-dee-dah] (*Lazio*, Italy) Good producer, especially for *Frascati*. The top wine is Colle Gaio.

Fontanafredda [fon-tah-nah-freh-dah] (*Piedmont*, Italy) Big producer with impressive *Asti* and very approachable (especially single-vineyard) *Barolo*.

Ch. Fontenil (*Bordeaux*, France) Michel Rolland is the name behind this *Fronsac* property. Predictably rich, oaky wines.

Domaine de Font Sane [fon-sen] (*Rhône*, France) Producer of fine *Gigondas*. Very traditional and full-bodied.

Castello di Fonterutoli (*Tuscany*, Italy) *Chianti* Classico producer of real class, which also produces great non-*DOC* blends: Concerto and Siepi.

Fontodi [Fon-toh-dee] (*Tuscany*, Italy) *Tuscan* producer with Flaccianello, a truly top class *IGT*. ★★★★★ Flaccianello della Pieve 2000 $$$

Foradori [Foh-rah-doh-ree] (*Trentino*, Italy) Specialist producer of *Teroldego* (Granato is the reserve wine) plus an inventive *Chardonnay-Pinot Bianco-Sauvignon* white blend.

Forman (*Napa Valley*, California) Rick Forman makes good *Cabernet* and *Merlot* and crisp *Chardonnay*.
★★★★★ Cabernet Sauvignon 1999 $$$

Forst [fawrst] (*Pfalz*, Germany) Wine town producing great concentrated *Riesling*. Famous for the *Jesuitengarten* vineyard.

Fortant de France [faw-tan duh frons] (*Languedoc-Roussillon*, France) Good-quality revolutionary brand owned by *Skalli* and specializing in varietal *Vin de Pays d'Oc*.

Château Fortia (*Rhône*, France) Improving ultratraditional *Châteauneuf-du-Pape* estate.

Les Forts de Latour [lay faw duh lah-toor] (*Pauillac*, *Bordeaux*, France) *Second label* of *Ch. Latour*. Like the *second labels* of other top châteaux; still often better than lesser *classed growth châteaux'* top wines. Very fine 2000.

Ch. Fourcas-Dupré [foor-kah doo-pray] (*Listrac Cru Bourgeois*, *Bordeaux*, France) Rapidly improving *Listrac*.

Ch. Fourcas-Hosten [foor-kah hos-ten] (*Listrac Cru Bourgeois*, *Bordeaux*, France) Once tough, now greatly improved *Listrac* property.

Fox Run Vineyards (*New York*) Successful Finger Lakes producer, with good sparkling wine, *Riesling*, and *Chardonnay*.

Foxen (*Santa Ynez*, California) Successful producer of single-vineyard *Pinot* and *Chardonnay*, now moving into *Syrah*.

Ch. de France (*Bordeaux*, France) Pessac-Léognan property benefitting from tighter selection and later picking. One to watch.

Franciacorta [fran-chee yah-kor-tah] (*Lombardy*, Italy) *DOC* for good, light, French-influenced reds but better noted for – often Champagne-price – sparklers. *Bellavista; Ca' Del Bosco; Cavalleri; Monte Rossa;* Uberti.

F

Ⅰ Franciscan Vineyards [fran-sis-kan] (*Napa Valley*, California) Now part of the huge US/Australian Constellation BRL Hardy, a reliable *Napa* winery whose Chilean boss, Augustin Huneeus, was one of the pioneers of naturally fermented wines with his *Burgundy*-like "Cuvée Sauvage" *Chardonnay*. Now also making wine in Chile – at *Veramonte*. ★★★★★ Oakville Estate Magnificent 1999 $$$ ★★★★★ Oakville Estate Merlot 2000 $$$

Ⅰ Ch. Franc-Mayne [fron' mayn] (*Bordeaux*, France) *St-Emilion Grand Cru Classé* with improving quality and deep pockets for investment.

Ⅰ Ch. de Francs [duh fron] (*Côtes de Francs, Bordeaux*, France) Well-run estate which makes great-value crunchy, blackcurranty wine and, with *Ch. Puygeraud*, helps to prove the worth of this little-known region.

Franken [fran-ken] (Germany) *Anbaugebiet* making characterful, sometimes earthy, dry whites, traditionally presented in the flagon-shaped "*Bocksbeutel*" on which the *Mateus* bottle was modeled. A key variety is the *Silvaner,* which explains the earthiness of many of the wines. Juliusspital; Gebiets-Winzergenossenschaft; Rudolf Fürst; Horst Sauer; Reiss; Hans Wirsching.

Franschhoek [fran-shook] (South Africa) Valley leading into the mountains away from Paarl. The best producers are mostly clustered at the top of the valley, around the picturesque town. Dieu Donne; Veenwouden; Graham Beck.

Ⅰ Frascati [fras-kah-tee] (*Latium*, Italy) Clichéd dry or semidry white from *Latium*. At its best it is soft and clean with a fascinating "sour cream" flavor. Drink within 12 months of *vintage*. *Fontana Candida*; Pallavincini.

Ⅰ Ca' dei Frati [kah day-yee frah-tee] (*Lombardy*, Italy) Fine producers of *Lugana* and *Chardonnay*-based sparkling wine. ★★★ 2000 'Brolettino' $$

Ⅰ Freemark Abbey (*Napa Valley*, California) Well-regarded producer of good *Cabernet*. ★★★★ Sycamore Vineyards Cabernet Sauvignon 1997 $$$

Ⅰ Freie Weingärtner Wachau [fri-eh vine-gehrt-nur vah-kow] (*Wachau*, Austria) Fine cooperative with great vineyards, dry and sweet versions of the *Grüner Veltliner* and gloriously concentrated *Rieslings* that outclass the efforts of many a big-name estate in Germany.

Ⅰ Freisa [fray-ee-sah] (Italy) Perfumed red wine grape with lovely cherryish, raspberryish flavors, popular with Hemingway and grown in *Piedmont* by producers like Gilli and *Vajra*. Drink young. *Bava; Aldo Conterno.*

Ⅰ Freixenet [fresh-net] (*Catalonia*, Spain) Giant in the *cava* field and proponent of traditional *Catalonia*n grapes in sparkling wine. Its dull, off-dry big-selling *Cordon Negro* made from traditional grapes is a perfect justification for adding *Chardonnay* to the blend. Now also a big investor in other regions and countries. ★★★ Reserva Real $$

Ⅰ Marchesi de' Frescobaldi [mah-kay-see day fres-koh-bal-dee] (*Tuscany*, Italy) Family estate with classy wines: *Castelgiocondo*, Mormoreto (*Cabernet Sauvignon*-based wine), the rich white Pomino Il Benefizio *Chardonnay*, *Pomino Rosso* using *Merlot* and *Cabernet Sauvignon*, and Nippozano in *Chianti*. Now in joint venture to make *Luce* with *Mondavi*. ★★★★ 1999 Montesodi Chianti Rufina $; ★★★ 1999 Mormoreto Chianti Rufina $$$$

Ⅰ Freycinet [fres-sih-net] (*Tasmania*, Australia) Small East Coast winery with some of Australia's best *Pinot Noir* and great *Chardonnay.*

Ⅰ Friuli-Venezia Giulia [free-yoo-lee veh-neht-zee-yah zhee-yoo-lee-yah] (Italy) Northerly region containing a number of *DOCs*: Colli Orientali, Collio, Friuli Grave and Aquileia and Isonzo, and single-variety wines like *Merlot*, *Cabernet Franc, Pinot Bianco, Pinot Grigio,* and *Tocai.* Some are dilute; others are complex masterpieces. Jermann; Bidoli; Puiatti; Feudi di Romans; Zof.

Ⅰ J Fritz (*Sonoma*, California) Serious producer of *Dry Creek Sauvignon Blanc* that actually does repay aging.

Frizzante [freet-zan-tay] (Italy) Semi-sparkling, especially *Lambrusco*.

Ⅰ Frog's Leap (*Napa Valley*, California) Winery with a fine sense of humor (their slogan is "Time's fun when you're having flies".). Tasty *Zinfandel*, "wild yeast" *Chardonnay*, and unusually good *Sauvignon Blanc*. ★★★★ Cabernet Sauvignon 1999 $$$

G

I Fronsac/Canon Fronsac [fron-sak] (*Bordeaux*, France). Among the oldest and hilliest parts of Bordeaux – and source of rich, intense wines. They are rarely subtle. However, they can often represent some of the best buys in *Bordeaux*. Canon Fronsac is thought by some to be the better of the pair. *Ch. Canon*; Cassagne; la Vieille; Arnauton; Mayne-Vieil; *Dalem*; Fontenil.

Frontignan [fron-tin-yo'n] (France) Source of sweet, fortified Muscat Vin Doux Naturel. Usually lacks the finesse of Muscat de Beaumes des Venise.

I Ch. de Fuissé [duh fwee-say] (*Burgundy*, France) Jean-Jacques Vincent makes wines comparable to some of the best of the *Côte d'Or*. The *Vieilles Vignes* can last as long as a good *Chassagne-Montrachet*; the other *cuvées* run it a close race. ★★★ 2000 Château de Fuissé Pouilly-Fuissé.

Fumé Blanc [fyoo-may blahnk] Name originally adapted from *Pouilly Blanc Fumé* by *Robert Mondavi* to describe his California oaked *Sauvignon*. Now widely used – though not exclusively – in the New World for this style.

Furmint [foor-mint] (*Tokaji*, Hungary) Lemony white grape, used in Hungary for *Tokaji* and, given modern winemaking, good dry wines. See *Royal Tokaji Wine Co* and *Disznókö*.

I Rudolf Fürst [foorst] (*Franken*, Germany) One of Germany's best producers of ripe, red, *Pinot Noir Spätburgunder*, and lovely floral *Riesling*. ★★★★ Bürgstadt Centgrafenberg Riesling Spätlese 2001 $$$

I Fürstlich Castell'sches Domänenamt [foorst-likh kas-tel-shes doh-mehnen-amt] (*Franken*, Germany) Prestigious producer of typically full-bodied dry whites from the German *Anbaugebiet* of *Franken*.

Fûts de Chêne (élévé en) [foo duh shayne] (France) Oak barrels (aged in).

Futures See En Primeur.

G

I Ch. la Gaffelière [gaf-fuh-lyehr] (*St. Emilion Premier Grand Cru, Bordeaux*, France) Lightish-bodied but well-made wines. Not to be confused with *Ch. Canon la Gaffelière*. Site of Roman viticultural remains.

I Dom. Jean-Noël Gagnard [jon noh-wel gan-yahr] (*Burgundy*, France) A *domaine* with vineyards across *Chassagne-Montrachet*. There is also some *Santenay*. ★★★★ Chassagne-Montrachet Morgeot 1999 $$$

I Jacques Gagnard-Delagrange [gan-yahr duh lag-ronzh] (*Burgundy*, France) A top-class producer who favors a light touch with oak. *Blain-Gagnard* and *Fontaine-Gagnard* are good estates owned by his daughters.

I Gaia [gai-ee-yahr] (*Nemea*, Greece) Up-and-coming modern estate.

Gaillac [gai-yak] (*South-West* France) Light, fresh, good-value reds and (sweet, dry and slightly sparkling) whites, produced using *Gamay* and *Sauvignon* grapes, as well as the indigenous *Mauzac*. The reds can rival *Beaujolais*. Ch. Clement Ternes; Labastide de Levis; Domaine de Gineste.

I Pierre Gaillard [gai-yahr] (*Rhône*, France) A top class producer of *Côte Rôtie, St. Joseph,* and *Condrieu*. ★★★★ Côte-Rôtie 2000 $$$

I Gainey Vineyard [gay-nee] (*Santa Barbara*, California) Classy *Merlot, Pinot,* and *Chardonnay*.

I Gaja [gai-yah] (*Piedmont*, Italy) In 1999, Angelo Gaja, the man who proved that wines from *Barbaresco* could sell for higher prices than top-class *clarets*, let alone the supposedly classier neighbors *Barolo*, announced that his highly prized – and priced – individual vineyard *Barbaresco* would henceforth be sold under the *Langhe* denomination. This would, he argued, focus attention on his excellent blended *Barolo* and *Barbaresco*. Whatever their legal handle, questioning the price of these wines is like querying the cost of a Ferrari. ★★★★★ Langhe Sori Tildin 1998 $$$$

Galestro [gah-less-troh] (*Tuscany*, Italy) The light white of the *Chianti* region. Antinori; Frescobaldi.

G

E & J Gallo [gal-loh] (*Central Valley*, California) Producer of 60 percent of the California harvest. The top end *Cabernet* and (particularly impressive) *Chardonnay* from individual "ranch" vineyards and Gallo's "Northern *Sonoma* Estate", a piece of land which was physically recontoured by their bulldozers. The Turning Leaf wines are good too, at their level, as are the California and Australian wines sold under the Garnet Point label. Ecco Domani is a new label for Italian-style wines. The basic range, though much improved and widely stocked, is still pretty ordinary, and the Carlo Rossi wines are strictly for those on a very tight budget. ✦✦✦✦ **Ernest & Julio Gallo Two Rock Vineyard Chardonnay 2000 $$$**; ✦✦✦✦ **Frei Ranch Cabernet Sauvignon 1997 $$**

Gamay [ga-may] (*Beaujolais*, France) Light-skinned grape traditional to *Beaujolais* where it is used to make fresh and fruity reds for early drinking, usually by the *carbonic maceration* method, and more serious *cru* wines that resemble light *Burgundy*. Also successful in California (*J Lohr*), Australia (*Sorrenberg*), and South Africa (*Fairview*).

Gamay [ga-may] (California) Confusingly unrelated to the *Gamay*.

Gamey Smell or taste oddly reminiscent of hung game – associated with *Pinot Noir, Tempranillo*, and *Syrah*. Sometimes partly attributable to the combination of those grapes' natural characteristics with careless use of *sulfur dioxide*. Another explanation can be the presence of a vineyard infection called *Brettanomyces*, feared in California but often unnoticed in France where gamey wines are (sometimes approvingly) said to "renarder" – to smell of fox.

Gamza [gam-zah] (Bulgaria) Local name for the Kadarka grape of Hungary.

Gancia [gan-chee-yah] (*Piedmont*, Italy) Reliable producer of *Asti* and good dry *Pinot* di *Pinot*, as well as *Pinot Blanc* sparkling wine.

Garage Wine/ry Tiny production, hand-made, ultraconcentrated wine named after Ch. Valandraud, which was made in the owner's garage.

Vin de Pays du Gard [doo gahr'] (*Languedoc-Roussillon*, France) Fresh, undemanding red and rosé wines from the southern part of the *Rhône*. Drink young, and quite possibly chilled.

Garganega [gahr-GAN-nay-gah] (Italy) White grape at its best – and worst – in *Soave* in the *Veneto*. In the right site and when not overcropped, it produces interesting almondy flavors. Otherwise the wines it makes are simply light and dull. Now being blended with *Chardonnay*.

Garnacha [gahr-na-cha] (Spain and France) See *Grenache*.

Garrafeira [gah-rah-fay-rah] (Portugal) Indicates a producer's *"reserve"* wine, which has been selected and given extra time in cask (minimum two years) and bottle (minimum one year).

Garvey [gahr-vay] (*Jerez*, Spain) Old-established sherry producer, most famous for good San Patricio fino.

Vincent Gasse [gass] (*Rhône*, France) Next to the La Landonne vineyard and producing superb, concentrated, inky black wines.

Gattinara [Gat-tee-nah-rah] (*Piedmont*, Italy) Red *DOC* from the *Nebbiolo* – varying in quality but generally full-flavoured and dry. Travaglini.

Domaine Gauby [Goh-Bee] (*Côtes de Roussillon*, France) Serious *Roussillon* reds and (*Muscat*) whites. The Muntada *Syrah* is the top *cuvée*.

Gavi [gah-vee] (*Piedmont*, Italy) Often unexceptional *Cortese*. Compared by Italians to white *Burgundy*, with which it and the more ambitious, creamily pleasant Gavi del Comune di Gavi and Gavi di Gavi share a propensity for high prices. La Chiara; San Bartolomeo; Produttori di Gavi; Pio Cesare.

Ch. le Gay [luh gay] (*Pomerol, Bordeaux*, France) Good *Moueix* property with intense complex wine.

Ch. Gazin [Ga-zan] (*Pomerol, Bordeaux*, France) Increasingly polished since the mid-1980s.

Geelong [zhee-long] (*Victoria*, Australia) Cool region pioneered by Idyll Vineyards (makers of old-fashioned reds) and rapidly attracting notice with Clyde Park and with *Bannockburn's* and *Scotchman Hill's* *Pinot Noirs*. Bannockburn; By Farr; Prince Albert; Scotchmans Hill; Shadowfax.

G

Geisenheim [gi-zen-hime] (*Rheingau,* Germany) Home of the German Wine Institute wine school, once one of the best in the world, but now overtaken by more progressive seats of learning in France, California, and Australia.

� **Ch. de la Genaiserie** [Jeh-nay-seh-Ree] (*Loire,* France) Classy, lusciously honeyed, single-vineyard wines from *Coteaux du Layon.*

Generoso [zheh-neh-roh-soh] (Spain) Fortified or dessert wine.

Genève [jer-nev] (Switzerland) Region best known for high quality, if often lightweight, *Gamay* and slightly sparkling "Perlan" *Chasselas.*

� **Gentilini** [zhen-tee-lee-nee] (*Cephalonia,* Greece) One of Greece's best new wave producers, Nick Cosmetatos makes impressive modern white wines, using both classic Greek grapes and French varieties.

� **JM Gerin** [ger-an] (*Rhône,* France) A producer of good modern *Côte Rôtie* and *Condrieu;* uses new oak to make powerful, long-lived wines.

� **Gerovassilou** [jeh-roh-vah-see-loo] (*Cephalonia,* Greece) Producer of successful new wave whites, including impressive *Viognier.*

� Gevrey-Chambertin [zheh-vray shom-behr-tan] (*Burgundy,* France) Best-known big red *Côte de Nuits commune;* very variable, but still capable of superb, plummy, cherryish wine. The top *Grand Cru* is *Le Chambertin* but, in the right hands, *Premiers Crus* like Les Cazetiers can beat this and the other *Grands Crus. Denis Bachelet; Albert Bichot; Alain Burguet;* Bourrée (Vallet); *Champy,* Charlopin; *Bruno Clair;* P. Damoy; *Joseph Drouhin; Dugat-Py; Dujac; Leroy; Château de Marsannay; Denis Mortet;* Henri Rebourseau; *Roty; Rossignol-Trapet; Armand Rousseau;* Marc Roy; Gérard Seguin.

🍇 **Gewürztraminer** [geh-voort-strah-mee-nehr] White (well, slightly pink) grape, making dry-to-sweet, full, oily-textured, spicy wine. Best in *Alsace* (where it is spelled Gewurztraminer, without the umlaut accent) but also grown in Australasia, Italy, the US, and Eastern Europe. Instantly recognizable by its parma-violets-and-lychees character. *Alsace; Casablanca.*

� **Geyser Peak** [Gih-Suhr] (*Alexander Valley,* California) Australian winemaker Darryl Groom (who now has his own Australian label) revolutionized Californian thinking with his *Semillon-Chardonnay,* and reds with an Australian attitude toward ripe *tannin.* Canyon Road is the good-value *second label.* ★★★★★ **Alexander Valley Reserve Meritage 1999 $$$**

� Ghemme [gem-may] (*Piedmont,* Italy) Spicy *Nebbiolo* usually unfavorably compared to its neighbor Gattinara. Cantalupo is the star producer.

� **Ghiaie della Furba** see *Capezzana.*

� **Giaconda** [zhee-ya-kon-dah] (*Bechworth, Victoria,* Australia) Small winery hidden away in the hills. Sells out of its impressive *Pinot Noir* and Burgundian *Chardonnay en primeur.* The *Cabernet* is fine too. ★★★ **Chardonnay 2000 $$$$**

� **Bruno Giacosa** [zhee-yah-koh-sah] (*Piedmont,* Italy) Stunning winemaker with a large range, including *Barolos* (Vigna Rionda in best years) and *Barbarescos* (Santo Stefano, again, in best years). Recent success with whites, including a *Spumante.*

� **Gie les Rameaux** [lay ram-moh] (*Corsica,* France) One of this island's top producers.

� **Giesen** [gee-sen] (*Canterbury,* New Zealand) Small estate, with particularly appley *Riesling* (plus a late harvest version) from *Canterbury,* and *Sauvignon* from *Marlborough.* ★★★★ **Marlborough Reserve Barrel Selection Chardonnay $$$**

� Gigondas [zhee gon-dass] (*Rhône,* France) *Côtes du Rhône commune,* with good-value, spicy/peppery, blackcurranty reds which show the *Grenache* at its best. A good competitor for nearby Châteauneuf. Dom des Bosquets; Brusset; de Cabasse; du Cayron; *Delas;* Font-Sane; Entrefaux; des Espiers; les Goubert; *Guigal;* Pochon; *Sorrel;* de Thalabert; *Vidal-Fleury.*

☐ **Ch. Gilette** [zheel-lette] (*Sauternes, Bordeaux,* France) Eccentric, unclassified but of classed-growth quality *Sauternes* kept in tank (rather than cask) for 20 or 30 years. Rare, expensive, worth it. The current vintage is the 1981!

G

Gimblett Road (*Hawkes Bay*, New Zealand). Recent appellation for New Zealand – including the best (though arguably not *all* the best land in *Hawkes Bay*. *Craggy Range*; Matariki; Trinity Hill.

Ginestet [jeen-nes-stay] (*Bordeaux*, France) Huge *Bordeaux* merchant.

Gippsland [gip-sland] (*Victoria*, Australia) Up-and-coming coastal region where *Bass Philip* and *Nicholson River* are producing fascinating and quite European-style wines. Watch out for some of Australia's finest *Pinot Noirs*.

♈ Vincent Girardin [van-son zhee-rahr-dan] (*Burgundy*, France) Dynamic *Santenay* producer and (since 1996) *négociant*, with vines in several other *communes*. ★★★★ Rully Blanc 1er Cru Les Cloux 2001 $$

Giropalette [zhee-roh-pal-let] Large machine which automatically and highly efficiently replaces the human beings who used to perform the task of *remuage*. Used by most *Champagne* houses which, needless to say, prefer to conceal them from visiting tourists.

♈ Camille Giroud [kah-mee zhee-roo] (*Burgundy*, France) Traditional *négociant* with small stocks of great mature wine that go a long way to prove that good *Burgundy* really doesn't need oak to taste good. Purchase in 2002 by a US consortium headed by superstar Napa wine producer Ann *Colgin* should – paradoxically – guarantee continuity.

Gisborne [giz-bawn] (New Zealand) North Island vine-growing area since the 1920s. Cool, wettish climate seems to suit fruit salady *Chardonnay*. An ideal partner for *Marlborough* in blends. *Corbans*; Kim Crawford; Matawhero; *Matua Valley*; Millton; Montana; Revington; Tohu Wines.

♈ Ch. Giscours [zhees-koor] (*Margaux 3ème Cru Classé, Bordeaux*, France) Recently-bought *Margaux* property which is only (since 1999) beginning to offer the quality associated with the vintages of the late 1970s. A good 2001.

♈ Louis Gisselbrecht [gees-sel-brekt] (*Alsace*, France) Recommendable grower and *negociant* which, like cousin Willy, has good vines in the Frankstein *Grand Cru*.

♈ Givry [zheev-ree] (*Burgundy*, France) *Côte Chalonnaise commune*, making typical and affordable, if rather jammily rustic, reds and creamy whites. French wine snobs recall that this was one of King Henri IV's favourite wines, forgetting the fact that a) he had many such favourites dotted all over France and b) his mistress – of whom he also probably had several – happened to live here. Bourgeon; Derain; *Joblot*; Lumpp; Mouton; Ragot; Clos Salomon; Steinmaier; Thénard.

♈ Glen Carlou [kah-loo] (*Paarl*, South Africa) Small-scale winery with rich, oily, oaky *Chardonnay*. ★★★★★ Glen Carlou Shiraz 2002 $$.

♈ Glen Ellen (*Sonoma Valley*, California) Dynamic firm producing large amounts of commercial tropical fruit juice-like *Chardonnay* under its "Proprietor's Reserve" label. Reds are better value.

Glenrowan [glen-roh-wan] (*Victoria*, Australia) Area near *Rutherglen* with a similar range of excellent *liqueur Muscats* and *Tokays*.

♈ Ch. Gloria [glaw-ree-yah] (*St. Julien Cru Bourgeois, Bordeaux*, France) One of the first of the super *Crus Bourgeois*. Now back on form.

♈ Golan Heights Winery [goh-lan] (Israel) California expertise is used to produce good Kosher *Cabernet* and *Muscat*. Labels include Gamla, Golan, and Yarden (used for the top wines).

♈ Goldwater Estate (*Auckland*, New Zealand) *Bordeaux*-like red wine specialist on *Waiheke Island* whose wines are expensive but every bit as good as many similarly-priced Californian offerings. The *Sauvignon Blanc* is fine too, if leaner than most New Zealand examples.

♈ La Gomerie [lah goh'm-ree] (*Bordeaux*, France) 100 percent Merlot garage wine produced by the owners of Ch. Beau-Séjour-Bécot.

♈ Gonzalez Byass [gon-thah-leth bee-yass] (*Jerez*, Spain) If *sherry* is enjoying a comeback, this company deserves much of the credit. Producer of the world's best-selling *fino, Tio Pepe* – and a range of fine, complex, traditional *sherries*. ★★★★★ Apostoles 30 Year Old Palo Cortado $$

G

Gordon Brothers (*Washington State*) Grapegrowers-turned-winemakers, and now a name to look for when shopping for well-made *Washington State Merlot* and *Chardonnay*

Gosset [gos-say] (*Champagne*, France) The oldest house in *Champagne* producing some marvellous and very long-lived *cuvées*, particularly the Celebris. ★★★★ 1995 Celebris $$$

Henri Gouges [Gooj] (*Burgundy*, France) Long-established *Nuits St. Georges* estate, producing some truly classic, long-lived wines. ★★★★★ Nuits-St.-Georges Les St. Georges 1999 $$$

Marquis de Goulaine [goo-layn] (*Loire*, France) One of the best producers of *Muscadet* – and a butterfly museum to boot.

Goulburn Valley [gohl-boorn] (*Victoria*, Australia) Small, long-established region, now known as Nagambie and reigned over by the respectively ancient and modern *Ch. Tahbilk* and *Mitchelton*, both of whom make great *Marsanne*, though in very different styles. Also Osicka; Plunkett; David Traeger; McPherson. ★★★★ Tahbilk Marsanne 2001 $$

Gould Campbell [goold] (*Douro*, Portugal) Underrated member of the same stable as *Dow's*, *Graham's*, and *Warre's*.

Goumenissa [goo-may-nee-sah] (Greece) Tough Macedonia reds.

Goundrey [gown-dree] (*Western* Australia) Winery in *Mount Barker* whose wines rarely match those of its neighbor Plantagenet, but are showing improvement. ★★★★ Reserve Chardonnay 2001 $$

Graach [grahkh] (*Mosel-Saar-Ruwer*, Germany) *Mittelmosel* village producing fine wines. Best known for its *Himmelreich* vineyard. *Deinhard; JJ Prüm; Max Ferd Richter; Von Kesselstadt.*

Grace Family Vineyards (*Napa*, California) Small quantities – occasionally fewer than 100 cases – of *Cabernet* whose rarity makes for prices of $300-400 per bottle. (If potatoes were harder to grow, they'd cost more, too.)

Viña Gracia [veen-yah gra-see-yah] (Chile) Rapidly-improving venture. Good Cabernet Reserva; look out for *Syrah* and *Mourvèdre* in the future. ★★★ Cabernet Sauvignon - Carmenère "Vision" 2002 $$

Graham [gray-yam] (*Douro*, Portugal) Sweetly delicate wines that can outclass the supposedly finer but heftier *Dow's*. Malvedos is erroneously thought of as the single *quinta*. ★★★★★ 1985 Late-Bottled Vintage $$

Alain Graillot [al-lan grai-yoh] (*Rhône*, France) Progressive-minded producer who should be applauded for shaking up the sleepy, largely undistinguished *appellation* of *Crozes-Hermitage*, using grapes from rented vineyards. All the reds are excellent, and La Guiraude is the wine from the top vineyard. ★★★★ 1999 Crozes Hermitage $$

Grampians (*Victoria*, Australia) New name for *Great Western*.

Ch. Grand-Corbin-Despagne [gro'n cor-ba'n day-span'y] (*Bordeaux*, France) *St-Emilion Grand Cru* that used to be a *Grand Cru Classé* and is determined to be so again. Quality improving year by year; value is excellent.

Gran Reserva [gran rays-sehr-vah] (Spain) Wine aged for a designated number of years in wood and, in theory, only produced in the best *vintages*. On occasion dried-out and less worthwhile than *Crianza* or *Reserva*.

Grand Cru [gron kroo] (France) Prepare to be confused. Term referring to the finest vineyards and the – supposedly – equally fine wine made in them. It is an official designation in *Bordeaux, Burgundy, Champagne*, and *Alsace*, but its use varies. In *Alsace* where there are 50 or so *Grand Cru* vineyards, some are more convincingly grand than others. In Burgundy, *Grand Cru* vineyards with their own *ACs*, e.g., *Montrachet*, do not need to carry the name of the village (e.g., *Chassagne-Montrachet*) on their label. Where these regions apply the designation to pieces of soil, in *Bordeaux* it applies to châteaux whose vineyards can be bought and sold. More confusingly, still *St. Emilion* can be described as either *Grand Cru, Grand Cru Classé* – or both – or *Premier Grand Cru Classé*. Just remember that in St. Emilion, the words *Grand Cru* by themselves provide absolutely no indication of quality at all.

G

Ch. Grand Mayne [Gron-mayn] (*St. Emilion Grand Cru, Bordeaux, France*) Producer of rich, deeply flavorsome, modern *St. Emilion*. A candidate for promotion to *Premier Grand Cru* status.

Ch. du Grand Moulas [gron moo-lahs] (*Rhône, France*) Very classy *Côtes du Rhône* property with unusually complex red wines.

Grand Vin [gron van] (*Bordeaux, France*) The first (quality) wine of an estate – as opposed to its *second label*.

Ch. Grand-Pontet [gron pon-tay] (*St. Emilion Grand Cru Classé, Bordeaux, France*) Rising star with showy wines.

Ch. Grand-Puy-Ducasse [gron pwee doo-kass] (*Pauillac 5ème Cru Classé, Bordeaux, France*) Excellent wines from an over-performing fifth growth *Pauillac* property.

Ch. Grand-Puy-Lacoste [gron pwee lah-kost] (*Pauillac 5ème Cru Classé, Bordeaux, France*) Top-class fifth growth owned by the Borie family of *Ducru-Beaucaillou* and now right up there among the *Super Seconds*.

Grande Rue [grond-roo] (*Burgundy, France*) Recently promoted *Grand Cru* in Vosne-Romanée, across the way from Romanée-Conti (hence the promotion). The Dom. Lamarche to which this *monopole* belongs is a long-term underperformer that is now beginning to show signs of improvement.

Grandes Marques [grond mahrk] (*Champagne, France*) Once-official designation for "big name" *Champagne* houses, irrespective of the quality of their wines. Now, although the "Syndicat" of which they were members has been disbanded, the expression is still quite widely used.

Grands-Echézeaux [grons EH-shay-zoh] (*Burgundy, France*) One of the best *Grand Crus* in *Burgundy*; and supposedly better than *Echézeaux*. The *Domaine de la Romanée-Conti* is a famous producer here.

Grange [graynzh] (*South Australia*) *Penfolds'* and Australia's greatest wine – "The Southern Hemisphere's only first growth" – pioneered by Max Schubert in the early 1950s following a visit to Europe. Although Schubert was aiming to match top *Bordeaux*, he used *Shiraz* and American (rather than French) oak barrels and a blend of grapes from 70-year-old vines sited in several South Australian regions. Now very popular in the US. It needs time for its true complexity to become apparent. ★★★★★ **1998 $$$$**

Dom de la Grange des Pères [gronj day pehr] (*Languedoc, France*) A competitor for *Mas de Daumas Gassac*. Vin de Pays de l'Hérault that's better than many from a smart appellation.

Grangehurst [graynzh-huhrst] (*Stellenbosch, South Africa*) Concentrated modern reds from a small winery converted from the family squash court! Expanding. Good *Cabernet* and *Pinotage*.

Granite Belt (*Queensland, Australia*) High altitude vineyards but still not cool as cool goes. Best for reds and *Semillon*.

Weingut Grans-Fassian [grans-fass-yan] (*Mosel, Germany*) Improving estate with some really fine, classic wine – especially at a supposedly basic level.

Grão Vasco [grow vash-koo] (*Dão, Portugal*) Large volume, reliable brand of *Dão* from *Sogrape*.

Yves Grassa [gras-sah] (*Southwest, France*). Pioneering producer of *Vin de Pays des Côtes de Gascogne* – moving from *Colombard* and *Ugni Blanc* into *Sauvignon* and *late-harvest* styles.

Elio Grasso [eh-lee-yoh grah-so] (*Piedmont, Italy*) Producer of fine single-vineyard *Barolo* (Casa Maté and Chiniera), *Barbera, Dolcetto*, and *Chardonnay*.

Silvio Grasso [sil-vee-yoh grah-so] (*Piedmont, Italy*) Another top class Grasso. Look out for the Bricco Luciani and Ciabot Manzoni *Barolos*.

Alfred Gratien [gras-see-yen] (*Champagne, France*) Good *Champagne* house, using traditional methods. Also owner of *Loire* sparkling winemaker Gratien et Meyer, based in *Saumur*.

G

🍇 **Grauerburgunder** [grow-urh-buhr-goon-duhr] (Germany) Another name for *Pinot Gris*. **Müller-Catoi; Wolf.**

🍷 **Dom. la Grave** [lah grahv] (*Graves, Bordeaux,* France) Small property in the *Graves* with a growing reputation for 100 percent *Sémillon* whites.

🍷 **La Grave à Pomerol** [lah grahv ah pom-rohl] (*Pomerol, Bordeaux,* France) One of the excellent Christian *Mouiex's* characteristically stylish estates that shows off *Pomerol's* plummy-cherry fruit at its best.

🍷 **Grave del Friuli** [grah-veh del free-yoo-lee] (*Friuli-Venezia Giulia,* Italy) *DOC* for young-drinking reds and whites. *Cabernet, Merlot,* and *Chardonnay* are increasingly successful.

🍷 **Graves** [grahv] (*Bordeaux,* France) Large region producing vast quantities of red and white, ranging from good to indifferent. The best whites come from *Pessac-Léognan* in the northern part of the region. Reds can have a lovely raspberryish character. **Ch. d'Archambeau; de Chantegrive; Clos Floridène; Lesparre; Rahoul; du Seuil; Villa Bel Air.**

🍷 **Josko Gravner** [grahv-nehr] (*Friuli-Venezia Giulia,* Italy) Innovative producer with brilliant oaked *Chardonnay* and *Sauvignon Blanc* produced in *Collio* but not under the rules of that denomination. The blended white Breg, which includes no fewer than six varieties, is good too, as is Rujino, a mixture of *Merlot* and *Cabernet Sauvignon.*

Great Western (*Victoria,* Australia) Old name for region noted for *Seppelt's* sparkling wines including the astonishing "Sparkling *Burgundy*" *Shirazes,* for *Best's* and for the wines of *Mount Langi Ghiran.* Now renamed *Grampians,* though I suspect it will take time for enthusiasts to get used to the new name.

🍇 **Grechetto** [grek-keh-toh] (Italy) Subtly spicy white grape used to fine effect in *Umbria* by *Adanti, Falesco,* Goretti, and Palazzone. **Sergio Mottura.**

🍷 **Greco di Tufo** [greh-koh dee too-foh] (*Campania,* Italy) From *Campania,* best-known white from the ancient Greco grape; dry, characterfully herby, southern wine. **Botromagno; Librandi; Mastroberardino; Feudi di San Gregoria.**

Greece This country is finally, if belatedly, beginning to exploit the potential of a set of grapes grown nowhere else. Unfortunately, as Greece begins to rid itself of its taste for the stewed, oxidized styles of the past, the modern wines are so popular in the stylish restaurants in Athens that they tend to be both expensive and hard to find overseas. **Amethystos; Antonopoulos; Boutari; Ch. Carras; Gaia; Gentilini; Gerovassilou; Hatzimichalis; Ktima; Lazarides; Papantonis; Skouras; Strofilia.**

🍷 **Green Point** (*Yarra Valley,* Australia) See *Dom. Chandon.*

🍷 **Green & Red** (*Napa Valley,* California) Rising star with good *Zinfandel.*

🍷 **Green on Green** (*Western Cape,* South Africa) Up and coming Sémillon label *from Jack & Knox.*

🍇 **Grenache** [greh-nash] Red grape of the *Rhône* (aka *Garnacha* in Spain) making spicy, peppery, full-bodied wine, provided yields are kept low. Also used to make rosés across Southern France, Australia, and California.

🍇 **Grenache Blanc** [greh-nash blon] Widely grown in Southern France and Spain, where it is used to make mostly dull, slightly peppery, white wine. Treated with love and care, however, it can add welcome spice to a blend.

🍷 **Ch. Gressier-Grand-Poujeaux** [gress-yay gron' poo-joh] (Bordeaux, France) Moulis Cru Bourgeois making wine of good structure and fruit.

🍷 **Marchesi de Gresy** [mah-kay-see day greh-see] (*Piedmont,* Italy) Good producer of single-vineyard *Barbaresco.* ✮✮✮✮ **Camp Gros 1997 $$$**

🍷 **Ch. Greysac** [gray-sak] (*Bordeaux,* France) Médoc *Cru Bourgeois* with a good, if slightly rustic style.

🍷 **Grgich Hills** [guhr-gich] (*Napa Valley,* California) Pioneering producer of *Cabernet Sauvignon, Chardonnay,* and *Fumé Blanc.* The name is a concatenation of the two founders – Mike Grgich and Austin Hills, rather than a topographical feature.

🍷 **Miljenko Grgich** [mell-yen-koh guhr-gich] (Croatia) The coast of Dalmatia gets the *Grgich Hills* treatment – and a Californian rediscovers his roots.

G

✤ **Grignolino** [green-yoh-lee-noh] (*Piedmont,* Italy) Red grape and modest but refreshing cherryish wine, e.g. the *DOCs* Grignolino d'Asti and Grignolino del Monferrato Casalese. Drink young. **Pio Cesare.**

✲ **Ch. Grillet** [gree-yay] (*Rhône,* France) *Appellation* consisting of a single estate and producer of improving *Viognier* white. The best producers in neighboring *Condrieu* still offer better value.

✲ **Marqués de Griñon** [green-yon] (*La Mancha, Rioja, Ribera del Duero,* Spain/Argentina) Dynamic exception to the dull *La Mancha* rule, making wines, with the help of *Michel Rolland,* which can outclass *Rioja.* The juicy *Cabernet Merlot* and fresh white *Rueda* have been joined by Durius, a blend from *Ribera del Duero,* an exceptional new *Syrah* and an extraordinary *Petit Verdot.* Look out too for new wines from Argentina.
★★★★★ Dominio de Valdepusa Syrah 2000 $$$

✲ **Griotte-Chambertin** [gree-yot] (*Burgundy,* France) see *Chambertin.*

✲ **Bernard Gripa** [gree-pah] (*Rhône,* France) Maker of top-notch *St. Joseph* – ripe, thick, *tarry* wine that could age forever.

✲ **Jean-Louis Grippat** [gree-pah] (*Rhône,* France) The domaine has been sold to Marcel *Guigal,* but Grippat was an unusually great white *Rhône* producer in *Hermitage* and *St. Joseph.* His reds in both appellations were less stunning, but worth buying in their subtler-than-most way. Look out for his Cuvée des Hospices. *St. Joseph* Rouge.

✲ **Gristina** [gris-tee-nah] (*New York State*) Pioneering Long Island winery which has established a deserved local reputation for its *Merlot* and its *Chardonnay.* Both stand comparison with pricier California fare.

✲ **Dom. Jean Grivot** [gree-voh] (*Burgundy,* France) Top-class *Vosne-Romanée* estate whose winemaker Etienne has one of the most sensitive touches in Burgundy. ★★★★★ Echézeaux 2000 $$$

✲ **Robert Groffier** [grof-fee-yay] (*Burgundy,* France) Up-and-coming estate with top-class wines from *Chambolle-Musigny.*

✲ **Groot Constantia** [khroot-kon-stan-tee-yah] (*Constantia,* South Africa) Government-run, 300-year-old wine estate and national monument that is finally beginning to make worthwhile – if not great – wines.
★★★ Pinotage 2001 $$

✲ **Groote Post** [khroot-ter post] (*Darling,* South Africa) Blazing a trail in the "new" region of Darling in the West Coast a few miles from the Atlantic, this young estate is already producing one of the Cape's top *Sauvignon Blancs* and promising *Pinot Noir.* ★★★★ Pinot Noir 2001 $$

✲ **Dom. Anne Gros** [groh] (*Burgundy,* France) Unfortunately for one's wallet, the best wines from this *Vosne-Romanée domaine* are as expensive as they are delicious – but they are worth every cent. ★★★★★ Richebourg 2001 $$$$

✲ **Jean Gros** [groh] (*Burgundy,* France) Slightly less impressive *Vosne-Romanée* producer, but the *Clos Vougeots* are good.

✲ **Michel Gros** [groh] (*Burgundy,* France) Another member of the Gros clan – on a roll at the moment with regular. gold medals for his well-made modern *Clos Vougeot, Nuits St Georges* and *Vosne Romanée* at the *International Wine Challenge.* ★★★★★ Clos Vougeot Grand Maupertuis $$$$ ★★★★★ Vosne Romanée 1er Cru Brûlées 2001 $$$$

✤ **Gros Lot/Grolleau** [groh-loh] (*Loire,* France) The workhorse black grape of the *Loire,* particularly in *Anjou,* used to make white, rosé, and sparkling *Saumur.*

✤ **Gros Plant (du Pays Nantais)** [groh-plon doo pay-yee non-tay] (*Loire,* France) Light, sharp white *VDQS* wine from the western *Loire.* In all but the best hands, serves to make even a poor *Muscadet* look good.

✲ **Grosset** [gros-set] (*Clare Valley,* South Australia) White (*Chardonnay, Semillon,* and especially *Riesling*) specialist now making great reds (the Gaia red *Bordeaux*-blend and lovely *Pinot Noir*). Give all wines time to develop. (Mrs. Grosset is responsible for the similarly brilliant *Mount Horrocks* wines). Both are leading the move to putting their wine into "*Stelvin*" screwcaps.

G

Grosslage [gross-lah-guh] (Germany) Wine district, the third subdivision after *Anbaugebiet* (e.g., *Rheingau*) and *Bereich* (e.g., *Nierstein*). For example, *Michelsberg* is a *Grosslage* of the *Bereich Piesport*.

☗ **Groth** [grahth] (*Napa Valley*, California) Serious producer of quality *Cabernet* and *Chardonnay*.

☗ **Grove Mill** (New Zealand) Young *Marlborough* winery with good *Sauvignon Blanc, Chardonnay*, and *Riesling*.

☗ **Ch. Gruaud-Larose** [groo-oh lah-rohz] (*St. Julien 2ème Cru Classé, Bordeaux*, France) Now under the same ownership as Chasse-Spleen, and right on form in 2000. The second wine is "Le Sarget".

🍇 **Gruner Veltliner** [groo-nuhr felt-lee-nuhr] Spicy white grape of Austria and Eastern Europe, producing light, fresh, aromatic wine – and for *Willi Opitz* an extraordinary *late harvest* version. Knoll; *Kracher;* Lang; Metternich-Sándor; *Opitz; Pichler; Prager;* Schuster; Steininger; Johann Topf Strasser.

☗ **Bodegas Guelbenzu** [guhl-bent-zoo] (*Navarra*, Spain) Starry new wave producer of rich red wines using local grapes and *Cabernet*. Has just left the Navarra DO, preferring to rely on the prestige of its brand to attract customers. ★★★★ Evo 2001 $$$

☗ **Guerrieri-Rizzardi** [gwer-reh-ree rit-zar-dee] (*Veneto*, Italy) Organic producer, with good rather than great *Amarone* and *Soave Classico*.

☗ **Guffens-Heynen** [goof-fens ay-na(n)] (*Burgundy*, France) Rising star in *Pouilly-Fuissé* and the man behind the *Verget* empire. Look out for wines (from Burgundy and the Jura) from his partner Jean Rijckaert.

☗ **E Guigal** [gee-gahl] (*Rhône*, France) Still the yardstick for *Rhône* reds, despite increased competition from *Chapoutier* and *Delas*. Extraordinarily pricey single-vineyard La Mouline, La Landonne, and La Turque wines from *Côte Rôtie* and Château d'Ampuis wines are still way ahead of the field, and the "Brune et Blonde" blend of grapes from two hillsides remains a benchmark for this *appellation*. (An appellation of which, Guigal now owns a substantial portion, following the purchase of the Grippat and de Vallouit estates). The basic red and white *Côtes du Rhône* are less exciting than they have been, but the *Condrieu* remains a great example of Viognier. ★★★★★ Côte-Rôtie La Landonne 1998$$

☗ **Guimaraens** [gee-mah-rens] (*Douro*, Portugal) See *Fonseca*.

☗ **Ch. Guiraud** [gee-roh] (*Sauternes Premier Cru Classé, Bordeaux*, France) *Sauternes* classed growth, recently restored to original quality. Good wines but rarely among the most complex sweet *Bordeaux*. An impressive 2001 (like most of its neighbors).

Gumpoldskirchen [goom-pohld-skeerk-ken] (Austria) Part of *Thermen* region noted for its spicy sweet wines made from *Rotgipfler* and *Zierfandler* grapes.

☗ **Weingut Gunderloch** [goon-duhr-lokh] (*Rheinhessen*, Germany) One of the few estates to make *Rheinhessen* wines of truly reliable quality. ★★★★ Jean Baptiste Riesling Kabinett 2000 $$

☗ **Gundlach-Bundschu** [guhnd-lakh buhnd-shoo] (*Sonoma Valley*, California) Good, well-made, juicy *Merlot* and spicy *Zinfandel*.

☗ **Louis Guntrum** [goon-troom] (*Rheinhessen*, Germany) Family-run estate with a penchant for *Silvaner*.

☗ **Ch. la Gurgue** [lah guhrg] (*Margaux Cru Bourgeois, Bordeaux*, France) *Cru Bourgeois* across the track from *Ch. Margaux*. Less impressive since the same owner's neighboring *Ch. Ferrière* has both improved and increased its production, but the 1999 and 2000 are both winners and the 2002 is good.

🍇 **Gutedel** [goot-edel] (Germany) German name for the *Chasselas* grape. Generally dull wine.

☗ **Friedrich-Wilhelm Gymnasium** [free-drikh vil-helm-gim-nahz-yuhm] (*Mosel*, Germany) Big-name estate generally making good, rather than great, wine.

H

℗ Weingut Fritz Haag [hahg] (*Mosel-Saar-Ruwer,* Germany) Superlative small estate with classic *Rieslings.* ✶✶✶✶ **Riesling Kabinett Mosel-Saar-Ruwer Brauneberger Juffer-Sonnenuhr 2001 $$$**

℗ Weingut Willi Haag [hahg] (*Mosel-Saar-Ruwer,* Germany) Until the 1960s, this was part of the same estate as *Fritz Haag,* and both domaines produce wines on the same slopes. Markus Haag who took over in 1995, is a winemaker to watch.

℗ Weingut Reinhold Haart [rine-hohld hahrt] (*Mosel,* Germany) *Piesport* star.

℗ Franz Haas (*Alto Adige,* Italy) One of Italy's growing band of innovators. His passion is complex and supple Pinot Noir, but he also makes stunning, highly scented, Moscato Rosa, *Petit Verdot,* and *Petit Manseng,* as well as novel blends such as his Manna Gewürztraminer/Chardonnay/Sauvignon. ✶✶✶✶✶ **Mitterberg Manna 2001 $$$**

Halbtrocken [hahlb-trok-en] (Germany) Off-dry. alternative to *Trocken.* Look for *QbA, Spätlese* or *Auslese* versions rather than *Kabinett* which can taste unripe.

Hallgarten [hal-gahr-ten] (*Rheingau,* Germany) Important town near *Hattenheim* producing robust wines including the (in Germany) well-regarded produce from *Schloss Vollrads.*

℗ Hamilton Russell Vineyards (*Walker Bay,* South Africa) Pioneer of impressive *Pinot Noir* and *Chardonnay* at a winery in Hermanus at the southernmost tip of the *Cape.* Now expanded to include a *second label –* Southern Right – to produce a varietal *Pinot*age, and a *Chenin*-based white. Ashbourne, the top wine, is pricey but recommendable, as is the recently launched Hanibal blend of Italian varieties and Pinot Noir.

℗ Handley Cellars (*Mendocino,* California) Fine sparkling wine producer with a particularly good pure *Chardonnay Blanc de Blanc.* The still *Chardonnay* is pretty impressive, too.

℗ Hanging Rock (*Victoria,* Australia) This winery makes Australia's biggest, butteriest sparkling wine and some pretty good reds and whites.

℗ Hanzell (*Sonoma,* California) One of the great old names of California wine, and a pioneer producer of *Chardonnay* and *Pinot Noir.* The former grape is still a major success story – in its traditional California style.

℗ Haras de Pirque (Chile) New *Maipo* estate with characterful, serious wines.

℗ BRL Hardy (*South* Australia) The second biggest wine producer in Australia, encompassing *Houghton* and *Moondah Brook* in *Western Australia, Leasingham* in the *Clare Valley, Redman* in *Coonawarra, Barossa Valley Estates* in *Barossa,* Hardy's itself, and *Ch. Reynella.* Recently taken over by the US giant Constellation Brands (*Franciscan, Ravenswood, Simi, Mt Veeder etc*) and thus now part of the biggest wine company in the world. *Hardy's* reliable range includes the commercial Nottage Hill, Stamps, Bankside, and Banrock Station, and multiregional blends, but the wines to look for are the top-of-the-line Eileen and Thomas Hardy. The *Ch. Reynella* wines from *McLaren Vale* fruit (and, in the case of the reds, using *basket presses*) are good, very lean examples of the region. Hardy's ventures in Italy (d'Istinto), France (la Baume), and Chile (Dallas Conte) are less impressive. ✶✶✶✶✶ **Eileen Hardy Shiraz 1999 $$$$**; ✶✶✶✶ **Leasingham Magnus Shiraz Cabernet Sauvignon 2000 $$**

℗ Hargrave Vineyard / Castello di Borghese (*Long Island,* New York) This 30-year-old winery put Long Island on the wine map with its Chardonnay and Merlot. It so impressed the owner of *Ch. Pichon-Lalande* when she visited that she apparently briefly considered making wine here. Since 1999 under new ownership and renamed Castello di Borghese.

Harlan Estate (*Napa Valley*, California) Fiercely pricey, small quantities of *Bordeaux*-style reds, made with input from *Michel Rolland*, and using grapes from hillside vineyards. One of the best of California's *garage wines*. Join the waiting list.

Hárslevelü [harsh-leh-veh-loo] (Hungary) White grape used in *Tokaji* and for light table wines.

Hartenberg Estate (*Stellenbosch*, South Africa) A name to watch, for rich, ripe reds (including an unusually good Shiraz) and the only example I've seen of Pontac, alias Teinturier du Cher, a seldom-grown red-fleshed French grape. Chardonnay and Riesling are fine, too.

Harveys (*Jerez*, Spain) Maker of the ubiquitous *Bristol Cream*. Other styles are unimpressive apart from the 1796 range and Club Classic.

Haskovo [hash-koh-voh] (Bulgaria) Along with the more frequently seen Stambolovo and Sakar, this is a name to look out for. All three are newly privatised cooperatives that can make good, rich, red wine.

Hattenheim [hat-ten-hime] (*Rheingau*, Germany) One of the finest villages in the *Rheingau*, with wines from producers such as *Balthasar Ress*, Von Simmern, *Schloss Rheinhartshausen*, and *Schloss Schönborn*.

Hatzimichalis [hat-zee-mikh-ahlis] (*Atalanti*, Greece) The face of future Greek winemaking? Hopefully. This self-taught producer's small estate makes variable but often top-notch *Cabernet Sauvignon*, *Merlot*, *Chardonnay*, and fresh dry Atalanti white.

Ch. Haut-Bages-Averous [oh-bahj-aveh-roo] (*Pauillac Cru Bourgeois*, *Bordeaux*, France) *Second label* of *Ch. Lynch-Bages*. Good-value black-curranty *Pauillac*.

Ch. Haut-Bages-Libéral [oh-bahj-lib-ay-ral] (*Pauillac 5ème Cru Classé*, *Bordeaux*, France) Classy small property in the same stable as *Chasse-Spleen*.

Ch. Haut-Bailly [oh bai-yee] (*Pessac-Léognan Cru Classé*, *Bordeaux*, France) Brilliant *Pessac-Léognan* property, recently sold, but still under the winemaking management of Véronique Sanders: Reliable, excellent-quality, long-lived red wines (unusually in this region, there are no whites). A stunning 1998 and 2000 and a very fine 2002.

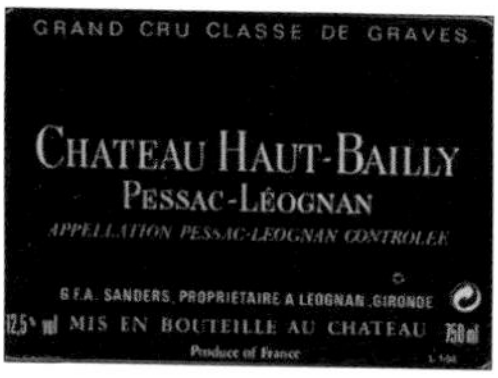
GRAND CRU CLASSE DE GRAVES
CHATEAU HAUT-BAILLY
PESSAC-LÉOGNAN
APPELLATION PESSAC-LEOGNAN CONTROLEE
S.F.A. SANDERS, PROPRIÉTAIRE A LEOGNAN, GIRONDE
MIS EN BOUTEILLE AU CHATEAU
750 ml
Produce of France

Ch. Haut-Batailley [oh-ba-tai-yee] (*Pauillac 5ème Cru Classé*, *Bordeaux*, France) Subtly-styled wine from the same stable as *Ducru-Beaucaillou* and *Grand-Puy-Lacoste*

Ch. Haut-Brion [oh bree-yon] (*Pessac-Léognan Premier Cru Classé*, *Bordeaux*, France) Pepys' favorite wine and still the only non-*Médoc* first growth. Situated in the *Graves* on the outskirts of *Bordeaux* in the shadow of the gas company. Wines can be tough and hard to judge when young, but at their best they develop a rich, fruity, perfumed character which sets them apart from their peers. 1996, 1998, 1999, and 2000 were especially good, as – comparatively – were 1993, 1994, and 1995. Even so, competition is heating up from stablemate, la *Mission-Haut-Brion*. The white is rare and often sublime.

Ch. Haut-Marbuzet [oh-mahr-boo-zay] (*St. Estèphe Cru Bourgeois*, *Bordeaux*, France) *Cru bourgeois* which thinks it's a *cru classé*. Immediately imposing wine with bags of oak. Decidedly new-wave *St. Estèphe*.

Haut-Médoc [oh-may-dok] (*Bordeaux*, France) Large *appellation* which includes nearly all of the well-known *crus classés*. Basic *Haut-Médoc* should – in theory – be better than plain *Médoc*.

Haut-Montravel [oh-mo'n rah-vel] (*South-West*, France) Rare, but potentially good alternative to *Monbazillac* and even *Sauternes*. See *Montravel*.

Haut-Poitou [oh-pwa-too] (*Loire*, France) A source of inexpensive *Sauvignon*.

Hautes Côtes de Beaune [oht-coht-duh-bohn] (*Burgundy*, France) Rustic wines from the hills above the big-name *communes*. Worth buying in good *vintages*; in poorer ones the grapes have problems ripening. The Cave des Hautes Côtes cooperative makes good examples.

H

Ⅎ **Hautes Côtes de Nuits** [oht-coht-duh-nwee] (*Burgundy*, France) This appellation produces mostly red wines that are slightly tougher than *Hautes Côtes de Beaune*.

Hawkes Bay (New Zealand) Major North Island vineyard area which, when it escapes the frequent threat of frost (a problem in 2002 and 2003) is producing top-class reds. Whites can be fine too, though rarely achieving the bite of *Marlborough*. *Babich;* Brookfields; Church Road; Cleview; *Craggy Range; Delegats; Esk Valley; Matua Valley,* Mills Reef; *Mission; Montana; Morton Estate; Ngatarawa; CJ Pask;* Sacred Hill; Sileni; *Te Mata;Trinity Hill; Vidal;Villa Maria;* Unison.

Ⅎ **Hedges** (*Washington State*) Producer of good, rich, berryish reds from a number of the best vineyards in Washington State.

Ⅎ **Dr. Heger** [hay-gehr] (*Baden,* Germany) A brilliant exponent of the *Grauerburgunder* which ripens well in this warm region of Germany.

Ⅎ **Heggies** [heg-gees] (*South* Australia) Impressive *Adelaide Hills* label in the same camp as *Yalumba.* Lovely Riesling, *Viognier, Merlot, Pinot Noir,* and sweet wines. ★★★★ Eden Valley Chardonnay 2002 $$

✤ **Heida** [hi-da] (Switzerland) Spicy Swiss grape variety, thought to be related to *Gewürztraminer.* When carefully handled, produces refreshing wines.

Ⅎ **Charles Heidsieck** [hide-seek] (*Champagne,* France) Innovative producer whose late winemaker Daniel Thibaut (*Bonnet, Piper Heidsieck*) introduced the clever notion of labeling non-*vintage* wine with a "mis en cave" bottling date. Wines are all recommendable. ★★★★★ 1990 Blanc des Millénaires $$$$; ★★★★★ 1982 Blancs de Blancs $$$$

Ⅎ **Heidsieck Dry Monopole** [hide-seek] (*Champagne,* France) Do not confuse with *Charles* or *Piper Heidsieck.* This is a subsidiary of *Mumm* and thus until 1999 controlled by Seagram. Now part of Allied Domecq (like *Montana* in New Zealand). Recent *vintages* have shown some improvement from previously unambitious levels. ★★★ Extra Dry $$$

Ⅎ **Gernot Heinrich** (*Burgenland,* Austria) Go-ahead producer in Gols, with his sights firmly set on structured dry wines.

Ⅎ **Heitz Cellars** [hites] (*Napa Valley,* California) One of the great names of California and the source of stunning Martha's Vineyard and Bella Oaks reds in the 1970s, but less impressive in more recent years. Post-1996 vintages of Martha's Vineyard are made from newly replanted (post-*phylloxera*) vines. Trailside Vineyard is a newish label for *Cabernet.*

Ⅎ **Helderberg** (*Stellenbosch,* South Africa) The mountain on which are situated some of the best vineyards in Stellenbosch, including *Vergelegen, Yonder Hill, Avontuur,* and *Cordoba.* Competes with *Simonsberg.*

Hengst (*Alsace,* France) Top-flight *Grand Cru* vineyard, especially good for *Riesling* and *Gewürztraminer.* Barmes-Buecher; Josmeyer; Zind Humbrecht.

Ⅎ **Joseph Henriot** [on-ree-yoh] (*Champagne,* France) Modern *Champagne* house producing soft, rich wines. Now also shaking things up and improving wines at its recently purchased *Bouchard Père et Fils négociant* and at the William Fèvre Chablis estate in *Burgundy.* ★★★★★ Champagne Cuvée des Enchanteleurs 1988 $$$$

Ⅎ **Henriques & Henriques** [hen-reeks] (*Madeira,* Portugal) One of the few independent producers still active in *Madeira.* Top quality. ★★★★★ 15 Year Old Verdelho $$$

Ⅎ **Henry of Pelham** (*Ontario,* Canada) One of Canada's better producers of Chardonnay – plus a rare recommendable example of the Baco Noir grape.

Ⅎ **Henschke** [hench-kee] (*Adelaide Hills,* Australia) One of the world's best. From the long-established Hill of Grace with its 140-year-old vines and (slightly less intense) Mount Edelstone *Shirazes* to the Abbott's Prayer *Merlot-Cabernet* from *Lenswood,* the *Riesling,* Cranes Chardonnay and Tilly's Vineyard white blend, there's not a poor wine here. The Henry's Seven Shiraz/Grenache/Viognier is a new wine to look out for. The reds last forever. ★★★★★ Henrys Seven 2001 $$$

℗ **Vin de Pays de l'Hérault** [Eh-roh] (*Languedoc-Roussillon*, France) Large region made famous by the Aimé Guibert's *Mas de Daumas Gassac*. Other producers such as *Grange-des-Pères* and Domaine Limbardie are following in his footsteps. ★★★★ Mas de Daumas Gassac Blanc 2002 $$

℗ **Hermitage** [ayr-mee-tazh] (*Rhône*, France) Supreme Northern *Rhône* *appellation* for long-lived pure *Syrah*. Whites are less reliable. *Belle Père & Fils; Michel Bernard; Chapoutier; Chave; Dom. Jean-Luc Colombo; Colombier; Bernard Faurie; Ferraton; Grippat; Guigal; Delas; Bernard Faurie; Jaboulet Aîné; Sorrel; Cave de Tain l'Hermitage; Marc Sorrel; Tardieu-Laurent; Vins de Vienne.*

℗ **James Herrick** [heh-rick] (*Languedoc-Roussillon*, France) Started by a dynamic Briton who brought an Australian philosophy to southern France, planting extensive *Chardonnay* vineyards and producing good-value varietal wine. Now part of Southcorp (*Penfolds* etc). ★★★ Syrah 2002 $

℗ **The Hess Collection** (*Napa Valley*, California) High-class *Cabernet* producer high in the *Mount Veeder* hills named after the owner's art collection (see *Vinopolis*). The lower-priced Hess Select *Monterey* wines are worth buying, too. ★★★★ Reserve Cabernet Sauvignon 1998 $$$

Hessische Bergstrasse [hess-ishuh behrg-strah-suh] (Germany) Smallest *Anbaugebiet* capable of fine *Eisweins* and dry *Silvaners* which can surpass those of nearby *Franken*.

℗ **Heuriger** [hoy-rig-gur] (Austria) Austria's equivalent of *Beaujolais* Nouveau – except that this newborn wine is white and sold by the carafe in cafés. Of interest if only as a taste of the way most wine used to be drunk.

℗ **Heyl zu Herrnsheim** [highl zoo hehrn-sime] (*Rheinhessen*, Germany) Organic estate in *Nierstein* with good *Riesling* from the Pettenthal vineyard.

℗ **Heymann-Löwenstein** [hay-mun lur-ven-shtine] (*Mosel-Saar-Ruwer*, Germany) A rising star with bone dry to lusciously sweet Rieslings.

℗ **Vinicola Hidalgo y Cia** [hid-algoh ee-thia] (*Jerez*, Spain) Speciality producer of impeccable dry "La Gitana" *sherry* and a great many own-label offerings. ★★★★ Palo Cortado Viejo $$

℗ **Cavas Hill** [kah-vas heel] (*Penedés*, Spain) Best-known for its sparkling wine, but also producing rich, fruity *Tempranillo* reds.

℗ **Hillebrand Estates** (*Ontario*, Canada) Highly promising *Riesling* and Bordeaux-blend red. ★★★ Trius Vidal Icewine 2000 $$.

℗ **Hill-Smith** (South Australia) Dynamic, but still very classy firm, under the same family ownership as *Pewsey Vale, Yalumba*, and *Heggies* Vineyard, and now active in Tasmania (Jansz sparkling wine), New Zealand (*Nautilus*), and California (Voss). ★★★★ NV Jansz $$$

℗ **Hillstowe** [hil-stoh] (*South Australia*) Up-and-coming producer in the *McLaren Vale*, using grapes from various parts of the region to produce stylish *Chardonnay, Sauvignon Blanc, Shiraz* and *Cabernet-Merlot*. ★★★ 1999 Udy's Mill Lenswood Chardonnay $$; ★★★ 1999 Mary's Hundred Shiraz $$$

Hilltops (*New South Wales*, Australia) Coolish-climate area previously known as Young. The pioneers are McWilliams, which established its Barwang estate and label here. Stand by for classy *Cabernet Sauvignon, Merlot*, and *Shiraz*. Demondrille; Barwang.

℗ **Hilltop Neszmely** [nej-may-lee] (*Hungary*) One of Hungary's most go-ahead producers of red and white wines and of *Tokaji*. ★★★★ Tokaji Azu 5 Puttonyos 1996 $$

Himmelreich [him-mel-raikh] (*Mosel*, Germany) One of the finest vineyards in *Graach*. See JJ Prum.

Franz Hitzberger [fruntz hits-ber-gur] (*Wachau*, Austria) A name to remember for reliable dry *Grüner Veltliner* and *Riesling*.

℗ **Paul Hobbs** (*Sonoma*, California) Former winemaker at *Simi*, and currently engaged as a consultant at *Catena* and *Valdivieso*, Paul Hobbs produces fine *Pinot Noir*, lean *Cabernet*, and rich *Chardonnay* from the memorably-named "Dinner Vineyard" and good Argentine wines under the Paul Hobbs Selections label. ★★★★ Cabernet Sauvignon Napa Valley 1999 $$$

H

Hochfeinste [hokh-fine-stuh] (Germany) "Very finest."

Hochgewächs QbA [hokh-geh-fex] (Germany) Recent official designation for *Rieslings* which are as ripe as a *QmP* but can still only call themselves QbA. This from a nation supposedly dedicated to simplifying what are acknowledged to be the most complicated labels in the world.

Hochheim [hokh-hihm] (*Rheingau*, Germany) Village whose fine *Rieslings* gave the English the word "*Hock*". ★★★★★ Kunstler Hochheimer Kirchenstück Riesling Auslese Trocken 2001 $$$

�“ **Reichsgraf zu Hoensbroech** [rike-sgrahf tzoo hoh-ern sbroh-urch] (*Baden*, Germany) A large estate specializing in *Pinot Blanc* (Weissburgunder) and *Pinot Gris* (Grauburgunder).

�“ **Höffstatter** [Hurf-shtah-ter] (*Alto Adige,* Italy) Star new wave producer with unusually good *Pinot Noir* and *Gewurztraminer.*

�“ **Hogue Cellars** [hohg] (*Washington State*) Highly dynamic *Yakima Valley* producer of good *Chardonnay, Riesling, Merlot,* and *Cabernet.*

�“ **Hollick** (*Coonawarra*, Australia) A good, traditional producer; the *Ravenswood* (no relation to the California *Ravenswood*) is particularly worth seeking out.

�“ **Ch. Hortevie** (*Bordeaux*, France) There aren't many *Crus Bourgeois* in *St-Julien*, and this one produces rich, dense, approachable wine.

�“ **Dom. de l'Hortus** [Or-Toos] (*Languedoc-Roussillon*, France) Exciting spicy *Syrah* reds from *Pic St. Loup* in the *Coteaux de Languedoc* that easily outclass many an effort from big-name producers in the *Rhône.*

�“ **Hosanna** [Oh-zah-nah] (*Pomerol, Bordeaux*, France) Christian Moueix's sleek new stablemate for *Pétrus* – produced from the best part of the *Certan-Guiraud* vineyard.

�“ **Hospices de Beaune** [os-peess duh bohn] (*Burgundy*, France) Hospital whose wines (often *cuvées* or blends of different vineyards) are sold at an annual charity auction, the prices of which are erroneously thought to set the tone for the *Côte d'Or* year. In the early 1990s, wines were generally substandard, improving instantly in 1994 with the welcome return of winemaker André Porcheret who, before leaving once again, proved controversial by (in 1997) making wines that struck some critics (not this one) as too big and rich. In any case, be aware that although price lists often merely indicate "Hospices de Beaune" as a producer, all of the wines bought at the auction are matured and bottled by local merchants, some of whom are a great deal more scrupulous than others.

�“ **Houghton** [haw-ton] (*Swan Valley*, Australia) Long-established subsidiary of *Hardy's*. Best known in Australia for its *Chenin*-based rich white blend traditionally sold down under as "White *Burgundy*" and in Europe as "HWB". The Wildflower Ridge commercial wines are good, as are the ones from *Moondah Brook*. Look out too for the more recently launched *Cabernet-Shiraz-Malbec* "Jack Mann", named after one of *Western Australia's* pioneering winemakers who was once quoted as saying that any wine that couldn't be enjoyed after being diluted 50–50 with water was too light-bodied. ★★★★★ Verdlho 2002 $$ ★★★★★ Jack Mann 1999 $$$

�“ **Weingut von Hovel** [fon huh-vel] (*Mosel-Saar-Ruwer*, Germany) A 200-year-old estate with fine *Rieslings* from great vineyards. These repay the patience that they demand.

�“ **Howard Park** (*Western Australia*) John Wade is one of the best winemakers in *Western Australia*. He is also one of the finest *Riesling* producers in the whole of Australia. Madfish Bay is the *second label.* ★★★ Madfish Cabernet Sauvignon Merlot Cabernet Franc 2000 $$

Howell Mountain [how-wel] (*Napa Valley*, California) Increasingly well-respected hillside region in the north of the *Napa Valley*, capable of fine whites and reds that justify its *AVA*. *Beringer; Duckhorn; Dunn; la Jota; Liparita; Turley.*

�“ **Huadong Winery** (*Shandong Province*, China) Joint venture producing the perfectly acceptable Tsing Tao brand of wines.

H

Ⅎ **Bernard Huber** (*Baden*, Germany) International oak-aged wines from the Pinot family: *Spätburgunder, Weissburgunder, Chardonnay*.

Ⅎ **Alain Hudelot-Noëllat** [ood-uh-loh noh-el-lah] (*Burgundy,* France) A great winemaker whose generosity with oak is matched, especially in his *Grand Cru Richebourg* and *Romanée St.Vivant*, by the intense fruit flavors of his wine.

Huelva [wel-vah] (*Extremadura,* Spain) *DO* of the *Extremadura* region, producing rather heavy whites and fortified wines.

Ⅎ **Gaston Huët** [oo-wet] (*Loire,* France) Organic winemaker Noël Pinguet produces top-quality individual vineyard examples of *Sec, Demi-Sec,* and *Moëlleux* wines. The non-*vintage* sparkling wine, though only made occasionally, is top class too.
★★★★ Vouvray Sec Clos du Bourg 2000 $$$

Ⅎ **Hugel et Fils** [oo-gel] (*Alsace,* France) Reliable *négociant*. Best are the *late harvest* and Jubilee wines. The wine "Gentil" revives the tradition of blending different grape varieties.

Hungary Country too long known for poor quality *Bull's Blood* and *Olasz Rizling*, rather than *Tokaji*. Red and white wines are both steadily improving, with efforts by the Liszt Winery's Gróf Zichy and Chateau Kajmád estates, Tibor Gal (who worked at *Ornellaia*) and Akos Kamocsay at *Neszmély*. The *Tokaj* quality battle has been won. The challenge lies in getting people to try and buy it. *Disznókö;* Egervin; Megyer; Kym Milne; Nagyrede; Neszmély ("Hilltop"); Pajsos; Royal Tokay; Hugh Ryman.

Hunter Valley (*New South Wales,* Australia) The best-known wine region in Australia is one of the least suitable places to make wine. When the vines are not dying of heat and thirst they are drowning beneath torrential harvest-time rains. Even so, the *Shirazes* and *Semillons* – traditionally sold as "Hermitage," "Claret," "Burgundy," "Chablis," and "Hunter Valley Riesling" – develop remarkably and taste like wines produced nowhere else. (Just show an unoaked Semillon with a natural strength of 11% to anyone who thinks they "know all about" rich, alcoholic, overly-woody Australian wines. Note also, that the Hunter is split into two halves (the Upper, where Rosemount is based) and more traditional Lower, and there are worthwhile subregions like Broke. Allandale; Allanmere; Brokenwood; Evans Family; Lake's Folly; Lindemans; McWilliams; Petersons; Reynolds; Rosemount; Rothbury Estate; Tyrrells; Wilderness Estate.

Ⅎ **Hunter's** (*Marlborough,* New Zealand) One of *Marlborough's* most consistent producers of ripe fruity *Sauvignon Blancs* and a high quality sparkling wine.
★★★ Miru Miru Malborough Brut $$

Ⅎ **Ch. de Hureau** [oo-roh] (*Loire,* France) One of the few producers to excel in all styles of *Saumur*, from rich red to sparkling white.

⚘ **Huxelrebe** [huk-sel-ray-buh] Minor white grape, often grown in England but proving what it can do when harvested late in Germany. **Anselmann (Germany); Barkham Manor; Nutbourne Manor (England).**

Hybrid [high-brid] Crossbred grape *Vitis vinifera* (European) x *Vitis labrusca* (North American) – an example is *Seyval Blanc*. Wines made from these grapes can be good, if rarely great. But they can be grown in cool regions like England, where *Vitis vinifera* has a tougher time.

Hydrogen sulfide Naturally occurring rotten egg-like gas produced by yeasts as a by-product of fermentation, or alternatively by *reductive* conditions. Before bottling, may be cured by *racking*. If left untreated, hydrogen sulfide will react with other components in the wine to form *mercaptans*. Stinky bottled wines may often be "cleaned up" by decanting or by the addition of a copper coin. Unfortunately, too many go unnoticed, especially in France where wines are still sometimes relaxedly described as smelling of foxes (*renarder*).

I

Ⓧ **Iambol** [yam-bohl] (*Southern Region*, Hungary) Large, former cooperative which now makes commercial **Merlot** and **Cabernet Sauvignon** reds, particularly for sale overseas under the Domaines Boyar label.

Icewine Increasingly popular Anglicization of the German term *Eiswein*, used particularly by Canadian producers making luscious (usually non *nobly-rotten*) spicily exotic wines from grapes of varieties like *Vidal*, frozen on the vine. Cave Springs; Cilento; Henry of Pelham; Inniskillin; Jackson Triggs; Konzelmann; Lakeview Cellars; Mission Hill; Pelee Island; Pillitteri; Royal de Maria

Ⓧ **IGT – Indicazione Geografiche Tipici** (Italy) Designation for quality non-*DOC/DOCG* wines previously sold as *Vino da Tavola*. Originally derided by just about everyone, but now recognised as the masterstroke that allowed Italy's producers to play by Old and New World rules simultaneously.

Ⓧ **Vin de Pays de l'Île de Beauté** [eel-duh-bow-tay] (*Corsica*, France) Designation that includes varietal wines (including *Pinot Noir*, *Cabernet*, *Syrah*, and *Merlot* as well as local grapes). Often better than the island's *ACs*.

Imbottigliato nel'origine [im-bot-til-yah-toh neh-loh-ree-zhee-nay] (Italy) Estate-bottled.

Imperial(e) [am-pay-ray-ahl] (*Bordeaux*, France) Bottle containing almost six and a half liters of wine (eight and a half bottles). Such bottles are sought by collectors for their rarity and the extra longevity they give their contents.

India Source of generally execrable table wine and surprisingly reliable sparkling wine, labeled as Marquis de Pompadour or *Omar Khayam*.

Ⓧ **Inferno** [een-fehr-noh] (*Lombardy*, Italy) Lombardy DOC. Nebbiolo red that needs aging for at least five years. ★★★ 1998 Caven "Al Carmine" $$

Ⓧ **Inglenook Vineyards** [ing-gel-nook] (*Napa Valley*, California) Once-great winery which, like *Beaulieu*, fell into the hands of the giant Grand Metropolitan. The Gothic building and vineyards now belong appropriately to Francis Ford Coppola. The now far-from-dazzling brand has been sold to the giant Canandaigua which has also recently bought *Franciscan* and *Simi*.

Ⓧ **Inniskillin** (*Ontario*, Canada) Pioneering winery which produces some good *Icewines* (from the Vidal grape), highly successful *Chardonnay*, improving *Pinot Noir*, a rare example of a good *Maréchal Foch*, and an extraordinary sparkling *Icewine*. ★★★★★ Vidal Sparkling Ice Wine $$$$

Institut National des Appellations d'Origine (INAO) (France) French official body which designates and (unsuccessfully) polices quality, and outlaws a number of manifestly sensible techniques such as irrigation and the blending of *vintages*, which are permitted elsewhere. Which is why *Appellation Contrôlée* wines are often inferior to – and sell at lower prices than – the newer *Vins de Pays*.

International Wine Challenge (England) Wine competition, held in London by WINE Magazine and in China, Hong Kong, Vietnam, and Singapore. (The author is founder-chairman.)

International Wine & Spirit Competition (England) Wine competition, held in London.

Ⓧ **Iphofen** (*Franken*, Germany) One of the finest places to sample wines made from the *Silvaner*. Modern wine drinkers may, however, prefer the *Rieslings*, which are fruitier and less earthy in style.

Ⓧ **IPR – Indicação de Proveniência Regulamentada** (Portugal) Designation for wines that fall beneath the top – *DOC* – grade and above the basic Vinho Regional.

Irancy [ee-ron-see] (*Burgundy*, France) Little-known light reds and rosés made near *Chablis* from a blend of grapes including the *Pinot Noir* and the little-known *César*. Recently elevated to AC status. *Brocard*; Simonnet-Fèbvre.

Ⓧ **Iron Horse Vineyards** (*Sonoma* Valley, California) One of the most consistent and best sparkling-wine producers in the New World. Reds and still whites are impressive too.

J

Irouléguy [ee-roo-lay-gee] (*Southwest*, France) Earthy, spicy reds and rosés, and improving whites from Basque country where names seem to include an abundance of the letter "x." *Dom. Brana*; Etxegaraya; Irouléguy Cooperative.

I **Isabel Estate** (*Marlborough*, New Zealand) Producer of reliably good, rather than great *Sauvignon*, but some rather more impressive Riesling, and a stunning late harvest wine. ★★★ Isabel Riesling 2002 $$

Isinglass [Ih-sing-glahs] *Fining* agent derived from sturgeon bladders.

I **Isole e Olena** [ee-soh-lay ay oh-lay-nah] (*Tuscany*, Italy) Brilliant pioneering small *Chianti* estate with a pure *Sangiovese Super-Tuscan*, *Cepparello*, Italy's first *Syrah* (which is similarly impressive), and a great *Chardonnay*. New cellars are worth visiting – and ask about the new project in Barolo-country.
★★★★ Cepparello 1999 $$$$

I **Isonzo** [Ih-son-zoh] (*Friuli-Venezia Giulia*, Italy) One of the best *DOCs* in this region, offering a wide range of varietal wines from some very progressive producers. Lis Neris-Pecorari; Ronco del Gelso; *Vie di Romans*. ★★★ 2001 Sauvignon I Feudi di Romans $$

Israel Once the source of appalling stuff, but the new-style varietal wines are increasingly impressive. *Golan Heights*; Carmel.

I **Ch. d'Issan** [dee-son] (*Margaux 3ème Cru Classé, Bordeaux*, France) Recently revived *Margaux* third growth with lovely, recognizable blackcurranty *Cabernet Sauvignon* intensity. Good in 2000.

🍇 **Italian Riesling/Riesling Italico** [ee-tah-lee-koh] Not the great *Rhine Riesling*, but another name for an unrelated variety, which also goes by the names *Welschriesling, Riesling Italico*, and *Laski Rizling*, and is widely grown in Northern and Eastern Europe. At its best in Austria.

Italy Tantalizing, seductive, infuriating. In many ways the most exciting wine nation in the world, though, as ever, in a state of change as it reorganizes its wine laws. See individual regions.

J

I **J** (Sonoma, California) Reliable California sparkling wine, launched by *Jordan* and now independently produced by Judy *Jordan*.

I **JP Vinhos** (Portugal) See *Peter Bright*.

I **Paul Jaboulet Aîné** [zha-boo-lay ay-nay] (*Rhône*, France) This once reliable firm is now a frequently disappointing producer of a wide range of Rhône wines. The Hermitage La Chapelle is the flagship wine.

I **Jackson Estate** (*Marlborough*, New Zealand) Neighbor of *Cloudy Bay* and producer of *Sauvignon*, which doesn't quite have that winery's lustre at the moment. The sparkling wine is good though. ★★★ 2001 Sauvignon Blanc $$

I **Jacob's Creek** (*South Australia*) Brilliantly commercial *South Australian* wines made by *Orlando* and taken up a major step by the recent introduction of a decent sparkling wine and classy trophy-winning "Limited Release" reds and whites. ★★★★ Limited Release Shiraz Cabernet $$

I **Jacquart** [zha-kahr] (*Champagne*, France) Large cooperative with some top-class wines. ★★★★ Brut de Nominée $$$

🍇 **Jacquère** [zha-kehr] The slightly citrusy grape of *Savoie*.

I **Jacquesson et Fils** [jak-son] (*Champagne*, France) A small *Champagne* house that deserves to be better known, particularly for its delicately stylish *Blanc de Blancs*. ★★★★★ Blanc de Blancs, Avize $$$

I **Jade Mountain** (*Napa*, California) Rhône varieties are the specialty, done with considerable stylishness. ★★★★ la Provençale California 2000 $$$

J

 ℐ **Louis Jadot** [zha-doh] (*Burgundy*, France) Good, occasionally great, *Beaune négociant* with a growing number of its own top-class vineyards in *Beaune*, *Chassagne-*, and Puligny-Montrachet. Jadot has also been a pioneering producer of *Rully* in the *Côte Chalonnaise*. Whites are most impressive.

 ℐ **Jaffelin** [zhaf-lan] (*Burgundy*, France) Small *négociant*, particularly good at supposedly "lesser" *appellations* – *Rully Blanc* and *Monthelie* are particularly good – but winemaker Bernard Repolt (who is now also responsible for the improving wines at *Bouchard Aîné*) is now showing his skills across the board.

 ℐ **Josef Jamek** (*Wachau*, Austria) Powerful, elegant dry whites that age well.

 ℐ **Joseph Jamet** [zha-may] (*Rhône*, France) Top-class *Côte Rôtie* estate, making wines that are more stylish than many in this *appellation*.

 ℐ **Jamieson's Run** (*Coonawarra*, Australia) *Mildara's* pair of prize-winning, good-value red and white wines. Just what commercial wines should be.

 ℐ **Dom. de la Janasse** [ja-nass] (*Rhône*, France) High-quality *Châteauneuf-du-Pape* estate, producing three individual wines under this *appellation*, plus a good *Côtes du Rhône* les Garrigues and unusually good whites, including a Viognier-based Vin de Pays. ★★★★ Vieilles Vignes 2000 $$$

 ℐ **Jansz** [yantz] (*Tasmania*, Australia) One of Australia's most successful sparkling wines. See *Yalumba* and *Pirie*.

 ℐ **Vin de Pays du Jardin de la France** [jar-da'n duh lah fronss] (*Loire*, France) Large *Loire* region that can produce alternatives to the region's *appellations*, but tends to offer light, unripe whites.

 ℐ **Robert Jasmin** [zhas-man] (*Rhône*, France) Traditionalist *Côte Rôtie* estate, producing great wine despite (or thanks to) his dislike of new oak.

 Jasnières [zhan-yehr] (*Loire*, France) Relatively seldom seen bone-dry and – even more seldom seen – *moelleux*, sweet *Chenin Blanc* wines from *Touraine*. Buy very carefully.

 ℐ **Jasper Hill** (*Bendigo*, Australia) Winery in Heathcote with a cult following for both reds and whites. The Georgia's Paddock is a pure *Shiraz*; Emily's Paddock, more unusually – for Australia, and indeed anywhere else – is a *Shiraz-Cabernet Franc*. ★★★★ Emily's Paddock 2000 $$$

 ℐ **Jaume Serra** [how-may seh-rah] (*Penedès*, Spain) Privately owned company which recently relocated from *Alella* to *Penedès*, and is doing good things with *Xarel-lo*. ★★★ Cava Jaume Serra Brut Vintage 1998 $$

 ℐ **Patrick Javillier** [zha-vil-yay] (*Burgundy*, France) Reliable, small merchant making meticulous village *Meursault*. ★★★★ 2000 Meursault Clos du Cromin 2000.

 ℐ **Henri Jayer** [zha-yay] (*Burgundy*, France) Now retired cult winemaker who is still represented on labels referring to Georges et Henri. Also an influence on the wines of *Méo-Camuzet*.

 ℐ **Robert Jayer-Gilles** [zhah-yay-zheel] (*Burgundy*, France) *Henri Jayer's* cousin, whose top wines – including an *Echézeaux* – bear comparison with those of his more famous relative. (His *Hautes Côtes de Nuits* wines, including the *Aligoté* – are good too). ★★★★ Echezeaux 1999 $$$

 Jerez (de la Frontera) [hay-reth] (Spain) Centre of the *sherry* trade, giving its name to entire *DO* area. *Gonzalez Byass; Lustau; Hidalgo; Barbadillo.*

 ℐ **Jermann** [zhehr-man] (*Friuli-Venezia Giulia*, Italy) Brilliant, if unashamedly showy, winemaker with a cult following who gets outrageous flavors – and prices – out of every white grape variety he touches. Look out for the *Vintage* Tunina blend of *Tocai*, *Picolit*, and *Malvasia*, and the "Dreams" white blend plus the Ribolla-based Vinnae and the single-vineyard Capo Martino. Also good at *Chardonnay*, *Pinot Gris*, *Pinot Blanc*, and the *Cabernets*. Ever the innovator, Jermann is now considering the installation of a bottling line that will allow him to use screwcaps. ★★★★★ Dreams 2001 $$$

 Jeroboam [dzhe-roh-bohm] Large bottle; in *Champagne* holding three liters (four bottles); in *Bordeaux*, four and a half (six bottles). Best to make sure before writing your check.

Jesuitengarten [yez-oo-witten-gahr-ten] (*Rheingau*, Germany)
One of Germany's top vineyards – well handled by *Bassermann-Jordan*.
★★★★★ Bassermann-Jordan Forster Jesuitengarten Riesling Eiswein 2001 $$

Jeunes Vignes [zhuhn veeñ] Denotes vines too young for their crop to
be sold as an *Appellation Contrôlée* wine – in other words, vines that have
not yet reached their fourth year.

Ⓘ **Dom. François Jobard** [fron-swah joh-bahr] (*Burgundy*, France) Great
white wine estate in *Meursault*.

Ⓘ **Dom. Joblot** [zhob-loh] (*Burgundy*, France) One of the top *domaines* in *Givry*.

Ⓘ **Charles Joguet** [zho-gay] (*Loire*, France) Recently-retired producer
of single-vineyard *Chinon* wines that last. The more basic wines still
produced by the estate are less impressive, but Joguet's remains one of the
names to remember in this region.

Johannisberg [zho-han-is-buhrg.] (*Rheingau*, Germany) Village making
superb *Riesling*, which has lent its name to a *Bereich* covering all the
Rheingau. ★★★★ Riesling Schloss Johannisberger 2000 $$

❋ **Johannisberg Riesling** [rees-ling] California name for *Rhine Riesling*.

Ⓘ **Johanneshof Cellars** [zhoh-hah-ness-hoff] (*Marlborough*, New Zealand)
Producer with unusually good *Pinot Gris* ★★★★ Pinot Gris 2001 $$

Ⓘ **Johannishof** [zhoh-hah-niss-hoff] (*Rheingau*, Germany) Exemplary
family-owned estate with fine examples of wines from *Johannisberg*
and *Rüdesheim*.

Ⓘ **Weingut Karl-Heinz Johner** [karl-hihntz yoh-nuh] (*Baden*, Germany)
Former winemaker at *Lamberhurst*, now making exceptional oaky *Pinot Noir*
in southern Germany. Also makes wine in New Zealand.

Ⓘ **Pascal Jolivet** [zhol-lee-vay] (*Loire*, France) Superstar producer of modern
Sancerre and *Pouilly-Fumé*.

Ⓘ **Nicolas Joly** [Zhoh-lee] (*Loire*, France) The biodynamic owner-winemaker
behind the *Coulée de Serrant* in *Savennières* – and probably the most famous
spokesman for biodynamic viticulture.

Ⓘ **Jordan** (*Stellenbosch*, South Africa) Young winery whose California-trained
winemakers first hit their mark with *Sauvignon* and *Chardonnay*, and are
now doing as well with *Cabernet* and *Merlot*. ★★★★★ Cabernet Sauvignon
2000 $$; ★★★★ Chenin Blanc 2002 $$

Ⓘ **Jordan** (*Sonoma Valley*, California) *Sonoma* winery surrounded by the
kind of hype more usually associated with *Napa*. Table wines – from the
Alexander Valley – are mostly good rather than great.

Ⓘ **Joseph** (*South Australia*) *Primo Estate's* label for its top wines (including
the excellent sparkling *Shiraz*) and olive oils. ★★★★ Joseph Moda
Amarone 2000 $$

Ⓘ **Josmeyer** [jos-mi-yur] (*Alsace*, France) Estate producing wines that are
more delicate and restrained than those of some of its neighbors.
★★★★ Riesling le Kottabe 2001 $$

Ⓘ **Weingut Toni Jost** [toh-nee yohst] (*Mittelrhein*, Germany) A new-wave
producer with (well-sited) vines in Bacharach, good reds, and a penchant
for experimenting (often successfully) with new oak barrels.

Ⓘ **La Jota** [lah hoh-tah] (*Napa Valley*, California) Heading for its quarter-
century, this small *Howell Mountain* estate continues to produces very
stylish reds, including an unusually good *Cabernet Franc*.
★★★★ 18th Anniversary Release Cabernet Sauvignon 1999 $$

Ⓘ **Judd's Hill** (*Napa Valley*, California) Young winery making an impact with
dazzling *Cabernets*.

Juffer [yoof-fuh] (*Mosel*, Germany) Famous vineyard in the village of
Brauneberg and producing delicious, typically slatey wines. ★★★★ *Fritz
Haag*, Brauneberger Juffer-Sonnenuhr Riesling Beerenauslese 2001 $$$

Jug wine (California) American term for quaffable *Vin Ordinaire*.

Ⓘ **Marcel Juge** [zhoozh] (*Rhône*, France) Producer of one of the subtlest,
classiest examples of *Cornas*.

J

Juliénas [joo-lee-yay-nas] (*Burgundy*, France) One of 10 *Beaujolais Crus*, producing classic, vigorous wine which often benefits from a few years in the bottle. E. Aujas; Jean Benon; Bernard Broyer; François Condemine; Georges Descombes; *Georges Duboeuf;* Eventail des Producteurs; Pierre Ferraud; Pascal Granger; Paul Granger; Ch. de Juliénas; Henri Lespinasse; Dom. Michel Tête; Raymond Trichard. ★★★★ Juliénas Cuvée Speciale 2000 Pascal Granger $

Weingut Juliusspital [yoo-lee-yoos-shpit-ahl] (*Franken*, Germany) Large estate whose profits benefit its hospital. Good *Riesling* and *Silvaner*. ★★★★ Wurzburger Innere Leiste Silvaner Spatlese 2001 $$

Jumilla [hoo-mee-yah] (Spain) *DO* region in northern Murcia, like *Priorat*, traditionally known for high-alcohol wines but – like *Priorat* – now making increasingly stylish ones. ★★★★ Bodegas Casa de la Ermita 2000 $$

Jurançon [zhoo-ron-son] (*Southwest*, France) Rich, dry, apricoty white wines and excellent sweet wines that are made from the *Gros* and *Petit Manseng*. Bellegarde; Dom. J-P Bousquet; *Brana;* Bru-Baché; Castera; *Cauhapé;* Clos Guirouilh; Clos Lapeyre; Cru Lamouiroux; Clos Uroulat. ★★★★★ Jurançon Sec 'Chant des Vignes' 2001 Domaine Cauhapé $$$

Justin (*San Luis Obispo*, California) A winery to watch, with stunning reds, including a great *Cabernet Franc* and Isosceles, a classy *Bordeaux* blend. ★★★★ Isosceles 2000 $$$$

Juvé y Camps [hoo-vay ee kamps] (*Catalonia,* Spain) The exception which proves the rule – by making and maturing decent cava from traditional grapes and excellent *vintage Brut*.

K

Kaapzicht Estate [kahp-tsikt] (South Africa) Steytler Pinotage is tops; the *Cabernet, Merlot, Pinotage, Shiraz* are good too. ★★★★★ 2000 Pinotage $$$

Kabinett (Germany) Now unfashionable first step in German quality ladder, describes – usually off-dry – wines made from naturally ripened grapes.

Kadarka [kah-dar-ka] (Hungary) Red grape that used to be the mainstay of *Bull's Blood*. Handled well and not overcropped it makes good weighty wine.

Kaefferkopf [kay-fur-kopf] (*Alsace*, France) Excellent vineyard never made a *Grand Cru* because its forte is blends, not varietals. ★★★ 2000 Kaefferkopf Kuehn $$

Kaiserstuhl-Tuniberg [ki-sehr shtool too-nee-behrg] (*Baden*, Germany) Supposedly the finest *Baden* Bereich (actually, it covers a third of *Baden's* vineyards) with top villages producing rich, spicy *Riesling* and *Sylvaner* from volcanic slopes. Dr. Heger, Bercher, Karl-Heinz Johner.

Kallstadt [kahl-shtaht] (*Pfalz*, Germany) Village containing the best-known and finest vineyard of Annaberg, making luscious full *Riesling*.

Kalin (Sonoma County, California) Producer of unusually long-lived *Pinot Noirs* and *Chardonnays*.

Kamptal [kamp-tal] (*Niederösterreich*, Austria) Up-and-coming region for rich dry white *Grüner Veltliners* and *Rieslings*, thanks largely to the efforts of star producer *Bründlmayer*. ★★★ 2001 Weingut Allram Zöbinger Heiligenstein Riesling, Kamptal $$$$

Kanonkop Estate [ka-non-kop] (*Stellenbosch*, South Africa) Famous for top-quality *Pinotage*, but the *Bordeaux*-style "Paul Sauer" is better. The light red blend, "Kadette," is good too. ★★★★ Kanonkop Paul Sauer 1999 $$

Karlsmühle [kahl-smoo-lur] (*Mosel-Saar-Ruwer*, Germany) Very high-class estate producing good Riesling in the heart of the *Ruwer*.

Karly (Anmador County, California) A name to remember if you enjoy rich, dark *Zinfandels* with loads of character. Sadie Upton is the best of the single-vineyard examples. Try the *Syrah* and the Orange *Muscat* too.

K

ℤ **Karthäuserhof** [kart-oy-ser-hof] (*Mosel-Saar-Ruwer,* Germany) *Ruwer* estate with great Eitelsbach Rieslings in naked bottles – apart from a stylish neck label.

ℤ **Katnook Estate** (*Coonawarra,* Australia) Small estate making the highly commercial Deakin Estate wines as well as plenty of such innovative stuff as a *late harvest Coonawarra Chardonnay* and top-class *Coonawarra Merlot* and *Cabernet.* ★ ★ ★ ★ **Merlot 2000 $$$**

ℤ **Katsatos** [kart-oy-ser-hof] (*Coonawarra,* Australia) Sm (Greece) One of the classiest new-wave *Cabernet Sauvignon* producers in Greece.

ℤ **Ch. Kefraya** [keh-frah-ya] (Lebanon) *Ch. Musar* is not the only Lebanese winery; this is another one worth taking seriously.

🍇 **Kekfrankos** [kek-frenk-kosh] Another name for *Blaufränkisch.*
Kellerei/Kellerabfüllung [kel-luh-ri/kel-luh-rap few loong] (Germany) Cellar/producer/estate-bottled.

ℤ **Kendall-Jackson** (*Clear Lake,* California) Jess Jackson has created one of the world's most dynamic wine companies and brands/estates such as Cardinale, Carmel Road, Lokoya, Legacy, Hartford Court, Stonestreet, Yangarra Park (Australia), Tapiz (Argentina), Calina (Chile), Villa Arceno (Tuscany). The best Kendall-Jackson wines, including the Great Estates range, come from a region called "True Coast" (Mendocino, Sonoma etc) over which Jackson (a former lawyer) has copyright.. The "Vintner's Reserve" *Chardonnay* and *Sauvignon,* of which millions of cases are produced, are off-dry. Reds and "Grand Reserve" wines are better, as are *Stonestreet,* Cardinale, La Crema etc – though subtlety is not a quality most could claim. ★ ★ ★ ★ **Grand Reserve Chardonnay 1999 $$$**

ℤ **Ken Forrester Vineyards** (*Stellenbosch,* South Africa) Former restaurateur Ken Forrester makes serious *Chenin Blanc* and *Sauvignon.* Reds are good too.

ℤ **Kenwood Vineyards** (*Sonoma Valley,* California) Classy *Sonoma* winery with good single-vineyard *Chardonnay*s and impressive *Cabernet*s (including one made from the author Jack London's vineyard). The other stars are the brilliant *Zinfandel* and *Sauvignon.*

🍇 **Kerner** [kehr-nuh] A white grape variety. A *Riesling*-cross that is grown in Germany and also widely in England. **Anselmann.**

ℤ **Weingut August Kesseler** [kes-sel-lur] (*Rheingau,* Germany) Maker of good Assmannshausen Spätburgunder and elegant *Rieslings* too.

ℤ **Weingut Reichsgraf von Kesselstatt** [rikh-sgraf fon kes-sel-shtat] (*Mosel-Saar-Ruwer,* Germany) Large, impressive collection of four *Riesling* estates spread between the *Mosel, Saar,* and *Ruwer.*

Kiedrich [kee-drich] (*Rheingau,* Germany) Hillside village vineyards that produce intense *Rieslings.*

Kientzheim [keents-him] (*Alsace,* France) Village noted for its *Riesling.*

ℤ **André Kientzler** [keent-zluh] (*Alsace,* France) Classy producer with better-than-average *Pinot Blanc.*

ℤ **JF Kimich** [kih-mikh] (*Pfalz,* Germany) Fast-rising star making rich, spicy wines typical of the *Pfalz.* Gewürztraminers are as good as *Rieslings.*

ℤ **King Estate** (*Oregon*) Huge, glitzy new winery whose own vineyards are in part of the state that has yet to produce top-class wine. Decent *Pinot Gris Reserve* and *Zinfandel* and pleasant *Reserve Pinot Noir.*

King Valley (*Victoria,* Australia) Popular high altitude region.

ℤ **Kingston Estate** (*Murray Valley,* South Australia) Controversial commercial producer in the Riverland.

ℤ **Kiona** [kih-yoh-nah] (*Washington State*) Small producer with a penchant for berryish reds and intensely flavored *late harvest* wines.

Kir (*Burgundy,* France) A mixture of sweet fortified Burgundian *Crème de* with simple and often rather *acidic* local white wine (*Aligoté* or basic *Bourgogne Blanc*) to produce a delicious summertime drink.

ℤ **Ch. Kirwan** [keer-wahn] (*Margaux 3ème Cru Classé, Bordeaux,* France) Coming out of the doldrums, but still doesn't warrant its third growth status.

K

 Kistler [kist-luh] (*Sonoma Valley*, California) Probably California's top *Chardonnay* producer, with uncompromising complex single-vineyard wines and fast-improving *Pinot Noirs*. *Burgundy* quality at *Burgundy* prices.

 Klein Constantia [kline kon-stan-tee-yah] (*Constantia*, South Africa) Small estate on the site of the great 17th-century *Constantia* vineyard. The star wine is the sweet "Vin de Constance" which is sadly hard to find outside South Africa. ★★★★ Cabernet Sauvignon 1999 $$

 Kloster Eberbach [klos-tur ay-bur-bark] (*Rheingau*, Germany) 12th Century Cistercian abbey now the HQ of the German Wine Academy.

Klüsserath [kloo-seh-raht] (*Mosel-Saar-Ruwer*, Germany) Small village best known for *Sonnenuhr* and Königsberg vineyards.

 Knappstein [nap-steen] (*Clare Valley*, South Australia) No longer associated with founder Tim (see *Knappstein Lenswood*) but producing good *Clare* wines. ★★★★ Riesling 2002 $$

 Emerich Knoll [knowl] (*Wachau*, Austria) Maker of stunning new-wave *Riesling* and *Grüner Veltliner* wines.

 Weingut Freiherr zu Knyphausen [fry-hair tzoo knip-how-sen] (*Rheingau*, Germany) Large, quality-conscious producer. Very fine *Rieslings*.

Koehler-Ruprecht [kurler-roop-recht] (*Pfalz*, Germany) Classy estate in Kallstadt, producing good *Riesling* and unusually fine *Spätburgunder*.

 Kollwentz-Römerhof [kohl-ventz roh-mair-hof] (*Burgenland*, Austria) Go-ahead producer with serious international-style reds and good *Chardonnay*.

 Konnsgaard [kons-gahd] (*Napa*, California) The former winemaker at *Newton*, and the unsung hero behind that winery's success, removes his light from under a bushel with his own top-class *Chardonnay*.

 Konocti Cellars [ko-nok-tih] (*Lake County*, California) Dynamic producer with good straightforward wines.

Kosher (mostly Israel) Wine made under complex rules. Every seventh vintage is left unpicked; non-Jews are barred from the winemaking process.

 Korbel [Kor-BEL] (*Sonoma*, California) Big producer of basic California sparkling wine. Better wines like Le Premier Reserve show what can be done.

 Kourtakis [koor-tah-kis] (Greece) One of Greece's growing number of dynamic wine companies with unusually recommendable whites and the characterful native *Mavrodaphnes*. ★★★ NV Samos Muscat Sweet White $

 Weinlaubenhof Weingut Alois Kracher [Ah-loys krah-kuh] (*Neusiedlersee*, Austria) Frequent trophy winner at the *International Wine Challenge*, and source of world-class, (very) *late harvest* wines including an unusual effort which blends the *Chardonnay* with the *Welschriesling*. ★★★★★ Welschriesling No.4. 2000 $$$

Krems/Kremstal [krems] (*Wachau*, Austria) Town and *Wachau* vineyard area producing Austria's most stylish *Rieslings* from terraced vineyards. ★★★ 1999 Sepp Moser Weissburgunder Beerenauslese, Kremstal $$

Kreuznach [kroyt-znahkh] (*Nahe*, Germany) Northern *Bereich*, boasting fine vineyards situated around the town of *Bad Kreuznach*.

 Dom. Kreydenweiss [cry-den-vice] (*Alsace*, France) Top-class organic producer with particularly good *Muscat*, *Pinot Gris*, and *Riesling*.

 Krondorf [kron-dorf] (*Barossa Valley*, Australia) Fosters-owned winery specializing in traditional, big *Barossa* style wines. ★★★ Show ReserveE Shiraz 1997 $$$

 Krug [kroog] (*Champagne*, France) The *Ch. Latour* of *Champagne*. Great vintage wine, extraordinary rosé, and pure *Chardonnay* from the *Clos de Mesnil* vineyard. The *Grande Cuvée* is theoretically the ultimate non-vintage, thanks to the greater proportions of aged *Reserve* wine. Now part of the *Moët/Mercier/Veuve Clicquot/Pommery/Ruinart* stable.

 Kruger-Rumpf [kroo-gur roompf] (*Nahe*, Germany) *Nahe* estate, demonstrating the potential of varieties like the *Scheurebe*.

 Kuentz-Bas [koontz bah] (*Alsace*, France) Reliable producer for *Pinot Gris* and *Gewurztraminer*. ★★★★ Gewurztraminer Collection 1999 $$$

L

🍷 **Kuhling-Gillot** [koo-ling gil-lot] (*Rheinhessen,* Germany) Producer who is now fast developing a reputation for rich and concentrated wines.

🍷 **Kumeu River** [koo-myoo] (*Auckland,* New Zealand) Master of Wine Michael Brajkovich is successful with a wide range of wines, but *Chardonnay* is his strongest suit. Until *Laroche* sealed some of its *Grand Cru Chablis* with screwcaps, Kumeu's was the best screwcapped Chardonnay in the world.

🍷 **Weingut Franz Künstler** [koonst-luh] (*Rheingau,* Germany) A new superstar producer with superlative *Riesling.* ★ ★ ★ ★ ★ Hochheimer Kirchenstück Riesling Auslese Trocken 2001 $$$

🍷 **KWV** (*Cape,* South Africa) Huge cooperative formed by the South African government at a time when surplus wine seemed set to flood the industry. Wines were previously only sold overseas, but they are now available in South Africa. Winemaking has improved recently – especially the wines sold under the Cathedral Cellars label. Perold is the name of a new, pricey, "super-premium" red which has yet to convince, but the old fortified KWV Jerpigos are a real treasure. ★ ★ ★ ★ ★ 1975 Jerpigo Muscatel $

L

🍷 **Ch. Labégorce** [la-bay-gors] (*Bordeaux,* France) Good traditional *Margaux.*

🍷 **Ch. Labégorce-Zédé** [la-bay-gors zay-day] (*Margaux Cru Bourgeois, Bordeaux,* France). An estate that belongs to the same Thienpont family as *Vieux Château Certan* and *le Pin.* A wine beyond its Bourgeois class.

🍷 **Labouré-Roi** [la-boo-ray rwah] (*Burgundy,* France) A highly successful and very commercial *négociant,* responsible for some quite impressive wines. See *Cottin Frères.* ★ ★ ★ ★ ★ Nuits St Georges 2001 $$$

🍇 **Labrusca** [la-broo-skah] *Vitis labrusca,* the North American species of vine, making wine which is often referred to as "foxy." All *vinifera* vine stocks are grafted on to *phylloxera*-resistant *labrusca* roots, though the vine itself is banned in Europe and its wines, thankfully, are almost unfindable.

🍷 **Ch. Lacoste-Borie** [la-cost-bo-ree] (*Pauillac, Bordeaux,* France) The reliable *second label* of *Grand-Puy-Lacoste.*

Lacryma Christi [la-kree-mah kris-tee] (*Campania,* Italy) Literally, "tears of Christ," the melancholy name for some amiable, light, rather rustic reds and whites. Those from Vesuvio are *DOC.* Grotta del Sole; Mastroberardino.

🍷 **Ladoix** [la-dwah] (*Burgundy,* France) Village (sometimes also referred to as Ladoix-Serrigny) including parts of *Corton* and *Corton-Charlemagne.* The village wines are not well-known and because of this some bargains are still to be found. Capitain-Gagnerot; Chevalier Père et Fils; Dubreuil-Fontaine; Gay; Launay; Maréchale; André Nudant.

🍷 **Patrick de Ladoucette** [duh la-doo-set] (*Loire,* France) Intense *Pouilly-Fumé,* sold as "Baron de L." Other wines are greatly improved.

🍷 **Michel Lafarge** [la-farzh] (*Burgundy,* France) One of the very best producers in *Volnay* – and indeed *Burgundy.* Fine, long-lived, modern wine. ★ ★ ★ ★ ★ Volnay Clos des Chênes 2001 $$$

🍷 **Ch. Lafaurie-Peyraguey** [la-foh-ree pay-rah-gay] (*Sauternes Premier Cru Classé, Bordeaux,* France) Much-improved *Sauternes* estate that has produced creamy, long-lived wines in the 1990s.

🍷 **Ch. Lafite-Rothschild** [la-feet roth-chihld] (*Pauillac Premier Cru Classé, Bordeaux,* France) Often almost impossible to taste young, this *Pauillac* first growth is still one of the monuments of the wine world – especially since the early 1980s. A brilliant 1998 and 2000, and arguably the wine of the vintage in 2001. The *second wine, Carruades,* is worth looking out for, too.

L

Ⓣ **Ch. Lafleur** [la-flur] (*Pomerol, Bordeaux*, France) *Christian Moueix's* pet *Pomerol*, often on a par with the wine *Moueix* makes at *Pétrus* – though in a more understated way.

Ⓣ **Ch. Lafleur-Gazin** [la-flur-ga-zan] (*Pomerol, Bordeaux*, France) Another good *Moueix* wine.

Ⓣ **Dom. des Comtes Lafon** [day comt la-fon] (*Burgundy*, France) The best domaine in *Meursault* (and one of the very best in the whole of Burgundy) with great vineyards in *Volnay*, a small slice of *Montrachet*, and a new venture with more affordable single-vineyard wines in the Mâconnais. The Côte d'Or wines last forever. Now biodynamic. ★★★★★ **Meursault Clos de la Barre 2000 $$$** ★★★★ **Mâcon Mill-Lamartine 2000 $$**

Ⓣ **Ch. Lafon-Rochet** [la-fon-ro-shay] (*St. Estèphe 4ème Cru Classé, Bordeaux*, France) Very classy modern *St. Estèphe*. Impressive in 1998.

Ⓣ **Alois Lageder** [la-gay-duh] (*Trentino-Alto Adige*, Italy) New-wave producer of the kind of wine the *Alto Adige* ought to make.

Lago di Caldaro [la-goh dih kahl-dah-roh] (*Trentino-Alto Adige*, Italy) Also known as the *Kalterersee*, using the local *Schiava* grape to make cool light reds with slightly unripe, though pleasant, fruit.

Ⓣ **Ch. Lagrange** [la-gronzh] (*St. Julien 3ème Cru Classé, Bordeaux*, France) A once underperforming third growth rejuvenated by Japanese cash and local know-how (for a while from Michel Delon of *Léoville-las-Cases*). Look out for *Les Fiefs de Lagrange*, the impressive *second wine*.

Ⓣ **Ch. Lagrange** [la-gronzh] (*Pomerol, Bordeaux*, France) Yet another *Moueix* property – and yet another good wine.

❄ **Lagrein** [la-grayn] (Italy) Cherryish red grape of northeast Italy.

Ⓣ **Marquis de Laguiche** [lah-geesh] (*Burgundy*, France) Owner of the largest chunk of Le Montrachet. The wines are made and sold by J. Drouhin.

Ⓣ **Ch. la Lagune** [la-goon] (*Haut-Médoc 3ème Cru Classé, Bordeaux*, France) Lovely accessible wines which last well and are worth buying even in poorer years. A great 2000.

Ⓣ **Weingut Andreas Laible** [ahn-dray-yas ly-blay] (*Baden*, Germany) Complex, racy wines from Scheurebe, Riesling, *Gewürztraminer*, and others.

Lake County (California) Vineyard district salvaged by improved irrigation techniques and now capable of some fine wines as well as *Kendall Jackson's* highly commercial efforts.

Ⓣ **Lake's Folly** (*Hunter Valley*, Australia) Max Lake, surgeon-turned-winemaker/writer/researcher has great theories about the sexual effects of sniffing various kinds of wine. He is also a leading Australian pioneer of *Chardonnay*, with an unusually successful *Hunter Valley Cabernet Sauvignon*. Wines are now made by Max's son, Stephen.

Ⓣ **Lalande de Pomerol** [la-lond duh po-meh-rol] (*Bordeaux*, France) Bordering on *Pomerol* with similar, but less fine wines. Still generally better than similarly priced *St. Emilions*. Some good-value *Petits-Châteaux*. **Ch. Garraud; Grand Ormeau.**

Ch. Lalande-Borie [la-lond bo-ree] (*St. Julien, Bordeaux*, France) In the same stable as *Ch. Ducru-Beaucaillou*. Reliable wines.

Ⓣ **Ch. Lamarque** [la-mahrk] (*Haut-Médoc Cru Bourgeois, Bordeaux*, France) Spectacular *château* with good, quite modern, wines.

Ⓣ **Lamborn Family** (*Napa Valley*, California) Small *Howell Mountain* producer, focusing on rich, concentrated, long-lived *Zinfandel*.

Ⓣ **Dom. des Lambrays** [lom-bray] (*Burgundy*, California) Under new ownership and promising further improvements in quality. Already very worthwhile, though. ★★★★★ **Clos des Lambrays Grand Cru 1999 $$$**

Ⓣ **Lambrusco** [lam-broos-koh] (*Emilia-Romagna*, Italy) Famous/infamous low-strength (7.5 percent) sweet, sparkling UK and North American version of the sparkling, dry, red wine favoured in Italy. The real thing is far more fascinating with its dry, unripe cherry flavor – comes with a cork rather than a screw-cap. Barbolini; F Bellei; Cavicchioli; Donelli; O Lini; Medici Ermete

L

Ⅎ **Lamoureaux Landing** [lam-moh-roh] (*New York State*) Impressive young *Chardonnay* specialist in the *Finger Lakes*.

Ⅎ **Bodegas LAN** (*Rioja*, Spain) [lahn] Bodega benefiting from a recent shake-up. Culmen de Lan is the top wine. ★ ★ ★ ★ **Viña Lanciano Reserva 1998 $$$**

Ⅎ **Landmark** (*Sonoma*, California) Small *Chardonnay* specialist with rich, fruity, buttery wines from individual "Damaris" and "Overlook" vineyards, and blends of Chardonnay from Sonoma, Santa Barbara, and Monterey.

Landwein [land-vine] (Germany) The equivalent of a French *Vin de Pays* from one of 11 named regions. Often dry.

Ⅎ **Ch. Lanessan** [la-neh-son] (*Haut-Médoc Cru Bourgeois, Bordeaux*, France). Recommendable *Cru Bourgeois* now more influenced by new oak than it used to be, but still quite traditional fare.

Langelois [lung-ger-loyss] (*Kamptal*, Austria). One of the best wine communes in Austria. Hiedler; *Bründlmayer*.

Langhe [lang-gay] (*Piedmont*, Italy) A range of hills; when preceded by "*Nebbiolo delle*," indicates declassified *Barolo* and *Barbaresco*. Also, the denomination now used by Angelo *Gaja* for his single-vineyard wines.

Ⅎ **Langlois-Château** [long-lwah-sha-toh] (*Loire*, France) Very good still and sparkling *Saumur* and *Saumur-Champigny*.

Ⅎ **Ch. Langoa-Barton** [lon-goh-wah-bahr-ton] (*St. Julien 3ème Cru Classé, Bordeaux*, France) *Léoville-Barton's* (slightly) less complex kid brother. Often one of the best bargain classed growths in *Bordeaux*. Well made in poor years.

Languedoc-Roussillon [long-dok roo-see-yon] (*Midi*, France) One of the world's largest wine regions (producing 10 percent of the planet's wine) and, until recently, a major source of the wine lake. But a combination of government-sponsored uprooting and activity by *flying winemakers* and (a few) dynamic producers is beginning to turn this into a worrying competitor for the New World. The region includes appellations like *Fitou, Corbières* and *Minervois, Faugères, St. Chinian, Coteaux de Languedoc, Côtes de Roussillon*, and a torrent of *Vin de Pays d'Oc*. Sadly, many of the best, more ambitious, wines are hard to find outside France where they are developing a cult following among consumers who relish the value they often offer.

Ⅎ **Lanson** [lon-son] (*Champagne*, France) Much-improved *Champagne* house with decent non-vintage "Black Label", good *Demi-sec*, and fine *vintage champagne*. ★ ★ ★ ★ ★ **Noble Cuvée 1989 $$$**

Ⅎ **Casa Lapostolle** [la-pos-tol] (*Colchagua Valley*, Chile) Instant superstar. Belongs to the owners of Grand Marnier and benefits from the expertise of *Michel Rolland*. Cuvée Alexandre *Merlot* reds have been a classy instant success, though the whites need more work. The Clos Apalta *Merlot*-Carmenère blend is one of the best of Chile's new-wave flagship reds. ★ ★ ★ ★ **Clos Apalta Rapel Valley 2000 $$$**

Ⅎ **Ch. Larcis-Ducasse** [lahr-see doo-kass] (*St. Emilion Grand Cru Classé, Bordeaux*, France) Wines rarely live up to the potential of its hillside site.

Ⅎ **Ch. Larmande** [lahr-mond] (*St. Emilion Grand Cru Classé, Bordeaux*, France) A property to watch for well-made ripe-tasting wines. A very good 2000

Ⅎ **Dom. Laroche** [la-rosh] (*Burgundy*, France) Highly reliable *Chablis* négociant with some enviable vineyards of its own, including top-class *Premiers* and *Grands Crus*. At more affordable prices, there are also reliable southern French *Vin de Pays d'Oc* (including a tasty new super-premium red effort) and innovative wines from Chile and (less impressively) California. Now a screwcap pioneer. ★ ★ ★ ★ ★ **Chablis Les Clos 2000 $$$.** ★ ★ ★ ★ **Chardonnay "Rio Azul" Michel Laroche - Jorge Corderch 2002 $$**

Ⅎ **Ch. Larrivet-Haut-Brion** [lah-ri-vay oh-bree-yo'n] (*Bordeaux*, France) Graves property that is improving under the consultancy of Michel Rolland.

Ⅎ **Viña de Larose** [veen-ya day lah-rose] (Chile) *Bordeaux* estate Ch. Larose-Trintaudon's New World venture, producing *Chardonnay* and blended red. ★ ★ ★ ★ **Leyenda Cabernet 1999 $$**

L

☣ **Ch. Lascombes** [las-komb] (*Margaux 2ème Cru Classé, Bordeaux*, France)
Subtle second growth *Margaux* which can exemplify the perfumed character
of this *appellation*, but has been underperforming until recently. A change of
owners has improved matters since 2000.

🍷 **Laski Riesling/Rizling** [lash-kee riz-ling] (Former Yugoslavia) Yugoslav
name for a white grape also known as the *Welsch, Olasz,* and *Italico* Riesling
and unrelated to the *Rhine Riesling*.

☣ **Ch. de Lastours** [duh las-toor] (*Languedoc-Roussillon*, France) Combined
winery and home for people with mental disabilities. Look out for the *cuvée*
Simone Descamps. ★★★★ Cuvée Fût de Chêne, la Grande Rompue 1998 $

Late harvest Made from (riper) grapes picked after the main vintage.
Should have at least some *botrytis*.

Late-bottled Vintage (Port) (LBV) (*Douro*, Portugal) Officially, bottled
four or six years after a specific (usually nondeclared) *vintage*. Until the late
1970s, this made for a *vintage port*-style wine that matured early, was light
and easy to drink, but needed to be decanted. Until recently, the only houses
to persevere with this style were *Warre's* and *Smith Woodhouse*, labeling their
efforts "*Traditional*" *LBV*. Almost every other LBV around was of the filtered,
"modern" style, tasted like *vintage character ports*, need no decanting, and
bear little resemblance to real *vintage* or even *crusted port*. Belatedly, a
growing number of producers are now confusingly offering "Traditional" as
well as modern LBV. For the moment, buyers can tell one style from the
other by reading the small print – and the word "Traditional".

Latium/Lazio [lah-tee-yoom] (Italy) The vineyard area surrounding
Rome, including *Frascati* and Marino. *Fontana Candida; Falesco.*

☣ **Louis Latour** [loo-wee lah-toor] (*Burgundy*, France) Underperforming
négociant who still pasteurizes his reds, treating them in a way no quality-
conscious New World producer would contemplate. Some whites, however,
including *Corton-Charlemagne*, can be sublime, and Latour deserves credit
for pioneering regions such as *Mâcon Lugny*, the *Ardèche*, and now Provence
where it is making its great new Domaine de Valmoissine *Pinot Noir*.
★★★★ Vin de Pays de Verdon Domaine de Valmoissine 2000 $$$

☣ **Ch. Latour** [lah-toor] (*Pauillac Premier Cru Classé, Bordeaux*, France)
Recently bought – from its British owners, Allied Domecq – by the same self-
made French millionaire who recently bought Christie's. First growth *Pauillac*
which can be very tricky to judge when young, but which develops
majestically. *Les Forts de Latour* is the – often worthwhile – second label. The
1999, 2000, and 2001 were among the very top wines of the vintage.

☣ **Ch. Latour-à-Pomerol** [lah-toor ah po-meh-rol] (*Pomerol, Bordeaux*, France)
A great-value, small (3,500-case) *Pomerol* estate under the same ownership as
Ch. Pétrus and the same *Moueix* winemaking team. It is a little less
concentrated than its big brother, but then it is around a quarter of the price.

☣ **Ch. Latour-Martillac** [la-toor mah-tee-yak] (*Graves Cru Classé, Bordeaux*,
France) Good, sometimes overlooked reds and whites.

Laudun [loh-duhn] (*Rhône*, France) Named village of *Côtes du Rhône*, with
peppery reds and attractive rosés. ★★★ 1999 Chateau de Bord Laudun $

☣ **Laurel Glen** (*Sonoma Mountain*, California) Small hillside estate with *claret*-
style reds that are respected by true Californian wine lovers. Terra Rosa is the
accessible *second label*.

☣ **Dominique Laurent** [Loh-ron] (*Burgundy*, France) A young *négociant*
founded a few years ago by a former pastry chef who has rapidly shown
his skills at buying and maturing top-class wines from several *appellations*.

☣ **Laurent-Perrier** [law-ron pay-ree-yay] (*Champagne*, France) Historically
one of the more reliable larger houses, though some recent bottlings have
seemed variable. ★★★★★ Grand Siècle Lumière du Millénaire 1993 $$$$

☣ **Lavaux** [la-voh] (Switzerland) A wine region in the Vaud, itself the second
most important wine region in Switzerland. This is a good place to taste
varied examples of *Chasselas* (known here as "*Fendant*") and *Pinot Noir*.

L

☲ **Ch. Laville Haut-Brion** [la-veel oh-bree-yon] (*Graves Cru Classé, Bordeaux,* France) Exquisite white *Graves* that lasts for 20 years or more.

☲ **Lawson's Dry Hills** (*Marlborough,* New Zealand) Producer of good *Sauvignon Blanc* and an unusually good *Gewürztraminer.*

☲ **Ch. Lazaridis** (Greece) One of Greece's best producers of red wines, making no use of the national appellation system. Nikos Lazaridi is the brother of...

☲ **Kostas Lazaridis** (Greece) An up-and-coming producer of various styles of wine, including an unusually good rosé. ★ ★ ★ ★ Syrah 2000 $$

Lazio [lat-zee-yoh] (Italy) See *Latium.*

☲ **Lazy Creek** (*Sonoma,* California) An Anderson Valley *Pinot Noir* producer to watch.

LBV (*Douro,* Portugal) See *Late-bottled Vintage.*

☲ **Leacock** (*Madeira,* Portual) Part of the *Madeira Wine Company.*

Lean Lacking body.

☲ **Leasingham** (*South Australia*) BRL Hardy subsidiary in the *Clare Valley* that makes top-flight reds and whites, including great *Shiraz, Cabernet,* and *Chardonnay.* ★ ★ ★ ★ ★ Magnus Shiraz Cabernet Sauvignon 2000 $$$

Lebanon Best known for the remarkable *Ch. Musar* from the *Bekaa Valley.*

☲ **Leconfield** [leh-kon-feeld] (*South Australia*) Reliable producer of intense *Coonawarra* reds. (Ralph Fowler, the man behind the award-winning recent vintages, has his own wine now and works for *Chapoutier,* Australia).

Lees or lie(s) The sediment of dead yeasts that fall in the barrel or vat as a wine develops. *Muscadet* – like some other white wines – is aged *Sur Lie.* Producers of modern *Chardonnay* also leave their wine in its lees, stirring it occasionally to maximize richness – the rich flavor provided by the yeasts.

☲ **Leeuwin Estate** [loo-win] (*Margaret River,* Western Australia) Showcase winery (and concert venue) whose vineyards were originally picked out by *Robert Mondavi.* The genuinely world-class ("art label") *Chardonnay* is one of Australia's priciest and longest-lived. Other wines are less dazzling.

☲ **Dom. Leflaive** [luh-flev] (*Burgundy,* France) Anne-Claude Leflaive has taken the domaine made famous by her father Vincent to new heights, possibly, she might argue, with the help of biodynamic methods. The various Montrachets (Chevalier, Batard etc.) are the stars here. All wines are hard to find, and well worth leaving for a few years in the cellar.
★ ★ ★ ★ ★ Puligny-Montrachet Les Pucelles 2000 $$$$

☲ **Olivier Leflaive** [luh-flev] (*Burgundy,* France) The *négociant* business launched by Vincent Leflaive's nephew in 1994. Mostly high-class white wines, with just the occasional red. (Wines can also be tasted in a bistro restaurant close to the cellars.)

☲ **Peter Lehmann** [lee-man] (*Barossa Valley,* Australia) The grand old man of the *Barossa,* Peter Lehmann and his son Doug make intense *Shiraz, Cabernet, Semillon,* and *Chardonnay* which make up in character (and value) what they lack in subtlety. Stonewell is the best red.
★ ★ ★ ★ Stonewell Shiraz 1998 $$$

☲ **J. Leitz** [lites] (*Rheingau,* Germany) Up-and-coming estate with rich *Riesling.*

🍇 **Lemberger** [lem-burg-gur] (Gemany) German and Washington State name for *Blaufrankisch.* In Germany it's found mostly in Württemberg.

Lemnos [lem-nohs] (Greece) Island for *Muscat* – sweet, fortified, and dry.

Length How long the taste lingers in the mouth.

Lenswood (*South Australia*) New region near *Adelaide,* proving its potential with *Sauvignon, Chardonnay, Pinot Noir,* and even (in the case of *Henschke's* Abbott's Prayer) *Merlot* and *Cabernet Sauvignon.* Pioneers include *Stafford Ridge, Shaw & Smith, Knappstein Lenswood,* and *Nepenthe.*

☲ **Lenswood** (*Lenswood,* South Australia) Label used by Tim Knappstein for excellent *Sauvignon, Semillon, Chardonnay, Pinot Noir,* and *Cabernets.*
★ ★ ★ ★ Pinot Noir 2000 1998 $$$

☲ **Lenz Vineyards** [lentz] (*Long Island,* New York) One of the best wineries on Long Island, with particularly recommendable *Merlot* and *Chardonnay.*

L

León [lay-on] (Spain) Northwestern region producing acceptable dry, fruity reds and whites.

℥ **Jean León** [zhon lay-ON] (*Catalonia*, Spain) American pioneer of Spanish *Chardonnay* and *Cabernet*, whose wines have greatly improved since its purchase by *Torres*. ★★★ Cabernet Sauvignon Reserve 1997 $$

℥ **Leone de Castris** [lay-oh-nay day kah-streess] (*Puglia*, Italy) A leading exponent of Salice Salentino, Copertino, Salento Chardonnay, and pink Salento rosato. A name to watch as this region gathers prestige.

℥ **Leonetti Cellars** [lee-oh-net-tee] (*Washington State*) One of the best red wine producers in the US. Now showing its skills with *Sangiovese* and an innovative "American" (Washington State/Dry Creek) *Merlot*. ★★★★ Merlot Columbia Valley 2000 $$

℥ **Ch. Léoville-Barton** [lay-oh-veel bahr-ton] (*St. Julien 2ème Cru Classé*, *Bordeaux*, France) Anthony Barton's daughter Liliane is now taking over here, and produces one of the most reliably classy wines in *Bordeaux*, without – unlike a great many of her neighbors – recourse to the machines that concentrate the juice to provide "bigger" flavors. Then, again, unlike them, she has the temerity to ask a reasonable rather than extortionate price for it. *Langoa Barton* is the sister property. Both made fine 2002s.

℥ **Ch. Léoville-las-Cases** [lay-oh-veel las-kahz] (*St. Julien 2ème Cru Classé*, *Bordeaux*, France) Impeccably made *St. Julien Super Second* whose quality now often matches its neighbor *Ch. Latour* – a fact that its owner Hubert Delon reflects in his prices. The *Clos du Marquis second label* is also good, as are his other properties, *Potensac* and *Nenin*. 2002 was good at all of these.

℥ **Ch. Léoville-Poyferré** [lay-pwah-feh-ray] (*St. Julien 2ème Cru Classé*, *Bordeaux*, France) Fast improving, thanks to the efforts of *Michel Rolland* here. The *second label* is Moulin Riche. ★★★★ 2000 $$$$

℥ **Dom. Leroy** [luh-rwah] (*Burgundy*, France) Organic domaine in *Vosne-Romanée* founded by the former co-owner of the *Dom. de la Romanée-Conti* and making wines as good as those of that estate. Prices are stratospheric, but the humblest wines are much better than other producers' *Grands Crus*. ★★★★ Bourgogne Blanc 1996 $$. ★★★★ Clos de Vougeot 1999 $$$$

℥ **Maison Leroy** [luh-rwah] (*Burgundy*) If you want to bu y a really great old bottle of *Burgundy*, no matter the cost, this is the place to come.

℥ **Ch. Lestage** [les-stahj] (*Bordeaux*, France) Cru Bourgeois making attractive, supple wines.

⚘ **Lexia** [lex-ee-yah] See *Muscat d'Alexandrie*.

℥ **Librandi** [lee-bran-dee] (*Calabria*, Italy) Another flagship winery from the fast-improving regions of southern Italy. There are terrific examples of the Cirò grape, as well as Gravello, a great blend of the local Gaglioppo and the *Cabernet Sauvignon*. ★★★★ Terre Lontane 2002 $$$

Lie(s) See *Lees/Sur Lie*.

Liebfraumilch [leeb-frow-mihlch] (Germany) Seditious exploitation of the *QbA* system. Good examples are pleasant; most are alcoholic sugar-water bought on price alone.

℥ **Lievland** [leev-land] (*Stellenbosch*, South Africa) Estate which has a reputation in South Africa as a high-quality speciality producer of *Shiraz* and *late harvest* wines.

℥ **Hubert Lignier** [Lee-nee-yay] (*Burgundy*, France) Producer of classic long-lived *Morey-St.-Denis*.

Limestone Coast (*South Australia*, Australia) Zone in the south-east of the state that includes *Padthaway* and *Coonawarra*.

℥ **Limestone Ridge** (*South Australia*) *Lindemans'* historically excellent *Coonawarra* red blend now back on form. ★★★★ Limestone Ridge Shiraz Cabernet Sauvignon 1999 $$$

Limousin [lee-moo-zan] (France) Oak forest that provides barrels that are high in wood *tannin*. Better, therefore, for red wine than for white.

L

Limoux [lee-moo] (*Midi*, France) (Relatively) cool-climate, chalky soil *appellation* that was recently created for *Chardonnay* which was previously sold as *Vin de Pays d'Oc*. Stories of tankers of wine being driven north by night to *Burgundy* have been hotly denied in the latter region – and given plenty of credibility by several recent Burgundian scandals. Now the site of a venture by the owners of *Ch. Mouton Rothschild* (Baron d'Arques). Also see *Blanquette*.

☿ **Lindauer** [lin-dowr] (*Marlborough*, New Zealand) Good-value Montana sparkling wine. ★★★ Lindauer Special Reserve **$$**

☿ **Lindemans** (*South Australia*) Once *Penfolds'* greatest rival, now (like so many other once-independent Australian producers) a fellow member of the same Southcorp giant. Noted for long-lived *Hunter Valley Semillon* and *Shiraz*, *Coonawarra Pyrus* and *Limestone Ridge* reds, and good-value multi-region blends, such as the internationally successful *Bin 65 Chardonnay*, *Bin 45 Cabernet*, and Cawarra wines.

☿ **Weingut Karl Lingenfelder** [lin-gen-fel-duh] (*Pfalz*, Germany) Great new-wave *Rheinpfalz* producer of a special *Riesling, Dornfelder, Scheurebe*, and an unusually successful *Pinot Noir*. ★★★ Bird Label Riesling 2001 **$$**

☿ **Jean Lionnet** [lee-oh-nay] (*Rhône*, France) Classy *Cornas* producer whose Rochepertius is a worthwhile buy. The *St. Péray* is an unusually good example of its *appellation* too.

☿ **Ch. Liot** [lee-yoh] (*Barsac, Bordeaux*, France) Good light and elegant *Barsac*.

Liqueur Muscat (*Rutherglen*, Australia) A wine style unique to Australia. Other countries make fortified *Muscat*s, but none achieve the caramelized-marmalade and Christmas-pudding flavors that *Rutherglen* can achieve. Campbell's; Mick Morris; Seppelt;Yalumba.

Liqueur d'Expédition [lee-kuhr dex-pay-dees-see-yon] (*Champagne*, France) Sweetening syrup for *dosage*.

Liqueur de Tirage [lee-kuhr duh tee-rahzh] (*Champagne*, France) The yeast and sugar added to base wine to induce secondary fermentation (and hence the bubbles) in bottle.

Liquoreux [lee-koh-ruh] (France) Rich and sweet.

Liquoroso [lee-koh-roh-soh] (Italy) Rich and sweet.

☿ **Ch. Lilian Ladouys** [lahd-weess] (*Bordeaux*, France) St-Estèphe *Cru Bourgeois* resurrected in the 1980s. Well-regarded by plenty of other people, but I find it disappointing.

☿ **Lirac** [lee-rak] (*Rhône*, France) Peppery, *Tavel*-like rosés, and increasingly impressive, deep berry-fruit reds. Ch. D'Aqueria; Bouchassy; Delorme; Ch. Mayne Lalande; André Méjan; Mordorée; Perrin. ★★★★ Grande Réserve 2001 Louis Bernard **$$**

☿ **Listel** [lees-tel] (*Languedoc-Roussillon*, France) Slowly improving firm with vineyards on beaches close to Sète. Best wines: rosé ("Grain de Gris") and sparkling *Muscat* (Pétillant de Raisin). ★★★ 2000 Cuvée Pierre Julian Rouge **$**

Listrac-Médoc [lees-trak] (*Bordeaux*, France) Small *Haut-Médoc* commune near *Moulis*, though quite different in style. Clay makes this *Merlot* country, though this isn't always reflected in the vineyards. Wines historically have tended to be tough even in warm vintages, and generally of greatest interst to those with very conservative tastes. But the 2000 vintage showed huge improvements. *Ch. Clarke*, (which benefits from newly planted Merlot vineyards) in particular, made a very good 2001. A region to watch. Clarke; Fonréaud; Fourcas-Dupré; Fourcas-Hosten.

☿ **Littorai** (*Sonoma*, California) Classy *Chardonnay* from *Russian River Valley* (Mais Canyon Vineyard) and *Sonoma Coast* (Occidental Vineyard) where the Hirsch vineyard produces some stylish *Pinot Noir*.

Livermore (Valley) [liv-uhr-mohr] (California) Traditionally overlooked, warm-climate vineyard area with fertile soil producing full rounded whites, including increasingly fine *Chardonnay*. *Randall Grahm* of *Bonny Doon* is now making wine here, too.

L

Y **Llano Estacado** [yah-noh es-ta-kah-doh] (*Texas*, USA) Texan pioneer. Signature red blend is good and Italian and Rhône varietals interesting.

Y **Los Llanos** [los yah-nos] (*Valdepeñas*, Spain) Commendable modern exception to the tradition of dull *Valdepeñas*, with quality mature reds.

Y **De Loach** [duh lohch] (*Sonoma*, California) Sadly had to look for protection against its creditors in 2003 – and now plans to reduce production. Wines remain recommendable. Look for the letters OFS – Our Finest Selection – on the *Chardonnay* and *Cabernet* – and for the individual vineyard *Zinfandels*. ★★★★ Russian River Valley Pinot Noir $$$

Y **Locorotondo** [loh-koh-roh-ton-doh] (Italy) A memorable name for perfectly acceptable white from the South.

Y **Carl Loewen** [lur-ven] (*Mosel-Saar-Ruwer*, Germany) Outstanding wines of classic proportions, with a particular name for sweet wines of Auslese level.

Y **J Lohr** [lohr] (*Santa Clara*, California) Affordable wines, particularly the Wildflower range, and now a selection of more classic noble styles. ★★★★★ Arroyo Vista Chardonnay $$

Loire [lwahr] (France) Varied region producing inexpensive, traditional dry whites such as *Muscadet*, classier *Savennières*, *Sancerre*, and *Pouilly-Fumé*; grassy summery reds (Chinon and Bourgueil); buckets of rosé – some good, most dreadful; glorious sweet whites (*Vouvray* etc.); and decent sparkling wines (also *Vouvray* plus *Crémant de Loire*).

Lombardy [lom-bahr-dee] (Italy) Region (and vineyards) around Milan, known mostly for sparkling wine but also for increasingly interesting reds, such as Valcalepio and *Oltrepò Pavese*, and the whites of *Lugana*.

Long Island (*New York State*) A unique microclimate where potato fields now yield classy *Merlot* and *Chardonnay* that are sadly underappreciated by New Yorkers, but many are discovering them on vacation in the Hamptons. Bedell; Bridgehampton; Gristina; Lenz; Palmer; Peconic; Pindar.

Y **Long Vineyards** (*Napa*, California) High-quality producer of long-lived *Cabernet Sauvignon*, *Chardonnay*, and *late-harvest Riesling*.

Y **Longridge** (*Stellenbosch*, South Africa) Designer winery tailoring three lines (Longridge, Bay View, and Capelands) to export markets.

Lontue [lon-too-way] (Chile) Good Merlot region. *Lurton; San Pedro; Santa Carolina.* ★★★★★ 1999 Single Vineyard Cabernet Franc Valdivieso $$

Y **Weingut Dr. Loosen** [loh-sen] (*Mosel-Saar-Ruwer*, Germany) New-wave *Riesling* producer. One of the best and most reliable in the *Mosel*. His *Wolf* wines from the *Pfalz* and *Eroica* joint venture with Chateau Ste Michelle are brilliant too. ★★★★ Dr L Riesling 2002 $$

Y **Lopez de Heredia** [loh-peth day hay-ray-dee-yah] (*Rioja*, Spain) Ultratraditional winery with Viña Tondonia white and *Gran Reserva* reds.

Y **Ch. Loudenne** [loo-denn] (Bordeaux, France) New owners are investing in this showpiece *Cru Bourgeois*, and wine quality started rising in 2000.

Y **Louisvale** [loo-wis-vayl] (*Stellenbosch*, South Africa) Once avowed *Chardonnay* specialists, now making good *Cabernet*-based reds.

Y **Loupiac** [loo-peeyak] (*Bordeaux*, France) *Sauternes* styles, but lighter. *Clos-Jean; Ch. du Cros; Loupiac-Gaudiet; Mazarin;* du Noble; de Ricaud.

Y **Ch. Loupiac-Gaudiet** [loo-pee-yak goh-dee-yay] (*Loupiac, Bordeaux*, France) A reliable producer.

🍇 **Loureiro** [loh-ray-roh] (Portugal) *Vinho Verde* grape.

Y **Ch. la Louvière** [lah loo-vee-yehr] (*Graves, Bordeaux*, France) Reliable, rich, modern whites and reds. The second wine is called "L" de Louvière.

Y **Fürst Löwenstein** [foorst ler-ven-shtine] (*Franken*, Germany) One of the very top producers of *Silvaner*.

Y **Van Loveren** [van loh-veh-ren] (*Robertson*, South Africa) Good value wine, especially classic fresh whites and fast-improving soft reds. ★★★ Van Loveren Shiraz Limited Release 2001 $$

Côtes du Lubéron [koht doo LOO-bay-ron] (*Rhône*, France) Light reds, pink and sparkling wines, and *Chardonnay*-influenced whites.

Luce [loo-chay] (Tuscany, Italy) Coproduction between *Mondavi* and *Frescobaldi*, who have combined forces to produce a good, if pricey, red. The cheaper *second label*, Lucente, can be a good buy for earlier drinking.

Lugana [loo-gah-nah] (*Lombardy*, Italy) Potentially appley, almondy whites made from the *Trebbiano*. Ca' dei Frati; Vigneti Villabella; Zenato.

Lugny [loo-ñee] (*Burgundy*, France) See *Mâcon*.

Luna (*Napa*, California) A name to remember for anyone looking for good Californian versions of Italian classics such as *Sangiovese*.

Pierre Luneau [loo-noh] (*Loire*, France) A rare beast: a top-class *Muscadet* producer. His experiments with new oak barrels have appealed to some US critics – I prefer the unwooded wines. Try the L d'Or.

Cantine Lungarotti [kan-tee-nah loon-gah-roh-tee] (*Umbria*, Italy) Highly innovative producer, and the man who single-handedly created the *Torgiano* denomination and introced *Cabernet Sauvignon* to Umbria. His daughters now produce two individual *Chardonnays* – Aurente and I Palazzi – and a fine red *IGT*, San Giorgio.

Jacques & François Lurton [loor-ton] Having begun at their father's *Ch. la Louvière* and *Ch. Bonnet*, Jacques and brother François make and sell wine worldwide. Look out for Hermanos Lurton labels from Spain and Bodega Lurton wines from Argentina. The Ch Merville Corbières proves they haven't lost their touch in France. ★★★★ **Gran Lurton Grande Reserve 2000 $$**

Ch. de Lussac [loo-sak] (*Lussac St. Emilion, Bordeaux*, France) A name to watch out for in *Lussac St. Emilion*.

Lussac St. Emilion [loo-sak sant-ay-mee-yon] (*Bordeaux*, France) *St. Emilion* satellite with potential. Ch. Villadiere.

Emilio Lustau [loos-tow] (*Jerez*, Spain) Top-class *sherry* producer with great *almacenista* wines. ★★★★★ **Lustau Old East India $$**

Lutomer [loo-toh-muh] (Slovenia) Area still known for its (very basic) Lutomer *Laski Rizling*, now doing better things with *Chardonnay*.

Luxembourg [luk-sahm-burg] This small principality makes pleasant, fresh, white wines from *Alsace*-like grape varieties, and generally dire fizz.

Ch. Lynch-Bages [lansh bazh] (*Pauillac 5ème Cru Classé, Bordeaux*, France) Reliably overperforming fifth-growth *Pauillac*. Haut-Bages Averous is the *second label*. The (very rare) white is worth seeking out too.

Ch. Lynch-Moussas [lansh moo-sahs] (*Pauillac 5ème Cru Classé, Bordeaux*, France) Slowly improving.

M

Macération carbonique [ma-say-ra-see-yon kahr-bon-eek] Technique of *fermenting* uncrushed grapes under a blanket of carbon dioxide gas to produce fresh fruity wine. Used in *Beaujolais* and elsewhere.

Machard de Gramont [ma-shahr duh gra-mon] (*Burgundy*, France) Producer of fine *Nuits-St.-Georges, Vosne-Romanée*, and *Savigny-lès Beaune*.

Macedonia (Greece) Relatively cool wine region growing a lot of black *Xynomavro* for spicy, earthy wines.

Mâcon/Mâconnais [ma-kon/nay] (*Burgundy*, France) Look for the suffix *Villages, Superieur*, or *Prissé, Viré, Lugny*, or *Clessé*. The region contains *St.-Veran* and *Pouilly-Fuissé*. For straight Mâcon you could try *Jadot* or *Duboeuf*, but Jean Thévenet Dom. de la Bongran from Clessé is of *Côte d'Or* quality. Bonhomme; Deux Roches; Comtes Lafon; Roger Lasserat; Manciat; Caves de Lugny; Cave de Prissé; Verget; J-J Vincent.

M

Maculan [mah-koo-lahn] (*Veneto,* Italy) A superstar producer of blackcurranty *Cabernet* Breganze, *Cabernet-Merlot* Fratta, oaked *Pinot Bianco-Pinot Grigio-Chardonnay* blend called Prato di Canzio, and the lusciously sweet *Torcolato.* ★★★★★ **Fratta 2000 $$$**

Madeira [ma-deer-ruh] (Portugal) Atlantic island producing fortified wines, usually identified by style: *Bual, Sercial, Verdelho,* or *Malmsey.* Most is ordinary; some is finer fare of unique marmalady character. *Blandy;* Cossart-Gordon; Barros e Souza; *Henriques & Henriques,* Leacock.

Maderization [mad-uhr-ih-zay-shon] Deliberate procedure in *Madeira,* produced by the warming of wine in *estufas.* Otherwise an undesired effect produced by high temperatures during transport and storage, resulting in a dull, flat flavor. A frequent problem in Asia – and unfortunately in the US, where wines are occasionally handled carelessly during the hot summer.

Madiran [ma-dee-ron] (*South-West,* France) Robust reds made from *Tannat; tannic* when young, but worth aging. Aydie; Barréjat; Berthoumieu; *Bouscassé;* Dom. du Crampilh; *Ch. Montus;* Producteurs de Plaimont.

Ch. Magdelaine [Mag-duh-layn] (*St. Emilion Premier Grand Cru, Bordeaux,* France) Impeccable, perfumed wines.

Duc de Magenta (*Burgundy,* France) Large *Burgundy* estate run by *Louis Jadot* and on the up quality-wise.

Maglieri [mag-lee-yeh-ree] (*McLaren Vale,* South Australia) Dynamic *Shiraz* specialist recently taken over by *Mildara-Blass.*

Magnum Large bottle containing the equivalent of two bottles of wine (one and a half liters in capacity). Wines age slower in big bottles, and fewer are produced. For both reasons, magnums tend to sell for more at auction.

Magrez-Fombrauge [mah-grehz-fohm-broh'j] (*St Emilion, Bordeaux,* France) *Garage wine* from the boss of *Malesan/Wiliam Pitters* (and winemaking-partner of Gérard Dépardieu).

Maipo [my-poh] (Chile) Historic region with many good producers. Reds are most successful, especially *Cabernet* and *Merlot,* and softer *Chardonnays* are also made. New varieties and enterprising organic vineyards are moving in, but vineyards close to Santiago, the capital, increasingly have to compete with the needs of housing developers. *Aquitania* (Paul Bruno); *Canepa; Carmen; Concha y Toro;* Cousino Macul; *Peteroa; Santa Carolina;* Santa Inés; *Santa Rita; Undurraga; Viña Carmen.*

Maître de Chai [may-tr duh chay] (France) Cellar master.

Majella (*Coonawarra,* Australia) Producer of big rich *Shirazes* and *Cabernet.*

Malaga [ma-la-gah] (Spain) A semimoribund Andalusian *DO* producing raisiny dessert wines of varying degrees of sweetness. Immensely popular in the 19th century; sadly very hard to find nowadays. **Lopez Hermanos.**

Malagousia [mah-lah-goo-shah] (Greece) Good quality peachy, aromatic, low-acid white grape.

Ch. Malartic-Lagravière [mah-lahr-teek lah-gra-vee-yehr] (*Pessac-Léognan Cru Classé, Bordeaux,* France) Previously slumbering estate, bought in 1994 by *Laurent Perrier.* Improving new-wave whites; reds need time.

Malbec [mal-bek] Red grape, now rare in *Bordeaux* but widely planted in Argentina, the *Loire* (where it is known as the *Côt*), *Cahors,* and also in Australia. Producing plummy, silky-peppery wines. **Catena; Agricola**

Malesan [ma-les-son] (France) Dynamic brand (mostly) for *Bordeaux,* launched by the spirits group William Pitters. Can be good. ★★★ **Malesan Eleve en Futs de Chene 2000 $$**

Ch. Malescasse [ma-les-kas] (*Haut-Médoc Cru Bourgeois, Bordeaux,* France) Since 1993, wines have benefitted from being made by the former cellarmaster of *Pichon-Lalande.*

Ch. Malescot-St.-Exupéry [ma-les-koh san tek-soo-peh-ree] (*Margaux 3ème Cru Classé, Bordeaux,* France) Rarely impressive wines.

Ch. de Malle [duh mal] (*Sauternes 2ème Cru Classé, Bordeaux,* France) Good *Sauternes* property near Preignac, famous for its beautiful *château.*

Malmsey [marlm-say] (*Madeira*, Portugal) The sweetest style of Madeira.
★★★★★ **Cossart Gordon Colheita 1989 $$$**

Malolactic fermentation [ma-loh-lak-tik] Secondary "fermentation" in which appley **malic acid** is converted into the "softer", creamier *lactic* acid by naturally present or added strains of bacteria. Almost all red wines undergo a malolactic fermentation. For whites, it is common practice in *Burgundy*. Malolactic fermentation is often used in New World countries, where natural acid levels are often low. An excess is recognizable as a buttermilky flavor.

⚡ **Ch. de la Maltroye** [mal-trwah] (*Burgundy,* France) Classy modern *Chassagne*-based estate. All the wines are made by *Dom. Parent*.

🍇 **Malvasia** [mal-vah-see-ah] *Muscatty* white grape vinified dry in Italy (as a component in *Frascati*), but far more successfully as good, sweet, traditional *Madeira*, in which country it is known as Malmsey. Not the same as Malvoisie.

La Mancha [lah man-cha] (Spain) Huge region of inland Spain south of Madrid, known for mostly dull and old-fashioned wines. However, it is currently producing increasingly clean, modern examples. Also the place where the *Marqués de Griñon* is succeeding in his experiments with new techniques and grapes, especially *Syrah*.

⚡ **Albert Mann** (*Alsace*, France) The Barthelmé brothers always manage to express true varietal character without overblown flavors and excessive alcohol. There are some very fine Grands Crus: Altenbourg, Furstentum, Schlossberg and Steingruber.

🍇 **Manseng (Gros M. & Petit M.)** [man-seng] (*Southwest*, France) Two varieties of white grape grown in southwestern France. Both are capable of apricot-and-cream concentration, and the latter is used in the great *vendange tardive* wines of *Jurançon*. *Dom. Cauhapé; Grassa*.
★★★★★ **Jurançon Sec "Chant des Vignes" 2001 Domaine Cauhapé $$**

⚡ **Josef Mantler** [yoh-sef mant-lehr] (*Krems*, Austria) Reliable producer of both Grüner and Roter Veltliner as well as good *Riesling* and *Chardonnay*.

Manzanilla [man-zah-nee-yah] (*Jerez*, Spain) Dry tangy *sherry* – a *fino* style, widely (possibly mistakenly) thought to take on a salty tang from the coastal *bodegas* of Sanlucar de Barrameda. *Barbadillo; Don Zoilo; Hidalgo*.
★★★★ **Hidalgo La Gitana Manzanilla Pasada/Pastrana $$**

⚡ **Maranges** [mah-ronzh] (*Burgundy*, France) *appellation* promising potentially affordable, if a little rustic, *Côte d'Or* wines. *Bachelet*; Pierre Bresson; Chevrot; Drouhin; Vincent Girardin; Claude Nouveau.

⚡ **Ch. Marbuzet** [mar-boo-zay] (*Bordeaux*, France) St-Estèphe Cru Bourgeois that was formerly the second wine of Ch. Cos d'Estournel.

Marc [mahr] (France) Residue of seeds, stalks, and skins left after grapes are pressed. Often distilled into fiery brandy, e.g., Marc de Bourgogne.

⚡ **Marcassin** (*Sonoma*, California) Helen Turley produces expressive – and, for some, sometimes a touch overblown – *Côte d'Or Grand Cru*-quality *Chardonnays* and *Pinot Noirs* in tiny quantities from a trio of vineyards.
★★★★ **Marcassin Estate Chardonnay 1998 $$$$**

Marches/Le Marche [lay Mahr-kay] (Italy) Region on the Adriatic coast, below Venice. Best known for *Rosso Conero* and good, dry, fruity *Verdicchio* whites. Boccadigabbia; *Fattoria Coroncino*; Fazi Battaglia; Garofoli; Gioacchino Garafolli; San Savino; Umani Ronchi; Vallerosa Bonci.

⚡ **Marcillac** [mah-see-yak] (*Southwest*, France) Full-flavored, though generally tough and rustic country reds, made principally from the *Fer*, possibly blended with some *Cabernet* and *Gamay*. Du Cros; Lacombe; Cave du Vallon-Valady.

🍇 **Maréchal Foch** [mah-ray-shahl fohsh] A *hybrid* vine producing red grapes in Canada and Eastern North America. *Inniskillin* makes a good example.

Maremma [mah-rem-mah] (*Tuscany*, Italy) Southern part of *Tuscany*, somewhat warmer than *Chianti* and the site of much new planting. Includes *Bolgheri, Morellino di Scansano* etc.

M

Margaret River (*Western* Australia) Cool(ish) vineyard area on the coast, almost at Australia's southwestern tip, now gaining notice for *Cabernet Sauvignon* and *Chardonnay*. Also one of Australia's only *Zinfandels*. *Brookland Valley; Cape Mentelle; Cullen; Devil's Lair; Evans & Tate; Leeuwin; Moss Wood; Pierro; Vasse Felix; Voyager Estate; Ch. Xanadu.*

Margaux [mahr-goh] (*Bordeaux*, France) Large, varied *commune* with a concentration of *crus classés* including *Ch. Margaux, Palmer*, and *Lascombes*. Sadly, other wines that should be deliciously blackberryish can disappoint partly thanks to the diverse nature of the soil, and partly through a readiness to sacrifice quality for the sake of yields. Matters improved in 2000, however: a good vintage here. 2002 was quite sucessful too.

Ch. Margaux [mahr-goh] (*Margaux Premier Cru Classé, Bordeaux*, France) Intense wines with cedary perfume and velvet softness when mature. 2001 was lighter than usual, but seems to have come together with time. The top *second label* is *Pavillon Rouge* and *Pavillon Blanc* is a fascinating white.

Henry Marionet [mah-ree-yoh-nay] (*Loire*, France) Top-class producer with great old-clone *Gamay* and distinctive whites made from the Romarantin.

Markham (*Napa Valley*, California) Unusually fairly priced reds and whites.

Marlborough [morl-buh-ruh] (*New Zealand*) Cool-climate South Island region at the north-western tip of the island, opposite Wellington: excellent *Sauvignon, Chardonnay*, improving *Merlot* and *Pinot Noir*, good sparkling wines. *Babich; Cellier le Brun; Cloudy Bay; Corbans Giesen; Grove Mill; Hunter's; Jackson Estate; Montana; Stoneleigh; Vavasour.*

Marojallia [mah-roh-jah-lee-yah] (*Bordeaux*, France) The first *garage wine* in *Margaux* – or the *Médoc* for that matter. Inevitably, from *Jean-Luc Thunevin*.

Marne et Champagne [mahr-nay-shom-pañ] (*Champagne*, France) Huge cooperative that owns the Besserat de Bellefon, *Lanson*, and Alfred Rothschild labels, and can provide good own-label wines. ★★★★★ **1995 Andre Simon Champagne Brut Vintage Marne et Champagne Diffusion $$$**

Marquis Philips (*McLaren Vale*, Australia) Australian-US joint-venture (the logo is an eagle-kangaroo cross) formed to make "wines that make you go wow" – and that's precisely what they do, particularly with US critics.

Ch. Marquis-de-Terme [mahr-kee duh tehrm] (*Margaux 4ème Cru Classé, Bordeaux*, France) Traditional property with quite tough wines.

Marsala [mahr-sah-lah] (*Sicily*, Italy) Rich, fortified wine from *Sicily* for use in recipes such as Zabaglione. *De Bartoli; Cantine Florio; Pellegrino; Rallo.*

Marsannay [mahr-sah-nay] (*Burgundy*, France) Northernmost village of the *Côte de Nuits* with a range of largely undistinguished but, for *Burgundy*, affordable *Chardonnay* and *Pinot Noir* (red and rosé). *Charles Audoin; Domaine Bruno Clair; Fougeray de Beauclair; Louis Jadot.*

Marsanne [mahr-san] (*Rhône*, France) Grape that is blended with *Roussanne* in northern *Rhône* whites. Also successful in the *Goulburn Valley* in *Victoria* for *Ch. Tahbilk* and *Mitchelton* and in California for *Bonny Doon*. Has a delicate, perfumed intensity when young, and fattens with age. Look for unoaked versions from Australia. *Bonny Doon; Guigal; Mitchelton; Tahbilk.*

Martinborough (*New Zealand*) Best-known part of the North Island region of *Wairarapa*. Good for *Pinot Noir* and *Chardonnay*. *Alana Estate; Ata Rangi; Dry River; Martinborough Vineyard; Palliser Estate; Voss.*

Martinborough Vineyard (*Martinborough*, New Zealand) Top Kiwi *Pinot Noir* and one of the best *Chardonnays*. ★★★★ **Pinot Noir 2000 $$$**

Martinelli (*Sonoma*, California) Century-old *Zinfandel* specialists, making rich intense reds from this variety and juicy *Pinot Noirs*.

Martinez [mahr-tee-nesh] (*Douro*, Portugal) Old port house that has just been ambitiously revived by owners Allied Domecq. ★★★★★ **Vintage Port 2000 $$$.**

M

✧ **Bodegas Martinez Bujanda** [mahr-tee-neth boo-han-dah] (*Rioja*, Spain) New-wave producer of fruit-driven wines sold as *Conde de Valdemar*. Probably the most consistently recommendable producer in *Rioja*.
★★★★ Rioja Gran Reserva 1985 $$

✧ **Martini** (*Piedmont*, Italy) Good *Asti* from the producer of the vermouth house that invented "lifestyle" advertising.

✧ **Louis Martini** (*Napa Valley*, California) Grand old winery with great vineyards, prticularly the Monte Rosso (great *Cabernet Sauvignon*). Now under the owership of *E&J Gallo*.

❦ **Marzemino** [mahrt-zeh-mee-noh] (Italy) Grape that makes spicy-plummy wines. ★★★ Vigna Fornas Marzenino 2001 $$

✧ **Mas Amiel** [mahs ah-mee-yel] (*Provence*, France) Wonderful rich *port*-like wine in the *appellation* of Maury.

✧ **Mas Brugière** [mas bro-gee-yehr] (*Languedoc-Roussillon*, France) Producer of top class, single-vineyard *Pic St. Loup*.

✧ **Mas de Daumas Gassac** [mas duh doh-mas gas-sac] (*Midi*, France) Groundbreaking *Vin de Pays* red from a blend including *Pinot Noir*, *Syrah*, *Mourvèdre*, and *Cabernet*. Good when young, but also lasts for ages. A *Viognier* white is similarly impressive. ★★★★ Blanc 2002 $$$

✧ **Mas Jullien** [mas joo-lye'n] (*Languedoc-Roussillon*, France) The most stylish wines in the *Coteaux du Languedoc* (or elsewhere in southern France). Classic individual reds and whites from classic southern traditional grapes.

✧ **Mas Martinet** [mas mahr-tee-neht] (*Priorato*, Spain) One of a pair of dazzling *Priorato* wines. The *second label* is Martinet Bru.

✧ **Bartolo Mascarello** [mas-kah-reh-loh] (*Piedmont*, Italy) Ultratraditional *Barolo* specialist whose rose-petally wine proves that the old ways can compete with the new. But they do call for patience.

✧ **Giuseppe Mascarello** [mas-kah-reh-loh] (*Piedmont*, Italy) Top-class *Barolo* estate (unconnected with that of *Bartolo Mascarello*), producing characterful wine from individual vineyards. Succeeds in tricky vintages. Great *Dolcetto*. ★★★★★ Barolo Bricco 1997 $$$

✧ **Gianni Masciarelli** [mash-chee-yah-reh-lee] (*Abruzzo*, Italy) One of the starriest makers of Montepulciano d'Abruzzo.

✧ **Masi** [mah-see] (*Veneto*, Italy) Producer with reliable, affordable reds and whites and single-vineyard *Valpolicella's*. Now also producing similar wines in Argentina under the Corbec and Paso Doble labels.
★★★★★ Costasera Amarone Classico 1999 $$$

✧ **La Massa** [mah-sah] (*Tuscany*, Italy) Top class *Chianti* producer with a spectacularly good 1996 Chianti Classico.

✧ **Massandra** [mahsan-drah] (*Crimea*, Ukraine) Famous as the source of great, historic, dessert wines, now a place for okay *Cabernet Sauvignon*.

✧ **Massaya** [mas-sie-yah] (Lebanon) Exciting new venture by a group of French producers including Hubert de Bouard of Ch. l'Angélus.
Master of Wine (MW) One of a small number of people (around 260) internationally who have passed a gruelling set of wine exams.

✧ **Mastroberadino** [maas-tro-be-rah-dino] (*Campania*, Italy) Top producer of rich *Taurasi* in Italy's south as well as fine Fiano di Avellino.

✧ **Matanzas Creek** [muh-tan-zuhs] (*Sonoma Valley*, California) Top-class complex *Chardonnay* (one of California's best), good *Sauvignon*, and high-quality accessible *Merlot*. Pay the extra for "Sonoma Valley" wines rather that ones from "California" (Under the same ownership as *Kendall Jackson*).

❦ **Mataro** [muh-tah-roh] See *Mourvèdre*.

✧ **Mateus** [ma-tay-oos] (Portugal) Pink and white off-dry *frizzante* wine sold in bottles that are traditional in Franken, Germany, and with a label depicting a palace with which the wine has no connection. A 50-year-old marketing masterpiece. The name is now also used for more serious reds.

✧ **Thierry Matrot** [tee-yer-ree ma-troh] (*Burgundy*, France) Top-class white producer with great white and recommendable red *Blagny*.

M

⟁ **Chateau Matsa** [maht-sah] (*Attica*, Greece) Good Greek new-wave producer.

⟁ **Matteo Correggia** [mah-tey-yoh coh-rey-djee-yah] (*Piedmont*, Italy) Producer excelling with Barbera d'Alba and Nebbiolo d'Alba.

⟁ **Matthew Cellars** (*Washington State*) Up-and-coming maker of *Cabernet* and *Sémillon*.

⟁ **Matua Valley** [ma-tyoo-wah] (*Auckland*, New Zealand) Reliable maker of great (*Marlborough*) *Sauvignon*, (Judd Estate) *Chardonnay*, and *Merlot*. Also producer of the even better *Ararimu* red and white. Shingle Peak is the second label. ★★★★★ **Ararimu Chardonnay 2001 $$$**

⟁ **Yvon Mau** [ee-von moh] (*Bordeaux & Southwest*, France) Highly commercial producer of *Bordeaux* and other, mostly white, wines from Southwest France. Occasionally good. ★★★ **Ch Ducla Entre Deux-Mers 2002 $**

⟁ **Ch. Maucaillou** [mow-kai-yoo] (*Moulis Cru Bourgeois, Bordeaux*, France) *Cru Bourgeois* in the *commune* of *Moulis* regularly producing approachable wines to beat some *crus classés*.

Maule [mow-lay] (Chile) Up-and-coming *Central Valley* region; especially for white wines but warm enough for red. el Aromo; Balduzzi; J Bouchon; Santa Carolina; Carta Vieja; Cremaschi Barriga; Domaine Oriental.

⟁ **Bernard Maume** [mohm] (*Burgundy*, France) Small *Gevrey-Chambertin* estate making long-lived wines.

⟁ **Bodegas Mauro** [mow-roh] (Spain) Just outside the *Ribera del Duero DO*, but making very similar rich red wines. ★★★★ **Vendimia Seleccionada, Viño de Mesa de Castilla y León 1997 $**

⟁ **Maury** [moh-ree] (*Languedoc-Roussillon*, France) Potentially rich sweet wine to compete with *Banyuls* and *port*. Sadly, too many examples are light and feeble.

🍇 **Mauzac** [moh-zak] (France) White grape used in southern France for *Vin de Pays* and *Gaillac*. Can be characterful and floral or dull and earthy.

🍇 **Mavrodaphne** [mav-roh-daf-nee] (Greece) Characterful indigenous Greek red grape, and the wine made from it. Dark and strong, needs aging to be worth drinking. **Kourtakis.**

🍇 **Mavrud** [mah-vrood] (Bulgaria) Rustic, characterful red grape and wine.

⟁ **Maximin Grünhaus** [mak-siee-min groon-hows] (*Mosel-Saar-Ruwer*, Germany) 1,000-year-old estate producing intense *Rieslings*.

⟁ **Maxwell** (*McLaren Vale*, Australia) Reliable producer of *Shiraz, Merlot*, and *Sémillon*, and good mead. ★★★ **Maxwell Ellen Street Shiraz 1999 $$**

⟁ **Mayacamas** [my-yah-kah-mas] (*Napa Valley*, California) Long-established winery on *Mount Veeder* with *tannic* but good old-fashioned *Cabernet*, and long-lived, rich *Chardonnay*.

⟁ **Mazis-Chambertin** [mah-zee shom-behr-tan] (*Burgundy*, France) Grand Cru vineyard in which some of Gevrey-Chambertin's best producers have land.

⟁ **McGuigan Brothers** (*Hunter Valley*, Australia) Commercial and occasionally impressive stuff from the former owners of *Wyndham Estate*. Too often, however, wines are too oaky and/or too sweet.

McLaren Vale (*South Australia*) Region renowned for European-style wines, but with varied topography, soil, and climate. D'Arenberg; Beresford; Chapel Hill; Hardy's; Kays Amery; Maglieri; Geoff Merrill; Penny's Hill; Pirramimma; Ch. Reynella; Shottesbrooke; Tatachilla; Wirra Wirra. ★★★★★ 2000 Tatachilla McLaren Vale Shiraz $$

⟁ **McWilliams** (*Hunter Valley*, Australia) Big, *Hunter Valley*-based, evidently non-republican, firm with great traditional ("Elizabeth") *Semillon* and ("Philip") *Shiraz*. Fortified wines can be good, too, as are the pioneering *Barwang* and improved *Brand's* wines. Distributed by *E&J Gallo*.

⟁ **Médoc** [may-dok] (*Bordeaux*, France) Area of *Bordeaux* immediately south of the *Gironde* and north of the town of *Bordeaux* in which the *Cru Classés* as well as far more ordinary fare are made. Should be better than basic *Bordeaux* and less good than *Haut-Médoc*. This is not always the case.

⟁ **Meerlust Estate** [meer-loost] (*Stellenbosch*, South Africa) Top *Cape* estate. Classy *Merlots* and a highly rated *Bordeaux*-blend called "Rubicon".

M

Gabriel Meffre [mef-fr] (*Rhône*, France) Sound *Rhône* and, now, southern France producer under the Galet Vineyards and Wild Pig labels.

Ch. Megyer [meg-yer] (*Tokaji*, Hungary) French-owned pioneer of *Tokaji* and *Furmint*.

Alphonse Mellot [mel-loh] (*Loire*, France) Dynamic, quality-driven producer. ★ ★ ★ 2001 Sancerre Blanc la Moussière Alphonse Mellot $$

Melnik [mehl-neek] (Bulgaria) Both a grape variety and a commune where rich reds are produced.

Melon de Bourgogne [muh-lon duh boor-goyn] (France) Grape originally imported from *Burgundy* (where it is no longer grown) to the *Loire* by Dutch brandy distillers who liked its resistance to frost. Now grown for *Muscadet*.

Charles Melton (*Barossa Valley*, Australia) Lovely still and sparkling *Shiraz* and world-class rosé called "Rose of Virginia", as well as Nine Popes, a wine based on *Châteauneuf-du-Pape*.

Mendocino [men-doh-see-noh] (California) Northern, coastal wine county known for unofficial marijuana farming and for laid-back winemakers who successfully exploit cool microclimates to make "European-style" wines. *Fetzer; Handley Cellars;* Hidden Cellars; *Lazy Creek; Parducci; Roederer.*

Mendoza [men-doh-zah] (Argentina) Source of good rich reds, traditional but bright-fruited, from firms including La Agricola; Bianchi; *Catena; Etchart;* Finca Flichman; *Lurton; Morande; Norton; la Rural;* San Telmo; *Trapiche;Weinert.*

Menetou-Salon [men-too sah-lon] (*Loire*, France) Bordering on *Sancerre*, making similar if earthier, less pricey *Sauvignon*, as well as some decent *Pinot Noir. Henri Pellé* makes the best. De Beaurepaire; R. Champault; Charet; Fournier; de Loye; Pellé; la Tour St Martin.

Dom. Méo-Camuzet [may-oh-ka-moo-zay] (*Burgundy*, France) Brilliant *Côte de Nuits* estate with top-class vineyards and intense, oaky wines, made, until his retirement, by the great *Henri Jayer.*
★ ★ ★ ★ ★ 1999 Nuits St Georges 1er Cru Aux Boudots

Mercaptans [mehr-kap-ton] See *Hydrogen sulphide.*

Mer Soleil [mehr soh-lay] (California) Producer of big, oaky, fruity, slightly old-fashioned Central Coast *Chardonnays.*

Melnik [mehl-neek] (Bulgaria) Both a grape variety and a commune where rich reds are produced.

Mercier [mehr-see-yay] (*Champagne*, France) Sister company of *Moët & Chandon*, and producer of improving but pretty commercial sparkling wine that, according to the advertisements, is the biggest seller in France.
★ ★ ★ Champagne Mercier demi-sec $$$

Mercouri [mehr-koo-ree] (*Peloponnese*, Greece) Starry new-wave producer with good reds and very successful Roditis.

Mercurey [mehr-koo-ray] (*Burgundy*, France) *Côte Chalonnaise* village, where *Faiveley* makes high-quality wine. Dom Brintet; Marguerite Carillon; Ch. de Chamirey; *Dom. Faiveley;* Genot-Boulanger; Michel Juillot; *Olivier Leflaive;* Meix-Foulot; *Pillot.* ★ ★ ★ 2000 Mercurey 1er Cru Les Byots Domaine Menand $$

Région de Mercurey [ray-jee-yo'n dur mehr-koo-ray] (Burgundy, France) Alternative name for the Côte Chalonnaise.

Meridian (*San Luis Obispo*, California) Unusually good-value *Pinot Noir* from *Santa Barbara.* The *Merlot* and *Chardonnay* are impressive too.

Meritage [may-rit-taj] (California) Term for red or white Bordeaux-style blends. ★ ★ ★ 1999 Jackson-Triggs Proprietors' Grand Reserve Meritage $$

Merlot [mehr-loh] Red variety used to balance the more *tannic Cabernet Sauvignon* throughout the *Médoc*, where it is the most planted grape (as it is in *Pomerol* and *St. Emilion*). Increasingly, though not spectacularly, successful in the *Languedoc*. California's best include *Newton, Matanzas Creek*, and (recently) *Duckhorn.* Australia, South Africa, and New Zealand have had few real stars, but there are impressive efforts from *Washington State* and Chile. At best, appealing, soft, honeyed, toffeeish wine.

Merricks Estate (*Mornington Peninsula*, Australia) Small *Shiraz* specialist.

Geoff Merrill (*McLaren Vale*, Australia) The ebullient moustachioed winemaker who has nicknamed himself "The Wizard of Oz". Impressive if restrained *Semillon*, *Chardonnay*, and *Cabernet* in *McLaren Vale* under his own label, plus easier-going Mount Hurtle wines (especially the rosé). ★★★★★ **Henley Shiraz 1996 $$$**

Merry Edwards (*California*, USA) Star consultant winemaker Edwards has established her own *Pinot Noir* vineyard, with (so far) excellent results.

Merryvale (*Napa Valley*, California) Starry winery with especially good Reserve and Silhouette *Chardonnay* and Profile *Cabernet*.

Louis Métaireau [meht-teh-roh] (*Loire*, France) The Cadillac of *Muscadet*, which comes here in the form of individual *cuvées*. Cuvée One is the star.

Méthode Champenoise [may-tohd shom-puh-nwahz] Term now outlawed by the EU but still used to describe the way all quality sparkling wines are made. Labour intensive because bubbles are made by secondary fermentation in bottle, rather than in a vat or by the introduction of gas. Bottles are given the "*dégorgement* process", more wine is added, and they are recorked.

Methuselah Same size bottle as an *Imperiale* (six liters). Used in *Champagne*.

Meursault [muhr-soh] (*Burgundy*, France) Superb *Chardonnay* with nutty, buttery richness. It has no *Grands Crus* but great *Premiers Crus* like Charmes, Perrières, and Genevrières. There is a little red, some sold as *Volnay-Santenots*. Ampeau; d'Auvenay; Coche-Dury; Drouhin; Henri Germain; Jobard; Comtes Lafon; Michelot; Pierre Morey; Jacques Prieur; Ch. de Puligny-Montrachet; Ropiteau; Roulot; Roux Père et Fils; Verget.

Ch. de Meursault [muhr-soh] (*Burgundy*, France) One of *Burgundy*'s few *châteaux* and worth a visit. The wines – better than most produced by its owner, *Patriarche* – are good too. ★★★★ **Meursault du Chateau 2001 $$$**

Mexico See *Baja California*.

Ch. Meyney [may-nay] (*St. Estèphe Cru Bourgeois, Bordeaux*, France) Improving *St. Estèphe* property, with quite rich-flavored wines.

Miani [mee-yah-nee] (*Friuli-Venezia Giulia*, Italy) Good *Bordeaux*-style reds, *Riesling*, and *Chardonnay* from Enzo Pontoni.

Peter Michael (*Sonoma*, California) UK-born Sir Peter Michael produces stunning *Sonoma*, *Burgundy*-like *Chardonnays*, *Sauvignon*, and *Cabernet*. ★★★★★ **Mon Plaisir Chardonnay 1998 $$$**

Louis Michel et Fils [mee-shell] (*Burgundy*, France) Top-class *Chablis* producer. ★★★★★ **Chablis 1er Cru Montmain 2000 $$$$**

Robert Michel (*Rhône*, France) Produces softer *Cornas* than most from this sometimes tough *appellation*: beautiful, strong yet silky wines.

Alain Michelot [mee-shloh] (*Burgundy*, France) Producer of perfumed, elegant *Nuits-St.-Georges* that can be enjoyed young – but is worth keeping.

Dom. Michelot-Buisson [mee-shloh bwee-son] (*Burgundy*, France) Wines are rarely subtle, but they never lack *Meursault* flavor.

Micro-Wine/Micro-Vin Term used to describe limited-production wines such as *Le Pin* and *Screaming Eagle*.

Mildara Blass [mil-dah-rah] (*South Australia*) Dynamic, market-driven company whose portfolio includes *Rothbury*, *Yarra Ridge*, *Yellowglen*, *Wolf Blass*, *Balgownia*, Mount Helen, *Stonyfell*, *Saltram*, and *Maglieri*. *Coonawarra* wines, including the very commercial *Jamieson's Run*, are best. Annie's Lane is also worthwhile.

Millton Estate (*Gisborne*, New Zealand) James Millton makes first-class organic *Chenin Blanc* and *Chardonnay* wine in *Gisborne*.

Milmanda [mil-man-dah] (*Conca de Barbera*, Spain) *Torres*' top *Chardonnay*.

Kym Milne Successful antipodean *flying winemaker* working with Vinfruco in South Africa, at Le Trulle in southern Italy, and at *Nagyrede* in Hungary.

Minervois [mee-nehr-vwah] (*Southwest*, France) Improving reds. Old-vine *Carignan* can be richly intense; *maceration-carbonique* wines from younger *Carignan* can compete with *Beaujolais*; *Mourvèdre* can be perfumed, and

M

Syrah, spicy. Look for the la Livinière sub-region, where Jean-Christophe Piccinini is based. Whites and rosés are considerably less interesting. Abbott's; Gérard Bertrand; Clos Centeilles; Ch. Coupe Roses; Dom. Cros; Gourgazaud; Ch. d'Oupia; Châ. de Paraza; Piccinini; Ste. Eulalie; la Tour Boisée;Villerambert-Julien.

Minöségi Bor [mee-ner-shay-gee bohr-] (Hungary) Quality wine; the local equivalent of AC.

Mis en Bouteille au Ch./Dom. [mee zon boo-tay] (France) Estate-bottled.

Misket (Bulgaria) Dullish, sometimes faintly herby white grape.

Mission (*Hawkes Bay*, New Zealand) Still run by monks nearly 150 years after its foundation, this estate is now one of the best in New Zealand.

Mission Hill (*British Columbia*, Canada) Dynamic producer of styles, ranging from *Riesling icewine* to *Merlot*. ★★★★ Estate Riesling Icewine 2001 $$$

Ch. la Mission-Haut-Brion [lah mee-see-yon oh-bree-yon] (*Pessac-Léognan Cru Classé, Bordeaux*, France) Rich reds that rival and occasionally even overtake its supposedly classier neighbor, *Haut-Brion*.

Mitchell (*Clare Valley*, Australia) Good producer of *Riesling* and of the Peppertree *Shiraz*. Also good for powerful *Grenache, Riesling, Semillon*, and sparkling *Shiraz*. ★★★★★ Marsanne 2002 $

Mitchelton (*Goulburn Valley*, Australia) Producer of good *Marsanne* and *Sémillon*. *Late harvest Rieslings* are also good, as is a *Beaujolais*-style red, "Cab Mac". The French-style Preece range – named after the former winemaker – is also worth seeking out. ★★★★ Airstrip Marsanne-Rousanne-Viognier 2002 $$

Mittelhaardt [mit-tel-hahrt] (*Pfalz*, Germany) Central and best *Bereich* of the *Rheinpfalz*.

Mittelmosel [mit-tel-moh-zul] (*Mosel-Saar-Ruwer*, Germany) Middle and best section of the *Mosel*, including the *Bernkastel Bereich*.

Mittelrhein [mit-tel-rine] (Germany) Small, northern section of the *Rhine*. Good *Rieslings* that sadly are rarely seen outside Germany. *Toni Jost*.

Mittnacht-Klack [mit-nakt-clack] (*Alsace*, France) Seriously high-quality wines with particular accent on "*vendange tardive*" and *late harvest* wines.

Moelleux [mwah-luh] (France) Sweet.

Moët & Chandon [moh-wet ay shon-don] (*Champagne*, France) The biggest producer in *Champagne*. *Dom Pérignon*, the top wine, and *vintage* Moët are fine, and Brut Imperial Non vintage usually reliable. Watch out too for a good *Brut* rosé. ★★★★★ Dom Perignon 1995 $$$$

Clos Mogador [kloh MOH-gah-dor] (*Priorato*, Spain) Juicy, modern, and more importantly, stylish red wine from the once ultratraditional and rustic region of *Priorat*. The shape of things to come.

Moillard [mwah-yar] (*Burgundy*, France) *Négociant* whose best wines are sold under the "Dom. Thomas Moillard" label.

Mauro Molino [moh-lee-noh] (*Piedmont*, Italy) Modern Barolo worth seeking out, and good Barbaresco. ★★★★ Barolo Vigna Conca 1998 $$$

Monbazillac [mon-ba-zee-yak] (*Southwest*, France) *Bergerac AC* using the white grapes of *Bordeaux* – Sémillon and Sauvignon, plus some Muscadelle – to make alternatives to *Sauternes*. Pierre Alard; Ancienne Cure; Belingard; Grande Maison;Tirecul-la-Gravière

Ch. Monbousquet [mon-boo-skay] (*St. Emilion Grand Cru Classé, Bordeaux*, France) Rich, concentrated wines. The 2000 was notable.

Ch. Monbrison [mon-bree-son] (*Margaux, Bordeaux*, France) *Cru Bourgeois* that has become a reliable, constant overperformer. A great 2001.

Mönchof [mern-chof] (*Mosel*, Germany) Top *Mosel* producer in *Urzig*.

Ch. de Moncontour [mon-con-toor] (*Loire*, France) Recommendable source of *Vouvray*.

M

Ⴢ **Robert Mondavi** [mawn-dah-vee] (*Napa Valley*, California) Pioneering producer of great Reserve *Cabernet* and *Pinot Noir*, and *Chardonnay*, and inventor of *oaky Fumé Blanc Sauvignon*. Owns *Arrowood* and Byron and co-owns *Opus One* (with *Ch Mouton Rothschild*). Also in joint ventures with *Caliterra* in Chile (*Seña*) and *Frescobaldi* in *Tuscany* (*Luce, Ornellaia*). Wanted to invest in S. France close to Mas de Daumas Gassac. The Woodbridge and Coastal range lack substance, but the top wines such as the To Kalon Cabernet and Carneros wines deserve credit for subtlety.

♔ **Mondeuse** [mon-durz] (France) Red grape found in Savoie; Refosco in Italy.

Ⴢ **la Mondotte** [mon-dot] (*St. Emilion, Bordeaux*, France) Ultra-intense rich micro-wine produced by the owner of Canon la Gaffelière.

Ⴢ **Mongeard-Mugneret** [mon-zhahr moon-yeh-ray] (*Burgundy*, France) A reliable source of excellent and sometimes stunningly exotic red *Burgundy*.

♔ **Monica (di Cagliari/Sardegna)** [moh-nee-kah] (*Sardinia*, Italy) Red grape and wine of *Sardinia* producing drily tasty and fortified spicy wine.

Ⴢ **Marqués de Monistrol** [moh-nee-strol] (*Catalonia*, Spain) Single-estate *Cava*. Also successfully producing noble varietals.

 Monopole [mo-noh-pohl] (France) Literally, exclusive – single ownership of an entire vineyard. Romanée-Conti and Château Grillet are good examples.

Ⴢ **Mont Gras** [mon gra] (*Colchagua*, Chile) Fast-improving winery.

Ⴢ **Clos du Mont Olivet** [Mo(n)-toh-lee-vay] (*Rhône*, France) Good *Châteauneuf-du-Pape* producer. *Cuvée du Pape* is the top wine.

Ⴢ **Les Producteurs du Mont Tauch** [mon-tohsh] (*Midi*, France) Southern cooperative with surprisingly good, top-of-the-line wines.

Ⴢ **Montagne St. Emilion** [mon-tan-yuh san tay-mee-yon] (*Bordeaux*, France) A "satellite" of *St. Emilion*. Often very good-value *Merlot-dominant* reds which can outclass supposedly finer fare from *St. Emilion* itself. Drink young. Ch. d'Arvouet; Beauséjour; Bonfort; Calon; Corbin; Faizeau; Fauconnière; Vieux Château Calon.

Ⴢ **Montagny** [mon-tan-yee] (*Burgundy*, France) Small hillside *Côte Chalonnaise* commune producing good, lean *Chardonnay* that can be a match for many *Pouilly-Fuissés*. Confusingly, unlike other parts of Burgundy, *Premier Crus* here are not from better vineyards; they're just made from riper grapes. Bertrand & Juillot; J-M Boillot; Cave de Buxy; Ch. de Davenay; Joseph Faiveley; Louis Latour; Olivier Leflaive; Bernard Michel; Moillard; Antonin Rodet; Ch. de la Saule; Jean Vachet.

Ⴢ **Montalcino** [mon-tal-chee-noh] (*Tuscany*, Italy) Village near Sienna known for *Brunello di Montalcino, Chianti's* big brother, whose reputation was largely created by *Biondi Santi*, whose wines no longer deserve the prices they command. *Rosso di Montalcino* is lighter. Altesino; Banfi; Costanti; Frescobaldi; Poggio Antico. ★★★★ 1997 Banfi Brunello di Montalcino Poggio Alle Juira $$$$

Ⴢ **Montana** (*Marlborough*, New Zealand) Impressively consistent, huge firm with tremendous *Sauvignons*, improving *Chardonnays*, and good-value *Lindauer* and *Deutz Marlborough Cuvée* sparkling wine. Reds are improving but still tend to be on the green side. Look out for the Church Road wines and the smartly packaged single-estate wines such as the Brancott *Sauvignon*. ★★★★★ 2000 Stoneleigh Rapaura Series Pinot Noir Marlborough $$

Ⴢ **Domaine du Mont d'Or** [mon dohr] (Valais, Switzerland) Good quality across the board from this estate.

Ⴢ **Monte Real** [mon-tay ray-al] (*Rioja*, Spain) Made by Bodegas Riojanos; generally decent, richly flavored, and *tannic Rioja*.

Ⴢ **Montecarlo** [mon-tay car-loh] (*Tuscany*, Italy) A wide variety of grapes are allowed here, including Rhône varieties such as the *Syrah* and *Roussanne* as well as the *Sangiovese* and the red and white *Bordeaux* varieties. Unsurprisingly, there are good IGTs too. Carmignani; Wandanna.

Ⴢ **Fattoria di Montechiari** [mon-tay-kee-yah-ree] (*Tuscany*, Italy) A fast-rising star in Montecarlo, producing rich, berryish, varietal reds under the Montechiari name using the *Cabernet Sauvignon*, *Sangiovese*, and *Pinot Noir*. The *Chardonnay* is worth looking out for too.

M

�). **Bodegas Montecillo** [mon-tay-thee-yoh] (*Rioja*, Spain) Classy wines including the oddly named Viña Monty. The Cumbrero Blanco white is good, too. ★★★★ **Rioja Reserva 1997 $$**

�. **Montée de Tonnerre** [mon-tay duh ton-nehr] (*Burgundy*, France) Excellent *Chablis Premier Cru*.

�. Montefalco Sagrantino [mon-teh-fal-koh sag-ran-tee-noh] (Umbria, Italy) Intense, characterful, cherryish red made from the local Sagrantino grape. Rosso di Montefalco is a Sagrantino/Sangiovese/Trebbiano blend.

�. **Ch. Montelena** [mon-teh-lay-nah] (*Napa Valley*, California) Its two long-lived *Chardonnays* (from Napa and the rather better Alexander Valley) make this one of the more impressive producers in the state. The vanilla-and-blackcurranty *Cabernet* can be impenetrable. I prefer the *Zinfandel*.

🍇 Montepulciano [mon-tay-pool-chee-yah-noh] (Italy) Very confusingly, this is both a grape used to make rich red wines in central and south-eastern Italy (Montepulciano *d'Abruzzi*, etc) and the name of a wine-producing town in *Tuscany* (see *Vino Nobile di Montepulciano*) which (yes, you guessed) uses a different grape altogether.

Monterey [mon-teh-ray] (California) Underrated region south of San Francisco, producing potentially good if sometimes rather grassy wines. **Estancia; Foggarty; Hess Colection; Jekel; Sterling; Redwood Trail.**

�. **The Monterey Vineyard** (*Monterey*, California) Generally reliable inexpensive varietal wines now sold overseas under the Redwood Trail label.

�. **Monte Rossa** [mon-teh ros-sah] (*Lombardy*, Italy) A really top class Franciacorta producer with two key wines in the Satèn and Cabochon cuvées.

�. **Viña Montes** [mon-tehs] (*Curico*, Chile) Leading Chilean enologist Aurelio Montes' go-getting winery with good reds, including the flagship Alpha M and improved *Sauvignon*. Montes Folly is the *Syrah*-based super-cuvée.

�. **Fattoria di Montevertine** [mon-teh-ver-TEE-neh] (*Tuscany*, Italy) Pioneer of modern *Tuscan* wine, and of the rediscovery of the *Sangiovese* grape. Le Pergole Torte is the long-lived top wine. Il Sodaccio is also fine.

�. **Montevetrano** [mon-teh-veh-trah-noh] (*Campania*, Italy) Innovative producer applying skilled winemaking to a novel blend of the local Aglianico and the *Cabernet Sauvignon* and *Merlot* – and making a world-class red.

�. **Monteviña** [mon-tay-veen-yah] (*Amador County*, California) *Sutter Home* subsidiary, making exceptionally good *Amador County Zinfandel* and reliable *Barbera*, *Cabernet*, *Chardonnay*, and *Fumé Blanc*. ★★★★ **Barbera 2000 $$**

�. Monthelie [mon-tuh-lee] (Burgundy, France) Often overlooked Côte de Beaune village producing potentially stylish reds and whites. The appropriately named Dom. Monthelie-Douhairet is the most reliable estate. *Coche-Dury; Jaffelin; Comtes Lafon; Olivier Leflaive; Leroy; Monthelie-Douhairet; Ch. de Puligny-Montrachet; Roulot.* ★★★ 1997 Ch. de Monthélie Eric de Suremain $$$

Montilla-Moriles [mon-tee-yah maw-ree-lehs] (Spain) *DO* region where *sherry*-type wines are produced in *soleras*. These are often so high in alcohol as to render fortification unnecessary. Good examples offer far better value than many sherries. Occasional successes achieve far more. Pérez Barquero; Albalá.

�. **Dom. de Montille** [duh mon-tee] (*Burgundy*, France) A lawyer-cum-winemaker whose *Volnays* and *Pommards*, if rather tough and astringent when young, are unusually fine and long-lived. Classy stuff.

�. Montlouis [mon-lwee] (Loire, France) Neighbor of *Vouvray* making similar, lighter-bodied, dry, sweet, and sparkling wines. **Berger; François Chidaine; Delétang; Levasseur; Moyer; la Taille aux Loups.**

�. Le Montrachet [luh mon-ra-shay] (Burgundy, France) This *Grand Cru* vineyard (also known as plain Montrachet) is shared between *Chassagne*- and *Puligny-Montrachet*, with its neighbors *Bâtard-M.*, Chevalier-M., Bienvenue-Bâtard-M., and Criots-Bâtard-M. Potentially the greatest, biscuitiest white *Burgundy* – and thus dry white wine – in the world. *Bouchard Père et Fils; Marc Colin; Drouhin (Marquis de Laguiche); Comtes Lafon; Leflaive (Olivier and Domaine); Ramonet; Domaine de la Romanée-Conti; Sauzet.*

M

Ⓣ **Montravel** [mon'-ravel] (Southwest France) Region with four separate *appellations*: Montravel itself, for dry *Sémillon/Sauvignon* and now for Bordeaux-style red; and *Côtes de Montravel* and Haut-Montravel, both of which produce semisweet, medium-sweet, and *late-harvest* whites. Ch du Bloy; Pique-Serre; Puy-Servain; la Roche-Marot.

Ⓣ **Ch. de Mont-Redon** [mo'n-rur-do'n] (*Rhône*, France) Large and excellent Châteauneuf-du-Pape estate; white has finesse and weight, too.

Ⓣ **Ch. Montrose** [mon-rohz] (*St. Estèphe 2ème Cru Classé, Bordeaux,* France) Back-on-track *St. Estèphe* renowned for its longevity. More typical of the *appellation* than *Cos d'Estournel* but sometimes (including 2002) less approachable in its youth. However, still maintains a rich, tarry, inky style.

Ⓣ **Ch. Montus** [mon-toos] (*Southwest,* France) Ambitious producer in *Madiran* with carefully oaked examples of *Tannat* and *Pacherenc de Vic Bilh*. *Bouscassé* is a cheaper, more approachable label.

Ⓣ **Moondah Brook** (*Swan Valley,* Australia) An atypically (for the baking *Swan Valley*) cool vineyard belonging to *Houghtons* (and thus *Hardys*). The stars are the wonderful tangy *Verdelho* and richly oaky *Chenin Blanc*. The *Chardonnay* and reds are less impressive.

Ⓣ **Moorilla Estate** [moo-rillah] (*Tasmania*, Australia) Long-established, recently reconstituted estate with particularly good *Riesling*.

Ⓣ **Mór** [moh-uhr] (Hungary) Region gaining a name for its dry whites.

Ⓣ **Moraga** (*Bel Air*, California) Multimillion dollar homes were demolished to create this steeply sloping seven-acre vineyard in the heart of Bel Air. So, the $100 price tag on its Bordeaux-like wine seems almost modest. The quality is good, too – thanks to the involvement of Tony Soter of *Etude*.

Ⓣ **Morande** [moh-ran-day] (Argentina/Chile) Impressive winemaker, producing wine often from pioneering varieties that are grown on both sides of the Andes. ★★★★ **Morande Terrarum Pinot Noir 2002 $$**

Ⓣ **Moreau-Naudet** [moh-roh noh-day] (*Burgundy,* France) Small, up-and-coming producer of *Chablis*. ★★★★ **Chablis 1er Cru Montée de Tonnerre 2000 $$**

Ⓣ **Morellino di Scansano** [moh-ray-lee-noh dee skan-sah-noh] (*Tuscany,* Italy) Cherry and raspberry, young-drinking red made from a clone of *Sangiovese*. *Barbi;* Cantina Cooperativa; Il Grillesino; Moris Farms; Motta; le Pupille.

Ⓣ **Dom. Marc Morey** [maw-ray] (*Burgundy,* France) Estate producing stylish white *Burgundy*. ★★★★ 2000 **Chassagne-Montrachet 1er Cru Les Vergers $$$**

Ⓣ **Dom. Pierre Morey** [maw-ray] (*Burgundy,* France) Top-class *Meursault* producer known for concentrated wines in good vintages. ★★★ **Meursault Charmes 2000 $$$**

Ⓣ **Bernard Morey et Fils** [maw-ray] (*Burgundy,* France) Top-class producer in *Chassagne-Montrachet* with good vineyards here and in *St. Aubin*. ★★★★ **Chassagne-Montrachet La Maltroie 2000 $$$**

Ⓣ **Morey-St.-Denis** [maw-ray san duh-nee] (*Burgundy,* France) *Côtes de Nuits* village which produces richly smooth reds, especially the *Grand Cru* "Clos de la Roche". Best producer is *Domaine Dujac*, which virtually makes this *appellation* its own. *Bruno Clair; Dujac; Faiveley;* Georges Lignier; *Hubert Lignier; Ponsot.*

Ⓣ **Morgon** [mohr-gon] (*Burgundy,* France) One of the 10 *Beaujolais Crus*. Worth maturing, as it can take on a delightful chocolate/cherry character. J-M Burgaud; Dom. Calon; *Georges Duboeuf (aka Marc Dudet);* F&J Calot; Bernard Collonge; Jean Descombes; *Sylvain Fessy;* Jean Foillard; Lapierre; Piron; Savoye.

🍇 **Morio Muskat** [maw-ree-yoh moos-kat] White grape grown in Germany and Eastern Europe and making simple, grapey wine.

Ⓣ **Moris Farms** (Italy) Splendid *Morellino di Scansano* and even better Avvoltore, *Sangiovese/Cabernet/Syrah.*

M

Mornington Peninsula (*Victoria*, Australia) Some of Australia's newest and most southerly vineyards on a perpetual upward crescent. Close to Melbourne and under threat from housing developers. Good *Pinot Noir*, minty *Cabernet*, and juicy *Chardonnay*, though other varieties are now proving successful. *Dromana*; Elgee Park; Merricks; *Paringa*; Stonier; T'Gallant.

Morris of Rutherglen (*Rutherglen*, Australia) Despite the takeover by *Orlando* and the retirement of local hero and champion winemaker, Mick Morris, this is still an extraordinarily successful producer of delicious *Liqueur Muscat* and *Tokay* (seek out the Show Reserve). Also worth buying is a weird and wonderful *Shiraz-Durif* sparkling red.

Denis Mortet [mor-tay] (*Burgundy*, France) Fast up-and-coming producer with intense, rich, dark, straight *Gevrey-Chambertin*, every bit as good as some of his neighbors' *Grands Crus*. ★★★ Chambertin 2000 $$$

Morton Estate (*Waikato*, New Zealand) Maker of fine *Sauvignon*, *Chardonnay*, and *Bordeaux* styles. ★★★★★ Stone Creek Sauvignon Blanc 2002 $$

Mosbacher [moss-bahk-kur] (*Pfalz*, Germany) High-quality estate producing spicy *Rieslings* in Forst.

Moscadello di Montalcino [moss-kah-del-loh dee mon-tal-chee-noh] (*Tuscany*, Italy) Once common sweet white that's now being revived. It comes in fizzy and passito versions, too.

Moscatel de Setúbal [mos-kah-tel day say-too-bahl] (Portugal) See *Setúbal*.

Moscato [mos-kah-toh] (Italy) The Italian name for *Muscat*, widely used across Italy in all styles of white wine from *Moscato d'Asti*, through the more serious *d'Asti*, to dessert wines like *Moscato di Pantelleria* and *Moscato Passito*. Also pink: *Mocato Rosa*.. Beni di Batasiolo; Donnafugata; M. Chiarlo; Contero

Moscato d'Asti [mos-kah-toh das-tee] (Italy) Delightfully grapey, sweet, and fizzy, low-alcohol wine from the *Muscat*, or *Moscato*, grape. Far more flavorsome (and cheaper) than designer alcoholic lemonade. Drink young.

Moscato (Passito) di Pantelleria [pah-see-toh dee pan-teh-leh-ree-yah] (*Sicily*, Italy) Gloriously traditional sweet wine made on an island off *Sicily* from grapes that are dried out of doors until they have shrivelled into raisins. ★★★★ Salvatore Murana, Khamma 2000 $$

Moscofilero [moss-koh-fee-leh-roh] (Greece) Aromatic, quite spicy white grape with good acidity. Good quality.

Mosel/Moselle [moh-zuhl] (Germany) River and term loosely used for wines made around the Mosel and nearby Saar and Ruwer rivers. Equivalent to the "*Hock*" of the Rhine. (Moselblumchen is the equivalent of Liebfraumilch.) Not to be confused with France's uninspiring *Vins de Moselle*. The wines tend to have flavors of green fruits when young but develop a wonderful ripeness as they fill out with age. *Dr. Loosen*; JJ Christobel; Jakoby-Mathy; Freiherr von Heddersdorff; Willi Haag; Heribert Kerpen; Weingut Karlsmuhle; Karp-Schreiber; *Immich Batterieberg*.

Lenz Moser [lents moh-zur] (Austria) Big producer with good wines from the Klosterkeller Siegendorf. ★★★ Siegendorf Weissburgunder Kabinett 2002 $$

Sepp Moser [Sep moh-zur] (Austria) Estate with vineyards in Apetlon and Rohrendorf and a fine range that includes dry *Gruner Veltliners* and luscious dessert wines. ★★★★ Weissburgunder Beerenauslese 1999 $$

Moss Wood (*Margaret River*, Australia) Pioneer producer of *Pinot Noir*, *Cabernet*, and *Semillon*. Wines last well and have a very French feel to them. Do not confuse with Moss Brothers. ★★★★ Glenmore Cabernet 2000 $$

La Motte Estate [la mot] (*Franschhoek*, South Africa) Best known for top *Shiraz*. ★★★ Shiraz 2000 $

Herdade de Mouchão [Hehr-dah-day dey moo sha-'oh] (*Alentejo*, Portugal) Estate producing high-quality reds in this up-and-coming region.

J.P. Moueix [mwex] (*Bordeaux*, France) Top-class *négociant*/producer, Christian *Moueix* specializes in stylishly traditional *Pomerol* and *St. Emilion* and is responsible for *Pétrus*, *La Fleur-Pétrus*, Bel Air, Richotey, and *Dominus* in California. (Do not confuse with any other Moueixs.)

M

ℤ **Moulin Touchais** [moo-lan too-shay] (*Loire,* France) Producer of intensely honeyed, long-lasting, sweet white from *Coteaux du Layon*.

ℤ **Moulin-à-Vent** [moo-lan-na-von] (*Burgundy,* France) One of the 10 *Beaujolais Crus* – big and rich at its best, like *Morgon,* it can benefit from aging. Charvet; Degrange; *Duboeuf;* Paul Janin; Janodet; Lapierre; *Ch. du Moulin-à-Vent;* la Tour du Bief. ★★★ 2000 Domaine de Champ de Cour $

ℤ **Ch. Moulin-à-Vent** [moo-lan-na-von] (*Moulis Cru Bourgeois, Bordeaux,* France) Leading *Moulis* property.

ℤ **Ch. du Moulin-à-Vent** [moo-lan-na-von] (*Burgundy,* France) Reliable producer of *Moulin-à-Vent*.

ℤ **Moulis** [moo-lees] (*Bordeaux,* France) Red wine village of the *Haut-Médoc;* traditionally offering more approachable good-value *Crus Bourgeois* than its neighbor *Listrac,* but now facing tougher competition. Ch. Anthonic; *Chasse-Spleen; Maucaillou;* Moulis; *Poujeaux.*

Mount Barker (Western Australia) Cooler-climate, southern region with great *Riesling, Verdelho,* impressive *Chardonnay,* and restrained *Shiraz.* Frankland Estate; *Goundrey; Howard Park; Plantagenet;* Wignalls.

ℤ **Mount Horrocks** (*Clare Valley,* Australia) Inventive *Shiraz* and *Riesling* producer that revived "Cordon Cut" winemaking which concentrates the flavor of the *Riesling* juice by cutting the canes some time before picking the grapes. A screwcap pioneer. ★★★★ **Cordon Cut Riesling 2002 $$**

ℤ **Mount Hurtle** (*McLaren Vale,* South Australia) See *Geoff Merrill.*

ℤ **Mount Langi Ghiran** [lan-gee gee-ran] (*Victoria,* Australia) A *Grampians* maker of excellent cool-climate *Riesling,* peppery *Shiraz,* and very good *Cabernet.* ★★★★ **Langi Shiraz 2000 $$**

ℤ **Mount Mary** (*Yarra Valley,* Australia) Dr. Middleton makes very Gallic *Pinot Noir, Cabernet Sauvignon* and *Chardonnay.* Not always great but among the most interesting wines in Australia. ★★★★ **Pnot Noir 1999 $$**

Mount Veeder (*Napa Valley,* California) Convincing hillside *appellation* producing impressive reds, especially from *Cabernet Sauvignon* and *Zinfandel.* Hess Collection; *Mayacamas;* Mount Veeder Winery; *Ch. Potelle.*

ℤ **Mountadam** (*High Eden Ridge,* Australia) Founded by Coonawarra pioneer David Wynn and his son Adam, but now a subsidiary of the giant LVMH which owns *Moët & Chandon, Krug,* and *Cloudy Bay,* this hilltop winery makes good, rather than great, Burgundian *Chardonnay* and *Pinot Noir* (both still and sparkling) and a blend called "The Red". Other labels include the *Eden Ridge* organic wines, *David Wynn* line, and Samuel's bay.

🍇 **Mourvèdre** [mor-veh-dr] (*Rhône,* France) Floral-spicy *Rhône* grape usually found in blends. Increasingly popular in France and California where, as in Australia, it is called *Mataro.* Also plays a big part in *Ch. Beaucastel.* Jade Mountain; *Penfolds;* Ridge.

Mousse [mooss] The bubbles in *Champagne* and sparkling wines.

Mousseux [moo-sur] (France) Cheap unremarkable sparkling wine.

ℤ **Mouton-Cadet** [moo-ton ka-day] (*Bordeaux,* France) A brilliant commercial invention by Philippe de Rothschild who used it to profit from the name of *Mouton-Rothschild,* with which it has no discernible connection. Until recently the quality and the value for money offered by these wines has been poor, but there have been improvements. The "Réserve" is now better than the basic, and the recently launched white *Graves Réserve* creditable in its own right. Even so, there are better buys to be found on the shelves.

ℤ **Ch. Mouton-Baronne-Philippe** see *Ch. d'Armailhac.*.

ℤ **Ch. Mouton-Rothschild** [moo-ton roth-child] (*Pauillac Premier Cru Classé, Bordeaux,* France) The only *château* to be elevated to a first growth from a second, Mouton can have gloriously rich, complex flavors of roast coffee and blackcurrant. Recent vintages were eclipsed by *Margaux, Lafite,* and *Latour,* but since 1998 there has been a return to quality. President Jacques Chirac sent six bottles of the 1989 as a peace offering to Tony Blair on his 50th birthday. A dozen might have been more appropriate.

M

Mudgee [mud-zhee] (*New South Wales*, Australia) Australia's first *appellation* region, a coolish-climate area now being championed by *Rosemount* as well as by *Rothbury*. Botobolar; Huntington Estate. ★★★★ Mountain Blue Shiraz-Cabernet Sauvignon 1999

ℤ **Muga** [moo-gah] (*Rioja*, Spain) Producer of good old-fashioned *Riojas*, of which Prado Enea is the best. ★★★★ **Prado Enea Gran Reserva 1995 $$**

ℤ **Mugneret-Georges/Mugneret Gibourg** [moon-yeh-ray jee-boor] (*Burgundy*, France) *Côte de Nuits* estate making outstanding quality.

ℤ **Jacques-Frederic Mugnier** [moo-nee-yay] (*Burgundy*, France) *Chambolle-Musigny* estate making long-lived wines from vineyards such as Bonnes-Mares and *Musigny*.

ℤ **Mulderbosch** [mool-duh-bosh] (*Stellenbosch*, South Africa) South Africa's answer to *Cloudy Bay*: exciting *Sauvignon* and *Meursault*-like *Chardonnay*, not to mention a red blend called Faithful Hound.

ℤ **Weingut Müller-Catoir** [moo-luh kah-twah] (*Pfalz*, Germany) Great new-wave producer using new-wave grapes as well as *Riesling*. Search out powerful Grauburgunder, Rieslaner, and *Scheurebe* wines.

ℤ **Egon Müller-Scharzhof** [moo-luh shahrtz-hof] (*Mosel-Saar-Ruwer*, Germany) Truly brilliant *Saar* producer. ★★★★ Scharzhofberger Spätlese 2001 Riesling $$$

🍇 **Müller-Thurgau** [moo-lur-toor-gow] (Germany) Workhorse white grape, which is a *Riesling* x *Sylvaner* cross. It is also known as *Rivaner*. Müller-Thurgau is used for making much unremarkable wine in Germany, but it also yields some gems for certain producers, such as *Müller-Catoir*. Very successful in England.

ℤ **Mumm/Mumm Napa** [murm] (*Champagne*, France/California) Maker of much improved Cordon Rouge *Champagne* and now slightly less good *Cuvée Napa* from California. Recently sold by Seagram to Allied Domecqw, who have greater ambitions.

ℤ **René Muré** [moo-ray] (*Alsace*, France) Producer of full-bodied wines, especially from the *Clos St. Landelin* vineyard.

ℤ **Klosterkellerei Muri Gries** [klos-ter-kel-lehr-rih moo-ree gree-ess] (*Alto Adige*, Italy) Lagrein specialist with seductive Kretzer pink, sturdy red Dunkel, and lovely Abtei Muri riserva.

Murfatlar [moor-fat-lah] (Romania) Major vineyard and research area that is currently having increasing success with *Chardonnay* (including some late-harvest sweet examples), and also with *Cabernet Sauvignon*.

ℤ **Murphy-Goode** (*Alexander Valley*, California) Classy producer of white wines that are quite Burgundian in style and sell at – considering this is California – affordable prices. Murphy-Goode also makes a high quality Cabernet Sauvignon.

ℤ **Bodegas Marqués de Murrieta** [mar-kays day moo-ree-eh-tah] (*Rioja*, Spain) Probably Spain's best old-style *oaky* white (sold as Castillo Ygay), and a traditional version of *Rioja* that is increasingly hard to find nowadays. The red, at its best, is one of the most long-lived, elegant example of this region's wines. You should definitely look out for the old Castillo Ygays from the 1960s with their distinctive old-style labels.

ℤ **Murrietta's Well** (*Livermore*, California) An innovative blend of *Zinfandel*, *Cabernet*, and *Merlot*.

ℤ **Ch. Musar** [moo-sahr] (*Ghazir*, Lebanon) Lebanon's leading winemaker, *Serge Hochar* makes a different red every year, varying the blend of *Cabernet*, *Cinsault*, and *Syrah*. The style veers between *Bordeaux*, the *Rhône*, and Italy, but certainly with Château Musar there's never a risk of becoming bored. Good vintages easily keep for a decade. The *Chardonnay*-based whites are less than dazzling, though, and the Rosé can be very old fashioned. ★★★★★ 1999 $$

M

🌿 **Muscadel** [mus-kah-del] Name used for the *Muscat* in South Africa. Mostly used for late harvest and fortified – *Jerpigo* – styles.

🌿 **Muscadelle** [mus-kah-del] Spicy ingredient in white *Bordeaux*. Confusingly used in *Rutherglen* in Australia to produce fortified wine known as *Tokay*.

🍷 **Muscadet des Coteaux de la Loire/Côtes de Grand Lieu/de Sèvre et Maine** [moos-kah-day day koh-toh dur lah lwar/koht dur gron lyur/dur say-vr' eh mayn] (*Loire*, France) Non-aromatic wines that are made from the *Melon de Bourgogne*. Worthwhile examples are matured for a brief period before being bottled (*"sur lie"*) on their dead yeasts or *lees*. The Côtes de Grand Lieu and the rare Coteaux de la *Loire* can be good, but Sèvre et Maine is less reliable. *Dom. de Chasseloir;* Bossard; Chéreau-Carré; Couillaud; Guindon; *de Goulaine;* Pierre Luneau; Metaireau; Marcel Sautejeau; Sauvion.

🌿 **Muscat** [mus-kat] Generic name for a species of white grape (aka *Moscato* in Italy) of which there are a number of different subspecies.

🌿 **Muscat à Petits Grains** [moos-kah ah puh-tee gran] Aka *Frontignan*, the best variety of Muscat and the grape responsible for *Muscat de Beaumes de Venise, Muscat de Rivesaltes, Asti, Muscat of Samos,* and *Rutherglen* Muscats.

🍷 **Muscat de Cap Corse/Frontignan/Mireval/Rivesaltes/St. Jean de Minervois** (*Languedoc-Roussillon*, France) Fortified Muscats of which Rivesaltes is the most common and St. Jean de Minervois possibly the best.

🌿 **Muscat of Alexandria** [moos-kah] Grape responsible for *Moscatel de Setúbal, Moscatel de Valencia,* and sweet South Australians. Also known as *Lexia*. It is also grown in South Africa (where it is known by both names) and satisfies the Afrikaner sweet tooth as Hanepoot.

🌿 **Muscat Ottonel** [moos-kah ot-oh-nel] *Muscat* variety grown in Middle and Eastern Europe.

🍷 **Musigny** [moo-zee-nyee] (*Burgundy*, France) Potentially wonderful *Grand Cru* from which *Chambolle-Musigny* takes its name. A tiny amount of white is produced here. *De Vogüé;* Groffier; Leroy; Mugnier; Prieur.
★★★★★ Domaine Mugnier 1999 $$$$

Must Unfermented grape juice.

MW See *Master of Wine.*

N

Nackenheim [nahk-ehn-hime] (*Rheinhessen*, Germany) Village in the *Nierstein Bereich* that is unfortunately best known for its nowadays debased *Grosslage*, Gutes Domtal. *Gunderloch;* Kurfürstenhof; Heinrich Seip.

🍷 **Fiorenzo Nada** [fee-yor-ren-zoh nah-dah] (*Piedmont*, Italy) Look for *Barbaresco, Dolcetto d'Alba,* and the Seifile, barrique-aged *Barbera/Nebbiolo.*

Nahe [nah-huh] (Germany) *Anbaugebiet* producing wines which can in the right circumstances combine delicate flavor with full body and taut structure. *Crusius; Schlossgut Diel;* Hermann Donnhoff; Hehner Kiltz; Kruger-Rumpf.

🍷 **Ch. Nairac** [nay-rak] (*Barsac 2ème Cru Classé, Bordeaux,* France) Lush, long-lasting wine sometimes lacking a little complexity. Fine in 2001.

🍷 **Nalle** (*Sonoma*, California) Great *Dry Creek* producer of some of California's (and thus the world's) greatest *Zinfandel*.

Naoussa [nah-oosa] (Greece) Region producing dry red wines, often from the *Xynomavro* grape. Boutari; Dalamaris; Kyr Yanni.

Napa [na-pa] (California) Named after the Native American word for "plenty", this is a region with plentiful wines ranging from ordinary to sublime. Too many are commercially hyped; and none is cheap. The average price of Napa Cabernet is now an almost unbelievable $52! Another problem

N

is that the region as a whole is far too varied in altitude and winemaking conditions to make proper sense as a single *appellation*. On the other hand the 20 or so smaller *appellations* that are found within Napa, such as *Carneros, Stag's Leap, Howell Mountain,* and *Mt. Veeder* deserve greater prominence – as do nearby regions like *Sonoma. Atlas Peak; Beaulieu; Beringer; Cain; Cakebread; Caymus; Chimney Rock; Clos du Val; Crichton Hall; Cuvaison; Diamond Creek; Dom. Chandon; Duckhorn; Dunn; Flora Springs; Franciscan; Frog's Leap; Heitz; Hess Collection; Ch. Montelena; Monteviña; Mumm; Newton; Niebaum-Coppola; Opus One; Ch. Potelle; Phelps; Schramsberg; Screaming Eagle; Shafer; Stag's Leap; Sterling; Turley.*

- **Napa Ridge** (California) Highly successful brand, most of whose pleasant, commercial wines are made from grapes that have been grown outside *Napa*. (Exports from this producer are less confusingly labeled as "Coastal Ridge".)
- **Nautilus Estate** [naw-tih-luhs] (*Marlborough*, New Zealand) *Yalumba's* New Zealand offshoot. Sparkling wine and *Sauvignon*.
  ★★★★ **Nautilus Sauvignon Blanc 2002 $$**
- **Navajas** [na-VA-khas] (*Rioja*, Spain) Small producer making impressive reds and *oaky* whites worth keeping. ★★★ **Crianza Tinto 1999 $$**
- **Navarra** [na-VAH-rah] (Spain) Northern Spanish *DO*, located not far from Pamplona and the western Pyrenees, traditionally renowned for rosés and heavy reds but now producing wines to rival those from neighboring *Rioja*, where prices are often higher. Look for innovative *Cabernet Sauvignon* and *Tempranillo* blends. *Chivite; Guelbenzu; Castillo de Monjardin; Vinicola Murchantina; Nekeas; Ochoa; Palacio de la Vega; Senorio de Sarria.*
  Navarro Correas [na-vah-roh koh-ray-yas] (Argentina) Big, oaky wines with loads of personality. ★★★ **Colleccion Privada Syrah 2000 $$**
- **Nebbiolo** [neh-bee-oh-loh] (*Piedmont*, Italy) Grape of *Piedmont*, producing wines with tarry, cherryish, spicy flavors that are slow to mature but become richly complex – epitomized by *Barolo* and *Barbaresco*. Quality and style vary enormously depending on soil. Aka *Spanna*.
- **Nederburg** [neh-dur-burg] (*Paarl*, South Africa) Huge commercial producer. The Edelkeur *late harvest* wines are the gems of the cellar. Sadly, the best wines are only sold at the annual Nederburg Auction.
  ★★★ **Nederburg Cabernet Sauvignon Reserve 1998 $$$**
- **Neethlingshof** [neet-lings-hof] (South Africa) Large estate with decent quality and an abundance of labels. Lord Neethling Reserve and Lord Neethling Laurentius are Bordeaux blends. ★★★ **Laurentius 1998 $$$**
  Négociant [nay-goh-see-yon] (France) Merchant who buys, matures, and bottles wine. See also *Eléveur*.
  Négociant-manipulant (NM) [ma-nih-pyoo-lon] (*Champagne*, France) Buyer and blender of wines for *Champagne*, identifiable by the NM number which is mandatory on the label.
- **Negroamaro** [nay-groh-ah-mah-roh] (*Puglia*, Italy) A Puglian grape whose name means "bitter-black" and produces fascinating, spicy-gamey reds. Found in *Salice Salentino* and *Copertino* and in increasingly impressive *IGT* wines.
  ★★★★ **Villa Quinziana Cantine Due Palme Squinzano 2001 $$**
  Nelson (New Zealand) Small region, a glorious bus ride to the north-west of *Marlborough*. Holmes; McCashin's; Neudorf; Seifried; Waimea.
  ★★★★ **Seifried Winemakers Collection Pinot Noir 2002 $$**
- **Nemea** [nur-may-yah] (Peloponnese, Greece) Improving cool(ish) climate region for reds made from Agiorgitiko. *Boutari; Semeli; Tsantalis.*
  Ch. Nenin [neh-na'n] (*Bordeaux*, France) Large *Pomerol* estate now under the same ownership as *Léoville-Lascases* and making a great 2001.
- **Nepenthe** [neh-pen-thi] (*Adelaide Hills*, South Australia) Instant star with dazzling *Chardonnay, Semillon, Sauvignon, Pinot Noir, Cabernet-Merlot,* and *Zinfandel.* ★★★★ **Riesling 2002 $$**
- **Ch. la Nerthe** [nehrt] (*Rhône*, France) One of the most exciting estates in *Châteauneuf-du-Pape*, producing rich wines with seductive, dark fruit.

N

Neuburger [noy-bur-gur] (Austria) A white grape that makes spicy, broad wines, sweet or dry, with more richness than finesse.

Neuchâtel [nur-sha-tel] (Switzerland) Lakeside region. Together with Les Trois Lacs, a source of good red and rosé, *Pinot Noir*, and *Chasselas* and *Chardonnay* whites. **Ch. d'Auvernier; Porret.**

Neudorf [noy-dorf] (*Nelson*, New Zealand) Pioneering small-scale producer of beautifully made *Chardonnay, Semillon, Sauvignon, Riesling,* and *Pinot Noir.*

Neumayer [noy-my-yer] (Traisental, Austria) Vigorous dry wines including *Grüner Veltliner* and *Riesling*, from a family estate.

Neusiedlersee [noy-zeed-lur-zay] (Austria) *Burgenland* region on the Hungarian border centred on the broad, shallow Neusiedl lake. Great *late-harvest* and improving whites and reds. Fieler-Artinger; *Kracher; Lang;Willi Opitz;* Tschida. ★★★★★ *Kracher,* Welschriesling Trockenbeerenauslese Nouvelle Vague No. 10 1999 $$$$

Neusidlersee-Hügelland [noy-zeed-lur-zay hoo-gurl-lend] (Austria) Region on the western side of the Neusiedlersee, where sweet whites can be made in a narrow strip near the lake, and good dry wines, up in the hills.

Nevers [nur-vehr] (France) Subtlest oak – from a forest in *Burgundy*.

New South Wales (Australia) Major wine-producing state, which is home to the famous *Hunter Valley*, along with the increasingly impressive *Cowra, Mudgee, Orange,* and *Murrumbidgee* regions. ★★★★ 2000 The Mill Shiraz $

New Zealand Instant superstar with proven *Sauvignon Blanc* and *Chardonnay* and – despite most expectations – increasingly successful *Merlots* and more particularly *Pinot Noirs*. Syrah can work well too occasionally, as can *Pinot Gris* and *Gewürztraminer. Cabernet Sauvignon,* however, rarely ripens properly. Vintages vary, however. See *Central Otago, Marlborough, Martinborough, Hawkes Bay, Nelson, Gisborne, Auckland.*

Newton Vineyards (*Napa Valley,* California) High-altitude vineyards with top-class *Chardonnay*, *Merlot*, and *Cabernet*, now being made with help from *Michel Rolland.*

Neszmély (Hungary) Progressive winery in Aszar-Neszmély producing good commercial white wines.

Ngatarawa [na-TA-ra-wah] (*Hawkes Bay,* New Zealand) Small winery that can make impressive reds and even better *Chardonnays* and *late harvest* whites. ★★★ 2000 Alwyn Merlot Cabernet 2000 $$$

Niagara (*Ontario,* Canada) Area close to the falls of the same name, and to the shores of lakes Ontario and Erie, where the *Vidal* is used to make good *Icewine. Chardonnay, Riesling,* and – though generally less successfully – red varieties such as *Pinot Noir* and *Merlot* are now used too by some eager producers. Watch this space. *Cave Springs; Ch. des Charmes; Henry of Pelham; Hilebrand; Jackson-Triggs; Inniskillin; Konzelmann; Magnotta; Reif;* Southbrook.

Nicholson River (*Gippsland,* Australia) The temperamental *Gippsland* climate makes for a small production of stunning *Chardonnays*, some of which are of a very Burgundian style.

Niebaum-Coppola [nee-bowm coh-po-la] (*Napa Valley,* California) You've seen the movie. Now taste the wine. The *Dracula* and *Godfather* director is very serious about the vineyards of an estate that now includes the appropriately Gothic *Inglenook* winery and has some of the oldest vines about. Inglenook makes intensely concentrated *Cabernets* that will definitely suit the patient. ★★★★ Rubicon 1999 $$$$

Niederösterreich [nee-dur-os-tur-rike] (Austria) Lower Austria: the region where over half of the country's vineyards are situated.

Niederhausen Schlossböckelheim [nee-dur-how sen shlos-berk-ehl-hime] (*Nahe,* Germany) State-owned estate producing highly concentrated *Riesling* from great vineyards.

N

I **Dom. Michel Niellon** [nee-el-lon] (*Burgundy*, France) One of the top five white *Burgundy* producers, making highly concentrated wines.
★★★★ Chassagne-Montrachet 2000 Blanc $$$

I **Niepoort** [nee-poort] (*Douro*, Portugal) Small, independent *port* house making subtle vintage, particularly impressive *colheita tawnies*, and terrific Redoma red and white table wine. ★★★★ Redoma Tinto 1997 $$$

Nierstein [neer-shtine] (*Rheinhessen*, Germany) The fine wines made here are obscured by the notoriety of the reliably dull Niersteiner Gutes Domtal. Balbach; *Gunderloch;* Heyl zu Herrnsheim; Franz Karl Schmitt; J & HA. Strub; Eugen Wehrheim ★★★★ Freiherr Heyl-zu-Herrnsheim, Nierstein Brudersberg Riesling Auslese Gold Capsule 2001 $$$

I **Nieto & Senetiner** [nee-yeh-toh eh seh-neh-tee-nehr] (*Mendoza*, Argentina) Reliable wines sold under Valle de Vistalba and Cadus labels.
★★★ 2001 Finca Las Marias Barbera $

I **Nigl** [nee-gel] (*Kremstal*, Austria) One of Austria's best producers of dry *Riesling* and *Grüner Veltliner*.

I **Weingut Nikolaihof** [nih-koh-li-hof] (*Niederösterreich*, Austria) Producers of top class *Grüner Veltliners* and *Rieslings*.

I **Nipozzano** [nip-ots-zano] (*Tuscany*, Italy) See *Frescobaldi*.

I **Nino Negri** [nee-noh neh-gree] (*Lombardy*, Italy) Casimiro Maule makes one of the best examples of *Valtellina Sfursat*.

I **Nobilo** [nob-ih-loh] (*Huapai*, New Zealand) Kiwi colony of the *BRL Hardy* empire making good *Chardonnay* from *Gisborne*, "*Icon*" wines from *Marlborough* including the commercial off-dry *White Cloud* blend.
★★★★ Icon Sauvignon Blanc 2002 $$

Noble rot Popular term for *botrytis cinerea*.

I **Vino Nocetto** (*Shendoah Valley, California*) Winery that has been unusually successful with Italian-style Sangiovese.

I **Normans** (*McLaren Vale*, Australia) Fast-improving *Cabernet* and *Shiraz* specialist. Now belongs to *Xanadu*. ★★★★★ Normans Chais Clarendon Barossa-McLaren Vale Shiraz 1999 $$

North Fork (New York State, USA) Long Island *AVA*, with most of *Long Island's* wineries.

I **Bodegas Norton** [naw-ton] (Argentina) This is one of Argentina's most recommendable producers, producing a wide range of *varietal* wines. The "Privada" wines are the cream of the crop. ★★★★ 2000 Cabernet Sauvignon $$

Nouveau [noo-voh] New wine, most popularly used of *Beaujolais*.

I **Nova** [meg-yer] (*Tokaji*, Hungary) French-owned pioneer of wines including *Tokaji* and *Furmint*.

I **Quinta do Noval** (*Douro*, Portugal) Fine and potentially finer estate. The ultrarare Nacional *vintage ports* are the jewel in the crown, made from ungrafted vines. Also of note are great *colheita tawny ports*.
★★★★ Silval 1997 $$

I **Albet i Noya** [al-bet-ee-noy-ya] (Spain) Innovative producer with red and white traditional and imported varieties. A superstar in the making.
★★★★ Reserva Marti Tempranillo 1997

Nuits-St.-Georges [noo-wee san zhawzh] (*Burgundy*, France) *Commune* producing the most *claret*-like of red *Burgundies*, properly tough and lean when young but glorious with age. Whites are good but ultra-rare. *Dom. de l'Arlot;* *Robert Chevillon; Jean-Jacques Confuron; Faiveley; Henri Gouges; Jean Grivot; Leroy;* *Alain Michelot; Patrice Rion; Henri & Gilles Remoriquet.*

I **Nuragus di Cagliari** [noo-rah-goos dee ka-lee-yah-ree] (*Sardinia*, Italy) Good-value, tangy, floral wine from the Nuragus grape. ★★★ Dolianova Perlas 2002 $$

NV Non-vintage, meaning a blend of wines from different years.

Nyetimber [nie-tim-bur] (England) Sussex vineyard exploiting England's potential for sparkling wine with promising efforts made from *Chardonnay*, *Pinot Noir*, and *Pinot Meunier*.

O

Oakville Ranch (*Napa Valley,* California) Potentially one of the *Napa's* most exciting red wine producers, but wines have so far been a little too tough.
Oaky Flavor imparted by oak casks which varies depending on the source of the oak (American is sweeter than French). Woody is usually less flattering.

Vin de Pays d'Oc [pay-doc] (*Languedoc-Roussillon,* France) The world's biggest wine region, encompassing *appellations* such as *Corbières* and *Minervois* and several smaller *Vins de Pays* regions. Pioneers here include *Mas de Daumas Gassac* and *Skalli.*

Bodegas Ochoa [och-oh-wah] (*Navarra,* Spain) Producer of fresh *Cabernet, Tempranillo, Viura* and sweet wines. ★★★ Dulce de Moscatel 2002 $

Ockfen [ok-fehn] (*Mosel-Saar-Ruwer,* Germany) Village producing some of the best, steeliest wines of the *Saar-Ruwer Bereich,* especially *Rieslings* from the *Bockstein* vineyard. St Urbanshof; Dr. Heinz Wagner

Oddero [od-DEHR-roh] (Piedmont, Italy) Producer with great vineyards and fine Barolo. ★★★★★ Barolo Vigna Rionda 1998 $$$

Oechsle [urk-slur] (Germany) Indication of the sugar level in grapes or wine.

Oeste [wes-teh] (Portugal) Western region in which a growing number of fresh, light, commercial wines are being made, of which the most successful has undoubtedly been Arruda.

Oestrich [ur-strihckh] (*Rheingau,* Germany) Source of good *Riesling.* Wegeler Erben; Peter Jacob Kuhn; Balthazar Ress; Spreitzer.

Ogier Cave des Papes [ogee-yay] (*Rhône,* France) *Châteauneuf du Pape* merchant whose range includes the excellent *Clos de l'Oratoire des Papes.*

Michel Ogier [ogee-yay] (*Rhône,* France) *Côte-Rôtie* producer, making less muscular wines than most of his neighbors.

Oïdium [oh-id-ee-yum] Fungal grape infection, shrivelling the berries and turning them gray.

Ojai Vineyard [oh-high] (*Santa Barbara,* California) The specialities here are a *Sauvignon-Semillon* blend and – more interestingly – a *Rhône*-like *Syrah.*
★★★★ Roll Ranch Vineyard Syrah 2000 $$

Okanagan (*British Columbia,* Canada) This is the principal wine region in the west of Canada. Rapidly proving to be as good – in parts – as Ontario. JacksonTriggs; Mission Hill; Quail's Gate; Peller Estates

Olasz Rizling [oh-lash-riz-ling] (Hungary) Name for the *Welschriesling.*

Ch. Olivier [oh-liv-ee-yay] (*Pessac-Léognan Cru Classé, Bordeaux,* France) A spectacularly beautiful estate which is finally joining the *Graves* revolution.

Oloroso [ol-oh-roh-soh] (*Jerez,* Spain) Style of full-bodied *sherry,* either dry or semisweet. Barbadillo; Gonzalez Byass; Hidalgo; Osborne; Lustau; Pedro Romero; Sandeman

Oltrepò Pavese [ohl-tray-poh pa-vay-say] (*Lombardy,* Italy) Still and sparkling *DOC* made from grapes such as the spicy red Gutturnio and white Ortrugo. Ca' di Frara; Tenuta il Bosco; Cabanon; Fugazza; Mazzolina; Bruno Verdi.

Omar Khayyam (Champagne India) [oh-mah-ki-yam] (*Maharashtra,* India) Pleasant *Champagne*-method wine. The producer's cheeky name, "*Champagne* India", annoys the Champenois, but they, in the shape of *Piper Heidsieck,* were happy enough to sell the Indians their expertise.

Ontario (Canada) The main wine region of eastern Canada, famous for Ice Wine and with increasingly good Chardonnay, Riesling, Cabernet Franc, Pinot Gris. Vineyards are in Lake Erie, Pelee Island, and Niagara Peninsula.

Willi Opitz [oh-pitz] (*Neusiedlersee,* Austria) Oddball pet food-manufacturer-turned-producer of a magical mystery tour of *late-harvest* and straw-dried wines (Schilfwein), including an extraordinary *botrytis* red labeled – to the discomfort of some Californians – "Opitz One."

Oppenheim [op-en-hime] (*Rheinhessen,* Germany) Village in *Nierstein Bereich* best known – unfairly – for unexciting wines from the Krottenbrunnen. Elsewhere produces soft wines with concentrated flavor.

Opus One (*Napa Valley,* California) Twenty-year-old coproduction between *Mouton-Rothschild* and *Robert Mondavi*. Opus one is a classy, *claret*-like, blackcurranty wine that sells at an appropriately classy, *claret*-like price.

Orange (*New South Wales,* Australia) Coolish region which, like *Cowra,* now competes with the *Hunter Valley.* Glenguin; Little Boomey; Logan; Meerea Park; Reynolds; Rosemount. ★★★★ Reynolds Orange Cabernet Merlot 2001 $$$

Orange Muscat Another highly eccentric member of the *Muscat* family, best known for dessert wines in California by *Quady* and in Australia for the delicious *Brown Brothers Late Harvest Orange Muscat* and *Flora.*

Oregon Fashionable cool-climate state, specialising in *Pinot Noir.* The *Chardonnay, Riesling, Pinot Gris,* and sparkling wines show promise too. *Adea; Adelsheim; Amity; Archery Summit; Argyle; Beaux Freres;* Bergström; Bethel Heights; Brick House; *Cameron; Chehalem;* Cristom; *Dom Drouhin;* Duck Pond; Elk Cove; *Erath; Eyrie;* Henry Estate; *King Estate; Ponzi;* Raptor Ridge; *Rex Hill; Sokol Blosser.*

Oremus [oh-ray-mosh] (Tokaj, Hungary) 1: a Tokaji estate owned by Vega Sicilia and making outstanding quality; 2: a grape, a cross between Furmint and Bouvier, increasingly giving way to another Furmint x Bouvier called Zeta. ★★★★ Oremus Tokaji Furmint Late Harvest 1999 $$$

Oriachovitza [oh-ree-ak-hoh-vit-sah] (Bulgaria) Major source of reliable *Cabernet Sauvignon* and *Merlot.*

Orlando-Wyndham (South Australia) Huge, French-owned (Pernod-Ricard) producer of the reliable *Jacob's Creek* and *Wyndham Estate* wines. Look for "Reserve" and "Limited Release" efforts. The Orlando RF range is good but the harder-to-find Gramps and Flaxmans wines are better.

Orléanais [aw-lay-yo-nay] (*Loire,* France) A vineyard area around Orléans in the Central Vineyards region of the *Loire,* specializing in unusual white *Chardonnay/Pinot Gris* and red *Pinot Noir/Cabernet Franc* blends.

Ch. Les Ormes-de-Pez [awm dur-pay] (*St. Estèphe Cru Bourgeois, Bordeaux,* France) Stablemate of *Lynch-Bages* and made with similar skill.

Tenuta dell'Ornellaia [teh-noo-tah del-aw-nel-li-ya] (*Tuscany,* Italy) *Bordeaux*-blend *Bolgheri Super-Tuscan* created by the brother of Piero Antinori and recently bought by *Robert Mondavi* and *Frescobaldi.* This is serious wine that is worth maturing. ★★★★★ Ornellaia 2000 $$$$

Ortega [aw-tay-gah] This is a recently developed grape variety that is well used by *Biddenden* and *Denbies.* Can make good *late-harvest* wine.

Orvieto [ohr-vee-yet-toh] (*Umbria,* Italy) White Umbrian *DOC* responsible for a quantity of dull wine. Orvieto *Classico* is better. Look out for Secco if you like your white wine dry; *Amabile* if you have a sweet tooth. *Antinori;* Bigi; La Carraia; Covio Cardetto; Palazzone.

Osborne [os-sbaw-nay] (*Jerez,* Spain) Producer of a good range of *sherries* including a brilliant *Pedro Ximenez* and now also a range of *ports.* ★★★★ Manzanilla $

Dom. Ostertag [os-tur-tahg] (*Alsace,* France) Poet and philosopher André Ostertag's superb *Alsace domaine.*

Overgaauw [oh-ver-gow] (South Africa) Heavyweight reds which benefit from bottle age. Look out for *Cabernet Sauvignon* and *Merlot.* The Tria Corda *Bordeaux* blend is worth seeking out. ★★★★ Tria Corda 2000 $$

Oxidation The effect (usually detrimental, occasionally – as in *sherry* – intentional) of oxygen on wine.

Oxidative The opposite to reductive. Certain wines – most reds, and whites like *Chardonnay* – benefit from limited exposure to oxygen during their fermentation and maturation, such as barrel aging.

Oyster Bay (*Marlborough,* New Zealand) See *Delegats.*

P

P

Paarl [pahl] (South Africa) Warm region in which *Backsberg* and *Boschendal* make appealing wines. Hotter and drier than neighboring *Stellenbosch*. *Charles Back/Fairview;* Boland Kelder; Diemersfontein; Dieu Donne; *KWV; Backsberg; Boschendal; Glen Carlou; la Motte;* Veenwouden; *Villiera; Plaisir de Merle*.

Pacherenc du Vic-Bilh [pa-shur-renk doo veek beel] (*Southwest*, France) Rare, dry, or fairly sweet white wine made from the *Petit* and *Gros Manseng*. A speciality of *Madiran*. ★★★ Saint Albert Producteurs Plaimont 2000 $$

Pacific Echo Recommendable sparkling wine, once called *Scharffenberger*.

Padthaway [pad-thah-way] (South Australia) Area north of *Coonawarra* specializing in *Chardonnay* and *Sauvignon*, though reds work well here too. *Angove's Hardys;* Henry's Drive; *Lindemans; Orlando; Penfolds;* Two Hands.

Pagadebit di Romagna [pah-gah-deh-bit dee roh-man-ya] (*Emilia-Romagna*, Italy) Dry, sweet, and sparkling whites from the Pagadebit grape.

Pago de Carrovejas [pah-goh deh kah-roh-vay-jash] (*Ribera del Duero*, Portugal) One of the best producers in Ribera del Duero.

Pahlmeyer (*Napa Valley*, California) One of California's most interesting winemakers, producing *Burgundian Chardonnay* and a *Bordeaux*-blend red.

Paitin [pie-teen] (*Piedmont*, Italy) The Sori Paitin vineyard in Barbaresco can offer Gaja quality at affordable prices.

Ch. Pajzos [pah-zhohs] (*Tokaj*, Hungary) Serious, French-owned producer of new-wave *Tokaji*. ★★★★ Tokay Aszú 5 Puttonyos 1993 $$$

Bodegas Palacio [pa-las-see-yoh] (*Rioja*, Spain) Underrated *bodega* with stylish, fruit-driven reds and distinctively oaky whites. Also helped by wine guru *Michel Rolland*. ★★★ Rioja Blanco 2001 $

Palacio de Fefiñanes [pah-las-see-yoh day fay-feen-yah-nays] (*Galicia*, Spain) Fine producer of *Rias Baixas Albariño*. ★★★★ 2001 Albariño $$

Palacio de la Vega [pah-lath-yo deh lah vay-gah] (Navarra, Spain) Good Tempranillo and international varieties. ★★★★ Conde de la Vega 2000 $$

Alvaro Palacios [pah-las-see-yohs] (*Catalonia*, Spain) Superstar *Priorat* estate producing individual wines with rich, concentrated flavors. L'Ermita is the (very pricey) top wine. Finca Dofi and Les Terrasses are more affordable.

Palate Nebulous term describing the apparatus used for tasting (i.e., the tongue) as well as the skill of the taster (e.g., "he has a good palate").

Podere Il Palazzino [poh-day-ray eel pal-lat-zee-noh] (Tuscany, Italy) Ripe, juicy *Chianti* aged in barrique. Try the Reserva, Grossa Sanese.

Palette [pa-let] (*Provence*, France) Usually overpriced *AC* rosé and creamy white, well liked by vacationers in St. Tropez

Palliser Estate [pa-lih-sur] (*Martinborough*, New Zealand) Source of classy *Sauvignon Blanc*, *Chardonnay* and – increasingly – *Pinot Noir* from *Martinborough*. ★★★★★Pinot Noir 2001 $$

Palmela [pal-may-lah] (Terras do Sado, Portugal) Region making attractive reds from Periquita, among others. ★★★ quinta da mimosa 2001 $

Ch. Palmer [pahl-mur] (*Margaux 3ème Cru Classé*, *Bordeaux*, France) Third-growth *Margaux* stands alongside the best of the *Médoc* and often outclasses its more highly ranked neighbors. Wonderfully perfumed.

Palo Cortado [pah-loh kaw-tah doh] (*Jerez*, Spain) Rare *sherry* pitched between *amontillado* and *oloroso*. *Gonzalez Byass; Hidalgo; Lustau; Osborne; Valdespino*. ★★★★★ Apostoles 30 Year Old Palo Cortado Muy Viejo $$$

Palomino [pa-loh-mee-noh] (*Jerez*, Spain) White grape responsible for virtually all fine *sherries* – and almost invariably dull white wine, when unfortified. Also widely grown in South Africa.

Quinta das Pancas [keen-tah dash-pan-kash] (Estremadura, Portugal) Modern estate with good Cabernet and Chardonnay and Touriga Nacional.

Marchese Pancrazi [mar-kay-say pan-crat-zee] (Tuscany, Italy) This property planted Pinot Noir thinking it to be Sangiovese – the nursery had sent the wrong vines. Now it makes rather good Pinot Nero.

P

Panther Creek (*Oregon*) Fine Pinot Noir producer in the Willamette Valley. The Shea Vineyard wines are worth cellaring for a while.

Ch. Pape-Clément [pap klay-mon] (*Pessac-Léognan Cru Classé, Bordeaux, France*) Great source of rich reds since the mid-1980s and, more recently, small quantities of delicious, peach-oaky white.

Paradigm (California, USA) Good new estate in Oakville. ★★★★ Oakville Cabernet Sauvignon 1999 $$

Parducci [pah-doo-chee] (*Mendocino,* California) Steady producer whose *Petite Sirah* is a terrific bargain. ★★★★ Chardonnay 2000 $$

Dom. Alain Paret [pa-ray] (*Rhône,* France) Producer of a truly magnificent *St. Joseph* and *Condrieu,* in partnership with one of the world's best-known winemakers. (Though, to be fair, this particular associate, Gérard Dépardieu does owe his fame to the movies rather than his efforts among the vines.) ★★★★ Condrieu Les Ceps du Nébadon 2001 $$

Paringa Estate (*Mornington, Victoria,* Australia) With *T'Galant, Dromana* and *Stoniers,* this is one of the stars of *Mornington Peninsula.* Fine *Shiraz.*

Parker Estate (*Coonawarra,* Australia) Small producer cheekily sharing its name with the US guru, and calling its (very pricey) red "First Growth".

Parkers Estate (*Sonoma,* California) New label unconnected to Parker Estate, and Robert Parker.

Parusso [pah-roo-soh] (*Piedmont,* Italy) Very fine single-vineyard Barolos (Munie and Rocche) and wines sold under the Langhe designation. ★★★★ 1997 Barolo Castiglione Falletto Parusso 'Mariondino'

Parxet [par-shet] (Alella, Spain) The only *cava* from *Alella,* and good dry white Marques de Alella, too. ★★★ NV Parxet Titiana $$

Pasado/Pasada [pa-sah-doh/dah] (Spain) Term applied to old or fine *fino* and *amontillado* sherries. ★★★ Hildago Manzanilla Pasada Pastrana $$

C.J. Pask [pask] (*Hawkes Bay,* New Zealand) *Cabernet* pioneer with excellent *Chardonnay* and *Sauvignon.* One of New Zealand's very best.

Paso Robles [pa-soh roh-blays] (*San Luis Obispo,* California) Warmish, long-established region, unaffected by coastal winds or marine fog, and good for *Zinfandel* (especially *Ridge*), *Rhône,* and Italian varieties. Plus increasingly successful *Chardonnays* and *Pinots.* ★★★★ 2000 EOS Cabernet Sauvignon $$

Pasqua [pas-kwah] (*Veneto,* Italy) Producer of fairly priced, reliable wines.

Passetoutgrains [pas-stoo-gran] (*Burgundy,* France) Wine supposedly made from two-thirds *Gamay,* one-third *Pinot Noir,* though few producers respect these proportions. Once the Burgundians' daily red – until they decided to sell it and drink cheaper wine from other regions.

Passing Clouds (*Bendigo,* Australia) "We get clouds, but it never rains ..." Despite a fairly hideous label, this is one of Australia's most serious wineries.

Passito [pa-see-toh] (Italy) Raisiny wine made from sun-dried grapes in Italy. This technique is now used in Australia by *Primo Estate.*

Ch. Patache d'Aux [pa-tash-doh] (*Médoc Cru Bourgeois, Bordeaux,* France) Château producing traditional, toughish stuff.

Frederico Paternina [pa-tur-nee-na] (*Rioja,* Spain) Loved by Hemingway.

Luis Pato [lweesh-pah-toh] (*Bairrada,* Portugal) One of Portugal's rare superstar winemakers, proving, among other things, that the *Baga* grape can make first-class spicy, berryish red wines. ★★★★★ Vinha Pan 1999 $$$

Patras [pat-ras] (Greece) Appellation for white *Roditis.*

Patriarche [pa-tree-arsh] (*Burgundy,* France) Improving merchant. Best wines are from the *Ch. de Meursault.* ★★★★ 1999 Volnay $$

Patrimonio [pah-tree-moh-nee-yoh] (*Corsica,* France) One of the best appellations in Corsica. Grenache reds and rosés and Vermentino whites. Aliso-Rossi; Arena; de Catarelli; Gentile; Leccia; Clos Marfisi; Orenga de Gaffory.

Patz & Hall (*Napa Valley,* California) Big, full-flavored *Chardonnays.*

Pauillac [poh-yak] (*Bordeaux,* France) One of the four famous "*communes*" of the *Médoc,* Pauillac is the home of *Châteaux Latour, Lafite,* and *Mouton-Rothschild,* as well as the two *Pichons* and *Lynch-Bages.*

P

ɪ **Domaine Paul Bruno** (Chile) Joint venture in *Maipo* by Paul Pontallier of *Ch. Margaux* and Bruno Prats (formerly) of *Cos d'Estournel*. Now beginning to find its feet after an unconvincing start.

ɪ **Paul Cluwer** (South Africa) Estate in *Elgin* with subtle Sauvignon, very good Pinot Noir, Chardonnay, and Gewurztraminer.

ɪ **Clos de Paulilles** [poh-leey] (*Languedoc-Roussillon*, France) Top-class producer of *Banyuls* and *Collioure*. ★★★★ Banyuls Rimage 2000 $$

ɪ **Neil Paulett** [paw-let] (South Australia) Small, top-flight *Clare Valley* producer. ★★★ Polish Hill River Chardonnay 2002 $$

ɪ **Dr. Pauly-Bergweiler** [bur-gwi-lur] (*Mosel-Saar-Ruwer*, Germany) Ultramodern winery with really stylish, modern, dry and late-harvest Riesling. ★★★★★ Graacher Himmelreich Riesling Eiswein 2001 $$$

ɪ **Ch. Pavie** [pa-vee] (*St. Emilion Premier Grand Cru Classé, Bordeaux*, France) Plummily rich *St. Emilion* wines that are beginning to rediscover their traditional delicacy of style.

ɪ **Ch. Pavie-Decesse** [pa-vee dur-ses] (*St. Emilion Grand Cru Classé, Bordeaux*, France) Neighbor to *Ch. Pavie*, but a shade less impressive.

ɪ **Ch. Pavie-Macquin** [pa-vee ma-kan'] (*St. Emilion Grand Cru Classé, Bordeaux*) Returned to form since the late 1980s – and the producer of a very good and unusually failrly priced 2002.

ɪ **Le Pavillon Blanc de Ch. Margaux** [pa-vee-yon blon] (*Bordeaux*, France) The (rare) all-*Sauvignon* white wine of *Ch. Margaux* which still acts as the yardstick for the growing number of *Médoc* white wines.

ɪ **Pazo de Barrantes** [pa-thoh de bah-ran-tays] (*Galicia*, Spain) One of the newest names in *Rias Baixas*, producing lovely, spicy *Albariño*. Under the same ownership as *Marques de Murrieta*. ★★★ Albariño 2001 $$

ɪ **Ca' del Pazzo** [kah-del-pat-soh] (*Tuscany*, Italy) Ultraclassy, *oaky Super-Tuscan* with loads of ripe fruit and oak.

Pécharmant [pay-shar-mon] (*Southwest*, France) In the *Bergerac* area, producing light, *Bordeaux*-like reds. Worth trying.

🍇 **Pedro Ximénez** (PX) [peh-droh khee-MEH-nes] (*Jerez*, Spain) White grape, dried in the sun to create a sweet, curranty wine, which is used in the blending of the sweeter *sherry* styles, and in its own right by *Osborne*, and by *Gonzalez Byass* for its brilliant Noe. Also produces a very unusual wine at *De Bortoli* in Australia. ★★★★★ Hidalgo La Gitana Napoleon $$

ɪ **Viña Pedrosa** [veen-ya pay-droh-sah] (*Ribera del Duero*, Spain) Producer of a modern blend of *Tempranillo* and classic *Bordelais* varieties. The Spanish equivalent of a *Super-Tuscan*. ★★★★ Gran Reserva 1996 $$

ɪ **Clos Pegase** [kloh-pay-gas] (*Napa Valley*, California) Showcase winery with improving but overpraised wines. ★★★ Cabernet Sauvignon 1999 $$$

ɪ **Pegasus Bay** (New Zealand) Well structured Riesling and supple Pinot Noir, plus elegant Chardonnay and good Cabernet blend.

ɪ **Pelissero** [peh-lee-seh-roh] (*Piedmont*, Italy) Oaky *Barberas*, rich, *Dolcetto*, pure *Favorita*, lovely single-vineyard *Barbaresco* and a fine *Barbera-Nebbiolo* blend on behalf of the curious Long Now Foundation (www.longnow.org).

ɪ **Dom. Henry Pellé** [on-ree pel-lay] (*Loire*, France) Reliable producer of fruitier-than-usual *Menetou-Salon*.

ɪ **Pellegrini** (*Long Island*, New York) Producer of fine *Merlot* on the North Fork of Long Island.

ɪ **Pelorus** [pe-law-rus] (*Marlborough*, New Zealand) Showy, big, buttery, yeasty, almost Champagne-style New Zealand sparkling wine from *Cloudy Bay*.

Pemberton (Western Australia) Up-and-coming cooler climate region for more restrained styles of *Chardonnay* and *Pinot Noir*. Houghton; Picardy, Plantagenet, Salitage; Smithbrook. ★★★★ Houghton Chardonnay 2001 $$

P

Ɨ **Peñaflor** [pen-yah-flaw] (Argentina) Huge, dynamic firm producing increasingly good-value wines. ★ ★ ★ ★ Elementos Shiraz Malbec 2001 $

Penedès [peh-neh-dehs] (Catalonia, Spain) Largest DOC of Catalonia with varying altitudes, climates, and styles ranging from cava to still wines pioneered by Torres and others, though some not as successfully. The current trend toward increasing use of varietals such as Cabernet Sauvignon, Merlot, and Chardonnay allows more French-style winemaking without losing any of the intrinsic Spanish character. Belatedly living up to some of its early promise. Albet i Noya; Can Feixes; Can Ráfols dels Caus; Freixenet; Cavas Hill; Juvé y Camps; Jean Leon; Monistrol; Puigi Roca; Torres.

Ɨ **Penfolds** (South Australia) Australia's most famous wine company with a high-quality line, from Rawson's Retreat to Grange. Previously a red wine specialist but now rapidly becoming a skillful producer of still white wines such as Eden Valley Rieslings and the improving Yattarna (good but not yet living up to its supposed role as the "White Grange"). Under the same ownership as Rosemount, Wynns, Seaview, Rouge Homme, Lindemans, Tullochs, Leo Buring, Seppelt, Coldstream Hills, and Devil's Lair. ★ ★ ★ ★ ★ RWT Barossa Valley Shiraz 2000 $$$

Ɨ **Penley Estate** (Coonawarra, Australia) High-quality Coonawarra estate with rich Chardonnay and very blackcurrant Cabernet. ★ ★ ★ ★ ★ Reserve Coonawarra Estate Grown Cabernet Sauvignon 2000 $$$

Ɨ **Peppoli** [peh-poh-lee] (Tuscany, France) One of Antinori's most reliable Chianti Classicos.

Ɨ **Comte Peraldi** [peh-ral-dee] (Corsica, France) High-class Corsican wine producer, now also making good wine in Romania.

Ɨ **Perez Pascuas** [peh-reth Pas-scoo-was] (Ribera del Duero, Spain) Producer of Viña Pedrosa, one of the top examples of Ribera del Duero.

Ɨ **Le Pergole Torte** [pur-goh-leh taw-teh] (Tuscany, Italy) Long-established pure Sangiovese, oaky Super-Tuscan. ★ ★ ★ ★ ★ Le Pergole Torte 1999 $$$

⚕ **Periquita** [peh-ree-kee-tah] (Portugal) Spicy, tobaccoey grape – and the wine J.M. da Fonseca makes from it. Its official name is Castelão Francês.

Perlé/Perlant [pehr-lay/lon] (France) Lightly sparkling.

Perlwein [pehrl-vine] (Germany) Sparkling wine.

Pernand-Vergelesses [pehr-non vehr-zhur-less] (Burgundy, France) Commune with jammy reds but fine whites, including some best buys. (Many producers also make Corton.) Arnoux; Champy; Chandon de Briailles; Dubreuil-Fontaine; Germain (Château de Chorey); Jadot; Laleure-Piot; Pavelot; Rapet; Dom. Rollin. ★ ★ ★ ★ Rémi Rollin Pernand-Vergelesses Blanc Sous Frétille 2000 $$$

Ɨ **André Perret** (Rhône, France) Producer of notable Condrieu and some unusually good examples of St. Joseph. ★ ★ ★ St Joseph 1999 $$$

Ɨ **Joseph Perrier** [payh-ree-yay] (Champagne, France) Family-run producer whose long-lasting elegant Champagnes have a heavy Pinot Noir influence.

Ɨ **Perrier-Jouët** [payh-ree-yay zhoo-way] (Champagne, France) Hitherto sadly underperforming Champagne house which, like Mumm, is benefitting from greater attention from new owners. Even so, sidestep the non-vintage for the genuinely worthwhile – and brilliantly packaged – Belle Epoque prestige cuvée white and rosé sparkling wine.

Ɨ **Elio Perrone** [eh-lee-yoh peh-roh-nay] (Piedmont, Italy) Good Barberas, Chardonnays and Dolcettos and truly spectacular Moscato.

Ɨ **Pesquera** [peh-SKEH-ra] (Ribera del Duero, Spain) Robert Parker dubbed this revolutionary estate the Ch. Pétrus of Spain. Look out for individual Janus and Millennium bottlings. ★ ★ ★ ★ ★ Janus 1994 $$$$

Pessac-Léognan [peh-sak lay-on-yon] (Bordeaux, France) Graves commune containing most of the finest châteaux. Unusually in Bordeaux, most estates here make both red and white wine. Ch. Bouscaut; Carbonnieux; Fieuzal; Domaine de Chevalier; Haut-Bailly; Haut-Brion; Larrivet-Haut-Brion; Laville-Haut-Brion; La Louvière; Malartic-Lagravière; la Mission-Haut-Brion; Smith-Haut-Laffite; la Tour-Haut-Brion.

P

Petaluma [peh-ta-loo-ma] (*Adelaide Hills*, Australia)
Recently purchased by a bif brewery, this high-tech
creation of *Brian Croser* is a role model for other
producers in the New World who are interested in
combining innovative winemaking with the fruit of
individually characterful vineyards. Classy *Chardonnay*s
and *Viogniers* from Piccadilly in the *Adelaide Hills*, *Clare
Rieslings* (particularly good *late harvest*), and *Coonawarra*
reds. Also owns *Smithbrook* and *Mitchelton*.
★★★★★ Tiers 2000 $$

Pétillant [pay-tee-yon] Lightly sparkling.

Petit Chablis [pur-tee shab-lee] (*Burgundy*, France) Theoretically, this is
a less fine wine than plain *Chablis* – though plenty of vineyards that were
previously designated as Petit Chablis are now allowed to produce wines sold as
Chablis. Hardly surprisingly, the ones that are left as Petit Chablis are often poor
value. *La Chablisienne; Jean-Paul Droin; William Fèvre; Dom des Malandes.*

Petit Verdot [pur-tee vehr-doh] (*Bordeaux*, France) Highly trendy and
excitingly spicy, if *tannic* variety traditionally used in small proportions in
red *Bordeaux*, in California (rarely) and now (increasingly often) as a pure
varietal in Australia (*de Bortoli*, *Leconfield*, *Pirramimma*), Italy, and Spain
(*Marqués de Griñon*). ★★★★ de Bortoli Deen Vat 4 2001 $$

Ch. Petit Village [pur-tee vee-lahzh] (*Pomerol*, *Bordeaux*, France) Classy,
intense, blackcurranty-plummy *Pomerol*. Worth keeping.

Petite Sirah [peh-teet sih-rah] Spicy, rustic red grape grown in California and
Mexico and as *Durif* in the *Midi* and Australia. Do not confuse with Syrah. *LA
Cetto; Carmen; EOS; Fetzer; Morris; Parducci; Ridge; Rosenblum; Turley.* ★★★★ EOS
Reserve Petite Sirah 2000

Petrolly A not unpleasant overtone often found in mature *Riesling*.
Arrives faster in Australia than in Germany.

Ch. Pétrus [pay-trooss] (*Pomerol*, *Bordeaux*, France) Until *Le Pin* came along,
this was the priciest of all *clarets*. Voluptuous *Pomerol* hits the target especially
well in the US, and is finding a growing market in the Far East. Beware of
fakes (especially big bottles) which crop up increasingly often.

Pewsey Vale [pyoo-zee vayl] (*Adelaide Hills*, Australia) Classy, cool-climate
wines. Under the same ownership as *Yalumba*, *Hill-Smith*, and *Heggies*.
★★★★ Pewsey Vale Contours Riesling 1997 $$

Peyre Rose [pehr rohz] (*Languedoc-Roussillon*, France) Truly stylish producer of
Coteaux du Languedoc Syrah that competes with examples from the Northern
Rhône – and sells at similar prices.

Ch. de Pez [dur pez] (*St. Estèphe Cru Bourgeois*, *Bordeaux*, France) Historic
estate, now fast-improving, especially since its purchase by *Louis Roederer*. In
good vintages, well worth aging.

Pfalz [Pfaltz] (Germany) Formerly known as *Rheinpfalz*, and *Palatinate*. Warm,
southerly *Anbaugebiet* noted for riper, spicier *Riesling*. Currently competing with
the *Mosel* for the prize of best of Germany's wine regions. *Bassermann-Jordan;
Bürklin-Wolf; A. Christmann; Kurt Darting; Lingenfelder; Pfeffingen; Müller-Cattoir;
Ruppertsberger Winzerverein; Vier Jahreszeiten; von Buhl; JL Wolf.*

Weingut Pfeffingen [Pfef-fing-gen] (Pfalz, Germany) Look out for excellent
Riesling and Scheurebe from well-sited vineyards.

Ch. Phélan-Ségur [fay-lon say-goor] (*St. Estèphe Cru Bourgeois*, *Bordeaux*,
France) Good-value property since the
late-1980s, with ripe, well-made wines.

Joseph Phelps (*Napa Valley*, California)
Pioneer *Napa* user of *Rhône* varieties
(*Syrah* and *Viognier*), and a rare source
of *late-harvest* Riesling. *Cabernet* is a
strength and the *Bordeaux-like* Insignia is
a star wine. ★★★★ Insignia 1999 $$$$

P

☒ **Philipponnat** [fee-lee-poh-nah] (*Champagne*, France) Small producer famous for Clos des Goisses. Other wines are currently disappointing.

☒ **RH Phillips** (*California*) Producer whose great value California wines deserve to be better known.

Phylloxera vastatrix [fih-lok-seh-rah] Root-eating louse that wiped out Europe's vines in the 19th century. Foiled by grafting *vinifera* vines onto resistant American **labrusca** rootstock. Pockets of pre-phylloxera and/or ungrafted vines still exist in France (in a *Bollinger* vineyard and on the south coast – the louse hates sand), Portugal (in *Quinta do Noval's* "Nacional" vineyard), Australia, and Chile. Elsewhere, phylloxera recently devastated *Napa Valley* vines.

Piave [pee-yah-vay] (*Veneto*, Italy) DOC in *Veneto* region, including reds made from a *Bordeaux*-like mix of grapes.

☒ **Ch. Pibarnon** [pee-bah-non] (*Bandol*, France) Top-class producer of modern *Bandol*. ★★★★ Chateau de Pibarnon 2000 $$$

☒ **Ch. Pibran** [pee-bron] (*Pauillac Cru Bourgeois, Bordeaux*, France) Small but high-quality and classically *Pauillac* property.

☒ **Picardy** (*Pemberton*, Western Australia) Impressive new *Pinot Noir* and *Shiraz* specialist by the former winemaker of *Moss Wood*.

☒ Pic St. Loup [peek-sa'-loo] (*Languedoc-Roussillon*, France) Up-and-coming region within the *Coteaux du Languedoc* for *Syrah*-based, *Rhône*-style reds, and whites. *Dom. l'Hortus;* Mas Bruguière; Ch. Lancyre; Ravaille; Ch. La Roque. ★★★★ Ermitage du Pic 2001 $$

☒ **FX Pichler** [peek-lehr] (*Wachau Cru*, Austria) Arguably the best dry ("*Trocken*") winemaker in Austria – and certainly a great exponent of the *Grüner Veltliner* and *Riesling* at their richly dry best.

☒ **Ch. Pichon-Lalande** [pee-shon la-lond] (*Pauillac 2ème Cru Classé, Bordeaux,* France) The new name for Pichon-Longueville-Lalande. Famed **super second** and tremendous success story, thanks to top-class winemaking and the immediate appeal of its unusually high *Merlot* content. A great 1996, but surprisingly a slightly less exciting 1998. Great in 2000.

☒ **Ch. Pichon-Longueville** [pee-shon long-veel] (*Pauillac 2ème Cru Classé, Bordeaux,* France) New name for Pichon-Longueville-Baron. An under-performing second growth *Pauillac* until its purchase by *AXA* in 1988. Now level with, and sometimes ahead of, *Ch. Pichon-Lalande*, once the other half of the estate. Wines are intense and complex. Les Tourelles, the *second label*, is a good-value alternative.

☆ **Picolit** [pee-koh-leet] (*Friuli*, Italy) Grape used to make both sweet and dry white wine. *Jermann* makes a good one.

☒ **Picpoul de Pinet** [peek-pool duh pee-nay] (South-West France) Underrated herby white that is particularly well made by Dom. St. Martin de la Garrigue.

Piedmont/Piemonte [pee-yed-mont/pee-yeh-mon-tay] (Italy) Ancient and modern northwestern region producing old-fashioned, tough *Barolo* and *Barbaresco* and brilliant, modern, fruit-packed wines. Also makes *Oltrepò Pavese, Asti,* and *Dolcetto d'Alba.* See *Nebbiolo*.

☒ **Bodegas Piedmonte** [pee-yehd-mohn-teh] (*Navarra*, Spain) Confusingly named (see above) cooperative producing good *Tempranillo, Cabernet,* and *Merlot* reds.

☒ **Pieropan** [pee-yehr-oh-pan] (*Veneto*, Italy) Leonildo Pieropan is *Soave's* top producer. He more or less invented single-vineyard (La Rocca, Calvarino, Colombare) wines here and is still a great exception to the dull *Soave* rule. Lovely, almondy wine that lasts. Great *Recioto* and *Passito* examples too. ★★★★ Recioto Le Columbare 1999 $$

☒ **Pieroth** [pee-roth] Huge company whose salesmen visit clients' homes offering wines that are rarely recommendable.

☒ **Pierro** [pee-yehr-roh] (*Margaret River,* Australia) Small estate producing rich, buttery, *Meursault*-like *Chardonnay*.

P

Piesport [pees-sport] (*Mosel-Saar-Ruwer,* Germany) Produced in the *Grosslage Michelsberg,* a region infamous for dull German wine, and bought by people who think themselves above *Liebfraumilch.* Try a single-vineyard – Günterslay or Goldtröpchen – for something more memorable. **Kurt Hain; Johann Haart; Reinhold Haart; St Urbanshof; Weller-Lehnert.**

℞ **Pieve di Santa Restituta** [pee-yeh-vay dee san-tah res-tit-too-tah] (Tuscany, Italy) Angelo Gaja's Tuscan venture, with harmonious, balanced Brunello *crus* Rennina and Sugarille. Promis is from young vines.

℞ **Pighin** [pee-gheen] (*Friuli,* Italy) Good, rather than great, Collio producer, with creditable examples of most of the styles produced here.

℞ **Pikes** (*Clare Valley,* South Australia) Top-class estate with great *Riesling, Shiraz, Sangiovese,* and *Sauvignon.*

℞ **Jean Pillot** [pee-yoh] (*Burgundy,* France) There are three estates called Pillot in *Chassagne-Montrachet.* This one is the best – and produces by far the finest red. ★★★★★ **Chassagne Montrachet 1er Cru Chenevottes 2000 $$$**

℞ **Le Pin** [lur pan] (*Pomerol, Bordeaux,* France) Ultrahyped, small, recently formed estate whose – admittedly delicious – wines sell at silly prices in the US and the Far East. The forerunner of a string of other similar honey-traps (see *Ch. Valandraud* and *la Mondotte*). Brilliant in 2001 and 2002.

℞ **Pindar Vineyards** (New York State, USA) Good commercial quality from Long Island, especially Mythology, a *Bordeaux* blend.

℞ **Pine Ridge** (*Napa Valley,* California) Greatly improved *Stags Leap* producer that is now also making good quality reds on *Howell Mountain.* The Oregon *Archery Summit* wines are also worth seeking out. ★★★★ **Andrus Reserve Napa Valley 1999 $$$**

Pineau de Charentes [pee-noh dur sha-ront] (*Southwest,* France) Fortified wine from the Cognac region.

℞ **Pingus** [pin-goos] (*Ribeiro del Duero,* Spain) One of the finest wines now being made in this region. The top wine, Dominio de Pingus, has a cult following – fans are ready to pay $200 per bottle.

🍇 **Pinot Blanc/Bianco** [pee-noh blon] Like *Chardonnay* without the fruit, and rarely as classy. Fresh, creamy, and adaptable. At its best in *Alsace* (Pinot d'Alsace), the Alto Adige in Italy (as *Pinot Bianco*), Germany and Austria (as *Weissburgunder*). In California it is a synonym for *Melon de Bourgogne.*

🍇 **Pinot Chardonnay** (Australia) Misleading name for *Chardonnay,* still used by *Tyrrells.* Don't confuse with *Pinot Noir/Chardonnay* sparkling wine blends such as the excellent *Seaview* and *Yalumba.*

🍇 **Pinot Gris/Grigio** [pee-noh gree] (*Alsace,* France) White grape of uncertain origins. Can be light and plain – especially in Italy where it is known as as *Pinot Grigio* and is often over-cropped – or intense and spicy-gingery – particularly when picked super-ripe in *Alsace* (where it is traditionally called *Tokay d'Alsace*), and Germany (where it is *Ruländer* or *Grauburgunder*). Currently flavor of the month in New Zealand and the US where sales are rising dramatically. Sadly, the greatest success is of dull Italian examples whose principal quality is that they don't taste like oaky, buttery Chardonnay. **Ernst Brun; Bott-Geyl; Dopff & Irion; Dry River; Kreydenweiss; Ostertag; Piper's Brook; Schleret; Sorg; Cave de Turckheim; Weinbach (Faller); Zind Humbrecht.**

🍇 **Pinot Meunier** [pee-noh-mur-nee-yay] (*Champagne,* France) Dark, pink-skinned grape. Also known as the Wrotham Pinot and "Dusty Miller," a name which, like Meunier (French for flour miller) refers to the dusty appearance of this variety. Plays an unsung but major role in *Champagne.* Can also be used to produce a still varietal wine. **Best's; Bonny Doon; William Wheeler.**

🍇 **Pinot Noir** [pee-noh nwahr] Black grape responsible for all red *Burgundy* and in part for white *Champagne.* Also successfully grown in the New World within sites whose climate is neither too warm nor too cold. **Oregon, Carneros, Central Otago; Yarra, Santa Barbara, Martinborough, Tasmania, Burgundy.**

P

🍇 **Pinotage** [pee-noh-tazh] (South Africa) Controversial *Pinot Noir* x *Cinsault* cross with a spicy, plummy character and a recognisable bitter note that is usually the flavor that lingers longest. Developed and first used in South Africa in the 1950s and now rarely found elsewhere, apart from occasional examples in New Zealand and California. Winemakers like Beyers Truter of Kanonkop and Beyerskloof love it dearly; others like Andre van Rensburg of Vergelegen think otherwise. (He likened it to excrement, though using blunter language.) Good old examples are brilliant but rare; most taste muddy and rubbery. New winemaking and international demand are making for more exciting wines. *Beyerskloof; Clos Malverne; Fairview; Grangehurst; Kanonkop; Longridge; Saxenburg; Simonsig; Warwick.* ★ ★ ★ ★ ★ **Longridge Pinotage 2001 $$$**

🍷 **Pio Cesare** [pee-yoh CHAY-ser-ray] (Piedmont, Italy) Slightly mixed quality, but the modern cru Barolos and Barbarescos are tops.

🍷 **Piper Heidsieck** [pi-pur hide-seek] (Champagne, France) Good, easy-going *Champagne* made by the producers of *Charles Heidsieck*. The "Rare" is worth looking out for. ★ ★ ★ ★ **Cuvée Reservée Rare $$$**

🍷 **Pipers Brook Vineyards** (Tasmania, Australia) Pioneering producer of fine *Burgundian Chardonnay, Pinot Noir*, and *Pinot Gris*. Ninth Island, the *second label*, includes an excellent unoaked *Chablis*-like *Chardonnay*. The new Pirie sparkling wine is good too. ★ ★ ★ ★ **The Lyre Single Site Pinot Noir 2000 $$$**

🍷 **E. Pira** [pee-rah] (Piedmont, Italy) Chiara Boschis's impressive small *Barolo* estate makes long-lived wines. Beware of confusion with other Piras. ★ ★ ★ ★ **Dolcetto d'Alba 2001 $$**

🍷 **Pirramimma** (Australia) McLaren Vale winery with especially good Petit Verdot. ★ ★ ★ ★ **1999 Shiraz $$**

🍷 **Producteurs Plaimont** [play-mon] (Southwest, France) Reliable *Côtes de St. Mont* cooperative, with *Bordeaux*-lookalike reds and good whites made from local grapes. See also *Pacherenc du Vic-Bilh* and *Madiran*.

🍷 **Plaisir de Merle** [play-zeer dur mehrl] (Paarl, South Africa) Paul Pontallier of *Ch. Margaux* helps to make ripe, soft reds and rich whites for *Stellenbosch Farmers' Winery* in this new showcase operation. ★ ★ ★ **2000 Chardonnay $$**

🍷 **Planeta** [plah-nay-tah] (Sicily, Italy) A name to watch among the growing number of starry producers in Sicily. Wines are well made and very fairly priced ★ ★ ★ ★ **Cabernet Sauvignon Burdese 2000 $$**

🍷 **Plantagenet** (Mount Barker, Western Australia) This is a good producer of *Chardonnay, Riesling, Cabernet*, and lean *Shiraz* in the southwest corner of Australia. Omrah is another label. ★ ★ ★ ★ **Omrah Merlot /Cabernet Sauvignon 2001 $$**

🍷 **Plumpjack** (Napa, California) Small Cabernet specialist that hit the headlines by having the courage to bottle some of its Reserve *Cabernet* in screwtop bottles (to avoid cork taint). Bidders at the 2000 Napa Valley Charity Auction were undeterred and paid a record sum for the wine.

PLANTAGENET
1998
Mount Barker/Pemberton
Pinot Noir
750ML•PRODUCT OF AUSTRALIA•14% VOL

🍷 **Il Podere dell'Olivos** [eel poh-deh-reh del-oh-lee-vohs] (California) Pioneering producer of Italian varietals.

🍷 **Poggio Antico** [pod-zhee-yoh an-tee-koh] (Tuscany, Italy) Ultrareliable *Brunello* producer. ★ ★ ★ ★ **Brunello di Montalcino 1998 $$**

🍷 **Pojer & Sandri** [poh-zhehr eh san-dree] (Trentino, Italy) Good red and white and, especially, sparkling wines.

🍷 **Pol Roger** [pol rod-zhay] (Champagne, France) Fine non-vintage that improves with keeping. The Cuvée Winston Churchill (named in honor of a faithful fan) is spectacular, and the *Demi-sec* is a rare treat.

🍷 **Erich & Walter Polz** [poltz] (Styria, Austria) Fine dry wines, including Pinot Blanc and Gris, and good Sauvignon Blancs. ★ ★ ★ ★ **Sauvignon Blanc Therese 2001 $$**

🍷 **Poliziano** [poh-leet-zee-yah-noh] (Tuscany, Italy) Apart from a pack-leading *Vino Nobile di Montepulciano*, this is the place to find the delicious Elegia and Le Stanze Vini da Tavola. ★ ★ ★ ★ ★ **Vino Nobile di Montepulciano 2000 $$**

P

☤ **Pomerol** [pom-meh-rohl] (*Bordeaux*, France) With *St. Emilion*, the *Bordeaux* for lovers of *Merlot*, which predominates in its rich, plummy wines. Also home to *garage* wines. None is cheap because production is often limited to a few thousand cases (in the *Médoc*, 20,000 is more common). Quality is more consistent than in *St. Emilion*. See *Pétrus*, *Moueix*, and individual châteaux.

☤ **Pomino** [poh-mee-noh] (*Tuscany*, Italy) Small *DOC* within *Chianti Rufina*; virtually a monopoly for *Frescobaldi* which makes a delicious, buttery, unwooded, white *Pinot Bianco/Chardonnay*, the oaky-rich Il Benefizio, and a tasty *Sangiovese/Cabernet*. ★★★ Pomino Benefizio 2000 $$

☤ **Pommard** [pom-mahr] (*Burgundy*, France) Variable *commune*, with slow-to-mature, solid and complex reds. *Comte Armand; Jean-Marc Boillot; de Courcel; Girardin; Dominique Laurent; Leroy; Château de Meursault; de Montille; Mussy; Dom. de Pousse d'Or*. ★★★★ Dom. de Courcel, Clos des Épenots 1999 $$

☤ **Ch de Pommard** [pom-mahr] (*Burgundy*, France) Estate recently purchased by the dynamic owners of Ch. Smith-Haut-Lafitte. Watch this space.

☤ **Pommery** [pom-meh-ree] (*Champagne*, France) The home of POP quarter bottles from which the fizz is drunk through a straw, and of top quality *Louise Pommery* white and rosé ★★★★★ Pommery Brut 1992 $$$

☤ **Pongracz** [pon-gratz] (South Africa) Brand name for the *Bergkelder's* (excellent) *Cap Classique* sparkling wine.

☤ **Dom. Ponsot** [pon-soh] (*Burgundy*, France) Top-class estate noted for *Clos de la Roche, Gevrey-Chambertin*, and (rare) white *Morey-St.-Denis*.

☤ **Ch. Pontet-Canet** [pon-tay ka-nay] (*Pauillac 5ème Cru Classé, Bordeaux*, France) Rich, concentrated, up-and-coming *Pauillac*. The same family owns the similarly fine *Lafon-Rochet*.

☤ **Ponzi** [pon-zee] (*Oregon*) The ideal combination: a maker of good *Pinot Noir, Chardonnay,* and even better beer.

Port (*Douro*, Portugal) Fortified wine made in the upper *Douro* valley. Comes in several styles; see *Tawny, Ruby, LBV, Vintage, Crusted,* and *White port*.

☤ **Viña Porta** [veen-yah por-ta] (*Rapel*, Chile) Dynamic winery that specializes in juicy *Cabernet* and *Merlot*. The *Chardonnay* is good too.

☤ **Quinta do Portal** [keentah doo por-tahl] (*Douro*, Portugal) Pricey table wine and port estate. ★★★★★ Douro Grande Reserva 2000 $$$

☤ **Ch. Potelle** (*Napa Valley*, California) French-owned *Mount Veeder* winery whose stylish wines have been served at the White House.

☤ **Ch. Potensac** [po-ton-sak] (*Médoc Cru Bourgeois, Bordeaux*, France) Under the same ownership as the great *Léoville-las-Cases*, and offering a more affordable taste of the winemaking that goes into that wine.

Pouilly-Fuissé [poo-yee fwee-say] (*Burgundy*, France) Variable white often sold at vastly inflated prices. Pouilly-Vinzelles, Pouilly-Loché, and other *Mâconnais* wines are often better value, though top-class Pouilly-Fuissé from producers like *Ch. Fuissé*, Dom. Noblet, or Dom. Ferret can compete with the best of the *Côte d'Or*. *Barraud; Corsin; Ferret; Ch. Fuissé; Lapierre; Noblet; Philibert; Verget;* Domaine Vessigaud.

☤ **Pouilly-Fumé** [poo-yee foo-may] (*Loire*, France) Potentially ultra-elegant *Sauvignon Blanc* with classic gooseberry fruit and "smoky" overtones derived from flint ("silex") subsoil. Like *Sancerre*, rarely repays cellaring. *Henri Bourgeois; Didier Dagueneau; Serge Dagueneau; Ladoucette; Michel Redde; Ch de Tracy*

☤ **Ch. Poujeaux** [poo-joh] (*Moulis Cru Bourgeois, Bordeaux*, France) Up-and-coming, reliable, plummy-blackcurranty wine.

Pourriture noble [poo-ree-toor nohbl] (France) See *Botrytis cinerea* or noble rot.

☤ **Dom. de la Pousse d'Or** [poos-daw] (*Burgundy*, France) One of the top estates in *Volnay*. (The *Pommard* and *Santenay* wines are good too.)

Prädikat [pray-dee-ket] (Germany) As in Qualitätswein mit Prädikat (*QmP*), the (supposedly) higher quality level for German and Austrian wines, indicating a greater degree of natural ripeness.

P

Franz Prager [prah-gur] (*Wachau,* Austria) Top-class producer of a wide range of impressive *Grüner-Veltliners* and now *Rieslings*.

Precipitation The creation of a harmless deposit, usually of *tartrate* crystals, in white wine, which the Germans romantically call "diamonds."

Premier Cru [prur-mee-yay kroo] In *Burgundy,* indicates wines that fall between *village* and *Grand Cru* quality. Some major *communes* such as *Beaune* and *Nuits-St.-Georges* have no *Grand Cru*. Meursault Premier Cru, for example, is probably a blend from two or more vineyards.

Premières Côtes de Blaye See *Côtes de Blaye*

Premières Côtes de Bordeaux [prur-mee-yehr koht dur bohr-doh] (*Bordeaux,* France) Up-and-coming riverside *appellation* for reds and (often less interestingly) sweet whites. *Carsin;* Grand-Mouëys; *Reynon*.

Prestige Cuvée [koo-vay] (*Champagne,* France) The top wine of a *Champagne* house. Expensive and elaborately packaged. Some, like *Dom Pérignon,* are excellent; others less so. Other best-known examples include *Veuve Clicquot's* Grand Dame and *Roederer's* Cristal.

Preston Vineyards (*Sonoma,* California) Winery making the most of *Dry Creek Zinfandel* and *Syrah*. A white Meritage blend is pretty good too, and there is an improving *Viognier*.

Pride Mountain (*Napa,* California) Small Napa label whose Merlot is worth seeking out. ★ ★ ★ ★ Napa Valley Cabernet Sauvignon 2000 $$$

Dom. Jacques Prieur [pree-yur] (*Burgundy,* France) Estate with fine vineyards. Increasingly impressive since takeover by *Antonin Rodet*.
★ ★ ★ ★ Musigny 2000 $$$$

Ch. Prieuré-Lichine [pree-yur-ray lih-sheen] (*Margaux 4ème Cru Classé, Bordeaux,* France) Recently (1999) sold and – in 2000 – much improved *château* making good if rarely subtle blackcurranty wine that benefits from input by *Michel Rolland*. One of the very few *châteaux* with a gift shop, and a helicopter landing pad on its roof. The 2001 vintage was controversial, striking some – including the editor of this guide – as too rich and dark for a Margaux.

Primeur [pree-mur] (France) New wine, e.g., *Beaujolais* Primeur (a.k.a. *Beaujolais Nouveau*) or, as in *en primeur,* wine which is sold in the barrel. Known in the US as futures.

Primitivo [pree-mih-tee-voh] (*Puglia,* Italy) Italian name for the *Zinfandel*. ★ ★ ★ ★ ★ Tenuta Albrizzi Cantine Due Palme 2001 $

Primo Estate [pree-moh] (South Australia) Imaginative venture among the fruit farms of the Adelaide Plains and McLaren Vale. Passion-fruity *Colombard,* sparkling *Shiraz,* and *Merlot* made *Amarone*-style, using grapes dried in the sun. The olive oil is good too. ★ ★ ★ ★ Moda Amarone 2000 $$

Principe de Viana [preen-chee-pay de vee-yah-nah] (*Navarra,* Spain) Highly commercial winery producing large amounts of good value red and white wine. The Agramont label is particularly worthwhile. ★ ★ ★ Senorial Rioja Crianza Principe de Viana 1999 $

Prinz zu Salm-Dalberg [zoo sahlm dal-burg] (*Nahe,* Germany) Innovative producer with good red *Spätburgunder* and (especially) *Scheurebe*.

Priorato/Priorat [pree-yaw-rah-toh/raht] (*Catalonia,* Spain) Highly prized/priced, sexy new-wave wines from a region once known for hefty alcoholic reds from *Cariñena* and *Garnacha* grapes. *Rene Barbier (Clos Mogador); Costers del Siurana; Mas Martinet;* Clos i Terrasses; J.M. Fuentes; Daphne Glorian; *Alvaro Palacios;* Mas dén Gil; Mas Igneus; Pasanau Germans; (Freixenet) Prior Terrae; Scala Dei; Vilella de la Cartoixa. ★ ★ ★ Coma Vella Mas dén Gil 2000 $$$

Propriétaire (Récoltant) [pro-pree-yeh-tehr ray-kohl-ton] (France) Vineyard owner-manager.

Prosecco (di Conegliano-Valdobbiàdene) [proh-sek-koh dee coh-nay-lee-anoh val-doh-bee-yah-day-nay] (*Veneto,* Italy) Fashionable soft, dry and sweet sparkling wine made from the *Prosecco* grape. Drink young. Di Conegliano is best. Bisol; Bortolin; Canevel; Produttori; Ruggeri; Zardetto.

Provence [proh-vons] (France) Region producing fast-improving wine with a number of minor *ACs*. Rosé de Provence should be dry and fruity with a hint of peppery spice. This is also the region where *Louis Latour* is making its new *Vin de Pays Pinot Noir*. See *Bandol, Coteaux d'Aix-en-Provence, Palette*.

Ⓣ **Provins** [proh-vah'] (*Valais*, Switzerland) Dynamic cooperative, making the most of *Chasselas* and more interesting varieties such as the *Arvine*.

Ⓣ **J.J. Prüm** [proom] (*Mosel-Saar-Ruwer*, Germany) Producer with fine *Wehlener* vineyards. ★★★★★ Graacher Himmelreich Riesling Spätlese 1997 $$$

Ⓣ **Dom. Michel Prunier** [proo-nee-yay] (*Burgundy*, France) Best estate in *Auxey-Duresses*. ★★★★ Auxey-Duresses Vieilles Vignes 2000 $$$

Ⓣ **Alfredo Prunotto** [proo-not-toh] (*Piedmont*, Italy) Good *Barolo* producer that belongs to *Antinori*. ★★★★★ Barolo Bussia 1998 $$$

Puerto de Santa María [pwehr-toh day san-tah mah-ree-yah] (Spain) Sherry town. Fino here can be softer and lighter than that from Jerez.

Puglia [poo-lee-yah] (Italy) Hot region, now making cool wines, thanks to *flying winemakers* like *Kym Milne*. Also see *Salice Salentino* and *Copertino*.

Ⓣ **Puiatti** [pwee-yah-tee] (*Friuli-Venezia Giulia*, Italy) Producer of some of Italy's best *Chardonnay, Pinot Bianco, Pinot Grigio*, and *Tocai Friulano*. The Archetipi are the cream of the crop. ★★★★ Bianco de Pinot Nero 1999 $$

Ⓣ **Puisseguin St. Emilion** [pwees-gan san tay-mee-lee-yon] (*Bordeaux*, France) Satellite of *St. Emilion* making similar, *Merlot*-dominant wines which are often far better value. Ch. Côte Montpezat; la Mariane.

Ⓣ **Puligny-Montrachet** [poo-lee-nee mon-ra-shay] (*Burgundy*, France) Aristocratic white *Côte d'Or commune* that shares the *Montrachet* vineyard with *Chassagne*. Should be complex, buttery *Chardonnay*. Carillon, Sauzet, Ramonet, Drouhin, and *Dom. Leflaive* are all worth their money. D'Auvenay; Louis Carillon; Chavy; Drouhin; Latour-Giraud; Leflaive (Olivier & Domaine); Marquis de Laguiche; Ch de Puligny-Montrachet; Ramonet.; Etienne Sauzet.

Putto [poot-toh] (Italy) See *Chianti*.

Puttonyos [poot-toh-nyos] (*Tokaji*, Hungary) The measure of sweetness (from 1 to 6) of *Tokaji*. The number indicates the number of puttonyos (baskets) of sweet *aszú* paste added to the base wine.

Ⓣ **Ch. Puygeraud** [Pwee-gay-roh] (*Bordeaux*, France) Perhaps the best property on the *Côtes de Francs*.

Pyrenees (*Victoria*, Australia) One of the classiest regions in *Victoria*, thanks to the efforts of *Taltarni* and *Dalwhinnie*. ★★★ 2000 Blue Pyrenees Shiraz $$

Ⓣ **Pyrus** [pi-rus] (Australia) *Lindemans Coonawarra* wine that's back on form.

Q

QbA *Qualitätswein bestimmter Anbaugebiet:* [kvah-lih-tayts-vine behr-shtihmt-tuhr ahn-bow-geh-beet] (Germany) Basic-quality German wine from one of the 13 *Anbaugebiete*, e.g. *Rheinhessen*.

QmP *Qualitätswein mit Prädikat:* [pray-dee-kaht] (Germany) *QbA* wine (supposedly) with "special qualities." The QmP blanket designation is broken into five quality rungs, from *Kabinett* to *Trockenbeerenauslese* plus *Eiswein*.

Ⓣ **Quady** [kway-dee] (*Central Valley*, California) Makes "Starboard" (served in a decanter), *Orange Muscat* Essencia (great with chocolate), *Black Muscat* Elysium, low-alcohol Electra, and Vya Sweet Vermouth.

Ⓣ **Quarles Harris** [kwahrls] (*Douro*, Portugal) Underrated *port* producer.

Ⓣ **Quarts de Chaume** [kahr dur shohm] (*Loire*, France) Luscious, but light, sweet wines, aging beautifully, from the *Coteaux du Layon*. The *Dom. des Baumard* is exceptional. Dom des Baumard; Piere Bise; Jo Pithon; Pierre Soulez; la Varière.

Ⓣ **Querciabella** [kehr-chee-yah-BEH-lah] (*Tuscany*, Italy) Top class *Chianti Classico* estate with a great *Sangiovese-Cabernet* blend called Camartina.

℞ **Quilceda Creek** [kwil-see-dah] (*Washington State*) Producer of one of the best, most blackcurranty *Cabernets* in the American Northwest.

℞ Quincy [kan-see] (*Loire*, France) Dry *Sauvignon*, lesser-known and sometimes good alternative to *Sancerre* or *Pouilly-Fumé*. ★ ★ ★ Villain Jacques Rouzé 2001 $

℞ **Quinault l'Enclos** [kee-noh lon-kloh] (*St. Emilion*, Bordeaux, France) Recently – 1997 – created, tiny-production wine from the same stable as la Croix de Gay and la Fleur de Gay, and produced from previously unvaunted land close to both *Pomerol* and the town of Libourne. Like most such wines, it's rich, dark, and concentrated.

Quinta [keen-ta] (Portugal) Vineyard or estate, particularly in the *Douro*, where "single Quinta" *vintage ports* are increasingly being taken as seriously as the big-name blends. See *Crasto*, *Vesuvio*, and *de la Rosa*.

℞ **Quintessa** (*Napa*, California) Exciting venture from Agustin Huneeus, the man behind *Franciscan* and *Veramonte*. ★ ★ ★ ★ **Rutherford 1999 $$**

℞ **Guiseppe Quintarelli** [keen-ta-reh-lee] (*Veneto*, Italy) Old-fashioned *Recioto*-maker producing quirky, sublime *Valpolicella*, recognizable by the apparently handwritten labels. Try the more affordable Molinara.

℞ **Quivira** (*Sonoma*, California) Great *Dry Creek* producer of intense *Zinfandel* and *Syrah* and a deliciously clever *Rhône*-meets-California blend that includes both varieties.

℞ **Qupé** [kyoo-pay] (*Central Coast*, California) Run by one of the founders of *Au Bon Climat*, this *Santa Barbara* winery produces brilliant *Syrah* and *Rhône*-style whites. ★ ★ ★ ★ **Bien Nacido Syrah 2000 $$$**

R

℞ **Ch. Rabaud-Promis** [rrah-boh prraw-mee] (*Sauternes Premier Cru Classé*, *Bordeaux*, France) Underperforming until 1986; now making top-class wines.

℞ **Rabbit Ridge** (*Sonoma*, California) Small producer with a fairly priced, very starry, Russian River Zinfandel.

Racking The drawing off of wine from its *lees* into a clean cask or vat.

℞ **Rafael Estate** [raf-fay-yel] (*Mendoza*, Argentina) Dynamic producer of great value *Malbec*-based reds with the assistance of *flying winemaker* Hugh Ryman.

℞ **A Rafanelli** [ra-fur-nel-lee] (*Sonoma*, California) Great *Dry Creek* winery with great *Cabernet* Sauvignon. The *Zinfandel* is the jewel in the crown though.

℞ **Olga Raffault** [ra-foh] (*Loire*, France) There are several Raffaults in *Chinon*; this is the best – and the best source of some of the longest-lived wines.

℞ **Le Ragose** [lay-rah-goh-say] (*Veneto*, Italy) A name to look out for in *Valpolicella* – for great *Amarone*, *Recioto*, and Valpolicella Classico (le Sassine). ★ ★ ★ ★ **Amarone della Valpolicella Marta Galli 1997 $$$**

℞ **Raïmat** [ri-mat] (*Catalonia*, Spain) Innovative *Codorníu*-owned winery in *Costers del Segre*. *Merlot*, a *Cabernet*/*Merlot* blend called Abadia, and *Tempranillo* are interesting though less impressive than in the past, and *Chardonnay* – both still and sparkling – is good. ★ ★ ★ ★ **Cabernet Sauvignon 1998 $$**

Rainwater (*Madeira*, Portugal) Light, dry style of *Madeira* popular in the US.

℞ **Ch. Ramage-la-Batisse** [ra-mazh la ba-teess] (*Haut-Médoc Cru Bourgeois*, *Bordeaux*, France) Good-value wine from the commune of St. Laurent.

℞ **Ramitello** [ra-mee-tel-loh] (*Molise*, Italy) Spicy-fruity reds and creamy citrus whites produced by di Majo Norante in Biferno on the Adriatic coast.

℞ **Adriano Ramos Pinto** [rah-mosh pin-toh] (*Douro*, Portugal) Dynamic family-run winery that belongs to *Roederer*. *Colheita tawnies* are a delicious specialty, but the *vintage* wines and *single quintas* (Bom Retiro, Ervamara) are good, as are the Dias Quintas table wines. ★ ★ ★ ★ **Vintage 200 $$** ★ ★ ★ **Duas Quintas Douro Tinto 2000 $$**

R

☩ **Dom. Ramonet** [ra-moh-nay] (*Burgundy,* France) Supreme *Chassagne-Montrachet* estate with top-flight *Montrachet, Bâtard,* and *Bienvenues-Bâtard-Montrachet* and fine complex *Premiers Crus.* Pure class; worth waiting for, too. ★★★★★ Chassagne-Montrachet Morgeot 2000 $$$$

☩ **João Portugal Ramos** [jwow por-too-gahl ramosh] (Portugal) One of this conservative country's best new-wave winemakers. ★★★ Trincadeira 2001 $

☩ **Castello dei Rampolla** [kas-teh-loh day-ee ram-poh-la] (*Tuscany,* Italy) Good *Chianti*-producer whose wines need time to soften. The berryish Sammarco *Vino da Tavola* is also impressive.

Rancio [ran-see-yoh] Term for the peculiarly tangy, and yet highly prized, *oxidized* flavor of certain fortified wines, particularly in France (e.g., *Banyuls*) and Spain.

Randersack [ran-dehr-sak] (*Franken,* Germany) One of the most successful homes of the *Silvaner,* especially when made by Weingut *Juliusspital.* ★★★ Juliusspital, Randersacker Pfülben Riesling Spätlese Trocken 2001 $$

Rangen [rang-gen] (*Alsace,* France) *Grand Cru* vineyard especially good for *Riesling,* but also *Gewurztraminer, Pinot Gris.* Zind Humbrecht

Rapel [ra-pel] (Central Valley, Chile) Important subregion of the *Central Valley,* especially for reds. Includes *Colchagua* and *Cachapoal.* Bisquertt; Casa Lapostolle; Caliterra; Canepa; Concha y Toro; Luis Felipe Edwards; Gracia; La Palmeria; MontGras; Montes; Merlot Gran Reserva; Viu Manent $$

☩ **Rapitalà** [ra-pih-tah-la] (*Sicily,* Italy) Estate producing a fresh, peary white wine from a blend of local grapes.

☩ **Kent Rasmussen** (*Carneros,* California) One of California's too-small band of truly inventive winemakers, producing great *Burgundy*-like *Pinot Noir* and *Chardonnay* and Italianate *Sangiovese* and *Dolcetto.* Ramsey is a second label. ★★★★ Pinot Noir 1999 $$$

Rasteau [ras-stoh] (*Rhône,* France) Southern village producing peppery reds with rich, berry fruit. The fortified *Muscat* can be good, too. Red: Bressy-Masson; des Coteaux des Travers; Dom des Girasols; de la Grangeneuve; Marie-France Masson; Rabasse-Charavin; La Soumade; François Vache. ★★★★ Les Peyrières Cave de Rasteau 2000 $$

☩ **Renato Ratti** [rah-tee] (*Piedmont,* Italy) One of the finest, oldest producers of *Barolo.* ★★★★ Barolo Marcenasco Conca 1998 $$$

Rauenthal [row-en-tahl] (*Rheingau,* Germany) *Georg Breuer* is the most interesting producer in this beautiful village. Other names to look for include *Schloss Schönborn* and *Schloss Rheinhartshausen.*

☩ **Ch. Rauzan-Gassies** [roh-zon ga-sees] (*Margaux 2ème Cru Classé, Bordeaux,* France) Compared to *Rauzan-Ségla,* its neighbor, this property is still underperforming magnificently. Better in 2001 and 2002.

☩ **Ch. Rauzan-Ségla** [roh-zon say-glah] (*Margaux 2ème Cru Classé, Bordeaux,* France) For a long time this used to be an underperforming *Margaux.* Now, since its purchase by Chanel in 1994, it has become one of the best buys in *Bordeaux.* Fine in 2001 and 2002.

☩ **Jean-Marie Raveneau** [rav-noh] (*Burgundy,* France) The long-established king of *Chablis,* with impeccably made *Grand* and *Premier Cru* wines that last wonderfully well. ★★★★ Chablis Montée de Tonnerre 2000 $$$

☩ **Ravenswood** (*Sonoma Valley,* California) *Zinfandel*-maker, now under the same ownership as BRL Hardy, Franciscan etc and making a lot more wine. Look out for individual-vineyard wines. The *Merlots* and *Cabernet* are fine, too. ★★★★ Ravenswood Lodi Zinfandel 2000 $$

☩ **Ravenswood** (South Australia) Label confusingly adopted by *Hollick* for its top *Coonawarra* reds (no relation to the above entry).

R

Raventos i Blanc [ra-vayn-tos ee blank] (*Catalonia,* Spain) Josep Raventos' ambition is to produce the best sparkling wine in Spain, adding *Chardonnay* to local varieties.

Ch. Rayas [rye-yas] (*Rhône,* France) The only chance to taste *Châteauneuf-du-Pape* made solely from the *Grenache.* Pricey but good.

Raymond (*Napa Valley,* California) Maker of tasty, intense *Cabernets* and *Chardonnays.*

Ch. Raymond-Lafon [ray-mon la-fon] (*Sauternes, Bordeaux,* France) Very good small producer whose wines deserve keeping.

Ch. de Rayne-Vigneau [rayn veen-yoh] (*Sauternes Premier Cru Classé, Bordeaux,* France) *Sauternes* estate, located at *Bommes,* producing a deliciously rich complex wine.

RD (*Récemment Dégorgée*) (*Champagne,* France) A term invented by *Bollinger* for their delicious vintage *Champagne,* which has been allowed a longer-than-usual period (as much as 15 years) on its *lees.*

Real Companhia Vinicola do Norte de Portugal [ray-yahl com-pah-nee-yah vee-nee-koh-lah doh nor-tay day por-too-gahl] (*Douro,* Portugal) The full name of the firm that is better known as the *Royal Oporto Wine Co.* The best wines are the *tawny* ports; these are sold under the Quinta dos Carvalhas label. The whole company is being revived by a new generation.

Rebholz [reb-holtz] (Pfalz, Germany) High quality estate making superb *Spätburgunder, Gewürztraminer, Chardonnay* and *Muskateller.*

Ignacio Recabarren [ig-na-see-yoh reh-ka-ba-ren] (Chile) Superstar winemaker and Casablanca pioneer.

Recioto [ray-chee-yo-toh] (*Veneto,* Italy) Sweet or dry alcoholic wine made from semidried, ripe grapes. Usually associated with *Valpolicella* and *Soave.* ★★★★★ Tommaso Bussola Recioto della Valpolicella Classico 1999 $$$

Récoltant-manipulant (RM) [ray-kohl-ton ma-nee-poo-lon] (*Champagne,* France) Term for an individual winegrower and blender, identified by what is known as the RM number on the label.

Récolte [ray-kohlt] (France) Vintage, literally "harvest."

Dom. de la Rectorie [rehc-toh-ree] (*Languedoc-Roussillon,* France) One of top names in *Banyuls,* and producer of fine *Collioure.*

Redman (South Australia) Improved *Coonawarra* estate with intense reds.

Redoma [ray-doh-mah] (*Douro,* Portugal) New-wave red and white table wines from the dynamic, yet reliable port producer Dirk *Niepoort.* Batuta is the super-cuvée. ★★★★★ Batuta 1999 $$$

Redwood Valley Estate See *Seifried.*

Refosco [re-fos-koh] (*Friuli-Venezia Giulia,* Italy) Red grape and its dry and full-bodied *DOC* wine. Benefits from aging. ★★★ Ronchi di Manzano $$

Regaleali [ray-ga-lay-ah-lee] (*Sicily,* Italy) Red and white made by the aristocratic Tasca d'Almerita estate, using local varieties.

Régisseur [rey-jee-sur] (*Bordeaux,* France) In *Bordeaux* (only), the cellar-master.

Régnié [ray-nyay] (*Burgundy,* France) Once sold as *Beaujolais Villages,* Régnié now has to compete with *Chiroubles, Chénas,* and the other *crus.* It is mostly like an amateur competing against professionals. Fortunately enough for Régnié, these particular professionals often aren't great. *Duboeuf* makes a typical example. *Duboeuf; Dubost; Piron; Sapin; Trichard.*

Reguengos (*Alentejo,* Portugal) Richly flavorsome reds pioneered by Esporão and the Reguengos de Monsaraz cooperative. ★★★ Cooperativa Agricola de Reguengos de Monsaraz 2001 $

Reichensteiner [rike-en-sti-ner] Recently developed white grape, popular in England (and Wales).

Reif Estate Winery [reef] (*Ontario,* Canada) Impressive *icewine* specialist.

Remelluri [ray-may-yoo-ree] (*Rioja,* Spain) One of the first examples in *Rioja* of a top-class, small-scale organic estate. Wines are more serious (and *tannic*) than most, but they're fuller in flavor, and built to last.

R

Remuage [reh-moo-wazh] (*Champagne*, France) Part of the *méthode champenoise*, the gradual turning and tilting of bottles so that the yeast deposit collects in the neck ready for *dégorgement*.

Renaissance (*California*, USA) Idealistic estate run on almost religious philosophical lines. Very good *Riesling* and *Roussanne*; subtle, elegant flavors across the board. ★★★ Renaissance Le Provencal 1999 $$$

Reserva [ray-sehr-vah] (Spain) Wine aged for a period specified by the relevant *DO*: usually one year for reds and six months for whites and pinks.

Réserve [reh-surv] (France) Legally meaningless, as in "Réserve Personelle," but implying a wine selected and given more age.

Residual sugar Term for wines that have retained grape sugar not converted to *alcohol* by yeasts during fermentation. Bone-dry wines have less than 2 grams per liter of residual sugar. In the US, many so-called "dry" white wines contain as much as 10, and some supposedly dry red *Zinfandels* definitely have more than a trace of sweetness. New Zealand Sauvignons are rarely bone dry, but their *acidity* balances and conceals any residual sugar.

Weingut Balthasar Ress [bahl-ta-zah rress] (*Rheingau*, Germany) Good producer in *Hattenheim*, blending delicacy with concentration. ★★★★ Hattenheimer Nussbrunnen Riesling Spätlese 2001 $$$

Retsina [ret-see-nah] (Greece) Wine made the way the ancient Greeks used to make it – resinating it with pine to keep it from spoiling. Today, it's an acquired taste for non-vacationing, non-Greeks. Pick the freshest examples you can find (though this isn't easy when labels mention no vintage).

Reuilly [rur-yee] (*Loire*, France) (Mostly) white *AC* for dry *Sauvignons*, good-value, if sometimes rather earthy alternatives to nearby *Sancerre* and *Pouilly-Fumé* and spicy *Pinot* rosé. *Henri Beurdin*; Bigonneau; *Lafond*.

Rex Hill Vineyards (*Oregon*) Recommendable *Pinot Noir* specialist.

Chateau Reynella [ray-nel-la] (*McLaren Vale*, Australia) *BRL Hardy* subsidiary, mastering both reds and whites. ★★★★ McLaren Vale Basket Pressed Shiraz 2000 $$

Ch. Reynon [ray-non] (*Premier Côtes de Bordeaux*, France) Fine red and especially recommendable white wines from *Denis Dubourdieu*.

Rheingau [rine-gow] (Germany) Traditional home of the finest *Rieslings* of the 13 *Anbaugebiete*; now overshadowed by *Pfalz* and *Mosel*. QbA/Kab/Spät: *Künstler*; *Balthasar Ress*; Domdechant Werner'sches; HH Eser.

Rheinhessen [rine-hehs-sen] (Germany) Largest of the 13 *Anbaugebiete*, now well known for *Liebfraumilch* and *Niersteiner*. Fewer than one vine in 20 is now *Riesling*; sadly, easier-to-grow varieties, and lazy cooperative wineries, generally prevail. There are a few stars, however. *Balbach*; Keller; Gunderloch.

Rhône [rohn] (France) Fast-improving, exciting, packed with increasingly sexy *Grenache*, *Syrah*, and *Viognier* wines. See *St. Joseph*, *Crozes-Hermitage*, *Hermitage*, *Condrieu*, *Côtes du Rhône*, *Châteauneuf-du-Pape*, *Tavel*, *Lirac*, *Gigondas*, *Ch. Grillet*, *Beaumes de Venise*.

Rias Baixas [ree-yahs bi-shahs] (*Galicia*, Spain) The place to find spicy *Albariño*. Burgáns; Fefiñanes; *Lagar de Cervera*; Martín Codáx; *Pazo de Barrantes*; Santiago Ruiz; Valdamor $$

Ribatejo [ree-bah-tay-joh] (Portugal) *DO* area north of Lisbon where *Peter Bright* and the cooperatives are beginning to make highly commercial white and red wine, but traditional *Garrafeiras* are worth watching out for, too.

Ribera del Duero [ree-bay-rah del doo-way-roh] (Spain) One of the regions to watch in Spain for good reds. Unfortunately, despite the established success of *Vega Sicilia* and of producers like *Pesquera*, *Pingus*, *Arroyo*, and *Alion*, there is still far too much poor winemaking. *Alion*; Ismael Arroyo; Arzuaga; Condado de Haza; Peñalba López; Pesquera; Pedrosa; Pingus; Hermanos Sastre; Valtravieso; *Vega Sicilia*.

Ribolla [rib-bol-lah] (Italy) White grape from the Northeast with nuttiness and good acidity but not a lot else. It becomes Robola in Greece.

R

Dom. Richeaume [ree-shohm] (*Provence*, France) Dynamic producer of good, earthy, long-lived, organic *Cabernet* and *Syrah*. The Cuvée Tradition is Rhône-like, with plenty of *Syrah* and *Grenache*, while the Columelle is more influenced by *Cabernet-Sauvignon* and new oak.

Richebourg [reesh-boor] (*Burgundy*, France) Top-class *Grand Cru* vineyard just outside *Vosne-Romanée* with a recognizable floral-plummy style. *Grivot; Anne Gros; Leroy; Méo-Camuzet; D&D Mugneret; Noëllat; Romanée-Conti.* ★★★★★ A.F. Gros Richebourg 2001 $$$$

Richou [ree-shoo] (*Loire*, France) Fine *Anjou* producer with reliable reds and whites and fine, affordable, sweet whites from Coteaux de l'Aubance.

Weingut Max Ferd Richter [rikh-tur] (*Mosel-Saar-Ruwer*, Germany) Excellent producer of long-lived, concentrated-yet-elegant *Mosel Rieslings* from high-quality vineyards. The *cuvée* Constantin is the unusually successful dry wine, while at the other end of the scale, the *Eisweins* are sublime. ★★★★ Brauneberger Juffer-Sonnenuhr Riesling Spätlese 2001 $$$

John Riddoch (South Australia) Classic *Wynn's* Coonawarra red. One of Australia's best and longest-lasting wines. (Not to be confused with the wines that *Katnook Estate* sells under its own "Riddoch" label.) ★★★★ 1998 $$$

Ridge Vineyards (*Santa Cruz*, California) Paul Draper, and Ridge's hilltop *Santa Cruz* and *Sonoma* vineyards, consistently produce some of California's very finest *Zinfandel, Cabernet, Mataro*, and *Chardonnay*. ★★★★★ Ridge Geyserville 2000 $$$

Riecine [ree-eh-chee-nay] (*Tuscany*, Italy) Modern estate with fine *Chianti* and an even more impressive la Gioia *Vino da Tavola*.

Rieslaner [rees-lah-nur] (Germany) A decent modern grape crossing, *Silvaner x Riesling* with a good curranty flavor when ripe.

Riesling [reez-ling] The noble grape responsible for Germany's finest offerings, ranging from light, floral, everyday wines, to the delights of *botrytis*-affected sweet wines, which retain their freshness for decades. Reaching its zenith in the superbly balanced, racy wines of the *Mosel*, and the richer offerings from the *Rheingau*, it also performs well in *Alsace*, California, South Africa, and Australia. Watch out for the emergence of the *Wachau* region as a leader of the Austrian *Riesling* pack.

Riesling Italico See *Italian Riesling*, etc.

Ch. Rieussec [ree-yur-sek] (*Sauternes Premier Cru Classé, Bordeaux*, France) Fantastically rich and concentrated *Sauternes*, often deep in color and generally at the head of the pack chasing *d'Yquem*. Owned by the Rothschilds of *Lafite*. R de Rieussec is the unexceptional dry white wine.

Rioja [ree-ok-hah] (Spain) Spain's best-known wine region, split into three parts. The Alta produces the best wines, followed by the Alavesa, while the Baja is the largest. Most Riojas are blends by large *bodegas*: small *Bordeaux*- and *Burgundy*-style estates are rare. New-wave Riojas are abjuring the tradition of long oak aging and producing fruitier, modern wines, and "experimental" *Cabernet* is being planted alongside the traditional *Tempranillo* and lesser-quality *Garnacha*. *Allende; Amézola de la Mora; Ardanza; Artadi; Baron de Ley; Berberana; Breton; Campillo; Campo Viejo; Contino; El Coto; Lopez de Heredia; Marqués de Griñon; Marqués de Murrieta; Marqués de Riscal; Marqués de Vargas; Martinez Bujanda; Montecillo; Ondarre; Palacio; Remelluri; La Rioja Alta; Riojanos.*

La Rioja Alta [ree-ok-hah ahl-ta] (*Rioja*, Spain) Of all the big companies in *Rioja*, this is the most important name to remember. Its Viña Ardanza, Reserva 904, and (rarely produced) Reserva 890 are all among the most reliable and recommendable wines in the region. ★★★ Vina Ardanza Reserva 1996 $$

Dom. Daniel Rion [ree-yon] (*Burgundy*, France) Patrice Rion produces impeccably made modern Nuits-St.-Georges and Vosne-Romanées. ★★★★ Nuits-St.-Georges Blanc Les Terres Blanches 2000 $$$

R

Ripasso [ree-pas-soh] (*Veneto*, Italy) Winemaking method whereby newly made *Valpolicella* is partially refermented in vessels that have recently been vacated by *Recioto* and *Amarone*. The old technique, which increases the *alcohol* and *body* of the wine, was revived and promoted by *Masi* (which now owns, but does not monopolise, the term). Masi's Campo Fiorin is a good example, but there are many others.*Allegrini; Tedeschi; Quintarelli.*

Marqués de Riscal [ris-kahl] (*Rioja*, Spain) Historic *Rioja* name now back on course thanks to more modern winemaking for both reds and whites. The Baron de Chirel is the recently launched top wine. ★★★★ **Gran Reserva 1996 $$**, ★★★★ **Baron de Chirel 1996 $$**

Riserva [ree-zEHr-vah] (Italy) *DOC* wines aged for a specified number of years – often an unwelcome term on labels of wines like *Bardolino*, which are usually far better drunk young.

Ritchie Creek (*Napa*, California) Small producer with dazzling Cabernet from the region of Spring Mountain.

Rivaner [rih-vah-nur] (Germany) The name used for *Müller-Thurgau* (a cross between *Riesling* and *Silvaner*) in parts of Germany and *Luxembourg*.

Rivera [ree-vay-ra] (*Puglia*, Italy) One of the new wave of producers who are turning the southern region of *Puglia* into a source of interesting wines. The red Riserva il Falcone is the star wine here. ★★★ **il Falcone Riserva 2000 $$**

Riverina [rih-vur-ee-na] (*New South Wales*, Australia) Irrigated *New South Wales* region which produces basic-to-good wine, much of which ends up in "*Southeast Australian*" blends. Late-harvest *Semillons* can, however, be surprisingly spectacular. *Cranswick Estate, McWilliams.*

Rivesaltes [reev-zalt] (*Languedoc-Roussillon*, France) Fortified dessert wine of both colors. The white made from the *Muscat* is lighter and more lemony than *Beaumes de Venise*, while the *Grenache* red is like liquid Christmas pudding and ages wonderfully. *Cazes;* Ch. de Corneilla; Força Réal; Ch. de Jau; Sarda-Malet.

Giorgio Rivetti [ree-VAY-tee] (*Piedmont*, Italy) Superstar producer of wonderfully aromatic Moscato d'Asti, *Barberesco*, and *Barbera*.

Riviera Ligure di Ponente [reev-ee-yeh-ra lee-goo-ray dee poh-nen-tay] (*Liguria*, Italy) Little-known northwestern region, close to Genoa, where local grapes like the *Vermentino* produce light aromatic reds and whites.

Rkatsiteli [r'kat-sit-tel-lee] (Russia, Eastern Europe) Widely grown neutral white grape with enough acidity to stand up to poor winemaking.

Robola [roh-boh-lah] (Greece) The *Ribolla* of Italy.

Robertson (South Africa) Warm area where *Chardonnays* and *Sauvignons* are taking over from the *Muscats* that used to be the region's pride. *Graham Beck; Springfield;* Robertson Winery; *Van Loveren;* Weltevrede.

Rocche dei Manzoni [rok-keh day-yee mant-zoh-nee] (*Piedmont*, Italy) The Nebbiolo-Barbera Bricco Manzoni is the top wine here, but the single-vineyard *Barolo* is good too and there's some lovely *Chardonnay*.

Rocca delle Macie [ro-ka del leh mah-chee-yay] (*Tuscany*, Italy) Reliable if unspectacular *Chianti* producer.

La Roche aux Moines [rosh oh mwahn] See *Nicolas Joly*.

Joe Rochioli [roh-kee-yoh-lee] (*Sonoma*, California) Brilliant *Russian River Pinot Noir* and *Chardonnay* producer whose name also appears on single-vineyard wines from *Williams Selyem*.

Rockford (*Barossa Valley*, Australia) Robert "Rocky" O'Callaghan makes a great intense *Barossa Shiraz* using 100-year-old vines and 50-year-old equipment. There's a mouthfilling *Semillon*, a wonderful Black *Shiraz* sparkling wine, and a magical *Alicante Bouschet* rosé, which is sadly only to be found at the winery.

Antonin Rodet [on-toh-nan roh-day] (*Burgundy*, France) Very impressive *Mercurey*-based *négociant*, which has also improved the wines of the *Jacques Prieur domaine* in *Meursault*. Ch. de Chamery; *de Rully.*

🍇 **Roditis** [roh-dee-tiss] (Greece) A pink-skinned grape with good acidity much used for retsina. It can, however, make interesting unresinated wine.

🍷 **Louis Roederer** [roh-dur-rehr] (*Champagne*, France) This is still a family-owned *Champagne* house, and still one of the most reliable of these; its delicious non-vintage wine benefits from being cellared for a few years. Roederer's prestige Cristal remains a most deliciously "wine-like" *Champagne*.

Roederer Estate [roh-dur-rehr] (*Mendocino*, California) No longer involved with the *Jansz* sparkling wine in *Tasmania* but making top-class wine in California, which is sold in the US as Roederer Estate and in the UK as Quartet.

🍷 **Roero** [roh-weh-roh] (*Piedmont*, Italy) *Nebbiolo* red and *Arneis* white (sold as Roero Arneis) which are now among Italy's most interesting wines. *Ceretto; Bruno Giacosa; Prunotto; Serafino; Vietti.* ★★★ 2001 Contea di Castiglione Roero Arneis Araldica Vini Piemontesi $$

Michel Rolland [roh-lon] Based in *Pomerol* and *St. Emilion*, Rolland is now an increasingly international guru-enologist, whose taste for ripe fruit flavors is influencing wines from *Ch. Ausone* to Argentina and beyond.

🍷 **Rol Valentin** [rohl-vah-lo'n-ta'n] (*Bordeaux*, France) *St-Emilion* garage wine with the expected concentration and price.

🍷 **Rolly-Gassmann** [rroh-lee gas-sman] (*Alsace*, France) Fine producer of subtle, long-lasting wines.

🍷 **Dom. de la Romanée-Conti** [rroh-ma-nay kon-tee] (*Burgundy*, France) Aka "DRC". Small *Grand Cru* estate. The jewel in the crown is the Romanée-Conti vineyard itself, though *La Tâche* runs it a close second. Both can be extraordinary, ultraconcentrated spicy wine, as can the *Romanée-St.-Vivant*. The *Richebourg, Echézeaux,* and *Grands Echézeaux* and *Montrachet* are comparable to those produced by other estates – and sold by them for less kingly ransoms.

Romania Traditional source of sweet reds and whites, now developing drier styles from classic European varieties. Unreliability is a constant problem, though *flying winemakers* are helping, as is the owner of the *Comte Peraldi* estate in *Corsica*. Note that Romania's well-praised *Pinot Noirs* are generally made from a different variety, mistaken for the *Pinot*.

🍇 **Romarantin** [roh-ma-ron-tan] (*Loire*, France) Interesting, limey grape found in obscure white blends in the *Loire*. See *Cheverny*. At its best from **Henri Marrionet.**

Römerlay [rrur-mehr-lay] (*Mosel*, Germany) One of the *Grosslagen* in the *Ruwer* river valley.

🍷 **Ronchi di Manzano** [ron-kee dee mant-zah-noh] (*Friuli-Venezia Giulia*, Italy) Famed in Italy for its *Merlot* (Ronc di Subule), this producer's most interesting wine may well be its rich white *Picolit*.

🍷 **Ronco del Gnemiz** [ron-koh del gneh-meez] (*Friuli-Venezia Giulia*, Italy) One of the world's few producers of great *Müller-Thurgau*, and some pretty good *Chardonnay* in the *Colli Orientali*.

🍷 **Ronco delle Betulle** [ron-koh deh-leh beh-too-leh] (*Friuli-Venezia Giulia*, Italy) Try the *Bordeaux*-blend Narciso here – or the *Tocai Friulano, Sauvignon, Pinot Bianco,* or *Grigio*. You won't be disappointed.

🍷 **Rongopai** [ron-goh-pi] (*Te Kauwhata*, New Zealand) Estate in a region of the North Island pioneered by *Cooks*, but which has fallen out of favor with that company and other producers. The speciality here is *botrytis* wines, but the *Chardonnay* is good, too.

🍷 **La Rosa** (Chile) One of the fastest-growing wineries in Chile, with new vineyards and great winemaking from *Ignacio Recabarren*. Las Palmeras is a highly reliable *second label*.
★★★★ la Palmeria Cabernet Sauvignon Reserve 2002 $$

🍷 **Quinta de la Rosa** (*Douro*, Portugal) Recently established estate producing excellent port and exemplary dry red wine, under guidance from David Baverstock, Australian-born former winemaker at *Dow's* and responsible for the wines of *Esporão*. ★★★★ Quinta de la Rosa 2001$$

R

Rosato (Italy) Rosé.

Ⓘ **Rosé d'Anjou** [roh-zay don-joo] (*Loire*, France) Usually dull, semisweet pink from the *Malbec*, *Groslot*, and (less usually) *Cabernet Franc*.

Ⓘ **Rosé de Loire** [roh-zay duh-lwahr] (*Loire*, France) The wine *Rosé d'Anjou* ought to be. Dry, fruity stuff. *Richou*; Cave des Vignerons de Saumur.

Ⓘ **Rosé de Riceys** [roh-zay dur ree-say] (*Champagne*, France) Rare and occasionally delicious still rosé from *Pinot Noir*. Pricey. Alexandre Bonnet.

Ⓘ **Rosemount Estate** (*Hunter Valley*, Australia) Now under the same Southcorp umbrella as *Penfolds*, *Lindemans* etc. Famous for its Show Reserve and Roxburgh *Hunter Chardonnay*. Now makes good wines in *Orange* and *Mudgee* (Mountain Blue).

Ⓘ **Rosenblum** (*Alameda*, California) Great *Zinfandels* from *Napa*, *Sonoma*, *Contra Costa*, and *Paso Robles* vineyards, plus great multi-regional blends. ★★★★ Sonoma County Hillside Syrah 2000 $$

Ⓘ **Rossese di Dolceaqua** [ros-seh-seh di dohl-chay-ah-kwah] (*Liguria*, Italy) Attractive, generally early-drinking wines made from the Rossese. Single-vineyard examples like Terre Bianche's Bricco Arcagna are more serious.

Ⓘ **Dom. Rossignol-Trapet** [ros-seen-yol tra-pay] (*Burgundy*, France) Once old-fashioned, now more recommendable estate in *Gevrey-Chambertin*.

Ⓘ **Rosso Conero** [ros-soh kon-neh-roh] (*Marches*, Italy) Big, *Montepulciano* and *Sangiovese* red, with rich, herby flavor. Good-value, characterful stuff. Fazi Battaglia; Umani Ronchi; Alberto Serenelli; Spinsanti; le Terrazze.

Ⓘ **Rosso di Montalcino** [ros-soh dee mon-tal-chee-noh] (*Tuscany*, Italy) *DO* for lighter, earlier-drinking versions of the more famous *Brunello di Montalcino*. Often better – and better value – than that wine. *Altesino*; *Caparzo*; Fattoria dei Barbi; Col d'Orcia; Talenti.

Ⓘ **Rosso Piceno** [ros-soh pee-chay-noh] (*Marches*, Italy) Traditionally rustic red made from a blend of the *Montepulciano* and *Sangiovese*. ★★★★ Saladini Pilastrii Vigna Montetinello 2000 $

Ⓘ **René Rostaing** [ros-tang] (*Rhône*, France) Producer of serious northern *Rhône* reds, including a more affordable alternative to *Guigal's* la Landonne.

Ⓘ **Rothbury Estate** (*Hunter Valley*, Australia) Founded by Len Evans, Svengali of Australian wine; the company is now a subsidiary of *Mildara*–Blass and Fosters. Rothbury is a great source of *Shiraz*, *Semillon*, and *Chardonnay* from the *Hunter Valley*, *Cowra Chardonnay* and *Marlborough Sauvignon*.

Ⓘ **Rotllan Torra** [rot-lahn tor-rah] (*Priorat*, Spain) Concentrated, weighty red wines made in the current mode, especially Amadis, Balandra.

Ⓘ **Joseph Roty** [roh-tee] (*Burgundy*, France) Superstar producer of a range of intensely concentrated but unsubtle wines in *Gevrey-Chambertin*. One of the first "new-wave" winemakers in Burgundy.

Ⓘ **Rouge Homme** (*Coonawarra*, Australia) Reliable *Coonawarra* producer. founded by Mr. *Redman*; now under the same ownership as *Penfolds*.

Ⓘ **Emmanuel Rouget** [roo-jay] (*Burgundy*, France) Rouget inherited *Henri Jayer's* superb vineyards. Top quality.

Ⓘ **Dom. Guy Roulot** [roo-loh] (*Burgundy*, France) One of the greatest *domaines* in *Meursault*. ★★★★ Meursault Perrières 2000 $$$

Ⓘ **Georges Roumier** [roo-me-yay] (*Burgundy*, France) Blue-chip winery with great quality at every level, from village *Chambolle-Musigny* to the *Grand Cru* Bonnes Mares, and (more rarely seen) white *Corton-Charlemagne*. ★★★★★ Chambolle-Musigny 2000 $$$$

Ⓘ **Round Hill** (*Napa*, California) A rare source of Californian bargains. Large-production, inexpensive *Merlots* and *Chardonnays*.

🍇 **Roussanne** [roos-sahn] (*Rhône*, France) With the *Marsanne*, one of the key white grapes of the northern *Rhône*. In the US, has been mistaken for *Viognier*. ★★★★ Bonterra Vineyards Roussanne 2002 $$

R

♆ **Armand Rousseau** [roos-soh] (*Burgundy,* France) *Gevrey-Chambertin* top-class estate with a line of *Premiers* and *Grands Crus.* Well-made, long-lasting wines. ★ ★ ★ ★ ★ Chambertin 1999 $$$$

♆ **Roussette de Savoie** [roo-sette] (*Savoie,* France) The local name for the equally local Altesse grape. Fresh, easy-drinking fare. ★ ★ ★ 2001 Roussette de Savoie Pierre Boniface Domaine de Rocailles $

Roussillon [roos-see-yon] (*Languedoc-Roussillon,* France) Vibrant up-and-coming region, redefining traditional varieties, especially *Muscat.*

♆ **Ch. Routas** [roo-tahs] (*Provence,* France) Impressive producer of intense reds and whites in the *Coteaux Varois.*

♆ **Royal Oporto Wine Co.** (*Douro,* Portugal) Large and now improving producer of occasionally high-quality wines, including very good table wines.

♆ **The Royal Tokaji Wine Co.** (*Tokaji,* Hungary) Pioneering part-foreign-owned company which – with other foreign investors – has helped to drag *Tokaji* into the late 20th (and early 21st) century with a succession of great single-vineyard wines.

♆ **Rozendal Farm** [rooh-zen-dahl] (*Stellenbosch,* South Africa) Impeccably made, organic, Bordeaux-style reds from a producer whose quality consciousness made him decide not to release the 1997 vintage.

♆ **Rubesco di Torgiano** [roo-bes-koh dee taw-jee-yah-noh] (*Umbria,* Italy) Modern red *DOCG*; more or less the exclusive creation of *Lungarotti.*

♆ **Rubino** [roo-bee-noh] (*Umbria,* Italy) Rich "Super-Umbrian" red from the la Pazzola estate. Matches many a *Super-Tuscan.*

Ruby (*Douro,* Portugal) Cheapest, basic *port*; young, blended, sweetly fruity.

♆ **Ruby Cabernet** [roo-bee ka-behr-nay] (California) A *Cabernet Sauvignon/Carignan* cross making basic wines in California, Australia, and South Africa.

♆ **Ruche** [roo-kay] (*Piedmont,* Italy) Raspberryish red grape from northern Italy producing early-drinking wines. Bava; Dacapo; Sant'Agata

Rüdesheim [rroo-des-hime] (*Rheingau,* Germany) Tourist town producing powerful *Rieslings. Georg Breuer; August Kesseler; Josef Leitz; Dr. Nagler; Balthasar Ress; Schloss Schönborn; Staatsweingüter Kloster Eberbach.* ★ ★ ★ ★ Weingut Dr. Nagler Rudesheimer Berg Rottland First Growth 2001$$

♆ **Rueda** [roo-way-dah] (Spain) *DO* in northwest Spain for clean, dry whites from the local *Verdejo.* Progress is being led most particularly by the *Lurtons, Marqués de Riscal,* and *Marqués de Griñon.*

♆ **Ruffino** [roof-fee-noh] (*Tuscany,* Italy) Big *Chianti* producer with impressive top-of-the-line wines, including the reliable Cabreo il Borgo and Modus IGTs. ★ ★ ★ ★ Modus 1999 $$$

Rufina [roo-fee-na] (*Tuscany,* Italy) A subregion within *Chianti.* Home to *Frescobaldi.* ★ ★ ★ ★ *Frescobaldi* Montesodi 2000 $

♆ **Ruinart** [roo-wee-nahr] (*Champagne,* France) High-quality sister to *Moët & Chandon,* with superlative *Blanc de Blancs.*

♆ **Ruländer** [roo-len-dur] (Germany) German name for *Pinot Gris.*

♆ **Rully** [roo-yee] (*Burgundy,* France) *Côte Chalonnaise commune* producing rich white and a red that's been called the "poor man's" *Volnay.* See *Antonin Rodet, Jadot,* and *Olivier Leflaive. Faiveley; V Girardin;* Jacqueson; Jadot; Olivier Leflaive; Antonin Rodet.

♆ **Rupert & Rothschild** (*Paarl,* South Africa) Up-and-coming joint venture between Edmond de Rothschild (Ch. Clarke) and the Rupert family (Rothmans). Wines are named after Baron Edmond and Baroness Nadine.

Ruppertsberg [roo-pehrt-sbehrg] (*Pfalz,* Germany) Top-ranking village with a number of excellent vineyards making vigorous fruity *Riesling. Bassermann-Jordan; Bürklin-Wolf;* A. Christmann; Kimich; Reichsrat von Buhl; Ruppertsberger Winzerverein "Hoheburg"; Werlé; J.L Wolf.

♆ **la Rural** [lah roo-rahl] (*Mendoza,* Argentina) Old-established producer, now making good, commercial wines. The Malbec is the strongest card.

♆ **Rusden** (*Barossa,* South Australia) Small, new estate gaining instant recognition in the US for its rich Barossa Cabernets and Grenaches.

R

Russe [rooss] (Bulgaria) Danube town best known in Britain for its reliable red blends but vaunted in *Bulgaria* as a source of modern whites.

Russian River Valley (California) Cult, cool-climate area to the north of *Sonoma* and west of *Napa*. Ideal for apples and good sparkling wine, and great *Pinot Noir* country. *Dehlinger; de Loach; Iron Horse; Kistler; Rochioli; Simi; Sonoma-Cutrer;* Joseph Swann; *Marimar Torres; Williams Selyem.* ★★★★★ Simi Reserve Chardonnay 2000 $$$

Rust [roost] (*Burgenland*, Austria) Wine center of *Burgenland*, famous for Ruster *Ausbruch* sweet white wine. *Feiler-Artinger*

🍷 **Rust-en-Vrede** (*Stellenbosch*, South Africa) Vastly improved estate, thanks to the efforts of a new generation.

🍷 **Rustenberg** (*Stellenbosch*, South Africa) On a roll since 1996 with investment in the cellars (which put an end to musty flavors encountered in previous vintages), this is now a leading light in the Cape. The lower-priced Brampton efforts are quite good, too. ★★★★ Peter Barlow 1999 $$

Rutherford (California) *Napa* region in which some producers believe sufficiently to propose it – and its geological "bench" – as an *appellation*.

Rutherglen (*Victoria*, Australia) Hot area on the *Murray River* pioneered by gold miners. Today noted for rich *Muscat* and *Tokay* dessert and *port*-style wines. The reds are often tough, and the *Chardonnays* are used by cool-region winemakers to demonstrate why *port* and light, dry whites are hard to make in the same climate. *All Saints; Campbells*; *Chambers; Morris;* Pfeiffer; Rutherglen Estates; *Seppelt; Stanton & Killeen.* ★★★★★ Seppelts DP63 Grand Rutherglen Muscat $$$

🍷 **Rutz Cellars** (*Sonoma*, California) Competing with Kistler to produce superlative Russian River Chardonnay, Rutz offers the chance to taste a different Chardonnay from the Dutton Ranch vineyard.

Ruwer [roo-vur] (*Mosel-Saar-Ruwer*, Germany) *Mosel* tributary alongside which is to be found the *Römerlay Grosslage*, and includes Kasel, *Eitelsbach*, and the great *Maximin Grünhaus* estate.

Hugh Ryman [ri-man] Former *flying winemaker* who now has his own brands: Santara, Kirkwood, Richemont, Rafael Estate.

🍷 **Rymill** [ri-mil] (South Australia) One of several *Coonawarra* wineries to mention *Riddoch* on its label (in its Riddoch Run) and a rising star. Rymill at least has the legitimacy of a family link to *John Riddoch*, the region's founder. The *Shiraz* and *Cabernet* are first class, as are the whites and the sparkling wine. ★★★★ MC2 Merlot Cabernet Franc Cabernet Sauvignon 1998 $$

S

Saale-Unstrut [zah-leh oon-shtruht] (Germany) Remember East Germany? Well, this is where poor wines used to be made there in the bad old days. Today, good ones are being produced, by producers like Lützkendorf.

Saar [zahr] (*Mosel-Saar-Ruwer*, Germany) The other *Mosel* tributary associated with lean, slatey *Riesling*. Villages include *Ayl, Ockfen*, Saarburg, Serrig, *Wiltingen*.

Sablet [sa-blay] (*Rhône*, France) Good *Côtes du Rhône* village.

🍷 **Sachsen** [zak-zen] (Germany) Revived former East German region where Klaus Seifert is producing good *Riesling*.

🍷 **St. Amour** [san ta-moor] (*Burgundy*, France) One of the 10 *Beaujolais Crus* – usually light and fruity. Billards; la Cave Lamartine; *Duboeuf;* Patissier; Revillon.

🍷 **Sadie Family** [sah-dee] (South Africa) Former Spice Route winemaker, Eben Sadie is one of the most exciting (*garage*) winemakers in the Cape and his Columella (5,000 bottle-production) one of the most exciting wines.

S

Ȳ **Weingut St Antony** (*Rheinhessen*, Germany) As good as Nierstein gets.

Ȳ St. Aubin [san toh-ban] (*Burgundy*, France) Underrated *Côte d'Or* village for (jammily rustic) reds and rich, nutty, rather classier white; affordable alternatives to *Meursault. Jean-Claude Bachelet; Champy; Marc Colin;* Hubert Lamy-Monnot; *Olivier Leflaive;* Henri Prudhon; *Ch de Puligny-Montrachet;* Roux Père et Fils; Gérard Thomas.

Ȳ St. Bris [san bree] (*Burgundy*, France) The VDQS *Sauvignon de St. Bris* has now become St. Bris appellation – and labels may no longer reveal the fact that the wine, from this village close to *Chablis,* is made from a different grape to every other white Burgundy. There are also good examples of the *Aligoté* grape here. *Jean-Marc Brocard; la Chablisienne;* Joel and David Griffe; Sorin Defrance.

Ȳ St. Chinian [san shee-nee-yon] (*Southwest*, France) Neighbor of *Faugères* in the *Coteaux du Languedoc,* producing midweight wines from *Carignan* and other *Rhône* grapes. Ch. des Albières; de Astide Rousse; Babeau; Mas Champart; Clos Bagatelle; Canet-Valette; Cazel-Viel; Coujan; Cooperative de Roquebrun; Mas de la Tour; Maurel Fonsalade; Laurent Miquel; Ch. Quartironi de Sars. ★★★★★ Laurent Miquel Saint Chinian Bardou 2001 $$

Ȳ **St. Clement** (*Napa Valley*, California) Japanese-owned winery whose best wine is the Oroppas red blend. In case you were wondering, the name isn't a Native American word, but that of the owner spelled backward.

Ȳ St. Emilion [san tay-mee-lee-yon] (*Bordeaux*, France) Large *commune* with varied soils and wines. At best, sublime *Merlot*-dominated *claret;* at worst dull, earthy, and fruitless. Some 170 or so *"Grand cru"* St. Emilions are made in better-sited vineyards and have to undergo a tasting every vintage to be able to use these words on their labels, and too few fail. *Grand Cru Classé* refers to 68 *châteaux,* of which two – Ausone and Cheval-Blanc – are rated as *"Premier Grands Crus Classés"* and 11 are *"Premiers Grands Crus Classés B."* These ratings are reviewed every decade. Supposedly "lesser" satellite neighbors – *Lussac, Puisseguin, St. Georges,* etc. – often make better value wine than basic St. Emilion. *Angélus; Ausone;* Beau-Séjour-Bécot; Beauséjour; Belair; Canon; Canon la Gaffelière; Cheval Blanc; Clos des Jacobins; Clos Fourtet; Figeac; Franc Mayne; Grand Mayne; Larcis Ducasse; Magdelaine; la Mondotte; Pavie; Tertre Rôteboeuf; Troplong-Mondot; Trottevieille; Valandraud.

Ȳ St. Estèphe [san teh-stef] (*Bordeaux*, France) Northernmost *Médoc commune* with clay soil and wines which can be a shade more rustic than those of neighboring *Pauillac* and *St. Julien,* but which are often longer-lived and more structured than some of the juicy, easy-to-drink *St. Emilions* and *Pomerols* that tend to win approval from critics. Calon-Ségur; Cos d'Estournel; Haut-Marbuzet; Lafon-Rochet; Marbuzet; Montrose; de Pez; Ormes de Pez; Phélan-Ségur.

Ȳ **St. Francis** (*Sonoma*, California) Innovative winery with great *Zinfandels,* and Reserve *Chardonnays* and *Cabernets.* The first Californian to introduce artificial corks to protect wine drinkers from faulty bottles.

Ȳ St. Georges-St.Emilion [san jorrzh san tay-mee-lee-yon] (*Bordeaux,* France) Satellite of *St. Emilion* with good *Merlot*-dominant reds, often better value than *St. Emilion* itself. Ch. Maquin St. Georges; St. Georges.

Ȳ **St. Hallett** (*Barossa Valley*, Australia) Superstar *Barossa* winery specializing in wines from old ("old block") *Shiraz* vines. Whites (especially *Semillon* and *Riesling*) are good too. ★★★★★ **Blackwell Shiraz 2001 $$$**

Ȳ **St. Hubert's** (*Victoria*, Australia) Pioneering *Yarra* winery with ultrafruity *Cabernet* and mouth-filling *Roussanne* whites.

Ȳ **Chateau St. Jean** [jeen] (*Sonoma*, California) Named after the founder's wife; now Japanese-owned and a source of good single-vineyard *Chardonnays,* late-harvest *Rieslings* and *Bordeaux*-style reds.

Ȳ St. Joseph [san joh-sef] (*Rhône*, France) Potentially vigorous, fruity *Syrah* from the northern *Rhône.* Whites range from flabby to fragrant *Marsannes.* Chapoutier; Chave; Courbis; Coursodon; Cuilleron; Delas; de Fauturie; Gacho-Pascal; Gaillard; Graillot; Gripa; Grippat; Perret; Pichon; St.-Désirat; Tardieu-Laurent; Trollo; Vernay.

S

☙ St. Julien [san-joo-lee-yen] (*Bordeaux*, France) Aristocratic *Médoc commune* producing classic rich wines, full of cedar and deep, ripe fruit. *Beychevelle; Branaire; Ducru-Beaucaillou; Gruaud-Larose; Lagrange; Langoa-Barton; Léoville-Barton; Léoville-Las-Cases; Léoville-Poyferré; Talbot.*

☙ St. Laurent [sant loh-rent] (Austria) *Pinot Noir*-like berryish red grape, mastered, in particular, by *Umathum*. ★★★★ Zahel St. Laurent Grand Reserve 2001 $$

☙ St. Nicolas de Bourgueil [san nee-koh-lah duh boor-goy] (*Loire*, France) Lightly fruity *Cabernet Franc*; needs a warm year to ripen its raspberry fruit, but then can last for up to a decade. Pretty similar to Bourgueil. Yannick Amirault; *Caslot;* Max Cognard; Delauney; *Druet; Jamet;* Mabileau; Vallée.

☙ St. Péray [san pay-reh] (*Rhône*, France) *AC* near *Lyon* for full-bodied white and *traditional method* sparkling wine, at risk from encroaching housing. J-F Chapoud; Auguste Clape; Bernard Gripa; Marcel Juge; Jean Lionnet; Alain Voge.

☙ Ch. St. Pierre [san pee-yehr] (*St. Julien 4ème Cru Classé, Bordeaux*, France) Reliable *St. Julien* under the same ownership as *Ch. Gloria.*

☙ St. Romain [san roh-man] (*Burgundy*, France) *Hautes Côtes de Beaune* village producing undervalued fine whites and rustic reds. Christophe Buisson; Chassorney; Cordier; Germain et Fils; Iain Gras; *Jaffelin;* Thévenin-Monthelie.

☙ St. Véran [san vay-ron] (*Burgundy*, France) Once sold as *Beaujolais Blanc;* affordable alternative to *Pouilly-Fuissé;* better than most *Mâconnais* whites. Ch. Fuissé is first class. *Barraud; Corsin;* Cordier; Dom des Deux Roches; *Duboeuf; Ch. Fuissé;* Roger Luquet; Merlin; Pacquet.
★★★★ Merlin, La Grande Bussiere 2000 $$

☙ Ste. Croix-du-Mont [sant crwah doo mon] (*Bordeaux*, France) Never as luscious, rich, and complex as the better efforts of its neighbor *Sauternes* – but often a far more worthwhile buy than wines unashamedly sold under that name. Ch Loubens; le Rame.

☙ Saintsbury (*Carneros*, California) Superstar *Carneros* producer of unfiltered *Chardonnay* and – more specially – *Pinot Noir.* The slogan: "Beaune in the USA" refers to the winery's Burgundian aspirations. The Reserve *Pinot* is top notch, while the easy-going Garnet is the good *second label.*
★★★★ Carneros Pinot Noir 2001 $$$

Sakar [sa-kah] (Bulgaria) Long-time source of much of the best *Cabernet Sauvignon* to come from *Bulgaria.*

☙ Castello della Sala [kas-tel-loh del-la sah-lah] (*Umbria*, Italy) Antinori's overpriced but sound *Chardonnay, Sauvignon.* Also good *Sauvignon*/Procanico blend.

☙ Ch de Sales [duh sahl] (*Pomerol, Bordeaux*) Good but generally unexciting wine for relatively early drinking. Also worth looking out for is Stonyfell, which matches rich Shiraz flavors with an appealingly "retro" label.

☙ Salice Salentino [sa-lee-chay sah-len-tee-noh] (*Puglia*, Italy) Spicy, intense red made from the characterful *Negroamaro.* Great value, especially when mature. *Candido;* due Palme; *Leone de Castris;* Taurino; Vallone.
★★★★★ Taurino Salice Salentino Reserva 1999 $$

☙ Salomon-Undhof [sah-loh-mon oond-hohf] (*Kremstal*, Austria) Top-class producer, with especially notable *Riesling.*

☙ Salon le Mesnil [sah-lon lur may-neel] (*Champagne*, France) Small, traditional subsidiary of *Laurent-Perrier* with cult following for pure long-lived *Chardonnay Champagne.* Only sold as a single-vintage cuvée.

Salta (Argentina) The world's highest vineyards.

☙ Saltram [sawl-tram] (South Australia) Fast-improving part of the *Mildara-Blass* empire. Rich, fairly priced *Barossa* reds and whites (also under the Mamre Brook label) and top-flight *"ports".* ★★★★★ 1999 Saltram No. I Shiraz $$$

☙ Samos [sah-mos] (Greece) Aegean island producing sweet, fragrant, golden *Muscat* once called "the wine of the gods." Kourtakis; Union of Cooperatives.

S

- **Cellier des Samsons** [sel-yay day som-son] (*Burgundy*, France) Source of better-than-average *Beaujolais*.
- **San Giusto a Rentennano** [san-jus-toh ah ren-ten-nah-noh] (*Tuscany*, Italy) Modern, international-style *Super-Tuscan* Percalo *Sangiovese* and *Merlot* La Ricolma, plus excellent *Chianti Classico*.
- **San Leonardo** [san lay-yoh-nar-doh] (*Trentino*, Italy) Look especially for the outstanding Bordeaux blend.
- San Luis Obispo [san loo-wis oh-bis-poh] (California) Californian region gaining a reputation for *Chardonnay* and *Pinot Noir*. Try *Edna Valley*.
- **Viña San Pedro** [veen-ya san-pay-droh] (*Curico*, Chile) Huge firm whose wines are steadily improving thanks to the efforts of French consultant *Jacques Lurton*. ★★★★ 1865 Carmenère 2000 $$$
- Sancerre [son-sehr] (*Loire*, France) At its best, the epitome of elegant, steely dry *Sauvignon*; at its worst, oversulfured and fruitless. Reds and rosés, though well regarded and highly priced by French restaurants, are often little better than quaffable *Pinot Noir*. Bailly-Reverdy; Jean-Paul Balland; *Henri Bourgeois*; *Cotat*; Lucien Crochet; Vincent Delaporte; Pierre Dézat; Fouassier; de la Garenne; Gitton; les Grands Groux; *Pascal Jolivet*; de *Ladoucette*; Serge Laporte; Mellot; Thierry Merlin-Cherrier; Paul Millerioux; Natter; Vincent Pinard; Jean-Max Roger; *Vacheron*; André Vatan; Domaine de la Villaudière.

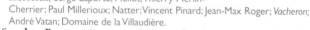

- **Sanchez Romate** (*Jerez*, Spain) Top quality sherry producer with delicious NPU (Non Plus Ultra) Amontillado. ★★★★ Pedro Ximénez Very Rare $$
- **Sandeman** (Spain/Portugal) Occasionally dazzling *port* and *sherry* producer. ★★★ Vau Vintage 2000 $$$
- **Sanford Winery** (*Santa Barbara*, California) *Santa Barbara* superstar producer of *Chardonnay* and especially distinctive, slightly horseradishy *Pinot Noir*. ★★★★ Talinda Oaks Chardonnay 2001 $$$
- **Sangiovese** [san-jee-yoh vay-seh] (Italy) The tobaccoey, herby-flavored red grape of *Chianti* and *Montepulciano*, now being used increasingly in *IGTs* and – though rarely impressively – in Australia, Argentina, Washington State, and California. *Antinori; Atlas Peak; Bonny Doon; Isole e Olena.*
- **Castello di San Polo in Rosso** [san-poh-loh in -ros-soh] (*Tuscany*, Italy) Reliable, quite traditional *Chianti Classico* estate.
- **Luciano Sandrone** [loo-chee-yah-noh sahn-droh-nay] (*Piedmont*, Italy) With fellow revolutionaries *Clerico*, *Roberto Voerzio*, and *Altare*, Luciano Sandrone has spearheaded the move to modern *Barolo*. Great *Dolcetto* too. ★★★★ Barolo Le Vigne 1998 $$$
- Sanlúcar de Barrameda [san loo-kar- day bar-rah-may-dah] (Spain) One of the three sherry towns, and the source of Manzanilla.
- Santa Barbara (California) Successful southern, cool-climate region for *Pinot Noir* and *Chardonnay*. *Au Bon Climat; Byron; Ojai; Qupé; Sanford.*
- **Viña Santa Carolina** [ka-roh-lee-na] (Chile) Greatly improved producer, thanks to *Ignacio Recabarren* and vineyards in *Casablanca*. Good reds. ★★★ Barrica Selection Syrah 2001 $$
- Santa Cruz Mountains [krooz] (California) Exciting region to the south of San Francisco. See *Ridge* and *Bonny Doon*.
- **Santa Emiliana** (*Aconcagua*, Chile) Large producer with good Andes Peak offerings from *Casablanca*, and wines from the new southern region of Mulchen.
- **Santadi** [san-tah-dee] (*Sardinia*, Italy) A co-op noted for good quality especially Terre Brune Carignano del Sulcis. ★★★ Terre Brune 1999 $$
- Santa Maddalena [san-tah mah-dah-LAY-nah] (*Alto Adige*, Italy) Light, spicy-fruity red made from the *Schiava*. Rarely found outside the region, but well worth seeking out. Cantina Produttori Sta. Maddalena; Gojer. ★★★★ Franz Gojer Santa Maddalena Classico Rondell $$

S

Ⓣ **Santa Rita** [ree-ta] (*Maipo*, Chile) The Casa Real is not only one of Chile's best and most fairly priced reds; it is also truly world class and the Carmenère-Cabernets "Triple C" a great value new arrival on the scene. ★★★★ Triple C Maipo Valley 1999 $$

Ⓣ **Santenay** [sont-nay] (*Burgundy*, France) Southern *Côte d'Or* village, producing pretty whites and good, though occasionally rather rustic, reds. Look for *Girardin* and *Pousse d'Or*. Roger Belland; Fernand Chevrot; Marc Colin; Colin-Deléger; *Girardin*; Olivier Leflaive; Bernard Morey; Lucien Muzet; Claude Nouveau; *Pousse d'Or*; Prieur Brunet.

Ⓣ **Caves São João** [sow-jwow] (*Bairrada*, Portugal) Small company which can produce high-quality *Bairrada*.

Sardinia (Italy) Traditionally the source of powerful reds (try *Santadi*) and whites, increasingly interesting *DOC* fortified wines, and new-wave modern reds to match the best *Super-Tuscans*. *Sella e Mosca*.

Ⓣ **Paolo Saracco** [pow-loh sah-rak-koh] (*Piedmont*, Italy) Competitor for the role of top *Moscato*-maker. Bianch del Luv *Chardonnay* is impressive too.

Ⓣ **Sarget de Gruaud-Larose** [sahr-jay dur groowoh lah-rohs] (*St. Julien*, *Bordeaux*, France) Reliable *second label* of *Ch. Gruaud-Larose*.

Ⓣ **Sassicaia** [sas-see-kai-ya] (*Tuscany*, Italy) World-class *Cabernet*-based *Super-Tuscan* with more of an Italian than a *claret* taste. No longer a mere *Vino da Tavola* since the *DOC* Bolgheri was introduced in 1994.

Ⓣ **Saumur** [soh-moor] (*Loire*, France) Heartland of variable *Chenin*-based sparkling and still wine, and potentially more interesting red *Saumur-Champigny*. Langlois-Château; Roches Neuves; Vatan; Cave des Vignerons de Saumur; Villeneuve. ★★★★ Saumur Rouge La Cabriole Alliance Loire 2002 $$

Ⓣ **Saumur-Champigny** [soh-moor shom-pee-nyee] (*Loire*, France) Crisp *Cabernet Franc* red; best served slightly chilled. Good examples are worth cellaring. *Bouvet-Ladubay*; *Couly-Dutheil*; *Filliatreau*; Foucault; *Ch. du Hureau*; Langlois-Château; Targé; Vatan; de Villeneuve. ★★★★ Ch. de Villeneuve, Vieilles Vignes 2002 $$

Ⓣ **Saussignac** [soh-sin-yak] (*Southwest*, France) Historically in the shadow both of *Sauternes* and nearby Monbazillac, this sweet-wine region is enjoying a minor boom at the moment and putting many a Sauternes to shame. Ch la Chabrier; des Eyssards; Ch Grinou; Dom. Léonce Cuisset; Dom de Richard, Ch. les Miaudoux, Tourmentine; le Payral; Clos d'Yvigne. ★★★★★ Ch. Grinou 2001 $$

Ⓣ **Sauternes** [soh-turn] (*Bordeaux*, France) Rich, potentially sublime, honeyed dessert wines from *Sauvignon* and *Sémillon* (and possibly *Muscadelle*) blends. Should be affected by *botrytis* but the climate does not always allow for this. Avoid generic examples; they are almost always disappointing. *Bastor-Lamontagne*; Clos Dady; *Doisy-Daëne*; Fargues; Filhot; Guiraud; Rieussec; Suduiraut; Yquem. ★★★★ Clos Dady 2001 $$$

🍇 **Sauvignon Blanc** [soh-vin-yon-blon] "Grassy", "catty", "asparagussy", "gooseberryish" grape widely grown but rarely really loved, so often blended, oaked, or made sweet. In France, at home in the *Loire* and *Bordeaux*. New Zealand gets it right – especially in *Marlborough*. In Australia, *Knappstein*, *Cullens*, *Stafford Ridge*, and *Shaw & Smith* are right on target. *Mondavi's* oaked *Fumé Blanc* and *Kendall Jackson's* sweet versions are successful but *Monteviña*, *Quivira*, *Dry Creek*, *Simi*, and – in blends with the *Semillon* – *Carmenet* are the stars. Chile makes better versions every year, despite starting out with a lesser variety. See *Caliterra*, *Casablanca*, *Canepa*, *Sta. Carolina*, and *Villard*. In South Africa, see *Thelema*, *Klein Constantia*, and *Neil Ellis*.

Ⓣ **Sauvignon de St. Bris** [soh-veen-yon-duh san bree] (*Burgundy*, France) Now defunct designation, replaced by *St Bris*.

Ⓣ **Etienne Sauzet** [soh-zay] (*Burgundy*, France) First-rank estate whose white wines are almost unfindable outside collectors' cellars and Michelin-starred restaurants. ★★★★★ Puligny-Montrachet Les Perrières 2000 $$$

S

🍇 **Savagnin** [sa-van-yan] (*Jura*, France) Unrelated to *Sauvignon*; a white *Jura* variety used for *Vin Jaune* and blended with *Chardonnay* for *Arbois*. Thought to be identical to Traminer, the non-aromatic form of *Gewürztraminer*.

🍷 **Savanha** [sa-vah-nah] (South Africa) Great Bordeaux-like Naledi Cabernet and Sejana Merlot; both concentrated but subtle and made by joint venture with producers from *Pomerol*.

🍷 **Savennières** [sa-ven-yehr] (*Loire*, France) Fine, if sometimes aggressively dry, *Chenin Blanc* whites. Very long-lived. *des Baumard; Bise; du Closel; Coulée de Serrant; d'Epiré; La Roche aux Moines; de Plaisance; Soulez.*

🍷 **Savigny-lès-Beaune** [sa-veen-yee lay bohn] (*Burgundy*, France) Distinctive whites (sometimes made from *Pinot Blanc*) and raspberry reds. At their best can compare with *Beaune*. *Simon Bize; Bruno Clair; Chandon de Briailles; Ch. de Meursault; Ecard; Girard-Voillot; Girardin; Pavelot; Tollot-Beaut.*

Savoie [sav-wah] (Eastern France) Mountainous region near Geneva producing crisp, floral whites such as Abymes, *Apremont, Seyssel*, and *Crepy*. Pierre Boniface; Dupasquier; Louis Magnien; A&M Quénard.

🍷 **Saxenburg** (*Stellenbosch*, South Africa) Reliable producer of ripely flavorsome wines. Particularly good *Pinotage, Shiraz*, and *Sauvignon Blanc*. ★★★★★ **Private Collection Shiraz 2000 $$**

🍷 **Cellers de Scala Dei** [sel-lehrs day skah-la day-yee] (*Priorat*, Spain) Long-established *bodega* currently making less exciting wine than the newcomers.

🍷 **Scavino** [ska-vee-noh] (*Piedmont*, Italy) Terrific juicy reds, including single-vineyard *Barolos, Barberas*, and *Dolcettos*.

🍷 **Willi Schaefer** [shay-fur] (*Mosel-Saar-Ruwer*, Germany) Excellent grower in the Mosel vineyard of Himmelreich in the village of Graach (Grosslage Münzelay). ★★★★★ **Wehlener Sonnenuhr Riesling Kabinett 2001 $$**

Scharzhofberg [sharts-hof-behrg] (*Mosel-Saar-Ruwer*, Germany) Top-class *Saar* vineyard, producing great *Riesling. Egon Muller; Reichsgraf von Kesselstadt.*

Schaumwein [showm-vine] (Germany) Low-priced sparkling wine.

🍇 **Scheurebe** [shoy-ray-bur] (Germany) Grapefruit-like *Riesling* x *Silvaner* cross, grown in Germany and England. In Austria, it is called Samling 88. *Kurt Darting; Hafner; Alois Kracher; Lingenfelder.* ★★★★ **Kracher Scheurebe No 5 2000 $$$**

🍇 **Schiava** [skee yah-vah] (*Alto Adige*, Italy) Grape used in *Lago di Caldaro* and *Santa Maddalena* to make light reds.

Schilfwein [shilf-vine] (Austria) Luscious "reed wine" – Austrian *vin de paille* pioneered by *Willi Opitz.* ★★★★ **Hans Tschida Traminer Schilfwein 2000 $$$**

🍷 **Schiopetto** [skee yoh-peh-toh] (*Friuli-Venezia Giulia*, Italy) Gloriously intense, perfumed *Collio* white varietals to rival those of *Jermann*.

Schloss [shloss] (Germany) Literally "castle"; in practice, vineyard or estate.

Schist [shist] Type of slaty soil very suitable for growing vines.

🍷 **Schloss Böckelheim** [shloss ber-kell-hime] (*Nahe*, Germany) Varied southern part of the Nahe. Wines from the Kupfergrube vineyard and the State Wine Domaine are worth buying.

🍷 **Schloss Johannisberg** [shloss yo-hah-nis-behrg] (*Rheingau*, Germany) Beautiful, princely estate, now back on track. ★★★ **Riesling 2000 $**

🍷 **Schloss Lieser** [shloss lee-zuh] (*Mosel*, Germany) Excellent small estate related to *Fritz Haag*.

🍷 **Schloss Reinhartshausen** [shloss rine-harts-how-zehn] (*Rheingau*, Germany) Successful with *Pinot Blanc* and *Chardonnay* (introduced following a suggestion by *Robert Mondavi*). The *Rieslings* are good too.

S

☿ **Schloss Saarstein** [shloss sahr-shtine] (*Mosel-Saar-Ruwer*, Germany) High-quality *Riesling* specialist in *Serrig*. ★★★★ 2001 Riesling Auslese **$$**

☿ **Schloss Schönborn** [shloss shern-born] (*Mosel-Saar-Ruwer*, Germany) Increasingly brilliant estate.

☿ **Schloss Vollrads** [shloss fol-rahts] (*Rheingau*, Germany) Old-established estate enjoying a renaissance under new ownership and management. ★★★ **Riesling Spatlese 2001 $$**

☿ **Schloss Wallhausen** [shloss val-how-zen] (*Nahe,* Germany) Prinz zu Salm-Dalberg's estate is one of the best in the Nahe, with fine dry Riesling.

Schlossböckelheim [shloss berk-el-hime] (*Nahe*, Germany) Village giving its name to a large *Bereich*, producing elegant *Riesling*. Staatsweingut Niederhausen.

☿ **Schlossgut Diel** [deel] (*Nahe*, Germany) Armin Diel is both wine writer and winemaker. Co-author of the excellent *German Wine Guide*, his Dorsheimer Goldloch wines are worth seeking out.

☿ **Dom. Schlumberger** [shloom-behr-jay] (*Alsace*, France) Great, sizeable estate whose subtle top-level wines can often rival those of the somewhat more showy *Zind-Humbrecht*.

☿ **Schramsberg** [shram-sberg] (*Napa Valley*, California) The winery that single-handedly put California sparkling wine on the quality trail. Wines used to be too big for their boots, possibly because too many of the grapes were from warm vineyards in *Napa*. The J. Schram is aimed at *Dom Pérignon* and gets pretty close to the target.

☿ **Scotchman's Hill** (*Victoria*, Australia) *Pinot Noir* specialist in *Geelong*. *Sauvignons* and *Chardonnays* have been less exciting.

☿ **Screaming Eagle** (*Napa Valley*, California) Minuscule winery, the size of many people's living room, which has been producing around 2000 bottles of intense *Cabernet* per year since 1992 in an attempt to make California's greatest wine. It is undeniably rich and seductive, but this is not the place to go looking for delicacy and complexity. Prices at auction are stratospheric, however. ★★★★ **Screaming Eagle 1999 $$$$**

☿ **Seaview** (South Australia) *Penfold's* brand for brilliantly reliable sparkling wine and (less frequently) *McLaren Vale* red table wines. Look out for the Edwards & Chaffey label, too. ★★★ **1997 Seaview Pinot Noir Chardonnay $$**

☿ **Sebastiani/Cecchetti Sebastiani** [seh-bas-tee-yan-nee] (*Sonoma Valley*, California) Sebastiani makes unexceptional wine from *Central Valley* grapes. The associated, but separate, Cecchetti Sebastiani, however, like *Gallo*, makes really good stuff in *Sonoma*. The Pepperwood Grove wines are good too.

Sec/secco/seco [se-koh] (France/Italy/Spain) Dry.

Second label (*Bordeaux,* France) Wine from a producer's (generally a *Bordeaux château*) lesser vineyards, younger vines, and/or lesser *cuvées* of wine. Especially worth buying in good vintages. See *Les Forts de Latour*.

☿ **Seghesio** [seh-gay-see-yoh] (California, USA) Estate with old-vine *Zinfandel* of great density and depth. ★★★★ **Sonoma County Zinfandel 2000 $$**

☿ **Segura Viudas** [say-goo-rah vee-yoo-dass] (*Catalonia*, Spain) The quality end of the Freixenet Cava giant.

☿ **Seifried Estate** [see-freed] (*Nelson*, New Zealand) Also known as *Redwood Valley Estate*. Superb *Riesling*, especially *late-harvest* style, and very creditable *Sauvignon* and *Chardonnay*. ★★★★ **Winemake'rs Collection Pinot Noir 2002 $$**

Sekt [zekt] (Germany) Very basic sparkling wine. Watch out for anything that does not state that it is made from *Riesling* – other grape varieties almost invariably make highly unpleasant wines. Only the prefix "Deutscher" guarantees German origin.

☿ **Selaks** [see-lax] (*Auckland,* New Zealand) Large company in Kumeu best known for the piercingly fruity *Sauvignon* originally made by a young man called Kevin Judd, who went on to produce *Cloudy Bay*. ★★★★ **Selaks Premium Selection Sauvignon Blanc 2002 $$**

S

Weingut Selbach-Oster [zel-bahkh os-tehr] (*Mosel-Saar-Ruwer*, Germany) Archetypical *Mosel Riesling* of great finesse and balance. ★★★★ Zeltinger Schlossberg Riesling Kabinet t2001 $$$

Sélection de Grains Nobles (SGN) [say-lek-see-yon duh gran nohbl] (Alsace, France) Equivalent to German *Beerenauslese*; rich, sweet *botrytized* wine from specially selected grapes. These wines are rare, expensive, and long-lived.

Sella e Mosca [seh-la eh mos-kah] (*Sardinia*, Italy) Dynamic firm with a good *Cabernet* called Villamarina, the rich *Anghelu Ruju*, and traditional *Cannonau* which is also blended with *Cabernet* to produce the highly impressive *Tanca Farra*.

Ch. de Selle (*Provence*, France) Serious wines, unflashy and rather expensive.

Fattoria Selvapiana [fah-taw-ree-ya sel-va-pee-yah-nah] (*Tuscany*, Italy) Fine estate with great, classic *Chianti Rufina*, *vin santo*, and olive oil. ★★★★ Bucerchiale Riserva 1999 $$$

Château Semeli [seh-meh-lee] (*Attica*, Greece) Producer of classy Cabernet and Nemea reds.

Sémillon [in France: say-mee-yon; in Australia: seh-mil-lon and even seh-mih-lee-yon] Peachy grape generally blended with *Sauvignon* to make sweet and dry *Bordeaux*, and vinified separately in Australia, where it is also sometimes blended with *Chardonnay*. Rarely as successful in other New World countries, where many versions taste more like *Sauvignon*. *Carmenet; Geyser Peak; McWilliams; Rothbury; Tyrrell; Xanadu.*

Seña [sen-ya] (Chile) A *Mondavi* and *Caliterra* coproduction. A Mercedes of a wine: impeccably put together, and improving with every vintage, but never quite as interesting as its top stablemates. ★★★★ 2000 Seña $$$$

Ch. Sénéjac [say-nay-jak] (*Bordeaux*, France) *Cru Bourgeois* that age well.

Seppelt (South Australia) Pioneer of great fortified wines and of the *Great Western* region where it makes still and sparkling *Shiraz* and Dorrien *Cabernet*. Other sparkling wines are recommendable too, and Salinger, after a dull patch, is right back on form. ★★★★ Salinger $$

Sequioa Grove [sek-koy-yah] (California, USA) Well structured wines, reliably good.

Serafini & Vidotto [seh-rah-fee-noh eh vee-dot-toh] (*Veneto*, Italy) Francesco Serafini and Antonello Vidotto make great Pinot Nero.

Sercial [sehr-see-yal] (Madeira) The driest style of Madeira. ★★★★ Barbeito 10 Years Old Reserve $$

Seresin [seh-ra-sin] (*Marlborough*, New Zealand) New venture launched by a British movie cameraman. Impeccable vineyards and really impressive *Chardonnay*, *Sauvignon*, and a promising *Pinot Noir*.

Servir frais (France) Serve chilled.

Setúbal [shtoo-bal] (Portugal) *DOC* on the *Setúbal Peninsula*. ★★★ JP Moscatel de Setúbal $

Setúbal Peninsula [shtoo-bul] (Portugal) Home of the *Setúbal DOC*, but now notable for the rise of two new wine regions, Arrabida and Palmela, where *JM Fonseca Succs* and *JP Vinhos* are making excellent wines from local and international grape varieties.The lusciously rich *Moscatel de Setúbal*, however, is still the star of the show.

Seyssel [say-sehl] (*Savoie*, France) *AC* region near Geneva producing light white wines that are usually enjoyed in après-ski mood when no one is overly concerned about value for money. Maison Mollex; *Varichon et Clerc.*

Seyval Blanc [say-vahl blon] *Hybrid* grape – a cross between French and US vines – unpopular with EU authorities but successful in eastern US, Canada, and England, especially at *Breaky Bottom*. ★★★ Breaky Bottom Brut, Cuvée Rémy Alexandre 1999 $$

S

🍷 **Shafer** [shay-fur] (*Napa Valley*, California) Top *Cabernet* producer in the *Stag's Leap* district, and maker of classy *Carneros Chardonnay* and *Merlot*.
⋆ ⋆ ⋆ ⋆ ⋆ **Stags Leap District Hillside Select Cabernet Sauvignon 1999 $$$**

🍷 **Shaw & Smith** (*Adelaide Hills,* Australia) Winery producing fine *Sauvignon* and *Merlot* and *Burgundian Chardonnays* that demonstrate how good wines from this variety can taste with and without oak.
⋆ ⋆ ⋆ ⋆ **Shaw & Smith Adelaide Hills Merlot 2001 $$$**

🍷 **Sherry** (*Jerez,* Spain) The fortified wine made in the area surrounding *Jerez*. Wines made elsewhere – Australia, England, South Africa, etc. – may no longer use the name. See also *Almacenista; Fino; Amontillado; Manzanilla; Cream Sherry. Barbadillo; Gonzalez Byass; Hidalgo; Lustau.*

🍇 *Shiraz* [shee-raz] (Australia, South Africa) The *Syrah* grape in Australia and South Africa, named after its (erroneously) supposed birthplace in Iran. South African versions are lighter than the Australians, but they are improving fast, while the latter are usually riper and oakier than efforts from the *Rhône*. The move to cooler sites is broadening the range of Australian *Shiraz*, however. *Hardy's; Henschke; Maglieri; Lindemans; Rockford; Rothbury; Penfolds; Picardy; Plantagenet; St. Hallett; Saxenburg;Wolf Blass.*

🍷 **Shooting Star** (Lake County, California) One of California's avid proponents of Cabernet Franc. The Zinfandel and Cabernet Sauvignon are good, too.

🍷 **Sichel & Co** [see-shel] ((Bordeaux, France) Merchant and owner, or part-owner, of châteaux including *Palmer, Angludet,* and with good Sirius brand.

Sicily (Italy) Historically best known for *Marsala* and sturdy "southern" table wines. Now, however, there is an array of other unusual fortified wines and a fast-growing range of new-wave reds and whites, many made from grapes grown nowhere else. *De Bartoli; Corvo; Donafugatta; Cosumano Planeta; Regaleali; Terre di Ginestra.*⋆ ⋆ ⋆ ⋆ **Cabernet Sauvignon Burdese 2000 $$**

🍷 **Sierra Vista** (California, USA) Subtle (for California) high quality Rhône varieties from this estate.

🍷 **Sieur d'Arques** [see-uhr dark] (*Languedoc-Roussillon,* France) High-tech *Limoux* cooperative with good *Blanquette de Limoux* sparkling wine and *Chardonnays* sold under the Toques et Clochers label. Now in joint venture with the owners of *Ch. Mouton Rothschild.*

🍷 **Ch. Sigalas-Rabaud** [see-gah-lah rah-boh] (*Bordeaux,* France) Fine Sauternes estate, producing rich, but delicate, wines.

🍷 **Siglo** [seeg-loh] (*Rioja,* Spain) Good brand of modern red (traditionally sold in a burlap "sack") and old-fashioned whites.

🍷 **Signorello** (*Napa Valley,* California) Small winery making *Burgundian Chardonnay* with yeasty richness, *Bordeaux*-style *Semillon* and *Sauvignon,* and stylish, blackcurranty *Cabernets.* ⋆ ⋆ ⋆ **Chardonnay 2000 $$$**

🍷 **Sileni** [sil-lay-nee] (*Hawkes Bay,* New Zealand) Large new venture with very promising *Chardonnay, Semillon, Merlot/Cabernet.*

Silex [see-lex] (France) Term describing flinty soil, used by *Didier Dagueneau* for his oak-fermented *Pouilly-Fumé.*

🍇 **Silvaner** German spelling for *Sylvaner.*

🍷 **Silver Oak Cellars** (*Napa Valley,* California) Superb specialized *Cabernet* producers favoring fruitily accessible, but still classy, wines which benefit from long aging in (American oak) barrels and bottled before release.

🍷 **Silverado** [sil-veh-rah-doh] (*Napa Valley,* California) Reliable *Cabernet, Chardonnay,* and *Sangiovese* winery that belongs to Walt Disney's widow. Note that there are three separate bottlings of the Cabernet: Napa, Limited Reserve, and Stags Leap.

🍷 **Simi Winery** [see-mee] (*Sonoma Valley,* California) Winery made famous by the thoughtful Zelma Long and her complex, long-lived Burgundian *Chardonnay,* archetypical *Sauvignon,* and lovely, blackcurranty *Alexander Valley Cabernet.* ⋆ ⋆ ⋆ ⋆ ⋆ **Russian River ValleyReserve Chardonnay 2000 $$$**

🍷 **Langwerth von Simmern** [lang-vehrt fon sim-mehrn] (*Rheingau,* Germany) A famous estate that is now showing signs of a revival.

☒ **Bert Simon** (*Mosel-Saar-Ruwer*, Germany) Newish estate in the *Saar* river valley with supersoft *Rieslings* and unusually elegant *Weissburgunder*.

☒ **Simonsberg** (*Stellenbosch*, South Africa) The mountain on which *Thelema's* vineyards are situated. ✭✭✭✭ Trilogy 2000 $$

☒ **Simonsig Estate** [see-mon-sikh] (*Stellenbosch*, South Africa) Big estate with a very impressive commercial range, and the occasional gem – try the *Shiraz*, *Cabernet*, *Pinotage*, *Chardonnay* the Kaapse Vonkel sparkler. ✭✭✭✭ Simonsig Merindol Syrah 1998 $$$

☒ **Sin Crianza** [sin cree-an-tha] (Spain) Not aged in wood.

☒ **Sion** [see-yo'n] (*Valais*, Switzerland) One of the proud homes of the grape the Swiss call the Fendant and outsiders know as *Chasselas*. Dull elsewhere, it can produce creditable (and even occasionally ageworthy) wines.

☒ **Ch. Siran** [see-ron] (*Margaux Cru Bourgeois, Bordeaux,* France) Beautiful *château* outperforming its classification and producing increasingly impressive and generally fairly priced wines.

☒ **Skalli** [skal-lee] (Languedoc-Roussillon France) Pioneering producer of quality *Vins de Pays* under the Fortant label. ✭✭✭✭ Robert Skalli Syrah 2001 $$

☒ **Skillogalee** [skil-log-gah-lee] (*Clare Valley*, Australia) Well-respected *Clare* producer, specializing in *Riesling*, but also showing his skill with reds. ✭✭✭✭ Skillogalee Clare Valley Shiraz 2000 $$

Skin contact The longer the skins of black grapes are left in with the juice after the grapes have been crushed, the greater the *tannin* and the deeper the color. Some non-aromatic white varieties (*Chardonnay* and *Semillon* in particular) can also benefit from extended skin contact (usually between six and 24 hours) to increase flavor.

☒ **Skouras** (*Peloponnese*, Greece) Eager producer, making good Nemea reds and Viognier whites.

Sliven [slee-ven] Bulgarian region offering good-value, simple reds and better-than-average whites. ✭✭✭ 2001 Blueridge Chardonnay Boyar Estates $

Slovakia Up-and-coming source of wines from grapes little seen elsewhere, such as the *Muscat* by Irsay Oliver.

Slovenia Former Yugoslavian home of *Laski Rizling* Other grapes show greater promise. ✭✭✭✭✭ Vinakoper, Capris Plemenito Rdece 1999

Smaragd [shmah-ragd] ((Austria) Highest quality category in *Wachau* for dry wines. See also Federspiel and Steinfeder.

☒ **Smith & Hook** (*Mendocino*, California) Winery with a cult following for its zippy, blackcurranty *Cabernet Sauvignon*. These lack the ripe, richness sought by most US critics, however.

☒ **Smith-Madrone** (*Napa*, California) Long-established winery that bucks the trend by using the *Riesling* (which is being uprooted elsewhere) to make good wine. *Chardonnay* is good too.

☒ **Smith Woodhouse** (*Douro*, Portugal) Part of the same empire as *Dow's*, *Graham's*, and *Warre's* but often overlooked. *Vintage ports* can be good, as is the house speciality *Traditional Late Bottled Vintage*. ✭✭✭✭✭ LBV 1994 $$

☒ **Ch. Smith-Haut-Lafitte** [oh-lah-feet] (*Pessac-Léognan Cru Classé, Bordeaux,* France) Estate flying high under its new ownership. Increasingly classy reds and (specially) pure *Sauvignon* whites. Grape seeds from the estate are also used to make an anti-aging skin cream called Caudalie. ✭✭✭✭ 2001 Rouge $$$

☒ **Smithbrook** (Western Australia) *Petaluma* subsidiary in the southerly region of *Pemberton*. ✭✭✭ 2000 Smithbrook Merlot $$

☒ **Soave** [swah-veh] (*Veneto*, Italy) Mostly dull stuff, but *Soave Classico* is better; single-vineyard versions are best. Sweet *Recioto* di Soave is delicious. *Pieropan* is almost uniformly excellent. *Anselmi;* La Cappuccina; Inama; *Masi; Pieropan;* Pra; Tedeschi; Zenato. ✭✭✭✭ del Castello, Monte Pressoni 2001 $$

☒ **Ch. Sociando-Mallet** [soh-see-yon-doh ma-lay] (*Haut-Médoc Cru Bourgeois, Bordeaux,* France) A *Cru Bourgeois* whose oaked, fruity red wines are way above its status.

S

Ⅰ **Sogrape** [soh-grap] (Portugal) Having invented *Mateus* Rosé half a century ago, this large firm is now modernizing the wines of *Dão* (with the new Quinta dos Carvalhais), *Douro* and *Bairrada*, and *Alentejo* (Vinha do Monte) bringing out flavors these once-dull wines never seemed to possess. *Sogrape* also owns the *port* houses of *Sandeman* and *Ferreira* and is thus also responsible for *Barca Velha*, Portugal's top red table wine.
★★★ Quinta de Azevedo, Vinho Verde 2002 $

Ⅰ **Sokol Blosser** (*Oregon*) Highly successful makers of rich *Chardonnay*. The *Pinot* is good, too. Wine names refer to the ages of the vines: e.g. 24 Year Old Twelve Row Block Pinot Noir 1999.

Ⅰ **Solaia** [soh-lie-yah] (*Tuscany*, Italy) Another phenomenal *Antinori Super-Tuscan* blend of *Cabernet Sauvignon*, *Franc* and *Sangiovese*. Italy's top red?

Solera [soh-leh-rah] (*Jerez*, Spain) Aging system involving older wine being continually "refreshed" by slightly younger wine of the same style.

Ⅰ **Bodegas Felix Solís** [fay-leex soh-lees] (*Valdepeñas*, Spain) By far the biggest, most progressive winery in *Valdepeñas*. ★★★ Viña Albali Gran Reserva 1996 $$

Somontano [soh-mon-tah-noh] (Spain) *DO* region in the foothills of the Pyrenees in Aragon, now experimenting with international grape varieties. *Enate*; *Pirineos*; *Viñas del Vero*.

Sonoma Valley [so-noh-ma] (California) Despite the *Napa* hype, this lesser-known region not only contains some of the state's top wineries, it is also home to *E&J Gallo's* superpremium vineyard and *Dry Creek*, home of some of California's best *Zinfandels*. The region is subdivided into the *Sonoma*, *Alexander*, and *Russian River Valleys*, and *Dry Creek*. Adler Fels; Arrowood; Carmenet; Ch. St Jean Clos du Bois; Dry Creek; Duxoup; E&J Gallo; Geyser Peak; Gundlach Bundschu; Cecchetti Sebastiani; Iron Horse; Jordan; Kenwood; Kistler; Laurel Glen; Matanzas Creek; Peter Michael; Quivira; Ravenswood; Ridge; St. Francis; Sonoma-Cutrer; Simi; Marimar Torres; Joseph Swan.

Ⅰ **Sonoma-Cutrer** [soh-noh-ma koo-trehr] (*Sonoma Valley*, California) Recently sold producer of world-class single-vineyard *Chardonnay* that can rival *Puligny-Montrachet*. The "Les Pierres" is the tops.

Ⅰ **Bruno Sorg** (*Alsace*, France) Excellent quality from this small estate.

Ⅰ **Marc Sorrel** [sor-rel] (*Rhône*, France) *Hermitage* producer who is – unusually – as successful in white as red. The "le Gréal" single-vineyard red is the wine to buy, though the "les Roccoules" white ages well.

Ⅰ **Pierre Soulez** [soo-layz] (*Loire*, France) Producer of *Savennières*, especially Clos du Papillon and Roche-aux-Moines *late harvest* wines.

Ⅰ **Ch. Soutard** [soo-tahr] (*St. Emilion, Bordeaux*, France) Traditional *St. Emilion* estate with long-lived wines that rely on far less oak than many.

South Africa Quality is improving, with riper, more characterful wine that apes neither France nor Australia. Below the top level, look for inexpensive, simple, dry and off-dry *Chenins*, lovely *late-harvest* and fortified wines, and surprisingly good *Pinotages*; otherwise very patchy.
Fairview; Flagstone; Grangehurst; Klein Constantia; Jordan; Kanonkop; Mulderbosch; Plaisir de Merle; Sadie; Saxenburg; Simonsig; Thelema; Vergelegen.

South Australia Home of almost all the biggest wine companies, and still producing over half of Australia's wine. The *Barossa Valley* is one of the country's oldest wine regions, but like its neighbors *Clare* and *McLaren Vale*, faces competition from cooler areas like *Adelaide Hills*, *Padthaway*, and *Coonawarra*.

Southeast Australia A cleverly meaningless regional description. Technically, it covers around 85 percent of Australia's vineyards.

Southwest France An unofficial umbrella term covering the areas between *Bordeaux* and the Pyrenees, *Bergerac*, *Madiran*, *Cahors*, *Jurançon*, and the *Vins de Pays* of the Côtes de Gascogne.

⚘ **Spanna** [spah-nah] (*Piedmont*, Italy) The *Piedmontese* name for the *Nebbiolo* grape and the more humble wines made from it.

Ⅰ **Pierre Sparr** (*Alsace*, France) Big producer offering a taste of *Chasselas*.

☘ **Spätburgunder** [shpayt-bur-goon-dur] (Germany) Alias of *Pinot Noir*.
Spätlese [shpayt-lay-zeh] (Germany) Second step in the *QmP* scale, *late-harvested* grapes making wine a notch drier than *Auslese*.

☘ **Fratelli Speri** [speh-ree] (*Veneto*, Italy) A fast-rising star with delicious Monte Sant'Urbano Amarone della Valpolicella Classico.

☘ **Spice Route** (South Africa) Label showing the skills of Charles Back of Fairview. Good value, reliable wines from Malmesbury. Top wines are labeled "Flagship". ★ ★ ★ ★ **Flagship Syrah 2001 $$$**

☘ **Domaine Spiropoulos** [spee-ro-poo-los] (*Peloponnese*, Greece) Fine producer of organic wine, including Porfyros, one of Greece's best modern reds.

☘ **Spottswoode** (*Napa Valley*, California) Excellent, small producer of complex *Cabernet* and unusually good *Sauvignon Blanc*. Deserves greater recognition.

☘ **Spring Mountain** (*Napa Valley*, California) Area and old winery with great vineyards and classy, *Cabernet* and *Syrah*. ★ ★ ★ ★ ★ **Napa Valley Syrah 1999**

☘ **Springfield Estate** (*Robertson*, South Africa) Fast improving producer, with crisp dry *Sauvignons*, and a good "methode ancienne" *Chardonnay*.
★ ★ ★ **2002 Life from Stone Sauvignon Blanc $$**

Spritz/ig [shpritz/ich] Slight sparkle/sparkling. Also *pétillant*.

Spumante [spoo-man-tay] (Italy) Sparkling.

☘ **Squinzano** [skeen-tzah-noh] (*Puglia*, Italy) Traditional, often rustic reds from the warm South. The *Santa Barbara* cooperative makes the best wines.

Staatsweingut [staht-svine-goot] (Germany) A state-owned wine estate such as Staatsweingüter *Eltville* (*Rheingau*), a major cellar in *Eltville*.

☘ **Standing Stones** (*New York State*) Recommendable Finger Lakes producer with an especially good Riesling.

☘ **Stafford Ridge** (*Adelaide Hills*, Australia) Fine *Chardonnay* and especially *Sauvignon* from *Lenswood* by Geoff Weaver, former winemaker of *Hardys*.

Stags Leap District (*Napa Valley*, California) Hillside region, specializing in blackcurranty *Cabernet Sauvignon*. S. Anderson; *Clos du Val*; Cronin; Hartwell; *Pine Ridge; Shafer; Silverado Vineyards; Stag's Leap; Steltzner.*

☘ **Stags Leap Winery** (*Napa* Valley, California) Greatly improved Cabernet Sauvignon specialist. Don't confuse with...

☘ **Stag's Leap Wine Cellars** (*Napa* Valley, California) Pioneering supporter of the *Stags Leap appellation*, and one of the finest wineries in California. The best wines are the Faye Vineyard, SLV, and Cask 23 *Cabernets*. Don't confuse with the Stags Leap Winery. ★ ★ ★ ★ ★ **Napa Valley S.L.V. Cabernet Sauvignon 1999 $$$**

☘ **Staglin** (*Napa Valley*, California) Classy producer of Bordeaux-like *Cabernet* and pioneering *Sangiovese*.

Stalky or stemmy Flavor of the stem rather than of the juice.

☘ **Stanton & Killeen** (*Rutherglen*, Australia) Reliable producer of *Liqueur Muscat*. ★ ★ ★ ★ **NV Muscat $$**

☘ **Steele** (*Lake County*, California) The former winemaker of *Kendall Jackson*; a master when it comes to producing fruitily crowd-pleasing *Chardonnays* from various regions, as well as more complex *Zinfandel*.

Steely Refers to young wine with evident *acidity*. A compliment when paid to *Chablis* and dry *Sauvignons*.

🍇 **Steen** [steen] (South Africa) Traditional (now less fashionable) name for (and possibly odd *clone* of) *Chenin Blanc*. Widely planted (over 30 percent of the vineyard area). The best come from *Hazendal* and *Fairview*.

☘ **Steiermark/Styria** (Austria) Sunny southern region where the *Chardonnay* is now being used (under the name of "Morillon") to produce rich, buttery, but often quite Burgundian wines.

☘ **Steinfeder** [shtine-fay-dur] (*Wachau*, Austria) Category for the lightest dry wines. See also *Federspiel*, *Smaragd*.

S

Stellenbosch [stel-len-bosh] (South Africa) A climatically and topographically diverse region that, like the *Napa Valley*, is taken far too seriously as a regional *appellation*. Hillside subregions like Helderberg make more sense. *Bergkelder; Delheim; Neil Ellis; Grangehurst; Hartenberg; Jordan; Kanonkop; Meerlust; Mulderbosch; Rustenberg; Saxenburg; Stellenzicht; Thelema; Warwick.* ★★★★★ Rustenberg Stellenbosch John X 2000 $$$

℣ **Stellenbosch Farmers' Winery** (*Stellenbosch*, South Africa) South Africa's biggest producer, with Sable View, Libertas, *Nederburg*, *Plaisir de Merle*.

℣ **Stellenzicht Vineyards** [stel-len-zikht] (*Stellenbosch*, South Africa) Sister estate of Neethlingshof, with a good *Sauvignon* and a *Shiraz* good enough to beat *Penfolds Grange* in a blind tasting. ★★★★ Syrah 2000 $$$

Stelvin Brand of screwcap, specifically designed for wine bottled by its French manufacturer. Long respected by open-minded professionals, Stelvins have had a new boost following the decision by top producers to use them.

℣ **Sterling Vineyards** (*Napa Valley*, California) Founded by Peter Newton (now at *Newton* vineyards) and once the plaything of Coca-Cola, this showcase estate now belongs to Canadian liquor giant Seagram. Among the current successes are the Reserve *Cabernet*, *Pinot Noir*, and fairly priced Redwood Trail wines. ★★★★ Napa Valley Reserve Cabernet Sauvignon 1999 $$$

℣ **Weingut Georg Stiegelmar** [stee-gel-mahr] (*Burgenland*, Austria) Producer of pricey, highly acclaimed, dry *Chardonnay* and *Pinot Blanc*, late-harvest wines, and some particularly good *Pinot Noir* and *St. Laurent*.

℣ **Stoneleigh** (*Marlborough*, New Zealand) Reliable *Marlborough* label, now part of *Montana*. ★★★★★ Chardonnay 2002 $$

℣ **Stonestreet** (*Sonoma*, California) Highly commercial wines from the *Kendall-Jackson* stable.

℣ **Stonier's** [stoh-nee-yurs] (*Mornington Peninsula*, Australia) Small *Mornington* winery, successful with impressive *Pinot Noir*, *Chardonnay*, and *Merlot*. (Previously known as Stoniers-Merrick; and now a subsidiary of *Petaluma*.)

℣ **Stony Hill** (*Napa Valley*, California) Unfashionable old winery with the guts to produce long-lived, complex *Chardonnay* that tastes like unoaked *Grand Cru Chablis*, rather than follow the herd in aping buttery-rich *Meursault*.

℣ **Stonyridge** (*Auckland*, New Zealand) Rapidly rising star on fashionable Waiheke Island, making impressive, if pricey, *Bordeaux*-style reds.

℣ **Storybook Mountain** (*Napa Valley*, California) Great individual-vineyard *Zinfandels* that taste good young but are built for the long haul. The *Howell Mountain* vines were replanted with *Cabernet Sauvignon*.

Structure The "structural" components of a wine include *tannin, acidity*, and *alcohol*. They provide the skeleton or backbone that supports the "flesh" of the fruit. A young wine with good structure should age well.

℣ **Ch. de Suduiraut** [soo-dee-rroh] (*Sauternes Premier Cru Classé, Bordeaux*, France) Producing great things since its purchase by French insurance giant, AXA. Top wines: "*Cuvée* Madame", "Crème de Tête". The 2001 was the Sauternes of the vintage.

Suhindol [soo-win-dol] (Bulgaria) One of *Bulgaria's* best-known regions, the source of widely available, fairly-priced *Cabernet Sauvignon*.

Sulfites US labeling requirement alerting those suffering from an (extremely rare) allergy to the presence of *sulfur dioxide*. Curiously, no such requirement is made of cans of baked beans and dried apricots, which contain twice as much of the chemical.

Sulfur dioxide/SO₂ Antiseptic routinely used by food packagers and winemakers to protect their produce from bacteria and *oxidation*.

℣ **Sumac Ridge** (*British Columbia*, Canada) Decent quality, especially *Sauvignon* and *Gewurztraminer*.

℣ **Super Second** (*Bordeaux*, France) *Médoc* second growths: *Pichon-Lalande, Pichon-Longueville, Léoville-las-Cases, Ducru-Beaucaillou, Cos d'Estournel*; whose wines can rival the first growths. Other overperformers include: *Rauzan-Ségla* and *Léoville-Barton, Lynch-Bages, Palmer, La Lagune, Montrose*.

T

Super-Tuscan (Italy) New-wave *Vino da Tavola/IGT* (usually red) wines, pioneered by producers like *Antinori*, which stand outside *DOC* rules. Generally *Bordeaux*-style blends or *Sangiovese* or a mixture of both.

Supérieur/Superiore [soo-pay-ree-ur/soo-pay-ree-ohr-ray] (France/Italy) Often relatively meaningless in terms of discernible quality. Denotes wine (well or badly) made from riper grapes.

Sur lie [soor-lee] (France) The aging "on its *lees*" – or dead yeasts – most commonly associated with *Muscadet*.

Süssreserve [soos-sreh-zurv] (Germany) Unfermented grape juice used to bolster sweetness and fruit in German and English wines.

♇ **Sutter Home Winery** (*Napa Valley*, California) Home of robust red *Zinfandel* in the 1970s, and responsible for the invention of successful sweet "white" (or, as the non-color-blind might say, pink) *Zinfandel*. *Amador County Zinfandels* are still good, but rarely exceptional. The M. Trinchero Founders Estate *Cabernet* and *Chardonnay* are worth looking out for.

♇ **Joseph Swan** (*Sonoma*, California) Small Burgundian-scale winery whose enthusiastic winemaker, Rod Berglund, produces great single-vineyard, often attractively quirky, *Pinot Noir* and *Zinfandel*.

Swan Valley (*Western Australia*) Hot old vineyard area; good for fortified wines and a source of fruit for *Houghton's* successful *HWB*. *Houghton* also produces cooler-climate wines in the microclimate of *Moondah Brook*.

♇ **Swanson** [swon-son] (*Napa Valley*, California) Top flight, innovative producer of *Cabernet*, *Chardonnay*, *Sangiovese*, *Syrah*, and *late-harvest Semillon*.
★★★★★ Alexis 1999 $$$

Swartland [svart-land] (*South Africa*) Western region, once considered a source of rustic red, but now – well some parts of it anyway – producing great modern reds and whites. ★★★★ 2000 Reebeck Reserve Shiraz $$

Switzerland Produces increasingly enjoyable wines from grapes ranging from the *Chasselas*, *Marsanne*, *Syrah*, and *Pinot Noir* to the local *Cornallin* and *Petite Arvine*. See *Dôle*, *Fendant*, *Chablais*. Also the only country to use screwcaps for much of its wine, thus facilitating recycling and avoiding the problems of faulty corks. Clever people, the Swiss.

♛ **Sylvaner/Silvaner** [sill-vah-nur] Non-aromatic white grape, originally from *Austria* but found particularly in *Alsace* and *Franken* where modern winemaking is bringing huge improvements. There are also promising efforts in South Africa. ★★★★★ Horst Sauer Sehnsucht, Escherndorf 2001 $$

♛ **Syrah** [see-rah] (*Rhône*, France) The red *Rhône* grape, an exotic mix of ripe fruit and spicy, smoky, gamey, leathery flavors. In Australia and S. Africa, it is called *Shiraz*. Increasingly popular in California, thanks to "*Rhône* Rangers" like *Bonny Doon* and *Phelps*. See *Qupé*, *Marqués de Griñon* in Spain and *Isole e Olena* in Italy, plus *Côte Rôtie*, *Hermitage*, *Shiraz*.

♇ **Szamorodni** [jam-moh-rod-nee] ((*Tokaj*, Hungary) Means 'as it comes' and denotes wine that is usually dry to sweetish. Makes a good aperitif.

T

TBA (Germany) Abbreviation for *Trockenbeerenauslese*.

♇ **La Tâche** [la tash] (*Burgundy*, France) Wine from the La Tâche vineyard, exclusively owned by the *Dom. de la Romanée Conti*. Frequently as good as the rarer and more expensive "La Romanée Conti".

Tafelwein [tah-fel-vine] (Germany) Table wine. Only the prefix "Deutscher" guarantees German origin.

♇ **Ch. Tahbilk** [tah-bilk] (*Victoria*, Australia) Old-fashioned winemaking in the *Goulbourn Valley/Nagambie*. Great long-lived *Shiraz* from 130-year-old vines, surprisingly good *Chardonnay*, and lemony *Marsanne* which needs a decade. The second wine is Dalfarras. ★★★★ Marsanne 2001 $$

T

- ☰ **Cave de Tain L'Hermitage** (*Rhône*, France) Reliable cooperative for *Crozes-Hermitage* and *Hermitage*.
- ☰ **Taittinger** [tat-tan-jehr] (*Champagne*, France) Producer of reliable non-vintage, and fine Comtes de *Champagne Blanc de Blancs* and Rosé.
  ★★★★★ **Taittinger Comtes de Champagne Blanc de Blancs 1995 $$$$**
- ☰ **Ch. Talbot** [tal-boh] (*St. Julien 4ème Cru Classé, Bordeaux*, France) Reliable, if sometimes slightly jammy, wine. In the same stable as Ch. Gruaud Larose. Connétable Talbot is the *second label*.
- ☰ **Talbott** (*Monterey*, California) Serious small producer of elegant *Chardonnay* and *Pinot Noir* that lasts.
- ☰ **Talley** (*San Luis Obispo*, California) Small producer of elegant *Chardonnay* and *Pinot Noir* that lasts. ★★★★ **Arroyo Grande Valley Chardonnay 2000 $$$**
- ☰ **Taltarni** [tal-tahr-nee] (*Victoria*, Australia) Fine *Shiraz Cabernets* from a beautiful *Pyrenees* vineyard. ★★★★ **Pyrenees Shiraz 2000 $$**
- 🍇 **Tamîïoasa Romaneasca** [tem-yo-asha roh-mah-nay-yas-ka] (Romania) Local name for *Muscat Blanc à Petits Grains*. Other Tamîïoasas are different sorts of Muscat.
- 🍇 **Tannat** [ta-na] (France) Rustic French grape variety, traditionally used in the blend of *Cahors* and in South America, principally in *Uruguay*.
- ☰ **Lane Tanner** (*California*, USA) *Santa Barbara* estate with fine *Pinot Noir*.
  Tannic See *Tannin*.
  Tannin Astringent component of red wine that comes from the skins, seeds, and stalks, and helps the wine to age.
- ☰ **Jean Tardy** (*Burgundy*, France) Excellent domaine based in *Vosne-Romanée*.
- ☰ **Tardy & Ange** [tahr-dee ay onzh] (*Rhône*, France) Partnership producing classy *Crozes-Hermitage* at the Dom. de Entrefaux.
- ☰ **Tarragona** [ta-ra-go-nah] (*Catalonia*, Spain) *DO* region south of *Penedés* and home to many cooperatives. Contains the better-quality *Terra Alta*.
- ☰ **Tarrawarra** [ta-ra-wa-ra] (*Yarra Valley*, Australia) Increasingly successful *Pinot* and *Chardonnay* pioneer in the cool-climate region of the *Yarra Valley*. *Second label* is Tunnel Hill. ★★★★★ **Tarrawarra Pinot Noir 1999 $$$**
  Tarry Red wines from hot countries often have an aroma and flavor reminiscent of tar. The *Syrah* and *Nebbiolo* exhibit this characteristic.
  Tartaric Type of acid found in grapes. Also the form in which acid is added to wine in hot countries whose legislation allows them.
  Tartrates [tar-trayts] Harmless white crystals often deposited by white wines in the bottle. In Germany, these are called "diamonds."
  Tasmania (Australia) Cool-climate island, showing potential for sparkling wine, *Chardonnay*, *Riesling*, and *Pinot Noir*. Freycinet; Heemskerk; Jansz; Moorilla; Piper's Brook; Pirie; Tamar Ridge. ★★★★ Jansz **$$**
  Tastevin [tat-van] Silver *Burgundy* tasting cup used as an insignia by vinous brotherhoods (*confréries*), as a badge of office by sommeliers, and as an ashtray by others. The *Chevaliers de Tastevin* organize tastings, awarding a mock-medieval Tastevinage label to the best wines. *Chevaliers de Tastevin* attend banquets, often wearing similarly mock-medieval gowns.
- ☰ **Taurasi** [tow-rah-see] (*Campania*, Italy) Big, old-fashioned *Aglianico*. Needs years to soften and develop a burned, cherry taste. *Mastroberardino*.
- ☰ **Cosimo Taurino** [tow-ree-noh] (*Puglia*, Italy) The name to look for when buying Salice Salentino. The red Patrigliono and Notapanaro and Chardonnay are worth looking for, too. ★★★★ **Salice Salentino Reserva 1999 $$**
- ☰ **Tavel** [ta-vehl] (*Rhône*, France) Dry rosé. Seek out young versions and avoid the bronze color revered by traditionalists. Ch. d'Aquéria; Dom. de la Forcadière; de la Mordorée; du Prieuré; Ch. de Trinquevedel; de Valéry.
  Tawny (*Douro*, Portugal) In theory, pale browny-red *port* that acquires its mature appearance and nutty flavor from long aging in oak casks. *Port* houses, however, legally produce cheap "tawny" by mixing basic *ruby* with *white port* and skipping the tiresome business of barrel-aging altogether. The real stuff comes with an indication of age, such as 10-

T

or 20-year-old, but these figures are approximate. A 10-year-old *port* only has to "taste as though it is that old." *Colheita ports* are tawnies of a specific vintage. *Noval; Taylor's; Graham's; Cockburn's; Dow's; Niepoort; Ramos Pinto; Calem.*

Taylor (Fladgate & Yeatman) (*Douro*, Portugal) With *Dow's*, a *Douro* "first growths". Outstanding *vintage port*, "modern" *Late Bottled Vintage*. Also owns *Fonseca* and *Guimaraens*, and produces the excellent *Quintas de Vargellas* and *Tera Feita Single-Quinta ports*. ★★★★★ Quinta de Terra Feita 1988 $$$

Te Mata [tay mah-tah] (*Hawkes Bay*, New Zealand) Pioneer John Buck proves what *New Zealand* can do with *Chardonnay* (in the Elston Vineyard) and pioneered reds with his Coleraine and (lighter) Awatea.

Te Motu [tay moh-too] ((New Zealand) Dense reds from *Waiheke Island*.

Fratelli Tedeschi [tay-dehs-kee] (*Veneto*, Italy) Reliable producer of rich and concentrated *Valpolicellas* and good *Soaves*. The *Amarones* are particularly impressive. ★★★★ Amarone Classico 1999 $$

Tement [teh-ment] (*Steiermark*, Austria) Producer of a truly world-class barrel-fermented *Sauvignon Blanc* which competes directly with top *Pessac-Léognan* whites. *Chardonnays* are impressive, too.

Dom. Tempier [tom-pee-yay] (*Provence*, France) *Provence* superstar estate, producing single-vineyard red and rosé *Bandols* that support the claim that the *Mourvèdre* (from which they are largely made) ages well. The rosé is also one of the best in the region.

Tempranillo [tem-prah-nee-yoh] (Spain) The red grape of *Rioja* – and just about everywhere else in Spain, thanks to the way in which its strawberry fruit suits the vanilla/oak flavors of barrel-aging. In *Navarra*, it is called *Cencibel*; in *Ribera del Duero*, Tinto Fino; in the *Penedés*, *Ull de Llebre;* in *Toro*, Tinto de Toro; and in Portugal – where it is used for *port* – it's known as *Tinto Roriz*. Widely found in Argentina (*Zuccardi*). Also being planted in Australia. ★★★★ Familia Zuccardi Q Tempranillo 2001 $$

Tenuta [teh-noo-tah] (Italy) Estate or vineyard.

Terlano/Terlaner [tehr-LAH-noh/tehr-LAH-nehr] (*Trentino-Alto Adige*, Italy) Northern Italian village and its wine: usually fresh, crisp, and carrying the name of the grape from which it was made.

Teroldego Rotaliano [teh-rol-deh-goh roh-tah-lee-AH-noh] (*Trentino-Alto Adige*, Italy) Dry reds, quite full-bodied, with lean, slightly bitter berry flavors which make them better accompaniments to food. *Foradori.*

Terra Alta [tay ruh al-ta] (*Catalonia*, Spain) Small *DO* within the much larger *Tarragona DO*, producing wines of higher quality due to the difficult climate and resulting low yields. Pedro Rovira.

Terrazas [teh-rah-zas] (*Mendoza*, Argentina) The brand name of Moët & Chandon's recently launched impressive red and white Argentinian wines.

Terre Rosse [teh-reh roh-seh] (*Liguria*, Italy) One of the best estates in Liguria, with good examples of *Vermentino* and Pigato.

Ch. Terrey-Gros-Caillou [teh-ray groh kih-yoo] (*Bordeaux*, France) Well made *Cru Bourgeois St-Julien*.

Ch. du Tertre [doo tehr-tr] (*Margaux 5ème Cru Classé, Bordeaux*, France) Recently restored to former glory by the owners of *Calon-Ségur*.

Ch. Tertre-Daugay [tehr-tr-doh-jay] (*St. Emilion, Grand Cru, Bordeaux*, France) Steadily improving property whose wines are cast in a classic mould and do not always have the immediate appeal of bigger, oakier neighbors.

Ch. Tertre-Rôteboeuf [Tehr-tr roht-burf] (*St. Emilion Grand Cru Classé, Bordeaux*, France) Good, rich, concentrated, crowd-pleasing wines.

Teruzzi & Puthod (Tuscany, Italy) Go-ahead producer based in San Gimignano. Very good whites.

Tête de Cuvée [teht dur coo-vay] (France) An old expression still used by traditionalists to describe their finest wine.

T

⚷ **Thackrey** (*Marin County,* California) Rich, impressively concentrated wines that seek to emulate the *Rhône,* but actually come closer to Australia in style.

⚷ **Thames Valley Vineyard** (*Reading,* England) Reliable and dynamic winery – and consultancy.

⚷ **Dr. H Thanisch** [tah-nish] (*Mosel-Saar-Ruwer,* Germany) Two estates with confuzingly similar labels. The best of the pair which has a *VDP* logo offers improved examples of *Bernkasteler* Doctor.

⚷ **Thelema Mountain Vineyards** [thur-lee-ma] (*Stellenbosch,* South Africa) One of the very best wineries in South Africa, thanks to Gyles Webb's skill and to stunning hillside vineyards. *Chardonnay* and *Sauvignon* are the stars, though Webb is coming to terms with his reds, too.

Thermenregion [thehr -men-ray-gee-yon] (Austria) Big region close to Vienna, producing good reds and sweet and dry whites.

⚷ **Jean Thevenet** [tev-nay] ((*Burgundy,* France) *Macon* producer who makes sweet white when he can. The domaine is called Domaine de la Bongran.

⚷ **Ch. Thieuley** [tee-yur-lay] (*Entre-Deux-Mers, Bordeaux,* France) With *Château Bonnet,* this is one of the leading lights of this region.
★★★ 2001 Francis Courselle $

⚷ **Michel Thomas** [toh-mah] (Loire, France) Producer of reliable modern Sancerre with rich flavors. ★★★★★ 2001 Sancerre $$

⚷ **Paul Thomas** (*Washington State*) Dynamic brand now under the same ownership as Columbia Winery, and producing a broad range of wines, including good *Chardonnay* and *Semillon* whites, and *Cabernet-Merlot* reds.

⚷ **Three Choirs Vineyard** (*Gloucestershire,* England) Reliable estate, named for the three cathedrals of Gloucester, Hereford, and Worcester. Try the "Barrique-matured" whites and the "New Release" *Nouveau.*

⚷ **Jean-Luc Thunevin** (*Bordeaux,* France) Producer of tiny-production, rich, concentrated "garage wines" such as *Valandraud* and *Marojallia.*

⚷ **Thurston Wolfe** (*Washington State*) Enthusiastic supporter of the local speciality, the mulberryish red Lemberger – and producer, too, of good fortified "port" and Black Muscat.

⚷ **Ticino** [tee-chee-noh] (Switzerland) One of the best parts of Switzerland to go looking for easy-drinking and (relatively) affordable reds, the best of which are made from *Merlot.* Interestingly, this region has also quietly pioneered White Merlot, a style of wine we will be encountering quite frequently in the next few years, as California grape growers and winemakers struggle to find ways of disposing of the surplus of this grape. Terre de Gudo.

⚷ **Tiefenbrunner** [tee-fen-broon-nehr] (*Trentino-Alto Adige,* Italy) Consistent producer of good varietal whites, most particularly *Chardonnay, Gewürztraminer* and *Moscato Rosa.*

⚷ **Tignanello** [teen-yah-neh-loh] (*Tuscany,* Italy) *Antinori's* Sangiovese-Cabernet *Super-Tuscan* is one of Italy's original superstars. Should last for a decade.

🍇 **Tinta Roriz** [teen-tah roh-reesh] (Portugal) See *Tempranillo*

⚷ **Tio Pepe** [tee-yoh peh-peh] (*Jerez,* Spain) *Gonzalez Byass's* Ultrareliable fino.

🍇 **Tocai** [toh-kay] (Italy) Lightly herby Venetian white grape, confuzingly unrelated to others of similar name. Drink young.

⚷ **Philip Togni** (Napa, California) Producer of big, hefty *Cabernet Sauvignons* that take a long while to soften, but are well worth the wait.

⚷ **Tokaji** [toh-ka-yee] (Hungary) Not to be confused with Australian *liqueur Tokay,* Tocai Friulano, or *Tokay d'Alsace, Tokaji Aszú* is a dessert wine made in a specific region of Eastern *Hungary* (and a small corner of *Slovakia*) by adding measured amounts (*puttonyos*) of *eszencia* (a paste made from individually-picked, overripe, and/or *botrytis*-affected grapes) to dry wine made from the local *Furmint* and *Hárslevelu* grapes. Sweetness levels, which depend on the amount of *eszencia* added, range from one to six *puttonyos,* anything beyond which is labeled *Aszú Eszencia.* This last is often confused with the pure syrup which is sold – at vast prices – as *Eszencia.* Wines are fresher (less *oxidized*)

T

since the arrival of outside investment, which has also revived interest in making individual-vineyard wines from the best sites. Some Tokaji is now sold as late harvest – "Kezoi szuretelesu" –, rather than *Aszu*. Disznókö; *Royal Tokaji Wine Co; Ch. Megyer; Nezsmely; Oremus; Pajzos;* Tokajkovago.

�». **Tokaj Trading House** (*Tokaj*, Hungary) The state-owned wine producing company, now modernizing.

Tokay [in France: to-kay; in Australia: toh-kye] A number of wine regions use Tokay as a local name for various grape varieties. In Australia it is the name of a fortified wine made by *Rutherglen* from the *Muscadelle*. In *Alsace* it is the local name for *Pinot Gris*. The Italian *Tocai* is not related to either of these. Hungary's Tokay (renamed *Tokaji*) is largely made from the *Furmint*.

☞ Tokay d'Alsace [to-kay dal-sas] (Alsace, France) See *Pinot Gris*.

☮ **Tollana** [to-lah-nah] (South Australia) Another part of the Southcorp (*Penfolds, Lindeman*, etc.) empire – and a source of great value.

☮ **Dom. Tollot-Beaut** [to-loh-boh] (*Burgundy*, France) *Burgundy* domaine in *Chorey-lès-Beaune*, with top-class *Corton* vineyards and a mastery over modern techniques and new oak. Wines have lots of rich fruit flavor. Some find them overly showy. ★ ★ ★ ★ ★ Corton 2001 $$$

☮ **Torbreck** (*Barossa*, Australia) Producer of Rhône-like reds that blend *Shiraz* with *Viognier*. Look for Runrig, Descendent and Juveniles, originally produced for one of the best bar-restaurants in Paris.

☮ **Torcolato** [taw-ko-lah-toh] (*Veneto*, Italy) See *Maculan*.

☞ Torgiano [taw-jee-yah-noh] (*Umbria*, Italy) Zone in *Umbria* and modern red wine made famous by *Lungarotti*. See *Rubesco*. ★ ★ ★ Torgiano Rubesco 1995

☮ **Michel Torino** [Toh-ree-noh] (*Cafayate*, Argentina) Reliable producer of various wine styles from Salta – and a leading light in the move toward organic wine in Argentina. ★ ★ ★ ★ Don David Cabernet Sauvignon 2001 $$

☞ Toro [to-roh] (Spain) Chasing Priorat and Ribera del Duero and its Portuguese neighbor the *Douro*, this up-and-coming region is now producing intense reds such as Fariña's *Collegiata* using *Tempranillo* grapes that are confusingly known here as Tinta de Toro. Bajoz; Dominio de Eguren; *Fariña;* Maurodos; Numanthia; Vega Saúco; Toresanas.

☮ **Torre de Gall** [to-ray day-gahl] (*Catalonia*, Spain) *Moët & Chandon's* Spanish sparkling wine – now known as Cava Chandon. As good as it gets using traditional *cava* varieties.

☮ **Torres** [TO-rehs] (*Catalonia*, Spain) *Miguel Torres* revolutionized Spain's wines with its Viña Sol, Gran Sangre de Toro, Esmeralda, and Gran Coronas, before doing the same for Chile. Today, while these all face heavier competition, efforts at the top end of the scale, like the *Milmanda Chardonnay*, Fransola *Sauvignon Blanc*, and Mas Borras ("Black Label") *Cabernet Sauvignon*, still look good. ★ ★ ★ ★ ★ Grans Muralles 1998 $$$

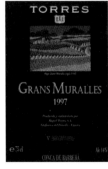

☮ **Marimar Torres** [TO-rehs] (*Sonoma*, California) *Miguel Torres'* sister is producing impressive *Pinot Noir* and *Chardonnay* from a spectacular little vineyard in *Russian River*. ★ ★ ★ Marimar Pinot Noir 1999 $$$

☮ **Miguel Torres** [TO-rehs] (*Curico*, Chile) Offshoot of the Spanish giant. Manso de Velasco is the star wine.
★ ★ ★ ★ Manso de Velasco Cabernet Sauvignon 1997 $$$

☮ **Torreón de Paredes** [tor-ray-yon day pah-ray-days] ((Chile) Erratic *Rapel* estate. Good Cabernet. ★ ★ ★ 2000 Torreon de Paredes Merlot Reserve $

☮ **Michel Torino** (Argentina) Organic estate currently on a roll.

☞ Torrontes [to-ron-tehs] (Argentina) Aromatic cousin of *Muscat*. Smells sweet even when the wine is bone dry. Etchart; la Agricola.

Toscana [tos-KAH-nah] (Italy) See *Tuscany*.

☮ **Ch. la Tour Blanche** [lah toor blonsh] (*Sauternes Premier Cru Classé*, *Bordeaux*, France) Wine school, producing fine, long-lasting Sauternes.

T

� **Ch. la Tour-Carnet** [lah toor kahr-nay] (*Haut-Médoc 4ème Cru Classé, Bordeaux*, France) Picturesque chateau whose wines are rarely spectacular.

� **Ch. la Tour-de-By** [lah toor dur bee] (*Médoc Cru Bourgeois, Bordeaux*, France) Reliable, in a traditional sort of way.

� **Ch. La Tour Figeac** [lah toor fee-jak] (*Bordeaux*, France) A St Emilion *Grand Cru Classé* to watch, with careful winemaking and good terroir.

� **Ch. La Tour Haut Brion** [lah toor oh-bree-yo'n] (*Bordeaux*, France) Until 1983 this was the second wine of Ch. *La Mission Haut-Brion*. Now it is an entirely separate wine, and is lighter, but still with great depth and style.

� **Ch. Tour-du-Haut-Caussan** [toor doo oh koh-sa'n] (*Haut-Médoc, Bordeaux*, France) Highly reliable modern estate.

� **Ch. Tour-du-Haut-Moulin** [toor doo oh moo-lan] (*Haut-Médoc Cru Bourgeois, Bordeaux*, France) Producer of sometimes *cru classé* quality wine.

� **Ch. la Tour-Martillac** [lah toor mah-tee-yak] (*Pessac Léognan, Bordeaux*, France) Organic *Pessac-Léognan* estate with juicy reds and good whites.

� **Touraine** [too-rayn] (*Loire*, France) Area encompassing the ACs *Chinon, Vouvray*, and *Bourgueil*. An increasing source of quaffable *varietal* wines – *Sauvignon, Gamay* de Touraine, etc. Dom de l'Aumonier; Bellevue; de la Besnerie; Briare; Paul Buisse; Charmoise; Clos Roche Blanche; de la Gabillière; Henry Marionnet; Dom. Pré BaronOctavie; Oisly & Thésée; Oudin Frères.

☦ **Les Tourelles de Longueville** [lay too-rel dur long-ur-veel] (*Pauillac, Bordeaux*, France) The *second label* of *Pichon-Longueville*.

☙ **Touriga (Nacional/Franca)** [too-ree-ga nah-see-yoh-nahl/fran-ka] (Portugal) Red *port* grapes, also (though rarely) seen in the New World. Now increasingly being used for exciting *varietal* wines in many parts of Portugal. Casa Santos Lima; Esporão; Maria Joana Castro Duarte; Olazabal; Quinta do Crasto; do Portal; do Vallado; Ramos Pinto; Roboredo Madeira; Vinhosauv

☦ **Tower Estates** (Australia) Dynamic new venture led by Len Evans, founder of Rothbury Estate and Emperor of Australia's wine competitions. Wines are produced in limited quantities in several different regions.

Tradition(al) Generally meaningless term, except in sparkling wines where the "méthode traditionelle" is the new way to say "*méthode champenoise*" and in Portugal where "Traditional *Late Bottled Vintage*" refers to *port* that unlike non-traditional LBV, hasn't been filtered. ("Tradition" in France can also refer to – often unappealingly – old-fashioned – usually unoaked – winemaking).

☦ **Traisen** [trih-sen] (Nahe, Germany) Star village of the Nahe, with Bastei and Rotenfels vineyards, and brilliant, fiery Rieslings.

☙ **Traminer** [tra-mee-nur; in Australia: trah-MEE-nah] A less aromatic variant of the *Gewürztraminer* grape widely grown in Eastern Europe and Italy, although the term is confusingly also used as a pronounceable, alternative name for the latter grape – particularly in Australia.

Transfer Method A way of making sparkling wine, involving a second fermentation in the bottle, but unlike the *méthode champenoise* in that the wine is separated from the lees by pumping it out of the bottle into a pressurized tank for clarification before returning it to another bottle.

☦ **Bodegas Trapiche** [tra-pee-chay] (Argentina) Huge, go-getting producer with noteworthy barrel-fermented *Chardonnay* and *Cabernet/Malbec*. ✦✦✦✦ Merlot Oak Cask 2001 **$**

Tras-os-Montes [tras-ohsh-montsh] (*Douro*, Portugal) Up-and-coming wine region of the *Upper Douro*, right up by the Spanish border. It's the source of *Barca Velha*. ✦✦✦ Casal de Valle Pradinhos 2000 $

☙ **Trebbiano** [treh-bee-yah-noh] (Italy) Ubiquitous white grape, known in France as *Ugni Blanc*.

☦ **Trebbiano d'Abruzzo** [treh-bee-yah-noh dab-root-zoh] (*Abruzzo*, Italy) A *DOC* region where they grow a clone of *Trebbiano*, confusingly called Trebbiano di Toscana, and use it to make unexceptional dry whites.

☦ **Trefethen** [treh-feh-then] (*Napa Valley,* California) Pioneering estate whose *Chardonnay* and *Cabernet* now taste oddly old-fashioned.

Trentino [trehn-tee-noh] (Italy) Northern DOC in Italy. Trentino specialities include crunchy red Marzemino, nutty white Nosiola, and excellent Vin Santo. Winemaking here often suffers from overproduction, but less greedy winemakers can offer lovely, soft, easy-drinking wines. **Càvit**; *Ferrari; Foradori; Pojer & Sandri*; San Leonardo; Vallarom; Roberto Zeni.

Trentino-Alto Adige [trehn-tee-noh al-toh ah-dee-jay] (Italy) Northern region confusingly combining the two DOC areas Trentino and Alto Adige.

⊼ **Dom. de Trévallon** [treh-vah-lon] (*Provence*, France) Superstar long-lived blend of *Cabernet Sauvignon* and *Syrah* that was sold under the *Les Baux de Provence appellation* but has now (because of crazily restrictive rules regarding grape varieties) been demoted to *Vin de Pays des Bouches du Rhône*.

⊼ **Triebaumer** [tree-bow-mehr] (*Burgenland*, Austria) Fine producer of late-harvest wines (including good Sauvignon) and well-made reds, including some unusually good examples of the *Blaufränkisch*.

⊼ **Dom. Frédéric-Emile Trimbach** [tram-bahkh] (*Alsace*, France) Distinguished grower and merchant with subtle, dry, complex wines. Top *cuvées* are the Frédéric Emile, Clos St. Hune, and Seigneurs de Ribeaupierre.
★ ★ ★ ★ Trimbach Pinot Gris Reserve 2000 $$

Trittenheim [trit-ten-hime] (*Mosel-Saar-Ruwer*, Germany) Village whose vineyards are said to have been the first in Germany planted with Riesling, making honeyed wine.

Trocken [trok-ken] (Germany) Dry, often aggressively so. Avoid Trocken *Kabinett* from such northern areas as the *Mosel*, *Rheingau*, and *Rheinhessen*. *QbA* (*chaptalized*) and *Spätlese* Trocken wines (the latter made, by definition, from riper grapes) are better. See also *Halbtrocken*.

Trockenbeerenauslese [trok-ken-beh-ren-ows-lay-zeh] (Austria/Germany) Fifth rung of the *QmP* ladder, wine from selected dried grapes which are usually *botrytis*-affected and full of natural sugar. Only made in the best years, rare and expensive, though less so in Austria than Germany.

⚘ **Trollinger** [trroh-ling-gur] (Germany) The German name for the Black Hamburg grape, used in *Württemberg* to make light red wines.

Tronçais [tron-say] (France) Forest producing some of the best oak for barrels.

⊼ **Ch. Tronquoy-Lalande** [trron-kwah-lah-lond] (*St. Estèphe Cru Bourgeois, Bordeaux*, France) Tough, traditional wines to buy in ripe years. Better than usual in 2000.

⊼ **Ch. Troplong-Mondot** [trroh-lon mondoh] (*St. Emilion Grand Cru Classé, Bordeaux*, France) Excellently-sited, top-class property whose wines now sell for top-class prices. However, 1999 and 2000 seemed a little less impressive than previous years. Better in 2002.

⊼ **Ch. Trotanoy** [trrot-teh-nwah] (*Pomerol*, *Bordeaux*, France) Never less than fine, and back on especially roaring form since the beginning of the 1990s to compete with *Pétrus*. Some may, however, prefer the lighter style of some of the 1980s than the denser wines on offer today.

⊼ **Ch. Trottevieille** [trrott-vee-yay] (*St. Emilion Premier Grand Cru, Bordeaux*, France) Steadily improving property.

⚘ **Trousseau** [troo-soh] (Eastern France) Grape variety found in *Arbois*.

⊼ **Tsantalis** [tsan-tah-lis] (*Nemea*, Greece) Increasingly impressive producer, redefining traditional varieties.

Tselepos [too-ree-ga nah-see-yoh-nahl/fran-ka] (Greece) Adventurous producer trying out *Gewurztraminer*, among other grapes. Good *Chardonnay* and *Cabernet-Merlot*.

Tualitin Vineyards [too-all-lit-tin] (*Oregon*, USA) Well-established property with good *Pinot Noir*.

⊼ **Tua Rita** [too-wah ree-tah] (*Tuscany*, Italy) Young estate making tiny quantities of wines using grapes from vines that previously went into *Sassicaia*. Giusto dei Notri is the *Bordeaux* blend; Redigaffi is the pure *Merlot*.

⊼ **Tulloch** [tul-lurk] (*Hunter Valley*, Australia) Faded Hunter name sold off by Penfolds etc in 2002.

T

Tunisia [too-nee-shuh] Best known for dessert *Muscat* wines.

🍷 **Cave Vinicole de Turckheim** [turk-hime] (*Alsace*, France) Cooperative whose top wines can often rival those of some of the region's best estates. ★★★★ Tokay Pinot Gris Herrenweg 2001 $$

🍷 **Turkey Flat** (South Australia) Small maker of intensely rich *Barossa Shiraz* and *Grenache*. ★★★★ Shiraz 1999 $$

🍷 **Turley Cellars** (*Napa Valley*, California) The wines here still show the hallmark Helen Turley qualities of intensity and ripeness almost a decade after her departure. This is a source of concentrated *Petite Sirahs* and *Zinfandels*, including small quantities from very old vines.

🍷 **Tursan** [toor-son] (Southwest France) Region, traditionally producing fairly tough reds and dull whites. Super-chef Michel-Guérard (inventor of "Cuisine Minceur") is revolutionizing the region at his Domaine de Bachen. (Reds are *Merlot-Tannat*; white are *Sauvignon-Manseng*.

Tuscany (Italy) Major region, the famous home of *Chianti* and *Brunello di Montalcino* and the new wave of *Super-Tuscan Vini da Tavola* and *IG* wines.

🍷 **Tyrrell's** (*Hunter Valley*, Australia) *Chardonnay* (confusingly sold as *Pinot Chardonnay*) pioneer, and producer of old-fashioned *Shiraz* and (probably most impressively), long-lived, unoaked, lemony *Semillon* and even older-fashioned *Pinot Noir*, which tastes curiously like old-fashioned *Burgundy*. ★★★★ Vat 1 Semillon 1995 $$

U

🍇 **Ugni Blanc** [oo-ñee blon] (France) Undistinguished white grape whose neutrality makes it ideal for distillation. It needs modern winemaking to produce a wine with flavor. In Italy, where it is known as the *Trebbiano*, it takes on a mantle of (spurious) nobility. Try Vin de Pays des Côtes de Gascogne.

🍇 **Ull de Llebre** [ool dur yay-bray] (Spain) Literally "hare's eye." See *Tempranillo*.

Ullage Space between surface of wine and top of cask or, in a bottle, the cork. The wider the gap, the greater the danger of oxidation. Older wines almost always have some degree of ullage; the less the better.

🍷 **Umani Ronchi** [oo-mah-nee ron-kee] (*Marches*, Italy) Innovative producer whose wines, like the extraordinary new Pelago, prove that *Tuscany* and *Piedmont* are no longer the only exciting wine regions in Italy. ★★★★ Vigneto San Lorenzo Rosso Conero 2000 $$$

Umathum [oo-ma-toom] (*Neusiedlersee*, Austria) Producer of unusually good red wines including a wonderful *St. Laurent*. Also top class late harvest wines . ★★★★ Trockenbeerenauslese 2001 $$$

Umbria [uhm-bree-ah] (Italy) Central wine region, best known for white *Orvieto* and *Torgiano*, but also producing the excellent red *Rubesco*.

🍷 **Viña Undurraga** [oon-dur-rah-ga] (*Central Valley*, Chile) Family-owned estate with a range of single varietal wines, including good *Carmenère*.

Unfiltered Filtering a wine can remove flavor – as can *fining* it with egg white or bentonite (clay). Most winemakers traditionally argue that both practices are necessary if the finished wine is going to be crystal-clear and free from bacteria that could turn it to vinegar. Many quality-conscious new-wave producers, however, are now cutting back on *fining* and/or filtering.

Ürzig [oort-zig] (*Mosel-Saar-Ruwer*, Germany) Village on the *Mosel* with steeply sloping vineyards and some of the very best producers, including *Christoffel*, *Mönchhof*, and *Dr. Loosen*. ★★★★★ Urziger Wurzgarten Riesling Kabinett Christoffel Berres 1996 $

🍷 **Utiel-Requena** [oo-tee-yel reh-kay-nah] (*Valencia*, Spain) *DO* of *Valencia*, producing heavy red and good fresh rosé from the Bobal grape.

V

⚱ **Dom. Vacheron** [va-shur-ron] (*Loire,* France) Reliably classy producer of *Sancerre* – including a better-than-average and ageworthy red.

⚱ **Vacqueyras** [va-kay-ras] (*Rhône,* France) *Côtes du Rhône* village with full-bodied, peppery reds which compete with (pricier) *Gigondas*. Dom des Amouriers; Cazaux; Combe; Couroulu; Fourmone; *Jaboulet Aîné;* Dom. de Mont Vac; Montmirail; *Perrin;* de la Soleïade; Tardieu-Laurent; Ch. des Tours; *Cave de Vacqueyras; Vidal-Fleury.* ★★★★★ Vacqueyras Les Christins 2001 Perrin $$

⚱ **Aldo Vajra** [vi-rah] (*Piedmont,* Italy) Producer of rich, complex *Barolo, Barbera* and the deliciously different, *gamey Freisa* delle Langhe. ★★★★ Barbera d'Alba 1999 $$$

Valais [va-lay] (Switzerland) Vineyard area on the upper *Rhône,* making good *Fendant* (*Chasselas*) which surmounts the usual innate dullness of that grape. There are also some reasonable – in all but price – light reds made from the *Pinot Noir.* Bonvin; Imesch; Provins.

Val/Valle d'Aosta [val-day-yos-tah] (Italy) Small, spectacularly beautiful area between *Piedmont* and the French/Swiss border. Better for tourism than wine.

⚱ **Vignerons du Val d'Orbieu** [val-dor-byur] (*Languedoc-Roussillon,* France) Huge, would-be innovative association of over 200 cooperatives and growers that now also owns Cordier in *Bordeaux,* which it is turning into a good brand of generic styles from that region. Examples of Val d'Orbieu's Corbières and Minervois can also be very reliable but, apart from the generally excellent Cuvée Mythique, too many of the other wines leave room for improvement. Reds are far better than whites.

⚱ **Valbuena** [val-boo-way-nah] (*Ribera del Duero,* France) The – relatively – younger version of *Vega Sicilia* hits the streets when it is around five years old.

⚱ **Ch. Valandraud** [va-lon-droh] (*St. Emilion, Bordeaux,* France) The original garage wine; an instant superstar created in 1991 by former bank teller Jean-Luc Thunevin in his garage as competition for *Le Pin.* Production is tiny, quality meticulous, and the price astronomical. Values quintupled following demand from the US and Asia, where buyers seem uninterested in the fact that these wines are – however delicious – actually no finer than *Médoc* classics costing far less. Now joined by l'Interdit de Valandraud, Virginie de Valandraud, and Axelle de Valandraud, and even a Kosher cuvée.

⚱ **Valdeorras** [bahl-day-ohr-ras] (*Galicia,* Spain) A barren and mountainous *DO* in *Galicia* beginning to exploit the *Cabernet Franc*-like local grape Mencia and the indigenous white Godello.

⚱ **Valdepeñas** [bahl-deh-pay-nyass] (*La Mancha,* Spain) *La Mancha DO* striving to refine its rather hefty strong reds and whites. Progress is being made, particularly with reds. Miguel Calatayud; Los Llanos; Felix Solis. ★★★★ Felix Solis, Viña Albali, Bataneros 2001 $$

⚱ **Valdespino** [bahl-deh-spee-noh] (*Jerez,* Spain) Old-fashioned *sherry* company that uses wooden casks to ferment most of its wines. Makes a classic *fino* Innocente and an excellent *Pedro Ximénez.* New ownership may change many things. ★★★★★ Tio Diego Amontillado $$

⚱ **Valdivieso** [val-deh-vee-yay-soh] (*Curico,* Chile) Dynamic winery with a range of good commercial wines, high-quality *Chardonnay* and (particularly) *Pinot Noir* and an award-winning blend of grapes, regions, and years called Caballo Loco whose heretical philosophical approach gives Gallic traditionalists apoplexy. ★★★★★ Caballo Loco no. 6 $$

⚱ **Abazzia di Vallechiara** [ah-bat-zee-yah dee val-leh-kee-yah-rah] (*Piedmont,* Italy) Following the lead of fellow actor Gérard Départieu, Ornella Muti now has her own wine estate, with some first class *Dolcetto.*

⚱ **Valençay** [va-lon-say] (*Loire,* France) *AC* within Touraine, near *Cheverny,* making comparable whites: light and clean, if rather sharp.

⚱ **Valencia** [bah-len-thee-yah] (Spain) Produces quite alcoholic red wines from the Monastrell and also deliciously sweet, grapey *Moscatel de Valencia.*

V

Edoardo Valentini [vah-len-tee-nee] (*Abruzzo*, Italy) Good, old-fashioned Montepulciano d'Abruzzo and unusually good Trebbiano d'Abruzzo.

Vallet Frères [va-lay frehr] (*Burgundy*, France) Small, traditional – not to say old-fashioned – merchant based in *Gevrey-Chambertin*. Also known as Pierre Bourrée. ★★★ Gevrey-Chambertin Clos de la Justice 1999 $$

Valpolicella [val-poh-lee-cheh-lah] (*Veneto*, Italy) Overcommercialized, light, red wine, which should be drunk young to catch its interestingly bitter-cherryish flavor. *Classico* is better; best is *Ripasso*, made by refermenting the wine on the *lees* of an earlier vat. For a different taste, buy *Amarone* or *Recioto*. *Allegrini; Berta.* Only these, and Ripasso wines, should be aged. *Masi, Allegrini; Bolla; Boscaini;* Brunelli; *dal Forno; Guerrieri-Rizzardi; Masi;* Mazzi; *Quintarelli; Le Ragose;* Serego Alighieri; *Tedeschi;* Villa Spinosa; *Zenato;* Fratelli Zeni.

Valréas [val-ray-yas] (*Rhône*, France) Peppery, fairly-priced red wine from a *Côtes du Rhône* village. *Clos Petite Bellane; Earl GAIA* ★★★★ Earl GAIA, Dom. de la Grande Bellane 2001 $

Valtellina [val-teh-lee-na] (*Lombardy*, Italy) Red *DOC* mostly from the *Nebbiolo* grape, of variable quality. Improves with age. The raisiny Sfursat, made from dried grapes, is more interesting. ★★★★ Caven, Al Carmine, Valtellina Superiore Inferno 1998 $$

Varichon et Clerc [va-ree-shon ay klayr] (*Savoie*, France) Good producer of sparkling wine.

Varietal A wine made from and named after one or more grape varieties, e.g., California *Chardonnay*. The French authorities are trying to outlaw such references from the labels of most of their *appellation contrôlée* wines.

Viña los Vascos [los vas-kos] (*Colchagua Valley*, Chile) Estate belonging to Eric de *Rothschild* of *Ch. Lafite*, and shamelessly sold with a *Lafite*-like label. The *Cabernet* Grande Reserve has improved, but the standard *Cabernet* is uninspiring and the white disappointing.

Vasse Felix [vas-fee-liks] (*Margaret River*, Australia) Very classy *Margaret River* winery belonging to the widow of millionaire Rupert Holmes à Court, specializing in juicy, high-quality (multi-regional) *Cabernet*, *Shiraz*, *Semillon*, and *Riesling*. ★★★★ Cabernet Sauvignon 2000 $$

Vaucluse [voh-klooz] (*Rhône*, France) *Côtes du Rhône* region with good *Vin de Pays* and peppery reds and rosés.

Vaud [voh] (Switzerland) Swiss wine area on the shores of Lake Geneva, famous for unusually tangy *Chasselas* (Dorin) and light reds.

Vaudésir [voh-day-zeer] (*Burgundy*, France) Possibly the best of the seven *Chablis Grands Crus*. ★★★★ William Fèvre Chablis Vaudésir 2001 $$$

Vavasour [va-va-soor] (*Marlborough*, New Zealand) Pioneers of the Awatere Valley subregion of *Marlborough*, with *Bordeaux*-style reds, and impressive *Sauvignons* and *Chardonnays*. Dashwood is the *second label*.

VDP (Germany) Association of high-quality producers. Look for the eagle.

VDQS (Vin Délimité de Qualité Supérieur) (France) Official, neither-fish-nor-fowl, designation for wines above *Vin de Pays* but humbler than *AC*.

Veenwouden [fehn-foh-den] (*Paarl*, South Africa) A chance to taste what happens when Michel Rolland of Bordeaux gets his hands on vineyards in South Africa. Hardly surprisingly, riper and richer-tasting Merlot than is traditionally associated with South Africa. ★★★ Merlot 2000 $$$

Vecchio [veh-kee-yoh] (Italy) Old.

Vecchio Samperi [veh-kee-yoh sam-peh-ree] (*Sicily*, Italy) Fine *De Bartoli Marsala* estate, making a dry aperitif similar to an *amontillado sherry*.

Vega Sicilia [bay-gah sih-sih-lyah] (*Ribera del Duero*, Spain) Spain's top wine is a long (10 years) barrel-matured, eccentric *Tempranillo-Bordeaux* blend called Unico. For a more affordable taste of the Vega Sicilia-style, try the supposedly lesser Valbuena.

Vegetal Often used of *Sauvignon Blanc*, like "grassy." Can be complimentary – though not in California or Australia, where it is held to mean "unripe".

Ⓘ **Velich** [veh-likh] (*Burgenland*, Austria) High-quality producers of a wide range of wines including recommendable Chardonnay.

Ⓘ **Caves Velhas** [kah-vash vay-yash] (Portugal) Large improving merchants who blend wine from all over the country, and saved the *Bucelas DO* from extinction. ★★★ Merlot 2001 $

Velho/velhas [vay-yoh/vay-yash] (Portugal) Old, as in red wine.

Velletri [veh-leh-tree] (Italy) Town in the Alban hills (*Colli Albani*), producing mainly *Trebbiano* and *Malvasia*-based whites, similar to *Frascati*.

Ⓦ **Veltliner** See *Grüner Veltliner*.

Vendange [von-donzh] (France) Harvest or vintage.

Vendange tardive [von-donzh tahr-deev] (France) Particularly in *Alsace*, wine from *late-harvested* grapes, usually lusciously sweet.

Vendemmia/Vendimia [ven-deh-mee-yah/ven-dee-mee-yah] (Italy, Spain) Harvest or vintage.

Ⓘ **Venegazzú** [veh-neh-gaht-zoo] (*Veneto*, Italy) Fine, understated *claret*-like Cabernet Sauvignon Vino da Tavola "Super-Veneto" to compete with those *Super-Tuscans*. Needs five years. The black label is better.

Veneto [veh-neh-toh] (Italy) North-eastern wine region, the home of *Soave*, *Valpolicella*, and *Bardolino*.

Venica e Venica [veh-ni-ca] (*Friuli-Venezia Giulia*, Italy) Two brothers who make some of the most flavorsome whites in Collio, including Sauvignon, Pinot Bianco, and Chardonnay.

Ⓘ **Veramonte** [vay-rah-mon-tay] (*Casablanca,* Chile) Venture by Augustin Huneeus of *Franciscan Vineyards*, producing impressive reds, especially the *Merlot* and *Carmenère*). Under the same ownership as *Simi, Sonoma-Cutrer, BRL Hardy* etc. ★★★★★ Primus Carmenère 1999 $$

Ⓦ **Verdejo** [vehr-de-khoh] (Spain) Interestingly herby white grape; confusingly not the *Verdelho* of *Madeira* and Australia, but the variety used for new-wave *Rueda*. ★★★ Telmo Rodriguez, Basa, Rueda Blanco 2002 $

Ⓦ **Verdelho** [in *Madeira*: vehr-deh-yoh; in *Australia*: vur-del-loh] (Madeira/Australia) Grape used for fortified *Madeira* and *white port* and for limey, dry table wine in Australia, especially in the *Hunter Valley*. *Capel Vale; Chapel Hill; Moondah Brook; Sandalford.* ★★★★★ Houghton Verdlho 2002 $$

Ⓦ **Verdicchio** [vehr-dee-kee-yoh] (*Marches*, Italy) Spicy white grape seen in a number of *DOCs*, the best of which is *Verdicchio dei Castelli di Jesi*. In *Umbria* it is a major component of *Orvieto*. ★★★★★ Monte Schiavo, "Le Giuncare" Verdicchio dei Castelli di Jesi Classico Riserva 2000 $$

Ⓘ **Verdicchio dei Castelli di Jesi** [vehr-dee-kee-yoh day-ee kas-tay-lee dee yay-zee] (*Marches*, Italy) Light, clean, and crisp wines to drink with seafood. Bucci; *Garofoli*; Monte Schiavo; Monacesca; *Umani Ronchi*.

Ⓦ **Verduzzo** [vehr-doot-soh] (*Friuli-Venezia Giulia*, Italy) Flavorsome white grape making a dry and a fine *amabile*-style wine in the *Colli Orientale*.

Ⓘ **Vergelegen** [vehr-kur-lek-hen] (*Somerset West*, South Africa) Hi-tech winery producing some of the Cape's finest wines (and absolutely NO *Pinotage*). ★★★★★ Vergelegen 2000 $

Ⓘ **Verget** [vehr-jay] (*Burgundy*, France) Young Mâconnais *négociant* producing impeccable white wines, from *Mâcon Villages* to *Meursault* and *Chablis*.

Ⓦ **Vermentino** [vayr-men-tee-noh] (*Liguria*, Italy) The spicy, dry white grape of the Adriatic and, increasingly, in modern southern French *Vin de Table*.

Ⓦ **Vernaccia** [vayr-naht-chah] (*Tuscany*, Italy) White grape making the Tuscan *DOCG* Vernaccia di San Gimignano (where it's helped by a dash of *Chardonnay*) and *Sardinian* Vernaccia di Oristano. At its best has a distinctive nut and spice flavor. Casale-Falchini; Panizzi; Teruzzi & Puthod. ★★★★ Giovanni Panizzi, Vernaccia di San Gimignano Riserva 2000 $$

Ⓘ **Georges Vernay** [vayr-nay] (*Rhône*, France) The great master of *Condrieu* who can do things with *Viognier* that few seem able to match.

V

☂ **Noël Verset** [vehr-say] (*Cornas, Rhône*) Top-class *Cornas* producer.

☂ **Quinta do Vesuvio** [veh-soo-vee-yoh] (*Douro*, Portugal) Single *quinta port* from the family that owns *Dow's, Graham's, Warre's*, etc. Unlike those wines, a vintage is offered almost every year. ★★★★★ Quinta do Vesuvio 2000 $$$$

☂ **Veuve Clicquot-Ponsardin** [vurv klee-koh pon-sahr-dan] (*Champagne*, France) The distinctive orange label is the mark of reliable non-vintage *Brut*. The *prestige cuvée* is called Grande Dame after the famous Widow Clicquot; the *demi-sec* is a lovely, honeyed wine; and the vintage rosé is now one of the best pink wines in the region. ★★★★★ la Grande Dame 1995 $$$$

Victoria (Australia) Wines range from the *Liqueur Muscats* of *Rutherglen* to the peppery *Shirazes* of *Bendigo* and the elegant *Pinot Noirs* of the *Yarra Valley*.

☂ **Vidal** [vee-dahl] (*Hawkes Bay*, New Zealand) One of New Zealand's top red wine producers. Associated with *Villa Maria* and *Esk Valley*. *Chardonnays* are the strongest suit. ★★★★★ Hawkes Bay Merlot-Cabernet Sauvignon 2001 $$

🍇 **Vidal** [vi-dal] (Canada) A *hybrid* and highly frost-resistant variety looked down on by European authorities but widely grown in *Canada* for spicily exotic *icewine*. *Iniskillin; Rief Estate*. ★★★★ HIllebrand Trius Icewine 2000 $$$

☂ **J. Vidal-Fleury** [vee-dahl flur-ree] (*Rhône*, France) High-quality grower and shipper that belongs to *Guigal*.

VIDE [vee-day] (Italy) Syndicate supposedly denoting finer estate wines.

☂ **Vie di Romans** [vee dee roh-mans] (*Friuli-Venezia Giulia,* Italy) If you thought the only winemaking Gallos were in California, meet Gianfranco Gallo's delicious *Tocai Friulano, Pinot Grigio*, and *Sauvignon Blanc*.

☂ **la Vieille Ferme** [vee-yay fairm] (*Rhône*, France) Organic red and white *Côtes du Ventoux* from the Perrin family of *Château de Beaucastel*. ★★★ La Vieille Ferme 2000 $

Vieilles Vignes [vee-yay veeñ] (France) Wine (supposedly) made from a producer's oldest vines. (In reality, while real vine maturity begins at 25, Vieilles Vignes can mean anything between 15 and 90 years of age.)

☂ **Vietti** [vee-yet-tee] (*Piedmont*, Italy) Impeccable single-vineyard *Barolo* (Rocche di Castiglione; Brunate; and Villero), *Barbaresco*, and *Barbera*. The white *Arneis* is pretty impressive, too.

☂ **Vieux Château Certan** [vee-yur-cha-toh-sehr-tan] (*Pomerol, Bordeaux*, France) Ultraclassy, small *Pomerol* property, known as "VCC'" to its fans, using a lot of Cabernet Franc to produce stylish complex wine. One of the stars of 2001.

☂ **Dom. du Vieux-Télégraphe** [vee-yuhr tay-lay-grahf] (*Rhône*, France) Modern *Châteauneuf-du-Pape* domaine now back on track after a dull patch. Great whites too.

☂ **Vignalta** [veen-yal-tah] (*Veneto,* Italy) Colli Eugeanei producer brewing up a storm with its Gemola (*Merlot-Cabernet Franc*) and Sirio (*Muscat*). ★★★★ Gemola 2000 $$

☂ **Vignamaggio** [veen-yah-maj-yo] (*Tuscany*, Italy) Chianti Classico estate, also producing "Obsession" a *Bordeaux* blend, and a *Cabernet Franc*.

☂ **Ch. Vignelaure** [veen-yah-lawrr] (*Provence*, France) Pioneering estate, now owned by David O'Brien, son of Vincent, the Irish racehorse trainer.

Vignoble [veen-yohbl] (France) Vineyard; vineyard area.

☂ **Villa Maria** (*Auckland*, New Zealand) One of New Zealand's biggest and best producers and a pioneer of Screwcaps. (Its *Pinot Noir* Reserve 2001 which won top wine of the 2002 Air New Zealand Competition was sealed with one.) *Riesling* and *Sauvignon are other* successes.

☂ **Villa Mathilde** [mah-til-day] (*Campania*, Italy) Good DOC Falerno del Massico white and red.

☂ **Villa Sachsen** [zak-zen] (*Rheinhessen*, Germany) Estate with good-rather-than-great, low-yielding vineyards in *Bingen*.

Ⓣ **Villa Russiz** [roos-sitz] (*Friuli-Venezia Guilia*, Italy) Very good Sauvignon and *Pinot Bianco*, even better Chardonnay Gräfin and Merlot Graf de la Tour.

Villages (France) The suffix "villages" e.g., *Côtes du Rhône* or *Mâcon* generally – like *Classico* in Italy – indicates a slightly superior wine from a smaller delimited area encompassing certain villages.

Villany [vee-lah-nyee] (Hungary) Warm area of Hungary with a promising future for soft, young-drinking reds. Vilyan is the best producer here.
★★★★ Vylyan Cabernet 1999 $

Ⓣ **Villard** [vee-yarr] (Chile) Improving wines from French-born Thierry Villard, especially *Chardonnays* from *Casablanca*.
★★★★ **1999 Chardonnay Reserve Esencia $$**

Ⓣ **Ch. Villemaurine** [veel-maw-reen] (*St. Emilion Grand Cru Classé*, *Bordeaux*, France) Often hard wines with overgenerous oak.

Ⓣ **Ch de Villeneuve** [veel-nurv] (*Loire*, France) Outstanding *Saumur* and *Saumur Champigny*.

Ⓣ **Villiera Estate** [vil-lee-yeh-rah] (*Paarl*, South Africa) Reliable range of affordable sparkling and still wines from the energetic Grier family. The *Sauvignons* and Cru Monro red and *Merlot* are the wines to buy.

Ⓣ **Viñas del Vero** [veen-yas del veh-roh] (*Somontano*, Spain) Modern producer of new-wave varietal wines, including recommendable Cabernet Sauvignon.

Vin de Corse [van dur kaws] (*Corsica*, France) *Appellation* within *Corsica*. Good sweet *Muscats* too. Gentile; *Peraldi*; Skalli; Toraccia.

Vin de garde [van dur gahrd] (France) Wine to keep.

Ⓣ Vin de l'Orléanais [van dur low-lay-yon-nay] (*Loire*, France) Small *VDQS* in the Central Vineyards of the *Loire*. See *Orléanais*.

Vin de Paille [van dur pie] (*Jura*, France) Traditional, now quite rare regional specialty; sweet, golden wine from grapes dried on straw mats.

Vin de Pays [van dur pay-yee] (France) Lowest/broadest geographical designation. In theory, simple country wines with regional characteristics. In fact, the producers of some of France's most exciting wines – such as *Dom. de Trévallon* and *Mas de Daumas Gassac* – prefer this designation and the freedom it offers. See *Côtes de Gascogne* and *Vin de Pays d'Oc*.

Ⓣ Vin de Savoie [van dur sav-wah] (Eastern France) Umbrella appellation encompassing mountainous subappellations such as *Apremont* and Chignon.

Vin de table [van dur tahbl] (France) Table wine from no particular area. Labels may not legally mention vintage, grape or region, so wines are theoretically unsaleable (unlike Italy's *Vino da Tavola* designation, from which the *Super-Tuscans*and IGTs were born). Even so, pioneers like les *Vins de Vienne* and *Dulong* are successfully making and selling good examples.

Ⓣ Vin de Thouarsais [twar-say] (*Loire*, France) VDQS for a soft, light red from the *Cabernet Franc*; whites from the *Chenin Blanc*.

Vin doux naturel [doo nah-too-rrel] (France) Fortified – so not really "naturel" at all – dessert wines, particularly the sweet, liquorous *Muscats* of the South, such as Muscat de Beaumes-de-Venise, *Mireval*, and *Rivesaltes*.

Vinea Wachau [vee-nay-hay vak-cow] (*Wachau*, Austria) Top Wachau growers' organisation whose quality designations – *Steinfeder*, *Federspiel* and *Smaragd* – apply to wines that meet the organisation's criteria.

Vin Gris [van gree] (France) Chiefly from *Alsace* and the *Jura*, pale rosé from red grapes pressed after crushing or following a few hours of skin contact.

Vin Jaune [van john] (*Jura*, France) Golden-colored *Arbois* specialty; slightly oxidized – like *fino* sherry. See *Ch. Chalon*.

Vin ordinaire (France) A simple local wine, usually served in carafes.

Vin Santo [veen sahn-toh] (Italy) Traditional white dessert wine made from bunches of grapes hung to dry in barns for up to six months, especially in *Tuscany* and *Trentino*. Can easily compete with top medium *sherry*. Best with sweet almond ("Cantuccine") biscuits. **Altesino; Avignonesi; Badia a Coltibuono; Capezzana; Berardenga; Felsina; Isole e Olena; Poliseano; Selvapiana.**

Vin vert [van vehrr] (*Languedoc-Roussillon*, France) Light *acidic* white wine.

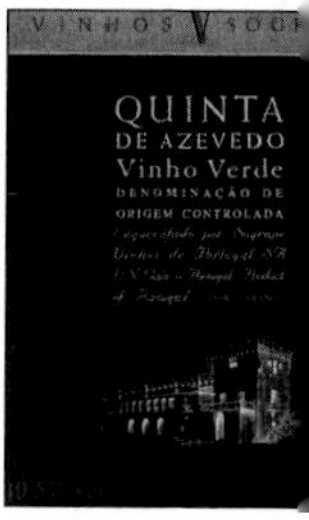

Vinsobres [van sohb-rruh] (*Rhône*, France) A weird name for a Côtes du Rhône Village. *Dom. des Aussellons; Haume-Arnaud; Dom du Coriançon; du Moulin.*

Vine Cliff (*Napa*, California) Estate with flavorsome, oaky *Cabernet* and *Chardonnay*. ★★★★ Reserve Merlot 1999 $$

Viña de Mesa [vee-ñah day may-sah] (Spain) Spanish for table wine.

Vinho Verde [vee-ñoh vehrr-day] (Portugal) Literally "green" wine, meaning young; can be red or white. At worst, dull and sweet. At best delicious, refreshing, and slightly sparkling. Drink young.

Vinícola Navarra [vee-nee-koh-lah na-vah-rah] (*Navarra*, Spain) Ultramodern winemaking and newly-planted vineyards beginning to come on stream. Owned by *Bodegas y Bebida*.

Vinifera [vih-nih-feh-ra] Properly *Vitis vinifera*: species of all European vines: the ones used globally for quality wine.

Vino da Tavola [vee-noh dah tah-voh-lah] (Italy) Table wine, but the *DOC* quality designation net is so riddled with holes that producers of many superb – and pricey – wines have contented themselves with this "modest" *appellation*. Now replaced by *IGT*.

Vino de la Tierra [bee-noh day la tyay rah] (Spain) Spanish wine designation that can offer interesting, affordable, regional wines.

Vino Nobile di Montepulciano [vee-noh noh-bee-lay dee mon-tay-pool-chee-ah-noh] (*Tuscany*, Italy) Potentially (though not often) truly noble, and made from the same grapes as Chianti. Can age well. Rosso di Montepulciano is the lighter, more accessible version. The *Montepulciano* of the title is the *Tuscan* town, not the grape variety. *Avignonesi; Boscarelli; Carpineto;* Casale; del Cerro; *Poliziano;* Tenuta Trerose. ★★★★★ Poliziano 2000 $$$

Vino novello [vee-noh noh-vay-loh] (Italy) New wine; equivalent to French *nouveau*.

Vinopolis London wine museum/theme park.

Vins de Vienne [van duh vee-yen] (*Rhône,* France) A merchant-cum-domaine recently created by Yves Cuilleron, Pierre Gaillard and François Villard, creating examples of the region's appellations, plus innovative wines such as the Sotanum Syrah Vin de Pays from newly planted vines close to Vienne, a Condrieu from semidried grapes and the Réméage Vin de Table. One to watch. ★★★★ Sotanum Vin de Pays des Collines Rhodaniennes 1999 $$

Vintage Year of production.

Vintage Champagne (*Champagne*, France) Wine from a single "declared" year.

Vintage Character (port) (*Douro*, Portugal) Stylishly packaged upmarket *ruby* made by blending various years' wines.

Vintage (port) (*Douro*, Portugal) Produced only in "declared" years, aged in wood, then in the bottle for many years. In "off" years, *port* houses release wines from their top estates as single-*quinta ports*. This style of *port* must be decanted, as it throws a sediment.

Vintners Quality Alliance / VQA (Canada) Quality symbol in Ontario and British Columbia. Treat Canadian non-VQA wine with suspicion.

Viognier [vee-YON-ñee-yay] (*Rhône*, France) Infuriating white variety which, at its best, produces floral, peachy wines. Once limited to the *Rhône* – *Condrieu* and *Ch. Grillet* – but now increasingly planted in southern France, California, and Australia. Benefits from a little – but not too much – contact with new oak. Some of the the Viognier grown in California is in fact *Roussanne*. *Calera; Duboeuf; Guigal; Heggies; Andre Perret; Georges Vernay.* ★★★★ 2001 The Last Ditch Viognier d'Arenberg McLaren Vale $

Viré-Clessé [vee-ray cles-say] (*Burgundy*, France) Newish *AC* centred on the two best white wine communes in *Mâcon*. New rules here have restricted the ability of *Thevenet* to make his sweet wine.

V

☒ **Virgin Hills** [*Victoria,* Australia] A single red blend that is unusually lean in style for Australia and repays keeping.

Visan [vee-so'n] (*Rhône,* France) *Rhône* village; decent reds, poor whites.

Viticulteur (-Propriétaire) (France) Vine grower (-vineyard owner).

🍇 **Viura** [vee-yoo-ra] (Spain) White grape of the *Rioja* region and elsewhere, now being used to greater effect. ★★★★ Marques de Murrieta Gran Reserva Cape Llania 1997 $

☒ **Dom. Michel Voarick** [vwah-rik] (*Burgundy,* France) Old-fashioned wines that avoid the use of new oak. Fine *Corton-Charlemagne.*

☒ **Dom. Vocoret** [vok-ko-ray] (*Burgundy,* France) Classy *Chablis* producer whose wines age well. ★★★ ★ Chablis 2000 $$

☒ **Gianni Voerzio** [vwayrt-zee-yoh] (*Piedmont,* Italy) Not quite as impressive as *Roberto* (see below), but a fine source of *Barbera, Freisa, Arneis,* and *Dolcetto.*

☒ **Roberto Voerzio** [vwayrt-zee-yoh] (*Piedmont,* Italy) New-wave producer of juicy, spicy reds, with a first-rate *Barolo.* ★★★★★ Barolo Cerequio 1998 $$$

☒ **Alain Voge** [vohzh] (*Rhône,* France) Traditional *Cornas* producer who also makes good *St. Péray.* ★★★★ Cornas Vieilles Vignes 2000 $$$

☒ **De Vogüé** [dur voh-gway] (*Burgundy,* France) *Chambolle-Musigny* estate whose brilliant red wines deserve to be kept – for ages.

Volatile acidity (VA) Vinegary character in wine; caused by bacteria.

☒ **Volnay** [vohl-nay] (*Burgundy,* France) Red wine village in the *Côte de Beaune* (the *Caillerets* vineyard, now a *Premier Cru,* was once ranked equal to *le Chambertin*). This is the home of fascinating, plummy, violety reds. Ampeau; d'Angerville; J-M Boillot; Bouchard Père et Fils; Joseph Drouin; Vincent Girardin; Camille Giroud; Francois Buffet; Michel Lafarge; Comtes Lafon; Leroy; Dom de Montille; Pousse d'Or; Régis Rossignol-Changarnier, Vaudoisey; Voillot.

☒ **Castello di Volpaia** [vol-pi-yah] (*Tuscany,* Italy) Top *Chianti* estate with *Super-Tuscans* Coltassala and Balifico. ★★★★ Balifico IGT 1999 $$

☒ **Vosne-Romanée** [vohn roh-ma-nay] (*Burgundy,* France) *Côte de Nuits* red wine village with *Romanée-Conti* among its many grand names, and other potentially gorgeous, plummy, rich wines from many different producers. Arnoux; Cacheux; Confuron-Cotetidot; Engel; Anne Gros; Faiveley; Grivot; Hudelot-Noëllat; Jayer-Gilles; Laurent; Leroy; Méo-Camuzet; Mongeard-Mugneret; Mugneret-Gibourg; Rion; Romanée-Conti; Rouget; Jean Tardy; Thomas-Moillard.

☒ **Voss** (*Sonoma,* California) Californian venture by *Yalumba,* producing lovely, intense *Zinfandel.* ★★★★ Napa Shiraz 1999 $$$

☒ **Voss Estate** (*Martinborough,* New Zealand) Estate, with fine Riesling, *Pinot Noir,* and Waihenga blend of *Cabernet Sauvignon* and *Franc and Shiraz.*

Vougeot [voo-joh] (*Burgundy,* France) *Côte de Nuits commune* comprising the famous *Grand Cru Clos de Vougeot* and numerous growers of varying skill. Amiot-Servelle; Bertagna; Bouchard Père et Fils; Chopin-Groffier; J-J Confuron; Joseph Drouin; Engel; Faiveley; Anne & François Gros; Louis Jadot; Leroy; Denis Mortet; Mugneret-Gibourg; Jacques Prieur; Prieuré Roch; Henri Rebourseau; Rion; Ch. de la Tour. ★★★★★ 1999 Domaine Méo-Camuzet Clos de Vougeot

☒ **la Voulte Gasparets** [voot gas-pah-ray] (*Languedoc-Roussillon,* France) Unusually ambitious estate with single-vineyard bottlings (Romain Pauc is the best) that show just how good *Corbières* can be from the best sites.

Vouvray [voov-ray] (*Loire,* France) Whites from *Chenin Blanc,* ranging from clean dry whites and refreshing sparkling wines to *demi-secs* and honeyed, very long-lived, sweet *moelleux* wines. Des Aubuisières; Champalou; Huët; Foreau; Fouquet; Gaudrelle; Jarry; Mabille; Clos de Nouys; Pichot; Vaugondy.

☒ **Voyager Estate** (*Margaret River,* Australia) Intense, concentrated wines, especially *Semillon, Chardonnay, Cabernet/Merlot.* ★★★★ Chardonnay 2000 $$

☒ **Champagne Vranken** (*Champagne,* France) Group that also just bought *Pommery.* The Vranken wines are not inspiring.

☒ **Vriesenhof** [free-zen-hof] (*Stellenbosch,* South Africa) Jan "Boland" Coetzee makes tough, occasionally classic *Cabernets* and *Pinotages* and improving *Pinot Noir.* Under the same umbrella as Paradyskloof and Talana Hill.

W

Wachau [vak-kow] (Austria) Major wine region producing some superlative *Riesling* from steep, terraced vineyards. Alzinger; *Pichler; Hirtzberger;* Jamek; *Nikolaihof; Prager; Freie Weingärtner Wachau.*

Wachenheim [vahkh-en-hime] (*Pfalz*, Germany) Superior *Mittelhaardt* village which should produce full, rich, unctuous *Riesling*.

Dr Wagner [vahg-nehr] (Mosel-Saar-Ruwer, Germany) Fine concentrated, taut Riesling. ★★★★ Ockfener Bockstein Riesling Kabinett 2001 $$$

Waiheke Island (*Auckland*, New Zealand) Tiny vacation island off Auckland producing some of New Zealand's best – and priciest – reds. *Goldwater Estate; Stonyridge; Te Motu.* ★★★ Te Motu Cabernet/Merlot 1999 $$$

Waipara Springs [wi-pah-rah] (*Canterbury*, New Zealand) Tiny producer offering the opportunity to taste wines from this southern region at their best.

Wairau River [wi-row] (*Marlborough*, New Zealand) Classic Kiwi *Chardonnays* and *Sauvignons* with piercing fruit character.

Wairarapa [why-rah-rah-pah] (New Zealand) Area in the south of the North Island that includes the better-known region of *Martinborough*. Benfield & Delamare; Gladstone; *Matua Valley;* Murdoch James; Nga Waka; *Palliser*

Walker Bay (South Africa) Promising region for *Pinot Noir* and *Chardonnay*. *Hamilton Russell; Bouchard-Finlayson.*

Warre's [waw] (*Douro*, Portugal) Oldest of the big seven *port* houses and a stablemate to *Dow's*, *Graham's*, and *Smith Woodhouse*. Traditional *port*, which is both rather sweeter and more *tannic* than most. The old-fashioned *Late-bottled Vintage* is particularly worth seeking out, too. Quinta da Cavadinha is the *single-quinta*.

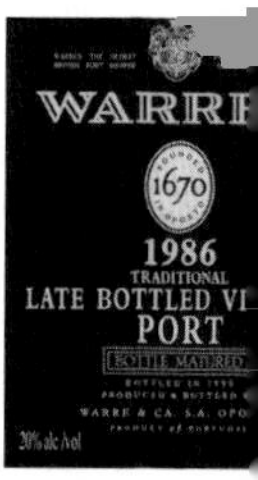

Warwick Estate [wo-rik] (*Stellenbosch*, South Africa) Source of some of South Africa's best reds, including a good *Bordeaux*-blend called Trilogy. *Cabernet Franc* grows extremely well here. ★★★★★ Trilogy 2000 $$

Washington State Underrated (especially in the US) state whose dusty irrigated vineyards produce classy *Riesling*, *Sauvignon*, and *Merlot*. *Col Solare; Columbia; Columbia Crest; L'Ecole No. 41; Hedges; Hogue; Kiona; Leonetti Cellars; Quilceda Creek;* Staton Hills; Ch. Ste. Michelle; *Paul Thomas;* Walla Walla Vintners; *Waterbrook;* Andrew Will; *Woodward Canyon.*

Waterbrook (*Washington State*) High-quality winery with stylish *Sauvignon Blanc*, *Viognier*, and *Chardonnay*, as well as berryish reds.

Jimmy Watson Trophy (*Victoria*, Australia) Coveted trophy for the best young (still-in-barrel) red at the Melbourne Wine Show. Often criticized for hyping stuff that is not necessarily representative of the bottled wine.

Wegeler Erben [vayg-lur ehr-burn] (Germany) Once owned by the Deinhard family; now part of sparkling wine giant Henkell. Wines include top *Mosels* such as *Bernkasteler Doctor* and Wehlener Sonnenuhr.

Wehlen [vay-lehn] (*Mosel-Saar-Ruwer*, Germany) *Mittelmosel village* making fresh, sweet, honeyed wines; look for the *Sonnenuhr* vineyard. JJ Prüm; SA Prüm; *Richter; Selbach-Oster; Wegeler Erben.*

Weingut Dr. Robert Weil [vile] (*Rheingau*, Germany) Suntory-owned, family-run winery with stunning dry and *late-harvest* wines.

Bodegas y Cavas de Weinert [vine-nurt] (Argentina) Excellent *Cabernet Sauvignon* specialist, whose soft, ripe wines last extraordinarily well.

Weingut [vine-goot] (Germany) Wine estate.

Weinkellerei [vine-keh-lur-ri] (Germany) Cellar or winery.

Dr Weins-Prüm [vines-proom] (*Mosel-Saar-Ruwer*, Germany) Fine *Riesling* from top sites. ★★★★ Erdener Prälat Riesling Auslese 2001 $$$

Weinviertel [vine-fehr-tel] (Austria) The largest Austrian wine region of all, seldom thrilling but often good for light whites.

- **Weissburgunder** [vice-bur-goon-dur] (Germany/Austria) The *Pinot Blanc* in Germany and Austria. Relatively rare, so often made with care.
- **Weissherbst** [vice-hairbst] (*Baden*, Germany) Spicy, berryish, dry rosé made from various different grape varieties.
- **Welschriesling** [velsh-reez-ling] Aka *Riesling Italico, Lutomer, Olasz, Laski Rizling*. Often dull grape, unrelated to the *Rhine Riesling*. Can make good dry wine in Austria; at its best when affected by *botrytis*.
- **Wendouree** (*Clare*, Australia) Small winery with a cult following (and full mailing-list) for its long-lived often *Malbec*-influenced reds.
- **Wente Brothers** (*Livermore*, California) Improving family company in *Livermore*. *Murrieta's Well* is still the strongest card.
- **Weingut Domdechant Werner'sches** [vine-goot dom-dekh-ahnt vayr-nehr-ches] (*Rheingau*, Germany) Excellent vineyard sites where *Hochheim* and *Riesling* grapes combine to produce traditional wines that age beautifully.
- Western Australia Very separate from the rest of the continent – some of the people here seriously dream of secession – this state has a very separate wine industry. Growing steadily southward from their origins in the warm Swan Valley, close to Perth, the vineyards now include *Margaret River* (focus of Western Australian winemaking and fine for *Cabernet* and *Chardonnay*), Pemberton (a good area for *Pinot Noir*), and Great Southern.
- **De Wetshof Estate** [vets-hof] (*Robertson*, South Africa) *Chardonnay* pioneer, Danie de Wet makes up to seven different styles of wine.
- **William Wheeler Winery** (*Sonoma*, California) Producer whose Quintet brings together *Pinot Meunier, Pinot Noir, Grenache*, and *Cabernet Sauvignon*.
- **White Cloud** (New Zealand) Commercial white made by *Nobilo*.
- *White port* (*Douro*, Portugal) Semidry aperitif, drunk by its makers with tonic water, which shows what they think of it. *Churchill's* make a worthwhile version.
- **Whitehall Lane** (*Napa Valley*, California) Producer of an impressive range of *Merlots* and *Cabernets*.
- Wien [veen] (Austria) Region close to the city of Vienna, producing ripe-tasting whites and reds. Mayer; Wieninger.
- **Fritz Wieninger** [vee-nin-gur] (Wien, Austria) Characterful wines with depth and elegance.
- **Wignall's** (*Western Australia*, Australia) *Pinot Noir* of originality and conviction.
- **Wild Horse** (*San Luis Obispo*, California) *Chardonnays, Pinot Blancs*, and *Pinot Noirs* are all good, but the perfumed *Malvasia Bianca* is the star.
- **Willakenzie Estate** (*Oregon*, USA) Newish, modern property with elegant wines of great promise.
- Willamette Valley [wil-AM-et] (*Oregon*) The heart of Oregon's *Pinot Noir* vineyards, on slopes that drain into the Willamette River.
- **William & Humbert** (*Jerez*, Spain) Very good Pando fino and Dos Cortados Palo Cortado, reliable Dry Sack medium amontillado.
- **Williams Selyem** [sel-yem] (*Sonoma*, California) Recently dissolved partnership producing fine *Burgundian*-style *Chardonnay* and *Pinot Noir*.
- Wiltingen [vill-ting-gehn] (*Mosel-Saar-Ruwer*, Germany) Saar village, making elegant, slatey wines. Well known for the *Scharzhofberg* vineyard.
- **Wing Canyon** (*Mount Veeder*, California) Small *Cabernet Sauvignon* specialist with vineyards in the hills of *Mount Veeder*. Intense, blackcurrany wines.
- Winkel [vin-kel] (*Rheingau*, Germany) Village with a reputation for complex delicious wine, housing *Schloss Vollrads* estate.
- *Winzerverein/Winzergenossenschaft* [vint-zur-veh-rine/vint-zur-geh-noss-en-shaft] (Germany) Cooperative.
- **Wirra Wirra Vineyards** (*McLaren Vale*, Australia) First-class *Riesling* and *Cabernet* that, in best vintages, is sold as The Angelus.
- **Hans Wirsching** [veer-shing] (*Franken*, Germany) Large estate with very good vineyards, producing structured, elegant wines. One of the more go-ahead producers in Franken.

Wither Hills (*Marlborough*, New Zealand) Instantly successful new venture from Brent Marris – former winemaker at *Delegat's*. Recently sold to *Lion Nathan*, brewery-giant-owners of *Petaluma* and *St Hallett*. The concentrated Pinot Noir is especially good. ★★★★ Sauvignon Blanc 2002 $$

WO (Wine of Origin) (South Africa) Official European-style certification system that is taken seriously in South Africa.

J.L. Wolf [volf] (*Pfalz*, Germany) Classy estate, recently reconstituted by *Dr. Loosen*. ★★★★ Forster Ungeheuer Riesling Spätlese Trocken $$$

Wolfberger [volf-behr-gur] (*Alsace*, France) Brand used by the dynamic Eguisheim cooperative for highly commercial wines.

Wolffer Estate (*New York*) Long Island winery gaining a local following for its *Merlot* and *Chardonnay*.

Wolff-Metternich [volf met-tur-nikh] (*Baden*, Germany) Good, rich *Riesling* from the granite slopes of *Baden*.

Woodward Canyon (*Washington State*) Small producer of characterful but subtle *Chardonnay* and *Bordeaux*-style reds that compete with some of the over-hyped efforts from California. *Semillons* are pretty impressive too. ★★★★ Klipsun Vineyard Cabernet Sauvignon 1999 $$$

Württemberg [voor-thm-behrg] (Germany) *Anbaugebiet* surrounding the Neckar area, producing more red than any other German region.

Würzburg [voor-ts-burg] (*Franken*, Germany) Great *Silvaner* country, though there are some fine *Rieslings* too. Some excellent steep vineyards. Bürgerspital; *Juliusspital*.

Wyken (*Suffolk*, UK) Producer of one of England's most successful red wines (everything's relative) and rather better *Bacchus* white.

Wyndham Estate (*Hunter Valley*, Australia) Ultracommercial *Hunter/Mudgee* producer that, like *Orlando*, now belongs to Pernod-Ricard. Wines – all of which bear memorably repetitive bin numbers – are distinctly drier than they used to be, but they are still recognizably juicy in style. Quite what that firm's French customers would think of these often rather jammy blockbusters is anybody's guess. ★★★★ Bin 999 Merlot 2001 $$

Wynns (*Coonawarra*, Australia) Subsidiary of *Penfolds*, based in *Coonawarra*, and producer of the *John Riddoch Cabernet* and Michael *Shiraz*, both of which are only produced in good vintages and sell fast at high prices. There is also a big buttery *Chardonnay* and (given the red wine reputation of this region) a surprisingly good *Riesling*. ★★★★ Wynns Coonawarra Estate Riesling 2002 $$

X

Xacoli [tcha-koh-lee] See Chacoli.

Xanadu [za-na-doo] (*Margaret River*, Australia) The reputation here was built on *Semillon*, but the *Cabernet* and *Chardonnay* are both good, too. A takeover by venture capitalists who are eager to buy more wineries (*Normans* is a recent aquisition) is helping to catapult Xanadu into the ranks of Australia's most dynamic producers. The wines are well-enough made to justify the commercial success. ★★★★★ Shiraz 2001 $$$

Xarel-lo [sha-rehl-loh] (*Catalonia*, Spain) Fairly basic grape exclusive to *Catalonia*. Used for *Cava*; best in the hands of *Jaume Serra*. ★★★ NV Jaume Serra Cava Brut Reserva $

Xynasteri [ksee-nahs-teh-ree] (Cyprus) Indigenous white grape.

Y

"Y" d'Yquem [ee-grek dee-kem] (*Bordeaux*, France) Hideously expensive dry wine of *Ch. d'Yquem*, which, like other such efforts by *Sauternes châteaux*, is of greater academic than hedonistic interest. (Under ludicrous Appellation Contrôlée rules, dry white wine from Sauternes properties has to be labeled as "Bordeaux Blanc" – like the region's very cheapest dry white wine.)

Yakima Valley [yak-ih-mah] (*Washington State*) Principal winegrowing region of *Washington State*. Particularly good for *Merlot, Riesling*, and *Sauvignon*. Blackwood Canyon; Chinook; *Columbia Crest; Columbia Winery; Hogue; Kiona;* Ch. Ste. Michelle; Staton Hills; Stewart; Tucker; Yakima River.

Yalumba [ya-lum-ba] (*Barossa Valley*, Australia) Associated with *Hill-Smith, Heggies, Pewsey-Vale,* and *Jansz* in Australia, *Nautilus* in New Zealand, and *Voss* in California. Producers of good-value reds and whites under the Oxford Landing label. Also produces more serious vineyard-designated reds, dry and sweet whites, and appealing sparkling wine, including *Angas Brut* and the excellent Cuvée One *Pinot Noir-Chardonnay*.
★ ★ ★ ★ ★ Yalumba Barossa Shiraz 2000 $$$

Yarra Ridge [ya-ra] (Australia) *Mildara-Blass* label that might lead buyers to imagine that its wines all come from vineyards in the *Yarra Valley*. In fact, like *Napa Ridge*, this is a brand that is used for wine from vineyards in other regions. European laws, which are quite strict on this kind of thing, also apply to imported non-European wines, so bottles labeled "Yarra" and sold in the EU will be from Yarra.

Yarra Valley [ya-ra] (*Victoria*, Australia) Historic wine district whose "boutiques" make top-class *Burgundy*-like *Pinot Noir* and *Chardonnay* (*Coldstream Hills* and *Tarrawarra*), some stylish *Bordeaux*-style reds, and, at *Yarra Yering*, a brilliant *Shiraz*. De Bortoli; *Dom. Chandon (Green Point); Coldstream Hills;* Diamond Valley; Long Gully; *Mount Mary;* Oakridge; St. Huberts; Seville Estate; *Tarrawarra; Yarra Yering; Yering Station.*

Yarra Yering [ya-ra yeh-ring] (*Yarra Valley*, Australia) Bailey Carrodus proves that the *Yarra Valley* is not just *Pinot Noir* country by producing a complex *Cabernet* blend, including a little *Petit Verdot* (Dry Red No.1) and a *Shiraz* (Dry Red No.2), in which he puts a bit of *Viognier*. Underhill is the *second label*. These have now been joined by Sangiovese, Viognier, and a "portsorts" fortified.

Yecla [yeh-klah] (Spain) Generally uninspiring red wine region.

Yellowglen (South Australia) Producer of uninspiring basic sparkling wine and some really fine top-end fare, including the "Y", which looks oddly reminiscent of a sparkling wine called "J" from Judy Jordan in California.

Yering Station (*Victoria*, Australia) High quality young *Yarra Valley* estate, with rich, but stylish *Chardonnay* and *Pinot Noir,* and now *Shiraz-Vignier*
★ ★ ★ ★ ★ Reserve Shiraz / Viognier 2001 $$

Yeringberg (*Victoria*, Australia) Imposing old *Yarra Valley* estate making *Rhône* style reds and whites that are worth looking out for.

Yonder Hill (*Stellenbosch*, South Africa) New winery making waves with well-oaked reds. ★ ★ ★ ★ ★ Merlot 2001 $$

Ch. Yon-Figeac [yo'n fee-jak] (*Bordeaux*, France) Not as fine as Château Figeac itself, but this Grand Cru Classé's wines are supple and fruity; very attractive, but not immensely long-lived.

Yonne [yon] (*Burgundy*, France) Northern *Burgundy* departement in which *Chablis* is to be found.

Young's (California, USA) *Barbera* and *Zinfandel* are the ones to look for.

Ch. d'Yquem [dee-kem] (*Sauternes Premier Cru Supérieur, Bordeaux,* France) Sublime *Sauternes*. The grape pickers are sent out several times to select the best grapes. Not produced every year.

Z

Zaca Mesa [za-ka may-sa] (*Santa Barbara,* California) Fast-improving winery with a focus on spicy *Rhône* varietals.

Zandvliet [zand-fleet] (*Robertson,* South Africa) Estate well-thought-of in South Africa for its *Merlot*. ★★★ Kalkveld Syrah 2000 $$

ZD [zee-dee] (*Napa,* California) Long-established producer of very traditional, Californian, oaky, tropically fruity *Chardonnay* and plummy *Pinot Noir*. Also the producer of the highly acclaimed *Abacus*.

Zeitgeist [Zight-Gihst] (*McBeal-Vally,* California) Huge, starry enterprise, launched by friends, and ex-City casualties, Bill Buffy and Ellen Frasier. The *Grand-Frère, Millionaire, Aile d'Ouest* cuvées have all gained high ratings, but the *Celebrité Evadée* remains a weak link, and by no means a good buy.

Zell [tzell] (*Mosel-Saar-Ruwer,* Germany) *Mosel Bereich* and village, making flowery *Riesling*. Famous for the once widely-available *Schwarze Katz* (black cat) *Grosslage*.

Zema Etate [zee-mah] (*South Australia*) High-quality *Coonawarra* estate with characteristically rich, berryish reds.

Zenato [zay-NAH-toh] (*Veneto,* Italy) Successful producer of modern *Valpolicella* (particularly *Amarone*), *Soave*, and *Lugana*. ★★★ Villa Flora Lugana 2002 $$

Zentralkellerei [tzen-trahl-keh-lur-ri] (Germany) Massive central cellars for groups of cooperatives in six of the *Anbaugebiete* – the *Mosel-Saar-Ruwer* Zentralkellerei is Europe's largest cooperative.

Fattoria Zerbina [zehr-bee-nah] (*Emilia-Romagna,* Italy) The eye-catching wine here is the Marzeno di Marzeno *Sangiovese-Cabernet,* but this producer deserves credit for making one of the only examples of Albana di Romagna to warrant the region's *DOCG* status.

Zevenwacht [zeh-fen-vakht] (*Stellenbosch,* South Africa) One of South Africa's better producers of both *Shiraz* and *Pinotage.* Has also been successful with *Sauvignon Blanc* and *Pinot Noir.*

Zibibbo [zee-BEE-boh] (*Sicily,* Italy) Light *Muscat* for easy summer drinking.

Zierfandler [zeer-fan-dlur] (Austria) Indigenous grape used in Thermenregion to make lightly spicy white wines. ★★★ 2000 Weingut Spaetrot Zierfandler Trockenbeerenauslese 2001 $$$$

Zilliken [tsi-li-ken] (*Saar,* Germany) Great *late-harvest Riesling* producer.

Zimbabwe An industry started by growing grapes in ex-tobacco fields is beginning to attain a level of international adequacy.

Dom. Zind-Humbrecht [zind-hoom-brekht] (*Alsace,* France) Extraordinarily consistent producer of ultraconcentrated, single-vineyard wines and good *varietals* that have won numerous awards from the *International Wine Challenge* and drawn *Alsace* to the attention of a new generation of wine drinkers. ★★★★ Gewurztraminer 2000 $$$

Zinfandel [zin-fan-del] (California, Australia, South Africa) Versatile grape, producing everything from dark, jammy, leathery reds in California, to (with a little sweet *Muscat*) pale pink "blush" wines, and even a little fortified wine that bears comparison with *port*. Also grown by *Cape Mentelle* and *Nepenthe* in Australia, and *Blaauwklippen* in South Africa and, as *Primitivo*, by many producers in southern Italy. Cline; Clos la Chance; De Loach; Edmeades; Elyse; Gary Farrell; Green & Red; Lamborn Family Vineyards; Ch. Potelle; Quivira; Rafanelli; Ravenswood; Ridge; Rocking Horse; Rosenblum; St. Francis; Steele; Storybook Mountain; Joseph Swan; Turley; Wellington. ★★★★★ Ridge Geyserville 2000 $$$

Don Zoilo [don zoy-loh] (*Jerez,* Spain) Classy *sherry* producer.

Zonin [zoh-neen] (*Veneto,* Italy) Dynamic company producing good wines in *Veneto, Piedmont,* and *Tuscany.*

Zweigelt [tzvi-gelt] (Austria) Berryish red wine grape, more or less restricted to Austria and Hungary. Angerer; Hafner; Kracher; Mariell; Müller; Umathum. ★★★★ Mariell Wetzlasberg 2000 $$$

International Wine Challenge 2003

THE WORLD'S BIGGEST CONTEST

Everything has to start somehow. The International Wine Challenge began life as a very different exercise to the hugely sophisticated event that took place in May 2003. 19 years earlier, in 1984, the wine writer and broadcaster Charles Metcalfe and I thought it might be interesting to compare a few English white wines with examples from other countries for a feature in **Wine International**, the magazine we had launched in the UK a few months earlier. So, we set out some 50 carefully camouflaged bottles in the basement of a London restaurant, and invited a group of experts to mark them out of 20. We never imagined that the home team would surprise everyone by beating well-known bottles from Burgundy, the Loire, and Germany – or that the modest enterprise we had immodestly called *"The International Wine Challenge"* would develop into the world's biggest, most respected wine competition.

The following year's *Challenge* attracted around 200 entries, while the third and fourth competitions saw numbers rise to 500 and 1,000 respectively. This annual doubling slowed down eventually, but by the end of the century we were within spitting distance of 10,000 entries, produced in countries ranging from France and Australia to Thailand and Uruguay. In 2003 there were no fewer than 9,400 individual wines.

ORIGINS IN LONDON

It is no accident that the *International Wine Challenge* was born in London. For centuries, British wine drinkers have enjoyed the luxury of being able to enjoy wines from a wide variety of countries. Samuel Pepys may have been a fan of Château Haut-Brion from Bordeaux, but plenty of other 18th-century sophisticates in London (and elsewhere in Britain) were just as excited about the sweet, late-harvest whites that were being produced at that time by early settlers in South Africa. More recently, as wine became steadily more popular, wines from California, Australia, New Zealand, and South America all found their way to these shores. Other arrivals were wines from regions like Languedoc-Roussillon in France and Southern Italy, that had often been overlooked. As the 21st century dawned, Britain's biggest supermarket chains boasted daunting ranges of 700–800 different wines. A well-run competition provided an invaluable means of sorting the best and most interesting of these bottles from the rest.

Above: every bottle is numbered and its identity hidden within specially-produced bags. Below: just some of the nearly 40,000 samples.

The Tasting Panels

If the diversity of the wines on offer in Britain created a need for the *International Wine Challenge*, the calibre of this country's wine experts provided the means with which to run the competition. The nation that spawned the Institute of Masters of Wine – the body whose members have to pass the world's toughest wine exam – is also home to some of the most respected wine critics and merchants on the planet. These are the men and women – some 370 of them – who, along with winemakers and experts from overseas such as Chris Gallo, Mireia Torres, and Charles Symington of Dow's port make up the tasting panels for the *Challenge*. So, a set of wines might well have been judged by a group

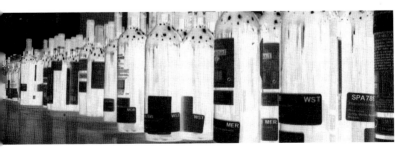

Above: One cork was pulled every 20 seconds over nine days of tasting. Below, the tasters at work: left – Helen McGinn, senior buyer for Tesco, Britain's biggest wine retailer, considers a red. Right - Chris Gallo of E&J Gallo and Mireia Torres of Torres discuss a white.

that included a traditional merchant, the buyer from a major supermarket chain, an Australian winemaker, a French sommelier, and a wine critic from Portugal. Considering these differences in background and experience, argument between the tasters is surprisingly rare. When agreement is impossible, Co-Chairmen Robert Joseph, Charles Metcalfe, and Derek Smedley MW are called in to adjudicate.

Two-round format

During the first of the two rounds of the competition, wines are assessed to decide whether or not they are worthy of an award – be it a medal or a seal of approval. At this stage, typicality is taken into account, and tasters are informed that they are dealing, for example, with a Chablis, a California Chardonnay or a Chianti.

Around a third of the wines will leave the competition with no award. A further 30 percent will get Seals of Approval; the remainder will be given Gold, Silver, or Bronze medals. The entries that have been thought to be medal-worthy in the first round, and the "seeded" entries that have already won recognition in the previous year's competition, then pass directly on to the second round. Now, the judges face the trickier task of deciding on the specific award each wine should receive – if any (they can still demote or throw wines out completely). The wines are still grouped by grape and region, but now their origins remain secret – there is no place for prejudices on behalf of or against a region or country. Modern winemaking methods can make spotting nationality quite tricky.

Super-Jurors

As a final check, after it has been open for an hour or so, every wine goes before a team of "Super-Jurors". These are mostly Masters of Wine (including 41 of the just over 232 who have passed the gruelling exam since it was first set nearly half a century ago), and professional buyers from leading merchants and retailers whose daily work involves the accurate assessment

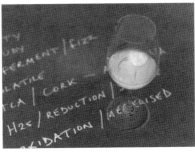

Apart from asssesing potential medal-winners the Super-Jurors also verified faults detected by other tasters. They confirmed that 4.9% were spoiled by bad corks, while 2.8% had other faults.

of hundreds of wines. The vital role of the Super-Jurors is both to ensure that tasters have not been overly harsh on wines that were reticent when first poured, or on wines with subtle cork taint that was initially unnoticed – and to watch out for entries that may have been over-estimated because of the immediate attraction of oakiness, for example. If two Super-Jurors agree, they can jointly up- or downgrade a wine.

TROPHY WINNERS

The Super-Jurors also decide which Gold medal winners deserve the additional recognition of a Trophy. These supreme awards can be given for any style, region, or nationality of wine. The judges are free to withhold trophies and to create them as they see appropriate (this year's Marsanne Trophy is a good example). The 2003 Trophy winners were as follows:

Cabernet/Merlot Viña Valdivieso Caballo Loco No 6
Shiraz/Syrah Graham Beck "The Ridge" Syrah 2000
  Viña Perez Cruz Syrah Reserva Limited Edition 2002
Italian Red Barone Ricasoli, Casalferro 2000
  Laithwaite's Private Cellars Edizione NV
Pinot Noir Domaine Michel Gros, Nuits-Saint-Georges 2001
  Domaine Carneros, Avant-Garde Pinot Noir 2001
Portuguese Red Esporão Touriga Nacional 2001
South-West French Red Château Peyros Greenwich 43N 2000
Spanish Red Mas d'en Gil Coma Vella Priorat 2000
Tempranillo Familia Zuccardi Q 2001
Zinfandel Ridge Geyserville 2000
Chardonnay Domaine Laroche Chablis Premier Cru Les Vaudevey 2001
  Clos du Bois Alexander Valley Reserve Chardonnay 2001
Grüner Veltliner Jurtschitsch-Sonnhof Alte Reben 2002

Italian White Monte Schiavo Verdicchio dei Castelli di Jesi Classico Riserva "Le Giuncare" 2000

Marsanne Rutherglen Estate Marsanne 2002

Pinot Gris Pierre Sparr Pinot Gris Réserve 2002

Riesling Horst Sauer, Escherndorfer Lump Riesling Spätlese Trocken 2002

Sauvignon Blanc Morton Estate Stone Creek Sauvignon Blanc 2002 Dom Ruinart Blanc de Blancs 1993

Sparkling Wine Charles Heidsieck Millésime Brut Rosé 1996

Late Harvest de Bortoli Noble One 2000

Dessert Wine Moncaro, Passito 2000

Fortified Muscat Seppelts DP63 Grand Rutherglen Muscat

Port Warre's Vintage Port 2000

Sherry Gonzalez Byass Apostoles 30-Year-Old Palo Cortado Muy Viejo

Top Trophy winners

Finest Red Barone Ricasoli, Casalferro 2000

Finest White Domaine Laroche Chablis Premier Cru Les Vaudevey 2001

Finest Sparkling (The Daniel Thibault Trophy) Dom Ruinart Blanc de Blancs 1993

Finest Fortified Warre's Vintage Port 2000

GOOD VALUE AWARDS

We are often asked if we take account of the price of the wines we are tasting. How can one judge a $5 California red in the same way as a $50 Napa Cabernet? In fact, knowing the cost of a wine is actually a hindrance: we all have our own notion of value and prestige; prices vary from one state or retailer to another and they go up or down after the competition. So, all of the medals listed on the following pages were earned irrespective of price.

But that's not to say that we're not interested in value for money. Once the medals and seals of approval have been distributed, we carefully compare the awards with approximate prices *(see chart on page 269)*. Entries that cost significantly less than the average for their level of medal get their own Good Value awards, over 750 of which are listed in the following pages, along with Gold medal winners.

Following a separate blind-tasting by the super-jurors of the most highly-rated and widely-available Good Value wines, the very best buys of all are named *Great* Value Wines of the Year. Look out for these; they tend to fly out of the shops very quickly and, of course, once a vintage or cuvée has sold out, it can never be replaced.

THE GREAT VALUE WINES OF THE YEAR

Red
Wolf Blass President's Selection Cabernet Sauvignon 2001, Australia
Wakefield Shiraz 2002, Australia
Grand 'Arte Trincadeira Red 2000, Portugal
Familia Zuccardi Q Tempranillo 2001, Argentina

White
d'Arenberg "The Hermit Crab" Marsanne-Viognier 2002, Australia
Pierre Sparr Pinot Gris Reserve 2002, France
Tesco Great Southern Riesling 2002, Australia
Domaine du Bois Viognier 2002, France

Rosé
Fetzer Vineyards Valley Oaks Syrah Rosé 2002, USA

Sparkling
Champagne Baron Fuenté, Rosé Dolores NV
Champagne Paul Langier Brut NV
Champagne Beaumont des Crayères NV

Fortified
Graham's Crusted Port Bottled 1999
Don Nuño Dry Oloroso
Dow's Crusted Port Bottled 1998

CATEGORY		STILL REDS AND WHITES	SPARKLING, PORT, AND MADEIRA	SWEET, FORTIFIED, MUSCAT, AND SHERRY
Gold medal	Ⓖ	Less than **$25**	Less than **$35**	Less than **$30**
Silver medal	Ⓢ	Less than **$15**	Less than **$25**	Less than **$18**
Bronze medal	Ⓑ	Less than **$10**	Less than **$18**	Less than **$15**
Seal of Approval	A	Less than **$8**	Less than **$12**	Less than **$10**

HOW TO USE THE AWARDS LIST

Every wine in this list gained an award at the 2003 *International Wine Challenge*. The wines are listed by country and style, with up to six headings: red, white, sweet, rosé, sparkling, and fortified.

Under each heading the wines are listed in price order, from the least to the most expensive. Wines of the same price are listed in medal order: Gold, Silver, and Bronze.

All Silver and Bronze medal winners and Seal of Approval wines listed are entries that were also given Good Value awards, following comparison of their average retail price and the average price for the award they received in the *International Wine Challenge*. Following consultation with leading retailers appropriate price limits were established for particular styles of wine. A Good Value sparkling wine or port, for example, might sell at a higher price than a red table wine with the same medal.

This list does not include the Silver and Bronze medal winners and Seal of Approval wines that did not win Good Value awards (for these, visit *internationalwinechallenge.com*). All of the 230 Gold medal winners and Trophy winners – the finest wines in the competition – do appear. For full details of the price limits that were used to allocate Good Value awards, turn to page 269.

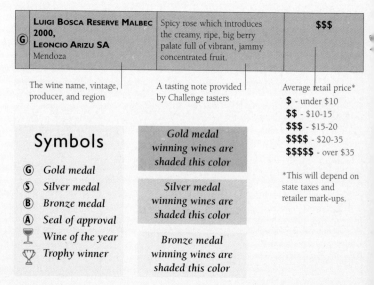

| ⓖ | **LUIGI BOSCA RESERVE MALBEC 2000,** **LEONCIO ARIZU SA** Mendoza | Spicy rose which introduces the creamy, ripe, big berry palate full of vibrant, jammy concentrated fruit. | **$$$** |

The wine name, vintage, producer, and region

A tasting note provided by Challenge tasters

Average retail price*
$ - under $10
$$ - $10-15
$$$ - $15-20
$$$$ - $20-35
$$$$$ - over $35

*This will depend on state taxes and retailer mark-ups.

Symbols

ⓖ *Gold medal*
Ⓢ *Silver medal*
Ⓑ *Bronze medal*
Ⓐ *Seal of approval*
🏆 *Wine of the year*
🏆 *Trophy winner*

Gold medal winning wines are shaded this color

Silver medal winning wines are shaded this color

Bronze medal winning wines are shaded this color

ARGENTINA

Chasing the Chileans hard, Argentina's wine industry is offering one of the few rays of light to this troubled economy of the New World when it comes to offering value for money. There are – inevitably – plenty of Cabernets, Merlots, and Chardonnays, but there are also some styles that are uniquely Argentine, such as the grapey Torrontes whites and the peppery reds made from the Malbec and the refreshingly juicy ones made from the Bonarda. It was interesting, too, to see an Argentine Tempranillo snatching a Gold medal from beneath the noses of the Spaniards.

ARGENTINA • SPARKLING

(B)	**GALA BRUT NV, CEPAS DE MENDOZA** Mendoza	Mature, gold color, rich bready nose, and a soft, deep palate of peppery, concentrated fruit.	**$$**

ARGENTINA • WHITE

(A)	**LA RIOJANA ARGENTINIAN WHITE NV, LA RIOJANA** La Rioja	Fresh wine with ripe citrus notes and refreshing acidity.	**$**
(A)	**TRIVENTO CHARDONNAY CHENIN 2002, BODEGAS TRIVENTO** Mendoza	Honeyed fruit allied to gentle acidity.	**$**
(A)	**LA BOCA TORRRONTES CHARDONNAY 2002, MEDRANO ESTATE** Mendoza	Aromatic wine with floral notes and soft finish.	**$**
(A)	**INTI TORRONTES CHARDONNAY 2002, LA RIOJANA** La Rioja	Perfumed with floral notes and sporting a rich a waxy finish.	**$**
(A)	**LA BOCA TORRONTES CHARDONNAY 2002, MEDRANO ESTATE** Mendoza	Crisp and aromatic with a slightly floral finish.	**$**
(A)	**TANGUERO CHARDONNAY 2002, FINCA FLICHMAN** Mendoza	Buttery with a refreshing citrus finish.	**$**

(A) ORIGIN CHARDONNAY CHENIN 2002, ORIGIN FINCA EUGENIO BUSTOS San Juan	Apple and citrus style with a good clean finish.	$
(A) OLA TORRONTES 2002, NIETO CARBO Y A SENETINER Mendoza	Crunchy citrus fruit allied to muscat-like perfume.	$
(A) TRIVENTO CHARDONNAY 2002, BODEGAS TRIVENTO Mendoza	Good pure fruit and decent mouthfeel.	$
(B) MALAMBO CHENIN BLANC CHARDONNAY 2001, BODEGAS ESMERALDA Mendoza	Vanilla tones overlay the warm tropical mango and pineapple fruit which displays good concentration.	$
(B) TRIVENTO VIOGNIER 2002, BODEGAS TRIVENTO Mendoza	Warm dried apricot on the nose. The palate has honeycomb, peaches and flowers.	$
(B) INTI PINOT GRIGIO 2002, LA RIOJANA La Rioja	Magical meld of delicate aromatic spring flowers and juicy drippingly ripe pear fruit.	$$

ARGENTINA • ROSE

(A) SLINKY ROSÉ 2002, LA RIOJANA La Rioja	Seductive fresh berry style. Slinky soft fruit-driven finish!	$

ARGENTINA • RED

(A) LAS LLANURAS MALBEC 2001, LES GRANDS CHAIS DE FRANCE Mendoza	Mulberry scented with a richly spiced palate.	$
(A) MENDOZA RED WINE 2002, PEÑAFLOR Mendoza	Juicy with soft structure and ripe berry fruit.	$
(B) ORIGIN MALBEC MERLOT 2002, ORIGIN WINES Mendoza	The breadth and fleshiness of Merlot goes hand in hand with dark, structural Malbec.	$

(B) **TRIVENTO SHIRAZ MALBEC 2002, BODEGAS TRIVENTO** Mendoza	Very dark prune, plum, and blackberry fruit on the nose and palate.	$
(A) **STOWELLS MALBEC TEMPRANILLO , STOWELLS** Mendoza	Jammy with a thick blueberry palate.	$
(A) **SLINKY SHIRAZ 2002, LA RIOJANA** La Rioja	Layered blackberry fruit and soft rich clear structure.	$
(A) **LA BOCA MALBEC BONARDA 2002, MEDRANO ESATE** Mendoza	Soft cherry-driven style with lovely round mouthfeel.	$
(A) **LA BOCA MALBEC 2002, MEDRANO ESTATE** Mendoza	Richly fruited with complex violet nuances.	$
(A) **LA PUERTA SYRAH 2002, VALLE DE LA PUERTA** La Rioja	Rich and ripe with an unctuous damson fruit palate.	$
(A) **TANGUERO SHIRAZ 2001, FINCA FLICHMAN** Mendoza	Sweet and supple with leather and smoke notes.	$
(A) **ORGANIC TEMPRANILLO CABERNET , LES CAVES DE LANDIRAS**	Shows berry and currant notes allied to soft tannins and a decent finish.	$
(A) **LA BOCA TEMPRANILLO 2002, MEDRANO ESTATE** Mendoza	Pure berry fruit aromas and a lush, spiced palate.	$
(A) **LA BOCA MALBEC SYRAH 2002, MEDRANO ESTATE** Mendoza	Spicy with berry and wood-smoke aromas.	$
(A) **TRIVENTO BONARDA 2002, BODEGAS TRIVENTO** Mendoza	Lush cherry style with good depth and silky tannin.	$
(A) **MALAMBO BONARDA 2002, BODEGAS ESMERALDA** Mendoza	Rich and concentrated with lovely mouthfeel.	$

(A)	**TRIVENTO SYRAH 2002, BODEGAS TRIVENTO** Mendoza	Spicy style with blackberry depth and richness.	$
(A)	**TRIVENTO MALBEC 2002, BODEGAS TRIVENTO** Mendoza	Intense and leathery with a rich mulberry palate.	$
(S)	**LAS MORAS SHIRAZ 2002, FINCA LAS MORAS** San Juan	Cranberries, bitter cherries, and leaves, with a soft, round, firm structure and a lengthy finish.	$$
(S)	**ELEMENTOS SHIRAZ MALBEC 2001, PEÑAFLOR** San Juan	Good ripening is evident, with evolved, mature aromas and flavors already beginning to develop.	$$
(B)	**PASCUAL TOSO MALBEC 2002, PASCUAL TOSO** Mendoza	Plums, prunes and inkwell aromas on the nose. The palate is a robust, full-bodied affair.	$$
(B)	**HIGH ALTITUDE CABERNET SAUVIGNON TEMPRANILLO 2002, BODEGAS ESCORIHUELA GASCON** Mendoza	Youthful violet color offsets a rich nose of ripe berries and a round, luxuriant palate.	$$
(B)	**SANTA JULIA SYRAH 2002, FAMILIA ZUCCARDI** Mendoza	All the rich aromatic intensity and well-defined black fruit one could ask for. Herbaceous notes.	$$
(B)	**LUIGI BOSCA VIÑA PARAISO MALBEC 2001, CASTELLANI** Mendoza	Powerful blackberries and prunes draped with savory notes and wrapped in a firm tannic structure.	$$
(B)	**SANTA ISABEL BONARDA 2002, NIETO CARBO Y A SENETINER** Mendoza	A rich, seductive nose. Firm sun-warmed blackberries reveal their charms on the palate.	$$
(A)	**SANTA JULIA OAK AGED TEMPRANILLO 2002, LA AGRICOLA** Mendoza	Richly spiced with sweet berry fruit and a creamy finish.	$$
(B)	**GRAFFIGNA MALBEC 2002, BODEGAS GRAFFIGNA** San Juan	Intense leathery black cherry fruit with inviting herbaceousness and a broad tannic structure.	$$
(S)	**TERRAZAS DE LOS ANDES ALTO MALBEC 2002, CASTELLANI** Mendoza	Fresh, warm strawberries and raspberries on the nose and a sweetly ripe, medium weight palate.	$$

(S)	**MENDOZA MALBEC 2002, ANUBIS** Mendoza	Graphite and tobacco leaves, bitter chocolate, and rain-soaked earth litter this complex wine.	$$
(S)	**LAS MORAS CABERNET SAUVIGNON SHIRAZ RESERVA 2001, FINCA LAS MORAS** San Juan	Bright ruby, with a cascade of fresh red berries and spice on the powerful palate.	$$
(G)	**TRIVENTO RESERVE SYRAH 2001, BODEGAS TRIVENTO** Mendoza	Dark fruit and smoky oak with prunes and star anise. Rich intensity and firm tannins.	$$
(S)	**FINCA EL RETIRO SYRAH 2001, FINCA EL RETIRO** Mendoza	Impossibly dark in color and huge, with masses of fierce cherry and fruitcake character.	$$
(G)	**Q TEMPRANILLO 2001, FAMILIA ZUCCARDI** Mendoza	Immensely deep, with huge extract and pronounced mulberry and cherry fruit. A powerful acidic lift.	$$

AUSTRALIA

The Australians had plenty to celebrate this year. Sales are booming throughout the world, and, in Britain, they actually managed to overtake those of France – both in value and volume. The quality and value for money at the bottom end of the scale are less impressive than they were, but the results at the International Wine Challenge confirmed that the Australians still seem to have the knack of delivering reliable wine almost across the board. Once again, they walked away with more Golds than any other country.

AUSTRALIA • SPARKLING

(A)	**BARRAMUNDI SPARKLING NV, CRANSWICK PREMIUM WINES** South Eastern Australia	Simple, crisp sparkler with lots of upfront, ripe fresh fruit appeal.	$$
(A)	**McGUIGAN BLACK LABEL SPARKLING CHARDONNAY 2001, McGUIGAN SIMEON** South Australia	Clean and refreshing with good acid balance.	$$

(A) **CURRABRIDGE BRUT NV, ALAMBE WINES** South Eastern Australia	Creamy style with waxy fruit and lively acidity.	$$
(A) **SANDFORD ESTATE S BRUT NV, WINGARA WINE GROUP** South Australia	Fresh, elegant nose and some creamy depth.	$$
(A) **BANROCK STATION SPARKLING CHARDONNAY 2001, BRL HARDY** South Australia	Fresh with citrus notes and a frothy grapefruit finish.	$$
(S) **NOTTAGE HILL SPARKLING CHARDONNAY 2000, BRL HARDY** South Australia	Baked pears, butter, and a racy palate of fresh fruit which boasts a delightful mousse.	$$
(A) **JACOB'S CREEK CHARDONNAY PINOT NOIR BRUT CUVÉE NV, ORLANDO WINES** South Eastern Australia	Lively, with some butter and yeast richness.	$$
(A) **LINDEMANS SPARKLING PINOT CHARDONNAY 1999, SOUTHCORP WINES** South Eastern Australia	Clean wine with light depth and complexity.	$$
(B) **SEAVIEW BRUT 2001, SEAVIEW WINES** South Eastern Australia	Delicious lime cordial fruit of good depth unfolds slowly on the elegant, restrained, persistent palate.	$$
(S) **EMERI SPARKLING DURIF NV, DE BORTOLI** New South Wales	Packed with cherries, flowers, and licorice. This smorgasbord is lush, sensual, and seductive.	$$
(S) **SEPPELTS SALINGER 2000, SOUTHCORP WINES** ACT	Persistent mousse, vivid aromas of nuts and honeyed apples, and a creamy citrus palate.	$$$
(B) **YELLOWGLEN PINOT NOIR CHARONNAY NV, BERINGER BLASS WINE ESTATES** South Australia	Soft, round, somewhat mature and complex. Energetic mousse lifts the juicy green plum palate.	$$$
(B) **JANSZ PREMIUM NV, JANSZ** Tasmania	Ripe white fruit flavors are given added roundness by the merest hint of residual sugar.	$$$
(B) **YELLOWGLEN BRUT VINTAGE 1999, YELLOWGLEN VINEYARDS** South Australia	Yeasty, bready, creamy notes on the nose. The palate has crisp, fresh herbal fruit.	$$$

(S) **GREEN POINT VINTAGE BRUT 1998, CHANDON ESTATES** Victoria	Nutty aromas and a gorgeous golden color provide the backdrop for a citrus fruit palate.	**$$$$**

AUSTRALIA • WHITE

(A) **BADGERS CREEK SEMILLON CHARDONNAY 2002, LES GRANDS CHAIS DE FRANCE** South Eastern Australia	Fresh with waxy lemon complexity.	$
(A) **MHV SCENIC RIDGE WHITE NV, REDELLO WINES** South Eastern Australia	Ripe, fruity white with nice sweetness to finish.	$
(A) **COLDRIDGE ESTATE CHARDONNAY 2002, MCGUIGAN SIMEON** South Eastern Australia	Soft, peachy wine with good fruit purity.	$
(A) **KALGOORIE COLOMBARD CHARDONNAY 2002, ANGOVES** South Eastern Australia	Fresh and simple with peach and citrus notes.	$
(S) **MHV SCENIC RIDGE SEMILLON NV, REDELLO WINES** South Eastern Australia	Sicilian lemons and juicy yellow apples on the palate, which is mouthcoating, powerful, and long.	$
(A) **MHV SCENIC RIDGE SEMILLON CHARDONNAY NV, REDELLO WINES** South Eastern Australia	Fresh fruit nose leads to a crunchy palate showing decent balance.	$
(A) **MASTERPEACE SEMILLON COLOMBARD CHARDONNAY 2002, ANDREW PEACE WINES** South Eastern Australia	Ripe with tropical notes and a rounded palate.	$
(A) **MOONDARRA SEMILLON CHARDONNAY 2002, MCGUIGAN SIMEON** South Eastern Australia	Lively wine with crisp fruit and decent balance.	$
(A) **MONDIALE SAUVIGNON BLANC NV, CALIFORNIA DIRECT** South Eastern Australia	Clean and grassy with ripe peach aromas.	$
(A) **N X G VINFIVE SEMILLON CHARDONNAY 2002, XANADU WINES** South Eastern Australia	Balanced with fresh citrus fruit and a waxy finish.	$

(A) **MHV Scenic Ridge Chardonnay NV, Redello Wines** South Eastern Australia	Rock melon and yellow stone fruit flavors assault the palate and linger on the finish.	$
(S) **Yaldara Farms Chardonnay 1999, McGuigan Simeon** South Eastern Australia	Ripe tropical fruits saturate the palate: melon, lemon, lime and succulent green plums.	$$
(B) **Hardys Stamp of Australia Riesling Gewurztraminer 2002, BRL Hardy** South Australia	A nose of rose petals is complemented by a fresh palate of crisp, mouthwatering citrus.	$$
(B) **Wildcard Chardonnay 2002, Peter Lehmann** South Australia	Tropical lemons, limes, and quince ooze from the clear, vibrant palate of this wine.	$$
(B) **Oxford Landing Chardonnay 2002, Yalumba** South Australia	Vanilla and butterscotch notes accentuate the crisp, refreshing honeydew, melon, and peach fruit.	$$
(B) **Jindalee Chardonnay 2002, Jindalee Wines** South Australia	Soft, silky, bright guava fruit boasts warm, creamy, buttery oak elements and good balance.	$$
(B) **Kirribilly Chardonnay 2003, Kirrihill Estates** South Eastern Australia	Touches of earth and grass serve only to enhance the upfront, honeyed, apple fruit palate.	$$
(B) **Reynolds Little Boomey Sauvignon Blanc 2002, Reynolds Vineyards** New South Wales	Definitely warm climate style with a ripe tropical nose and a peachy palate that runs on with a zing.	$$
(B) **Little Boomey Chardonnay 2001, Reynolds** New South Wales	Delicate pineapple, peach, and vanilla nose and bags of soft stone fruit on the palate.	$$
(B) **Penfolds Rawsons Retreat Riesling 2002, Southcorp Wines** South Eastern Australia	A fine honeysuckle, flower, and mineral nose. Beautifully balanced with a crisp citric acidity.	$$
(B) **Kanarie Creek Chardonnay 2001, Angoves** South Australia	A restrained, scented nose of peaches and apricots and a creamy palate of stone fruit.	$$
(B) **N X G Vinfive Reserve Chardonnay 2001, Xanadu Wines** South Eastern Australia	Golden apple aromas on nose; restrained palate of peaches and cream with a caramel edge.	$$

(G)	**THOMAS MITCHELL MARSANNE 2002, MITCHELTON WINES** South Eastern Australia	Honeysuckle, tropical fruit and an intriguing hint of almonds. Excellent ripeness coupled with crisp acidity.	$$
(B)	**DEAKIN ESTATE CHARDONNAY 2002, WINGARA WINE GROUP** Victoria	Delicate floral and straw aromas and bright citrus fruit and melon flavours; crisp and balanced.	$$
(S)	**SANDFORD ESTATE SEMILLON CHARDONNAY 2001, WINGARA WINE GROUP** Victoria	Ripe, unoaked yet almost creamy palate of candied lemons and perfumed white fruit.	$$
(S)	**WISEMAN'S CROSSING SAUVIGNON BLANC VERDELHO 2002, ROSSETTO WINES** South Eastern Australia	Peaches, lime cordial, bananas, and pink rose petal notes. Fresh yet concentrated.	$$
(G)	**RUTHERGLEN ESTATE MARSANNE 2002, RUTHERGLEN ESTATE** Victoria	An apple and caramel nose and bright zesty acidity. Well-structured, with good fruit concentration.	$$
(B)	**XANADU SECESSION SEMILLON CHARDONNAY 2001, XANADU WINES** Western Australia	The richness of Semillon blends seamlessly with the crisp, fresh white fruit of Chardonnay.	$$
(G)	**PETER LEHMANN RIESLING 2002, PETER LEHMANN** South Australia	Lean and austere with lime and mineral aromas and a palate which displays good concentration.	$$
(G)	**TESCO FINEST* GREAT SOUTHERN RIESLING 2002, TESCO** Western Australia	Racy limes, ripe juicy grapefruit, and lemon meringue pie appear on the gorgeous palate.	$$
(S)	**Y RIESLING 2002, YALUMBA** South Australia	Flavors of lime and delicate, ethereal apple blossom on the crisp palate.	$$
(S)	**WYNNS COONAWARRA ESTATE RIESLING 2002, SOUTHCORP WINES** South Australia	Peach and pineapple fruit. Ripe and warm, but lifted by a fine streak of acidity.	$$
(S)	**CARLYLE CLASSIC RUTHERGLEN MUSCAT NV, PFEIFFER WINES** Victoria	Marmalade and toffee with layers of spice, nuts, treacle and orange peel. Amazingly complex.	$$
(G)	**HOUGHTON VERDELHO 2002, BRL HARDY** Western Australia	A mineral-laden, honeyed, citric wine with mouthfilling flavors of melon fruit and lime.	$$

(S) **CHATEAU TAHBILK MARSANNE 2001, TAHBILK WINES** Victoria	Very tropical, with lemongrass and peaches and a honeyed, creamy richness to the texture.	$$
(S) **ANNIE'S LANE SEMILLON 2002, BERINGER BLASS WINE ESTATES** South Australia	Lemons and limes and white flowers on the nose. The palate is textured and long.	$$
(S) **YALUMBA Y VIOGNIER 2002, YALUMBA** South Australia	Well-defined stone fruits on the nose and palate, with touches of honey and summer flowers.	$$
(S) **KNAPPSTEIN RIESLING 2002, KNAPPSTEIN WINES** South Australia	Delicate lime and blossom notes. Peachy, fruit salad flavors cut by a tangy acidity.	$$
(S) **THE OLIVE GROVE CHARDONNAY 2002, D'ARENBERG WINES** South Australia	Enticing biscuit and roast nut aromas enhance lime and lemon fruit on the intense palate.	$$
(S) **XANADU SEMILLON SAUVIGNON BLANC 2002, XANADU WINES** Western Australia	Waxed lemons and green plums intermingle on this bright, zesty yet silky blend.	$$
(S) **MCLAREN VALE CHARDONNAY 2002, TATACHILLA WINES** South Australia	Delicate melon and banana on nose and palate, a soft creamy mouthfeel and bold oak.	$$
(S) **MATILDA PLAINS SAUVIGNON BLANC 2002, MATILDA PLAINS** South Australia	Fresh pears, gooseberries and vegetal tones on the nose. The palate is concentrated and long.	$$
(S) **WINDY PEAK RIESLING 2002, DE BORTOLI** Victoria	Youthful yet complex lime cordial, peaches and white guava on the crisp, intense palate.	$$
(G) **TIM ADAMS CLARE VALLEY RIESLING 2002, TIM ADAMS WINES** South Australia	Elderflower and nettle nose with a hint of kerosene. Racy and crisp with fresh acidity.	$$$
(G) **THE HERMIT CRAB 2002, D'ARENBERG WINES** South Australia	Perfumed and lively, this has plenty of citrus and banana flavors with overtones of pineapple.	$$$
(G) **NEPENTHE RIESLING 2002, NEPENTHE WINES** South Australia	Lots of cool lime, grapefruit, and apple flavors with a tangy minerality on the finish.	$$$

G	**STARVEDOG LANE SAUVIGNON BLANC 2002, RAVENSWOOD LANE** South Australia	Tropical citrus with bright acidity to balance the concentration and hold the long finish.	**$$$**

AUSTRALIA • RED

A	**STOWELLS SHIRAZ MATARO , STOWELLS** South Eastern Australia	A creamy nose leads to a thick bramble fruit palate of fair depth and intensity.	**$**
B	**BADGERS CREEK SHIRAZ CABERNET 2002, LES GRANDS CHAIS DE FRANCE** South Eastern Australia	Appealing blend of blueberries, strawberries and vanilla, with faint echoes of undergrowth.	**$**
B	**HAIR OF THE DINGO CABERNET SHIRAZ NV, KINGSLAND WINES & SPIRITS** South Eastern Australia	A forward nose of blackberries and a mouthful of ripe cassis robed in deepest violet.	**$**
A	**JACARANDA HILL SHIRAZ 2002, ANGOVES** South Australia	Jammy with blackberry and sugar apple notes.	**$**
A	**MAYRAH ESTATES CABERNET SAUVIGNON NV, CALIFORNIA DIRECT** South Eastern Australia	Supple with sweet berry and vanilla oak notes.	**$**
A	**COLDRIDGE ESTATE MERLOT 2002, MCGUIGAN SIMEON** South Eastern Australia	Sweet chewy black bramble fruit and aromatic herbs feature on the nose and palate.	**$**
B	**BUCKINGHAM ESTATE SHIRAZ 2002, CELLARMASTER WINES** South Australia	Spice box nose and ripe, lush, medium-bodied palate of blackberries.	**$**
S	**TORTOISESHELL BAY MOURVEDRE SHIRAZ 2002, CASELLA WINES** New South Wales	Peppery and rich in fruit. An attractive strawberry nose and palate and a round finish.	**$**
S	**MOONDARRA SHIRAZ 2002, MOONDARRA** South Eastern Australia	Sophisticated leather and black fruit of fabulous concentration. An impossibly long finish crowns it all.	**$**
B	**MOONDARRA SHIRAZ CABERNET 2002, MCGUIGAN SIMEON** South Eastern Australia	Deep ruby red color. Cassis, woody notes and exotic eucalyptus on the nose and palate.	**$**

(B)	**EVOLUTION OLD VINE RED NV, CALIFORNIA DIRECT** South Eastern Australia	This beauty offers just-picked blueberries and subtle smoky notes on a medium-bodied palate.	$
(A)	**KALGOORIE SHIRAZ CABERNET 2002, ANGOVES** South Eastern Australia	Rich cassis and blackberries with a creamy finish.	$
(A)	**SOMERTON SHIRAZ CABERNET MERLOT 2002, MIRANDA WINES** South Eastern Australia	Rounded and balanced with lush fruit. Supple finish.	$
(A)	**RANSOME'S VALE SHIRAZ PETIT VERDOT NV, CALIFORNIA DIRECT** South Eastern Australia	Brooding with intense black fruit flavors.	$
(A)	**N X G VINFIVE CABERNET MERLOT 2002, XANADU WINES** South Eastern Australia	Opulent style with a currant driven palate.	$
(S)	**FAMILY RESERVE DURIF 2002, DE BORTOLI** South Eastern Australia	Mocha and crushed vanilla beans grace the nose of this intense, inky purple wine.	$
(B)	**DB SHIRAZ DE CABERNET 2002, DE BORTOLI** New South Wales	Rich, sweet bramble fruit in the mouth and a delightful herbaceousness in the background.	$
(A)	**MHV SCENIC RIDGE SHIRAZ MERLOT NV, REDELLO WINES** South Eastern Australia	Plumcake style with good fruit richness.	$
(B)	**BANROCK STATION SHIRAZ MATARO 2002, BRL HARDY** South Australia	Deeply colored and richly flavored with mocha, toast, and black bramble fruits.	$
(B)	**FIREFLY SHIRAZ 2002, MIRANDA WINES** South Eastern Australia	Purple-red color pleases the eye. The palate has very appealing loganberry fruit.	$
(B)	**YELLOW TAIL SHIRAZ 2002, CASELLA WINES** South Eastern Australia	Intense blueberry and raspberry aromas and flavors on the nose and on the ripe palate.	$$
(B)	**MHV SCENIC RIDGE AUSTRALIAN CABERNET SAUVIGNON NV, REDELLO WINES** New South Wales	Saturated ruby color, gamey, savory notes and generous spice feature on this round, rich wine.	$$

(B)	**PETER LEHMANN GRENACHE 2001, PETER LEHMANN** South Australia	Light, slightly medicinal nose but persistent red fruit and a good dry and clean finish	**$$**
(S)	**STONEY VALE SHIRAZ CABERNET 2002, YALDARA WINES** South Eastern Australia	This full-bodied, fleshy wine has raspberries, leather, and spice on the nose and palate.	**$$**
(S)	**JACOB'S CREEK SHIRAZ CABERNET 2001, ORLANDO WINES** South Eastern Australia	Full of berries and cherries, this is ripe and forward. Subtle oak and gentle tannins.	**$$**
(S)	**MASTERPEACE SHIRAZ CABERNET SAUVIGNON 2002, ANDREW PACE WINES** South Eastern Australia	Very good balance is achieved between leafy herbaceous elements and rich cushiony velvet red fruit.	**$$**
(B)	**BANROCK STATION PETIT VERDOT 2002, BRL HARDY** South Australia	The bright ripe strawberry fruit packs a brisk peppery punch. Leafy, juicy, and medium-bodied.	**$$**
(B)	**BANROCK STATION SHIRAZ 2002, BRL HARDY** South Australia	Elegant, juicy berry and redcurrant fruit, a soft palate of rounded tannins and gentle acidity.	**$$**
(B)	**HARDYS STAMP OF AUSTRALIA GRENACHE SHIRAZ 2002, BRL HARDY** South Australia	Soft fruit and a dry finish, with a good level of sweetness on the palate.	**$$**
(B)	**JACOB'S CREEK GRENACHE SHIRAZ 2002, ORLANDO WINES** South Eastern Australia	Light style with lifted berry fruit; a very user friendly easy drinking soft wine.	**$$**
(B)	**JINDALEE SHIRAZ 2002, JINDALEE WINES** South Australia	A nose of forest fruits and a touch of seaweed. Generous, with a minty background.	**$$**
(B)	**MASTERPEACE SHIRAZ 2002, ANDREW PEACE WINES** South Eastern Australia	A very generously spiced Shiraz with bags of black fruit and whiffs of saddle leather.	**$$**
(B)	**MASTERPEACE SHIRAZ CABERNET 2002, ANDREW PEACE WINES** South Eastern Australia	A surfeit of ripe cassis fruit is buttressed by firm, generous tannins and fresh acidity.	**$$**
(B)	**JULIANS PETIT VERDOT 1999, MCGUIGAN SIMEON** South Australia	Very pronounced undergrowth and tree bark on the nose accents the fresh peppery fruit.	**$$**

(B) **BURRA BROOK SHIRAZ 2002, SOUTHCORP WINES** South Eastern Australia	Gratifying blackberry fruit palate with good balance between fruit concentration and fresh, mouthwatering acid.	$$
(B) **KIRRIBILLY MERLOT 2003, KIRRIHILL ESTATES** South Eastern Australia	Delicate scents of vanilla, earth and mint. The palate is well-balanced and packed with fruit.	$$
(B) **ORIGIN CABERNET SAUVIGNON 2002, CRANSWICK** South Eastern Australia	Sweetly ripe, generously oaked, full-bodied red berry fruit. Big, with an exceedingly long finish.	$$
(S) **VARIETAL CABERNET SAUVIGNON 2002, MIRANDA WINES** South Eastern Australia	Black cherry fruit with a hint of herbaceousness and pepper notes on the opulent palate.	$$
(S) **VARIETAL SHIRAZ 2002, MIRANDA WINES** South Eastern Australia	Ephemeral scents of patchouli linger over the blackberry fruit palate. Medium-bodied palate of forest fruits.	$$
(S) **EAGLEHAWK CABERNET SHIRAZ MERLOT 2001, BERINGER BLASS WINE ESTATES** South Eastern Australia	What a powerhouse! Black plums laced with spices, ripe juicy raspberries, and vegetal notes.	$$
(S) **ECHO POINT SHIRAZ 2001, CRESTVIEW ESTATE** South Australia	Full of ripe, soft, brambly, plummy fruit with just a hint of tobacco and spice.	$$
(S) **BARRAMUNDI RESERVE MERLOT 2002, CRANSWICK PREMIUM WINES** South Eastern Australia	Fresh damsons and redcurrants, cedar, mint, and hints of vanilla. Powdery tannins sustain the finish.	$$
(S) **YANGARRA PARK MERLOT 2001, KENDALL-JACKSON** South Eastern Australia	An aromatic nose of menthol, vanilla, and toast, and a palate supported by youthful tannins.	$$
(S) **THOMAS MITCHELL SHIRAZ 2001, MITCHELTON WINES** Victoria	Fruit-driven style, without new oak. A warm, minty nose and ripe, blackberry fruit on the palate.	$$
(S) **LITTLE BOOMEY CABERNET SAUVIGNON MERLOT 2001, REYNOLDS WINES** New South Wales	A magnificent licorice and black cherry bouquet and a lush palate of cassis and minerals.	$$
(B) **MOONDARRA SHIRAZ RESERVE 2002, McGUIGAN SIMEON** South Eastern Australia	Blackcurrants, raspberries, and toasty notes decorate the nose. The palate is concentrated and long.	$$

Ⓑ	**RUTLAND VALLEY SHIRAZ 2002, BEELGARA ESTATES** South Eastern Australia	Notes of eucalyptus lurk behind the ripe red berry nose. The palate is concentrated.	$$
Ⓢ	**SECESSION SHIRAZ CABERNET SAUVIGNON 2002, XANADU WINES** Western Australia	A powerful structure supports the glowing velvet fleshy loganberries on the palate. Etched with soft spice.	$$
Ⓢ	**SECESSION SHIRAZ CABERNET SAUVIGNON 2001, XANADU WINES** Western Australia	Rich raspberries, blackcurrants, mulberries, and damp earth all make an appearance on nose and palate.	$$
Ⓢ	**THE BLACK SHIRAZ 2002, ROSSETTO WINES** New South Wales	Leather, licorice, cracked pepper, smoke and tarry nuances line the intense palate.	$$
Ⓢ	**YALDARA GRENACHE 2001, McGUIGAN SIMEON** South Eastern Australia	Rendered by earthiness, a hint of spice and delicate echoes of incense and minerality.	$$
Ⓢ	**WISEMAN'S CROSSING PETIT VERDOT SHIRAZ 2002, ROSSETTO WINES** South Eastern Australia	With bell pepper and cut grass on the nose and strawberry fruit on the palate.	$$
Ⓢ	**PROMISED LAND SHIRAZ CABERNET 2001, WAKEFIELD ESTATE** South Australia	Oak-perfumed berry fruit and a hint of leather, with a lingering finish.	$$
Ⓖ	**LEASINGHAM MAGNUS SHIRAZ CABERNET SAUVIGNON 2000, BRL HARDY** South Australia	Spicy, cedary notes together with plums and cherries. The chocolate oak brings out the fruit.	$$
Ⓖ	**MARY'S CELLAR SHIRAZ 2002, HILLSTOWE WINES** South Australia	Smoky minerals balance super-ripe, savory fruit and heathery, herbal flavors. Unique, and technically excellent.	$$
Ⓖ	**BLEASDALE SHIRAZ CABERNET 2001, BLEASDALE** South Australia	Ripe and concentrated in a forward style. Minty currants and mouthfilling berries on the palate.	$$
Ⓢ	**STONEHAVEN STEPPING STONE CABERNET SAUVIGNON 2001, BRL HARDY** South Australia	Saturated with voluptuous cassis, forest fruits, toast and vanilla, and boasting a lasting finish.	$$
Ⓢ	**HOUGHTON CABERNET SAUVIGNON 2000, BRL HARDY** Western Australia	Cassis and chocolate on the nose; ripe berries and generous spice on the youthful palate.	$$

(S) **WAKEFIELD ESTATE MERLOT 2002, WAKEFIELD ESTATE** South Australia	Damsons, eucalyptus, and spice on the nose, and plenty of weighty, structured redcurrant fruit flavors.	$$
(S) **Y SHIRAZ 2001, YALUMBA** South Australia	A complex mint and chocolate nose and a palate laden with forest fruit elements.	$$
(S) **GRENACHE SHIRAZ MOURVEDRE 2002, RUTHERGLEN ESTATE** Victoria	The summer pudding nose is forward and sophisticated. The fruit is super-ripe.	$$
(S) **RUTHERGLEN ESTATE SHIRAZ 2002, RUTHERGLEN ESTATE** Victoria	Inky violet color. Graphite, leather, black cherries and tree bark on the nose.	$$
(S) **OLD WINERY CABERNET MERLOT 2001, TYRRELL'S** New South Wales	A nose of capiscum, violets, and black fruit, together with red berries and creamy oak.	$$
(S) **ESTATE CABERNET SAUVIGNON 2001, PALANDRI WINES** Western Australia	Fresh raspberries and cracked white pepper, leaves and spice on the youthful, yet complex, palate.	$$
(S) **PENFOLDS KOONUNGA HILL SHIRAZ CABERNET 2001, SOUTHCORP WINES** South Eastern Australia	Smooth, ripe berry fruit and good, firm tannins. Attractive complexity and real length.	$$
(S) **DEEN VAT 4 PETIT VERDOT 2001, DE BORTOLI** New South Wales	Bittersweet cherries robed in finest dark chocolate. Some herbaceousness and a firm structure.	$$
(S) **WYNDHAM ESTATE BIN 999 MERLOT 2001, ORLANDO WYNDHAM** South Eastern Australia	Elegant, beguiling ripe cherries and plums, with seductive hints of pepper and ripe tannins.	$$
(S) **NOTTAGE HILL RESERVE CABERNET SAUVIGNON 2001, BRL HARDY** South Australia	Peppery, coffee nose with a rich palate of vibrant fruit and a tight tannic structure.	$$
(S) **WESTEND ESTATE SHIRAZ PETIT VERDOT 2002, WESTEND ESTATE** New South Wales	Notes of pepper and capiscum together with the ripe redcurrant fruit. Intense and well structured.	$$
(S) **MCLAREN VALE GRENACHE SHIRAZ 2001, TATACHILLA WINES** South Australia	Masses of powerful fruit and silky tannins on the palate. Drinking beautifully now.	$$

(S) **WIRREGA VINEYARD SHIRAZ 2002, HEARTLAND WINES** South Australia	Black cherry fruit, menthol, and mocha oak. Full and rich with sweet tannins.	**$$**
(G) **WAKEFIELD SHIRAZ 2002, WAKEFIELD ESTATE** South Australia	An enormous mouthful of ripe fruit, menthol, plums, and pepper with ripe, textured tannins.	**$$**
(G) **YALUMBA BAROSSA SHIRAZ 2000, YALUMBA** South Australia	Layers of ripe fruit and oak on the full, ripe palate of intensity and concentration.	**$$$**
(G) **MCLAREN VALE SHIRAZ 2001, TATACHILLA WINES** South Australia	Packed with ripe blackcurrant fruit, smoky, peppery notes, and well-integrated vanilla oak. Very good intensity.	**$$$**
(G) **MCLAREN VALE SHIRAZ 2001, BERESFORD** South Australia	Big, oaky shiraz with mocha, vanilla flavors and typically McLaren Vale eucalyptus and pepper overtones.	**$$$**
(G) **XANADU SHIRAZ 2001, XANADU WINES** Western Australia	Eucalyptus and mint nose with fruit aromas of morello cherry. Fleshy, fruity and very supple.	**$$$**
(G) **BUSH VIEW MARGARET RIVER SHIRAZ 2001, EVANS & TATE** Western Australia	Rich eucalyptus and mint chocolate aromas. Plenty of sweetly ripe red and blackberry fruit.	**$$$**
(G) **WINEMAKER'S RESERVE SHIRAZ 2001, WILLOW BRIDGE ESTATE** Western Australia	A perfumed nose with spicy peppery notes. Soft-textured palate of spice, cherries and toasty oak.	**$$$**
(G) **TINTARA CABERNET SAUVIGNON 1999, BRL HARDY** South Australia	Full of red berry confit, with smoky, spicy oak. Rich and ripe, dry and crisp.	**$$$**
(G) **STONEHAVEN LIMESTONE COAST CABERNET SAUVIGNON 1999, BRL HARDY** South Australia	Damson, dark juicy prune and mint. Concentrated and round with cosy vanilla and caramel oak.	**$$$**
(G) **RESERVE SHIRAZ CABERNET 2001, MCLEAN'S FARM WINES** South Australia	Laced with chocolate and vanilla new oak, and charmingly perfumed with forward, ripe cassis fruit.	**$$$**
(G) **LISA MCGUIGAN TEMPUS TWO PEWTER SERIES SHIRAZ , MCGUIGAN SIMEON** South Australia	Lots of light, juicy fruit on the nose and a powerful palate with excellent depth.	**$$$**

DIRECTORS CUT SHIRAZ 2002, HEARTLAND (G) South Australia	Bramble and blackcurrant fruit on the ripe yet fresh, taut and classically styled palate.	$$$
BAROSSA SHIRAZ 2001, HERITAGE WINES (G) South Australia	Notes of leather and beguiling red berries. Soft, ripe tannins and white and black pepper.	$$$
KILLIBINBIN SHIRAZ 2001, KILLIBINBIN WINES (G) South Australia	Bramble fruits and currants, spicy notes, good depth, well-integrated oak and fabulous balance.	$$$$
RAILWAY SHIRAZ 2000, HAMILTON'S EWELL VINEYARDS (G) South Australia	There's real vibrancy of primary fruit here, given complexity by spice, oak, and leather.	$$$$
WOLF BLASS PRESIDENT'S SELECTION CABERNET SAUVIGNON 2001, BERINGER BLASS South Australia (G)	Blackberries, pencil lead, and pepper on a powerhouse palate featuring bitter chocolate and redcurrants.	$$$$
STARVEDOG LANE SHIRAZ 1999, RAVENSWOOD LANE (G) South Australia	Stunning young peppery aromas with mint, spice and layers of toasted fruit. Fresh and lively.	$$$$
THE TWENTY EIGHT ROAD 2001, D'ARENBERG WINES (G) South Australia	Fresh and minty with violets and currants. Full body, round tannins and a savory maturity.	$$$$
MCLAREN VALE SHIRAZ 2000, PENNY'S HILL (G) South Australia	Big modern style with plenty of warm oak to emphasise the macerated black cherry fruit.	$$$$
BLACKWELL SHIRAZ 2000, ST HALLETT (G) South Australia	A driven nose of rose hip, black plums and liquorice introduce this intense, complex wine.	$$$$
BIN 138 SHIRAZ GRENACHE MOURVÈDRE 2001, PENFOLDS WINES (G) South Australia	Packed with succulent, spicy fruit and clear pepperiness, coconut and chocolate. Firm tannins.	$$$$
NORMANS CHAIS CLARENDON SHIRAZ 1999, XANADU WINES (G) South Australia	Rosemary and black pepper. A sassy, plummy, leathery mouthful with chunky tannins and solid weight.	$$$$
RESERVE SHIRAZ VIOGNIER 2001, YERING STATION (G) Victoria	Intense, perfumed fruit complemented by ripe tannins and a keen white pepper astringency.	$$$$

(G) **ANNIE'S LANE COPPER TRAIL SHIRAZ 1999, BERINGER BLASS WINE ESTATES** South Australia	Big and rich, with black fruit, leather and spices on a big framework of tannins.	$$$$
(G) **WALTER'S CABERNET 1999, BREMERTON WINES** South Australia	Deep garnet pink color with a curranty style and a touch of creamy, vanilla oak.	$$$$
(G) **REIVER SHIRAZ 2001, MITOLO WINES** South Australia	Huge extract and an abundance of blackberry and bilberry fruit with a touch of mint.	$$$$
(G) **THE STOCKS SHIRAZ 2001, WOODSTOCK WINERY** South Australia	A deep, complex character with smoky gamey notes as well as blueberries, cassis and chocolate.	$$$$
(G) **THE STOCKS SHIRAZ 2000, WOODSTOCK WINERY** South Australia	Lots of vanilla cream oak flavors balancing the up-front berry and cassis fruit and spice.	$$$$
(G) **REUNION SHIRAZ 1998, RAVENSWOOD LANE** South Australia	Licorice and black pepper give complexity to the dense, sturdy structure and chewy tannins.	$$$$
(G) **LANGHORNE CREEK AREA RED BLEND 2000, DORRIEN ESTATE WINERY** South Australia	Eucalyptus, mint and spicy black cherry fruit intertwine with oak lurking in the background.	$$$$
(G) **RESERVE COONAWARRA ESTATE GROWN CABERNET SAUVIGNON 2000, PENLEY ESTATE** South Australia	Sweet and opulent with masses of ripe berry fruit and warming chocolate, mocha oak.	$$$$
(G) **SALTRAM NO 1 SHIRAZ 1999, BERINGER BLASS WINE ESTATES** South Australia	Positively royal purple in color, with a subtle bramble, spice and pepper and smoke nose.	$$$$
(G) **THE DEAD ARM SHIRAZ 2001, D'ARENBERG WINES** South Australia	Deep and rich with an amazing array of chocolate, vanilla, pepper and dark, black fruit.	$$$$$
(G) **ST HENRI SHIRAZ 1999, PENFOLDS WINES** South Eastern Australia	Blueberries, herbs, blackberries, and liquorice cascade forth. The soft tannins support the fruit beautifully.	$$$$$
(G) **STONEWELL BAROSSA SHIRAZ 1998, PETER LEHMANN** South Australia	Sweet liquorice fruit, leathery spice, and pepper undertones. Balanced sweet oak, fine tannins and weight.	$$$$$

(G) Wolf Blass Platinum Label Clare Valley Cabernet Sauvignon 2000, Beringer Blass South Australia	Dense, concentrated, perfectly ripe fruit and layers of subtle flavors that run through the palate.	$$$$$
(G) Wolf Blass Platinum Label Shiraz 2000, Beringer Blass Wine Estates South Australia	Very fine tannins, fantastic fruit and pure cassis flavors that just keep going on and on.	$$$$$
(G) Bin 707 Cabernet Sauvignon 1999, Penfolds Wines South Eastern Australia	Classic Oz minty aromatics coupled with soft, ripe fleshy fruit and an immense classy finish.	$$$$$
(G) RWT Barossa Valley Shiraz 2000, Penfolds Wines South Australia	Packed with intense bright cherry plum fruit. The herbaceous character adds a layer of complexity.	$$$$$
(G) Houghton Jack Mann Cabernet Sauvignon 1999, BRL Hardy Western Australia	Subtle herbal and mineral aromas. New oak, ripe sweetness, a sound structure and grippy tannins.	$$$$$
(G) Eileen Hardy Shiraz 1999, BRL Hardy South Australia	Deep, powerful, and rich with spiced black berry fruit and a touch of eucalyptus mintiness.	$$$$$
(G) Barossa Valley Estates E+E Black Pepper Shiraz 1999, BRL Hardy South Australia	Very complex with well used oak, good acidity, and solid tannins, and some immense length.	$$$$$
(G) Grange 1998, Penfolds Wines South Eastern Australia	Powerful, very concentrated, and crammed to the hilt with licorice, pepper, spice and cassis.	$$$$$

AUSTRALIA • SWEET

(B) Cranswick Estate Botrytis Semillon 2001, Cranswick Premium Wines South Eastern Australia	Intoxicating nose of golden syrup, limes and honey. Rich and textured, yet fresh. Well balanced.	$
(S) Botrytis Semillon Myall Road 1999, Bimbadgen Estate New South Wales	A beautifully concentrated array of peaches, apricots, and oranges on nose and palate.	$$$
(S) Family Reserve Late Harvested Noble Riesling 1999, Brown Brothers Victoria	Intense, evolved aromas of raisins. A rich and honeyed palate is sustained by crisp acidity.	$$$

G	**NOBLE ONE 2000, DE BORTOLI** New South Wales	An intensely sweet, rich nose with glycerol smoothness and luscious peach syrup on the palate.	$$$$

AUSTRALIA · FORTIFIED

B	**CAMPBELLS RUTHERGLEN WINES MUSCAT NV, CAMPBELLS RUTHERGLEN WINES** Victoria	Intensely luscious wine, full of tangy caramel character and a touch of candied citrus peel.	$$
S	**LIQUEUR MUSCAT NV, MICK MORRIS** Victoria	A sensual, unctuous, rich concoction, laden with marmalade, raisins, orange rind, and a whiff of flowers.	$$
G	**SEPPELTS DP63 GRAND RUTHERGLEN MUSCAT NV, SOUTHCORP WINES** Victoria	Wonderfully complex; woody, rich, sweet, nutty with a touch of coffee and masive intensity.	$$
G	**SHOW LIQUEUR MUSCAT NV, DE BORTOLI** New South Wales	An intense blend of coffee, spice, walnuts and caramel flavors with astonishing depth and complexity.	$$$
S	**LIQUEUR MUSCAT NV, BROWN BROTHERS** Victoria	Delicious, high alcohol, orange treacle with notes of coffee and smoky burnt brown sugar.	$$$

Wines are listed in approximate price order (though this can vary widely depending where they are on offer). All of the wines in the Guide are good value, by definition, but the best buys carry the "Great Value Wine of the Year" symbol. These were the bottles that performed best in their their price band in a blind tasting by the International Wine Challenge top tasters – the super-jurors. Buy them when you can; they tend to sell out very quickly.

CHILE

Chile's wine industry may be one of the oldest in South America, but it came of age in the 1990s, when a number of ambitious producers – local and from overseas – began to show that the wines here could compete with the best from across the world. New and freshly exploited regions are helping – Casablanca and Aconcagua in particular – as are a growing understanding of the grapes that grow best here and the kind of open-mindedness that helped to create the Gold medal winning non-vintage Caballo Loco.

CHILE • WHITE

(A)	**MHV SAN ANDRES CHILEAN WHITE 2002, VIÑA SAN PEDRO** Central Valley	Light style with crisp fruit and a short finish.	$
(B)	**MHV SAN ANDRES SAUVIGNON BLANC CHARDONNAY 2002, VIÑA SAN PEDRO** Central Valley	Green herbaceous elements of Sauvignon blend effortlessly with white-fleshed Chardonnay.	$
(S)	**MHV SAN ANDRES CHARDONNAY 2002, VIÑA SAN PEDRO** Central Valley	Full-bodied and robust yet balanced and harmonious, with a palate of pear, pineapple, and melons.	$
(B)	**STOWELLS CHARDONNAY 2002, STOWELLS** Aconcagua	Ripe pineapple, guava, and citrus feature in this clear, fresh, medium-weight wine.	$
(B)	**CANEPA SEMILLON 2002, VIÑA CANEPA** Rapel	Soft texture, candied lemon fruit plus a hint of musk equals a seductive wine indeed.	$
(B)	**VISTAMAR SAUVIGNON BLANC 2002, VISTAMAR WINES** Central Valley	All the classic Sauvignon elements: vivid green berries, good concentration and fresh acidity.	$
(B)	**LOS CAMACHOS CHARDONNAY 2002, VIÑA SAN PEDRO** Central Valley	Very inviting crunchy and juicy yellow apple fruit on the nose and palate.	$
(B)	**PACHAMAMA CHILEAN CHARDONNAY 2002, VIÑA MORANDÉ** Central Valley	Very attractive, clear crisp starfruit and melon drip from the ripe, mouthwatering, tropical palate.	$

(A)	**STOWELLS SAUVIGNON BLANC , STOWELLS** Curicó	Gooseberry driven style with fine balancing acidity.	$
(A)	**CASA TECOPILLA SAUVIGNON BLANC 2002, VIÑA SAN PEDRO** Curicó	Fresh with grass and asparagus notes.	$
(A)	**VISTAMAR CHARDONNAY 2002, VISTAMAR WINES** Central Valley	Clean and pure with fruit depth and balance.	$
(A)	**CASCADA WHITE 2002, VIA WINE GROUP** Central Valley	Zesty wine with good acidity and freshness.	$
(A)	**TIERRUCA 2003, VIÑEDOS ERRAZURIZ OVALLE** Curicó	Crisp with decent fruit and a grassy finish.	$
(B)	**ANTU MAPU SAUVIGNON BLANC 2002, COVICA** Maule	The mouthwatering fruit is ripe and tropical, with a soft, mouthcoating texture.	$
(A)	**COPPER CHARDONNAY 2002, VIÑA CONCHA Y TORO** Central Valley	Clean and fresh with peach and lemon zest.	$
(B)	**CHILEAN CHARDONNAY 2002, VIÑA MORANDÉ** Central Valley	Very appealing lemon yellow. A rather tropical palate of pineapple, guava and starfruit.	$
(B)	**35 SOUTH CHARDONNAY 2002, VIÑA SAN PEDRO** Central Valley	Mangosteen, starfruit and banana all get a look-in on this round tropical wine.	$
(B)	**ANAKENA CHARDONNAY 2002, ANAKENA** Aconcagua	Clear, bright golden yellow colour. Pineapples, pears and lemons feature on the ripe palate.	$$
(B)	**TERRAMATER CHARDONNAY 2002, TERRAMATER** Central Valley	Rich toast and butterscotch on the nose. The palate is round, full and intense.	$$
(B)	**CASA LEONA CHARDONNAY 2002, LA ROSA** Rapel	Very impressive concentration, length and balance, with ripe pear and apple flavors.	$$

(B)	**CANEPA CHARDONNAY 2002, VIÑA CANEPA** Rapel	Ripe yellow tropical fruit emanates from the lifted nose and beguiling palate.	$$
(S)	**DON CAYETANO CHARDONNAY 2002, VIÑA LUIS FELIPE EDWARDS** Rapel	Comes up trumps with fresh juicy pineapples, greengage fruit and piles of pears.	$$
(S)	**CASAS DEL BOSQUE SAUVIGNON BLANC 2002, CASAS DEL BOSQUE** Aconcagua	The freshness is unparalleled. Juicy green and white berry fruit explodes on nose and palate.	$$
(S)	**CHILENSIS SAUVIGNON BLANC 2002, VIA WINE GROUP** Aconcagua	Excellent balance and restraint. Invigorating acidity weaves skillfully in and out of the fruit.	$$
(B)	**CASILLERO DEL DIABLO CHARDONNAY 2002, VIÑA CONCHA Y TORO** Aconcagua	Star-bright. A robust, buttered toast, grapefruit, lime, and lemon nose and palate.	$$
(B)	**CASILLERO DEL DIABLO VIOGNIER 2002, VIÑA CONCHA Y TORO** Aconcagua	Juicy peaches and vibrant yellow crocuses on the nose and warm, robust palate.	$$
(B)	**VALDIVIESO SAUVIGNON BLANC 2003, VIÑA VALDIVIESO** Central Valley	Freshly picked gooseberries and hints of guava vie for attention on nose and palate.	$$
(S)	**ANAKENA RESERVADO CHARDONNAY 2002, ANAKENA** Rapel	Peach and apple flesh seduces with deep, intense flavors, good grip, and fresh, lifted acidity.	$$
(A)	**ECHEVERRIA RESERVA CHARDONNAY 2001, VIÑA ECHEVERRIA** Curicó	Nuts and vanilla feature on the nose, while herbs and delicate lemons define the palate.	$$
(S)	**CHARDONNAY RIO AZUL 2002, MICHEL LAROCHE & JORGE CORDERCH** Aconcagua	Grapefruit and green plum flavors. A waxy texture, depth of concentration and persistent finish.	$$
(S)	**MONTGRAS RESERVA CHARDONNAY 2002, MONTGRAS WINERY** Rapel	The intensity of fresh yellow fruit on the palate belies its elegant, tightly-knit structure.	$$$

Wines are listed in approximate price order (though this can vary widely depending where they are on offer). All of the wines in the Guide are good value, by definition, but the best buys carry the "Great Value Wine of theYear" symbol. These were the bottles that performed best in their their price band in a blind tasting by the International Wine Challenge top tasters – the super-jurors. Buy them when you can; they tend to sell out very quickly.

CHILE • RED

(A)	**MHV San Andres Cabernet Sauvignon Merlot 2002, Viña San Pedro** Central Valley	Soft and unassuming with cassis persistence.	$
(A)	**35 South Cabernet Sauvignon Merlot 2002, Viña San Pedro** Central Valley	Plum and currant notes. Soft heart.	$
(A)	**35 South Cabernet Sauvignon Shiraz 2002, Viña San Pedro** Curicó	Spicy with good fruit intensity.	$
(A)	**Casa Tecopilla Cabernet Sauvignon 2002, Viña San Pedro** Curicó	Redcurrant and blackberry nose and palate.	$
(A)	**Vistamar Merlot 2002, Vistamar Wines** Central Valley	Deeply colored and scented with oak, this wine offers fresh blackberry aromas and grippy tannins.	$
(A)	**Quintas Las Cabras Cabernet Sauvignon 2002, Viña La Rosa** Rapel	Intense ripe cassis on the lifted nose and full-bodied palate.	$
(A)	**Chile Con Cabernet NV, Kingsland Wines & Spirits** Central Valley	Meaty by name. Meaty by nature!	$
(A)	**Gato Negro Cabernet Sauvignon 2002, Viña San Pedro** Central Valley	Blackberry and mint driven style.	$
(B)	**Santa Helena Gran Vino 2002, Viña Santa Helena** Central Valley	An elegant nose of blackcurrants with a hint of leafiness complements the structured cherry palate.	$
(S)	**Sunrise Carmenère 2002, Viña Concha y Toro** Central Valley	Firm woody notes and ripe red cherry fruit on the juicy, punchy palate.	$
(S)	**Tierra Arena Cabernet Sauvignon 2002, Aguirre** Limara Valley	This offering is round and supple and crammed with currants, plums, and raspberries. Mouthwatering and long.	$

(B) CHILEAN MERLOT 2002, VIÑA MORANDÉ Central Valley	Pure, rich cassis fruit nose with compelling grassy elements and a mouthwatering, youthful blackcurrant palate.	$
(B) 35 SOUTH SHIRAZ 2002, VIÑA SAN PEDRO Central Valley	Smoldering leaves, toast, red cherries and thyme mix freely in this beautiful wine.	$
(B) 35 SOUTH CABERNET SAUVIGNON 2002, VIÑA SAN PEDRO Central Valley	Intriguing elements of undergrowth complement black cherries and cassis on the smooth, structured palate.	$
(S) TERRAMATER SHIRAZ CABERNET 2001, TERRAMATER Central Valley	Sweet vanilla and toffee oak provide structure to the ripe, peppery, summer pudding fruits.	$$
(S) CHILENO SHIRAZ CABERNET 2001, VIÑA VENTISQUERO Central Valley	Savory character and smoky bacon aromas. Peppery and ripe with raspberry fruit and vanilla oak.	$$
(B) TERRAMATER ZINFANDEL SHIRAZ 2001, TERRAMATER Central Valley	Pepper and cinnamon on the nose. Raspberries and strawberries on the palate.	$$
(B) CANEPA WINEMAKER'S SELECTION MALBEC 2002, VIÑA CANEPA Maipo	Ripe rich black fruit is inlaid with ground graphite. Admirable balance and integration.	$$
(B) ANTU MAP CARMENÈRE 2002, COVICA Maule	Youthful redcurrant fruit and leaves on the nose and firm, fleshed yet angular palate.	$$
(B) CASILLERO DEL DIABLO CARMENÈRE 2002, VIÑA CONCHA Y TORO Rapel	Wild strawberries and bramble vine leaves. Some vegetal elements on the round, ripe palate.	$$
(B) TRIO PINOT NOIR 2001, VIÑA CONCHA Y TORO Aconcagua	Earth, berries and hints of the farmyard appear on nose and palate.	$$
(B) ERRAZURIZ SYRAH CABERNET SAUVIGNON 2002, VIÑA ERRAZURIZ Maipo	The compact cassis and raspberry fruit possesses fresh acidity, excellent ripeness and firm supporting tannins.	$$
(S) CASILLERO DEL DIABLO SYRAH 2002, VIÑA CONCHA Y TORO Central Valley	A delicate floral top note. Velvety ruby-red cherries and liquorice on the palate.	$$

(A)	**DON CAYETANO CARMENÈRE 2002, VIÑA LUIS FELIPE EDWARDS** Rapel	Spicy red with a soft plum and cassis finish.	**$$**
(A)	**DON CAYETANO MERLOT 2002, VIÑA LUIS FELIPE EDWARDS** Rapel	Round, mouth-pleasing wine. Sweet berry finish.	**$$**
(A)	**DON CAYETANO CABERNET SAUVIGNON 2002, VIÑA LUIS FELIPE EDWARDS** Rapel	Spicy and earthy with a touch of chocolate oak.	**$$**
(S)	**TERRARUM RESERVE PINOT NOIR 2002, VIÑA MORANDÉ** Aconcagua	Classic savory farmyard notes are displayed alongside tree bark, vanilla and ripe cherries.	**$$**
(S)	**TERRAMATER RESERVA SHIRAZ 2001, TERRAMATER** Maipo	Great fruit typicity and a structured body. Balance and concentration complete this exemplary wine.	**$$**
(S)	**YALI CARMENÈRE RESERVA 2001, VIÑA VENTISQUERO** Maipo	Youthful herbaceous notes enliven the ripe, mouthwatering redcurrant fruit.	**$$**
(B)	**CASILLERO DEL DIABLO MERLOT 2002, VIÑA CONCHA Y TORO** Rapel	Bags of intense fresh red berries liberally laced with spice and boasting a long finish.	**$$**
(S)	**LA PALMERIA MERLOT RESERVA 2002, VIÑA LA ROSA** Rapel	Fresh plums underpinned by earth, blackcurrant leaves and vanilla. No small amount of ripe tannin.	**$$**
(S)	**CABERNET SAUVIGNON RESERVA 2001, VIÑA SEGÚ** Maule	Firm cassis berries of very soft, rich ripeness on the full-bodied, radiant palate.	**$$**
(S)	**RESERVA CABERNET SAUVIGNON COLCHAGUA VALLEY ESTATE 2001, VIÑEDOS TERRANOBLE** Talca	Warm spices, touches of smoke and ripe berry fruit are knitted together on the finish.	**$$**
(S)	**YALI CABERNET SAUVIGNON GRAN RESERVA 2001, VIÑA VENTISQUERO** Central Valley	Leafy, intensely ripe blackcurrant fruit. Full, textured and concentrated, with a firm tannic grip.	**$$**
(S)	**PRIVATE RESERVE SYRAH 2001, VIÑA CANEPA** Rapel	A restrained style with a great deal of harmony, fine tannins and bright acidity.	**$$**

(S)	**RESERVE CABERNET SAUVIGNON 2000, VIÑA VALDIVIESO** Central Valley	Rich and meaty, with succulent blackcurrant fruit, ripe tannins, leather, and chocolate.	$$
(G)	**SYRAH RESERVA LIMITED EDITION 2002, VIÑA PEREZ CRUZ** Maipo	A fresh, modern wine with youthful purity and ripe tannins - certain to improve with time.	$$$
(G)	**LEGADO DE ARMIDA CABERNET SAUVIGNON RESERVA 2001, SANTA INES** Maipo	A huge wine with loads of vibrant cassis, mocha, caramel and a layer of mint.	$$$
(G)	**LEGADO DE ARMIDA SYRAH RESERVA 2001, SANTA INES** Maipo	Monstrously big, yet refreshing. Black cherries, fruit pastilles and blackcurrant, spice and white pepper.	$$$
(G)	**LIMITED EDITION SYRAH RESERVA 2001, DE MARTINO**	A rich, ripe attack leads to blackcurrant fruit complemented by subtle oak and broad tannins.	$$$
(G)	**TERRACED SHIRAZ 2001, VIÑA LUIS FELIPE EDWARDS$**	A complexity of ripe fruit, toasty, vanilla oak and just a touch of interesting earthiness.	$$$
(G)	**ARBOLEDA CABERNET SAUVIGNON 1999, CALITERRA** Maipo	Rich raspberry nose with an underlying smoky, savory style. Silky tannins and ripe forest fruit.	$$$
(G)	**MONTGRAS LIMITED EDITION SYRAH 2001, MONTGRAS WINERY** Rapel	Broad, dark spicy fruit, crisp acidity and solid tannins. Powerful, with spices and blackberries.	$$$
(S)	**MONTGRAS LIMITED EDITION CABERNET MERLOT 2000, MONTGRAS WINERY** Rapel	Warm, ripe red fruit, scents of tar, herbs and vanilla, and a firm tannic structure.	$$$
(G)	**ECHEVERRIA FAMILY RESERVE CABERNET SAUVIGNON 1999, VIÑA ECHEVERRIA** Curicó	Warm, generous redcurrant fruit and smoky oakiness, with leather and smoke on the long finish.	$$$
(G)	**ERRAZURIZ SINGLE VINEYARD SYRAH 2001, VIÑA ERRAZURIZ** Aconcagua	A deep, rich smokiness and bright crunchy berry fruit, crushed black pepper and spicy ripeness.	$$$
(G)	**CABALLO LOCO NO 6 , VIÑA VALDIVIESO** Central Valley	A deep, intense spicy black fruit and cassis compote overlaid with eucalyptus and smoky oak.	$$$$

(G)	**Caballo Loco No 5 NV, Viña Valdivieso** Central Valley	Deep, lifted cassis fruit, blackberries, mocha and capiscum aromas. The palate is refined and concentrated.	$$$$

CHILE • SWEET

(G)	**Undurraga Late Harvest 2001, Viña Undurraga** Maipo	Magnificent honey, orange peel, spices and lychees in syrup. The finish seems to last forever.	$$

FRANCE

This was no better a year for France's wine producers than for the other exporters who confronted anti-French sentiment in the US following the Iraqi conflict, and growing competition globally from other countries. The 2002/3 statistics looked quite grim, with market share falling around the world as consumers lose patience with the unreliability of France's appellation contrôlée wines. Perhaps for this reason, the proven quality of the French winners from the International Wine Challenge has attracted growing attention in the UK and elsewhere.

FRANCE • SPARKLING

(A)	**Cremant du Jura Chardonnay NV, La Compagnie des Grands Vins du Jura** Jura	Light and refreshing with a citrussy finish.	$$
(A)	**Congratulations! NV, Ackerman Laurance** Loire	Clean and balanced with a sherbet dip finish.	$$
(B)	**Veuve Amiot Rosé Sparkling Saumur Brut NV, CFGV** Loire	A certain rusticity in no way diminishes the ripe, scented charms of this Loire sparkler.	$$
(A)	**Clairette de Die Jaillance NV, Cave de Die Jaillance** Rhône	Fresh and fruity with a lively palate and creamy finish.	$$

(A)	**SAUMUR SPARKLING BRUT NV, ACKERMAN LAURANCE** Loire	Lively wine with chalky minerality and a fresh citrus finish.	**$$**
(B)	**CREMANT DE BOURGOGNE BLANC DE NOIRS NV, BLASON DE BOURGOGNE** Burgundy	Aromas and flavors of ripe strawberries feature on the round palate of some complexity.	**$$$**
(G)	**ROSÉ DOLORES NV, CHAMPAGNE BARON FUENTÉ** Champagne	Fine mousse rises lazily in this delicate salmon-colored wine. Nutmeg, redcurrants and a silky texture.	**$$$$**
(S)	**GRANDE RÉSERVE NV, CHAMPAGNE BEAUMONT DES CRAYÈRES** Champagne	Classic green apples, toasted nuts and biscuits on the nose. A creamy, mature, full-bodied palate.	**$$$$**
(S)	**MHV THE HOUSE CHAMPAGNE NV, CHAMPAGNE P&C HEIDSIECK** Champagne	Classic champagne: lemons and grapefruit, classic biscuity notes, and a balanced, harmonious palate.	**$$$$**
(S)	**MHV CHAMPAGNE PAUL LANGIER BRUT NV, CHAMPAGNE P&C HEIDSIECK** Champagne	Frothy mousse and a palate of biscuits and ripe raspberries with a rich, mouthfilling texture.	**$$$$**
(S)	**WAITROSE BRUT NV, CHAMPAGNE P&C HEIDSIECK** Champagne	Palest tawny gold, with fine mousse. Ripe apples, biscuits and a remarkable depth and finesse.	**$$$$**
(G)	**CARTE D'OR 1998, CHAMPAGNE DRAPPIER** Champagne	A hint of lemons, bready development, and subtle autolysis on the full, rich palate.	**$$$$**
(G)	**CHARLES HEIDSIECK BLANC DE MILLENAIRES 1990, CHAMPAGNE P&C HEIDSIECK** Champagne	Deliciously soft and candied, with a hint of herbacousness and a yeasty ovaltine overtone.	**$$$$$**
(G)	**CHARLES HEIDSIECK MILLÉSIME BRUT ROSÉ 1996, CHAMPAGNE P&C HEIDSIECK** Champagne	Rich and creamy, with a coppery color, strawberry fruit, and a deep, nutty palate.	**$$$$$**
(G)	**CONSECRATION DU SIÈCLE BRUT CUVÉE DE PRESTIGE 1993, CHAMPAGNE J DE TELMONT** Champagne	It is very refined and shows superb balance of freshness, savoriness, acidity, fruit, and concentration.	**$$$$$**
(G)	**GANDE RESERVE MILLÉSIME 1991, BOUCHE PERE ET FILS** Champagne	Very rich and ripe, full of depth and complexity, with a honeyed, toasty nuttiness.	**$$$$$**

(G)	**BRUT SELECT CORDON BLEU NV, CHAMPAGNE DE VENOGE** Champagne	Clean and delicate, with a tightrope balance of appley, yeasty character and crisp acidity.	$$$$$
(G)	**BLANC DE CHARDONNAY 1996, CHAMPAGNE DUVAL-LEROY** Champagne	Rich breadiness on the nose and lemon marmalade flavors complementing the autolysis. Full-bodied and concentrated.	$$$$$
(G)	**GAUTHIER BRUT MILLÉSIME 1993, MARNE ET CHAMPAGNE DIFFUSION** Champagne	Dry and stylish, with a complex depth of maturing flavors on the weighty palate.	$$$$$
(G)	**YELLOW LABEL BRUT NV, VEUVE CLICQUOT** Champagne	Once again Veuve Cliquot proves its reputation with this powerful, rich wine. Biscuity and appley.	$$$$$
(G)	**CHARLES HEIDSIECK BRUT RÉSERVE MIS EN CAVE EN 1996 NV, CHAMPAGNE P&C HEIDSIECK** Champagne	All hail this masterful wine crafted by legend Daniel Thibault. Tight, rich, and very long.	$$$$$
(G)	**RUINART BRUT ROSÉ NV, CHAMPAGNE RUINART** Champagne	Crisp and firm, with a big raspberry and lime attack easing onto a long finish.	$$$$$
(G)	**BRUT 1992, CHAMPAGNE POMMERY** Champagne	An underlying power and richness, maturity, elegance, balance and ripeness to the fragrant grapefruit palate.	$$$$$
(G)	**BRUT DE NOMINÉE NV, CHAMPAGNE JACQUART** Champagne	Deep, toasty, honeyed nose and great fruit complexity on the weighty, intense, luxuriantly velvety palate.	$$$$$
(G)	**RUINART BRUT VINTAGE 1995, CHAMPAGNE RUINART** Champagne	Very good development, powerful weight and stunningly poised, sweetly ripe strawberry and lemon fruit.	$$$$$
(G)	**CUVÉE DES ENCHANTELEURS 1988, CHAMPAGNE HENRIOT** Champagne	Honeyed fruit and earthy notes intermingle with ripe crisp apples on the elegant, mature palate.	$$$$$
(G)	**FEMME DE CHAMPAGNE BRUT 1995, CHAMPAGNE DUVAL-LEROY** Champagne	Youthful grapefruit and pineapple fruit of great delicacy is offset by nutty mature aromas.	$$$$$
(G)	**NOBLE CUVÉE 1989, CHAMPAGNE LANSON** Champagne	Honeyed brioche nose with savory overtones. A honeyed, fleshy palate of fantastic concentration.	$$$$$

(G)	**BELLE EPOQUE BRUT 1996, CHAMPAGNE PERRIER-JOUËT** Champagne	Plenty of berry fruit and a touch of raspberries. Delicious development and savory notes.	$$$$$
(G)	**LA GRANDE DAME BRUT 1995, VEUVE CLICQUOT** Champagne	Youthful banana and candied currant fruit and yeasty, creamy, fresh bread aromas.	$$$$$
(G)	**CUVÉE DOM PÉRIGNON 1995, MOËT & CHANDON** Champagne	Driven as much by its depth and intensity as it is by its fruit character.	$$$$$
(G)	**CUVEÉ LOUISE 1989, CHAMPAGNE POMMERY** Champagne	The poised palate is layered with an elegant creaminess, redcurrants, honeycomb, toast and marzipan.	$$$$$
(G)	**COMTES DE CHAMPAGNE BLANC DE BLANCS BRUT 1995, CHAMPAGNE TAITTINGER** Champagne	Ebullient mousse. Pure white ripe fruit with a rich, mature yeasty character and excellent balance.	$$$$$
(G)	**DOM RUINART ROSÉ 1988, CHAMPAGNE RUINART** Champagne	Compelling elements of marmite and mushrooms lurk beneath the bright primary wild strawberry fruit.	$$$$$
(G)	**DOM RUINART BLANC DE BLANCS 1993, CHAMPAGNE RUINART** Champagne	Excellent richness of soft, delicate lemon fruit which is elegant, finely structured, generous and long.	$$$$$
(G)	**CHARLES HEIDSIECK CUVÉE CHAMPAGNE CHARLIE 1985, CHAMPAGNE P&C HEIDSIECK** Champagne	It's a treat to find such rich nutty, honeyed depth possessing such vibrant freshness.	$$$$$
(G)	**CHARLES HEIDSIECK BLANC DE BLANCS 1982, CHAMPAGNE P&C HEIDSIECK** Champagne	Twenty years and still going strong. Beefy, elegant, creamy and toasty, with fragrant buttered apples.	$$$$$
(G)	**CUVÉE DOM PÉRIGNON ROSÉ 1993, MOËT & CHANDON** Champagne	Raspberries explode on the palate. Great weight and vibrant acidity make it suited to food.	$$$$$

FRANCE • WHITE

(A)	**CELLIER DES DAUPHINS PRESTIGE BLANC CÔTES DU RHÔNE 2002, CELLIER DE DAUPHINS** Rhône	Ripe peach and pineapple aromas and a palate of fresh green apples.	$

(A)	**MHV Maison Blanc Vin de Table NV, Dominique Baud$**	Ripe, round and fruity. Clean finish.	$
(A)	**Skylark Hill Vin de Pays du Comte Tolosan NV, Les Chais Beaucairois** South West	Balanced, with fresh Granny Smith acidity and some fruit intensity.	$
(A)	**Vin de Pays du Comte Tolosan NV, Les Chais Beaucairois** South West	Bright with crisp appley fruit and fine acidity.	$
(A)	**MHV Marcel Hubert Medium Dry White Vin de Table Français NV, Dominique Baud**	Round style with mouth-pleasing fruit and sweetness.	$
(A)	**MHV Maison Blanc Medium Dry Vin de Table Français NV, Dominique Baud$**	Clean, peachy, easy-drinking style. Off-dry finish.	$
(A)	**MHV Vin de Pays de Gers NV, Prodis$**	Good, clean white with apple fruit and citrus appeal.	$
(A)	**Vin de Pays des Coteaux de l'Ardèche Blanc NV, Les Vignerons Ardechois** Rhône	Zesty with clean, fresh fruit flavors.	$
(A)	**Baron d'Arignac Blanc de Blancs 2002, Les Grands Chais de France** South West	Light, bright and white with good simple flavors.	$
(A)	**Conte de Fees Muscadet 2002, Prodis$**	Crisp with a creamy palate and mineral finish.	$
(B)	**Henri Vallon Muscadet de Sèvre-et-Maine 2002, Jean Beauquin** Loire	Mellow pear and apple fruit on the nose and on the light-bodied palate.	$
(B)	**Winter Hill Blanc Vin de Pays d'Oc 2002, Foncalieu** Languedoc-Roussillon	A refreshing alternative white from southern France. Lifted floral and white fruit aromas.	$
(A)	**Virgnie de France Sauvignon Blanc 2002, Les Domaines Virginie** Languedoc-Roussillon	Fresh, vivid fruit and a mouthwatering acidity make this pleasant indeed.	$

(A) **J St-Honore Vin de Pays du Jardin de la France Chardonnay 2002, Vinival** Loire	Balanced with ripe white fruits and fine acidity.	$
(A) **J St-Honore Vin de Pays du Jardin de la France Chenin Blanc 2002, Vinival** Loire	Light, fresh, and summery. Clean finish.	$
(S) **Marc Ducourneau Vin de Pays des Côtes de Gascogne 2002, Plaimont** South West	Many elements meld on the nose: elderflowers, peaches, quartz, and lemons. Very attractive.	$
(S) **Grange du Midi Marsanne Vin de Pays d'Oc 2002, LGI** Languedoc-Roussillon	Highly perfumed with appley aromas. Very floral on the palate with spice and banana.	$
(S) **Domaine du Bois Viognier 2002, Viña Morandé** Languedoc-Roussillon	The soft ripe apricot palate boasts impressive concentration, power, length and fresh acidity.	$
(B) **Chardonnay Marsanne Vin de Pays d'Oc , Stowells** Languedoc-Roussillon	Fig and nut aromas work beautifully with the juicy white fruit on the palate.	$
(B) **Frederic Roger Sauvignon Blanc 2002, Frederic Roger** Languedoc-Roussillon	Nettles and starfruit grace this bright tropical Sauvignon Blanc from the south of France.	$
(B) **Tour Verité Sauvignon Blanc 2002, André Quancard André** Bordeaux	Nettles, greengages and daisies on the nose. The palate is vibrant, fresh, and invigorating.	$
(A) **Lily Côtes de Gascogne 2002, Groupement de Producteurs Vignoble de Gascogne** South West	Fresh with grass and hay aromas. Crisp finish.	$
(A) **Domaine de Bergon 2002, VT Languedoc** Languedoc-Roussillon	Fruity wine with lemon and spice notes.	$
(A) **Sauvignon Blanc Lurton 2002, Ackerman Laurance** Loire	Zesty with a crisp palate and balanced finish.	$
(A) **Colombelle 2002, Les Producteurs Plaimont** South West	Light style with bright acidity and crunchy fruit.	$

(A) PRIEURE ST ANDRÉ OAK AGED BORDEAUX SAUVIGNON 2002, ANDRÉ QUANCARD ANDRÉ Bordeaux	Grassy wine with good oak influence.		$
(A) CHÂTEAU ROCHELONGUE 2002, LES CAVES DE LANDIRAS Bordeaux	Grassy nose leads to a crisp, balanced palate.		$
(A) ORGANIC VERMENTINO CHARDONNAY , LES GRANDS CHAIS DE FRANCE$	Aromatic wine with a ripe and spicy finish.		$
(A) VIN DE PAYS DES CÔTES DE GASCOGNE 2002, YVON MAU South West	Clean and grassy with piercing fresh acidity.		$
(A) FRUITS OF FRANCE CHARDONNAY 2002, PAUL BOUTINOT Languedoc-Roussillon	Light with fresh lemon and nectarine aromas.		$
(A) FRUITS OF FRANCE VIOGNIER 2002, PAUL BOUTINOT Languedoc-Roussillon	Perfumed with apricot and nectarine aromas.		$
(A) FORTANT DE FRANCE VIN DE PAYS D'OC SAUVIGNON BLANC 2002, ROBERT SKALLI$	Very pleasing crisp white fruit and pleasing herby aromas.		$
(A) FORTANT DE FRANCE VIN DE PAYS D'OC CHARDONNAY 2002, ROBERT SKALLI	Pleasant tropical banana and honeydew melon aromas and flavors.		$
(A) OLD TART TERRET SAUVIGNON BLANC 2002, PAUL BOUTINOT South West	Bright with clean lines and a vibrant, fruity finish.		$
(B) LA FONT CHARDONNAY 2002, LES VINS MAS-APLIN Languedoc-Roussillon	Subtle roast almond and toast aromas enliven the invigorating nose of ripe yellow fruit.		$
(B) MERCHANTS BAY SAUVIGNON BLANC SEMILLON 2002, INTERNATIONAL WINE SERVICES Bordeaux	Classic cut grass and waxed lemon aromas. A palate of fresh yet buttery fruit.		$
(B) MUSCADET DE SÈVRE-ET-MAINE SUR LIE CHÂTEAU LA TOUCHE 2002, VINIVAL Loire	Toasted walnuts accent the ripe yet light-bodied yellow fruit on nose and palate.		$

	Wine	Description	Price
B	**SAINT SAVIN 2002, JEAN MARC DULONG** Bordeaux	A touch of rich toasty oak rounds out the verdant green fruit palate.	$
B	**DOM BRIAL 2001, CAVES DES VIOGNIERS DE BAIXAS** Midi	A correct, well made wine with a refreshing grapeyness and a lift of bright acidity.	$
A	**MHV PREMIÈRES CÔTES DE BORDEAUX NV, BOUEY & FILS** Bordeaux	Flowers and honey on the developed nose, and an edgy palate of racy lemon fruit.	$
S	**DOMAINE DU TARIQUET CHENIN BLANC 2002, DOMAINE DU TARIQUET** South West	Fresh apples on nose and palate, which has a touch of cream on the finish.	$$
S	**LES JAMELLES SAUVIGNON BLANC 2002, BADET CLEMENT** South West	Crisp, crunchy white fruit in the mouth and chalky notes on the lifted, aromatic nose.	$$
B	**LA BAUME CHARDONNAY 2002, BRL HARDY** Languedoc-Roussillon	Good complexity to the richly oaked crystalline tropical fruit on nose and balanced palate.	$$
B	**WINTER HILL RESERVE CHARDONNAY 2002, FONCALIEU** Languedoc-Roussillon	Very full-bodied pear and apple fruit palate. Fresh invigorating acidity lasts for the duration.	$$
B	**VIOGNIER VIN DE PAYS D'OC 2001, BARON PHILIPPE DE ROTHSCHILD** Languedoc-Roussillon	Deep lemon yellow. Warm apricots and peaches feature on the nose and palate.	$$
B	**CHÂTEAU CHANTELOUP BORDEAUX BLANC SEC 2002, VIGNOBLES MICHEL PION** Bordeaux	Floral hints round out the nose and palate of fresh white pears and ripe gooseberries.	$$
B	**CHÂTEAU DUCLA ENTRE-DEUX-MERS 2002, YVON MAU** Bordeaux	Crisp, refreshing and clear, this is unoaked white Bordeaux at its most quintessential.	$$
B	**ORIGIN LOIRE SAUVIGNON BLANC 2002, ORIGIN** Loire	Very good grassy nettly fruit sits on the mid-palate enveloped in fresh acidity.	$$
B	**LA MOULINE VIOGNIER 2002, CAVE DE PUISSERGUIER** Languedoc-Roussillon	Juicy yellow apples, guava, banana and lemons all feature. Intense and expressive.	$$

(S)	**TOURAINE SAUVIGNON BLANC 2002, DOMAINE DE L'AUMONIER** Loire	Extremely pretty nettle and white berry fruit aromas and flavors on the nose and palate.	$$
(S)	**ALSACE ONE 2002, PIERRE SPARR & FILS** Alsace	Positively seductive, optimally ripe pink fruit on the nose. The palate lingers on and on.	$$
(S)	**SICHEL SIRIUS 2002, MAISON SICHEL** Bordeaux	Freshly cut grass vies with lifted lemon fruit on the nose. Soft, warm spice.	$$
(G)	**PINOT GRIS RÉSERVE 2002, PIERRE SPARR & FILS** Alsace	Perfumed and honeyed. Ripe and rich with a nutty character and a sweet, silky palate.	$$$ ♔♔
(G)	**JURANÇON SEC CHANT DES VIGNES 2001, DOMAINE CAUHAPÉ** South West	Full of honey, grapefruit and flowers. Intense, complex and exotic with a warm lemony palate.	$$$
(G)	**RIESLING GRAND CRU GOLDERT 2001, ZINCK WINES** Alsace	A wonderful array of tea roses, mangoes and lime, and a maturing, honeyed weight.	$$$$
(G)	**CHABLIS PREMIER CRU LES VAUDEVEY 2001, DOMAINE LAROCHE** Burgundy	Chalky, steely and grassy on the nose with a buttery intensity on the taut palate.	$$$$ ♔
(G)	**CHABLIS PREMIER CRU LES VAILLONS VIEILLES VIGNES 2001, DOMAINE LAROCHE** Burgundy	Quintessentially clean, lean steely style of Chablis with a perfumed minerality. A fresh acid streak.	$$$$
(G)	**CHABLIS GRAND CRU LES CLOS 2000, DOMAINE LAROCHE** Burgundy	Ripe melon fruit and almonds with a creamy savory note and a poised, rich palate.	$$$$$

FRANCE • ROSE

(A)	**ORGANIC CINSAULT GRENACHE 2002, LES GRANDS CHAIS DE FRANCE**	Clean, fresh and fruity. In the pink.	$
(A)	**JP CHENET CINSAULT GRENACHE VIN DE PAYS D'OC 2002, LES GRANDS CHAIS DE FRANCE**	Berry fruit driven with good freshness.	$

FRANCE • RED

(A)	**MHV Maison Rouge Dry Vin de Table Français NV, Dominique Baud**	Baked red-fruit style. Supple finish.	$
(A)	**Vignobles du Peloux Minervois 2001, Vignobles du Peloux** Languedoc-Roussillon	Spicy wine with hints of herb and wild scrub on the finish.	$
(A)	**Calvet Claret 2002, Benoit et Valérie Calvet** Bordeaux	Supple and ripe with user-friendly tannins.	$
(A)	**MHV Marcel Hubert Medium Dry Red Vin de Table Français NV, Dominique Baud**	Berry laden wine with a sweet finish.	$
(A)	**Vignobles du Peloux Corbières 2002, Vignobles du Peloux** Languedoc-Roussillon	Ripe, earthy red with rich fruit and a spicy finish.	$
(A)	**J St-Honore Vin de Pays Syrah 2002, Vinival** Languedoc-Roussillon	Leather and tar aromas allied to supple black fruit.	$
(A)	**L'Avielle Roche Claret NV, Prodis** Bordeaux	Easy-quaffing style with juicy fruit and soft structure.	$
(A)	**Winter Hill Classic Red 2002, Foncalieu** Languedoc-Roussillon	Morello cherries and coffee notes spill from a fresh, juicy palate wrapped in soft tannins.	$
(A)	**Winter Hill Rouge 2002, Foncalieu** Languedoc-Roussillon	A sweet nose of blackberries and spice is paired with a soft, dry, integrated palate.	$
(A)	**Pont Neuf Côtes du Rhône 2001, Princes de France** Rhône	Mature open and structured fruit	$
(S)	**Old Git Red Côtes du Ventoux 2002, Paul Boutinot** Rhône	Mineral notes, pepper and spice on the palate, with a clean finish of some length.	$

(B)	**LE BRASSET GRENACHE SYRAH OLD VINE SELECTION 2001, DOMAINES PAUL MAS** Languedoc-Roussillon	A grip and ripe fruit combination that continues all the way to the clean finish.	$
(A)	**STOWELLS MERLOT NV, STOWELLS** Languedoc-Roussillon	Sweet, lifted, perfumed nose of fresh red berries is married to a soft, attractive palate.	$
(A)	**STOWELLS CELLAR SELECTION MERLOT 2001, STOWELLS** South West	Clear spiced juicy plums dance on the palate.	$
(A)	**MERLOT CAROLINE DE BEAULIEU SELECTION 2002, CIRA** Languedoc-Roussillon	Plenty of red plum fruit on the fresh, vivid mid-palate.	$
(A)	**LE FAUVE MERLOT 2002, TERROIR CLUB** Languedoc-Roussillon	Plum and spice flavors and a structure of substance.	$
(A)	**LE FAUVE SYRAH 2002, TERROIR CLUB** Languedoc-Roussillon	Dark and thickly fruited with integrated tannin.	$
(A)	**B DE BERTIAC 2002, ANDRÉ QUANCARD ANDRÉ** Bordeaux	Fruit-rich with berry and cassis aromas.	$
(A)	**TOUR VERITÉ RED 2002, ANDRÉ QUANCARD ANDRÉ** Bordeaux	Light style with clean lines and a balanced finish.	$
(A)	**DOMAINE DE SUBREMONT ROUGE 2001, JEAN-LOUIS POUDOU** Languedoc-Roussillon	Herb strewn with pungent blackberry flavors.	$
(A)	**WINEMAKER SELECTION MINERVOIS CUVÉE PRESTIGE 2000, LES GRANDS CHAIS DE FRANCE** Alsace	Inky with ripe tannins and plump fruit.	$
(A)	**CHÂTEAU CAMPOT LAFON 1999, LES CAVES DE LANDIRAS** Bordeaux	Berry driven with light depth and complexity.	$
(A)	**VIN DE PAYS DE L'AUDE 2002, YVON MAU** Bordeaux	Earthy with plum and cassis flavors.	$

(A)	**DULONG X Y 2001, JEAN MARC DULONG** Bordeaux	Decent blackfruit intensity. Warming finish.	$
(A)	**FRUITS OF FRANCE MERLOT 2002, PAUL BOUTINOT** Languedoc-Roussillon	Juicy style with integrated tannins.	$
(A)	**FORTANT DE FRANCE VIN DE PAYS D'OC MERLOT 2002, ROBERT SKALLIS**	Plum fruit permeates nose and palate.	$
(A)	**FORTANT DE FRANCE VIN DE PAYS D'OC CABERNET SAUVIGNON 2001, ROBERT SKALLIS**	Ripe cassis fruit lines the palate and bounces from the nose.	$
(A)	**CHÂTEAU HAUT PRADOT BORDEAUX 2002, ANDRÉ QUANCARD ANDRÉ** Bordeaux	Cassis and mint aromas allied to supple structure.	$
(B)	**LAZY LIZARD SYRAH 2001, PAUL BOUTINOT** Languedoc-Roussillon	There is a nice complexity of gamey, farmy fruit and fresh currant and blackberry fruit.	$
(B)	**VIRGNIE DE FRANCE SYRAH 2002, LES DOMAINES VIRGINIE** Languedoc-Roussillon	Lifted marjoram and bay leaf aromas accent ripe red apples and plums on the palate.	$
(S)	**DOMAINE DE LAUREL 2002, CAVE LES VINS DE ROQUEBRUN** Languedoc-Roussillon	Herbes de Provence on the richly fruited ripe raspberry nose. Concentrated, balanced and long.	$
(B)	**WINTER HILL RESERVE SYRAH 2002, FONCALIEU** Languedoc-Roussillon	Ripe loganberries sit beautifully in a freshly-woven basket of supporting fruit tannins.	$$
(B)	**WINTER HILL RESERVE CABERNET SAUVIGNON 2002, FONCALIEU** Languedoc-Roussillon	The restrained dark fruit is classically styled and laced with spicy oak. Medium-bodied and concentrated.	$$
(B)	**VIN DE PAYS D'OC CABERNET SAUVIGNON 2001, BARON PHILIPPE DE ROTHSCHILD** Languedoc-Roussillon	Cassis, tree bark and tobacco on the nose. The palate is packed with fresh, vibrant fruit.	$$
(B)	**FITOU MONT TAUCH 2002, MONT TAUCH** Languedoc-Roussillon	Red berries, scents of rosemary and thyme, restrained minerality and good ripeness.	$$

B	**FRENCH KISS CORBIÈRES 2002, MONT TAUCH** Languedoc-Roussillon	Rich wild strawberry fruit oozes from the palate of this fresh, juicy wine.	$$
B	**BEAUJOLAIS LA BAREILLE 2002, MAISON THORIN** Beaujolais	Ephemeral blueberry and bubblegum aromas on the nose. Redcurrant fruit palate.	$$
B	**VINTAGE CLARET OAK AGED BORDEAUX SUPÉRIEUR 2001, YVON MAU** Bordeaux	Deep garnet red, with cherries, spice and hints of undergrowth on the supple, structured palate.	$$
B	**CHÂTEAU BEAU MAYNE 2002, DOURTHE** Bordeaux	Deep vibrant ruby red, and bursting with crunchy dark ripe plums and fresh juicy redcurrants.	$$
S	**BETOULET MERLOT ALICANTE 2001, CELLIER LAURENT CABARET** Languedoc-Roussillon	Lifted aromas of damsons and freshly crushed mint leaves; vibrant, velvety, ripe cherry fruit palate.	$$
S	**GINESTET MASCARON 2001, GINESTET** Bordeaux	Dark purple-red. A compelling, leafy nose, with a full, structured palate of lush blackcurrants.	$$
S	**ERMITAGE DU PIC-SAINT-LOUP 2001, PIERRE RAVAILLE** Languedoc-Roussillon	Soft scents of the maquis add complexity to the structured, intense blackcurrants and loganberries.	$$
S	**DOMAINE DE LA GRANDE BELLANE VALREAS CÔTES DU RHÔNE 2001, EARL GAIA** Rhône	Clear bright red damson fruit with plenty of cracked black pepper and delicate sandalwood.	$$
S	**ILE LA FORGE SYRAH 2001, DOMAINES PAUL MAS** Languedoc-Roussillon	A fragrant wine with blackberry and bramble fruit, integrated oak and firm structure.	$$
S	**BEAUJOLAIS VILLAGES TRADITION 2002, DOMAINE MANOIR DU CARRA** Beaujolais	What could be more seductive than this panopoly of vivid yet light-bodied flowers and fruits?	$$
S	**ROBERT SKALLI SYRAH 2001, LES VINS SKALLI** Languedoc-Roussillon	Bramble and blackcurrant fruit on the nose and palate. Good tannin/fruit balance and decent length.	$$
G	**ABBOTTS PLANTANUS 2001, ABBOTTS** Languedoc-Roussillon	Pure, clean, bouncy fruit with a plummy, jammy quality and a chewy tannic palate.	$$

(S)	**DARRIAUD LES HAUTS DU MONT VENTOUX BARRIQUE 2000, LA CHAPELLE DE CRAY** Rhône	A deep color and balanced, fleshy quality. The tannin and acidity bode well for aging.	$$
(S)	**CUVÉE TRADITION MADIRAN 2000, DOMAINE CAPMARTIN** South West	Very dark, with layers of morello morello cherries, blackcurrant fruit and a chunky structure.	$$
(S)	**TERRE ROMAINE SYRAH 2001, LAITHWAITE'S PRIVATE CELLARS** Rhône	Expressive fruit, an elegant structure and dark with blackcurrants, mint and powerful tannins.	$$
(S)	**CHÂTEAU DE LANDURE CUVÉE DE L'ABBÉ FREGOUSE 2000, CHÂTEAU DE LANDURE** Languedoc-Roussillon	Scented blackberry leaves and delicate vanilla hints on the nose. Expressive yet tightly-knit.	$$
(S)	**CÔTES DU RHÔNE BELLERUCHE 2001, M CHAPOUTIER** Rhône	Wonderful cedar oak aroma. Sturdy with rich bramble and spice notes, with firm, ripe tannins.	$$
(S)	**COSTIÈRES DE NÎMES GRANDE RÉSERVE 2001, LOUIS BERNARD** Languedoc-Roussillon	Big, warm grenache with black peppery fruit and chocolatey new oak. Ripe, dark and sweet.	$$
(S)	**CAVE DE RASTEAU LES PEYRIÈRES 2000, CAVE DE RASTEAU** Rhône	Medium intensity mulberry fruit on the nose, with a dry, savory palate and firm tannins.	$$
(S)	**DOMAINE DE FONTBERTIÈRE MINERVOIS LA LIVINIERE 1998, BIG FRANK CHLUDINSKI** Languedoc-Roussillon	Scents of the maquis on a warm summer wind. Ripe red fruit, spice and leather.	$$
(S)	**TERROIR DU TRIAS BEAUMES-DE-VENISE 2000, CAVE DES VIGNERONS DE BEAUMES-DE-VENISE** Rhône	The integration of oak is total, and a delicious counterpoint to sweet fruit.	$$
(S)	**ABBOTTS CUMULUS 2000, ABBOTTS** Languedoc-Roussillon	Attractive meaty, savory and perfumed tight palate with firm, young tannins.	$$
(G)	**CHÂTEAU DE LA GARDE BORDEAUX SUPÉRIEUR 2000, CHÂTEAU DE LA GARDE** Bordeaux	Youthful cassis and cedar aromas with subtle new oak. Ripe and opulent with fine tannins.	$$$
(G)	**CHÂTEAU PEYROS GREENWICH 43N 2000, LEDA** South West	Almost pitch black with heady fruit, floral overtones, chewy tannins and concentration. Very long finish.	$$$

(G) **LES VIGNES D'ANTAN 2000, DOMAINE LIGNON** Languedoc-Roussillon	Bright, chewy cherry aromas and peppery touches of fresh capsicum and spice. Concentrated and soft.	$$$
(G) **SAINT CHINIAN BARDOU 2001, LAURENT MIQUEL** Languedoc-Roussillon	Blackcurrant and tar flavors and a smattering of pepper, all supported by velvet tannins.	$$$
(G) **VACQUEYRAS LES CHRISTINS 2001, PERRIN** Rhône	Ripe, attractive raspberries and cream. Sweet spice, elegant structure, good balance and savory, smoky oak.	$$$
(G) **VOSNE ROMANÉE 1ER CU AUX BRÛLEES 2001, DOMAINE MICHEL GROS** Burgundy	A fresh, lively wine with explosive strawberry fruit and a slight truffliness. Elegant and balanced.	$$$$
(G) **CLOS VOUGEOT GRAND MAUPERTUIS GRAND CRU 2001, DOMAINE MICHEL GROS** Burgundy	An intense muscular style of Burgundy with a gamey, meaty complexity and chunky fruit.	$$$$
(G) **CUVÉE DU VATICAN 2001, DIFFONTY** Rhône	Massive, intense dark cherry and hedgerow fruit. The fruit and acidity are poignantly juxtaposed.	$$$$
(G) **CHÂTEAU LA VIEILLE CURE 1999, CHÂTEAU LA VIEILLE CURE** Bordeaux	An expressive cassis and blackberry nose with a touch of spice. Layered, fleshy fruit.	$$$$
(G) **LE JUGE 2000, DOMAINE DE CAPION** Languedoc-Roussillon	Aromatic, with an array of flavors from bramble and spice through to leather and saddlesoap!	$$$$
(G) **NUITS-SAINT-GEORGES 2001, LABOURÉ ROI** Burgundy	Expressive black forest fruit supported by firm, ripe tannins and an immense length.	$$$$
(G) **PREMIUM LA CLAPE 2000, CHÂTEAU CAMPLAZENS** Languedoc-Roussillon	Heaps of brambly, raspberry, plummy fruit aromas with licorice and black plum fruit.	$$$$
(G) **CHÂTEAU GRANGE NEUVE 2000, GROS & FILS** Bordeaux	Fleshy, ripe black fruit, mint and cassis fruit and very fine, tight tannins.	$$$$$
(G) **DOMAINE FERRATON CÔTE RÔTIE 1999, DOMAINE FERRATON PÈRE ET FILS** Rhône	Peppery and spicy with a touch of smoked bacon. Understated oak and restrained tannins.	$$$$$

G	**NUITS-SAINT-GEORGES 2001, DOMAINE MICHEL GROS** Burgundy	The floral nose leads into complex cherry flavors with fine tannins and old vine density.	$$$$$
G	**CORTON-RENARDES GRAND CRU 2000, DOMAINE MAILLARD PERE ET FILS** Burgundy	Perfumed, mature aromas of beetroot and caramel. Depth, concentration, refinement, and admirable persistence.	$$$$$

FRANCE • SWEET

S	**DOMAINE HAUT-RAULY MONBAZILLAC 2001, PIERRE ALARD** South West	Ripe and dense, honeyed, and creamy. The luscious palate of marmalade is youthful yet complex.	$
S	**SAUSSIGNAC CUVÉE FLAVIE 2001, CHÂTEAU DES EYSSARDS** South West	Delicate honey and apricot on the nose. Intense, waxy palate of nuts and candied oranges.	$$$
S	**CÔTES DE BERGERAC MOËLLEUX 2001, CLOS DALMAIN** South West	Crystalline lemons on the nose. The palate spills over with sweetness buttressed by firm acidity.	$$$
G	**CHÂTEAU GRINOU SAUSSIGNAC 2001, CHÂTEAU GRINOU** South West	Dried apricots, fragrant pear flavors and hints of cinnamon spice. Zingy, fresh, lifted acidity.	$$$$

GERMANY

The efforts of a new generation of winemakers are finally beginning to pay off, as Germany's modern whites (and a few reds) win critical acclaim at the International Wine Challenge, and as bottles find their way onto the tables of upmarket restaurants. The key to Germany's success lies in producing dry wines that are ripely attractive as well as classic sweet and off-dry wines – and packaging them in bottles whose labels don't require a degree in wine and deciphering Gothic text.

GERMANY • WHITE

A	**NIERSTEINER GUTES DOMTAL AUSLESE 2001, RUDOLF MÜLLER** Rheinhessen	Luscious nose leads to an opulent palate showing complex quince and honey flavors.	$

(A)	**KENDERMANN RIESLING KABINETT 2002, REH KENDERMANN** Mosel-Saar-Ruwer	Balanced with lovely fruit purity and a clinical finish.	$
(A)	**FIRE MOUNTAIN RIESLING 2001, ZGM** Pfalz	Fruit purity allied to good acidity and honeyed sweetness.	$
(A)	**DEVIL'S ROCK RIESLING NV, BINDERER ST URSULA** Pfalz	Fresh, clean and pure. Off-dry finish.	$
(A)	**SCHMITT SÖHNE PINOT GRIGIO 2001, SCHMITT SÖHNE** Pfalz	Spicy style with peach and citrus aromas.	$
(A)	**KENDERMANN CLASSIC RIESLING 2002, REH KENDERMANN** Pfalz	Lemony wine with fine acidity and a luscious finish.	$
(A)	**KENDERMANN LANGENBACH SPÄTLESE 2002, REH KENDERMANN** Rheinhessen	Honeyed nose leads to super-ripe palate balanced by piercing acidity.	$
(A)	**FIRE MOUNTAIN RIESLING 2002, ZGM** Pfalz	Lively fruit, a touch of sweetness and balancing acidity.	$
(A)	**KENDERMANN DRY RIESLING 2002, REH KENDERMANN** Pfalz	Pure style with a mineral and zest finish.	$
(B)	**CARL REH CLASSIC RIESLING 2002, REH KENDERMANN** Mosel-Saar-Ruwer	Very attractive candied lemon and tangerine fruit on the nose and palate. Zippy acidity.	$
(A)	**KENDERMANN RIESLING SPÄTLESE 2002, REH KENDERMANN** Mosel-Saar-Ruwer	Ripe and honeyed with good balance and a sweet finish.	$
(B)	**CARL REH RIESLING TROCKEN 2002, REH KENDERMANN** Mosel-Saar-Ruwer	Delicate tropical pineapple notes feature on the nose, while lemon drops radiate from the palate.	$$

Wines are listed in approximate price order (though this can vary widely depending where they are on offer). All of the wines in the Guide are good value, by definition, but the best buys carry the "Great Value Wine of the Year" symbol. These were the bottles that performed best in their their price band in a blind tasting by the International Wine Challenge top tasters – the super-jurors. Buy them when you can; they tend to sell out very quickly.

(G)	**URZIGER WÜRZGARTEN RIESLING KABINETT 1996, CHRISTOFFEL BERRES** Mosel-Saar-Ruwer	Rich and perfumed with fragrant flowers and spice. Displaying maturity and possessing an immense length.	$$
(S)	**DURKHEIMER MICHELSBERG 2002, DARTING ESTATE** Pfalz	Complex array of white pepper, mandarin oranges and lemons, with a refreshing blast of acidity.	$$
(S)	**URZIGER WÜRZGARTEN RIESLING SPÄTLESE 1993, CHRISTOFFEL PRÜM** Mosel-Saar-Ruwer	Great complexity of lime and floral fruit overlaid with petrolly kerosene notes of impending maturity.	$$
(S)	**DR L RIESLING 2002, DR LOOSEN** Mosel-Saar-Ruwer	Elegant flowers and limes on the nose, and a palate of perfumed Sicilian lemons.	$$
(S)	**SCHEUREBE TROCKEN 2002, WEINGUT WITTMANN** Rheinhessen	A wonderful fresh lemon scent on the nose and a touch of spice for warmth.	$$
(S)	**HOCHHEIMER BERG RIESLING KABINETT 2001, DOMDECHANT WERNER'SCHES WEINGUT** Rheingau	Limes, sherbet and floral lavender notes. Just off-dry with a keen balancing acidity.	$$
(G)	**ESCHERNDORFER LUMP RIESLING SPÄTLESE TROCKEN 2002, WEINGUT HORST SAUER** Franken	Tremendous floral aromatics and zippy lime fruit with a touch of underlying bedrock minerality.	$$$$
(G)	**GRAACHER HIMMELREICH RIESLING SPÄTLESE 1997, JJ PRÜM** Mosel-Saar-Ruwer	Rich developed aromas of petrol and perfumed spice, clean, concentrated fruit, and zingy, balanced acidity.	$$$$
(G)	**SEHNSUCHT 2001, WEINGUT HORST SAUER** Franken	A waxed lemon, marzipan and apricot nose with a hint of florality. Full-bodied and balanced.	$$$$$

GERMANY • ROSÉ

(A)	**CARL REH ROSÉ 2002, REH KENDERMANN** Rheinhessen	Fresh with strawberry and cherry notes.	$

Wines are listed in approximate price order (though this can vary widely depending where they are on offer). All of the wines in the Guide are good value, by definition, but the best buys carry the "Great Value Wine of the Year" symbol. These were the bottles that performed best in their their price band in a blind tasting by the International Wine Challenge top tasters – the super-jurors. Buy them when you can; they tend to sell out very quickly.

GERMANY • SWEET

Ⓖ	**FRANKEN RIEMENSCHNEIDER UNTEREISENHEIMER SONNENBERG SPÄTLESE 2000, WINZERGENOSSENSCHAFT**	Honeyed lemon vanilla nose with great complexity, richness and vivacious acidity.	$$$$
Ⓖ	**GRAACHER HIMMELREICH RIESLING EISWEIN 2001, DR PAULY-BERGWEILER** Mosel-Saar-Ruwer	Rich and intensely sweet, with piercing acidity. Great candied lime, orange zest and marmalade complexity.	$$$$$

HUNGARY

The only country in Eastern Europe to produce top class wines as well as bottles that offer good value daily drinking, Hungary has benefited from extensive foreign investment in Tokaji and renewed local efforts to revive the fortunes of Eger Bikaver (Bull's Blood). The numbers of truly impressive wines are still small, however, as these results from the International Wine Challenge show. But they are worth exploring because they include styles such as Tokaji and Irsay Oliver that are not produced anywhere else in the world.

HUNGARY • SPARKLING

Ⓐ	**CHAPEL HILL SPARKLING PINOT NOIR CHARDONNAY NV, BALATONBOGLAR$**	Apple and pear style with decent acid balance.	$$
Ⓐ	**CHAPEL HILL SPARKLING CHARDONNAY NV, BALATONBOGLAR$**	Sherbet nose and a lively citrus palate.	$$
Ⓐ	**CHATEAU VINCENT CRYSTAL DRY 2000, VINARIUM** Buda	Clean and fresh with a bone dry finish.	$$
Ⓐ	**CHATEAU VINCENT EXTRA BRUT 2000, VINARIUM** Buda	Lemon sponge nose and a biscuity finish.	$$

HUNGARY • WHITE

(A)	**NAGYREDE UNOAKED CHARDONNAY 2002, NAGYREDE** Nagyrede	Zesty nose leads to a fresh and uncluttered palate.	$
(B)	**CHAPEL HILL IRSAI OLIVÉR 2002, BALATONBOGLAR$**	Lemon yellow. Delicate cashew notes add interest to the juicy pear fruit palate.	$
(A)	**RIVERVIEW PINOT GRIGIO 2002, HILLTOP NÉSZMELY$**	Spicy wine with peach and citrus notes.	$
(A)	**RIVERVIEW SAUVIGNON BLANC 2002, HILLTOP NÉSZMELY** North Transdanubia	Fresh and bright and packed with gooseberry and grass aromas.	$
(B)	**VIRGIN VINTAGE SAUVIGNON BLANC 2002, HILLTOP NÉSZMELY** North Transdanubia	Crisp cool-climate white pears spill from the classically styled palate. Clean and green.	$$
(B)	**VIRGIN VINTAGE CHARDONNAY 2002, HILLTOP NÉSZMELY** North Transdanubia	Yellow plums and white flowers on the nose. The palate is round yet not heavy.	$$
(B)	**CHAPEL HILL CHARDONNAY SINGLE VINEYARD SELECTION 2002, BALATONBOGLAR** South Transdanubia	Crystalline tropical pears on the nose are given an added dimension by notes of spice.	$$

HUNGARY • ROSÉ

(A)	**RIVERVIEW CABERNET SAUVIGNON ROSÉ 2002, HILLTOP NÉSZMELY** North Transdanubia	Light and breezy style. Summer pudding flavors on the finish.	$

HUNGARY • RED

(A)	**RIVERVIEW CABERNET SAUVIGNON 2000, HILLTOP NÉSZMELY** North Transdanubia	Pepper, cedar and blackcurrants shine on the sweetly ripe, round, integrated and well-balanced palate.	$

Ⓐ **SZEKSZÁRDI BULLS BLOOD 2001, HUNGAROVIN** South Transdanubia	Powerful wine with fruit depth and balance.	$

HUNGARY • SWEET

Ⓖ **TOKAJI ASZÚ 5 PUTTONYOS 1956, CROWN ESTATES OF HUNGARY** Tokaj-Hegyalja	Floral aromas and notes of beeswax and honey lace an intense orange peel and marmalade palate.	$$

ITALY

Increasingly the most exciting wine-producing country in the world, Italy continues to impress tasters at the International Wine Challenge with the range of its wines – and the choice that's now offered between classics and new styles, and between super-premium wines and inexpensive efforts from the recently developed wine regions of the south and Sicily. One development this year was the continued improvement of Italy's whites such as the Gold medal Verdicchio.

ITALY • SPARKLING

Ⓢ **MOMBELLO ASTI NV, CAPETTA** Piemonte	A generous sprinkling of rose petals on the nose and a palate of ripe fruit.	$
Ⓐ **CAPETTA ASTI DOCG NV, CAPETTA** Piemonte	Good aromatics allied to pure fruit and fresh acidity.	$
Ⓐ **ASTI SANTERO NV, SANTERO** Piemonte	Floral nose leads to a light and refreshing palate.	$
Ⓐ **DOMANI ASTI NV, FRATELLI MARTINI** Piemonte	Perfumed with a light and spritzy finish.	$

(A) GAVIOLI LAMBRUSCO GRASPAROSSA DI CASTELVETRO 2002, DONELLI VINI Emilia Romagna	Soft and fruit rich with a spritzy finish.	**$**
(B) ASTI CANTI NV, FRATELLI MARTINI SECONDO LUIGI Piemonte	Beautiful bright lemon yellow color, fresh scented fruit and a pleasing off-dry palate.	**$$**
(B) ASTI LE MONFERRINE NV, ARALDICA VINI PIEMONTESI Piemonte	Excellent mousse, tropical fruit and minerals on the nose and palate of ripe pineapples.	**$$**
(B) BENI DI BATASIOLO MOSCATO D'ASTI 2002, BATASIOLO Piemonte	Comely honeycomb and pear aromas on the nose and a sweet yet fresh palate.	**$$**
(B) LAMBRUSCO DELL' EMILIA AMABILE 2002, DONELLI VINI Emilia Romagna	Deep ruby purple color, rich concentrated fruit with lively mousse and a pleasingly long finish.	**$$**
(A) CONGRATULATIONS! 2001, CONCILIO Trentino-Alto Adige	Light and fruity with a refreshing finish.	**$$**
(A) CONGRATULATIONS! 2002, CONCILIO Trentino-Alto Adige	The fresh nose leads to a light and frothy palate.	**$$**
(B) LAMBRUSCO REGGIANO ARTE E CONCERTO 2002, MEDICI ERMETE Emilia Romagna	Youthful violet color, very good bitter cherry fruit depth, soft tanins, and a lengthy finish.	**$$**
(S) MOSCATO D'ASTI 2002, CONTERO Piemonte	Streams of miniscule bubbles and a delicate golden color. Elegant ginger and lemon peel aromas.	**$$**
(B) MONTI FURCHI ASTI SPUMANTE TERRE DA VINO 2002, TERRE DA VINO Piemonte	Deep golden color, aromatic muscat nose and superlative acid/sugar balance on the palate.	**$$$**
(B) FONTANAFREDDA ASTI DOCG NV, FONTANAFREDDA Piemonte	Very attractive mousse, pale yellow color and sweet sharp apples on the soft, balanced palate.	**$$$**

Wines are listed in approximate price order (though this can vary widely depending where they are on offer). All of the wines in the Guide are good value, by definition, but the best buys carry the "Great Value Wine of the Year" symbol. These were the bottles that performed best in their their price band in a blind tasting by the International Wine Challenge top tasters – the super-jurors. Buy them when you can; they tend to sell out very quickly.

ITALY • WHITE

(B)	**MHV VINO DA TAVOLA BIANCO 2002, SARTORI** Veneto	Ground almonds and lilies on the nose, and sweet pear fruit on the palate.	$
(A)	**MHV SOAVE 2002, SARTORI** Veneto	Clean style with a peach and almond finish.	$
(A)	**MHV ORVIETO CLASSICO 2002, SCHENK$**	Aromatic with almond and honey notes.	$
(B)	**TERRA VIVA BIANCHO TERRE DI CHIETI ORGANIC 2002, PERLAGE** Marche	White hedgerow flowers, faint whiffs of bitter almonds, and a crisp white fruit palate.	$
(B)	**VILLA PINOT BIANCO DELLE VENEZIE 2001, RACKE INTERNATIONAL**	Ripe white fruit is packed into the impressively textured, concentrated palate.	$
(A)	**TERRA VIVA PINOT GRIGIO ORGANIC 2002, PERLAGE** Veneto	Balanced, with fresh green fruit and lively, brisk acidity.	$
(A)	**CHIARO DI LUNA BIANCO DI CUSTOZA VENIER 2002, GRUPPO ITALIANO VINI** Veneto	Crisp wine with nice aromatics and a clean finish.	$
(A)	**PINOT GRIGIO DELLE VENEZIE VENIER 2002, GRUPPO ITALIANO VINI** Veneto	Lemon-fresh with a round and spicy finish.	$
(A)	**LE SELCI CHIANTI 2001, GRUPPO ITALIANO VINI** Tuscany	Spiced cherry wine with a savory finish.	$
(B)	**MHV SICILIAN ORGANIC INZOLIA 2002, CANTINE VOLPI** Sicily	A true original. Ripe succulent yellow fruit and sweet bubblegum aromas collide.	$
(B)	**PINOT GRIGIO VENETO 2002, LA GIOIOSA** Veneto	Verdant fields, fruit salad and understated nutmeg on the nose and palate.	$

(B) **MONTESICCI BIANCO IGT 2002, DOLIANOVA** Sardinia	Fresh yet somehow slightly unctuous, this straw-colored wine has apples, nutmeg, and flowers.	$
(S) **CANALETTO PINOT GRIGIO GARGANEGA DEL VENETO IGT 2002, CASA GIRELLI** Veneto	This stunning, light-bodied yet profound offering has white flowers, crisp green apples, cashews, and minerals.	$$
(B) **VIOCH DI PLAIA 2002, CONSTELLATION WINES** Sicily	A satisfying mouthful of white wildflowers, sun-warmed grasses, and ripe yellow fruit.	$$
(B) **SARTORI SOAVE CLASSICO 2002, SARTORI** Veneto	Almonds, pear and minerals shine on the palate, which has the faintest creamy quality.	$$
(B) **TRENTINO PINOT GRIGIO 2002, LA VIS** Trentino-Alto Adige	White flowers, cashews and a hint of minerality on the delicate, light-bodied nose and palate.	$$
(B) **FARNESE VINI TREBBIANO D'ABRUZZO 2002, FARNESE VINI** Abruzzi	Delicate, yet with a slightly mouthcoating texture to the pear and apple fruit palate.	$$
(B) **MONCARO LE VELE 2002, MONCARO** Marche	Pretty peach and floral aromas lead to a soft, textured palate of fresh ripe fruit.	$$
(S) **NADARIA ALCAMO BIANCO DOC 2002, CUSUMANO** Sicily	The fresh acidity sustains the sun-drenched pear and apple palate. Highly original.	$$
(S) **ANGIMBÈ IGT SICILIA 2002, CUSUMANO** Sicily	Lemons, cashews and minerals on the nose, and a powerfully extracted palate of white fruit.	$$
(S) **VERDICCHIO DEI CASTELLI DI JESI CLASSICO 2002, SARTARELLI** Marche	The delicacy of the floral nose and complexity of the white fruit palate are impressive.	$$
(G) **VERDICCHIO DEI CASTELLI DI JESI CLASSICO DOC RISERVA LE GIUNCARE 2000, MONTE SCHIAVO** Marche	Delicate flowers, peaches and green apples on the nose, and a palate of admirable concentration.	$$$
(G) **MONCARO PASSITO 2000, MONCARO** Marche	Orange peel and tropical dried apricot flavors. Unctuous and silky, full-bodied yet delicate and elegant.	$$$$

(G)	**Vinnaioli Jermann Dreams 2001, Vinnaioli Jermann** Friuli-Venezia Giulia	Ripe melon fruit flavors and an almondy, toasty oak undertow that lingers on the finish.	**$$$$$**

ITALY • RED

(A)	**Kwik Save Valpolicella Sanvito DOC 2001, Pasqua Vigbeti e Cantine** Veneto	Cherry fruit linked to silky tannin in a torrid love affair.	$
(A)	**Rosso Tavola Canti 2002, Fratelli Martini Secondo Luigi$**	Supple red color and a palate with ripe fruit and soft tannin.	$
(S)	**Sistina Montepulciano d'Abruzzo DOC 2001, Citra Vini** Abruzzi	Tight plummy nose with a flourish of minerality and a palate packed with red fruit.	$
(A)	**Cantele Alto Varo 2002, Cantele** Puglia	Intense and fruit-rich with a terracotta finish.	$
(A)	**MHV Valpolicella NV, Sartori** Veneto	Clean and fruity with a soft finish.	$
(A)	**MHV Tuscan Red 2000, Castellani** Tuscany	Ripe, juicy wine with a smooth finish.	$
(A)	**Rosso Piceno DOC Superiore 2000, Moncaro** Marche	Rich with baked fruit aromas and a spicy finish.	$
(A)	**Domani Valpolicella 2002, Casa Girelli** Veneto	Good ripe cherry fruit and a nice savory finish.	$
(A)	**Di Notte Valpolicella Valpantena DOC 2002, Pasqua Vigneti e Cantine** Veneto	Ripe red raspberry fruit laced with very delicate cinnamon, nutmeg and mocha.	$
(A)	**Mezzomondo Montepulciano d'Abrruzzo 2002, MGM Mondo del Vino** Abruzzi	Jammy, spicy wine with a good earthy finish.	$

(A) **IL PADRINO SANGIOVESE DI PUGLIA 2002, MGM MONDO DEL VINO** Puglia	Food wine with decent berry-fruit structure.	$
(A) **IL PADRINO SANGIOVESE DI SICILIA 2002, MGM MONDO DEL VINO** Sicily	Fruit-rich with supple tannin and a spicy finish.	$
(A) **MHV SICILIAN ORGANIC NERO D'AVOLA 2002, CANTINE VOLPI** Sicily	Deep and plummy with a lovely ripe core and powerful finish.	$
(A) **MHV BARDOLINO NV, SARTORI** Veneto	Soft and juicy style with good red fruit purity.	$
(A) **ALTENA BARBERA D'ASTI 2001, ARALDICA VINI PIEMONTESI** Piemonte	Berry nose leads to a bramble-patch palate.	$
(S) **IL PADRINO SYRAH DI SICILIA 2002, MGM MONDO DEL VINO** Sicily	Vivid, upfront loganberry and redcurrant fruit on the nose and palate. Mocha and vanilla tones.	$
(B) **PRIMITIVO SALENTO CALEO 2001, CASA VINICOLA BOTTER** Puglia	The excellent ripeness of the red berry fruit is lifted by fresh acidity and spice.	$
(B) **CANALETTO PRIMITIVO 2002, CASA GIRELLI** Lazio	Very impressive red damson fruit concentration on the nose and the mid-weight palate.	$
(B) **CANALETTO PRIMITIVO DI PUGLIA IGT 2001, CASA GIRELLI** Puglia	A leafy damson nose and a fresh, juicy palate. A pleasing easy-drinker.	$
(G) **VILLA ICONA SANGIOVESE 2002, TERRE CORTESE MONCARO** Marche	A wonderful complexity of earthy, mineral notes and terrific redcurrant fruit spiked with vanilla.	$$
(S) **MARC XERO SANGIOVESE 2001, FARNESE** Tuscany	Chewy red cherry fruit, chocolate and warm summer field notes on the nose.	$$
(B) **TOMMOLO CHIUSA GRANDE 2001, CHIUSA GRANDE** Tuscany	Outstanding aromatic definition: tobacco, chocolate, and loganberries. The palate is balanced and intense.	$$

(B) **DA LUCA PRIMITIVO MERLOT 2001, MGM MONDO DEL VINO** Puglia	Fantastic game and bitter chocolate overtones. Plum and prune fruit with a firm tannic grip.	**$$**
(B) **FARNESE VINI SANGIOVESE 2002, FARNESE VINI** Abruzzi	A deep, cherry-flavored, medium-weight palate and a gorgeous ruby color.	**$$**
(S) **ROSSO SALENTO 2001, ALIANTE** Puglia	Ephemeral incense, a generous handful of strawberry fruit and a firm web of woody tannins.	**$$**
(S) **VILLA PAOLINI SANGIOVESE 2002, VILLA PAOLINI** Sicily	Smoky, savory aromas back the baked fruit character and chocolate mocha oak adds complexity.	**$$**
(G) **TENUTA ALBRIZZI 2001, CANTINE DUE PALME** Puglia	Opulent, ripe and full of redcurrant, prune and chocolate oak flavors. Rich, deep and long.	**$$**
(S) **CLEMENTE VLL 2000, CASTELLI DEL GREVEPESA** Tuscany	Dark cherry notes and licorice aromas with bright acidity and dry, powdery tannins.	**$$**
(S) **LANGHE EREMO 2000, FONTANAFREDDA** Piemonte	Soft, bright cherry fruit. Very well balanced with a silky supple tannin backdrop.	**$$**
(S) **MONTEPULCIANO D'ABRUZZO VIGNA CORVINO 2001, AZIENDA AGRICOLA CONTESA DI ROCCO** Abruzzi	Rich red berry fruit with ink, tobacco, raspberry leaves and smoke. Intense and robust.	**$$**
(S) **VIGNA OTTIERI MOLISE ROSSO 2001, FEUDI DI SAN GREGORIO** Molise	Delicate toast and vivid black pepper spike the nose and palate of lush red cherries.	**$$**
(S) **TERRAGNOLO SALENTO PRIMITIVO 2000, APOLLONIO** Puglia	Dark, and full of bitter chocolate, strawberries, and scented oak on the nose and palate.	**$$**
(S) **BOTTEGA VINAI LAGREIN DUNKEL TRENTINO DOC 2000, CA 'VIT** Trentino-Alto Adige	Blueberries, damsons, Christmas cake spices and the scent of the forest linger on the nose.	**$$**
(G) **MANDRAROSSA BENDICÓ 2000, CANTINE SETTESOLI** Sicily	Big color, firm fruit, masses of cherry and damson fruit backed up with well-integrated oak.	**$$**

(G) **VIRTUOSO PRIMITIVO DI PUGLIA IGT 2000, CASA GIRELLI** Puglia	Rich vanilla oak combines with intense herbaceous bramble fruit and smoky, leathery flavors.	$$$
(G) **LAITHWAITE'S EDIZIONE 3 VINO DA TAVOLA NV, FARNESE VINI** Puglia	This Montepulciano blend is rich and oaky with dark, supple tannins and savory, dense fruit.	$$$
(G) **SANGIOVESE DI ROMAGNA DOC RISERVA 2000, UMBERTO CESARI** Emilia Romagna	A kaleidoscope of dark plums, raisins and smoke, cherry and chocolate on the complex palate.	$$$
(G) **TAURASI CAPUTO DOCG 1999, CANTINE CAPUTO** Campania	Soft redcurrant and licorice fruit with chewy tobacco and plum flavors complemented by firm tannins.	$$$$
(G) **VINO NOBILE DI MONTEPULCIANO VIGNETTI ALLA CERRAIA 2000,** Tuscany	Mountains of prunes, blackberries and cherries on the palate. Hints of mocha, bark and toast.	$$$$
(G) **BARBERA D'ASTI CROERE 2000, TERRE DA VINO** Piemonte	A deep purple wine with a scarlet tint, bursting with ripe black cherries and prunes.	$$$$
(G) **LA MALORA LANGHE NEBBIOLO 2000, TERRE DA VINO** Piemonte	An immense monster, with inky cherry fruit and savory bacon flavors buttressed by firm tannins.	$$$$
(G) **COSTASERA AMARONE CLASSICO 1999, MASI AGRICOLA** Veneto	Big evolved toffee apple and vanilla flavors, ripeness, savory depth and a powerful structure.	$$$$
(G) **VINO NOBILE DI MONTEPULCIANO 2000, POLIZIANO** Tuscany	Modern, with firm oak tannins underlying the rich, concentrated cherry and plum stone fruit.	$$$$
(G) **BRUNELLO DI MONTALCINO DOCG 1998, CASANOVA DI NERI** Tuscany	Big, smoky and rich, with a great complexity of figs, mushrooms, smoky fruit and mocha.	$$$$$
(G) **AMARONE DELLA VALPOLICELLA CLASSICO 2000, TOMMASI VITICOLTORI** Veneto	A masterpiece from Dario Tommasi. Spiced red fruits tumble from the rich, textured palate.	$$$$$
(G) **RICASOLI CASALFERRO 2000, CASTELLO DI BROLIO RICASOLI** Tuscany	Violets blossom above a dense wall of silky, intense juicy cherries and licorice. Supremely graceful.	$$$$$

(G)	**GHIAIE DELLA FURBA 2000, CAPEZZANA** Tuscany	All the extract, color and depth of black fruit with graphite. Big, young and chewy.	$$$$$
(G)	**BRUNELLO DI MONTALCINO DOCG TENUTA NUOVA 1998, CASANOVA DI NERI** Tuscany	Delicate notes of roses and violets, with luscious fruit, grippy tannins, and coffee flavors.	$$$$$
(G)	**TAULETO SANIGOVESE RUBICONE 1999, UMBERTO CESARI** Emilia Romagna	Bold and rich with intense, rustic, herbaceous fruit. Plenty of flavor and grippy tannins.	$$$$$
(G)	**ALLEGRINI AMARONE 1999, ALLEGRINI** Veneto	Textured and generously spiced red berries, figs and cinnamon, chewy dried cherries and white pepper.	$$$$$
(G)	**FLACCIANELLO DELLA PIEVE 2000, TENUTA FONTODI** Tuscany	Packed with herbs and oak which comprise the taut tannin and acid scaffolding.	$$$$$
(G)	**TURRIGA IGT 1998, ARGIOLAS** Sardinia	Cherry, bitter chocolate, black pepper and rich vanilla all with a huge handshake of tannins.	$$$$$

NEW ZEALAND

New Zealand continues to establish itself as a producer of top quality white wine in styles and prices that were once firmly associated with premium French regions such as Sancerre and Burgundy. The big news now is that reds – especially Pinot Noir from the South Island region – are improving rapidly, and beginning to change the view outsiders have of New Zealand. Screwcaps are a growing enthusiasm.

NEW ZEALAND • SPARKLING

(B)	**LINDAUER SPECIAL RESERVE NV, MONTANA WINES** East Coast	Unusual tawny color, brilliant mousse and rich creamy pineapple fruit of good concentration and evolution.	$$$

NEW ZEALAND • WHITE

(S) **MATUA VALLEY CHARDONNAY 2002, MATUA VALLEY WINES** North Island	Chalky mineral notes underlay the fresh sweet and sour tropical lemon and greengage palate.	**$$**
(B) **MONTANA MARLBOROUGH RIESLING 2002, MONTANA WINES** Marlborough	Very attractive zingy lemon and lime fruit and a sweet peachy quality on the nose.	**$$**
(S) **WINEMAKERS SERIES TE KAUWHATA SAUVIGNON BLANC 2002, LINCOLN VINEYARDS** Waikato	Stunning golden green color. Deep basket of gooseberry fruit lined with nettles and thyme.	**$$**
(S) **HAWKE'S BAY SAUVIGNON BLANC 2002, VIDAL ESTATE** Hawke's Bay	Bags of juicy gooseberries, key limes and herbs on the intense nose and palate.	**$$**
(S) **MARLBOROUGH SAUVIGNON BLANC 2002, MATUA VALLEY WINES** Marlborough	Aromatic, lifted scents of cut grass, green plums and hints of minerality.	**$$**
(S) **SHINGLE PEAK SAUVIGNON BLANC 2002, SHINGLE PEAK WINES** Marlborough	Very sophisticated nettley green fruit shines on the nose and palate of this balanced Sauvignon.	**$$**
(G) **RESERVE DRY RIESLING 2002, SHERWOOD ESTATE** Marlborough	Green, herbaceous notes over lime and apple; creaminess, and a crisp seam of acidity.	**$$**
(S) **MARLBOROUGH RIESLING 2001, BABICH WINES** Marlborough	Cool, composed limes and lemons on the nose, and a nervy palate of juicy fruit.	**$$**
(S) **BABICH MARLBOROUGH PINOT GRIS 2002, BABICH WINES** Marlborough	Creamy oatmeal, citrus, pears and apples, greengages and a little spice to the velvet palate.	**$$**
(G) **ORMOND ESTATE CHARDONNAY 2000, MONTANA WINES** Gisborne	Discreet oak mingles with lemon, apple, melon and honey fruit. Ripe, pure and refreshing.	**$$$**
(G) **SHEPHERDS RIDGE SAUVIGNON BLANC 2002, BRENT MARIS** Marlborough	Packed with greengage, passionfruit and melon; held together with a mineral edge and zealous acidity.	**$$$**

(G)	**STONE CREEK SAUVIGNON BLANC 2002, MORTON ESTATE WINES** Marlborough	Gooseberry, apple and asparagus flavors are balanced by a hint of richness and racy acidity.	$$$
(G)	**VAVASOUR SAUVIGNON BLANC 2002, VAVASOUR WINES** Marlborough	Delicate almonds, grass and currant leaves on nose. Very good length and depth of flavor.	$$$
(G)	**MANSION HOUSE BAY SAUVIGNON BLANC 2002, MANSION HOUSE WINES** Marlborough	A rich fruit style with zesty gooseberry, creamy lemon and herbal flavors. Spritzy and fresh.	$$$
(G)	**ARARIMU CHARDONNAY 2001, MATUA VALLEY WINES** Wairarapa	Honeyed and rich with a touch of sweetness and a creamy palate, with attractive restraint.	$$$$$

NEW ZEALAND • RED

(G)	**RESERVE CABERNET SAUVIGNON MERLOT 2001, DELEGAT'S WINE ESTATE** Hawke's Bay	Inky black and hugely concentrated, overlaid with coffee, deep cassis fruit and elegant vanilla oak.	$$$
(G)	**HAWKE'S BAY MERLOT CABERNET SAUVIGNON 2001, VIDAL ESTATE** Hawke's Bay	An explosion of cassis and red berry fruit, layers of smoky oak and ripe berries.	$$$
(G)	**PALLISER ESTATE PINOT NOIR 2001, PALLISER ESTATE** North Island	Complex truffled nose leads to a rich berry palate. A long, spicy and powerful finish.	$$$$
(G)	**HELMSMAN CABERNET MERLOT 2000, SACRED HILL** Hawke's Bay	Sweet blackcurrant fruit and cedar notes. Ripe and rich, with a spiced jam finish.	$$$$

Wines are listed in approximate price order (though this can vary widely depending where they are on offer). All of the wines in the Guide are good value, by definition, but the best buys carry the "Great Value Wine of the Year" symbol. These were the bottles that performed best in their their price band in a blind tasting by the International Wine Challenge top tasters – the super-jurors. Buy them when you can; they tend to sell out very quickly.

PORTUGAL

One of the big success stories of the 2003 International Wine Challenge, Portugal is finally, after many years of slumber, beginning to establish a name for its non-fortified table wines as well for its port and Madeira. Initially, the tendency was to use "international" grape varieties such as Cabernet Sauvignon and Merlot, but this year's successes exploited the potential of traditional Portuguese grapes like the Touriga Nacional for producing good, individual table wines. Reds are still generally more successful than whites, but, following the success of the Albariños from the other side of the border in Spain, we're looking forward to seeing some developments with the Alvarinho in Vinho Verde country.

PORTUGAL • WHITE

(A) **DFJ VINHOS ALTA CORTEA 2001, DFJ VINHOS** Estremadura	Bright with vibrant fruit and fine acidity.	**$**
(S) **DFJ VINHOS SEGADA 2002, DFJ VINHOS** Ribatejo	Concentration and delicacy. Pears, lemons and crisp juicy green apple fruit on nose and palate.	**$**
(S) **QUINTA DE AZEVDEO VINHO VERDE 2002, SOGRAPE VINHOS DE PORTUGAL** Vinho Verde	Elderflowers, cucumber, white roses and sliced green apples sing on the nose and palate.	**$$**
(B) **ESPIGA BRANCO QUINTA DA BOAVISTA 2002, CASA SANTOS LIMA** Estremadura	A compelling straw color, mouthwatering fresh white fruit and delicate echoes of undergrowth.	**$$**
(S) **ESPORÃO MONTE VELHO WHITE 2002, ESPORÃO** Alentejo	Fragile mineral shards pierce the pillow of ripe mangosteen and pineapple on the nose.	**$$**

PORTUGAL • RED

(G) **ENCOSTAS DE ESTREMOZ 2001, MARIA JOANA CASTRO DUARTE** Alentejo	Damson and floral nose and masses of warm, red jammy fruits and blackcurrant, plummy notes.	**$**

(A)	**DFJ VINHOS RAMADA RED 2002, DFJ VINHOS** Estremadura	Ripe and smoky with supple tannic structure.	$
(A)	**TERRA DE LOBOS 2001, CASAL BRANCO SOCIEDADE DE VINHAS** Ribatejo	Blackberry and damson rich. Soft finish.	$
(A)	**SERRAS DE AZEITAO 2001, JP VINHOS** Terras do Sado	Intense with vibrant fruit and an earthy finish.	$
(A)	**BAGA GRAN CASTAS 2001, BRIGHT BROTHERS** Beiras	Baked style with fruit intensity and some depth.	$
(B)	**DFJ VINHOS SEGADA RED 2001, DFJ VINHOS** Ribatejo	A full-bodied offering of redcurrants and blackberries spiked with notes of vanilla and toast.	$
(G)	**TOURIZ QUINTA DA BOAVISTA 2001, CASA SANTOS LIMA** Estremadura	Full of powerful cassis fruit and layers of complex flavors that create an amazing depth.	$$
(S)	**DFJ VINHOS VEGA RED 2000, DFJ VINHOS** Douro	Red and black bramble fruits intermigle with scents of hot wet stones and tobacco wisps.	$$
(B)	**DFJ VINHOS FONTE DO BECO RED 2000, DFJ VINHOS** Terras do Sado	Enjoy this ripe, full-bodied wine now, as its black cherry fruit is at its peak.	$$
(B)	**DFJ VINHOS TINTA RORIZ MERLOT RED 2000, DFJ VINHOS** Estremadura	A plummy yet structured palate of ripe, mouthwatering red fruit and spice.	$$
(B)	**DFJ VINHOS BELA FONTE TOURIGA FRANCA TINTA RORIZ RED 2001, DFJ VINHOS** Beiras	Vanilla and clove spice accent the appealing, balanced palate of blue and black fruit.	$$
(S)	**DFJ VINHOS TINTA MIUDA CABERNET SAUVIGNON 2000, DFJ VINHOS** Estremadura	Bursting with blackcurrant fruit, firm woody tannins, good intensity and a long finish.	$$
(S)	**DFJ VINHOS TOURIGA FRANCA MERLOT 2001, DFJ VINHOS** Estremadura	Purple red glassful of elegant damsons and robust blackcurrant fruit. Excellent balance and long finish.	$$

(B) **ESPORÃO MONTE VELHO RED 2002, ESPORÃO** Alentejo	Lifted red damsons and faint joss stick aromas on the nose. Robust and concentrated.	**$$**
(B) **DFJ VINHOS PEDRAS DO MONTE RED 2000, DFJ VINHOS** Terras do Sado	Liberally sprinkled with ground white pepper, rosemary and ripe redcurrants which burst in the mouth.	**$$**
(G) **GRAND' ARTE TRINCADEIRA RED 2000, DFJ VINHOS** Ribatejo	Inky black with a tight nose of smoky, gamey fruit. Dark fruits and bitter chocolate.	**$$**
(S) **QUINTA DO CRASTO DOURO RED 2001, QUINTA DO CRASTO** Douro	Search hard to extrapolate how the complex array of spices and aristocratic fruit will evolve.	**$$**
(S) **QUINTA DE LA ROSA DOUROSA 2001, QUINTA DE LA ROSA** Douro	Nutmeg and vanilla grace the nose, which displays compelling minerality and rich blackberry fruit.	**$$**
(S) **DFJ VINHOS GRAND' ARTE TOURIGA FRANCA 2001, DFJ VINHOS** Estremadura	Such aristocratic restraint coupled with such intensity is a formula that's hard to beat.	**$$**
(S) **DFJ VINHOS CASA DO LAGO RESERVA 2000, DFJ VINHOS** Ribatejo	A degree of evolution adds dimensionality to the palate of elegant red berry fruit.	**$$**
(G) **QUINTA DA URZE TINTA RORIZ 2001, CASA AGRICOLA ROBOREDO MADEIRA** Douro	Lifted scents of truffles, graphite, leather, plums and raspberries vie with warming spice for attention.	**$$$**
(G) **ESPORÃO ARAGONES 2001, ESPORÃO** Alentejo	Big, spicy fruit and huge extract both in color and depth of concentration.	**$$$**
(G) **ESPORÃO TOURIGA NACIONAL 2001, ESPORÃO** Alentejo	Immense, sweet black plum fruit and soft oak. A brute of great weight and complexity.	**$$$**
(G) **RESERVA DOURO 2000, QUINTA DO VALLADO** Douro	Elderberries, tobacco, violets, minerals and a strong tannic backbone, which bodes well for the future.	**$$$$**
(G) **DOURO TOURIGA NACIONAL 2001, QUINTA DO CRASTO** Douro	A floral, damson nose full of honeysuckle, roses, toast complements the massive sun-warmed fruit palate.	**$$$$**

G	**DUAS QUINTA RESERVA 2000, RAMOS PINTO** Douro	Bold, brassy wine with masses of rich cassis fruit and that indefinable dusty port-like character.	$$$$
G	**DOURO GRANDE RESERVA 2000, QUINTA DO PORTAL** Douro	Primary ripe fruit flavors and some developing savory, meaty characters with background chocolatey oak.	$$$$
G	**QUINTA DO VALE MEÃO DOURO 2000, F OLAZABAL & FILHOS** Douro	Splendid - dense with cherry and damson fruit, integrated oak, good weight and a powerful finish.	$$$$$

PORTUGAL • FORTIFIED

B	**ESCUDIERO PORT NV, CDC WINES & SPIRITS** Douro	Fantastic blend of ripe juicy red berries, licquorice and spicy black plums.	$
G	**QUINTA DO CASTELINHO 1997, CASTELINHO VINHOS** Douro	Delicate candied orange peel, raisins, damson and licorice. A spicy palate backed by ripe chocolate.	$$
G	**MOSCATEL DO DOURO 1989, ADEGA COOPERATIVA DE FAVAIOS** Douro	Fresh grapey aromas with toast and brown sugar. Honeyed, nutty and complex rainbow of flavors.	$$
B	**THE NAVIGATORS RUBY PORT NV, REAL COMPANHIA VELHA** Douro	Positively dripping with red cherries and cinnamon spice. Its upfront appeal is hard to resist.	$$
B	**THE NAVIGATORS TAWNY PORT NV, REAL COMPANHIA VELHA** Douro	Beautiful amber color. The nose is laden with sun-dried fruit, honey and roasted nuts.	$$
B	**CRUZ FINE VINTAGE CHARACTER PORT NV, GRAN CRUZ PORTO** Douro	This beautiful port has ripe blackberries and blueberries on the nose and palate.	$$
A	**TAWNY PORTO CRUZ NV, GRAN CRUZ PORTO** Douro	Rich and ripe with a fruitcake finish.	$$
B	**THE NAVIGATORS VINTAGE CHARACTER PORT NV, REAL COMPANHIA VELHA** Douro	Impressive concentration and balance. The black fruit palate is enlivened by refreshing acidity.	$$

(B)	**CROFT TRIPLE CROWN NV, THE FLADGATE PARTNERSHIP** Douro	Who tipped the spice box into this lush, velvet tangle of bramble fruit?	**$$**
(S)	**WARRES WARRIOR SPECIAL RESERVE 1994, WARRES** Douro	Very intense red and black forest fruits line the palate, which boasts richness, balance, and finesse.	**$$$**
(B)	**CROFT DISTINCTION PORT NV, THE FLADGATE PARTNERSHIP** Douro	Cream and nutmeg blend with black plums, mulberries and calligraphy ink on the nose.	**$$$**
(A)	**SANDEMAN PARTNERS' RUBY PORTO NV, SANDEMAN** Douro	Damson and plum style with lovely spice and sweetness to finish.	**$$$**
(S)	**BLANDY'S ALVADA 5 YEAR OLD RICH MADEIRA NV, MADEIRA WINE COMPANY** Madeira	Copper colored, with lifted notes of roasted nuts, butterscotch and orange peel. Luscious, lingering palate.	**$$$**
(G)	**DOÑA ANTÓNIA PERSONAL RESERVE NV, A FERREIRA** Douro	Blackberry and fruit cake character. Displaying good maturity, with balanced acidity and rich, unctuous sweetness.	**$$$**
(B)	**DOWS LBV PORT 1997, SILVA & COSENS** Douro	Sweet and rich are the bywords for the fruit with its restrained aromatics and flavors.	**$$$**
(S)	**FONSECA BIN 27 PORT NV, THE FLADGATE PARTNERSHIP** Douro	Exotically perfumed, with ripe mulberries, loganberries, smoke, grass and flowers on the nose and palate.	**$$$**
(S)	**BLANDY'S DUKE OF CLARENCE RICH MADEIRA NV, MADEIRA WINE COMPANY** Madeira	Deepest amber, with green flashes. The luxuriant palate has apricots, honeycomb and molasses in abundance.	**$$$**
(B)	**QUINTA DO CRASTO LBV PORT 1998, QUINTA DO CRASTO** Douro	Beginning to advance towards its peak, with an intense web of spicy red fruit.	**$$$**
(B)	**AVERYS INVESTITURE VINTAGE CHARACTER PORT NV, BARROS ALMEIDA** Douro	Blackcurrants and white pepper on the nose. The palate offers ripe fruit and clove spice.	**$$$**
(B)	**DO VALE DA MINA LBV PORT 1997, VAN ZELLER** Douro	A light port with velvety, figgy fruit and a little maturity in its softening structure.	**$$$**

(B)	**SANDEMAN LBV PORTO 1997, SANDEMAN** Douro	Soft, seductive red fruit with fabulous texture, good ripeness and generous spice.	**$$$**
(B)	**COSSART GORDON 5 YEAR OLD BUAL NV, MADEIRA WINE COMPANY** Madeira	A mature, robust Madeira with burnt toffee, nuts, raisins, oranges and a lifted, vivacious acidity.	**$$$**
(G)	**CRUZ LATE BOTTLED VINTAGE 1992, GRAN CRUZ PORTO** Douro	A noseful of bright aromatic red berries; on the palate, dried fruits and almonds.	**$$$**
(S)	**TAYLOR'S LBV PORT 1997, THE FLADGATE PARTNERSHIP** Douro	Black and red super-ripe fruit on the nose with maturing spicy flavors on the palate.	**$$$**
(S)	**QUINTA DO NOVAL TRADITIONAL LBV PORT 1997, QUINTA DO NOVAL** Douro	Very intense sun-warmed red berry flavors and inky mineral aromas nestle compatibly together.	**$$$**
(G)	**VISTA ALEGRE 2000, VALLEGRE VINHOS DO PORTO** Douro	Damson, jam and licorice fruit, complemented by toasty spice and chocolate. Ripe and beautifully concentrated.	**$$$$**
(G)	**PRESIDENTIAL 30 YEAR OLD PORTO NV, C DA SILVA VINHOS** Douro	Chestnut color, with an array of caramel, nuts and honey on the lifted, perfumed nose.	**$$$$**
(G)	**PORTO POÇAS LBV 1997, MANUEL D POÇAS JUNIOR VINHOS** Douro	Deep and black and tight and mysterious with ripe blackcurrant fruit and rich pepper notes.	**$$$$**
(G)	**ROZES VINTAGE PORTO 1999, SPR VINHOS** Douro	Profoundly velvety flesh, and a sophisticated tight structure. Burly blackberries and rich, feminine raspberries.	**$$$$**
(B)	**COSSART GORDON 5 YEAR OLD MALMSEY NV, MADEIRA WINE COMPANY** Madeira	Warm ripe nose with woody notes. The palate is robust, yet rendered with searing acidity.	**$$$$**
(S)	**GRAHAM'S SIX GRAPES UNFILTERED RESERVE NV, W&J GRAHAM** Douro	Meaty, savory notes, cherry fruit and layers of mocha oak on a tight tannic platform.	**$$$$**
(G)	**DOW'S CRUSTED PORT BOTTLED 1998 NV, SILVA & COSENS** Douro	A concentrated, brooding wine, almost black, and quite tight on the ripe Christmas cake palate.	**$$$$**

(S) **QUINTA DO INFANTADO LBV PORT 1998, QUINTA DO INFANTADO** Pinhao	A fantastic basket of red cherries, drippingly fresh and warmed by the sun.	$$$$
(B) **TAWNY 10 YEARS OLD PORT NV, CHURCHILL GRAHAM** Douro	Deep marmalade brown color, nutty raisined nose and mouthfilling, well integrated, medium-bodied palate.	$$$$
(G) **COSSART GORDON MALMSEY COLHEITA 1989, MADEIRA WINE COMPANY** Madeira	Intoxicating Christmas cake, candied peel and a solidity and depth you could dive into.	$$$$
(G) **SMITH WOODHOUSE LBV PORT 1994, SMITH WOODHOUSE** Douro	Vibrant licorice and spiced fruit and an intense, concentrated complexity that never seems to end.	$$$$
(S) **COSSART GORDON BUAL COLHEITA 1990, MADEIRA WINE COMPANY** Madeira	Classic rancio and caramel aromas. The palate has soft toffee essence and a dry finish.	$$$$
(G) **WARRE'S LBV PORT 1992, WARRE'S** Douro	Ripe and rich. All elements are well integrated on the leathery, smoky, fruitcake palate.	$$$$
(G) **TAYLOR'S QUINTA DE TERRA FEITA 1988, THE FLADGATE PARTNERSHIP** Douro	Sweet and raisiny with firm acidity, soft fruit and a plethora of nutty caramel flavors.	$$$$
(S) **COSSART GORDON 10 YEAR OLD BUAL NV, MADEIRA WINE COMPANY** Madeira	A tumult of marmalade, popcorn, toast and mandarin oranges. A palate as sweet as molasses.	$$$$
(G) **BARBEITO SERCIAL RESERVE 10 YEAR OLD NV, VINHOS BARBEITO MADEIRA** Madeira	Richly concentrated, with molasses, vanilla pods and even a touch of pineapple. Textured and intense.	$$$$$
(G) **DOW'S QUINTA DO BOMFIM 1995, SILVA & COSENS** Douro	Silky smooth with violets, prunes figs and raisins, smoke and flowers embedded in the finish.	$$$$$
(G) **15 YEAR OLD VERDELHO NV, HENRIQUES & HENRIQUES** Madeira	It is rich and ripe with powerful spice and toffee notes and a beguiling nutty warmth.	$$$$$
(G) **WARRE'S VINTAGE PORT 1994, WARRE'S** Douro	Mint and eucalyptus notes, and a developed raisiny, leathery complexity. A promising future ahead.	$$$$$

Quinta do Infantado Vintage Porto 2000, Quinta do Infantado Pinhao	Masses of damson and licorice fruit on the nose with spicy, chocolate oak aromas.	$$$$$	
Quinta do Portal Vintage Port 2000, Quinta do Portal Douro	The sheer depth of color is hypnotic and the ripe damson aromas go on and on.	$$$$$	
Smith Woodhouse Vintage Port 1985, Smith Woodhouse Douro	Masses of ripe berries and licorice, caramel and mineral aromas. Stunningly complex, with huge length.	$$$$$	
Martinez Vintage 2000, Martinez Douro	Still a little closed and brooding, but there is a complex world tucked away inside.	$$$$$	
Churchill Graham Vintage Port 1997, Churchill Graham Douro	Spicy chocolate flavors and baked plum and damson fruit work well with the firm tannins.	$$$$$	
Warre's Vintage Port 2000, Warre's Douro	Lush, rich and ripe, and as black as night. Peppery and slightly minerally notes.	$$$$$	
Calém Quinta da Pego 2000, AA Calém and Filho Douro	This really is amazing, and in time it will become stunning. Very full-bodied and round.	$$$$$	
Symington's Quinta do Vesuvio 2000, Sociedade Agricola Quinta do Vesuvio Douro	Cool mint and eucalyptus with a touch of chocolate on the rich, concentrated blackberry palate.	$$$$$	
Graham's LBV Port 1985, W&J Graham Douro	The lustrous dark amber hue hints at age, manifested in the coffee and burnt sugar nose.	$$$$$	
Graham's 40 Year Old Tawny NV, W&J Graham Douro	The judges simply raved about this intense, opulent glassful of toffee, and candied orange peel.	$$$$$	

Wines are listed in approximate price order (though this can vary widely depending where they are on offer). All of the wines in the Guide are good value, by definition, but the best buys carry the "Great Value Wine of the Year" symbol. These were the bottles that performed best in their their price band in a blind tasting by the International Wine Challenge top tasters – the super-jurors. Buy them when you can; they tend to sell out very quickly.

SOUTH AFRICA

After a period when South Africa's wines were over-praised by far too many well-meaning critics on one side or the other of the political divide, they are now beginning to live up to their potential. The key to South Africa's success lies in new thinking from a young generation of winemakers who are prepared to throw out some of the assumptions of the past – as well as thousands of hectares of virused vines that never ripened properly. Another view that is getting some careful inspection is the notion that Chenin Blanc and Pinotage are the Cape's strongest cards. In fact, the results of the International Wine Challenge support the widely held view that Sauvignon and Shiraz really occupy this role.

SOUTH AFRICA • SPARKLING

(A)	**INANDA BRUT NV, WESTCORP INTERNATIONAL** Olifantsriver	Frothy and fun with a good clean elderflower finish.	$$
(B)	**GRAHAM BECK BLANC DE BLANCS 1997, GRAHAM BECK** Robertson	Mature and toasty, with soft mousse, a zesty yet creamy palate and a long finish.	$$$

SOUTH AFRICA • WHITES

(A)	**MHV ROUWKES DRIFT SOUTH AFRICAN CHENIN BLANC 2002, AFRICAN TERROIR** Western Cape	Apples and cream style. Fresh finish.	$
(B)	**KUMALA CHARDONNAY SEMILLON 2002, WESTERN WINES** Western Cape	Lifted ginger and butter aromas happily married to fresh fruit salad flavors on the palate.	$
(A)	**STOWELLS CHENIN BLANC, STOWELLS** Coastal	Clean wine with fresh fruit and lively acidity.	$
(A)	**KAYA CHENIN BLANC 2003, COPPOOLSE FINLAYSON** Western Cape	Water white color. Ripe apples and pear drops on the nose and light-bodied palate.	$

(A)	**VAN LOUVEREN PINOT GRIS 2002, VAN LOUVEREN** Robertson	Apricot nose leads to a rich and spicy palate.	$
(A)	**BELLINGHAM CHADONNAY COLOMBARD 2002, DOUGLAS GREEN BELLINGHAM** Western Cape	Big, juicy-melon style. Peachy finish.	$
(A)	**KUMALA CHENIN BLANC CHARDONNAY 2002, WESTERN WINES** Western Cape	Melon and honey driven. Sugary finish.	$
(A)	**UNDER THE TABLE CHARDONNAY CHENIN BLANC NV, KINGSLAND WINES & SPIRITS** Western Cape	Honeyed style with a touch of vanilla oak.	$
(A)	**FIRSTCAPE CHARDONNAY SEMILLON 2002, FIRSTCAPE VINEYARDS** Western Cape	Waxy style with good citrus freshness.	$
(S)	**DOUGLAS GREEN BELLINGHAM CHARDONNAY 2002, DOUGLAS GREEN BELLINGHAM** Western Cape	Limes and lemons shine on the youthful palate, which is at once creamy and crisp.	$$
(S)	**BRADGATE CHENIN BLANC SAUVIGNON BLANC 2002, JORDAN WINERY** Stellenbosch	Bright golden yellow color. Vanilla and pears feature on this dry and satisfyingly crisp Chenin.	$$
(S)	**EXCELSIOR CHARDONNAY 2002, EXCELSIOR ESTATE** Robertson	Toffee, ripe peach and toast flavors. The richness and fine acidity lengthens the finish.	$$
(S)	**TWO OCEANS CHARDONNAY 2002, DISTELL** Stellenbosch	Very refined, yet intense palate dripping with pineapple fruit and rendered by fresh acidity.	$$
(B)	**CAPE PROMISE CHARDONNAY 2002, STELLENBOSCH** Stellenbosch	Full of caramel and butterscotch, it has a creamy honeyed palate and tropical fruit character.	$$
(B)	**KATHENBERG CHENIN BLANC 2002, WINECORP** Western Cape	Peaches and lemons rise from the warm tropical nose of this appealing, concentrated, balanced offering.	$$
(S)	**THANDI CHARDONNAY 2001, THANDI**	Hints of biscuit on the nose, and lemon drops and pineapples on the long finish.	$$

(S) **JORDAN CHENIN BLANC 2002, JORDAN WINERY** Stellenbosch	Full-bodied, intense, very elegant soft apricots. The rich fruit is lifted by fresh, zesty acidity.	$$
(S) **BERGSIG ESTATE CHARDONNAY 2002, BERGSIG ESTATE** Western Cape	Fresh white and yellow tropical fruit is admirably restrained, yet the finish lasts and lasts.	$$
(G) **FREE RUN SAUVIGNON BLANC 2002, FLAGSTONE WINERY** Western Cape	A lean, elegant creamy white pepper and asparagus nose. Good balance and ripe gooseberry freshness.	$$
(S) **VERGELEGEN CHARDONNAY 2002, VERGELEGEN** Stellenbosch	Vibrant lemon fruit and vanilla palate which is round, textured and boosted by crisp acidity.	$$
(S) **SINCERELY SAUVIGNON BLANC 2002, NEIL ELLIS WINES** Coastal	Crisp, refined grassy aromas and fresh vivid greengage flavors. Balanced, integrated and elegant.	$$
(G) **BOSCHENDAL CHARDONNAY 2002, BOSCHENDAL** Paarl	Almost figgy in its richness. Buttery and creamy, weighty and big, yet elegant and complex.	$$

SOUTH AFRICA • REDS

(A) **SWARTLAND PINOTAGE 2002, SWARTLAND** Swartland	Berry-rich with soft tannins and sweet violet perfume.	$
(A) **SOUTH AFRICAN CINSAULT RUBY CABERNET 2002, LGB WINES** Worcester	Spiced berry style with violet perfume.	$
(S) **DUMISANI PINOTAGE SHIRAZ 2002, WINECORP** Western Cape	Savory bacon fat aromas lurk behind the voluptuous red and black plum fruit palate.	$
(A) **LONG MOUNTAIN RUBY CABERNET 2002, LONG MOUNTAIN WINE COMPANY** Western Cape	Sweet-fruited with interesting violet aromas.	$
(B) **TWO OCEANS SHIRAZ 2002, TWO OCEANS DISTELL** Western Cape	Vibrant strawberry fruit on the nose and palate has a certain lifted, aromatic, spicy quality.	$

(B) **GOATS DO ROAM RED 2002, WINES OF CHARLES BACK** Coastal	A round, well-integrated, medium-bodied wine saturated with red and black fruits and soft tannins.	$
(G) **REMHOOGTE MERLOT 2000, REMHOOGTE WINE ESTATE** Stellenbosch	Bags of character and a complexity of cedar and tobacco overlaid with rich, plummy jam.	$$
(B) **BOLAND KELDER SHIRAZ 2001, BOLAND KELDER** Paarl	Brambly, with a forward, smooth palate possessing rich concentration and a firm structure.	$$
(G) **PORCUPINE RIDGE CABERNET SAUVIGNON 2002, BOUKENHOUTSKLOOF** Western Cape	Eucalptus and ripe berry fruit with taut, spicy, cedary, pencil shaving, mocha and vanilla aromas.	$$
(S) **ZEVENWACHT ESTATE PINOTAGE 2002, ZEVENWACHT ESTATE** Stellenbosch	Ripe, rich, classic plummy red fruit and savory bacon fat. Muscular tannic structure. Long finish.	$$
(S) **SENTINEL MERLOT 2001, COPPOOLSE & FINLAYSON** Coastal	Aromatic perfume on the nose. Well-balanced, plummy flavors set off with oak and crisp acid.	$$
(S) **STELLENZICHT SYRAH 2000, STELLENZICHT ESTATE** Stellenbosch	A subtle, perfumed, ripe and compact palate with evolved tannins and excellent depth.	$$
(S) **OAK VILLAGE BARREL SELECTION SHIRAZ 2001, VINFRUCO** Coastal	Cinnamon spice complements earthy ripe fruit. Supporting tannins keep the structure in place.	$$
(S) **ARIANE 2001, BEAUMONT WINES** Overberg	The long, intense palate offers cherries and chocolate, with nuances of cinnamon, nutmeg and cloves.	$$
(G) **FAIRVIEW PEGLEG CARIGNAN 2002, WINES OF CHARLES BACK** Coastal	Deep purple inky blackberry fruit, licorice and spice, velvety tannins and a splendid finish.	$$$
(G) **JORDAN CABERNET SAUVIGNON 2000, JORDAN WINERY** Stellenbosch	Distinctive cedar wood and mulberry fruit aromas. Soft and ripe, with a hint of herbaceousness.	$$$
(G) **YONDER HILL MERLOT 2001, YONDER HILL** Stellenbosch	A classy wine still in its youth, with plummy fruit and a touch of mint.	$$$

(B) **GOATS DO ROAM RED 2002, WINES OF CHARLES BACK** Coastal	A round, well-integrated, medium-bodied wine saturated with red and black fruits and soft tannins.	$
(G) **REMHOOGTE MERLOT 2000, REMHOOGTE WINE ESTATE** Stellenbosch	Bags of character and a complexity of cedar and tobacco overlaid with rich, plummy jam.	$$
(B) **BOLAND KELDER SHIRAZ 2001, BOLAND KELDER** Paarl	Brambly, with a forward, smooth palate possessing rich concentration and a firm structure.	$$
(G) **PORCUPINE RIDGE CABERNET SAUVIGNON 2002, BOUKENHOUTSKLOOF** Western Cape	Eucalptus and ripe berry fruit with taut, spicy, cedary, pencil shaving, mocha and vanilla aromas.	$$
(S) **ZEVENWACHT ESTATE PINOTAGE 2002, ZEVENWACHT ESTATE** Stellenbosch	Ripe, rich, classic plummy red fruit and savory bacon fat. Muscular tannic structure. Long finish.	$$
(S) **SENTINEL MERLOT 2001, COPPOOLSE & FINLAYSON** Coastal	Aromatic perfume on the nose. Well-balanced, plummy flavors set off with oak and crisp acid.	$$
(S) **STELLENZICHT SYRAH 2000, STELLENZICHT ESTATE** Stellenbosch	A subtle, perfumed, ripe and compact palate with evolved tannins and excellent depth.	$$
(S) **OAK VILLAGE BARREL SELECTION SHIRAZ 2001, VINFRUCO** Coastal	Cinnamon spice complements earthy ripe fruit. Supporting tannins keep the structure in place.	$$
(S) **ARIANE 2001, BEAUMONT WINES** Overberg	The long, intense palate offers cherries and chocolate, with nuances of cinnamon, nutmeg and cloves.	$$
(G) **FAIRVIEW PEGLEG CARIGNAN 2002, WINES OF CHARLES BACK** Coastal	Deep purple inky blackberry fruit, licorice and spice, velvety tannins and a splendid finish.	$$$
(G) **JORDAN CABERNET SAUVIGNON 2000, JORDAN WINERY** Stellenbosch	Distinctive cedar wood and mulberry fruit aromas. Soft and ripe, with a hint of herbaceousness.	$$$
(G) **YONDER HILL MERLOT 2001, YONDER HILL** Stellenbosch	A classy wine still in its youth, with plummy fruit and a touch of mint.	$$$

SPAIN

While there is no denying the fact that Spain is going through an extraordinary wine revolution – in regions like Priorat, Ribera del Duero, and Toro, many of the new wines are hard to find, and more spoken about than drunk. This year, some of these new stars performed very well at the International Wine Challenge, but so too did some examples from classic areas such as Rioja and Penedes. Whites are still less impressive than reds (though this could be considered an international phenomenon), but progress is being made in the Rias Baixas in the north of the country with the extraordinary Albariño, a grape that could do for Spain what the Grüner Veltliner is now doing for Austria.

SPAIN • SPARKLING

(B)	**GRAN PALAS CAVA BRUT NV, VINITIS**	Gorgeous bitter almond, pear drop and floral nose. Crisp, refreshing palate with a lively mousse.	$$
(A)	**GRAN PALAS CAVA SEMI SECO NV, VINITIS**	Light and elegant with apple, pear and citrus notes.	$$
(A)	**CASITO CAVA NV, ARCO BODEGAS UNIDAS** Catalonia	Pristine fruit allied to dancing acidity.	$$

SPAIN • WHITE

(A)	**MHV VALENCIA DRY WHITE 2002, BODEGAS MURVIEDRO** Valencia	Fruity wine with a good clean finish.	$
(A)	**MHV VALENCIA MEDIUM WHITE 2002, BODEGAS MURVIEDRO** Valencia	Off-dry style showing ripe fruit and balance.	$
(A)	**SANTERRA DRY MUSCAT 2002, BODEGAS MURVIEDRO** Valencia	Perfumed nose showing lovely grapey muscat character.	$

(B) **ESPIRAL MACABEO CHARDONNAY 2002, PIRINEOS** Aragón	Fresh, clear lemon and pear fruit is punctuated by butterscotch and toast.	$
(A) **VIÑA DEL SOPIE 2002, BODEGAS MARCO REAL** Castilla y León	Ripe with fruit richness balanced by good acidity.	$
(A) **CAMPO NUEVO WHITE 2002, BODEGAS PRINCIPE DE VIANA** Navarre	Clean with piercing fresh fruit and lively acidity.	$
(B) **MOSCATEL ORO NV, DE MULLER** Catalonia	A fresh lemony nose with a good concentration on the palate and a sparkling finish.	$
(B) **AURA ARS VINUM VEROEJO 2002, BODEGAS AURA** Castilla y León	Good concentration and acidity ensure the yellow fruit palate is well-balanced.	$$
(B) **BASA RUEDA BLANCO 2002, TELMO RODRIGUEZ** Navarre	Very nice green and white berry fruit on nose and palate. Fresh and vibrant.	$$
(S) **CHARDONNAY CUVÉE ALLIER 2001, BODEGAS NEKEAS** Navarre	Packed with tropicals: mango, pineapple, banana and lemons. The rich fruit sustains the spicy oak.	$$

SPAIN • ROSE

(A) **VIÑA ALBALI ROSADO 2002, FELIX SOLIS** Castilla-La Mancha	Warming, with good extract, sweet fruit and a soft structure.	$
(A) **CAMPO NUEVO ROSADO 2002, BODEGAS PRINCIPE DE VIANA** Navarre	Raspberry style with light structure and finish.	$

SPAIN • RED

(A) **GRAN TEMPRANILLO 2002, CORVINCA** Aragón	Ripe juicy red berries line the fresh, robust palate.	$

(A)	**MHV VALENCIA RED 2002, BODEGAS MURVIEDRO** Valencia	Redcurrant nose leads to a spiced berry palate.	$
(S)	**SANTA CRISTA GRAN LOPEZ 2002, SANTA CRISTA CRIANZAS Y VINEDOS** Aragón	A gorgeous supple texture envelops the generous red fruit. Notes of vanilla and white pepper.	$
(A)	**CASTILLO DE REQUENA TINTO 2002, ROMERAL VINICOLA** Valencia	Juicy with ripe berry and mulled spice notes.	$
(A)	**GRANDUC TEMPRANILLO GARNACHA 2001, GRANDUC** Castilla-La Mancha	Ripe with sweet tannins and rich fruit flavors.	$
(A)	**FOUR WINDS 2002, BODEGAS MARCO REAL** Navarre	Ripe and jammy with redcurrant and raspberry notes.	$
(A)	**SANTERRA TEMPRANILLO 2001, BODEGAS MURVIEDRO** Valencia	Lush and spicy with winberry and custard notes.	$
(S)	**YOUNG VATTED TEMPRANILLO 2002, BODEGAS CENTRO ESPAÑOLAS** Castilla-La Mancha	Textured red fruit on the nose and palate with a sophisticated mineral edge.	$
(A)	**BULLAS MONASTRELL SHIRAZ 2001, BULLAS** Murcia	Supple with lush fruit and creamy tannins.	$
(A)	**THE WILDERNESS TEMPRANILLO 2002, FINCA LUZON** Murcia	Lightly perfumed with richness and berry depth.	$
(A)	**ALBOR 2002, BODEGAS CADEVI** Castilla-La Mancha	Strawberries and cream flirt on nose and palate.	$
(A)	**BERBERANA DRAGON TEMPRANILLO 2001, ARCO BODEGAS UNIDAS** Castilla y León	Ripe and supple with a nice lick of vanilla oak to finish.	$
(A)	**MARCO REAL 2002, BODEGAS MARCO REAL** Navarre	Sweetly perfumed with berry and clove notes.	$

(B) ESPIRAL TEMPRANILLO 2001, BODEGAS PIRINEOS Aragón	A powerful wine with big plum and cassis fruit sustaining the ripe tannins with ease.	$
(B) VIÑA ALBALI BATANEROS 2001, FELIX SOLIS Castilla-La Mancha	Smooth, silky red berry fruit with a touch of spice box on the nose.	$$
(B) BAJOZ JOVEN 2002, VIÑA BAJOZ Castilla y León	Bright ruby red. Cracked black pepper and leather notes lift the juicy red vine fruits.	$$
(B) MURVIEDRO CRIANZA 1999, BODEGAS MURVIEDRO Valencia	Ripe juicy bramble fruit with hints of vanilla and toast, black pepper and firm tannins.	$$
(B) PRIMI 2002, BODEGAS LUIS GURPEGUI MUGA Rioja	Silky vanilla swathes ripe redcurrant fruit on the nose. The palate is ripe yet youthful.	$$
(S) RAMON ROQUETA TINTO TEMPRANILLO 2002, BODEGAS ROQUETA Catalonia	Vanilla pods and cloves soften the vibrant red fruit, which has texture and concentration.	$$
(S) VEGA DEL RAYO SELECCIONADA 2000, BODEGAS CARLOS SERRES Rioja	Savory characteristics add another dimension to the appetising juicy red cherry fruit palate.	$$
(S) GRAN FEUDO RESERVA 1998, BODEGAS JULIAN CHIVITE Navarre	A palate of red fruit which is weighty yet not heavy, concentrated yet not extracted.	$$
(S) CASA CASTILLO VENDIMIA 2001, CASA CASTILLO Murcia	Plenty of ripe, dark berry fruit character balanced by rounded tannins and hefty concentration.	$$
(S) BOBAL TEMPRANILLO 2001, ROZALEME Valencia	Red and black summer fruits, vanilla pods, a powerful structure and youthful cherry flavors.	$$
(S) BODEGAS NAVAJAS TINTO CRIANZA 1999, BODEGAS NAVAJAS Rioja	The silky, mouthcoating berry fruit has a touch of pepper and a jolt of vanilla.	$$
(S) GRAN FEUDO VIÑAS VIEJAS RESERVA 1998, BODEGAS JULIAN CHIVITE Navarre	Yet another modern classic, with ripe berry fruit, elegance and a fine length.	$$

(S) **GUELBENZU AZUL 2001, BODEGAS GUELBENZU** Castilla y León	Floral aromas and soft melange of silky red berries possessing good richness, concentration and length.	$$
(G) **MARQUÉS DE GRINON DOMINIO DE VALDEPUSA SYRAH 2000, ARCO BODEGAS UNIDAS** Montes del Toledo	This is still a bit of an athletic youngster, amazingly intense, concentrated, deep and dark.	$$
(S) **AÑARES RESERVA 1998, BODEGAS OLARRA** Rioja	Red cherry fruit. toast, spice box, tobacco and blueberries linger on the finish.	$$$
(S) **BARON DE LEY RESERVA 1998, BODEGAS BARON DE LEY** Rioja	Rich raspberry fruit and firm, integrated tannins. Smooth texture and excellent balance overall.	$$$
(G) **DIONISIO RUIZ IJALBA 2001, VIÑA IJALBA** Rioja	Sweet, ripe fruit is supported by a new oak chorus of vanilla and coconut.	$$$$
(G) **MAS D'EN GIL COMA VELLA 2000, VITICULTORS MAS D'EN GIL** Priorat	Graceful fruit, exotic incense and a sprinkling of minerals, leather, tobacco and cherry fruit.	$$$$
(G) **GRANS MURALLES 1998, MIGUEL TORRES** Catalonia	Mature, rich and ripe with concentrated forest fruits and well-integrated toasty oak. Terrific texture and mouthfeel.	$$$$$

SPAIN • FORTIFIED

(A) **LIRICO MOSCATEL DE VALENCIA 2001, GANDIA** Valencia	Perfumed with orange blossom aromas and a caramel finish.	$
(S) **BYASS CABRERA FINE PALE CREAM NV, GONZÁLEZ BYASS** Andalucia	A great example of nutty fruit and good balance. Elegant and hugely enjoyable.	$
(B) **BYASS CABRERA FULL RICH CREAM NV, GONZÁLEZ BYASS** Andalucia	A well-developed nutty bouquet with prune character and a warm round sweet conclusion.	$
(A) **BYASS CABRERA MANZANILLA DRY NV, GONZÁLEZ BYASS** Andalucia	Fresh and lively with a lingering salty tang.	$

(A) **LUSTAU MOSCATEL DE CHIPIONA NV, EMILIO LUSTAU** Andalucia	This rich glass of honey and candied orange peel is seductive indeed.	$$
(S) **LA GITANA MANZANILLA NV, BODEGAS HIDALGO LA GITANA** Andalucia	Infusions of tea, balsamico and flowers. Ripe fruit with a fresh tang of acidity.	$$
(B) **BARBADILLO CUCO OLOROSO SECO NV, BODEGAS BARBADILLO** Andalucia	Golden-brown hued, this wine smells of nuts with an orange or two lurking beneath.	$$
(B) **BYASS ELEGANTE NV, GONZÁLEZ BYASS** Andalucia	Rich, complex with a well structured palate filled with raisins and oranges.	$$
(S) **BYASS ALFONSO OLOROSO SECO NV, GONZÁLEZ BYASS** Andalucia	Butterscotch, caramel, toast and a broad candied fruit palate with hints of citrus.	$$$
(S) **BYASS TÍO PEPE NV, GONZÁLEZ BYASS** Andalucia	Straw yellow, with woody notes, clear white tangy fruit and a crisp, mouthwatering finish.	$$$
(G) **HIDALGO VERY OLD DRY AMONTILLADO NV, VINICOLA HIDALGO** Andalucia	This packs a punch of nut, coffee, toffee, spicy, fruitcake and peel flavors.	$$$
(S) **HIDALGO PASADA PASTRANA MANZANILLA NV, BODEGAS HIDALGO LA GITANA** Andalucia	With a delicate staw yellow, impressive richness and ethereal tangy lightness, this is a winner.	$$$
(S) **LUSTAU ALMACENISTA MANZANILLA PASADA DE SANLUCAR NV, EMILIO LUSTAU** Andalucia	An aged, smooth, dry style with incredible richness, beginning to display classic flor aromas.	$$$
(S) **LUSTAU ALMACENISTA AMONTILLADO DEL PUERTO NV, EMILIO LUSTAU** Andalucia	This mature sherry offers fresh daisies, pear fruit and fine woody aromas on the nose.	$$$
(S) **LUSTAU ALMACENISTA PALO CORTADO DE JEREZ NV, EMILIO LUSTAU** Andalucia	This splendid Palo Cortado features richness balanced by fine acidity, weighty fruit and herbaceous notes.	$$$
(G) **PEDRO XIMÉNEZ NAPOLEON NV, VINICOLA HIDALGO** Andalucia	This has a luscious richness, treacle and toffee with a streak of bright acidity.	$$$

(G)	**LUSTAU ALMACENISTA MANZANILLA AMONTILLADO NV, EMILIO LUSTAU** Andalucia	A warm, nutty, powerful Amontillado with the texture of golden syrup and white fruit flavors.	$$$
(G)	**LUSTAU PUERTO FINO NV, EMILIO LUSTAU** Andalucia	A delicious tang and grip of acid, fresh youthful citrus fruit and a salty finish.	$$$
(G)	**LUSTAU DON NUÑO DRY OLOROSO NV, EMILIO LUSTAU** Andalucia	This runs the gamut from candied lemon peel through to rancio, marmalade, nuts and fruitcake.	$$$
(G)	**LUSTAU ALMACENISTA AMONTILLADO DE JEREZ 1/30 NV, EMILIO LUSTAU** Andalucia	Complex, maturing aromas, rancio notes and underlying coffee and caramel. Vibrant acidity and persistence.	$$$
(S)	**LUSTAU ALMACENISTA AMONTILLADO DE JEREZ NV, EMILIO LUSTAU** Andalucia	The luminous golden color and yeast, white apple and warm hay aromas are just beautiful.	$$$
(S)	**LUSTAU OLOROSO PATA DE GALLINA NV, EMILIO LUSTAU** Andalucia	Very rich, weighty plethora of molasses, honeycomb and golden syrup on the nose and palate.	$$$
(S)	**LUSTAU PAPIRUSA MANZANILLA NV, EMILIO LUSTAU** Andalucia	This delicate, fresh, dry Manzanilla has crisp green and white fruit liberally laced with herbs.	$$$
(S)	**EL ALAMO OLOROSO CREAM , PEDRO ROMERO** Andalucia	Fantastic savory character with some sweetness, a persistent length and a long, warming finish.	$$$
(G)	**VIÑO 25 GF JEREZ VIEJISIMO AMONTILLADO NV, BODEGA GASPAR FLORIDO** Andalucia	This old amontillado has astounding complexity. Nutty and almondy with a touch of candied peel.	$$$$
(G)	**BYASS MATUSALEM OLOROSO DULCE NV, GONZÁLEZ BYASS** Andalucia	Sweet concentrated raisin flavors and Pedro Ximénez intensity, balanced by freshness and zippy acidity.	$$$$
(G)	**BYASS APOSTOLES 30 YEAR OLD PALO CORTADO MUY VIEJO NV, GONZÁLEZ BYASS** Andalucia	Honeyed and opulent with burnt toffee flavors and flavors of nuts and dried citrus peel.	$$$$$
(G)	**BYASS DEL DUQUE AMONTILLADO MUY VIEJO NV, GONZÁLEZ BYASS** Andalucia	Immensely concentrated and positively unctuous. It has a rich, deep nutty palate and fresh acidity.	$$$$$

(G)	**Byass Noe NV, González Byass** Andalucia	Burnt caramel, dried apricots and intense sweetness with overtones of raisin and fruitcake.	**$$$$$**
(G)	**Lustau Single Cask Amontillado Year 2000 Special Edition 2000, Emilio Lustau** Andalucia	There is caramel on the nose and palate and dried fruit, candied peel and nuts.	**$$$$$**

USA

The USA – which in wine terms effectively means the states on the west coast of North America – now produces some of the finest wines in the world. Unfortunately, that quality comes at a price that is often a lot higher than you might have to pay elsewhere. This helps to explain why a lot of top California wines rarely reach British, or other, shores these days. And why Australia's good value wines are enjoying such huge success among US wine drinkers. The award-winning wines on the following pages, however, do all offer both quality and value – both in the US and elsewhere.

USA • SPARKLING

(G)	**Le Rêve Blanc de Blancs 1996, Domaine Carneros** California	Rich, classy and elegant with a great future potential. Fantastic fizz that deserves its accolades.	**$$$$$**

USA • WHITE

(A)	**Laguna Canyon Chenin Blanc NV, California Direct** California	Peachy wine with a clean, honeyed finish.	**$**
(B)	**The Boulders Viognier 2001, Kingsland Wines & Spirits** California	Juicy, concentrated, rich and full-bodied, with white and pink-fleshed fruit in abundance.	**$$**
(G)	**Alexander Valley Reserve Chardonnay 2001, Clos du Bois** California	There is plenty of bright vanilla oak balancing the ripe melon and tropical fruit.	**$$$$**

(G)	**LAGUNA RANCH VINEYARD CHARDONNAY 2000, E & J GALLO** California	The Laguna Ranch is ultraripe, with melon fruit and buttered toast adding weight and depth.	$$$$
(G)	**TWO ROCK VINEYARD CHARDONNAY 2000, E & J GALLO** California	Nutty and rich with immense concentration of flavors ranging from lemons and melons to hazelnuts.	$$$$
(G)	**SIMI RUSSIAN RIVER VALLEY RESERVE CHARDONNAY 2000, SIMI WINERY** California	A leesy character and creamy rounded softness with a good hit of toffee and toasty oak.	$$$$
(G)	**ARROYO VISTA CHARDONNAY 2000, J LOHR WINERY** California	Deep gold, a rich buttery nose and ripe powerful tropical and apple fruit flavors.	$$$$
(G)	**NORTHERN SONOMA ESTATE BOTTLED CHARDONNAY 1999, E & J GALLO** California	This Russian river gem is big, deep and tropical, with a touch of acacia blossom.	$$$$$

USA • ROSÉ

(G)	**FETZER VALLEY OAKS SYRAH ROSÉ 2002, FETZER VINEYARDS** California	Bright, palest ruby colour. Rich vivacious succulent fruit on the forward nose and palate.	$$	

USA • RED

(A)	**ROCKY CREEK SHIRAZ CABERNET SAUVIGNON 2002, ZIMMERMAN GRAEFF** California	Simple, upfront wine with good black fruit purity.	$
(B)	**VENDANGE ZINFANDEL 2000, CONSTELLATION WINES** California	Black pepper and crushed bramble fruit and leaves on the nose and palate.	$$
(B)	**THE BOULDERS PETITE SYRAH 2001, KINGSLAND WINES & SPIRITS** California	Vegetal raspberry nose with plenty of juicy fruit on the palate and nice balancing acidity.	$$
(B)	**SIERRA VALLEY ZINFANDEL 2001, E & J GALLO** California	Unfettered ripe sun-warmed raspberries. The balanced, juicy palate has smooth textured fruit.	$$

(S)	**FETZER VALLEY OAKS SHIRAZ 2000, FETZER VINEYARDS** California	Warm oaky style with jammy berry fruit, plenty of tannins and a lift of acidity.	**$$**
(G)	**LA CREMA CARNEROS PINOT NOIR 1999, KENDALL-JACKSON** California	Perfumed, lifted sweet ripe fruit, subtle spiced oak and a savory, mature, up-front character.	**$$$$**
(G)	**SONOMA COUNTY ZINFANDEL 2000, GEYSER PEAK WINERY** California	Bramble fruits, white pepper, red plums and leather. The richness is mitigated by fresh acidity.	**$$$$**
(G)	**AVANT-GARDE PINOT NOIR 2001, DOMAINE CARNEROS** California	Floral nose with pungent herbaceous aromas. The palate is ripe and jammy with fair depth.	**$$$$**
(G)	**FRANCISCAN NAPA VALLEY MERLOT 2000, FRANCISCAN OAKVILLE ESTATE** California	Luscious new oak and ripe, broad, almost sweet, fruit. A big, friendly, ripe wine.	**$$$$**
(G)	**ALEXANDER VALLEY RESERVE CABERNET SAUVIGNON 1999, CLOS DU BOIS** California	A joyous blast of framboise and cassis on the nose and creamy layered cherry flavors.	**$$$$**
(G)	**RIDGE GEYSERVILLE 2000, RIDGE** California	This is a big wine with a deep color and ripe damson and loganberry fruit.	**$$$$$**
(G)	**MAGNIFICAT 1999, FRANCISCAN OAKVILLE ESTATE** California	Plum and black cherry fruit aromas, and red berries and forest fruits fill the palate.	**$$$$$**
(G)	**RESERVE MERITAGE 1999, IRONSTONE VINEYARDS** California	Smooth, round and plummy, with tobacco notes and an elegant creaminess on the palate.	**$$$$$**
(G)	**CAIN CELLARS FIVE 1998, CAIN CELLARS** California	Almost opaque in color, mellow and harmonious with developed aromas of ripe berry fruit.	**$$$$$**
(G)	**PINOT NOIR KNOX ALEXANDER 2000, AU BON CLIMAT** California	The plummy, spicy nose leads to an intense, focused palate with rich cinnamon spice flavors.	**$$$$$**

Wines are listed in approximate price order (though this can vary widely depending where they are on offer). All of the wines in the Guide are good value, by definition, but the best buys carry the "Great Value Wine of the Year" symbol. These were the bottles that performed best in their price band in a blind tasting by the International Wine Challenge top tasters – the super jurors. Buy them when you can; they tend to sell out very quickly.

OTHER COUNTRIES

The world is full of countries that now make good wine – and the number of countries and regions is growing with every year. The following pages include some of the most interesting and successful wines from these countries in the International Wine Challenge. We encourage you to explore them if you get the opportunity rather than faithfully heading back to a source of wine you already know.

AUSTRIA

AUSTRIA • WHITE

(G)	**SCHILFWEIN MUSKAT OTTONEL 2000, WEINGUT HANSTSCHIA ANGERHOF** Burgenland	Packed with elegant grapey flavors and hints of attractive orange blossom. Opulent and full-bodied.	$$$$$
(G)	**GRÜNER VELTLINER ALTE REBEN 2002, WEINGUT JURTSCHITSCH-SONNHOF** Niederösterreich	Pale and angular, but deliciously floral with notes of bramble, white pepper and ripe lemons.	$$$$$

AUSTRIA • RED

(G)	**BATONNAGE 2001, CLUB BATONNAGE** Burgenland	Rich, meaty, spicy aromas and soft generous fruit enveloped in warm integrated oak.	$$$$$

AUSTRIA • SWEET

(G)	**SAMLING BOUVIER TBA 1997, WEINGUT MUNZENRIEDER** Burgenland	A dense, waxy, fragrant wine with pronounced botrytis, aromatic orange blossom and marmalade character.	$$$$
(G)	**WELSCHRIESLING No 4 2000, WEINLAUBENHOF KRACHER** Burgenland	Rich and untuous with elegant opulence. Notes of orange peel and burnt caramel.	$$$$$

BULGARIA

BULGARIA • WHITE

(A)	**TIRVANA CHARDONNAY NV, DOMAINE BOYAR** Southern Region	Easy-drinking wine with enough fruit to satisfy.	$
(A)	**TUK TAM SAUVIGNON BLANC 2002, VINPROM** Sub-Balkan Region	Light bodied with ripe gooseberry notes.	$

BULGARIA • RED

(A)	**TIRNEVA CABERNET SAUVIGNON NV, DOMAINE BOYAR** Southern Region	Juicy style with integrated tannins.	$
(A)	**VALLEY OF THE ROSES CABERNET SAUVIGNON 2001, VINPROM SVISCHTOV** Northern Region	Simple wine with nice fruit and easygoing tannins.	$
(A)	**TUK TAM CABERNET SAUVIGNON MERLOT 2002, VINPROM** Sub-Balkan Region	Clean, fresh and simple with good fruit purity.	$
(A)	**BLUERIDGE MERLOT 2001, BOYAR ESTATES** Southern Region	Rich and ripe with plummy depth.	$
(A)	**TUK TAM OAKED CABERNET SAUVIGNON 2002, VINPROM** Sub-Balkan Region	Solid cassis flavors with a lick of oak.	$

Wines are listed in approximate price order (though this can vary widely depending where they are on offer). All of the wines in the Guide are good value, by definition, but the best buys carry the "Great Value Wine of the Year" symbol. These were the bottles that performed best in their their price band in a blind tasting by the International Wine Challenge top tasters – the super-jurors. Buy them when you can; they tend to sell out very quickly.

CANADA

CANADA • SWEET

G	**GRAND RESERVE RIESLING ICEWINE 2000, JACKSON TRIGGS VINTNERS** British Columbia	Very fresh and sweet, with a crisp acidity to lift the richness of the superb finish.	$$$$$
G	**SILVER RIESLING ICE WINE 1999, INNISKILLIN** Ontario	Delicious rhubarb nose, ripe and appealing with a complex, developing finish. Luscious weight and sweetness.	$$$$$

CYPRUS

CYPRUS • WHITE

A	**MOUNTAIN VINES CYPRUS SEMILLON 2001, SODAP** Troodos South	Zesty and fresh with good fruit and acidity.	$

CYPRUS • FORTIFIED

B	**COMMANDARIA ST JOHN , KEO LTD**	A deep, dark, hedonistic wine of great raisined richness. Sweet warm honeycomb in a glass.	$

Wines are listed in approximate price order (though this can vary widely depending where they are on offer). All of the wines in the Guide are good value, by definition, but the best buys carry the "Great Value Wine of the Year" symbol. These were the bottles that performed best in their price band in a blind tasting by the International Wine Challenge top tasters – the super-jurors. Buy them when you can; they tend to sell out very quickly.

ENGLAND

ENGLAND · SPARKLING

(A) **THREE CHOIRS CLASSIC CUVÉE NV, THREE CHOIRS VINEYARDS** Gloucestershire	Balanced with ripe pear fruit allied to fresh acidity.	**$$**

GREECE

GREECE · WHITE

(S) **CHATEAU JULIA ASSYRTIKO 2001, DOMAINE CONSTANTIN LAZARIDI** Adriani	Seductive aromas of freshly cut hay and wildflowers grace the pear and elderflower nose.	**$$**

GREECE · RED

(S) **ARGILOS SOUTHERN SLOPES NEMÉA 2000, DOMAINE HARLAFTIS** Peloponnese	Noble Agiorgitiko at its finest: silky, sweetly ripe fruit etched with cloves and vanilla.	**$$**
(G) **AMETHYSTOS CAVA 1999, DOMAINE CONSTANTIN LAZARIDI** Thrace	Soft, harmonious and generously fruited, with plenty of supporting tannins and finely integrated oak.	**$$$$**

Wines are listed in approximate price order (though this can vary widely depending where they are on offer). All of the wines in the Guide are good value, by definition, but the best buys carry the "Great Value Wine of the Year" symbol. These were the bottles that performed best in their their price band in a blind tasting by the International Wine Challenge top tasters – the super-jurors. Buy them when you can; they tend to sell out very quickly.

HOLLAND

HOLLAND • FORTIFIED

(S)	**ROSSINI VERMOUTH BIANCO NV, CDC WINES & SPIRITS**	Nutmeg, cloves, cinnamon and chamomile flowers all appear on the rich, full-bodied palate.	$
(S)	**ROSSINI VERMOUTH ROSSO NV, CDC WINES & SPIRITS**	A nose of sweet burnt sugar, damp earth, summer flowers, spice box and tree bark.	$

OTHER EASTERN EUROPEAN

ROMANIA • WHITE

(A)	**RIVER ROUTE PINOT GRIGIO 2002, CARL REH WINERY**	Fruity with fine acidity and a decent finish.	$
(A)	**RECAS PINOT GRIGIO 2002, CRAMELE RECAS**	Ripe and spicy with a slightly waxy finish.	$

SLOVENIA • RED

(G)	**CAPRIS PLEMENITO RDECE 1999, VINAKOPER** Primorska	Herbs, cassis, plums, cherries, tobacco and vanilla pods. Restrained, elegant cool climate black cherry fruit.	$$$$

RETAILERS

Under current legislation, the shipping of wine from one state to another is still illegal in several parts of the country. There are also local restrictions on sales of alcohol in stores that sell food. In some ways, these rules, and the so-called "three-tier system" of licenses that prevent retailers from selling wine they have imported themselves, are advantageous to the kind of small, local outlets that have been swept aside by supermarkets in other parts of the world. It has, however, also done much to slow the evolution of the United States into a wine drinking nation like, for example, Australia and Britain. The reduction in the number of wholesalers in the US – there are now 10% of the number 20 years ago – is also helping to cut down the range of interesting imported wines that are available in any given state. This in turn makes it all the more desirable to allow wine drinkers the freedom to ship wines from a well-stocked state to one with a smaller selection. Hopefully, more liberal attitudes will eventually prevail. Readers who would like to help them to do so should show their support by signing up at *www.freethegrapes.org*

ARIZONA
Colonial Wines & Spirits
501 223 3120.
c-trim@swbell.net
Good buys from Italy, Germany, and Portugal.

House Wine & Cheese
480 922 3470.
wineandcheese@earthlink.com
Stacks of domestic boutique wines, specially imported cheeses, and unique handmade chocolates.

Village Wine Cellar
480 556 8989.
jock@vwcaz.com
Young, hyper-avid retailer with well-chosen offerings from around the world.

CALIFORNIA
301 Wineshop & Club
516 374 2240.
A Wine Spectator Grand Award winner. .

Adventures in Wine
415 467 0130.
merrick@adventuresinwine.com

Ashbury Market
415 566 3136.
wine@ashburymarket.com
A favorite destination in the city for great deli food and even greater wine and beer.

Beltramos
888 710 9463.
sales@beltramos.com
Over 4,000 wines in stock at all times.

David Berkley
916 929 4422.
info@dberkley.com
Regular dinners, tastings, and seminars.

Beverages & More
888 77 BEVMO.
customer.service@bevmo.com
Chain, with 25 stores.

Briggs Wine & Spirits
310 395 9997.
Family owned and operated for 22 years.

Calistoga Wine Stop
707 942 5556.
calistogawinestp@aol.com
The oldest continually owned wine store in the Napa Valley.

Coit Liquor
415 986 4036.
tony@coitliquor.com
A large selection of wines from around the world.

Corti Bros
916 736 3803.
Darrell Corti is one of California's most experienced and respected wine retailers.

D & M Wine & Liquor Co.
800 637 0292.
wine@dnai.com
Six different clubs are run here, including Champagne, Single Malt, Armagnac, Cognac, and Calvados.

Dee Vine Wines
415 398 3838.
dade@dvw.com
Fine wines from Germany, Burgundy, Bordeaux, and Champagne.

Draeger's Supermarkets Inc.
650 685 3725.
draegers@aol.com

Duke of Bourbon
818 341 1234.
duke@dukeofbourbon.com
Hard-to-find California wines.

Enoteca Wine Shop
📞 707 942 1117.
Antique wine implements sold in-store.

Epicurus
📞 310 395 1352.
rpicone756@aol.com
Wines from California and around the world – including some old and rare.

Fireside Cellars
📞 310 3932888.
santos@firesidecellars.com

Golden West International
📞 415 931 2300.
info@golden-west-wine.com
Specialists in Champagne and Port, California Cabernet and Chardonnay, Zinfandel, and Bordeaux wines.

Green Jug Fine Wine & Spirits
📞 818 887 9463.
greenjug@earthlink.net
Extensive range of wines from around the world.

Hi-Time Wine Cellars
📞 800 331 3005.
hitimeclrs@aol.com
Tasting bar and wine classes on location.

K & L Wine Merchants
📞 650 364 8544.
orders@klwines.com
A good retailer of old and new Bordeaux and California wines.

Los Olivos
📞 805 688 4409.
bob@sbwines.com
Pinot Noir and Syrah specialist.

Kermit Lynch Wine Merchant
📞 510 524 1524.
klwmsl@aol.com
Long-established merchant with a cult following for great French wines.

Mission Wines
📞 626 403 9463.
info@missionwines.com
Specializing in boutique and hard-to-find wines.

Oakville Grocery Co.
📞 800 973 6324.
mdanielak@oakvillegrocery.com
Specialty gourmet food and wines with many ultrapremium California wines.

Old Bridge Cellars
📞 707 258 9552/800 922 2234.
info@oldbridgecellars.com
Unashamed Australia obsessives.

Old Doc's
📞 559 224 3627.
olddocswnz@aol.com
Vast selection of premium Californians.

Pebble Beach Market
📞 831 622 8771.
winfielj@pebblebeach.com
Predominantly upscale California reds.

Premier Cru
📞 510 655 6691.
sales@premiercru.net
Specialized Burgundy merchant with an extensive range of fine and rare wines.

Red Carpet Wine & Spirits
📞 818 247 5544.
jim@redcarpetwine.com
One of the finest tasting bars in southern California.

Roberts of Woodside
📞 650 851 1511.
john@robertsmarket.com
Roberts offers the choice between great deli items, fresh smoothies, top class Bordeaux, and a great website.

St. Helena Wine Merchants
📞 707 963 7888.
gsmith@napanet.net
The Yates family offers a comprehensive range of California wines.

Subterraneum
📞 510 451 3939.
joe@subterraneum.com

Twenty-Twenty Wine Merchant
sales@2020wines.com
Wide range with fine and rare wine focus on France, Italy, and California.

Vin Vino
📞 650 324 4903.
A tremendous range of unusual French wines

Vintage Wine & Spirits
📞 415 388 1626.
vintagewines@pacbell.net

Wally's Fine Wines & Spirits
📞 310 475 0606.
mail@wallywine.com
Wine and food baskets are a specialty.

Weimax Wines & Spirits
📞 650 343 0182.
gerald@weimax.com
They cater for those hard-to-find bottles.

Wine Cask
📞 805 966 9463.
winestore@winecask.com
The largest selection of Santa Barbara County wines to be found.

The Wine Club
📞 415 512 9086

Wine Exchange of Sonoma
📞 707 938 1794.
Rare California, Oregon, and Washington wines.

The Wine Exchange
800 769 4639.
wines@winex.com
A very competitively priced discount store.
The Wine House
415-3559463.
winesf@aol.com
John Carpenter's well-established retailer enjoys a cult following among San Francisco wine lovers.
The Wine Rack
408 253 3050.
An emphasis on California boutique wines.
The Wine Stop
800 283 WINE.
Specializing in fine California wines.
Woodland Hills Wine Co.
800 678 9463.
wine@whwineco.com
Large store with a stock of more than $8 million.

COLORADO
Applejack Liquors
303 233 3331.
slightfoot@applejack.com
Argonaut Wine & Liquor
303 831 7788.
Good Italians, Australians, and South Americans.
Chamber's Wine & Liquor
303 751 6935.
Good hard-to-get specialties.
Mayfair Liquors Inc.
303 322 0810.
lmouton61@aol.com
Specialists in fine and rare Californians.
Pringle's Fine Wines & Spirits
970 221 1717.

CONNECTICUT
Amity Wine & Spirit Co.
203 397 WINE.
203 792 2152.
The largest retailer in the state with the largest range of French wines.
Horseneck Wines & Liquor
203 869 8944.
A broad range from all over the world.

DELAWARE
Wine & Spirit Co. of Greenville
302 658 5939.

DISTRICT OF COLUMBIA
Bell Wine & Spirit
202 223 4727.
bellwine@msn.com

Calvert Woodley
202 966 4400.
calvertwoodley@erols.com
Specialize in rare, mature Bordeaux and international wines.
Chevy Chase Wines & Spirits
202 363 4000.
corkcrew@aol.com
Wines from all over the world and a broad range of spirits.
Central Liquor
202 737 2800.
centrallic@aol.com
Strength in depth here, with a large single-malt Scotch selection.
MacArthur Beverages
202 338 1433.
wine@bassins.com
Schneider's of Capitol Hill
202 543 9300.
cellar@cellar.com
One of the largest selections of old and rare Bordeaux, Burgundy, and Cabernets from elsewhere.

FLORIDA
67 Wine & Spirits
954 428 6255.
Top French and dessert wines.
B-21
888 B21 WINE
info@b-21.com
Bern's Fine Wines & Spirits
813 250 9463.
Great domestic wines, Burgundy, and Bordeaux.
Sunset Corners
305 271 8492.
Large gourmet food department.
Wine Watch
954 523 9463.
andy@winewatch.com

GEORGIA
Mink's Fine Wine & Spirits
770 952 2337.
minks@mindspring.com
Tower Wine & Spirits
404 881 0902.

HAWAII
Fujioka's Wine Merchant
808 739 9463.
mail@fujiokawine.com
Good Burgundy and Champagne.
Vintage Wine Cellar
808 523 9463.
vwchawaii@aol.com

IDAHO
The Boise Consumer Co-op
208 342 6652.
todd_g@boisecoop.com

ILLINOIS
Binny's Beverage Depot
847 674 4200.
The Corkscrew Wine Emporium
217 698 1112.
crkscru@thecorkscrew.com
International House of Wine and Cheese
800 323 0346.
winehouse@rsg.org
Mainstreet
708 354 0355. / 1-888 354 0355.
Sam's Wine & Spirits
800 777 9137.
sams@samswine.com
Largest independent wine store in the US.
Schaefer's
847 673 5711.
mail@schaefers.com
Good stocks of fine and rare wines from around the world.

INDIANA
John's Spirits & Fine Wine
317 637 5759.
Strong on Australian wines, including collectables.

KANSAS
Jensen Retail Liquor
785 841 2256.

KENTUCKY
The Party Source
859 291 4007.
bellevue@thepartysource.com
Over 5,000 wines and a range of gourmet foods.

LOUISIANA
Dorignac's Food Center
504 837 6548.
butch@dorignac.com
Good domestic and imported producers.
Martin Wine Cellar
504 899 7411 or 1 800 298 4274.
wine@martinwine.com

MAINE
Clayton's Gourmet Market
207 846 1117.
Specializing in hard-to-find wines from Australia, France, Italy, and Spain.

MARYLAND
Calvert Discount Liquors
410 628 2320.
Finewine.com
301 987 5933.
Mills Wine & Spirits Mart
410 263 2888.
Wells Discount Liquors
410 435 2700.
wellswine@aol.com
Bordeaux specialist.

MASSACHUSETTS
All Star Wine Liquors
617 332 9400.
Strong on California and Australia.
Bauer Wine & Spirits
617 262 0363.
bauerwine@aol.com
Emphasis on New World, Spain, and Italy.
Brookline Liquor Mart
617 734 7700
Dub's Discount Liquors & Fine Wines
508 339 3454.
cabernet@dubsonline.com
A large selection of rare and hard-to-find wines.
Federal Wine & Spirits
617 367 8605.
fedwine@aol.com
Marty's Liquors
617 332 1230.
martywine@earthlink.net
One of the finest wine stores in Massachusetts.
Merchants Wine & Spirits
617 523 7425.

MICHIGAN
G.B. Russo & Son
616 942 2980.
Also offers gourmet food.
Village Corner, Inc.
734 995 1818.
winerat@villagecorner.com
Haskell's Inc.
612 333 2434.
tfarrell@haskells.com
They have provided wines for the White House.
Hennepin Lake Liquors
612 825 4411

MISSOURI
Gomer's Fine Wines & Spirits
816 942 6200.
Largest single outlet in Missouri.

The Wine Chateau
636 532 6069.
info@thewinechateau.com
An intimate venture offering fine wines from around the world,

The Wine and Cheese Place
314 962 8150.
info@wineandcheeseplace.com
Fine cheeses.

The Wine Merchant Ltd
800 770 8466.
winemerchantltd@aol.com
Good French specialists.

MONTANA
City Vineyard
406 867 1491.
WIth gourmet foods, personalized gift baskets, and a wine bar.

The Liquor Store
406 293 4856.
Largest selection of fine wines in northwestern Montana.

NEBRASKA
The Winery
800 884 WINE.
Hard to find California wines.

NEW HAMPSHIRE
The Wine Cellar
603 883 4114.
winecell@aol.com

NEW JERSEY
Carlo Russo's Wine & Spirit World
201 444 2033.
russowine@aol.com
Emphasis is on all wine regions.

Corkscrewed of Cherry Hill
856 874 1090.

Wine Library
973 376 0005.

NEW YORK
67 Wine & Spirits
212 724 6767.
service@67wine.com
A range that spans the globe.

Abarbanel Wine Company
415 566 3136.
lisa@kosher-wine.com

Acker Merrall & Condit
212 787 1700.
ackerstore@aol.com
Wide-ranging specialists in everything including auctions.

Armonk Wines & Spirits
914 273 3044.
Global selection.

Astor Wines & Spirits
212 674 7500.
customerservice@astoruncorked.com
Fantastic sake selection.

Beacon Wines & Spirits
212 877 0028
www.beaconwines.com
One of the largest stores in Manhattan.

Bedford Wine Merchants
888 315 8333.
awunderlich@bedfordwines.com
Specialize in US, with good Bordeaux and Burgundy.

Beekman Liquors
212 759 5857.
bliquors@beekmanliquors.com
Some rare Bordeaux and other inaccessible items.

Best Cellars
212 426 4200.
bcnewyork@bestcellars.com
Features 100 of the world's greatest wine value selections, organized by taste and mostly priced under $15.

Burgundy Wine Company
212 691 9092.
info@burgundywinecompany.com
Specialists in Burgundy and Rhône.

The Chelsea Wine Vault Ltd.
212 462 4244.
chelseawinevault@erols.com
Good French, Italian, and Spanish wines.

Crossroads Wines
212 924 3060.
Full of esoteric wines from regions others tend to ignore.

Deprez Wines
914 271 3200.
Range has plentiful Zinfandels and over 80 California Merlots.

Diplomat Wines & Spirits
212 832 5080.
3,500 international wines close to the UN.

Dodd's Liquor City
914 762 5511.
Specialize in California boutique wines.

Embassy Wines and Spirits.
212 838 6551.
Tastings, courses, and parties.

Flagstone Winery
917 496 7700.
garnetwin@aol.com

Garnet Wines & Liquors
212 772 3211.
garnetwin@aol.com

Heights Chateau Wines & Spirits

[718 330 0963.

jrundel@aol.com

An emphasis on "undiscovered" good-value wines from new and exciting producers.

Liquor Square Inc.

[315 445 0539.

Largest wine and spirit retailer in Central New York.

Liquorama Wine Cellars

[845 229 8177.

The main areas of specialty here include Zinfandels and single malts.

Manley's Wines & Spirits Inc.

[212 242 3712

www.manleyswine.com

Website boasts owner Ken's G-gauge model railroad built in the roof of the store.

Marketview Liquor

[716 427 2480.

mktview@aol.com

Morrell & Company

[800 96 WINES.

larryc@morrellwine.com

Long established Manhattan specialist store.

Park Avenue Liquor Shop

[212 685 2442.

info@parkaveliquor.com

Many hard-to-find vineyards, vintages, and distillers in stock.

Premier Wines & Spirits

[716 873 6688.

office@premierwines.com

Award-winning national retailer.

Raeders Wine Merchants

[516 747 0004.

Rosenthal Wine Merchant

[809 910 1990

info@madrose.com

Terry Robards' Wines & Spirits

[518 523 9072.

Domestic and imported wines from one of the best known wine writers in the US.

Rochambeau Wines & Liquors

[914 693 0034.

rochambeauwines@aol.com

Specialists in Bordeaux and Burgundy.

Sherry-Lehmann, Inc.

[212 838 7500.

inquiries@s-lmail.com

More than twelve million dollars' worth of smart wines from all over the world.

Silver Spirits

[800 998 4411.

mail@silver-spirits.com

Wines from across the world.

D. Sokolin Co.

[631 283 0505.

sokolin@sokolin.com

Comprehensive and competitively priced Bordeaux and Burgundy wines.

Union Square Wines & Spirits

[212 675 8100.

usqwine@bellatlantic.net

Fine store with over 4,000 wines, a large range of premium spirits, and a mezzanine area available for rent.

Frederick Wildman & sons

[212 355 0700.

usqwine@bellatlantic.net

Zachys

info@zachys.com

A New York legend with top wines across the board (especially Italian).

NORTH CAROLINA
Asheville Wine Market

[828 253 0060

admin@ashevillewine.com

Small estate producers bring quality to the list.

Carolina Wine Company

[919 852 0236.

wines@carolinawine.com

Emphasis is on France, Italy, Spain, and Germany.

NORTH DAKOTA
Happy Harry's Bottle Shop

[701 780 0902.

They have hard-to-find wines, wine and food pairing courses, and a selection of fine cigars.

OHIO
Dorothy Lane Market

[937 434 1294.

ttemplin@dorothylane.com

Upmarket grocery store with an emphasis on fine food and great wine.

Gentile's, The Wine Sellers

[614 891 3284.

Featuring a small art gallery and an in-store deli.

Jungle Jim's International Market

[513 829 1919.

jungle@junglejims.com

Wine of the month and wine and food pairing available with cooking classes.

Pat O'Brien's Fine Wines & Gourmet Food

[216 831 8680.

Good range of wines and a fine selection of gourmet foods.

OKLAHOMA
Edmond Wine Shop
(405 341 9122.

thewineshop@msn.com

Emphasis on California, Southern France, and Italy. Also offer cellar consultation.

OREGON
Brentwood Wine Company
(503 638 9463.

info@brentwoodwine.com

An internet company specializing in fine and rare wines for auction, but also selling wine and other accessories online.

Oregon Wine Company
(503 472 6454.

wine@oregon.com

Flexible specialists in wines from the Pacific Northwest.

Oregon Wine Merchants
(541 687 9463.

The place to go for rare Oregon Pinot Noirs, Northwest wines, and Burgundy.

Mt. Tabor Fine Wines
(503 235 4444.

They stock hard-to-find boutique wines from the Northwest, and excellent Bordeaux and Burgundy.

TENNESSEE
Arthur's Wine & Liquor
(901 763 3772.

The mid-South's finest retailer of European wines.

Mt. Moriah Liquors Inc.
(901 794 9463.

winehawk@mtmoriah.com

Specialists in classy French and California wines.

TEXAS
Austin Wine Merchant
(512 499 0512.

email@theaustinwinemerchant.com

Excellent selection of French wines with an emphasis on Burgundy and Bordeaux.

La Cave Warehouse
(214 747 9463.

francois@lacavewarehouse.com

Reasonably priced, single-vineyard French wines with a rare selection of matured Bordeaux.

The Cellar
(512 328 6464.

wine@thecellaraustin.com

Expertise lies in California wines.

Gabriel's Wine & Spirits
(210 654 1123.

Houston Wine Merchant
(713 524 3397.

woa@houstonwines.com

Good selection of California boutique wines.

Po Go's Wine & Spirits
(214 350 8989.

grandcru@pogoswine.com

Global boutique wine specialists.

Joe Saglimbeni Fine Wines
(210 349 5149.

mail@jsfinewine.com

Apart from California, they have a great range of Italian, Spanish, and French wines.

Sigel's Beverages, L.P.
(214 350 1271.

email@sigels.com

California boutiques are the specialty.

Spec's Liquor Stores
(713 526 8787.

Wiggy's
(512 474 9463.

A library of older vintages in the vaults.

VIRGINIA
Arrowine
(703 525 0990.

drosen@arrowine.com

Wine dinners and weekly tastings.

Cecile's Finewine.com
(703 356 6500.

support@finewine.com

They have a great selection of Spanish wines.

La Cantina Wine Merchants
(206 525 4340.

Specialists in French wines, especially Burgundy.

McCarthy & Schiering Wine Merchants
(206 282 8500.

msqa@sprynet.com

Specialists in the Northwest, France, Italy, Spain, and Australia.

Pete's Wine Shops
(206 322 2660.

Supermarket with an excellent deli and more than 1,800 wines.

Pike and Western Wine Shop
(206 441 1307.

wines@pikeandwestern.com

Specializes in wines of the Pacific Northwest.

WISCONSIN
Steve's Liquor & More
(608 833 5995.

WINE LOVER'S
GUIDE TO
THE WORLD

Sélections   Maison Eyquard   Vins Fin

VENTES
EXPÉDITIONS

WHAT THIS CHAPTER CONTAINS

The following chapter will help you to find almost everything you are likely to need to enjoy wine. There are 200 restaurants, bars, shops, and schools across the world. This is followed by details of a wide range of online retailers and suppliers of wine courses, vacations, cellars, racks, and chillers.

Key: 🍴 *Serves food* 🍷 *Serves wine. Price bands:* **$, $$, $$$**

RESTAURANTS & WINE BARS

ARGENTINA

BUENOS AIRES

Gran Bar Danzon 🍴 🍷
Libertad y Santa F, Buenos Aires.
📞 +54 11 4811 1108

Chic candle-lit spot with designer leather sofas and a wall-to-wall wine bar. **$**

The Winery 🍴 🍷
Av. LN Alem 880, Buenos Aires.
📞 +54 11 4894 8201

One of four great new wine-bars/restaurants/gourmet-food-&-wine shops. The places to sample new wave Malbecs and whites made from the Torrontes. **$**

AUSTRALIA

ADELAIDE

Grange 🍴 🍷
Hilton Adelaide, 233 Victoria Sq. SA
📞 +61 08 8217 2000

Superstar chef Cheong Liew dispenses masterful fusion cuisine to go with an impressive wine list.. **$$$**

Magill Estate 🍴 🍷
87 Penfold Rd Adelaide, SA
📞 +61 08 8301 5551

Enjoy the best view in town (especially at night), and the best selection of Grange, Australia's most sought-after wine in the surroundings of Penfold's original winery and vineyard. **$$$**

Star of Greece 🍴 🍷
Esplanade Pt, Willunga, SA
📞 +61 08 8557 7420

A short drive from Adelaide, this converted beachside snack bar on a spectacular part of the coast is home-from-home to local and visiting winemakers. Lunch lasts all day. All wines are good but explore bottles from the nearby McLaren Vale. **$$**.

Universal Wine Bar 🍴 🍷
285 Rundle St, Adelaide, SA
📞 +61 08 8232 5000
Started by Michael Hill-Smith, Australia's first Master of Wine (now co-owner of Shaw & Smith). Now in other hands, but still an Adelaide institution. Good fresh Mediterranean food and new wines. **$$**

BRISBANE

Grape Food & Wine Bar 🍴 🍷
85 Merthyr Rd, New Farm, Brisbane, QLD
📞 +61 07 3358 6500

A frequent winner of Australia's top awards for its list. Choose from 200 local and imported wines; 45 by the glass. There are tutored tastings and wine dinners too. **$**

CANBERRA

Caffe della Piazza 🍴 🍷
19 Garema Place, Canbera, ACT
📞 +61 02 6248 9711

Canberra's best wine bar offers the chance to sample many wines by the glass as well as to dine in relaxed style while eavesdropping on the politicians. **$$**

MARGARET RIVER

Wino's 🍴 🍷
85 Bussel Highway, Margaret River, WA
📞 +61 08 9758 7155

*Four hours' south of Perth, in the heart of
a truly top wine region, this is a great wine
bar, owned and run by winemakers. Taste
efforts from here and other parts of WA..*
$/$$

MELBOURNE

Circa 🍴 🍷
The Prince, 2 Acland St, St Kilda, VIC
📞 +61 09 536 1122

*In gorgeous, grimy downtown St Kilda,
this elegant Melbourne culinary landmark
has one of the most expansive wine lists in
Australia presented by expert staff.* **$$**

Melbourne Wine Room 🍴 🍷
The George, 125 Fitzroy, VIC
📞 +61 03 9525 5599

*Busy, noisy bar and stylish, minimalist
restaurant serving Med-Aussie style
cooking. The wine list is a perfect
introduction to Australia's vineyards.* **$/$$**

Walter's 🍴 🍷
Shop Ur1, Southgate, Southbank,
Melbourne. VIC
📞 +61 03 9690 9211

*Overlooking the waterfront, and offering
the most exciting wines in Australia. The
food is good too. Eat on the terrace.* **$$**

Jimmy Watsons 🍴 🍷
333 Lygon Street, Carlton, Melbourne. VIC
📞 61 03 9347 3985

*Local institution: wine bar and restaurant
that share their name with the most
famous prize in Australian wine.* **$/$$**

MILDURA

Stefano's Cantina 🍴 🍷
Grand Hotel, Mildura, VIC.
📞 +61 03 5023 0511

*In small town, television star Stefano de
Pieri offers delicious yet informal food and
Australian and European wines galore.* **$$**

PERTH

Altos 🍴 🍷
424 Hay St, Subiaco, WA
📞 +61 08 9382 3292
*In the trendy suburb of Subiaco, this is the
place to learn all about Western Aussie
wines – possibly alongside their off-duty
producers.* **$/$$**

Friends 🍴 🍷
Hyatt Centre, 20 Terrace Rd, E. Perth, WA
📞 +61 08 9221 0885

*The best wine list in Perth – and one of the
most stylish places to eat. Book a table
with a view over the river.* **$$**

SYDNEY

Australian Wine Centre 🍷
1 Alfred Place, Sydney, NSW.
📞 +61 02 9247 2755

*Old bottles of Grange or new vintages from
Tasmania. Taste at the wine bar; pause for
a snack. Buy to take to a BYO restaurant –
or have wines shipped home.* **$/$$**

Banc/WineBanc 🍴 🍷
53 Martin Place, Sydney, NSW.
📞 +61 2 9233 5300

*In the heart of the business district, this
restaurant and wine-and-jazz bar are now
a must-visit for anyone interested in Aussie
wine trends. Take advantage of the 600
wines on offer, but also look out for special
tastings.* **$$**

Bel Mondo/Antibar 🍴 🍷
Level 3, Argyle Stores, 18-24 Argyle St,
The Rocks, Sydney, NSW
📞 +61 02 92413700

*Stefano Manfredi's Italian-Australian
restaurant and bar tucked away behind
the tourist traps of the Rocks, offer 550
wines on their lists – 40 by the glass –
and some great cooking.* **$/$$**

Forty-One 🍴 🍷
Lvl 41, Chiffley Tower, Sydney, NSW
📞 +61 02 9221 2500

*The views would be a good enough reason
to be here, but the cooking and wine are
among the best in Australia.* **$$$**

Restaurant VII 🍴 🍷
7 Bridge Street, Sydney, NSW
📞 +61 02 9221 2500

Japan meets France and Australia brilliantly (a competitor for Tetsuya, here). Stupendous wines. Pricey though. **$$$**

AUSTRIA

VIENNA

Eckel 🍴 🍷
Sieveringer Straße 46, Vienna
📞 +43 01 320 3218

First class modern Austrian wines, especially from the Wachau abound here. Try to get a table in the garden on a hot day. A perfect Viennese experience. **$$**

Wein & Co 🍷
Jasomirgottstraße 3-6, Vienna
📞 +43 01 535 0916

A terrific wine shop and bar where you can try before you buy. **$/$$**

BELGIUM

BRUSSELS

Amadeus 🍴 🍷
Rue Veydt 13, Brussels
📞 +32 02 538 3427

A magical candle-lit haven in a former framemaker's workshop. Bistro food, French wines. Good Sunday brunch. **$**

Le Pain et le Vin 🍴 🍷
Chaussée d'Alsemberg 812a, Brussels
📞 +32 02 332 1740

Delicious Mediterranean food in a relaxed restaurant with a delightful terrace. Both bread and wine are worth the detour. **$$**

BERMUDA

Fourways Inn 🍴 🍷
Fourways Inn Cottage Colony, 1 Middle Rd, Paget.
📞 +1441 236 6517

Great wines from across the world are on offer in the great setting of the 1727 restaurant. **$$/$$$**

BRAZIL

RIO DE JANEIRO

Cafe Laguiole 🍴 🍷
63 Rua Sete de Setembro, Centro, Rio de Janeiro.
📞 +55 21 2509 7215

Fine Brazilian/French cooking are matched by one of the best, most varied wine lists in South America. **$$/$$$**

CAMBODIA

SIEM REAP

Grand Hotel d'Angkor 🍴 🍷
1 Vithei Charles de Gaulle, Khum Svay Dang Kum, Siem Reap
📞 +855 63 963 888

Far enough away from the more awful Angkor Wat tourist hotels, the restaurant here offers the Raffles food-and-wine experience in Cambodia. **$$/$$$**

CANADA

LAKE LOUISE

Post Hotel Dining Room 🍴 🍷
200 Pipestone Road, Lake Louise, Alberta.
📞 +1 403 522 3989

This retreat in the Canadian Rockies offers some 900 wines at an altitude of 1500 metres. **$$$**

MONTREAL

Les Caprices de Nicolas 🍴 🍷
2072 Rue Drummond, Montreal, Quebec.
📞 +1 514 282 9760

Over 700 wines, innovative takes on French dishes and a huge cheese board. **$$$**

Vinfro Lounge 🍴 🍷
1222 Mackay St, Montreal.
📞 +1 514 935 4000

Over 50 kinds of cheese are served in the "Red Room" and cosier "Wine Cellar Room" to accompany an extraordinarily wide range of wines. **$$**

NORTH HATLEY (NR. QUEBEC)

Auberge Hatley 🍴 🍷
325 Virgin Hill Road, North Hatley, Quebec.
📞 +1 819 842 2451

On the shores of Lake Massawippi, this grand country inn offers vegetables from its own hothouse and over 1000 wines. **$$$**

QUEBEC

Ristorante Michelangelo 🍴 🍷
3111 Chemin Saint-Louis, Ste-Foy, Quebec.
📞 +1 418 651 6262

Charming art deco surroundings and one of the most extensive wine lists in North America. **$$$**

TORONTO

360 The Restaurant at the CN Tower 🍴 🍷
301 Front St. W. Toronto, Ontario.
📞 +1 416 362 5411

Enjoy a stellar view and the chance to choose from almost 600 wines. **$$$**

North 44)° 🍴 🍷
2537 Yonge St., Toronto, Ontario
📞 +1 416 487 4897

The)° is part of name of this elegant Toronto hotspot. Around 20 wines are served by the glass. **$$**

VANCOUVER

Brix 🍴 🍷
1138 Homer St, Yaletown
📞 +1 604 915 9463

Both tapas and fondue are on offer at this popular brick-walled Yaletown gathering point. **$$**

Sooke Harbour House 🍴 🍷
1528 Whiffen Spit Rd, Sooke, BC.
📞 +1 250 642 3421

Focus on the fish here – and wash it down with local wine, or a wide range of offerings from North America and the classic regions of Europe. **$$**

WHISTLER

Bearfoot Bistro 🍴 🍷
4121 Village Green, Whistler BC.
📞 +1 604 932 3433

Another reason to visit this skiing resort. Ten chefs and 14,000 bottles of 1,300 different wines. Ask for tasting glasses to go with the tasting food platters. **$$**

CHILE

SANTIAGO

Agua Comer y Beber 🍴 🍷
Nueva Costanera 3467, Vitacura
📞 +56 2 374 1540

South American specialties and an all-Chilean wine list in a trendy setting. **$$**

Kilometre 11680 🍴 🍷
Dardignac 0145, Bellavista
📞 +56 2 777 0410

The name refers to the distance between Paris and Santiago. The food is bistro-style French and the wine list considered to be one of the best in the city. **$/$$**

CHINA

BEIJING

Courtyard 🍴 🍷
95 Donghuamen Ave, Wang Fu Jing
📞 +86 010 6526 8883

A top class fresh, modern restaurant by any standards, with an art gallery showing new Chinese work on offer as well. Fusion food and a wide-ranging wine list in a short stroll from the Forbidden City. **$$/$$$**

SHANGHAI

M on the Bund 🍴 🍷
7/F 20 Guangdong Rd, Shanghai
📞 +86 21 635 09988

A glorious rooftop view over the river – and great fusion cooking from the sister restaurant to the similarly recommendable M at the Fringe *in Hong Kong. And a long list of wines from across the world.* **$$**

CUBA

HAVANA

El Floridita 🍴 🍷
Calle Obispo 557 esq. Monserrate
La Habana Vieja
📞 +53 7 571 300-1

*A Hemingway favorite. Try a Cuban wine
with the local food. Or one fermented
locally with Italian grape juice.* **$$**

CYPRUS

LIMASSOL

Barolo Food & Wine 🍴 🍷
248 Ayiou Andreou St., Limassol.
📞 +357 25 760 767

*Cypriot red and white wine is improving,
but the surest bet here is the traditional
sweet Commandaria with your
pudding.* **$$**

CZECH REPUBLIC

PRAGUE

Ostroff 🍴 🍷
Strelecky ostrov 336, Prague
📞 +420 2 2491 9235

*Sample local wines such as the
aromatically grapey Irsay Oliver with the
local dishes.* **$$**

Prazské Selátko 🍴 🍷
Karlovo nám 34, Prague
📞 +420 0229 8891

*The name means "Prague Piglet" - which
gives you a hint of what you may find on
your plate. Try a local Röter Veltliner; you
won't find bottles easily elsewhere.* **$/$$**

DENMARK

COPENHAGEN

Krogs Fiskerestaurant 🍴 🍷
38 Gammel Strand, Copenhagen.
📞 +45 3 315 8915

*A waterfront restaurant with great fish
(even by Danish standards) and fine
European classics to drink.* **$$**

Le Sommelier 🍴 🍷
63-65 Bredgade, Copenhagen.
📞 +45 3 311 4515

*The name and cooking are classically
Gallic, but the wine list is absolutely
cosmopolitan in its scope.* **$$**

GLOSTRUP

la Cocotte 🍴 🍷
Glostrup Park Hotel, 41 Hovedvejen,
Glostrup.
📞 +45 4 396 0038

*Fusion food is the keynote here, with wines
that cover the globe, though Italy is a
particular strength.* **$$$**

DUBAI

The Agency Wine Bar 🍴 🍷
Emirates Tower Hotel, Sheikh Zayed
Road, Dubai
📞 +971 4 330 0000

*In one of the tallest towers in Dubai, this is
a chic place to rendez-vous and sample a
wines by the glass and bottle.* **$$**

EGYPT

CAIRO

La Bodega 🍴 🍷
157 Sharia 26 July, Cairo
📞 +20 02 735 6761

*A popular spot with ex-pats looking for
non-Egyptian wine that has been well
chosen and stored.* **$$**

EIRE

CONG
The George V Room 🍴 🍷
Ashford Castle, Cong, County Mayo
📞 +353 92 46003

*A French-style castle that was the home of
the Guinness family. "Classic Irish"
cooking and superb wines.* **$$$**

DUBLIN

Bon Appetit 🍴 🍷
9 St James Terrace, Malahide
📞 +353 1845 03 14

Classic European cooking, with plenty of local fish. Wines are from Old and New World and include some well-chosen South Africans. **$$**

Dobbin's Wine Bistro
15 Stephen's Lane, Mount St Upper, Dublin 2
 +353 1 676 4679

Frequent winner of Wine List of the Year awards, with aound 600 wines by the bottle and 10 or so by the glass to go with some very serious cooking. **$$/$$$**

FINLAND
VASA

Bacchus
4 Strandgatan, Vasa.
+358 6 357 1326

Fish and game are the specialties here – and much use is made of local berries. Wines are mostly French, with an accent on Alsace, Eastern France, and Languedoc Roussillon. **$$**

FRANCE
BEAUNE

l'Athenéum
7 Rue de l'Hotel Dieu, Beaune
+33 03 80 22 12 00

The 1,500 books in almost all languages could just make this the best wine book and gift shop in the world.

le Bistro Bourguignon
8 Rue Monge, Beaune
+33 03 80 22 23 24

Burgundy by the glass, good country food, live jazz... all this makes this an essential first stop for any visitor. **$/$$**

Ma Cuisine
Passage Sainte-Hélène, Beaune
+33 03 80 22 30 22

Tucked away to the side of the central square, Place Carnot, this is a favorite with winemakers. Classic Burgundian food and wine from the list or the shop next door. **$$**

BORDEAUX

Bistro du Sommelier
163 Rue Georges Bonnac, Bordeaux
+33 05 56 96 71 78

The place to find the Bordelais at play. Modern French food with mostly local wine at unusually fair prices. **$$**

Chateau Cordeillan Bages
Pauillac.
+33 05 56 59 24 24

Once a wine estate, now a Relais & Chateaux hotel and restaurant. Belongs to the owners of nearby Ch. Lynch Bages. Vinous tuition is available on request here and at a wine school in Bordeaux itself. **$$$**

Le Lion d'Or
Place de la République, Arcins
+33 05 56 58 96 79

Known to local chateau owners and merchants as Chez Barbier after its gloriously grumpy (until you know him) chef-owner. Drink great Bordeaux or phone ahead and take your own bottle. **$/$$**

LYON

le 110 Vins
3 Rue St Georges, Lyon
+33 04 78 37 99 64

A Lyonnais classic, with 110 wines from the Beaujolais and Mâconnais to the North, and the Rhône to the south. **$$**

Les Oliviers
20 rue Sully, Lyon.
+33 04 78 89 07 09

Creative mediterranean cooking (opt for the bargain "menu du marché" and a choice of 120 wines. **$$**

NICE

Vin sur Vin
18 bis rue Biscarra, Nice.
+33 04 93 92 93 20

A friendly wine shop/bistro with a selection of French wines and a strong emphasis on the rising stars of Southern France **$$$**

PARIS

Astier 🍴 🍷
44 Rue Jean-Pierre-Timbaud, Paris, 11e.
☎ +33 01 43 57 16 35

Closed at weekends and as tightly packed as any restaurant can be, this is one of the cheapest places to enjoy good bistro food and cheese board, and serious wine. **$$$**

Au Bascou 🍴 🍷
38 Rue Réaumur, Paris 3e
☎ +33 01 42 72 69 25

Basque by name and Basque by nature. Great tasty food to enjoy with wines you might never see elsewhere. **$$**

Baratin 🍴 🍷
3, Rue Joueye Rouve, Paris 20e
☎ +33 01 43 49 39 70

Argentine-born owner-chef Raquel specialises in hearty French dishes – and hearty French wines to go with them. **$$**

les Bouchons de François Clerc
🍴 🍷
22 Rue de la Terrasse, Paris 17e
☎ +33 01 42 86 82 82
12, Rue de l'Hotel Colbert, Paris 5e
☎ +33 01 43 54 15 34
7, Rue du Boccador, Paris 8e
☎ +33 01 47 23 57 80
6, Rue Arsène Houssaye, Paris 8e
☎ +33 01 42 89 15 51

A collection of wine-focused restaurants with modern Mediterranean food and some of the best value bottles in France. **$$**

Chateaubriand 🍴 🍷
129 Ave Parmentier, Paris 11e
☎ +33 01 43 57 45 95

Simplicity is the hallmark here; a perfect counterpoint to a range of impeccably-chosen French wines. **$$**

Juvenile's 🍴 🍷
47 Rue de Richelieu, Paris 1er.
☎ +33 01 42 97 46 49

Tim Johnston offers one of the most eclectic menus and wine lists and decors . Ask for a "blind" wine - it could be a great Rhône – or a brilliant bottle from the Barossa. **$$$**

Les Enfants Rouges 🍴 🍷
9, Rue Beauce, Paris 3e
☎ +33 01 48 87 80 61

Former-banker Dany's new venture is a perfect little bistro, with wonderfully honest wines (especially from the Rhône). Ask nicely and she may sing. **$/$$**

Lavinia 🍷
3-5 Bd. de la Madeleine, Paris 1er
☎ +33 01 42 97 20 20

A Spanish-owned venture that seeks to be – and almost certainly is – the biggest and best wine shop in the world. There's a great wine bar here too. **$/$$$**

Taillevent 🍴 🍷
15 Rue Lamennais, Paris 8e
☎ 33 1 44 95 15 01

Over 300 great (and fairly-priced) wines are on offer here to go with some of the best cooking in the city. **$$$**

Willy's Wine Bar 🍴 🍷
13 Rue des Petits Champs, Paris 1er
☎ +33 01 42 61 05 09

Mark Williamson's wine-bar/restaurant is a Parisian landmark for ex-pats, visitors, and locals with a taste for modern French-accented cooking and unusual wine. **$$**

STRASBOURG

Au Crocodile 🍴 🍷
10 Rue de l'Outre, Strasbourg.
☎ +33 388 32 13 02

There are nearly 2,000 wines on the list here – from France and every other corner of France. Great Alsatian cooking too. **$$**

GERMANY

AMORBACH

Kulinarisches Restaurant Abstub
🍴 🍷
Schafhof Amorbach, Amorbach.
☎ +49 9373 97330

Classic European cooking is matched by classic European wine in wine country close to the River Rhine. **$$$**

BERLIN

Vau

Jägerstrasse 54-55, Berlin.
+49 202 97 30

Justifiably hyped: the place to explore modern German food and wine **$$$**

COLOGNE

Vintage

31-35 Pfeilstrasse, Cologne
+49 2 21 920 710

A tremendous range of French and German wines is matched by fairly priced Mediterranean cooking. Try some of the new wave German reds. **$$**

DUSSELDORF

La Terrazza

30 Konigsallee, Dusseldorf
+49 211 327540

A haven for fans of Italian food and wine, with bottles you never see elsewhere. **$$**

FRANKFURT

Zum Schwarzen Stern

Römerberg 6, Frankfurt
+49 69 29 19 79

A favorite with visiting wine merchants. Superb German wines galore. **$$/$$$**

HAMBURG

Restaurant Haerlin

Hotel Vier Jahreszeiten, 9-14 Neuer Jungfernstieg, Hamburg
+49 40 3494 3310

Classic French cooking is matched by wines from across the planet. **$$**

MUNICH

Bogenhauser Hof

Ismaninger Str. 85, Munich
+49 89 98 55 86

Elegance is the keynote here: the cooking focuses on simple preparation of fine ingredients. A beautiful old building with a sunny terrace. **$$**

Geisel's Vinothek

Schützenstrasse 11, Munich
+49 89 551 370

There aren't many reasons to visit this part of the city, but the quality of the Italian cooking and the range of wines on offer here make this a must-visit destination. **$$**

Restaurant Königshof

Hotel Königshof, 2 Karlsplatz, Munich
+49 89 55 136 142

One of the best wine ranges of German wines is on offer in this hotel – as well as some glorious Bordeaux and Burgundies. The cooking is traditional French/German.

GREECE

PIRAEUS

Varoulko

4 Deligiorgi, Piraeus
+30 210 411 2043

Up a side street in the port of Piraeus, this Michelin-starred restaurant offers terrific food (though don't ask for a menu – you will enjoy what you are given) and 240 local and imported wines. **$$$**

HONG KONG

Vong

Mandarin Oriental Hotel, 5 Connaught Rd, Central.
+852 2825 4028

Fusion food with a view over the city and harbour from the 25th floor of this hotel. The bar great for Champagne by the glass. Evolving in 2003. **$$/$$$**

Boca

G/F, 85 Peel St.. Central, Hong Kong
+852 2548 1717

Friendly, busy bar wih good wines by the glass, tapas, and dim sum. **$**

W's Entrecote

303 Times Sq. Hong Kong
+852 2506 0133

Wine authority Wilson Kwok's steak restaurant offers an appropriately well-chosen range of French wines. **$$**

HUNGARY

BUDAPEST

Gundel 🍴 🍷
Állatkerti út 2. Budapest
📞 +36 1 86 4040

A Budapest, landmark, this century-old restaurant has recently been revived under chef Kálmán Kalla. Worth visiting for the goose liver, classic paintings – and the range of great Hungarian wine.s. **$$**

ICELAND

REYKJAVIK

Sommelier 🍴 🍷
Hvervisgata 46, Reykjavik
📞 +354 511 4455

Probably the best place to go looking for good wine in this country. The food is innovative and recommendable too, and the service enthusiastic. **$$$**

Vinbarrin 🍴 🍷
Kirkjuhvoll 101, Reykjavik
📞 +354 552 4120

A regular haunt for Icelandic wine lovers. Expect varied fare. **$$**

INDIA

MUMBAI

Athena 🍴 🍷
41/44 Minoo Desai Marg Colaba, Mumbai.
📞 +91 22 202 8699

Trendy young restaurant belonging to Champagne Indage, producers of (good) local sparkling wine, and offering a range of 180 wines from across the world. **$$**

NEW DELHI

Latino 🍴 🍷
The Park Hotel, 15 Parliament St.
📞 +91 11 2374 3000

Siuated in a chic new wave hotel, this bar/restaurant offers tapa-style snacks called "picks" and one of the city's better selections of wines. **$$$**

La Rochelle & Wine Bar 🍴 🍷
The Oberoi, Dr. Zakir Hussain Marg. New Delhi.
📞 +91 11 24363030

Great international and Indian food and wine. Sunday Jazz Champagne brunches. (The Mumbai Oberoi La Rochelle is similar). **$$$**

ISRAEL

JERUSALEM

Vino Vero 🍴 🍷
6 Hillel St, Jerusalem
📞 +972 2 622 1812

Wine bar with over 100 wines including new wave efforts hard to find overseas. **$$**

ITALY

ALBEROBELLO

Il Poeta Contadino 🍴 🍷
27 Via Indipendenza, Alberobello, Puglia
📞 +39 0 80 432 1917

Food and wine that reflect the region at its best, in a stunningly beautiful village. **$$**

FLORENCE

Enoteca Pinchiorri 🍴 🍷
87 Via Ghibellina, Florence
📞 +39 0 55 242 757

Restaurant-cum-vinous cathedral, with over 4,500 wines. Very pricey, very full of tourists, but still worth the visit. **$$$**

Beccofino 🍴 🍷
Piazza degli Scarlatti, Florence
📞 +39 055 29007

"Simpatico" wine bar and restaurant. that is well liked by Tuscan winemakers. **$/ $$**

MILAN

Cantine Isola 🍷
Via A.. Sarpi, Milan
📞 +39 02331 5249

Fine French and Italian wines from 8.30am-8.30pm, Tuesday-Friday. The best bottles come out on Friday. No food. **$/ $$**

Peck
Via Hugo Victor, 4, Milan
+39 02 86 1040

*A local landmark in the shape of a
brilliantly stocked wine shop and
restaurant. $/ $$$*

NAPLES

La Cantina di Triunfo
Riv. di Chiaia 64, Castel Dell'Ovio e Chiaia
+39 081 66 8101

*A family-run restaurant offering classic
Neopolitan cuisine and Italian wine. Take
cash; credit cards are unwelcome. $/$$*

ROME

Dolce Vino
Via Pier Vettori, 36, Rome
+39 06 657 44777

*A wine bar that is highly popular with
Tuscan winemakers. $/$$*

Il Simposio dell' Enoteca Constantini
Il Piazza Cavour 16, Rome
+39 06 321 1502

*A wine bar with classic Italian cooking and
500 wines from the 5000 on offer in the
shop next door. $$*

Wine Academy of Roma
Vicolo del Bottino 8, Rome
+39 06 69 90878

The place to learn all about Italian wine.

SIENA

Enoteca Italiana
Piazza Matteotti 30, Siena
+39 0577 228811

*Wine mecca in the old fortress with 1,000
wines. Closes at 8pm nightly, including
Saturday and Sundays evenings. $$*

SOVANA

La Taverna Etrusca
Piazza del Pretorio 16, Sovana,
Maremma
+39 0564 616183

*In the up-and-coming Tuscan region of the
Maremma, this restaurant has plenty of
good wines and truly outstanding food. $$*

TURIN

Taberna Libraria
Via Bogino 5, Turin
+39 011 836515

*A young food-and-wine bookshop/wine
bar that has become an instant success in
this region. $/$$*

VENICE

Enoteca San Marco
Frezzeria-San Marco, 1610 Venice.
+39 041 5285242.

*Recently opened bar-restaurant with a good
range of wines from the Veneto. $$*

VERONA

Bottega del Vino
3 Via Scudo di Francia, Verona 37121
+39 0 45 800 4535

*The vinous heart of this glorious old town,
with walls covered by empty bottles and a
cellar packed with great full ones, mostly,
but not all, from Italy. Book in advance
during the tourist/opera season. $$*

JAPAN

TOKYO

Aux Amis du Vin, Maronouchi
 Maronouchi 2-4-1, Maronouchi
Bldg. 35fl, Tokyo
+81 5 5220 4011

*One of the best views in the city – from the
35th floor, plus fairly priced classic French
food and even more fairly-priced older
vintages of French wines. Most wine lovers'
Tokyo favorite. $$*

L Vino
Roppongi 7-7-8. Tokyo
+81 33 5771 2439

*Jiro Kinoshita's little bar offers tremendous
Australian wines (including some that are
hard to find in Sydney) and Italian snack
food until the early hours. $/$$*

Restaurant Wine Lounge S
Nishi-Shinbashi 3-15-12
Minato-Ku Tokyo
+81 3 5733 3212

World's top sommelier Tasaki Shinya offers over 50 wines at only ¥3,900. **$$**

AOC Yoyogi
Yoyogi 1-43-2, Tokyo
+81 3 5308 7588

A wine bar focusing on fairly-priced French food and organic wines. **$$**

JORDAN

AMMAN

Royal Club
Radisson SAS Amman, Al Hussein Bin Ali Street, Amman.
+962 6560 7200

Imaginative continental food, excellent service, and an extensive wine list. **$$$**

KOREA

SEOUL

Grand Café / Vinotheque
Grand Intercontinental, 159-8
Samseong-Dong, Gangnam-Gu, Seoul
+82 2 559 7614

300 wines, wine-and food pairings and Thursday BYO with no corkage to pay. **$$**

LATVIA

RIGA

Vina Seta
Kalku 2, Riga
+371 2 722 2566

The best place to drink wine in Riga – and to sample the best of Latvia's sparkling wine. **$$**

LEBANON

BEIRUT

Eau de Vie
Phoenicia Inter-Continental, Minet El Hosn, Beirut
+961 1 369 100

Offering great views from the roof of this hotel, French cooking and sushi, 200 whiskies, and a fine range of (the increasingly impressive) Lebanese and imported wine. **$$$**

LIECHTENSTEIN

VADUZ

Hotel Restaurant Real
Staedtle 21, Vaduz
+423 232 22 22

An ultra-smart hotel with a great restaurant and cellar. **$$$**

Torkel
Hintergasse 9, Vaduz
+423 232 44 10

Country inn belonging to the Prince and offering Liechtenstein wine that rarely travels far from the Principality. Groups of 10 or more can also taste local wine by appointment in the royal cellars (+423 232 1018) **$$**

LUXEMBOURG

Chiggeri Restaurant
5 Rue du Nord, Vielle Ville 2229.
+352 22 99 36

There are over 2000 wines to choose from in this delightful old-town building. **$$**

MACAO

Robuchon a Galera
Hotel Lisboa, 2-4 Avenida de Lisboa
+853 377 666

A surprising place to find a great name of Gallic cuisine – and some similarly great Gallic wines. **$$$**

MALAYSIA

KUALA LUMPUR
Cilantro Restaurant and Wine Bar
 Mi Casa Hotel Apartments
368B Jalan Tun Razak
+60 3 2161 8833

A walk-in cigar humidor and wine cellar plus masterful fusion cuisine. Book well in advance. **$$/$$$**

MEXICO

MEXICO CITY

La Hacienda de Los Morales
🍴 🍷 525 Vasquez de Mella,
Col. del Bosque, Mexico City 11510
☎ +52 5 096 3054

The place to find some genuinely impressive Mexican wine plus some similarly fine Mexican cooking. **$$**

MOROCCO

CASABLANCA

A Ma Bretagne 🍴 🍷
Boulevard de l'Atlantique
Sidi Abderrahman
☎ +212 22 36 21 12

Gérard Dépardieu has just invested in an ambitious Moroccan wine venture (in addition to his French vineyards). Try some of the new wave wines here – with some good Gallic dishes. **$$**

MARRAKECH

Villa Rosa 🍴 🍷
64 Avenue Hassan II, Marrakech
☎ +212 44 43 08 32

Modern French/Italian food and wine are served in a stylish room or on the terrace. A place that makes it easy to linger. **$$**

NETHERLANDS

AMSTERDAM

Dorrius 🍴 🍷
Niewezijds Voorburgwal 5, Nieuwe Zijde
Amsterdam
☎ +31 20 420-2224

The interior decor of this 1890 restaurant was skillully relocated to the Crowne Plaza in 1992. Fine Dutch food and wide ranging wines (but try the extraordinary selection of Jenever gins too). **$$/$$$**

Cafe Roux 🍴 🍷
Grand Amsterdam, Oudezijds
Voorburgwal 197, Oude Zidje,
Amsterdam
☎ +31 20 555 3560

If you are looking for reasonably-priced unpretentious French food and wine, this is probably the best place to find it in Amsterdam. **$$**

ROTTERDAM

En Verre 🍷
Van Vollenhovenstraat 15, Westelijk
Handelskrrein, Rotterdam
☎ + 31 10 241 05 10

Wednesday night is tasting night (and often packed), while for the rest of the week in this wine bar there are tapas and a choice of 200 wines. **$**

THE HAGUE

Restaurant Hotel Savelberg 🍴 🍷
4 Oosteinde, Voorburg The Hague
☎ +31 70 387 2081

Dress up before approaching this grand 18th century country house, but the effort will be worth it. Impeccable food and wine. **$$$**

NEW ZEALAND

AUCKLAND

Gaults at George 🍴 🍷
☎ 44 Parnell Rd, Auckland
☎ +64 9 358 2600

Great seafood from one of New Zealand's best chefs, and great New Zealand wines in a smart part of town. **$$**

Otto's 🍴 🍷
40 Kitchener Street (the Metropolis
Building), Auckland
☎ +64 9 300 9545

Local wines and fresh modern flavors abound in the grand surroundings of this converted old courthouse. **$$**

BLENHEIM

Herzog Winery 🍴 🍷
81 Jeffries Rd, Blenheim, Marlborough
☎ +64 3 572 8770

A rapidly up-and-coming winery, with a set-price restaurant and a good range of Marlborough wines. **$$**

HAWKES BAY

Terrôir
Craggy Range Winery, 253 Waimarama
Rd, Havelock Nth, Hawkes Bay
+64 6 873 0143

*A new impressive winery offers a modern
indoor-outdoor restaurant and fine
Kiwi/Gallic cooking.* **$$**

WELLINGTON

Logan Brown
92 Cuba Street, Wellington
+64 4 801 5114

*Top class cooking in the former National
Bank building, plus a wine list with just
about every Kiwi Pinot Noir and a few
foreign wines to boot. And you can take
your own bottle for $3 corkage!.* **$$**

NORWAY

OSLO

Bagatelle
3 Bygdoy Alle, Oslo.
+47 22 12 14 40

*The wines here are French – and skillully
chosen and fairly priced – but the cuisine
shows a deliciously wide range of
influences.* **$$**

PANAMA

Chalet Suisse
Calle Eusebio A Morales, El Cangrejo,
Panama
+507 263 8541

*The place to compare Bordeaux and
Californian Cabernet over a tasty dish of
Swiss cooking.* **$$/$$$**

PERU

LIMA

Manos Morenos
Pedro de Osma 409, Lima.
+51 1 467-4902

*Traditional Criolla cuisine in an elegant
modern setting. Peruvian wine is worth
trying – when in Peru.* **$$**

POLAND

KRAKOW

Cyrano de Bergerac
Slawkowska 26, Krakow.
+48 12 411 7288

*Good French cooking, with a better
selection of wines than is generally to be
found elsewhere in this beautiful city.* **$$**

WARSAW

Fukier
Stary Ryenek, 27, Warsaw
+48 22 831 1013

*Traditional Polish food served in a candle-
lit wine cellar in the Old Town.* **$$**

PORTUGAL

BUCACO

Bussaco Palace Hotel
Mata do Bussaco, Coimbra
+351 231 937970

*Disney-like former royal palace with old
Bucaco wine unavailable elsewhere.* **$$$**

LISBON

Coisas do Arco do Vinho
Centro Cultural de Belém, Lisbon.
+351 21 364 20 31

*The best wine shop in Lisbon, and a good
place to find local New Wave reds.* **$/$$$**

Nariz de Vinho Tinto
Rua do Conde 75, Lapa, Lisbon.
+351 21 395 3035

*Top class food, wine, and cigars (and olive
oils) from a restaurant that belongs to the
owner of Portugal's* Epicuro *magazine.* **$$**

OPORTO

D'Oliva
Rua Brito e Cunha, Oporto
+351 22 935 1005

*New restaurant in a converted warehouse
in the fishing area of Matosinhos. Great wine
list, recommended by port shippers.* **$$**

ROMANIA

BUCHAREST

Cronos
27-131, Calea 13 Septembrie, Bucharest
+40 1 410 2223

A chance to sample Romanian wines, and local dishes, at a reasonable price **$/$$**

RUSSIA

MOSCOW

First Restaurant
Sofiskaya 34, Moscow
+7 095 951 3598

A fashionable new restaurant close to the Kremlin, with a great wine list . **$$/$$$**

U Yara Wine Club
Leningradsky pr. 33, Moscow
+7 095 945 31 68

Run by a Frenchman who, for a small corkage fee, allows customers to bring in wine from the adjacent shop. **$$**

ST. PETERSBURG

Senat-Bar
Dekabristov str 21, St. Petersburg
+7 812 312 3205

City centre restaurant with a painted vaulted ceiling and good Russian/European food and wine. Bill Clinton ate here. **$$**

SINGAPORE

Les Amis
Scotts Road #02-16 Shaw Centre.
+65 6733 2225

Restaurant and wine bar in a colonial house. Exceptional French cuisine and a truly great list of wines. **$$$**

Provignage, The Wine Cave
30 Robertson Quay #01-12/13
Riverside View.
+65 6834 1490

Designed to resemble an underground cellar, this wine bar offers food and over 120 wines from around the world. **$$**

SOUTH AFRICA

CAPE TOWN

Constantia Uitsig
Spaanschemat River Rd, Constantia
+27 21 794 4480

A spectacular setting, plus spectacular Mediterranean-style cooling are on offer here, as well a good local wines. **$$**

The Cellars
Hohenort Hotel, 93 Brommersvlei Rd, Constantia
+27 21 994 2137

A luxury hotel in an old Cape Dutch winery with extraordinary gardens, fine cooking and a great wine list. **$$/$$$**

Vaughan Johnson
V&A Waterfront, Pierhead, Cape Town
+27 21 419 2121

Facing more competition now, but still the Cape's best known wine retailer **$/$$$**.

HERMANUS

B's Steakhouse
No. 5 Hemel & Aarde Village, National Rd, Sandbaai.
+27 21 887 5844

The meat is good and well cooked, but the proximity of the ocean makes fish the better option. With a local Pinot Noir. **$$**

JOHANNESBURG

The Saxon
36 Saxon Rd, Sandhurst, Johannesburg.
+ 27 11 292 6000

Modern cooking and wide-ranging wines in the place Mandela wrote Long Walk to Freedom. **$$**

STELLENBOSCH

Wijnhuis
Cnr Andringa & Church Sts, Stellenbosch.
+27 21 887 5844

Eat in the restaurant here, or simply taste and browse among 300 bottles of wine. **$$**

SPAIN

BARCELONA

Lavinia
Avda. Diagonal 605, Barcelona
☎ +34 93 363 4445

One of the world's best wine shops. **$/$$$**

Va de Vi 🍴 🍷
Lanys Vells 16, Barcelona
☎ +34 93 319 2900

The name means "about wine". Great setting in old stables. Fine ham. **$$**

la Vinateria del Call 🍴 🍷
Sant Demènec del Call 9, Barcelona
☎ +34 93 302 6092

Candle-lit spot close to the cathedral, with wines, tapas, and more serious dishes. **$$**

JEREZ

Juanito 🍴 🍷
Calle Pescadería Vieja 8-10, Jerez de la Frontera
☎ +34 95 633 4838

A Jerez favorite, with well-cooked local food and every sherry imaginable. **$/$$**

MADRID

Lavinia
José Ortega y Gaset 16, Madrid
☎ +34 91 426 0604

Shop offering 2000 ancient and modern Spanish and imported wines. **$/$$$**

La Cava Real 🍴 🍷
Espronceda 34, Madrid
☎ +34 91 442 5432

Bar/restaurant, associated with a wine club, offering over 50 wines by the glass. **$**

VALENCIA

Enoteca 🍴 🍷
Calle Vicente Iborra 3, Valencia
☎ +34 96 315 2072

Successful Barrio del Carmen venture with 120 local and imported wines. **$$**

SWEDEN

GOTEBORG

Sjomagasinet 🍴 🍷
Klippans Kulturreservat, Goteborg.
☎ +46 31 775 5920

Good seafood with classic French wines at – by Swedish standards – fair prices. **$$**

MALMO

Sankt Markus Wine Celler 🍴 🍷
Malmborgsgatan 7, Malmo
☎ +46 40 7030 6820

Fine modern cooking (especially seafood), skillul wine selection and service. **$$**

STOCKHOLM

The WineBar at Gondolen 🍴 🍷
Stadsgården 6, Stockholm
☎ +46 8 5569 6066

Forty wines by the glass, ten of which change daily, chosen by top sommeliers. **$$**

SWITZERLAND

BASEL

Lloyd's Tasting Factory 🍴 🍷
Spalenberg 53, Basel
☎ +41 61 263 2500

Former bank with 20 wines by the glass to enjoy with cheese or charcuterie. **$/$$**

GENEVA

Le Trianon 🍴 🍷
Le Mirador Resort & Hotel, Mont Pelerin, Lake Geneva.
☎ +41 21 925 1111

Ultra-fine French food, to go with ultra-fine French (and some Swiss) wines. **$$$**

ORMALINGEN

Langasthof & Vinothek, Farnsburg
🍴 🍷 Farnsburg, Ormalingen
☎ +41 61 985 90 30

One of the great wine lists, with over 2,000 different bottles. Fine Swiss cuisine. **$$$**

ZURICH

Caduff's Wine Loft
Kanzlestrasse 126, Zurich
+41 1 240 2255

A bright, modern restaurant with a tempting range of local and imported wines. Ask to visit the cellar. **$$**

Riesbächli
57 Zollikerstrasse, Zurich
+41 1 422 23 24

Just in case you were impressed by the Farnsburg Langasthof & Vinothek's 2,000+ wine list, here's a cellar with over 3,000. The (classic) food is good too. **$$$**

TAIWAN

TAIPEI

Blanc
342 Fuhsing Rd, Taipei.
+886 2 2516 3251

Candle-lit (some would say dark), Mediterranean bistro with one of Taipei's most interesting wine lists. **$$**

Eslite
243 TuhHua Rd, S B1.Taipei
+886 2 2775 5977 ext 756

Book shop and wine shop with one of the best, and most fairly-priced French wine ranges in Asia. **$/$$$**

Paris 1930
The Landis Taipei Hotel
41 Min Chuan East Road, Sec. 2
+886 2 2597 1234

One of the most serious restaurants in Taipei for wine lovers. **$$$**

THAILAND

BANGKOK

Doc Cheng's
Merchant Court Hotel, 202
Ratchadapisek Road
+66 2694 2222

Exciting fusion dishes accompanied by a mostly New World wine list. **$$$**

PHUKET
The Boathouse
2/2 Moo 2 Patak Rd, Tumbon Karon,
Amphur Muang, Phuket.
+66 76 330 015

Great Thai and European cooking and French wine in a magical setting. **$$**

TURKEY

ISTANBUL

Galata Eski Ingiliz Karakolu
Galata Kulesi Sokak 61, Istanbul
+90 212 245 18 61

Housed in a former English prison, this good restaurant offers a rare opportunity to sample Turkey's better wines. **$$**

UNITED KINGDOM

BELFAST

Nick's Warehouse
35-39 Hill St, Belfast, County Antrim.
+44 028 9043 9690

Former warehouse-turned-best wine bar in Northern Ireland. Good organic food, too **$**

BIRMINGHAM

Hotel du Vin
Church St, Birminmgham
+44 0121 200 0600
Ship St, **Brighton**.
+44 01273 718588
The Sugar House, Narrow Lewins Mead,
Bristol.
+44 0117 925 1199
Crescent Rd, **Tunbridge Wells**, Kent.
+44 (0) 1892 512044
Church St, **Winchester** Hants.
+44 01962 841414

Unique set of hotels and restaurants with stylish accommodation, good Mediterranean food and well-chosen wines. **$$**

BRIGHTON
Hotel du Vin (see Birmingham)

BRISTOL
Hotel du Vin (see Birmingham)

CARDIFF

Tides, Marco Pierre White 🍴 🍷
St. David's Hotel & Spa, Havannah St,
Cardiff
📞 +44 029 2045 4045

London's superstar restaurateur has lent his skills to the smartest restaurant in Wales where good wine can be hard to find. **$$$**

CHAGFORD

Gileigh Park Hotel 🍴 🍷
Chagford, Devon
📞 +44 01647 432 367

Country hotel 25 miles from Exeter with laudably fair wine prices (600 wines with a maximum $40 mark-up) Californian wines are a specialty. **$$**

DODDISCOMBLEIGH

The Nobody Inn 🍴 🍷
Doddiscombleigh, Devon
📞 +44 01647 252394

A cosy traditional village pub with comfortable rooms and an astonishing range of wines and whiskies. **$/$$$**

EDINBURGH

Ducks at le Marché Noir 🍴 🍷
2/4 Eyre Pl. Edinburgh
📞 +44 0131 558 1608

Malcolm Duck's range of wines is one of the most impressive in Scotland. **$$**

Valvona & Crolla 🍴 🍷
9 Elm Rw. Edinburgh
📞 +44 0131 556 6066

An extraordinary specialist Italian deli and wine shop offering family-style Italian cooking. **$$**

GLASGOW

Ubiquitous Chip 🍴 🍷
2 Ashton Lane, Glasgow
📞 +44 0141 337 1302

Restaurant, bar, and shop with Scotland's biggest wine range and a cult following. Fine food and malt. **$$**

LEEDS / LIVERPOOL

Simply Heathcote (see Manchester)

LONDON

Andrew Edmunds 🍴 🍷
46 Lexington Street, Soho
📞 +44 0207 437 5708

A friendly restaurant with a cult following among wine lovers who appreciate the unpretentiously good cooking and the ludicrously fair pricing policy. **$$**

Berry Bros & Rudd
3 St. James's St, London SW1
📞 +44 0207 396 9600

Great 300 year-old wine merchant. **$/$$$**

Capital / L'Metro 🍴 🍷
22-24/28 Basil St, London SW3.
📞 +44 0207 589 5171

Fine modern cooking and well-chosen wine close to Harrods. The L'Metro wine bar next door is a good choice too.

Chez Bruce 🍴 🍷
2 Bellevue Rd, London SW17.
📞 +44 0208 672 0114

Australian Bruce Poole's friendly South London restaurant offers great cooking and well chosen international wines. **$$**

Cork & Bottle 🍴 🍷
44-46 Cranbourn St, London WC2.
📞 +44 0207 734 7807

Hidden beneath a sex shop, this is one of London's oldest and best wine bars. **$/$$**

l'Etranger 🍴 🍷
36 Gloucester Rd, London SW7.
📞 +44 0207 584 1118

An instant hit, with good, modern cooking and a very innovatively chosen wine list, great wine service and fair prices.. **$$/$$$**

Moro 🍴 🍷
34 Exmouth Mkt, London EC1
📞 +44 0207 833 8336

Modern Spanish cooking, plus terrific modern Spanish wines. **$$**

Noble Rot 🍴 🍷
3-5 Mill St, Mayfair, London W1.
📞 +44 0207 629 8877

Airy restaurant wih a serious wine list and a popular Moroccan-style basement bar. **$$**

Ransome's Dock 🍴 🍷
35-37 Parkgate Rd, London SW11
📞 +44 0207 223 1611

A favorite with London's wine trade. Modern cooking, a casual atmosphere and wonderfully eclectic wines. **$$**

The Real Greek 🍴 🍷
4-15 Hoxton Mkt, London N1
📞 +44 0207 7739 8212

Terrific Greek food and new wave Greek wine. Service is patchy. **$$**

Tate Gallery 🍴 🍷
Tate Britain, Millbank, London, SW1
📞 +44 0207 7887 8825

Only open at lunchtime, but worth the detour for unusually fairly-priced wine and good modern British cooking. **$$**

Vinopolis 🍴 🍷
Bank End, London SE1
📞 +44 0870 4444 777

Wine theme-park (building) with exhibits, wine bars, the Hess art collection, and shops, close to Tate Britain. **$/$$**

MANCHESTER

Simply Heathcotes 🍴 🍷
Canal Wharf, Water Lane, **Leeds** Yorks..
📞 +44 0113 244 6611
Beetham Plaza, 25, the Strand,
Liverpool Yorks.
📞 +44 0151 236 3535
Jackson's Row, Deansgate, **Manchester ,**
Lancs..
📞 +44 0161 835 3536
📞 04-106 Higher Rd, Longridge,
Preston. Lancs..
📞 +44 01772 784969
23 Winckley Sq. **Preston,** Lancs..
📞 +44 01772 252732

Paul Heathcote's restaurants all offer the same range of well-chosen wines to go with recommendable modern British food. **$$**

PRESTON

Simply Heathcote (see Manchester)

TUNBRIDGE WELLS

Hotel du Vin (see Birmingham)

WINCHESTER

Hotel du Vin (see Birmingham)

UNITED STATES

ATLANTA

Bone's 🍴 🍷
3130 Piedmont Road Atlanta, GA
📞 +1 404 237 2663

Choose from reasonably priced wines by the glass or break the bank at one of the country's best steak houses. **$$**

BOSTON

The Federalist 🍴 🍷
5 Beacon St., Boston, MA
📞 +1 617 670 2515

Quite simply, a restaurant with the most extensive wine list in Boston.

CHICAGO

Cru Cafe & Wine Bar 🍴 🍷
888 N Wabash Ave. Chicago, IL
📞 +1 312 337 4001

Highly popular hang-out for anyone wanting a single glass of wine, or an instructive "flight" of several. **$$**

Everest 🍴 🍷
440 S. La Salle St. Chicago, IL
📞 +1 312 663 8920

Try for a window seat here on the roof of the Stock Exchange and test your knowledge of Alsatian wines--some 300 are offered on a list totalling 800. **$$$**

Randolph Wine Cellars/ TLC
1415 W. Randolph, Chicago, ILL
📞 +1 312 942 1313

A great wine store offering "flights" of wines with cheese or charcuterie. **$$**

DALLAS/FORT WORTH

Old Warsaw 🍴 🍷
2610 Maple Ave, Dallas TX
📞 +1 214 528 0032

*A romantic and culinary favorite since
1948, with a dazzling French and
Californian wine list.* **$$**

DENVER

Palace Arms 🍴 🍷
The Brown Palace Hotel, 321 17th St.,
Denver CO
📞 +1 303 297 3111

*900 wines are offered in this antique-filled
restaurant evoking the Napoleonic era.* **$$**

HOUSTON

Rotisserie for Beef & Bird 🍴 🍷
2200 Wilcrest St., Houston, TX
📞 +1 713 977 9524

*There are over 1,000 wines to pick from in
this bastion of authentic American cuisine.*
$$/$$$

LAS VEGAS

Aureole 🍴 🍷
Mandalay Bay Hotel & Casino, 3950 Las
Vegas Blvd., Las Vegas, NV
📞 +1 702 632 7401

*Make your choice, and a "wine angel"
will be hoisted up a 42 foot tower made of
10,000 bottles to fetch it.* **$$/$$$**

LOS ANGELES

Opaline 🍴 🍷
7450 Beverly Blvd, Los Angeles, CA
📞 +1 323 857 6725

*The hottest spot in town for wine lovers
with good modern Californian cooking ,
plenty of unusual bottles at $25-45 and 15
by the glass.* **$$**

Patina 🍴 🍷
5955 Melrose Ave., Los Angeles, CA
📞 +1 323 467 1108

*Award-winning food and wine list in the
heart of the Hollywood studio district.* **$$**

MIAMI BEACH

The Forge 🍴 🍷
432 41st Street, Miami Bech FLA
📞 +1 305 538 8533

*A place to peruse both celebrities and the
longest wine list in Miami.* **$$$**

NAPA

Copia 🍴 🍷
500 First Street, Napa, CA
📞 +1 707 963 4444

*The American Center for Wine, Food, and
the Arts offers a museum, tastings, and a
restaurant named after Julia Child.* **$$**

Tra Vigna 🍴 🍷
050 Charter Oak, St. Helena CA
📞 +1 707 963 4444

*80 wines by the glass and succulent Tuscan
fare in the heart of the Napa Valley.* **$$/$$$**

NEW YORK

Flute 🍷
40 E. 20th St. New York, NY
📞 +1 212 529 7878

*Terrific Champagne bar with affordable
fizz galore.* **$/$$**

Grammercy Tavern 🍴 🍷
42 East 20th Street , New York, NY
📞 +1 212 477 0777

*Danny Meyer's sister establishment to the
Union Square Cafe. Innovative cooking
and great wines.* **$$/$$$**

Montrachet 🍴 🍷
239 W. Broadway, New York, NY
📞 +1 212 219 2777

*This Nieporent brothers hotspot has the
best Burgundy list in the city and a cellar
with some 35,000 bottles.* **$$$**

Morrell Wine Bar & Café 🍴 🍷
Rockefeller Plaza, New York, NY.
📞 +1 212 262 7700

*50 wines are poured by the glass, from the
2000 bottles on the list . If you fall in love
with one, buy it in the store next door.* **$$**

La Goulue
746 Madison Ave. FL 1, New York, NY.
+1 212 988 8169

*Art deco French bistro with over 30 years'
history. Good Gallic food and wine.* **$$$**

Punch & Judy
26 Clinton St. New York, NY
+1 212 982 1116

*Redbrick, red couches, and red wine in a
lounge with over 30 wines by the glass.* **$$**

Rhone
63 Gansevoort St, New York, NY
+1 212 367 8440

*Sample French wine until 4am at this bar
in the gritty meat-packing district.* **$$**

Union Square Cafe
21 E. 16th St, New York, NY
+1 212 243 4020

*Quite possibly the best restaurant in New
York – and certainly one of the best ranges
of wine. Also convenient for shopping at
the Union Square Wine Shop.* **$$/$$$**

PORTLAND

Ponzi Wine Bar
100 Seventh Street, Dundee, OR
+1 503 554 1500

*45 minutes out of Portland, a winery-
owned bar in Pinot Noir country.* **$$**

SAN FRANCISCO

Bacar
448 Brannan St, San Francisco.
+1 415 904-4100

*Enjoy brasserie food with an Asian twist,
some 200 wines by the glass (including
many unavailable elsewhere), and live
jazz. The world's greatest wine bar?* **$$**

Chez Panisse
1517 Shattuck Ave., Berkeley, CA
+1 510-548-5525

*Alice Waters' institution (the original
Alice's Restaurant) offers the freshest
ingredients available and a concise but
imaginative wine list.* **$$/$$$**

SCOTTSDALE

Mary Elaine's
6000 E. Camelback Scottsdale, AZ.
+1 480 423 2530

*A self-proclaimed "Arizona Wine Oasis"
with more than 1,800 wines.* **$$/$$$**

SEATTLE

Campagne
86 Pine St, Seattle WA
+1 206 728 2800

*Restaurant and cafe offering top Bordeaux
and Burgundy (try with the oeuf meurette)
and plentiful local offerings.* **$$/$$$**

TUCSON

Anthony's in the Catalinas
6440 N. Campbell, Tucson, AZ
+1 520 299 1771

*Enjoy wonderful views and the chance to
choose from over 1,600 wines.* **$$**

WASHINGTON DC

Galileo Da Roberto Donna
1110 21st. N. W., Washington, DC
+1 202 293 7191

*Sample some of Washington's most
innovative Italianate cooking (especially in
the "Laboritorio" or on the terrace) to the
tune of Italy's finest wines.* **$$/$$$**

VIETNAM

HANOI

Press Club
59A Ly Thai To, Hanoi
+84 4 934 0888

*The best wine range in Hanoi, to enjoy
with western and Vietnamese food.* **$$**

OTHERS

These Wine Lover's Guide to the World
*restaurants, bars, and shops have all been
drawn from the steadily growing selection on*
wlgtw.com *. For the chance of receiving a
free copy of the 2005* Good Wine Guide,
*please submit recommendations you think
should appear within it.*

LIVE AUCTIONEERS

**Acker Merrall & Condit Fine
Wine Auctions**
☏ 212 724 9800. FAX 212 799 1984.
ⓦ www.ackerwines.com
@ ackerbids@aol.com

Butterfields / Fine and Rare
☏ 415 861 7500. FAX 650 654 6804.
ⓦ www.butterfields.com

The Chicago Wine Co.
☏ 847 647 8789. FAX 847 647 7265.
ⓦ www.tcwc.com
@ tcwc@aol.com
Live and online auctions.

Christie's New York
☏ 212 636 2270. FAX 212 636 4954. ⓦ
www.christies.com

US Wine Auctions
☏ 877 722 1600. FAX 302 395 9200.
ⓦ www.uswineauctions.com
@ appraisals@uswineauctions.com

Morrell & Co. Fine Wine Auctions
☏ 212 307 4200. FAX 212 247 5242.
ⓦ www.morrellwineauctions.com
@ Morrellvin@aol.com

Sotheby's, New York/Chicago
☏ 212 774 5330. FAX 212 774 5347.
ⓦ www.sothebys.com
@ wine@sothebys.com

Zachys
☏ 914 723 0241. FAX 914 723 1033.
ⓦ www.zachys.com
@ info@zachys.com

WINE RACKS, CELLARS & FITTINGS

Apex
☏ 800 462 2714. FAX 425 644 1049.
ⓦ www.apexwinecellars.com
@ apex@isomedia.com

Design Build Consultants, Inc.
☏ 203 861 0111. FAX 203 861 0112.
ⓦ www.customwinecellars.com
@ evang@evang.com

New England Wine Cellars
☏ 800 863 4851. FAX 860 672 6347.
ⓦ www.newcellars.com

Songal Designs
☏ 800 449 4451.
ⓦ www.songaldesigns.com

Stellar Cellar, Inc.
☏ 800 230 0111.
ⓦ www.stellarcellar.com
@ stellarcellar@bigplanet.com

The Ultimate Wine Cellars
☏ 203 263 7770.
ⓦ www.theultimatewinecellar.com
@ winecellar@wtco.net

Vinotemp Intl.
☏ 800 777 8466.
ⓦ www..vinotemp.com

Vintage Cellars
☏ 800 876 8789.
ⓦ www.vintagecellars.com
@ vintage@znet.com

Vintage Keeper, Inc.
☏ 888 274 8813.
ⓦ www.vintagekeeper.com

Westside Winecellars
☏ 888 694 9463.
ⓦ www.westside-group.com
@ westside-group@mindspring.com

Wine & All That Jazz
☏ 800 610 7731.
ⓦ www.winejazz.com
@ info@winejazz.com

Wine Appreciation Guild
☏ 800 231 9463.
ⓦ www.wineappreciation.com

Wine Cellar Concepts
☏ 703 356 3742. FAX 703 356 3747.
ⓦ www.winecellarconcepts.com

Wine Cellars Plus
☏ 877 725 WINE.
ⓦ www.cellarsplus. com

Wine Cellar Innovations
☏ 800 229 9813. FAX 513 979 5280.
ⓦ www.winecellarinnovations.com

Wine Chillers of California
☏ 800 331 4274.
@ winechillers@earthlink.net

The Wine Enthusiast
☏ 800 356 8466. FAX 800 833 8466.
ⓦ www.wineenthusiast.com

Wine Racks & More
☏ 336 784 1100.

TEMPERATURE/HUMIDITY

CMT, Inc. Habitat Monitor
☏ 978 768 2555. FAX 978 768 2555.
ⓦ www.habitatmonitor.com

Instrument Mart On-line
ⓦ www.instrumentmart.com

FRIDGE CONVERSION KITS

BH Enterprises
☏ 925 943 7311/800. 973 9707.
ⓦ www.winestat.com

WINE STORAGE

55 Degrees (Napa Valley, CA)
☎ 707 963 5281. FAX 707 963 5281.
🖥 www.fiftyfivedegrees.com
@ wine@fiftyfivedegrees.com

Acker Merrall & Condit (NYC)
☎ 212 787 1700. FAX 212 799 1984.
@ ackerbids@aol.com

Bel-Air 2020 Wine Merchants (Los Angeles, CA)
☎ 310 447 2020. FAX 310 475 2836.
🖥 www.Belair2020wine.com

Caves of Carlyle (Manhattan, NYC)
☎ 212 977 4900. FAX 212 977 2501.

Cawinewarehouse.com (San Rafael, CA)
☎ 415 455 1181. FAX 415 455 1182.
🖥 www.cawinewarehouse.com

Chelsea Wine Vault (NYC)
☎ 212 462 4244.
🖥 www.chelseawinevault.com

City Cellars at City Storage (San Francisco, CA)
☎ 415 436 9900. FAX 415 436 9194.
🖥 www.citystorage.com
@ storage@citystorage.com

International Wine Storage
☎ 305 856 1208. FAX 305 858 6124.

K&L Wine Merchants (Redwood City, CA)
☎ 800 247 5987. FAX 650 364 4687.
🖥 www.klwines.com

Kent Wine Cellars (Chicago, IL)
☎ 773 528 5445.
🖥 www.kentcellars.com

L.A. Fine Arts & Wine Storage (Los Angeles, CA)
☎ 310 447 7700. FAX 310 447 7070.
🖥 www.lafineart.com

La Cave Warehouse (Dallas, TX)
☎ 214 747 9463. FAX 214 741 4857.
🖥 www.lacavewarehouse.com

La Cave Wine Storage (Millbrae, CA)
☎ 800 660 2283. FAX 650 692 6087.

My Cellar (Philadelphia, NJ)
☎ 215 625-3928. FAX 215 592 4744.

Sam's Wines & Spirits (Chicago, IL)
☎ 800 777 9137. FAX 312 664 7037.
🖥 www.samswine.com
@ sams@samswine.com

Subterraneum Private Wine Storage (Oakland, CA)
☎ 510 451 3939. / 888 277 7777.
FAX 510 451 5753.
🖥 www.subterraneum.com

The Strongbox Wine Cellar (Chicago, IL)
☎ 312 787 2800. / 773 248 6800.
🖥 www.winestorage.com
@ info@winestorage.com

Wine Cellar Club (Irvine, CA)
☎ 949 252 1828. FAX 949 474 5008.
🖥 www.winecellarclub.com
@ winestor@aol.com

Wine Services Inc. (Long Island, NY)
☎ 800 955 WINE. FAX 516 722 8770.
🖥 www.a1stop.com/wine

TRANSPORTATION

Western Carriers Inc.
☎ 800 631 7776.
🖥 www.westerncarriers.com
@ wine@westerncarriers.com

Wine by Air International
☎ 650 508 9631. FAX 650 508 9632.
🖥 www.winebyairintl.com
@ winebyair@aol.com

ACCESSORIES

GENERAL ACCESSORIES

IWA
☎ 800 527 4072. FAX 214 349 8712.
🖥 www.iwawine.com

Wine Appreciation Guild
☎ 800 231 9463. / 650 866 3020.
FAX 650 866 3029.
🖥 www.wineappreciationguild.com

Wine Cellar Solutions
☎ 888 649 9463.
🖥 www.winehome.com

The Wine Enthusiast
☎ 800 356 8466. FAX 800 833 8466.
🖥 www.wineenthusiast.com

GLASSES

Absolutely Riedel
☎ 516 234 5314.
FAX 516 234 5583.

ABC Fine Wine & Spirits
☎ 407 851 0000. FAX 407 857 5500.
🖥 www.finewineandspirits.com
@ info@abcfws.com

Brown Derby International Wine Center
☎ 800 491 3438.
FAX 417 883 3073.
🖥 www.brownderby.com
@ bdwine@dialnet.net

L'Esprit et le Vin
☎ 212 695 7558. FAX 212 695 9438.
@ selex-inc@msn.com

Wine Stuff
☎ 516 234 5314.
W www.winestuff.com

SOFTWARE

Apex
☎ 800 462 2714.
W www.apexwinecellars.com

Cellar Savant
☎ 800 594 5228.
W www.cellarsavant.simplenet.com

Magnum
☎ 408 448 5344.
W www.tonycleveland.com

Wineformation
☎ 303 210 2028.
W www.wineformation.com

Wine Guild
☎ 800 231 9463. / 650 866 3020.
W www.wineappreciation.com

Wine Professor
☎ 607 257 7610. FAX 607 257 7610.
W www.wineprofessor.com

Wine Technologies
W www.winetech.com

WINE VACATIONS/TOURS

Absolute Australia
☎ 212 627 8258. FAX 212 627 4090.
W www.absoluteaustralia.com

Avalon Tours
☎ 949 673 7376. FAX 949 673 6533.
W www.avalon-tours.com

The Best of New Zealand
☎ 310 988 5880. FAX 310 829 9221.
@ info@bestofnz.net

Butterfield & Robinson
☎ 416 864 1354. FAX 416 864 0541.
W www.butterfield.com

Classic Encounters
☎ 212 972 0031. FAX 914 723 9166.
W www.classicencounters.com

France in your glass
☎ 206 325 4324. FAX 206 325 1727.
W www.inyourglass.com

Gabriele's Travels to Italy
☎ 888 287 8733.
W travelingtoitaly.com

Gascony Tours (European Culinary Adventures)
☎ 800 852 2625. FAX 978 535 5738.
@ juliahoyt@aol.com

Grape Adventures
☎ +FAX 978 440 9754.
W www.grapeadventures.com

Napa Valley Wine Train
☎ 800 427 4124
@ reservations@winetrain.com

New Europe Adventures
☎ 216 486 8324 FAX 440 269 8471
W www.neweuropeadventures.com
@ info@neweuropeadventures.com

The Parker Company
☎ 800 280 2811. FAX 781 596 3125.
W www.theparkercompany.com
@ italy@theparkercompany.com

TuscanFood and Wine Odyssey
☎ 619 989 9416.
W www.tuscany-adventures.com

Wine Destinations
707 224 8500. FAX 707 224 8483.
W www.winedestinations.com

Wine & Dine Tours
☎ 707 963 8930. FAX 707 963 2301.
W www.wineanddinetour.com

Wine Tours, Inc.
☎ 510 888 9625.
W www.winetoursinc.com
@ winetour@world-access.com

Wine Tours Australia and New Zealand
☎ 858 550 9696. FAX 858 550 9644.
W www.winetoursaustralia-nz.com

LEARNING ABOUT WINE

Institute of Masters of Wine
☎ 011 44 171 236 4427.

International Wine Center
☎ 212 627 7170. FAX 212 627 7116.
@ iwcny@aol.com

Society of Wine Educators
☎ 301 776 8569. FAX 301 776 8578.
W http://wine.gurus.com

Wine & Spirit Education Trust
☎ 011 44 171 236 3551.

Wine School/l'Ecole du Vin (Robert Joseph)
W www.wine-school.com / www.lecoleduvin.com

Christie's Wine Course
☎ 011 44 020 7581 3933.

The world of wine online is changing so rapidly that the following list can only offer a snapshot of what you may find if you go looking for wine on the web. But it should give you a pretty good start. For the latest news about the world of Wine on the Web see pages 16 and 17 at the beginning of this guide.

ONLINE RETAILERS

www.auswine.com.au
A wide range of Australian wines shipped worldwide.

www.bbr.com
Traditional merchant with a great site and a good query-answering service. Worldwide delivery.

www.bestcellars.co.uk
UK-based online retailer with good value offers across the board.

www.casevalue.com
UK based site with attractively-priced mixed case offers, including many winners from the International Wine Challenge.

www.cawineclub.com
California wine club.

www.chateau-online.com
French wines shipped throughout Europe. Sophisticated and French-focused.

www.clarets.com
Not just claret. California outfit that ships worldwide.

www.connseries.com
US site from the California Wine Club specialising in limited-production, critically highly-rated wines.

www.e-winegifts.com
The Saratoga Wine Exchange's online presence. Ships wines and gifts across the US (local laws permiting).

www.esquin.com
Superstore and wine club from the oldest wine merchant in Seattle.

www.everywine.co.uk
UK site offering 30,000 wines. The place to look before all else fails.

www.finestwine.com
Global supply of collectable wines, including top Bordeaux.

www.libation.com
Wine and beer delivered worldwide. Serious wines, including top Californians and Italians.

www.madaboutwine.com
UK-based general retailer. Informative site with good bin-end offers.

www.majestic.co.uk
Online presence of UK retailers, Majestic. Worth look at for bargains.

www.oddbins.com
A late but welcome arrival, the UK's most popular wine retailer offers good, unusual wines across the board.

www.nicks.com.au
Popular Melbourne wine merchant that ships worldwide. Informative site, worth looking at for news of new wines and vintages.

www.pippin.com.
Good US-based retailer with wide ranging wines and a recommendable newsletter.

www.ranchocellars.com
Online Californian business with 3,000 wine on offer.

www.liquors.pippin.us
Over 2,100 wines and spirits on offer in several states.

www.tesco.com.
Huge UK retail chain with the world's biggest online grocery business. Only supplies UK and Eire.

www.thedrinkshop.com
UK-based wine retailer that also ships to the US. A source for unusual wines that are not easy to find elsewhere.

www.utterdelight.com.
Good US-based retailer with wide ranging wines and a recommendable newsletter.

www.vino.com.
US-based wine and spirit retailer, only selling in N. America.

www.vintageandvine.com
Links to good retailers in Australia. Useful for obscure wines.

www.virginwine.com
Top UK-based site – and the one that has seen most of its competitors fail.

www.waitrose.com
Top-end UK-based supermarket with a good selection of wines across the board.

www.wine-searcher.com
Links to wine retailers across the globe.
Allows intersting price comparisons.
www.wineaccess.com
Useful links to independent US wine
retailers.
www.winalert.com
Over 60,000 wines are on offer from 100
US retailers.

www.wineandco.com
French-based retailer. Delivers to UK.
www.wine.com (includes evineyard.com)
Wines, gifts, accessories, and wine links.
www.winebroker.com
Fine wine specialists with a wide range
of serious wine on the net.
www.winex.com
A good catalog of wine across the board.

WINERIES

www.bestwinesites.com
A good list of links for North America
and Europe, with an excellent list of
wineries.
www.cawinemall.com
Comprehensive directory of California
web wineries by region or grape variety.
www.champagnes.com
An introduction to Champagne and its
producers.
www.vinosearch.com
Wines and wineries across the globe.
www.winecollection.com
An online collection of France's wineries
and wines.

www.wines.com
Details of over 1 400 Australian and
New Zealand wineries, with wines across
the board.
www.winetitles.com.au
An Australian based website with an
excellent range of selected wineries
from across the world. A useful place to
go looking for hard-to-find wines.
www.wineweb.com
An extensive list of wines and wineries
from across the world.
www.worldwine.com
Lots of links - not only to wineries, but
all aspects of wine.

ONLINE AUCTIONEERS

www.auctionvine.com
Business-to-collector auction that is now
part of Bretwood.
www.brentwoodwine.com
US-based auction site with fixed price
sales, too.
www.cellarexchange.com
US-based auction house offering
commission-free auctions for both
buyers and sellers.
www.tcwc.com
The Chicago Wine Company. Veteran
terrestial auctioneer based in the US and
mainly selling there.
www.bidnewyork.com
The online auction of New York
specialist Morrel Wine Fine Wine
Auctions.
www.magnumwines.com
Specialty wines, especially large format
bottles – as the name suggests. US-
based.
www.uvine.com
Online wine exchange based in the UK,
but operating globally. Mostly aimed at
professionals.

www.wine-auction-central.com
US-based auction site with wide-ranging
wines from all over the world.
www.winebazaar.com
A wine auction based in the US that
offers commission-free seles and
purchases.
www.winebid.com
Auctions in the US, UK, and
Australia..The biggest and probably best
auctioneer. Now selling more classic
French wine.
www.winecommune.com.
US-based auction, only shipping within
the US.
www.winesellar.com
US-based auctions that have been online
since 1999. The manager is called
Parker, so his recommendations should
go down well.
www.winetrader.com.au
Australian based operation with all the
top names..
www.zachys.com.
Top US-based specialist now has a
thriving auction on its website.

NEWS, REVIEWS, & GENERIC SITES

www.4wine.com
US-dominant link to worldwide wines.
www.ambrosiawine.com
Very popular vinous search engine and
chatroom.
www.bestwinesites.com
Good source of wine information on the
web. US-focused, but international.
www.decanter.com
The UK wine magazine online. A good
free wine-pricing service.
www.erobertparker.com
The guru Robert Parker @ home. A
mecca for enthusiasts, especially after
the new vintage of Bordeaux is released.
www.connectingdrinks.com
The route to Wine International, Wine
& Spirit International, and Drinks
International magazines online.
www.drinkwine.com
Stylish, California-oriented meeting spot
for Napa lovers.
www.foodandwine.com
Food and Wine Magazine online.
www.gangofpour.com
Loads of information about wine.
www.grapevineweekly.com
An online magazine with lots of links.
www.harpers-wine.com
UK-based site aimed at wine
professionals. Good for news and views.
www.hotwine.com
A link to winesites, plus poetic quotes.
www.interaxus.com
Wine reviews.
www.intlwinechallenge.com
The wine competition's official website,
now linked to www.wineint.com.
www.intowine.com
Winemaking and wine-and-the-Bible.
www.jancisrobinson.com
The UK-based wine authority's "purple
pages" have a strong following globally.
www.purplepages.com
Directory of wine-related websites. See
above.
www.smartwine.com
Market news for the investor.
www.thewinenews.com
News and reviews.
www.vine2wine.com
Links to over 2,000 wine sites.
www.wineanorak.com
Top class informative site based in the
UK but of international inerest. A wide
range of information.

www.winebrats.org
New-wave and emphatically unstuffy.
www.winebusiness.com
Good, news-based site for professionals
around the world.
www.winecellar.com
A complete source of wine links.
www.winecollector.com
Swap and chat about collectable bottles.
www.wineculture.com
A hip guide to wine on the web.
www.wineenthusiastmag.com
Articles and the latest news as well as
good accessories.
www.wineinfonet.com
A multi-language portal with links to a
wide range of sites. Good search engine.
www.intwin.com
An online magazine with lots of links.
www.ineint.com
The recently launched online presence
of Wine International Magazine
(previously Wine Magazine). Good
encyclopedia.
www.wine-investor.com
How to spend your cash.
www.winemag.co.za
South Africa's wine magazine.
www.wineplace.com
Winemaking galore. Hints and tips.
www.wineontheweb.com
The talking online wine magazine.
www.winepros.com
Australian-based site with experts
including James Halliday.
www.wineratings.com
Wine reviews and advice.
www.wine-searcher.com
Search the web for all aspects of wine.
www.winesense.com
Wine appreciation and women in wine.
www.winexwired.com
Online presence of *Wine X* Magazine.
Very hip approach to wine.
www.thewinenews.com
Features, reviews, recommendations.
www.winespectator.com
The *Wine Spectator's* online magazine.
Good for news.
www.worldwine.com
A website dedicated to wine links.
www.wlgtw.com
Wine Lover's Guide to the World. If you
liked the restaurants and bars in this
Guide, this is the place to look for more.
Or to recommend some of your own.

REGIONAL SITES

www.argentinewines.com
Argentina's new-wave wines.

www.bordeaux.com
A virtual tour of the wine and wineries
of Bordeaux.

www.coonawarra.com
Australia's most famous winemaking
region on the web.

www.germanwines.de
Multilingual official site.

www.indagegroup.com
Promoting India's wine.

www.ivp.pt
The Port Wine Institute's official website
and bulletin board.

www.liwines.com
Long Island wine country.

www.madeirawine.com
All about Madeira's wines and history.

www.nywine.com
New York uncorked.

www.nzwine.com
The official site of New Zealand wine.

www.portwine.com
Everything you need to know about port.

www.sonomawine.com
Sonoma County Wineries Association.

www.washingtonwine.org
All about wine in Washington.

www.wine.ch
The Swiss wine page.

www.wine.co.za
A guide to South African wines.

www.winecountry.com
The gateway to wines of California.

www.wineinstitute.org
Californian wineries with lots of links to
heaps of information.

www.wine.it
Wines of Italy.

www.wines-france.com
User-friendly guide to French wines.

ONLINE WINE EDUCATION

www.WineEducation.com
Certified Wine Educator, Stephen Reiss.

www.wine.gurus.com
Society of Wine Educators'
home page.

www.robertjoseph-wineschool.com
An online diploma wine course.

www.wineprofessor.com
Food and wine pairing, wine
labels, etc.

ONLINE CHATROOMS & CLUBS

www.4wine.com
Lists a multitude of chat rooms.

www.auswine.com.au
The Australian Wine Centre's virtual
shop with a forum, and a chat room.

www.drinkwine.com
Bulletin board and extensive listing of
associations.

www.evineyard.com
Offers live talk and a lively wine club.

www.iglou.com/wine/chat
Join a crowd of other wine lovers and
compare notes.

www.secretcellars.com
A virtual wine club that brings
California's small vineyards to your door.

www.vineswinger.com
Plentiful chat rooms and busy forums.

www.winebrats.org
Access to various wine chat rooms.

www.wineculture.com
A resource of various chat rooms.

www.wineinstitute.org
Lists discussion groups and chat rooms
focusing on California wine.

www.winelovers-page.com
Wine chat room.

www.winerave.com
Website with its own wine chat room –
arguably the liveliest on the net.

www.wines.com
Questions can be posed to wine experts.

www.winesite.com
Links to international wine clubs.

www.winespectator.com
Forum and online interviews.

www.zinfans.com
For lovers of the Zinfandel – in its every
form.

*Please email recommendations of other sites
to robertjoseph@robertjosephonline.com.In
return, I will send copies of my book* French
Wines *to senders of the most useful tips.*

INDEX

This index can be used as a supplement to the A–Z of Wine (pages 97–262).

A

Abbott's 197
Acacia 125
Accordini 102
Adams, Tim 132
Adouzes, Ch. des 153
Agricola, la 104
Aguilas, Pierre 139
Aguilhar, Ch. d' 137
Aiguilhe, Ch. d' 139
Aiguilloux 137
Akarua 108
Albalá199
Albert Morot 111
Albrecht 101
Alexander Valley Vineyards 101
Alianca 100, 147
Allandale 172
Allanmere 172
Allegrini 102
Allemand, Thierry 137
Allexant 131
Alliet, Philippe 131
Alquier , Gilbert 153
Alsace 161
Altare 144
Altesino 119, 198
Amarine, Ch. de l' 138
Amblard 139
Ambroise, Bertrand 138
Amethystos 165
Amiot, Pierre 128
Amiot-Servelle 133
Amirault 117
Amour, St 110
Ampeau 113, 196
Ampuis, Ch. d' 136, 139
Ancienne Cure 197

André, Pierre 130
Angeli 103
Angelo, D' 100
Angerville, d' 101
Angludet 142
Anheuser, Paul 107
Anne, Ste. 140
Anselmann 172, 179
Anthonic, Ch. 202
Antinori 131, 159
Antonin, St 153
Antonopoulos 165
Anubis 104
Aqueria, Ch. d' 187
Aquitania 190
Archambeau, Ch. d' 165
Arena, Antoine 123
Arenberg, D' 194
Argiano 119
Arjolle, dom d' 140
Arlay, Ch d' 104, 140
Armangia, l' 105
Arnault et Fils 103
Arnauton 159
Arnoux 101, 111, 131, 133
Aromo, el 194
Arrowood 101
Arvouet, Ch. d' 198
Ashton Hills 99
Ata Rangi 192
Atlas Peak 205
Aubert 122
Audoin, Charles 192
Aujas 178
Aujoux 156
Auriol, St 137
Auvenay, d' 115, 196
Avize 175
Aydie 190

B

Babich 169, 192
Bablut 103
Bachelet 128, 161, 191
Balbi 104
Balduzzi 194
Balgownie 111
Banfi 198
Bannockburn 160
Bara, Paul 114, 118
Barancourt 118
Barbadillo 155, 176, 191
Barbi 119, 200
Barbolini 182
Barca Velha 147
Barge 139
Barjac, de 137
Barkham Manor 172
Barmes-Buecher 169
Barossa Valley Estate 109
Barréjat 190
Barros e Souza 190
Bart, Dom 156
Bartoli, De 192
Basedow 109
Basilium 100, 109
Bassermann-Jordan 144
Bastide de Levis 140, 159
Baudare, Ch. 140
Baudoin 103, 139
Baudoux 100
Baudry Bernard 131
Baumard, Dom. des 139
Bava 105, 144, 153, 158
Beaucastel, Ch. de 130, 140
Beaulieu Vineyard 125, 148
Beaulieu 205
Beaulieu, Ch. de 140
Beaumont 142
Beaurenard 130, 140
Beaurepaire, de 195
Beauséjour 198
Beck, Graham 158

Becker 101, 107
Bedell 188
Begalli 102
Belcier, de 139
Belingard, Ch. 112, 197
Bellavista 157
Belle Père & Fils 142, 171
Bellegarde 178
Bellei 182
Bellevue la Forêt 140
Bellier, Caves 131
Beltrame, Tenuta 104
Beni di Batasiolo 201
Benon, Jean 178
Bera 105
Bercher 178
Beresford 194
Berger 199
Beringer 172, 205
Bernard, Louis 140
Bernard, Michel 171
Bernarde, dom. la 140
Bernardins, Dom. des 110
Berrod 156
Bersano 105
Bertagna 133
Berthaut, Vincent 156
Berthet-Bondet 129
Berthoumieu 190
Bertinerie, Ch. 139
Bertrand, Gérard 197
Bethany 109
Beyer, Léon 101
Bianchi 195
Bichot, Albert 127, 161
Bidoli 158
Biffar, Josef 144
Billaud-Simon 127
Biondi-Santi 119
Bise 103
Bisquertt 134
Black Ridge 127
Blanchard 129
Blanck, Paul 101
Blandy's 119, 190

Bloy, Ch du 200
Boas Quintas 144
Boccadigabbia 191
Boillot 198
Bonfort 198
Bonhomme 189
Bonneau du Martray 101, 138
Bonneau, Henri 130
Bonneford, Patrick & Christophe 136, 139
Bonnet , Ch. 151
Bonny Doon 192
Bonzara 135
Borba 100
Borgo Conventi 135
Borgo del Tiglio 135
Bosc, Paul 122
Bosca, Luigi 104
Boscaini 108
Bosquet des Papes 130, 161
Bosquets, dom des 161
Bossard 204
Botmaskop 145
Botobolar 203
Botromagno 165
Bott-Geyl 101
Boucard 117
Bouchard Père et Fils 115, 133, 199
Bouchard, Pascal 127
Bouchassy 187
Bouchon 194
Bouley 111
Bourdy 104, 140
Bourgeon 162
Bourrée (Vallet) 161
Bouscassé 190
Bousquet 178
Boussé, Denis 101
Boutari 165, 204
Bouvet-Ladubay 103
Bowen Estate 137
Boxler, Albert 101
Brana 178
Brana, dom 175
Brauneberger Juffer 177

Breaky Bottom 151
Bresson, Pierre 191
Breuil, Ch. du 103, 139
Brial 140
Brice 118
Bridgehampton 188
Bridgewater Mill Shiraz 2000 119
Brigaldara 102
Briggs, August 125
Brintet, dom 195
Brocard 127, 174
Brokenwood 172
Brookfields 169
Brookland Valley 192
Brouilly 110
Broustet, Ch. 109
Broyer, Bernard 178
Bru-Baché 178
Bruisyard 151
Brulesécaille 139
Bründlmayer 106, 183
Brunel, Lucien & André 130
Brunelli, Luigi 102
Bruno, Paul 190
Brusset 122, 140,. 161
Burgaud 139, 200
Burguet, Alain 128, 161
Buring, Leo 132
Burn, Ernest J & F 101
Bussola, Tommaso 102
Buxy, Cave de 198
Buzet 120
By Farr 160

C

Ca' dei Frati 189
Ca' Del Bosco 157
Cabasse 140, 161
Cabrières 130
Cabrol 121
Cady 139
Cailot 110

C

Cain 205
Caix, Ch. de 121, Ch. de
Cakebread 205
Caldaro, Cant. Vit. di 102
Calissanne 139
Caliterra 125, 143
Calon 198
Calon, dom 200
Calot 200
Caminade, la 121
Campbell's 187
Camplazens, Ch 132
Campuget, de 138
Canale 104
Canepa 190
Canon la Vieille, Ch. 159
Canon-Moueix Ch. 123
Canorgue, Ch. de la 140
Cantarelles, Dom. des 138
Cap de Faugères 139
Caparra & Siciliani 132
Caparzo, Tenuta 119
Cape Mentelle 192
Capitain-Gagnerot 101, 181
Caraguilhes 137
Carillon 113, 129, 195
Carmel 175
Carmen 190
Carmignani 198
Carneros Creek 125
Carobbio 131
Carr Taylor 151
Carras, Ch. 165
Carsin 121
Carta Vieja 194
Cartuxa 100
Casa de Santar 144
Casa Lapostolle 134
Casablanca 161
Caslot-Galbrun 117
Castell'in Villa 131
Castellare 131
Castello dei Rampolla 131
Castello di Ama 131
Castello di Neive 108

Castello di Salle 99
Castello di Volpaia 155
Castera 178
Catarelli, dom de 123
Catena (+Zapata) 104, 195
Catena 195
Cattin, Joseph 101
Cauhapé 178, 191
Cavalleri 157
Cave Diose 132
Cave Springs 122, 174
Caves Velhas 120
Cavicchioli 182
Cayla 121
Caymus 205
Cayron, du 161
Cèdre, du 121
Celli 100
Cellier le Brun 192
Celliers St. Martin 137
Cerbaiona 119
Ceretto 105
Cesari, Umberto 100
Chablisienne, la 127
Chain of Ponds 99
Chamirey, Ch. de 195, Ch. de
Champ de Mars 139
Champault 195
Champet 139
Champy 133, 161
Chandelles 137
Chandon de Briailles 101, 138
Chandon 104
Chantegrive, de 165
Chapel Hill 107, 194
Chapoutier 110, 130, 137, 142, 171
Chappaz 105
Charbonnière, la 130
Chard Farm 127
Charet 195
Charlopin 161
Charmes-Godard 139
Charvet 202
Chasseloir, Dom. de 204
Chasse-Spleen 142, 202

C

Chassorney, Dom 106
Château de Marsannay 161
Chateau des Charmes 122
Chave 171
Chavy-Chouet 113
Chenaie, Ch. 153
Chénas 110
Chênes 140
Chéreau-Carré 204
Chevalier Père et Fils 181
Chevrot 191
Cheysson, Emile 131
Chiara, la 160
Chiarlo 201
Chidaine, François 199
Chignard 156
Chiltern Valley 151
Chimney Rock 205
Chirat, Gilbert 136
Chiroubles 110
Chorey, Ch. de 131, 111
Christmann 144
Christobel 201
Christoffel 151
Church Road 169
Churchill's 142
Cilento 174
Cimicky, Charles 109
Citran 142
Clair Daü 115
Clair, Bruno 128, 156, 161, 200
Clape, Auguste 137
Clarke 187
Claverie, la 139
Clearview 169
Clement Ternes, Ch. 159
Clerc, Henri 113
Climens, Ch. 109
Clos Centeilles 197
Clos Dalmain 112
Clos de Gamot 121
Clos de Paulilles 108, 135
Clos des Mont-Olivet 130
Clos des Papes 130
Clos du Bois 101

Clos du Val 205
Clos Floridène 165
Clos Guirouilh 178
Clos la Coutale 121
Clos Lapeyre 178
Clos Nicrosi 123
Clos Salomon 162
Clos Ste. Magdeleine 126
Clos Triguedina. 121
Clos Uroulat 178
Closel 103
Closel, Dom. du 103
Closerie, la 153
Clos-Jean 188
Cloudy Bay 192
Clusel-Roch 139
Coche-Dury 106, 199
Cocument, 140
Cognard 117
Col d'Orcia 119
Colin, Marc 129, 199
Colin-Deleger 110, 129
Collards 105
Collier Falls 148
Collonge, Bernard 200
Colombier 142, 171
Colombo, dom 171
Colombo, Jean-Luc 137
Combier 142
Commanderie e Peyrassol 140
Comte Armand 106
Comte Senard 101
Comtes Lafon 189, 196, 199
Concha y Toro 99, 125, 190
Condamine 140
Condemine, François 178
Confuron, Jean-Jacques 133
Conterno 153
Conterno Aldo 144, 158
Contero 201
Conti 100
Contratto 105
Coopers Creek 105
Corbans Giesen 192
Corbans 162

C

Corbin 198
Cortaccia, Cant. Prod. di 102
Corte Gardoni 131
Corte Sant' Alda 102
Cortes de Cima 100
Cortese 144
Cossart Gordon 119, 190
Costanti 119, 198
Côte de Brouilly 110
Côte Montpezat 139
Cotton 119
Coudoulet) 140
Couillaud 204
Coulaine, Ch. de 103,
Couly-Dutheil 131
Coupe Roses, Ch. 197
Courbis 137
Couret 140
Courtade, la 140
Court-les-Muts 112
Cousino Macul 190
Coutet, Ch. 109
Coyeux, Dom. de 110
Craggy Range 162
Craggy Range 169
Crampilh, Dom. du 190
Crasto, do 147
Crawford, Kim 162
Crema, la 125
Cremaschi Barriga 194
Crichton Hall 205
Cros, Ch. du 188
Cros, dom 197
Cros, du 191
Cru Lamouiroux 178
Crusius 204
Cuilleron 139
Cuilleron Yves 136
Cullen 192
Cuvaison 125, 205
Cuvee du Roi Clovis 119
Cuvée Fût de Chêne 184
d'Ameilhaud, dom d'l 122
d'Auvenay, Dom 106

D

Dalem 159
Damoy 161
Damoy, Pierre 128
Dampt 127
Davenay, Ch. de 198
Daviau 103
Defaix 127
Deffends 139
Defrance, Michel 156
Degrange 202
Deinhard 163
Deiss, Marcel 101
Delarche, Marius 101
Delas 130, 142, 161, 171
Delaunay 117, 131
Delay 140
Delegats 169
Delesvaux 139
Delétang 199
Deletto 105
Delorme 187
Dépardieu, Gerard 136
Derain 162
Derey Frères 156
Descendientes de J. Palacios 113
Descombes, Georges 178
Descombes, Jean 200
Descottes 139
Deshenrys 140
Désirat, St Cooperative 135
Deslesvaux 103
Després 156
Deux Roches 189
Devil's Lair 192
Di Majo Norante 99
Diamond Creek 205
Diconne, Jean-Pierre 106
Diel, Schlossgut 204
Dieu Donne 158
Dino Illuminati 99
Dirler, Jean-Pierre 101

Disznókö 172
Doisy-Daëne, Ch. 109
Doisy-Dubroca, Ch. 109
Domaine Bruno Clair, dom 192
Domaine Carneros 125
Domaine Chandon 125
Domaine de Gineste, dom 159
Domaine de la Chanteleuserie, dom
    117
Domaine de la Romanée-Conti, dom
    199
Domaine. Chandon 205
Don Zoilo 191
Doña Maria 147
Donatien Bahuaud 103
Donelli 182
Donnafugata 201
Dopff au Moulin 101
Dow's 142
Dr Loosen, Dr 151
Dr. H. Thanisch, Dr 118
Dr. Heger, Dr 107, 178
Dr. Loosen, Dr 112, 201
Droin 127
Dromana 201
Drouhin (Marquis de Laguiche) 199
Drouhin 101, 115, 128, 131, 133, 191,
    196
Drouhin, Joseph 110, 127, 133, 161
Druet 117
Dry Creek 148
Dry River 192
Duas Quintas 147
Duboeuf 110, 119, 138, 139. 156, 202
Duboeuf, Georges 131, 178, 200
Dubois 111
Dubost 110
Dubreuil-Fontaine 138, 181
Duckhorn 172, 205
Dugat-Py 128, 161
Dugois 104
Dujac 115, 128, 133, 134, 149, 161, 200
Dumazet, Pierre 136
Dunn 2, 172
Duque de Viseu 144

Durand, Eric & Joël 137
Durand-Perron 129
Duras Cooperative 139
Durban 110
Durup 127
Durvieu 137
Duval-Leroy 114
Duxoup 148

E

E&E 109
Echeverria 143
Edmeades 102
Egervin 172
Egly-Ouiriet 114
Ehrenstette 107
Elderton 109
Elgee Park 201
Elvo Cogno 144
Engel 128, 133, 149
Entrefaux 161
Errazuriz 99, 125
Esclans, d' 140
Esk Valley 169
Esmeralda 104
Espiers 161
Espigne, Ch. d' 156
Esporão 100
Estancia 199
Estanilles 153
Estève, St 137
Etang des Colombes 137
Etchart 104, 195
Etoile, Ch de l' 152
Etoile, L' 108
Etxegaraya 175
Eulalie, Ste. 197
Evans & Tate 192
Evans Family 172
Eventail des Producteurs 178
Eveque, l' 140
Eyssards 112

F

Fabiano Masi 108
Faivelay 128, 133, 138, 195, 198200,
Faizeau 198
Falesco 184
Falfas 139
Faller 101
Farnese 99
Fattoria Coroncino 191
Fattoria Paradiso 100
Fauconnière 198
Faurie, Bernard 171
Faury, Philippe 136
Fayau 121
Fayolle 139
Fazi Battaglia 191
Fefiñanes 100
Feiler-Artinger 106, 120
Felluga 135
Felton Road 108, 127
Fenouillet, de 110
Féraud-Brunel 122
Ferme Blanche, la 126
Ferraton 171
Ferraud, Pierre 178
Ferrucci 100
Fesles, Ch. de 103, 115
Fessy, Sylvain 119, 200
Fetzer 195
Feudi di Romans 158
Feudi di San Gregoria 165
Finca Flichman 195
Finca la Anita 104
Fisher 125
Fitz-Ritter 107
Fleurie 110
Florio, Cantine 192
Foggarty 199
Fogliati, Giorgio 105
Foillard 110
Foillard, Jean 200
Fojo , do 147

Fonréaud 187
Font de Michelle 130
Fontana Candida 158, 184
Fontanafredda 105
Fontanel 140
Fonte, da 147
Fontenil 159
Fontenille 151
Fonterutoli Felsina 131
Font-Sane 161
Força Réal 140
Forefathers 101
Forges 139
Forlini e Cappellini 132
Fortia la Gardine 130
Fortuna, la 143
Fougas 139
Fougeray de Beauclair 115, 156, 192
Fourcas-Dupré 187
Fourcas-Hosten 142, 187
Fournier 195
Fox Run 155
Cazin, François 131
Francs, de 139
Frankland Estate 202
Freie Weingärtner 106
Freiherr von Heddersdorff 201
Frescobaldi 131, 159, 198
Fronton, 140
Fruitière Viticole 104
Funtanin 105
Fürst, Rudolf 158

G

Gaggioli 135
Gagnard, Jean-Noel 110, 129
Gagnard-Delagrange 110
Gaia 165
Gaierhof 102
Gaillard, Pierre 136
Gaivosa, da 147
Gaja 108

Gall, Tibor 150
Gallet 139
Gallo Sonoma 148
Gancia 105
Garafolli, Gioacchino 191
Garofoli 191
Garraud, Ch. 182
Gasse 139
Gauby 140
Gaudard 103
Gaudronnière, Ch de la 131
Gautoul 121
Gavelles, Dom. des 117
Gavoty 140
Gay 131, 181
Gay, Michel 101
Gebiets-Winzergenossenschaft 158
Gelin, Pierre 156
Genaiserie 103
Geneletti, Michel 152
Génot-Boulanger 111, 195
Gentaz-Dervieux 139
Gentilini 165
Geoffroy, André 156
Gerard Villano 136
Gerin 139
Gerin, Michel 136
Germain 111
Germain, Henri 129, 196
Germanier 102
Gerovassilou 165
Geyser Peak 101
Gibbston Valley 127
Giesen 123
Gigault 139
Girardin, Vincent 191
Gitana Manzanilla, la 191
Gloria 142
Godineau 139
Godineau, dom 115
Godwin 101
Goisot, G&J-H 101
Golan Heights 175
Goldsmidt 101
Goldwater Estate 105

Gonzalez Byass 155, 176
Gorgo 113
Goubert, les 140, 161
Goulaine, de 204
Goundrey 202
Gourgazaud 197
Gradoli 100
Graham's 142
Grai, Giorgio 102
Graillot, Alain 142
Grand Caumont 137
Grand Maupertuis 166
Grand Moulas 140
Grand Ormeau 182
Grande Maison 197
Grande Maye 139
Grande Rompue, la 184
Grandes Vignes, les 115
Grandes Vinos y Viñedos Aviet 104
Grands Vignes, Dom Les 103
Grangeneuve , Dom. de 139
Granger Pascal 178
Granger, Paul 178
Grant Burge 109
Grassa 140, 191
Gravner 135
Grézan 153
Grille, Ch. de la 131
Grillesino, Il 200
Grinou 112
Grippat 171
Gristina 188
Grivot 149
Grivot, Jean 133
Groffier 115, 128, 204
Groom 109
Gros, Anne 133
Gros, Jean 133
Grosett 99, 132
Grotta del Sole 181
Grove Mill 192
Gruppo Cevico 100
Guerrieri Rizzardi 131
Guerry 139
Gueyze, Ch. de 120

G

Guigal 130, 139, 140, 161, 171, 192
Guigal, Graham 136
Guimoniere 139
Guindon 204
Gunderloch 204
Gurgue, la 142
Guyard 156
Guyon, Antonin 101

H

Haag, Fritz 118, 177
Haag, Willi 201
Haas, Franz 102
Hallett, St 109
Handley Cellars 195
Hanstschia Angerhof 106
Hardy's 109, 137, 194
Hatzimichalis 165
Hauterive, de 121
Haute-Serre 121
Haut-Marbuzet 142
Haut-Sociondo 139
Heathcote 111
Heggies 99
Hehner Kiltz 204
Helena, St. 123
Hélène 137
Helmut Lang 120
Henriques & Henriques 119, 190
Henry of Pelham 122, 174
Henschke 99, 109
Herdade de Mouchao 100
Heritage 109
Hermann Donnhoff 204
Heron Hill 155
Hervé Richard 136
Hess Colection 199, 202
Hidalgo 155, 176, 191
Hidden Cellars 195
Hiedler 183
Hillebrand 122
Hobbs, Paul 125

Hoff, Steve 109
Hofstätter 102
Holler 106
Höpler 120
Horst Sauer 158
Howard Park 202
Hugel 101
Hunter's 192
Huntington Estate 203

I

Iby, Anton 120
Imesch.Gonzalez Byass 102
Immich Batterieberg 201
Inniskillin 122, 174
Irouléguy Cooperative 175
Isole e Olena 131
Isolette , Ch. de l' 140

J

Jaboulet Aîné 130, 137, 140, 171
Jaboulet Aîné, Paul 110
Jackson Estate 192
Jackson Triggs 122, 174
Jacques, Ch. des 110
Jade Mountain 202
Jadot 101, 115
Jaffelin 199
Jaillance 132
Jakoby-Mathy 201
Jamet 139
Janin 110
Janin, Paul 202
Janodet 202
Jasmin 139
Jasper Hill 111
Jau, Ch. de 135
Jau, de 140
Jaubertie, la 112

Javillier, Patrick 101
Jayer, Henri 149
Jayer-Gilles 101
Jechtingen 107
Jekel 199
Jermann 135, 158
Jim Barry 132
Jobard 113, 196
Joblot 162
Joguet, Charles 131
Johner, Karl-Heinz 107, 178
Joliet, Philippe 156
Jonqueyres, les 139
Jordan 101
Josmeyer 101
Josmeyer 169
Jota, la 172
Juge 137
Juge, du 121
Juillot, Michel 195
Juliénas 110
Juliénas, Ch. de 178
Juliusspital 158
Juris 106
Jurtschitsch 106

Kreydenweiss 101
Krondorf 109
Kruger-Rumpf 204
Ktima 165
Kuentz-Bas 101
Kumeu River 105
Kunstler 172
Kurfürstenhof 204
Kurt Darting 107
Kym Milne 172
Kyr Yanni 204

K

Kaesler 109
Kamptal 178
Karp-Schreiber 201
Katnook 137
Kays Amery 194
Kerpen, Heribert 112, 201
Kientzler, André 101
Kistler 125
Knappstein 132
Knoll 106, 167
Kollwentz-Römerhof 120
Konzelmann 122, 174
Kourtakis 194
Kracher 120, 167
Kracher, Alois 106

L

Labégorce 142
Labégorce-Zédé 142
Labourons, Ch. 156
Lacombe 191
Lafarge, Michel 111
Lagar de Cervera 100
Lageder, Alois 102
Lagrezette 121
Laible, Andreas 149
Lake's Folly 172
Lakeview Cellars 174
Laleur-Piot 138
Lamaroux Landing 155
Lamartine 121
Lambardi 119
Lancaster 101
Lang 167
Lang, Alois 106
Lapeyronie 139
Lapierre 200, 202
Lapierre, Hubert 131
Large 110
Largeot, Daniel 101, 111
Laroche 127
Lastours. de 137
Latuc 121
Launay 181
Launay, Raymond 128
Laurens, Cave Cooperative de 153

Laurent 111, 115
Laurent 149
Lazarides 165
Lazy Creek 195
Leacock 190
Leasingham 132
Lebreton 103
Lebreton 103
Lecheneault 133
Ledru.Banfi 118
Leeuwin 192
Leflaive (Olivier and Domaine) 101
     199
Leflaive, dom 110
Leflaive, dom 113
Lehmann, Peter 109
Lemercier, Jacques 137
Lemos & Van Zeller 147
Lenz 188
Leoncio Arizu 104
Lepaumier 156
Leroy 128, 133, 138, 161, 199, 204
Lerys 156
Lesparre 165
Lespinasse, Henri 178
Levasseur 199
Librandi 132, 165
Lignier, G 134
Lignier, Hubert 200
Lindemans 137, 172
Lini 182
Lionnet, Jean 137
Liparita 172
Liquière, la 153
Lis Neris-Pecorari 175
Logis de la Bouchardière 131
Lopez Hermanos 190
Lornet 104
Los Vascos 134
Louis Bernard 187
Louis Chèze, Louis 136
Louis Jadot, Louis 106, 156, 192
Louis Latour, Louis 138, 198
Louis Michel, Louis 127
Louis Rémy, Louis 133

Loupiac-Gaudiet 188
Loye, de 195
Lugny, Caves de 189
Lumpp 162
Luneau, Pierre 204
Lurton 104, 188, 195
Lustau 101, 102, 176, 189
Lustau 155

M

Macle, Jean 129
Macrostie 125
Maddalena 102
Maddalena, Sta 102
Madone, dom de la 156
Madonia 100
Maglieri 194
Magnotta 122
Maillard 111, 131, 138
Maldoror 139
Maltroye, Ch. de la 110
Maltroye, Ch. de 129
Malvira 105
Manciat 189
Mann, Albert 101
Manos 121
Marbuzet 142
Marcassin 101, 125
Marchese di Gresy 108
Maréchale 181
Marenco 118
Marfil 100
Marqués de Alella 100
Martin Codex 100
Martinborough Vineyard 192
Martini 105
Martino, Armando 100
Martray, Laurent 119
Mas Amiel, dom 108
Mas Blanc, dom du 135
Mas Blanc, Dom. du 108
Mas de Bressades 138

M

Mas Ste.-Berthe 139
Masciarelli, Gianni 99
Masi 102
Massa, la 131
Mastroberardino 165
Mastroberardino 181
Mastrojanni 119
Matariki 162
Matawhero 162
Matrot, Thierry 113
Matua Valley 105, 162, 169
Maucaillou 202
Max Ferd Richter 118, 163
Mayacamas 202
Mayne Lalande, Ch. 187
Mayne-Vieil 159
Mazarin 188
McPherson 163
McWilliams 172
Meaume, Bernard 128
Medici Ermete 182
Megyer 172
Meix-Foulot 195
Méjan, André 187
Melness 123
Melton 109
Memoires 121
Méo Camuzet 133
Merricks 201
Merrill, Geoff 194
Metaireau 204
Météore. de 153
Métrat 156
Mètrat, Andrè 131
Metternich-Sándor 167
Meunier St. Louis 137
Meyer-Fonné 101
Meyney 142
Méziat, Bernard 131
Michaud 119
Michel, Bernard 198
Michel, Robert 137
Michelot 196
Mick Morris 187
Mildara 137

Mills Reef 169
Millton 162
Mireille, de 140
Mission Hill 122, 174
Mission 169
Mitchells 132
Mitchelton 192
Mittnacht-Klack 101
Moillard 198
Monbrison 142
Mönchhof 151
Mondavi 125
Mongeard-Mugneret 149
Mont Tauch 137, 156
Montana 162, 169, 192
Montbo 152
Monte Rossa 157
Monteillet, de 136
Montes 143
Montez, Antoine 136
Monthelie-Douhairet 199
Montus, Ch. 190
Morande 99, 104, 195
Mordorée 187
Mordorée, la 130
Moreau-Naudin 127
Morey 129
Morey, Pierre 110
Morey, Pierre 196
Morgon 110
Moris Farms 200
Mortet, Denis 128, 161
Morton Estate 169
Moss Wood 192
Motta 200
Mottura, Sergio 165
Moulin Couderc 153
Moulin des Groyes 139
Moulin Pey-Labrie. 123
Chancellor, Ch. 123
Moulin-à-Vent 110
Moulin-à-Vent, Ch. du 202
Moulis 202
Mount Horrocks 132
Mount Ida 111

M

Mount Veeder Winery 202
Mountadam 99
Mourges du Grès, Ch. 138
Mouton 162
Moyer 199
Mt Difficulty 108
Mt Difficulty 127
Mt Edward 127
Mugneret-Gibourg 133, 149
Mugnier 204
Müller-Catoi 165
Mumm Cuvée Napa 125
Münzenrieder 106, 120
Muré, René 101
Murphy-Goode 101

N

Nages, de 138
Nagyrede 172
Nairac, Ch. 109
Nalle 148
Navarro Correas 104
Nepenthe 99
Nerthe, la 130
Neszmély ("Hilltop") 172
Neumayer 106
Ngatarawa 169
Nicolaihof 106
Nicolay, Peter 151
Nicolis e Figli 131
Nicolis , Angelo 102
Niedermayer 102
Niellon, Michel 110, 129
Niepoort 147
Nittnaus 120
Noble, du 188
Norton 104, 195
Notaio, Cantine del 100
Nouveau, Claude 191
Nouvelles, de 156
Nudant 138
Nudant, André 101, 181

Nutbourne Manor 172
Nyetimber 151

O

O 109
Obispo Gascon 108
Ogereau 103
Ogier 139
Olivier Leflaive 106, 195, 198, 199
Olssens 108, 127
Opitz 120, 167
Opitz, Willi 106
Oratoire St-Martin 122
Oriental, dom 194
Orlando 109, 137
Ornaisons, d' 137
Osicka 163
Ostertag 101
Ott 140
Oupia, Ch. d' 197
Overnoy 104

P

Paitin 108
Pajsos 172
Palais du Révérend , les 137
Pallavicini 158
Palliser Estate 192
Palmer 188
Palo Cortado Viejo 171
Papantonis 165
Paracombe 99
Paraza ch. de 197
Parducci 195
Parenchère, de 139
Parent, Alain 136
Paringa 201
Parker Estate 137
Parxet 100

Pascal 140
Pask, CJ 169
Passavant, Ch. de 103
Passing Clouds 111
Passot,.Alain 131
Paternoster 100
Patz & Hall 125
Pauly-Bergweiler 112
Pavilion-Mercure, Dom. du 142
Payral 112
Pazo de Barrantes 100
Pech-Céleyran 132
Pech-Latt 137
Pech-Redon 132
Peconic 188
Pegasus Bay 123
Pegaü, du 130
Pelee Island 122, 174
Pelissero 108
Pellé 195
Pellegrino 192
Peller Estates 122
Penfolds 99, 109, 132, 137, 202
Penley Estate 137
Pennautier 121
Penny's Hill 194
Pera Manca 100
Pérez Barquero 199
Pérez Caramés 113
Perret, André,, 136
Perrin 140
Perrin 187
Perrot-Minot 133
Petaluma 132
Petaluma 137
Peteroa 190
Petersons 172
Peyregran 153
Pez, de 142
Pezzi-King 148
Phélan-Ségur 142
Philibert, Denis
Pibarnon, Ch. de 108
Pibran 142
Piccinini 197

Pichler 106
Pichler 167
Pichon, Phillipe & Christophe 136
Picq, Gilbert 127
Pierre Bise, Ch. 139
Pierre 197
Pierre-Bise 103
Pierro 192
Pike 132
Pilliteri 122, 174
Pillot 129
Pillot. 195
Pindar 188
Pine Ridge 125
Pinget 144
Pinte , la 104
Pio Cesare 160, 166
Pique-Serre 200
Piron 119, 200
Pirramimma 194
Pithon 103
Pitray 139
Pivot 110, 138
Plaimont 140
Plaisance, Ch. la 139
Plantagenet 202
Plunkett 163
P-M Chermette 156
Pochon 142, 161
Pociarello.St
Poderina, la 119
Poggio Antico 119, 198
Pojer & Sandri 102
Pollenza, la 132
Ponsot 133, 134
Ponsot 200
Porta dos Cavaleiros 144
Portal, de 147
Portalupi 108
Portalupi 113
Portaz, Marc 103
Potelle, Ch. 202
Potensac 142
Poujeaux 142
Poujeaux 202

P

Poupille 139
Prade, la 139
Pradeaux 108
Prager 106
Prager 167
Prieur 204
Prieur, Jacques 111, 133, 138, 196
Prieuré de Cenac 121
Prieuré Roch 133
Prince Albert 160
Prince de Mérode 101
Prissé, 189
Producteurs de Plaimont 190
Produttori di Gavi 160
Provins 105
Prum, JJ 112, 163
Prunier, Michel 106
Prunier, Vincent 106
Prunotto, Alfredo 108
Puffeney 104
Puglia 100
Puiatti 135, 158
Puligny-Montrachet, Ch. de 196, 199
Pupille, le. 200
Putille Montigilet, de 103
Puygeraud 139
Puy-Servain 200

Q

Quady 102
Quartz Reef 127
Quénard, A&M 131
Quinta da Boavista 100
Quinta de Pancas 100
Quinta do Carmo 100
Quinta do Cotto 147
Quinta dos Roques 144
Quintarelli 102
Quivira 148

R

Rabbit Ridge 148
Rabiega 140
Rafanell 148
Ragot 162
Rahoul 165
Rallo 192
Rameaux, Gie Les 100
Ramey 125
Ramonet 110, 129, 199
Raousset, Ch de 131
Rapet Père et Fils 111
Raphet, Jean 128, 133
Rattray, Mark 123
Raveneau 127
Ravenswood (Hollick) 137
Rayas 130
Raz, de 112
Rebourseau, Henri 128, 133, 161
Rectorie, de la 135
Rectorie, Dom. de la 108
Redoma 147
Redondo 100
Redwood Trail 199
Regnié 110
Reichsrat von Buhl 144
Reif Estate 122
Reiss 158
René Dauvissat, René 127
René 103, 115
Repimplet 139
Réserve des Célestins 130
Revelette, Ch. 139
Revington 162
Reynella, Ch. 194
Reynolds 172
Reynon 121
Ricasoli, Barone 131
Ricaud, de 188
Richaud 122, 140
Richeaume 140
Richel, B&C 103

Richou 103
Ridge 202
Riecine 131
Rijckaert 104
Rino Varaldi 108
Rion, dom 133
Rippon 127
Robert Ampeau, Robert 106, 111
Robert Niero, Robert 136
Robin 139
Roc, le 140
Rocca di Castagnoli 131
Rocca, Albino 108
Roc-de-Cambes 139
Rochaix 105
Rochelles 103
Roche-Marot, la 200
Rochepertuis, Michel 137
Rochet-Lamother 121
Rochettes, Ch. des 139
Rockaway 101
Rockford 109
Rodet, Antonin 198
Roederer 102
Roederer.La Agricola 195
Roger Lasserat 189
Roland 119
Rolet 104
Rolland, de 156
Rolly Gassmann 101
Romanée-Conti, de la 149
Romano dal Forno 102
Ronco del Gelso 175
Ropiteau 196
Rosa, de la 147
Rosemount 101, 172
Rosemount 137
Rossignol-Trapet 161
Rostaing 139
Rothbury Estate 172
Roty 128, 161
Rouge Gorge, du 153
Rouge Homme 137
Rouget 149
Roulerie, de la 139

Roulot 196
Roulot, Guy 106
Roulot. 199
Roumier 115
Rousseau 133
Rousseau, Armand 128, 161
Rousset 139
Rouvière, Ch. la 108
Roux Père et Fils 129, 196
Roy, Marc 161
Royal de Maria 174
Royal Tokay 172
Rozets, de 139
Ruet 119
Ruffino 131
Rural, la 104, 195
Ryman, Hugh 172

S

S. Mosnier 127
Sablonettes 139
Sablonettes, Dom. des 103
Sacred Hill 105, 169
Sain Bel Co-operative 139
Sainte-Marie 151
Saintsbury 125
Salitis 121
Salnesu 100
Salvagnac 137
Salvatore Murana 201
San Bartolomeo 160
San Michele Appiano 102
San Pedro 188
San Savino 191
San Telmo 104, 195
Sanchez Romate 102
Sandoni 135
Sansonniere, Dom de la 103
Santa Ana 104
Santa Carolina 125, 188, 190, 194
Santa Emiliana 125
Santa Inés 190

S

Santa Rita 125, 190
Santi 131
Sasonniere 115
Saugère 139
Saule, Ch. de la 198
Sautejeau, Marcel 204
Sauvion 204
Sauzet 110, 113, 199
Savoye 200
Scagliola 108
Schäfer, Karl 107
Schiopetto 135
Schlumberger 101
Schoffit 101
Schuster 167
Scotchmans Hill 160
Seghesio 101
Segonzac 139
Seguin, Gérard 161
Seip, Heinrich 204
Selbach -Oster 112
Selvapiana 131
Seppelt 187
Serafino 105
Serette 137
Servin 127
Seuil, du 165
Sevenhill 132
Shadowfax 160
Shafer 125
Shaw & Smith 99
Sherwood Estate 123
Shottesbrooke 194
Sileni 169
Silver Oak 101
Simi 101
Simonnet-Fèbvre 174
Siran 142
Skouras 165
Sociando-Mallet 142
Sogrape 100
Sorg, Bruno 101
Sorrel 142, 161, 171
Sorrel, Marc 171
Soucherie 103

Soucherie, Ch. 139
Soulez, Pierre 103
Soulez, Yves 103
Soumade, la 110, 140
Sousa, Jose de 100
Sparr, Pierre 129
Spinetta, la 108
St Jean, Ch. 101
St. Pierre, de 137
Steele 102
Steininger 167
Steinmaier 162
Sterling 199
Stoneleigh 192
Stonestreet 101
Stoney Ridge 122
Stonier 201
Stonyridge 105
Stoppa, la 135
Strofilia 165
Sumac Ridge 122
Swanson 125

T

T'Gallant 201
Tahbilk. Alana Estate 192
Taille aux Loups, la 199
Tain Cooperative 137, 142
Tain l'Hermitage Cave de 171
Talenti 119
Tardieu-Laurent 122, 130, 137, 171
Tatachilla 194
Tayac 139
Te Mata 169
Tedeschi 102
Tedeschi 113
Teisserenc 140
Tempé, Marc 101
Tempier, dom 108
Termeno, Cant. Prod. di 102
Terrazas 104
Terres Dorées, Dom des 110

Testuz 100
Tête, Michel 178
Thalabert, de 161
Thames Valley Vineyards 151
Thénard 162
Thirty Bench 122
Thivin, Ch. 138
Thomas-Moillard 111, 138
Three Choirs 151
Thurnhof 102
Tiefenbrunner 102
Tigné, Ch. de 103
Tirecul-la-Gravière 197
Tissot 104
Tissot 120
Tissot, A&M 104
Tizzano 135
Tohu Wines 162
Tollot-Beaut 101, 111, 131, 138
Toni Jost 197
Topf Strasser, Johann 167
Torbrek 109
Torino 104
Torres, Miguel 143
Tosa , la 135
Tour Boisée, la 197
Tour de Bon, dom 108
Tour des Gendres 112
Tour du Bief, la 202
Tour Haut-Caussin, la 142
Tour St Martin, la 195
Tour Vieille 108
Tour Vieille, la 135
Tour, Ch. de la 133
Tour-de-Mirambeau 151
Tours, Ch. des 119
Tourtes 139
Traeger, David 163
Trapet, Jean 128
Trapiche 104, 195
Travaglini 160
Tremblay 127
Trichard, Raymond 178
Triebaumer, Ernst 106
Trimbach 101

Trinity Hill 162, 169
Truchard 125
Tschida, Johan 106
Tuilerie de Pazac 138
Turcaud 151
Turkey Flat 109
Turley 101, 148, 172
Two Paddocks 127
Tyrrells 172

U

Uberti 157
Uccellina 100
Umani Ronchi 191
Umathum 106, 120
Undurraga 134, 190
Unison 169

V

Vachet, Jean 198
Vaisse, Andre 156
Vajra 109
Vajra 144
Vajra, GD 108
Val d'Orbieu
Val di Suga 119
Valcombe 138
Valdamor 100
Valdivieso 143
Vale , do 147
Vale da Raposa 147
Valentini, Eduardo 99
Val-Joanis 140
Vallado , do 147
Vallado 147
Vallerosa Bonci 191
Vallona 135
Vallon-Valady, Cave du 191
Vallouit, I de. 139

V

Vanniéres 140

Vannières, Ch. 108

Varière, Ch. la 115, 103

Varière, la 139

Vasse Felix 192

Vavasour 192

Veenwouden 158

Venica & Venica 135

Ventenac. 121

Veramonte 125

Verget 127, 189, 196

Vernay , Georges 136

Vernay 139

Vernay, G 135

Verset, Noël 137

Vial Magnères 108

Vidal 169

Vidal-Fleury 110, 161, 139

Vie di Romans 175

Vieille Ferme 140

Vieille Ferme, la 140

Vietti 108, 109

Vieux Château Calon. 198

Vieux Chateau Champs de Mars 139

Vieux Micoulier, du 139

Vieux Télégraphe 130

Vigne di San Pietro, le 113

Vignelaure, Ch. 139

Vignerons Catalans 124, 140

Vignerons de Beaupuy, les 140

Vignerons de la Méditerranée 137

Vignerons des Garrigues, les 140

Vigneti Villabella 189

Vigot 149

Viguerie de Beulaygue 140

Vilaine, A&P de 101

Villa Banfi 119

Villa Bel Air 165

Villa Lanata 153

Villa Maria 169

Villa Russiz 135

Villa Vignamaggio 131

Villadiere 189

Villand, Francois 136

Villard 125

Villemajou 137

Villerambert-Julien 197

Viña Carmen 190

Viña Casablanca 125

Vincent, J-J 189

Vineland Estates 122

Vino Noceto 102

Vins de Vienne 171

Vins de Vienne, les 122

Violette, Ch. de la 103

Viticoltori Alto-Adige 102

Viviani 102

Voarick, Michel 101

Vocoret 127

Voerzio 105

Voerzio, Gianni 109

Voerzio, Roberto 108, 109

Voge, Alain 137

Vogüé, de 115, 204

Von Kesselstadt 112, 163

von Plettenberg 107

Voss 192

Voulte Gasparets, la 137

Voyager Estate 192

W

Wachter 120

Wagner 155

Waipara Springs 123

Waipara West 123

Wandanna 198

Water Wheel 111

Weaver, Geoff 99

Wegeler Erben 112

Weinbach 101

Weinert 104

Weingut Karlsmuhle 201

Wendouree 132

Wignalls 202

Wilderness Estate 172

William Fèvre 127

Williams Selyem 102

Wirra Wirra 194
Wirsching, Hans 158
Wolf Blass 109
Wolf 165
Wolf, JL 144
Wolf-Metternich 149
Wynns 137

X

Xanadu 192

Y

Yalumba 109. 137, 187

Z

Zapara 195
Zenato 102, 113, 189
Zerbina 100
Zimmerlin 107
Zind Humbrecht 101, 169
Zof 158
Zonin.Jalon 104

WINE ON THE WEB

Apart from our lists of recommended websites
on pages 16–17 and 395–397,
if you enjoy

the Robert Joseph Good Wine Guide

visit

vintage-intelligence.com

for news, comment, tasting notes, competitions, an electronic
Wine Atlas, and links to over 200 wineries and retailers
throughout the world,

www.robertjoseph-wineschool.com

and, of course,

www.dk.com

for details of other
DK Publishing titles.